THE KING OF FIFTH AVENUE

ALSO BY DAVID BLACK
Like Father, A NOVEL

David Black

THE KING
of
FIFTH AVENUE

*The Fortunes
of August Belmont*

The Dial Press   New York

Published by
The Dial Press
1 Dag Hammarskjold Plaza
New York, New York 10017

Manufactured in the United States of America
First printing
Design by Francesca Belanger

Library of Congress Cataloging in Publication Data

Black, David, 1945–
The King of Fifth Avenue.

Bibliography: p.773
1. Belmont, August, 1816–1890.   2. United States—Foreign
relations—1861–1865.   3. Diplomats—United States—Biography.
4. Bankers—New York (City)—Biography.   I. Title.
E415.9.B45B56   973.6′092′4   [B]   80–28741
ISBN 0–385–27194–8   AACR2

For Deborah and Susannah
And for Naomi

Acknowledgments

I owe a great debt of gratitude to Mr. and Mrs. August Belmont, who shared their manuscript collection with me and let me quote freely from it. Their hospitality, generosity, and kindness made research a pleasure. Without their help, this book could not have been written. They have my affectionate thanks.

I also must thank Gene Rachlis for first suggesting the book; Diane Giddis for her advice and support in the first few years of research; Megan Rosenfeld for her hospitality on my frequent research trips to Washington, D.C.; Sam Merrill for the use of his portable copier; and Naomi Black and Martha McKee Keehn for their invaluable help in the later stages of the project.

August Belmont, Jr., Mrs. Frank Lineberry, and Mrs. Rahel Liebeschütz were kind enough to share material in their collections with me and to allow me to quote from various letters and documents. Mrs. Harold Tinney graciously entertained me and my family in Newport, Rhode Island.

A number of other people helped in various ways: Tom and Linda Blackwell, George and Lone Blecher, David and Margo Burgess, Lewis and Cathy Cole, Jane Dickson, Benjamin Keehn, Monika Napoleon, William O'Rourke, Harry Stein, Linda Stevens, Anna Van, Robert Ward, Stefani Tashjian-Woodbridge, and David Woodbridge. Jay Acton's support for the project was also crucial.

Irving Katz's book *August Belmont: A Political Biography* added considerably to my understanding of Belmont's position in nineteenth-century American politics.

For readability, in some quotes I have removed brackets from around words inserted for the sake of clarity. I also have removed ellipses. In neither case is the meaning of the quoted material distorted. Generally, spelling has been modernized and corrected. In anecdotes about August Belmont's friend William Travers, who was called the Stuttering Wit of Wall Street, I have followed the often illogical spelling given in contemporary accounts and have allowed him to stutter according to the sources. In the notes at the end of the book, where it is clear that quotes are from a source already cited, I have omitted duplicating citations.

Joyce Johnson worked extraordinarily hard going over a long manuscript a number of times word by word, an intelligent, meticulous, and sensitive job of editing. I am very grateful to her.

It is commonplace for an author to thank his wife for her support and assistance, but it is no less true for being typical. The help that my wife, Deborah, gave to this project was crucial. The book is in great measure a product of her patience, faith, and love.

He taught New Yorkers how to eat, how to drink, how to dress, how to drive four-in-hands, how to furnish their houses, how to live generally according to the rules of the possibly somewhat effete, but unquestionably refined, society of the Old World. It is no exaggeration to say that on the whole of this continent there is not another house of which the appointments are as perfect as those of Mr. Belmont's. He is not a mere gastronome, a collector of works of art, or a blind adept of fashion. He is an artist in his household. From the livery of his coachman to the menu of his daily breakfast and the disposition of the knickknacks on the mantelpiece of a spare room of his countryhouse, everything is to him an object of sincere artistic solicitude.

New York Sun, *1877*

PART ONE

❦ *CHAPTER ONE* ❦

THE FAMILY had no name. German Jews at the end of the eighteenth century were known by just their given names and patronymics, which were enough to identify them within the ghettos like the one at Alzey where there were only a dozen households. Isaac Simon, everyone knew, was the son of Ephraim Simon. His grandfather was Joseph Jessel, a man so pious everyone in the neighboring towns had called him Rabbi Jessel of Alzey. And his great-grandfather was Simhah, son of Ephraim, who had come to Alzey a century before from Beckelheim, where he had been the leader of the Jewish community.

Isaac Simon sold groceries and draperies, lent money, and worked his farm. He planted corn, potatoes, and kidney beans; tended apple, pear, plum, cherry, and walnut trees; and cultivated grapevines. On warm evenings, he sat in the courtyard behind his house with his wife, Rosa, and their four children. The breeze smelled of ripe grapes, of hay and manure, of the balsams and carnations that grew in the window boxes, of the acrid goose-droppings that along with thousands of feathers covered the ground, of cooked cabbage, of rotting slops, and of the poppies in the meadows beyond the town.

Alzey was small. In Isaac Simon's father's time there had been only sixty-three families, Jew or Gentile, in the whole district. And it was old—a village that had survived on the site where a Roman town had stood a millennium before. The countryside around Alzey, the Rhenish Palatinate, was known as the Paradise of Germany. But it was a patchwork paradise, protected by a congress of gods—Norse, Roman, Christian, Jewish—whose worshipers at various times had lived in the region; a fairy-tale world of winding paths climbing through thick woods to overgrown towers and crumbling walls where—the Gentiles whispered—

kobolds and dwarfs hid in the leafy shadows. It was a world where charms and spells propped up prayer, because like all paradises it had been infiltrated by evil. In fact, only a dozen miles away from Alzey, at Münster-am-Stein, on top of a scar of red porphyry, were the ruins of Rheingrafestein, a fortress that—they said—was created in a single night by the Devil. And just beyond Münster-am-Stein, in Kreuznach, was the house on Karlstrasse where the Devil had come to collect the soul of Dr. Faustus.

A few miles beyond Kreuznach was Bingen, whose streets on market days were crowded with jugglers, wandering musicians, and traveling players. Up the Rhein from Bingen, past cliffs craggy with castles, was Lorch, the town from which the family of Isaac Simon's daughter-in-law Gertrude came. She was married to Isaac Simon's eldest son, Aaron Isaac. As Isaac Simon grew older he depended more and more on his children to take care of him. He did less and less business himself and intended to spend the rest of his life peacefully, patriarch of a growing family.

There was always a chance that the anti-semitism of his Gentile neighbors might flare up as it had in the past. Many of the old ghetto laws were still in force. As recently as the middle of the century, in 1748, the elector Karl Theodor had declared that no more than three Jewish families could live in Alzey, adding that "since there were already more than that number, no additional families would be allowed to settle there until the number had been diminished by death to fewer than three." And when Isaac Simon visited Frankfurt, about forty miles to the northeast of Alzey, he had to step aside and doff his hat if any Gentile, even a child or a beggar, demanded, "Jew, remember your manners."

But the situation of Jews in Germany was better than it had been when Isaac Simon's great-grandfather, Simhah, had settled in Alzey. It was certainly better than it had been four and a half centuries before in the Year of the Terror, 1349, when Jews, held responsible for the Black Plague, had been butchered in the town. By Isaac Simon's time at the end of the eighteenth century some of the restrictions were ignored; others were mildly enforced. In the cities a few Jews were entering the universities or under special protection were practicing professions and trades that had been closed to Jews for centuries. Travel outside the ghettos was not too difficult as long as you paid the Jew-tax and got a limited passport at Alzey's town hall, a sixteenth-century building in the center of the village. There was no reason why Isaac Simon could not expect to spend his last years supported by his sons, sitting in his courtyard, perhaps reading one of the new editions of the Talmud, recently printed in Frankfurt, or indulging in a game of cards.

Occasionally a wandering mystic would arrive in Alzey raving about the long-dead Messiah, Sabbati Zevi—who a hundred years before had promised deliverance from the ghetto and a return to the Holy Land—or preaching the gospel of other more recent Jewish saviors. It seemed more likely that if Jews were to be rescued from the ghettos it would be by revolutionaries, not prophets. Itinerant Jewish peddlers, after swinging their packs from their backs and haggling over the prices of their trinkets, spread rumors of the revolution in France, which had issued a Declaration of the Rights of Man and Citizen. They told of how the Portuguese Jews of Bayonne, Bordeaux, and Provence had been emancipated; of how fifty-three of the sixty districts represented in the Paris Commune had voted in favor of the enfranchisement of all Jews in their land; and of how on September 27, 1791, the French National Assembly had declared all French Jews to be citizens. In one of the battles between Germany and France that followed the French Revolution, French bombardment of Frankfurt had destroyed the walls around the ghetto. The physical barriers had been leveled. The social barriers soon would be down as well.

But although the French might be liberators, they were still French; and Isaac Simon was still German. In the last decade of the eighteenth century he loaned Alzey 30,000 florins to ransom the town from some invading French soldiers. Of these, 9,500 were repaid. The remaining 20,500 florins were used to establish a fund that provided a salary for Alzey's rabbi, flour for three families that could not afford to make matzoh on Passover, dowries for poor Jewish girls, and expenses for the town's first synagogue, which Isaac Simon's brother Elias built in 1791—the year after Isaac Simon's eldest son, Aaron Isaac, died.

Aaron Isaac left behind him one son, Simon, who was a year old, and another son who was born a few months after Aaron Isaac's death. Aaron's widow, Gertrude, named the second child Aaron for her dead husband. While Simon and Aaron were still infants she left them with her father-in-law, Isaac Simon, and went to Frankfurt. There she married a man named Hajum Lehman Hanau, whose sister soon would marry one of the five sons of Mayer Amschel Rothschild. Rothschild was famous in Frankfurt's Jew Street. Not only had he become rich enough in the secondhand trade to buy a new house, a three-story building with an indoor pump and a terrace in the back, but he was known at court because he sold antique coins to and cashed London drafts for William of Hanau, the new Landgrave of Hesse-Cassel.

Isaac Simon, his comfortable retirement interrupted by the obligation to raise two grandchildren, decided to groom the older of the two boys to take over the family business. He made sure Simon learned Hebrew and German and how to keep accounts. By the time Simon was eighteen he had read Schiller and given in to a passion for puzzles, which he collected in his homework notebooks. He worked hard and learned the formalized maneuvers of trade that had developed in Germany over generations. Like his grandfather he studied the government and laws that the new French overseers were establishing and that were altering the ways people in their district had always lived and done business. In 1808 Napoleon ordered all Jews in France and in the German territories France controlled to take surnames. When the French commissioners came to Alzey, Isaac Simon chose for his family the French name Belmont.

When Simon was twenty-two he had so mastered the local laws, the Napoleonic Code, and his grandfather's business that Isaac Simon gave the boy his power of attorney. Alzey's Jewish community, recognizing the young man's energy, prudence, and intelligence, made him president of the synagogue that his great-uncle Elias had built.

When he was twenty-three Simon married Frederika Elsass from Mannheim. She was a year older than he. She had dark hair, striking large, elongated, almost Oriental eyes and once was described as being "just as beautiful as she was charming and kind." Her dowry of 12,000 florins was high. Her parents were satisfied with their new son-in-law. He was modern and aggressive; he did not wear a beard; and he had candid eyes that looked boldly around his world. He was not an old ghetto Jew who ducked his head and shaded his glance for fear of provoking Gentiles; on the other hand he was not an assimilated German.

In 1813 old Isaac Simon died. On December 8 of the same year, at noon, his great-grandson was born. The child's twenty-four-year-old father, Simon, wrapped up the baby and as was the custom brought him to the mayor, who in the presence of two witnesses wrote in the birth register the baby's name: Aaron Belmont.

Simon decided to increase and modernize the business, which his grandfather had left him and which he would leave to his son, Aaron. To the one-eighth of the estate he had inherited, he added all the rest of old Isaac

Simon's farmlands, which he bought from his brother and other relatives. He planted oats, wheat, barley, cabbage, and grapes. He abandoned his grandfather's merchandising business and expanded the banking activities. He lent money to peasants whose crops had been poor and to the gentry living in Alzey's castle who needed ready cash. He collected local debts on commission for businessmen and bankers who lived as far away as Cologne and Aachen. Stubborn, ambitious, and as learned as most lawyers, he spent years dragging resistant debtors through higher and higher courts, a man climbing a pyramid of law to get his 5 percent interest—although he lost almost every suit he was involved in.

He wasted nothing, bought the cheapest, thinnest paper, and to save on postage covered every blank space on his letters, every margin and corner, so completely that some of them became unreadable. Years later, explaining why he had not sent his daughter a birthday present, he would write, "The description of your birthday and holiday and the many praises and presents you received clearly shows how much people recognize your worth. It is even more important that your father also through some token shows his appreciation. But I really did not know what I could buy here in Alzey which could have surprised you. Obviously, I could have sent money . . . , but from my grandfather, Isaac Belmont, I inherited a frugality which has been reinforced over the years. . . . I know your character, dear Babette, and I also know that you are not inclined to save a lot of money; and so, to calm you down, I confess myself to be your debtor. And this summer when, if God wills it, I visit you, I will pay off this debt. Just as my debtors often beg me, so I now beg you to be patient."

To Babette's husband, Stephan Feist, his explanation of his parsimoniousness was simpler: "I have never been a friend of luxury and splendor and less of spending great amounts of money." He did not even hire Jacob Engelhard, his full-time farmhand and coachman, until 1816. Before that he managed to plow, plant, and harvest doing what he could himself, using temporary workers for what he could not do.

In June 1815 Simon fell ill and had to go to Heidelberg for a cure. The Duke of Wellington had just defeated Napoleon near a small village south of Brussels called Waterloo. Alzey was filling up with Allied soldiers, who were being billeted with families in the area. Frederika, discovering that eight or nine men had been assigned to their house on St. George Street, complained. The house wasn't large enough; she was alone. There was nothing the mayor could do. "They treat all the Jews thus," she wrote to Simon. She missed her husband, and she didn't understand why he had to stay in Heidelberg. "The way I see it," she wrote, "being away does you more harm than good." If the doctor would let him come home, she could take care of him, he wouldn't be restless, and he would have peace and quiet. She was so eager for him to return she had investigated ways he could travel and timetables. He could get the coach from Heidelberg on Wednesday. Or he could even take a one-horse carriage, which, she explained, was "not too expensive."

Putting a pen in little Aaron's fist she guided the baby's hand, making him write, "I also greet you, dear father, a thousand times, and kiss you, and hope you're getting better." She had the baby sign the letter with the name they had begun calling him: "Your loving son, August Belmont."

A traveler who passed through the countryside around Alzey early in the nineteenth century described how children in the villages played "in the dust, beside the endless swarm of geese." Geese were everywhere. "Some of them, in flocks, were flying up and down, and making no little clangour." Others sat in the stream that ran down the side of the street in a gutter, "forming dams with their bodies, in which they nibbled, and ducked, and washed themselves. The whole long street, from bottom to top, was full of these geese." Sometimes the little children, their arms outstretched, would waddle toward the birds, which would honk and flutter away. Sometimes the birds, their necks outstretched and their beaks clacking, would waddle toward the children, who would shriek and toddle for cover.

On warm, sunny days the townswomen threw open the upper windows in the houses and draped over the sills eiderdowns and red-striped mattresses to air them out. Other women gossiped around the public pump and stone trough in the middle of the village or, barefoot, scrubbed laundry in the river. All along the bank linens would be stretched out on the grass to bleach and dry.

In the vineyards, once the mild spring weather had come, men and women cut back the grapevines, stripping off the new side-shoots and shortening the main stems. In the orchards they pruned the fruit trees. In the fields cows dragged harrows through the recently plowed soil. As the days grew longer, children were allowed to play outside through twilight until nine in the evening. After the youngsters went to bed, adults might stroll through the village in the moonlight, which would turn the houses into silvery silhouettes. On the first day of Passover, Jewish children played with nuts into the early spring morning and, excited by the holiday, might not get to sleep until outside the windows the village turned blue with dawn. In some small towns, where Jews and Gentiles mingled casually, the Gentiles sometimes brought their Jewish neighbors loaves of bread to mark the end of Passover.

As the restrictions of the ghetto faded and Jews were able to enter more and more easily into the Gentile world around them, the sense of being outsiders paradoxically increased. Once Jews no longer were set apart by inflexible laws, it became obvious—especially to a child growing up with no memory of the grimmer restraints of ghetto life—that they were set apart in other ways.

In March, on Summer-day, the few Jewish children in the Rhenish villages, unable to participate in the Gentile merrymaking, watched the Christian children skipping through the streets carrying "wands adorned with ribbons" and singing "the summer in with a song, which bears a striking resemblance to the oldest song in the English language, beginning, 'Ye somer ist ycomen in, Loud sing cuckoo . . .'" The Jewish children knew that the two men, "one dressed in moss and straw, as Winter" and the other dressed in ivy, green leaves, and new violets, as Summer, would romp through the town without knocking on their doors. On Easter the Jewish children could not join the Christian children who scattered through the village searching under bushes and in the long grass for colored eggs, which their parents told them were laid by rabbits. In June on Saint John's Day, when the Christian children again collected eggs in flower-decorated baskets and sang "Garden, garden, Brunnen egg/ For St. John's Day today we beg" as they danced from house to house, the Jewish children, shut away in homes that suddenly must have seemed very quiet, were left to their customary chores.

In the fall the Jews celebrated their New Year months before the New Year celebrated by their Gentile neighbors; and as the Gentiles went about their ordinary daily rounds the Jews observed their Yom Kippur fast. Even the Sabbaths were out of sync. On Saturday, while most of the village worked, the Jewish families prayed and spent the day quietly. They sang songs at dinner and entertained guests. After the meal a woman might read "the popular commentaries on the Bible written in Judeo-German," while her husband might teach their son how to play chess or might spend a mild afternoon "sitting on a bench outside the house . . . asleep with a cat at his feet." Families and friends strolled along the riverbank as, ahead of them in the marshy grasses, one by one the frogs fell silent and then plopped into the slow-moving water. Or they wandered through the meadows, lazily listening to the hum of bees and the *bump-thud, bump-thud* of the stampers, the beams used for grinding flour, in the Gentile mills, an iambic reminder that this Sabbath was not shared by the majority of the villagers. On Sundays while most of the village prayed and rested the Jews returned to work.

After the seemingly endless labors of autumn the Jews of Alzey built in their courtyards sukkahs, bough-covered booths to commemorate the Feast of Tabernacles, while the Gentiles caroused through the village streets celebrating the harvest with bawdy songs and drunken waltzing. In the winter the town pump was packed in straw to keep it from freezing, and rolls of straw wrapped in brightly colored cloth tubes were jammed along windowsills to keep out the twinkling clouds of snow that the wind puffed into the rooms through the cracks. Inside the Jewish homes of Alzey, instead of being lit by the few flickering lamps that ordinarily illuminated the dark December nights, the rooms blazed with Chanukah lights. The menorah candles were lit; gifts were exchanged; and children played dreidel and guessing games and challenged each other with arithmetical puzzles—while outside, the village was being festooned with Christmas decorations. Once Chanukah had ended and the Jewish families had settled back into the quiet routine of winter, they could hear from the other parts of the village the Christmas carolers singing through the streets.

On bright winter days the sun seemed to shatter on the snow, and splinters of light hurt the eyes of villagers who, muffled up in great cape-like coats, tromped through the drifts of the town. At night clouds crossing the moon cast moving purple shadows on the fields around Alzey. In the morning after a new snowfall tracks of weasels, foxes, or wild dogs might lead down from the woods, through the streets of the village, and back up into the woods.

In February the dreams and nightmares that had been incubating in the long winter nights finally hatched. The Gentiles woke from their hibernation, transformed by costumes and masks into mythological and legendary figures, and the town erupted into Carnival. While Venus, Charon, Faust, Don Juan, Mephistopheles, Hans Wurst, and Father Rhine paraded through the streets, inside Jewish homes biblical characters danced from room to room. The story of Esther was read from the Megillah. Young folk dressed to look their parts acted out the roles of Esther, Mordecai, King Ahasuerus, and Haman. A Rhenish David might slay Goliath before his appreciative parents. Men and women, to whoops and giggles, strutted about in one another's clothes. Everyone got drunk.

But the festival, as happy and boisterous as it was, rarely spilled beyond the limits of the Jewish community.

It must have seemed at best a merry retreat, an almost secret celebration, to a Jewish child living in a world where on Gentile holidays whole towns exploded into mirth. And there was no escaping the comparison. "I scarcely know of a single afternoon's walk in which I did not encounter some festive throng adorned with flags and flowers, and joyously wending their way through . . . the villages in obedience to some time-honored custom," a visitor to the region wrote about the Germans' addiction to holidays. "On these gala occasions the houses are literally flaming with flags and banners; the air resounds to the varied strains of vocal and instrumental music; pavilions with whirling horses, cake-stalls, beer-saloons, gardens; streets and windows seem absolutely to swarm with the brightest, happiest faces ever gathered together in any country upon earth; and the most fantastic tricks that ever were played before high Heaven became the great business of life." Of Gentile life.

The Jews sat in their homes waiting for the merriment, like a summer storm, to pass. A Jewish child like August Belmont, no longer cloistered behind ghetto walls, peering out at the rest of the world having fun, might reward himself for being excluded from the Gentile merrymaking by feeling special; and feeling special, he could easily grow up convinced he could do something extraordinary.

CHAPTER TWO

IN APRIL 1819, when August was almost five and a half years old, his mother gave birth to a girl she and Simon called Elizabeth, nicknamed Babette. Fourteen months later Frederika had another child, a boy they named Joseph. The house on St. George Street no longer seemed so lonely. Then, on June 9, 1821, at two o'clock in the morning, Frederika died. Joseph outlived her by one month.

Nine months after Frederika's death Simon brought August, now eight years old, to Frankfurt to leave him with his grandmother, Gertrude. August could get a better education in Frankfurt than in Alzey. Besides, Gertrude's husband, Hajum Hanau, was still connected to the Rothschild family, whose banking business had expanded into an empire. Rothschild brothers were established in London, Paris, Vienna, and, as of that year,

Naples. Four years earlier Prince Metternich's secretary had called the Rothschilds the richest people in Europe. Not only had the family been given a coat of arms in 1817, but within a year of August's arrival in Frankfurt the Emperor of Austria would make the five Rothschild brothers barons. August would grow up in an atmosphere that could help both his future career and Simon's current business.

The carriage ride from Alzey to Frankfurt was a jouncing trip along rutted roads and through villages that were busy in the spring weather with the familiar rustic life August was leaving behind. The moving blue and white spots on the hillside were workers trimming the vines. In far-off fields farmers and cows pantomimed plowing. Along the roadside boys who were not being carted off to live in a city wandered, playing like Rhenish fauns on pipes made of bark.

On the outskirts of Frankfurt the carriage passed apple orchards and mulberry trees. Coaches, wagons, people on horseback, traveling to and from the city, crowded the raised road, which was hemmed in on either side by stone walls. Along the paths beside the highway walked beggars with staffs, peddlers with packs, farmers, tinkers, and wandering madmen. The closer to the city, the more jammed the road and the paths became.

As the Main approached Frankfurt the green water turned dirty. Horses carrying wet riders trudged up the middle of the river, dragging flat barges parallel to the shore. On the slopes along the other bank of the Main were villas larger and more extravagant than any in Alzey.

Frankfurt was ringed by gardens that, instead of being cultivated for crops, were devoted to flowers—huge, carefully tended areas having no purpose other than to please. People dressed in the most elegant outfits sauntered among the budding plots or lounged on the benches. Beyond the gardens, within the city itself, the carriage jolted along streets that were so narrow in some places they seemed to be tunnels because of the gables looming overhead. Gaudily decorated booths sold things from all over the world: cotton from Manchester, Meissen china, Viennese pipes, Lyon silk. Whips cracked; and as aristocrats' coaches racketed past, caught for a moment in the coaches' windows were tableaux of men, women, and children so perfectly composed they seemed to exist in another world, a world without barnyard smells, without drudgery, without pain, without death.

Everything moved so fast in this city; everybody was hurrying—and talking in languages August had never heard: Italian, Polish, Russian, Bohemian, English. So much babble; so many people. "The city itself is generally old," wrote an English visitor to Frankfurt in the early nineteenth century; "much of it is crazy.

"Of the fifty thousand inhabitants who form the population of Frankfurt, about seven thousand are Jews," he continued.

> They inhabit chiefly a quarter of the town, which, though no longer walled in, as it once was, to separate them from the rest of the community, repels the Christian intruder, at every step, with filth much too disgusting to be particularized. In the driving of their traffic they are as importunate as Italian beggars. Laying in wait in his little dark shop, or little tattered booth, or, if these be buried in some obscure and sickening alley, prowling at the corner where it joins some more frequented street, the Jew darts out on every passenger of promise. . . . Unless thrown off at once, he sticks to you through half a street, whispering the praises of his wares mingled with your own; for, curving the spare, insignificant body into obsequiousness, and throwing into the twinkling gray eye as much condescension as its keenly expressed love of gain will admit, he conducts the whole oration as if he were sacrificing himself to do you a favor of which nobody must know. When all the usual recommendations of great bargains fail, he generally finishes the climax with "On my soul and conscience, Sir, they are genuine smuggled goods."

August, having grown up in one of the wealthiest families, Jew or Gentile, in Alzey, son of a proud modern owner of a freehold estate, must have found the poor Jewish quarter of Frankfurt as alien as the English traveler had. Those things that were not strange because they were mean were undoubtedly strange because they were grand. Unlike the simple synagogue in Alzey, Frankfurt's synagogue was splendid. "What first strikes the eye, on entering," wrote another English traveler, who visited Frankfurt a few years after August had arrived, "is the immense multitude of lights—innumerable gilt chandeliers, each one with innumerable branches, were suspended from the roof by richly-wrought iron chains."

During the first weeks in his grandmother's house in Frankfurt, August must have felt lonely and confused and wistful for a world that probably seemed, the longer he was away, more and more ideal. But he had been sent to the city to get a good education; he could not return to live in Alzey for many years. Since he couldn't go back, he would have to find that ideal world somewhere else. He would have to create it for himself—just as the rich people riding through town in their private carriages, protected by their flawless grace within their perfect tableaux, seemed to have done.

Before returning to Alzey, Simon had enrolled August in the *Philanthropin*, a Jewish school run by Dr. Michael Hess, an admirer of Voltaire and the Encyclopedists, a progressive who had opened his classes to Christian children in 1811 in an attempt at integrating the cultures to eliminate prejudice. Like a number of liberal Jewish parents who sent their children to Dr. Hess's school, Simon thought the Hebrew lessons were useless exercises. August could have had sufficient religious training in Alzey. But the Bible was a work of literature as well as a holy book, and Dr. Hess wanted his students to be able to read it in Hebrew. He was obviously not bound by the old orthodoxy. The school did not teach the Talmud, and the Sabbath "Hour of Devotion" was nonsectarian. Both Jews and Christians attended, and the sermons were not religious worship but ethical instruction.

Although August was untidy, ungovernable, and rowdy, he was—Dr. Hess observed—very bright. If he seemed at times savage compared to his classmates, he had after all grown up in a provincial village, not a cosmopolitan city like Frankfurt. He also had for a model a mulish, contentious, litigious father who refused to pay his bills. Simon had agreed to the yearly tuition of 60 florins, but school expenses kept increasing. August had been promoted to a higher form, he was eating dinner at the *Philanthropin,* and by 1825 his annual bill was 200 florins. He also had asked Dr. Hess to give him private lessons in Latin.

Simon balked. The bumper crops of the past few seasons had sent produce prices tumbling. No one was paying the 5 percent interest on his loan. Even Alzey's gentry, who were deeply in debt to Simon, were trying to sell their castle, not for the 50,000 florins it was worth but for only 20,000 florins. Money was so tight by 1828 that although Simon had relented, allowing August a weekly allowance of 10 kronen "if he uses it well," he had objected to the 16 florins a month August wanted to spend on lessons in yet another language, English.

Simon couldn't understand what attracted his son to all these foreign tongues. Eventually, if August settled down and stopped being so wild, which Simon sometimes doubted, the boy would return to Alzey to take over the family business. Even if August established himself in Frankfurt, Simon wasn't convinced he'd need to speak anything quite as exotic as English.

"Your insistence on this issue borders on the absurd," Simon wrote his son. Then, typically backing off, mollifying and temporizing, he added, "At any rate, there's no rush. I want to check into this and do what's best."

If the 16 florins for English lessons irked Simon, the 200 florins for tuition infuriated him. He could not even consider drawing on his capital in such economically ticklish times. As his half-brother, Isaac Hanau, owed him 1,800 florins, Simon asked him to pay the school. Isaac couldn't or wouldn't. Dr. Hess stopped August's private Latin lessons and canceled his dinner privileges. Intending to sue Simon if need be, Dr. Hess engaged Dr. Jacob Demburg, a lawyer Simon had used to prosecute many of his own suits. Dr. Demberg pressed Simon for the tuition as diligently as he pressed Simon's debtors for their late 5 percent interest. Simon gave notice at the *Philanthropin*. In the summer of 1828, when August was fourteen years old, he was dragged from school before he even had a chance to take his final exams.

During his seven years at the *Philanthropin,* August rarely returned to Alzey. When he did, the visits were short. Alzey must have seemed a sleepy, backward place to August now: the hand-packed lumps of cheese sitting on the windowsills, like rows of soft eggs, to dry; the greenish-yellow glowworms floating through the twilight; the geese gabbling under-foot and stinking up the town with their droppings; everything bucolic—and a little dull compared to life in Frankfurt. Although when he was away from Alzey, August may have been homesick for the town in which he had been born, he could never settle there.

He also had grown away from his father. He resented Simon's stinginess, undoubtedly was embarrassed by the fight over his tuition, and must have known that his father suspected he was becoming a spendthrift or, worse, a good-for-nothing like his uncle, Aaron, who now called himself Joseph Florian. There was bad blood in the family. August could have inherited some.

But if August had been difficult at school, perhaps he'd been forced to keep up a tough front to shield himself from classmates who may have known that his father wasn't willing to pay his tuition. Now he was out of school. His grandmother Gertrude got him a job with her husband's relations, the Rothschilds. Although August was only sweeping floors, polishing furniture, and running errands, it was a chance to make a fresh start. He was determined to succeed.

He was neat. He was punctual. In September 1828, a few weeks after beginning work, he wrote to his father, "I thank you very much for the sound advice and the admonitions you were kind enough to give me, and I shall try to comply with your wishes and thereby gain the satisfaction of my dear grandmother and my uncle [Isaac Hanau] as well as that of my employers."

Proudly he added, "Until now I have done rather well at the office." And he informed his father, "In addition to English lessons, I have made arrangements for arithmetic and writing" lessons. "Now, I am trying to find two fellow-students—I've already found one—to join me in French lessons. Thus," he concluded a little archly, "I shall comply with the orders of Baron Carl von Rothschild, who recommended I take the above-mentioned classes."

His father could object to his taking English when he was at Dr. Hess's *Philanthropin,* but he couldn't disagree with Carl von Rothschild, especially not when he himself was asking August to deliver letters about certain business matters to the Baron.

In October, August's grandmother died. August grieved, but he knew "if there really is reward and punishment after death (which we must not doubt), she will surely receive the rewards which she so fully deserves."

Although he was only a month from his fifteenth birthday, August in consoling his father sounded more like an older brother than a son. "Surely, it is a hard fate to lose one's mother," he wrote. "But, on the other hand, you must be comforted by the thought that in us she did not leave any forsaken and defenseless orphans."

He was in a way declaring himself a man. He could do no less. He was estranged from his father; he had lost his grandmother; his uncle Isaac was seriously ill. He was no longer a schoolboy. He couldn't afford a schoolboy's childishness.

In the office Amschel von Rothschild, oldest of the five famous brothers and head of the Frankfurt branch of the House of Rothschild, sat in the open on a raised platform, doing business in front of his clerks and secretaries, who scribbled and scuttled at his feet. August watched and listened.

He kept to his schedule: up at five o'clock in the morning; twice a week trudging across town in painfully tight boots—he could not afford a new larger pair—to get to his French lesson; into the Rothschild's office in the Fahrgasse, where during the summer he sweated in his heavy winter pants. "I beg you," he wrote his father, "be kind enough and send me by return mail two ducats. For these I shall have two pairs of light trousers made immediately as I am *really in great need* of them." Hoping to please his father enough to ease the money from him and to remind him that he worked in an international banking firm where suitable attire could be a good business investment, he added, "In order to save postage, will you be kind enough to address your letters to me in care of Messrs. A. Rothschild and Sons, without post-paying them."

In his unseasonable trousers August was not a very fashionable figure. He tended to keep to himself, staying in with Isaac Hanau when he was not at work or at classes. "During the Whitsun Holidays," he wrote, "I was home almost all the time and went out only once to take a walk on the Promenade" where folks strolled, showing off their holiday clothes.

He had neither time nor money to waste on weekend trips to the local resorts. On the occasional lonely Sundays he spent in the public gardens, he must have felt as he had years before in Alzey, when he used to watch the Gentile children frolicking on their holidays. He developed no lasting friendships with boys his own age. The youths he had gone to school with were, most of them, still studying at the *Philanthropin*. Cliquish as adolescents are, they undoubtedly did not want to spend time with a former schoolmate who because of circumstance could no longer be really part of their crowd. And August, already involved in the adult world of business, probably felt superior to his old classmates who were still confined in school. He had no romantic life. He did not have many chances to associate with girls he could have pursued; and he may have been too proud and ambitious to settle for those whom Frankfurt's matchmakers may have been suggesting to his uncle and his father.

In the winter the Main froze. Instead of partying in the public gardens, Frankfurt weekended on the ice. "Boys and girls, big and little, young men and old men, were flying over the crystal element in full glee," wrote an American visitor. "Smart buckish gentlemen were pushing before them ponderous old ladies who were seated in sledges or sliding-chairs. Pretty blooming damsels of vigorous form were flying hither and thither, laughing and joking with amazing zest. Whole schools of students were turned out to enjoy the exercise, with their teachers leading the way."

Men's long blue cloaks flipped in the wind, flashing crimson linings. Grinning exhausted skaters climbed into their coaches and bundled under deer- , wolf- , bear- , and foxskins. August couldn't even spare the few kreutzers' admission to the ice. Watching other young men and women flirting and playing, he may have determined that someday he would not only join in the fun but he would lead it.

Winter ended. The thaw came. Icicles dripped and shrank away or clattered to the ground. Snow loosened by mild breezes slipped in large chunks from roofs. The streets were slushy. August's tight boots got wet, dried stiff, and felt tighter.

August sent to his father the bits of international gossip he picked up at the office. "The riots at Hamburg, which for the most part were started against the Jews by the rabble, have ended," he wrote. "At Dresden, too, the masses demolished the town hall and the police headquarters and also burned the archives. . . . Also at Chemnitz, an industrial town in Saxony, the workers set fire to several factory buildings and destroyed the machinery. There are rumors all over that the King of Saxony, taking into consideration the dangerous situation, has abdicated in favor of his brother."

The July Revolution of 1830 in Paris had triggered insurrections across the Continent from Belgium to Poland. The Hapsburg rulers in Italy had to escape to Vienna. In Frankfurt the high cost of bread and meat was causing unrest. August walked through streets patrolled by both the army and detachments of citizen volunteers. He read the manifestos and political cartoons that had been posted by the rebels. He thought it "would be a great boon for the people" if the government would not just reduce but suspend the tolls, which were helping to force prices up. But if he was understanding of the reasons for the rebellion, he was not sympathetic to revolt.

"Thank God," he wrote Simon, "real calm is reigning here, and it doesn't look like it will be disturbed by anything."

He continued to learn from Amschel von Rothschild how the behemoth shiftings of the governments affected the finely calibrated fluctuations of the financial markets. If "Prussia and Austria recognized Philip I," he thought, that would have "a very good effect on government bonds." If the French Chamber of Deputies "by-passed the Duke of Bordeaux and . . . elected the Duke of Orleans king," that would cause "securities to go up." On occasion he worked all night at the office. His diligence paid off. In 1832 he was made a confidential clerk, a position that allowed him to examine in even more detail the alchemic mysteries of high finance. In 1833 he was sent on a mission to Naples. A year later he was promoted to private secretary.

August bought fashionable clothes now: blue coats with velvet collars, marcella waistcoats, white, close-fitting trousers made of elasticized cloth, coats frogged and braided like uniforms, Cossack trousers, fur-collared overcoats snug at the waist and flaring out below, silver stickpins, voluminous cravats, and silk top hats.

Now on Sundays when he walked in the public gardens and saw people guzzling beer or gorging on cheese, brown bread, and handfuls of nuts, he was an alien among them, not because he couldn't afford to join them, but because with the Rothschilds as models he felt superior. So much more was possible in life than being a good burgher who worked hard during the week and got red-faced and drunk on his Sunday outings.

He traveled to Paris and Rome. He visited art galleries, went to plays and concerts, glimpsed life in the great salons, and sampled unusual food, all the while schooling himself in the flatteries that lubricated business transactions and the courtesies that, like the epicycles in Ptolemaic cosmology, made up the complex universe of money and power he was exploring.

In Italy he spoke his newly acquired Italian; in France he learned French. He cultivated himself with as much care as his father worked the fields in Alzey. His future self—his intelligence, his business sense, his bearing—was the product he would market. As his father became more a gentleman farmer August became more a gentleman. He could never return to Alzey and settle with Simon on the family freehold. Land may have been a means of bettering oneself in earlier generations; but in this new world of international finance the intangibles—the profits you could conjure from the currencies, which seemed to exist in ledgers only as Platonic ideas, pure and ideal realities—were more important than the tangible produce his father and grandfather and great-grandfather had traded in Bingen and Worms.

The world was changing. People were even flying through the air. In 1836 the three Englishmen who had taken off in a balloon from Vauxhall Gardens in London had floated over the English Channel and landed just thirty miles from Frankfurt. The world beyond Alzey—beyond Frankfurt —was exciting. August, like the balloonists sailing higher and higher over Europe, rose through society to the stratosphere where Rothschilds drank the best wine, ate the finest foods, gave the most opulent balls, raced the fastest horses, bought the most exquisite paintings, and mingled with kings.

As August rode in a coach through the streets of Frankfurt, finally perfectly poised in his own tableau, glancing out at the people he passed who were going about their humdrum lives, it must have seemed a little as it had been in Alzey on the Jewish Sabbath, when he would feel special because his family was not working on a day almost everyone else in the village was.

In 1837 the Rothschilds asked August to go to Havana to investigate how the Cuban economy—and certain Rothschild interests—were being affected by the civil war being fought in Spain. In February, August confided to Babette, "I am planning to visit you this month or next to bid you farewell for a while. Probably, my dear little sister, you're startled by this news, but it can't be helped. In a month, I leave for the Americas."

CHAPTER THREE

AUGUST, only twenty-three years old, arrived in New York City, where he was to change ships, on Sunday evening, May 14, 1837. From the harbor the city was a shadowy silhouette, a ragged outline of chimneys and steeples, of three- , four- , five- , and six-story buildings beyond the masts on the many ships riding at anchor. The night wind carried the clank of turning capstans, the ringing of ships' bells, the voices of sailors singing chanteys, and the hollow snap of canvas buckling in the breeze.

But the city itself seemed oddly quiet, even for a Sunday night. Along the docks there was little activity. In town the people abroad on the streets seemed subdued, like mourners at a funeral or citizens of a city suffering from plague.

On Monday morning the banks were closed. Shops were doing little or no business. Some streets were deserted, others nearly so. A carriage clattered past, a porter loitered next to his wheelbarrow. A ragman pushed a cart, his bells tinkling in the eerie stillness. A few pigs rooted out rotten onions or split apples from the muck in the gutters before trotting up Broadway. Frowning businessmen "pass and repass" with "hurried steps, care-worn faces, rapid exchanges of salutation," according to the British novelist Frederick Marryat, who was visiting New York when August arrived. "Here two or three are gathered on one side, whispering and watching that they are not overheard; there a solitary, with his arms folded and his hat slouched, brooding. . . . Mechanics . . . are pacing up and down with the air of famished wolves."

The week before, the Panic had started. The boom in land, securities, and cotton speculation had collapsed. All year the country had been suffering from tightening credit, rising unemployment, and inflation. Coal mines in Pennsylvania had closed. There would be no fuel for next winter. People talked of revolution and civil war. In February on a freezing, blustery day a New York mob broke into two shops and dumped hundreds of barrels of flour and wheat into the streets. When the mayor tried to stop them with a speech, he was pelted with flour, wheat, dirt, and stones. He finally had to call out the military to stop the riot.

Radicals accused businessmen of hoarding goods to drive up prices, but businesses were failing. "So they go—smash, crash," wrote a young New Yorker in his diary early in April. "Where in the name of wonder is there to be an end to it? Near 250 failures so far."

On Wednesday, May 4, the president of the Merchants' Bank was found in his bed dead of apoplexy. The rumor was he had committed suicide. On Thursday twenty more businesses failed. Early Friday morning a crowd gathered in front of the Dry Dock Bank, waiting for the doors to open so they could get their money. By Monday there was a general run on all the banks in New York City. People jammed toward the tellers, shouting, "Pay! Pay!" In two days $1,200,000 was withdrawn from the banks, which had to stay open until nine o'clock at night to take care of their angry customers. By Friday the banks would be broke; so, on the Wednesday before August landed in New York, they suspended specie payments.

August went to Wall Street to find out what was happening from the Rothschilds' American agents, J. L. and S. I. Joseph & Co.; but J. L. and S. I. Joseph & Co. no longer existed. Not only had they gone out of business on March 17, with liabilities of $7 million, but earlier in that same week at one fifteen in the morning their new, still unfinished office building, which was renting space at exorbitant rates, caved in. The crash of falling granite, a physical hint of what would soon happen to the economy, shook every building on Wall Street.

It took almost a month to cross the Atlantic. If August were to wait for instructions from his employers about what to do with their American interests, he might not get word for weeks.

He canceled his Havana trip, and for two days and two nights—only taking time out at one o'clock Tuesday morning to jot a quick note to his sister telling her he had arrived safely—he worked on a report to send to the Rothschilds. Someone had to replace the Josephs. Gambling on his employers' approval, August rented a small room at 78 Wall Street, where he established August Belmont & Company. If the gamble failed, he might be out of a job in a foreign country, which was in the midst of a crash. But if it succeeded, if the Rothschilds sanctioned what he had done, he would no longer be a private secretary. He would be a merchant banker, the Rothschilds' American agent—in a new city, where no one knew his history. He would no longer be the boy from Alzey who had grown up in his grandmother's house in Frankfurt and gone to work as an apprentice for the Rothschilds. He could not re-create himself—he already had done that to a great extent in his years as a private secretary— but he could settle in a world where the self he had created, the August Belmont who was an intimate of the Rothschilds, a fashionable young man, a connoisseur of food and wine, was the only self anyone had ever known. Years later gossips would accuse August of having misrepresented who he was and where he had come from; but he never lied about his origins. If when he first arrived in New York he was a little mysterious, it was because he was trying to escape not his past but its isolation.

August's first week in New York was a succession of cloudy, rainy, humid, and unseasonably cool days, all so gloomy that when it finally cleared on Saturday, a Columbia College student jotted in his diary, "Miraculous! A clear day! And a glorious one too." But in the afternoon "it clouded up very quickly and blew hard for a minute or so with a drop or two of rain . . . then cleared off as quickly with the most beautiful rainbow I ever saw, a perfect arch from horizon to horizon—well defined and bright throughout and the brighter from the black clouds on which it was relieved."

The changeable weather, which even New Yorkers were finding extreme, must have made the country seem to August as surprising and odd as it was rumored in Germany to be, a quicksilver world as volatile as the people who inhabited it. While Americans were not quite the "uncivilized race" that some Germans assumed they were, they may have seemed to fit their stereotype of having a "prodigal disregard of money," even in the midst of a financial crisis.

After the first shocks of fear, greed, and panic, people adapted to the disaster. "Public amusements are going on as usual," said a New Yorker at the time of the crash. "Our merchants are certainly the most extraordinary people in the world; and, if every other resource were to fail them, would not hesitate one moment, instead of payment, to take and offer drafts payable in the moon. That's what I call the genius of a mercantile community."

Because all coins had disappeared from circulation once the banks had stopped specie payments, trade was carried out in the lunar economics of barter and promises. "Go to the theater and places of public amusement, and, instead of change, you receive an I.O.U.," wrote Marryat. "At the hotels and oyster-cellars it is the same thing. Call for a glass of brandy and water and the change is fifteen tickets, each 'good for one glass of brandy and water.' At an oyster shop, eat a plate of oysters, and you have in return seven tickets, good for one plate of oysters each. It is the same everywhere—The barbers give you tickets, good for so many shaves; and were there beggars in the streets, I presume they would give you tickets in change, good for so much philanthropy."

Stores issued their own scrip, which everyone called "shin-plasters." One young man Marryat described delighted in the crash. He had a twenty-dollar bill no one could—or would—break. Everyone gave him credit. To pay for his rent, meals, and amusements, he flashed his bank note. He was a rich man on twenty dollars.

With credit being given so casually, anyone who had solid money behind him could become wealthy simply by doing what August's father had done in Alzey. A storekeeper who needed money would sell the debts his customers owed him for much less than they were worth. When the economy picked up, the new owner of the debts could collect full—or almost full—payment. Or foreclose and take property instead.

But even that, as lucrative as it could be, was small-time wheeling and dealing compared to what August could do backed by the Rothschilds' wealth and reputation. "Seven-eighths of all business firms in the States have gone into bankruptcy," August wrote to Babette. "This pitiful condition preoccupies me very much and absorbs all my attention, time, and strength."

The boom and subsequent collapse of the economy ended the casual way banking and securities trading had been carried out in New York City. "The banks had offices fitted up with the simple appointments needed for the transaction of a moderate business," a New Yorker who was a teen-ager in the early 1830s remembered.

> The few clerks employed had abundant yawning time between breakfast and dinner. . . . The paying teller . . . generally found leisure for a friendly chat with his customers. . . . Business transactions were then conducted in a slow and cautious manner; men laid their plans ahead, so that the cashier was not infrequently

applied to for the promise of a discount at some distant day. . . . Few individuals came into the market with private European bills of exchange. . . . The few brokers who congregated in Wall Street had desks in basement rooms. . . . In the windows of two or three of the most prominent of these basements were to be seen packages of the bills of country banks. . . . This wild-cat money was procured by the brokers at a stipulated rate of discount, and resold by them at a slight advantage to mechanics and manufacturers, who . . . paid it out at par to their employees. Small stacks of foreign and domestic coin lay side by side with these paper tokens, and these jointly represented the stock in trade; in other words, the window sill held the entire capital of the concern.

Using Rothschild credit August could buy at severely depressed rates these wildcat, privately issued banknotes as well as securities, commodities, and property. Building-lots in the city, for example, were selling for about a tenth of their previous prices. Using the modern international banking techniques learned from the Rothschilds, August could shift money and commodities from market to market, from country to country, buying and selling in increasingly complex spirals of credit—cotton to England, cloth to America—until the commodities became not physical goods but merely representations of money, and the money became not physical cash, or even the core of credit, but an idea, an idealized counter in a mental exercise, a game that created a system of relationships: New Orleans, where the cotton is sold, is connected—via Manchester, where the cotton is spun into cloth—to New York, where the cloth is bought.

After a while even the relationships themselves became secondary to their movement and play. Multiplying branches diverged and intersected and sent off multiplying branches of their own. The money paid to a sailor for his part in shipping cotton to England was splurged on a rum binge in Liverpool. The money paid to the Liverpool barkeep was used to replenish his rum stock. The money paid to the Jamaican-rum distiller was spent on a new cotton shirt. International finance was a web connecting field workers in Alabama, sailors in New York, barkeeps in Liverpool, distillers in the West Indies, and mill workers in Manchester, a web connecting finally everyone to everyone else, a Jack-built house kept stable by faith in the system.

And the world had faith in the Rothschilds. There was no way that August, one of the few men in New York in the late 1830s who had mastered the mechanics of this new international finance, could fail in his speculations—as long as the Rothschilds supported his enterprise.

Every month there were only three sailings each of the London and Liverpool packet boats. August, exhilarated and tense, must have waited anxiously for the boat bringing the Rothschilds' decision. The letter finally came. The Rothschilds gave August Belmont & Company their blessing and August a $10,000-a-year salary, a fortune in a busted town.

The New York August adopted was a seaport packed into the bottom sixth of Manhattan Island, a city with a population of about 300,000, six times larger than that of Frankfurt. It extended from the Battery in the south all the way up to the newly developed Twenty-third Street in the north. Broadway, New York's major thoroughfare, a street averaging eighty feet in width, ran the length of the city, about three miles.

The Battery, a park at the toe of the island, was more modest than the gardens surrounding Frankfurt but was pleasantly laid out, with a promenade along the seawall and graveled paths and grassy plots bordered by trees whose trunks were protected by collars made of vertical wooden slats. The oaks, elms, and planes cast moving shadows, like the shadows of hands passing back and forth in front of a magic lantern, on strolling couples, who occasionally paused in the green darkness of the low bowers before emerging again into the flickering sunlight.

Although by 1837 the Battery was no longer a fashionable haunt of New York's best families, on hot summer days it was one of the most comfortable spots in the city. Crowds chatting in French and German as well as in dozens of English and American accents ambled along the promenade overlooking the harbor, where small market-boats and local steamers and ships with sails bellying out crossed back and forth, going up and down the North and East rivers and out into the Bay toward the Narrows and the ocean. "A more beautiful sight can hardly be imagined than the dawn breaking with possibly two or three of these magnificent packet ships in sight of each other at once and a mid-ocean race as a natural sequence," a reporter for the *New York Mirror* wrote at the time. "The sun bursts through the morning mists tinging the clouds with gold. Dancing white caps fleck the dark blue waters. . . . The graceful yachtlike hulls . . . send a spume of foam athwart their bows."

In Castle Garden, a semicircular former fortress that sat out in the harbor, people attended concerts, walked in the yard that had been planted with flowers and shrubs, and bought ice cream, lemonade, and sponge cake in its restaurant.

A German nobleman who walked on Broadway along the few blocks between the Battery and Wall Street one summer morning described "the sun's lurid glare, produced by a thick heavy mist—the usual companion of a sultry day in America—gave to the sleeping city the appearance of a general conflagration." His comparison no doubt was sparked by the great fire of 1835, which had destroyed seventeen blocks, about twenty acres, in the Wall Street area. The blaze, ignited by a gas-pipe explosion, burned from nine o'clock in the evening, December 17, until late the following day. At night, people as far away as New Haven reported seeing the red glow in the sky caused by the flames. By 1837 the ruined neighborhood was almost entirely restored.

Visitors to New York at the time repeatedly mentioned how new everything was and how odd this newness seemed. Everywhere in the city, especially around Twenty-third Street, where the city was expanding into the fields and farms and suburbs, buildings were going up—or rather, because of the crash, were standing half-finished. In fact, the whole city seemed half-finished, waiting for someone to come along and guide its growth, give it shape. It was not like Frankfurt, an old city that, suffering from a kind of municipal arthritis, found it hard to move, difficult to change. Even New Yorkers, particularly the old Knickerbockers, found this passion for progress remarkable. "The whole of New York is rebuilt about once in ten years," one of the city's former mayors, Philip Hone, wrote in his diary in the late 1830s. In order to grow, the city was destroying its past.

Along Broadway were chandlers' shops, hotels, warehouses, and stores, their windows filled with bolts of calico, cotton, Italian and French silks, Chinese and Indian satins, boots, pianos, parasols, imported toys, preserves in brandy, and coffins of various sizes, seven feet to two feet, that stood along the walls face-to-face, like pieces of a macabre chess set waiting to be deployed on a board. Although most people took their meals at home, a growing number of restaurants and chophouses, "the creations . . . of a foreign element in the city," according to a Knickerbocker of the time, were catering to businessmen, politicians, actors, journalists, and travelers. In the clatter of dishes and clicking of knives and forks, customers bolted their food without pausing to talk to their companions. Boys taking orders, a Scottish visitor recalled, "were gliding up and down, and across the passage" in a restaurant, "inclining their heads for an instant, first to one booth, then to another, and receiving the whispered wishes of the company, which they straightway bawled out in a loud voice." Waiters hurried back and forth bringing plates piled with food and retrieving empty greasy ones, which as they grabbed them trailed trickles of gravy or clear bloody juice from roast beef cooked rare—a novelty popularized in New York by restaurants like Clark and Brown on Maiden Lane.

All along the street were oyster stalls and, down a few steps in dim, briny-smelling basements, oyster cellars like the famous one at 5 Broad Street, Downings', where politicians gobbled phlegm-colored slippery saddle rocks and bluepoints. New York burned with an oyster passion, and New Yorkers bragged they had twenty ways of cooking them— although Philadephians claimed they had twenty-one. Everyone ate oysters, and sometimes it seemed as though everyone sold them. If there were no cellars or stalls around, all you had to do was wait. In a few moments a cart would rattle up, well supplied with oysters, biscuits, pepper, and ginger beer.

In front of the shops, over the sidewalks, ran galleries, some open to the sky, others shaded by awnings. From the crossbeams and pillars hung advertisements on fluttering colored papers and placards flapping in the breeze. Shopkeepers leaned against the pillars and loitered in their door-ways. An Englishman who considered settling in America found them cold and indifferent. While he did not disapprove of their independence, he did not like their style. They kept their hats on indoors and "sit or lie along their counters, smoking segars, and spitting in every direction."

In the streets among the pigs and chickens, porters wearing on their chests brass plates inscribed with their license numbers wheeled handcarts through the horse-drawn traffic. Boys hawked penny news-papers. Over their shoulders milkmen balanced yokes with buckets dan-gling from both ends. They trudged from house to house, calling out a cry that over the years had been transformed from "Milk, ho!" into a word-less musical shout. Bakers, breadbaskets perched on shoulders, jostled through the crowds announcing, "Bread, bread." Every peddler had his own street song: "Sweet potatoes, Carolina potatoes," "Here's your fine ripe watermelons," "Pineapples, fine pineapples," "Hot corn, hot corn," "Fine, ripe strawberries," "Clams, clams, clams, here's your Rockaway Beach clams, here's your fine sand clams."

"Was there ever such a sunny street as this Broadway?" Charles Dickens wrote after his American trip a few years later.

> The pavement stones are polished with the tread of feet until they shine again; the red bricks of the houses might be yet in the dry, hot kilns; and the roofs of those omnibuses look as though, if water were poured on them, they would hiss and smoke. . . .

No stint of omnibuses here! Half-a-dozen have gone by within as many minutes. Plenty of hackney cabs and coaches too; gigs, phaetons, large-wheeled tilburies, and private carriages. . . . Negro coachmen and white; in straw hats, black hats, white hats, glazed caps, fur caps; in coats of drab, black, brown, green, blue, nankeen, striped jean and linen.

Pedestrians moved to and fro along the sidewalks, crossing and crisscrossing the busy streets, stepping around pigs and dogs, pausing for the icemen who passed carrying blocks of ice with pieces of straw sticking to the melting surfaces. Men in black coats and top hats. Women in bright, rustling skirts. "Heaven save the ladies," Dickens wrote, "how they dress! We have seen more colors in these ten minutes, than we should have seen elsewhere, in as many days. What various parasols! what rainbow silks and satins! what pinking of thin stockings, and pinching of thin shoes, and fluttering of ribbons and silk tassels, and display of rich cloaks with gaudy hoods and linings."

A block north of Wall Street on the west side of Broadway stood the City Hotel, for years considered not only the best hotel in New York but the best in the United States. Businessmen from the area would briefly interrupt their work to eat in the plain, light, airy dining room and gulp a glass of port, Madeira, or sherry from what was thought to be the best wine cellar in the city—a cellar that, lacking French and German wines, Europeans like August found woefully incomplete.

Half a dozen blocks up Broadway from the City Hotel was the new Astor House, a hotel six stories high, a gigantic labyrinth with six hundred beds. Next to it was the City Hall Park. In the surrounding streets many of the city's best families owned homes, modest three- and four-story houses with front stoops. Park Place, Beekman Street, Barclay, Chambers, Warren, Murray. This was where August wanted to live. This was the world he wanted to enter. In exploring the neighborhood, August, like other newcomers, probably wandered into the City Hall and found, as the British novelist Marryat had, a large room filled with "interesting pictures and busts of the Presidents, mayors of the city, and naval and military officers, who have received the thanks of Congress and the freedom of the city." These were the people August's new country honored. These were the first among the first citizens. The most striking portrait, "the most spirited," according to Marryat, was that of Commodore Oliver Hazard Perry, who had become a hero at the Battle of Lake Erie the year August was born. The Perry family had the kind of position in society August wanted.

❧ *CHAPTER FOUR* ❧

AT FIRST August kept to himself. No one knew where he lived, although it was rumored he slept in the back of his office. He spent most of his time straightening out the Rothschilds' affairs, saving whatever could be saved from the mess left by the collapse of J. L. and S. I. Joseph & Co. and establishing his own firm on Wall Street. He had money to loan; people borrowed. He had money to invest; he bought. August Belmont and Company flourished.

Being the Rothschilds' American agent gave August clout in business but not in society. Not yet. Despite its size, energy, and growth New York was still a provincial Knickerbocker town. The old Dutch and English families, the Knickerbockers, were just discovering the fashionable life August had known in Europe as a private secretary of the Rothschilds. But the process of discovery was slow. The Knickerbockers tried the new styles with the hesitancy of a family bathing in a chilly late-May ocean: the youngsters rushed forward, stopped, retreated, rushed forward again; the older folks cautiously followed.

Some women were beginning to experiment with the colorful silks and satins that so impressed Dickens, but many still wore simple untrimmed dresses and "rag-like" shawls, which one not overly somber contemporary Knickerbocker later complained "completely concealed any charm of figure or grace of outline . . . a timid maiden might possess." Their bonnets, he thought, looked like coal-scuttles and acted as blinders. Their parasols, fringed with heavy silk that netted the dust kicked up by passing horses, were planted atop "ponderous ivory handles." They carried silk or embroidered velvet handbags and handkerchiefs "bordered with lace, the quality of which was supposed to definitely fix the financial status of the family." To advertise that status a woman held her handkerchief pinched at "its exact center between forefinger and thumb," a flag of fashion.

Knickerbocker men, he remembered, shied from any deviation in tradition and preferred to dress in black, which "was worn for promenade"—a walk up Broadway never continuing north of Bleeker Street, the boundary of a polite stroll—as well as for

> parlor, church, ball, and business. . . . No gentleman considered
> himself . . . presentable who was not attired in a high, black

beaver . . . which pressed like a vise on the head; a broad, black satin stock, so wide and unyielding that the ground could only be seen three paces to the front . . . ; a sharp-pointed, standing shirt collar . . . —no girl could kiss the wretched wearer without endangering her eyesight . . . ; a black frock coat, a marvel of disproportion and discomfort, . . . and black pantaloons, so tight . . . and so securely fastened by straps beneath the boot as to entirely destroy the free action of the knee. . . . This discomfort was materially enhanced by a pair of . . . boots, high-heeled, narrow, and pointed, which were only got into after a great deal of labor, assisted by boot-hooks and soap. Black gloves and a black cane about completed the costume.

Meals were simple, meat overcooked. Parties and balls were rare, masked balls virtually unknown. The Publicks occasionally given in the second-floor Ladies' Dining Room of the City Hotel were modest dances for the students of the Knickerbockers' dancing teacher, John Charruaud. Cotillions were tolerated; waltzing was distrusted.

"You see, sir, . . . our young ladies are very fond of dancing" explained a New Yorker in the mid-1830s; "and . . . , when once commencing, they are sure to go on the whole evening. Well, sir, they take a partner,—a young fellow who is quite as fond of dancing as they are,—and then they dance, or *waltz,* as you call it, round and round, until they both get as warm as possible; and then, sir—. . . Why, then they go into a cold room, or into the open air, and catch cold."

Most socializing was done at teas and evening at-homes. Private ballrooms were unheard of. Dancing was done—when it was done at all—in the parlors. Refreshments were modest—although one New Yorker who had been a young man in the 1830s found "The recollection of the ordeal . . . frightful even now. One hand was occupied in steadying a cup of boiling-hot tea or coffee, the other required to firmly grasp a plate piled with cake and sweetmeats, while close beside the bewildered beau sat a demure demoiselle expecting to be entertained with a limpid flow of conversation." By ten o'clock in the evening everyone would leave—often on foot, since most of the visitors lived in the same neighborhood. Only about two dozen families kept two-horse carriages. No one kept a four-horse coach. On the way home the partygoers would hear the hollow *tock-tock-tock* of the watchman—called a leatherhead because he wore a leather cap—hitting his club against the curb as the clocks tolled, before calling out the hour and assuring the Knickerbockers that "All is well."

The world of the Knickerbockers was small and safe. The children grew up together, went to school together, married each other, grew old together, and were buried in the same cemeteries. They shopped at the same stores, went to the same churches, followed the same routines, admired the same virtues (thrift, sobriety, industry, and modesty), condemned the same vices (idleness, luxury, recklessness, and ostentation), and shared the same opinions—from where in the pantry to put the tin spice-boxes (on the first shelf above the floor) to where one could find the best turtle soup (at Peter Bayard's near Battery Park on State Street).

At the two museums, Peale's and the American, opposite City Hall Park, Knickerbocker children goggled at wax criminals, ostrich eggs dangling from the ceilings, and mummies in sarcophagi. For amusement Knickerbocker parents went to the museums to hear lectures or to laugh at Yankee Hill imitating a Down Easter or Daddy Rice playing Jim Crow. The more sophisticated went to the Park Theater, just up Park Row from the American Museum, to see Charles Kean, Edmund Kean's son, play Hamlet, or to the Bowery Theater to see Junius Brutus Booth play Iago.

On warm afternoons young Knickerbocker men and women might saunter up Broadway the half-dozen blocks north of City Hall Park to Contoit's New York Garden, one of the few places a proper Knickerbocker couple could go without censure. Having entered the shady, cool, narrow café they would walk along the path between the green and white booths, nodding to friends and trying to ignore the June bugs that whirred into their faces from the leafy branches of the trees serving for a ceiling. Contoit's vanilla and lemon ice cream was famous throughout the city for its sweetness and thickness. For a quarter the waiter, in a white jacket and apron, would pour cognac into the dish on the sly. By the time the couple had finished their refreshments it would be twilight. Outside the Garden the gas streetlamps would be lit, and the orange-tipped blue flames would be casting fuzzy haloes around the lamps' octahedron-shaped glasses. With the souring taste of ice cream still in their mouths, the couple would go home.

The Knickerbockers felt comfortable in New York. It was their city. Its history was their history. Its customs were their customs. Even its eccentrics were their eccentrics—like the Gingerbread Man who prowled up and down Broadway, eating gingerbread that he kept in the pockets of his swallowtail coat, and the Lime Kiln Man, a gaunt specter who slept in a lime kiln by night and was found dead there one day. The Knickerbockers mingled and intermarried, at first because they were virtually the only culture in New York—and then because they weren't.

In the twenty years before August arrived in New York the city had tripled its population. Immigrants from Ireland and Germany swarmed into town bringing new customs—like Christmas-tree decorating, a novelty that arrived about the same time August did—and settling in pockets of poverty like Five Points, an area a few blocks northeast of City Hall Park. The streets there were covered in ankle-deep muck and reeked even worse than Broadway of rotting garbage. Ten-pin bowling alleys, dance cellars, gambling rooms, were crowded with both those who lived in the neighborhood and those who out of curiosity or compulsion were drawn to it. In the center of Five Points, New York's first true tenement, an old brewery stood on a lane appropriately named Murderers' Alley because a murder a day was committed in the vicinity.

This was a New York alien to the old Knickerbocker world. A few decades before, there had been almost no crime in the city. Travelers had remarked on the absence of even rowdiness. But by the late 1830s gangs like the Swamp Angels, the Roach Guards, the Dead Rabbits, and the Bowery Boys, most of them connected to volunteer fire companies, roamed up and down Bowery, the city's second major thoroughfare, the promenade of the poor.

The Knickerbockers, finding distinctions among the gangs as irrelevant as the gang members found distinctions among the Knickerbockers, called all young toughs Bowery Boys; and the Boys, with their hair close-cut in the back and long, curled with bear-grease, in the front; with their shiny flat black hats, their loose collars, their colorful satin or velvet vests, their long frock coats, and their flared pantslegs, flaunted a sense of style that fascinated young Knickerbocker men, who would sneak out to slum at fire-company dances in the Tammany Hall Ball-Room, where they often were chased into the streets. If there was no dance at the Tammany Hall Ball-Room, the young Knickerbocker men, bored by the decorous teas and at-homes, might risk a visit to the Apollo Ball-Room, a forbidden public dance hall a few blocks up Broadway from Contoit's New York Garden, at Canal Street, where they could flirt with dressmakers and milliners, who seemed more exciting than the polite Knickerbocker girls they were used to.

But the young Knickerbockers' fascination with the alien was not limited to New York's new foreign working-class world. From well-to-do immigrants like August they heard stories of the wondrously corrupt high-life of the European capitals. Imitating the worldly young Europeans who were arriving in New York, they began growing whiskers, dining not at the proper hour of noon but at three in the afternoon, and sporting London clothes and French manners.

"His air, gait, and voice are affected, the latter being almost screwed to a childish treble," said an American in the late 1830s, describing the new species of New York dandy; "his conversation is copiously sprinkled with foreign idioms, and he has the vanity of inviting the young ladies of his acquaintance to smell his hair, which he assures them is *scented with real Persian perfume!*"

The young Knickerbocker girls, also aware of the worlds beyond the small, stuffy Knickerbocker society of their parents, were mesmerized by the social whirls on the other side of the Atlantic Ocean and spellbound by the tales that August, having lived in the eddies of those whirls, could tell. "How our ladies' hearts beat when they think of Europe and its pleasures!" complained one American.

The older Knickerbockers were right to fear the influx of immigrants and new customs that were crowding the traditional Dutch and English society out of certain parts of the city and smothering it in others. Although the wealthier Knickerbockers for years had recognized themselves as an aristocracy, it was a modest aristocracy, a mere congenial interlocking of families. But as immigration increased—in May 1837, the month August had arrived, 5,750 immigrants landed in New York—and as the city changed, the wealthy Knickerbockers began to realize they did make up a previously unacknowledged kind of American elite—now beleaguered, seduced by new ideas, and needing to be schooled by sophisticated immigrants like August in the manners appropriate to the beau monde of a major port, a new world capital. In defending itself, in embracing the role of an American nobility, this elite would transform itself into a society having little in common with the old Knickerbocker world it was trying to preserve.

August's business—cotton speculation, Bank of Arkansas notes, $140,000 worth of Missouri securities—did so well that less than a year after he had arrived in New York the Rothschilds wrote, "We are happy to see that you have concluded considerable business for our account."

Despite his success, August felt uneasy in his adopted land. The country was rough. Young, August thought. And a bit uncivilized. "The arts and sciences have not yet reached a very high measure of perfection here," he wrote Babette at the end of summer. He mused about how important it was for a businessman to become rich enough to be a patron of the arts. "The fine arts strive for protection by the wealthy," he thought, "and there have not yet been amassed here those colossal fortunes which would make it possible to contribute by their abundance to the refinement of taste and morals."

But capital was breeding capital. Fortunes were accumulating. Although at the turn of the century there had not been a single millionaire in New York—even the word *millionaire* had not yet been invented—within three years of August's arrival in the city there would be forty. If the city's culture languished, it was because in America, where—as August told Babette—"everything turns on business," business seemed to be an end in itself. New York's new wealth did not support the kind of culture that in Europe was the main incentive of accumulating a fortune, because the old Knickerbockers disapproved of the pleasures money could buy, and the young Knickerbockers, who had the will to spend, lacked the taste to spend well.

August was frustrated. He finally had money to buy a private coach-and-four in which he could ride like the aristocrats he had seen when he had first gone to Frankfurt, but he lived in a city where no one owned a coach-and-four. Even the Italian Opera, which had struggled through a few bleak seasons in the mid-1830s, finally had closed. The year before August arrived, the Opera House, which everyone agreed was the most beautiful theater in America and equal to any opera house in Europe, was sold at auction. It was barbaric—a city without an Italian opera company —although Philip Hone explained that it was not culture that the Knickerbockers had resisted but the aristocratic pretentions of an opera-going public. In particular the old Knickerbockers did not like the idea of private boxes, which, Hone said, "cost $6,000 each. . . . and the use of them is all that the proprietors get for their money; but it forms a sort of aristocratical distinction." Hone and other of his peers liked "this spirit of independence which refuses its countenance to anything exclusive."

Surrounded by Knickerbockers who were wealthy and distrusted wealth and by immigrants who were poor and distrusted Knickerbockers, August felt out of place, isolated and lonely. He had little contact with New York's Jewish community, which could have offered a familiar milieu. The established Jewish families were mostly Sephardim, Spanish and Portuguese Jews, who went to the synagogue Shearith Israel, which had been established almost two centuries earlier when there had been fewer than a hundred Jews in New York. They felt superior to the newer Jewish immigrants, who were mostly Ashkenazim, Jews from central and eastern Europe. Clannish and cliquish, the Sephardim were as disconcerted by the flood of Jewish immigrants as the Knickerbockers were by the flood of Irish and German immigrants.

The Sephardim thought the Ashkenazim were uncivilized. The German Jews thought the Sephardic Jews were arrogant and the Polish Jews were boorish. The Polish Jews thought the German Jews were ignorant and held themselves aloof from the Russian Jews. The conflicts among the various groups intensified as more and more Jewish immigrants crowded into the city. Just before the turn of the century, during the mid-1790s, there had been about 350 Jews in New York. The year before August arrived there were 2,000. Three years after his arrival there were 7,000. Under the pressure of numbers, the Jewish community split like tapped shale. Before 1825 there had been only one synagogue in New York. By 1839 there were six, each congregation divorcing itself from the parent synagogue because of irreconcilable differences.

August, who a few years later would describe himself as having "liberal views regarding religious beliefs" that "keep me at a distance from the old requirements of the Jewish Talmud," found his "co-religionists in this country too disagreeable." Bored by the staid old Knickerbocker society, unaccepted by and unaccepting of the snobbish Sephardim, and disliking the generally uneducated Ashkenazim, August, through a set of European expatriates, fell in with a crowd of wild young Knickerbockers who both admired and distrusted his sophistication.

Most of this set lived at the American Hotel near City Hall Park, the hotel at which former President Andrew Jackson, Henry Clay, and Colonel Davy Crockett had stayed when they had visited the city. People still remembered the boisterous feast the Young Whigs gave the colonel at the American. The singing, the toasting, and the shouting had kept the neighbors on that side of the park up late into the night. The American did not have the modern luxuries that the new Astor House had introduced—gas lamps, free soap, and hot water on every floor—but it had a certain tone the stylish young men liked.

They hung out at Niblo's Garden, a café like Contoit's, about a dozen blocks north of City Hall Park, on Broadway between Prince and Houston streets. They raced horses up Third Avenue, which was called "the Macadamized Road," stopping on the way for brandy and cigars at Cato's House a couple of miles north of the city's Twenty-third Street uptown limit, or at the Hazard House about a mile farther north on

Yorkville Hill. From the Hazard House they dashed the downhill mile to the Red House, whipping the horses as fast as they could go, because the last to arrive on the Red House's wide piazza had to pay for everyone else's brandy. After lounging for an hour or so a few of the young men might arrange an impromptu race on the Red House's track—which for years was dominated by a horse named Flora Temple, "the queen of the trotting turf," until she was easily beaten by a Long Island mare named Lady Suffolk. The turning point of the day's drive into the country was Bradshaw's Hotel, about a mile from the Red House on the northern tip of Manhattan Island near the Harlem Bridge, where everyone stopped for another brandy and another cigar before racing back to town on the Bloomingdale Road, which as it entered the city connected to Broadway.

These wild young Knickerbockers bet not only on horses but on clandestine cockfights, rat-baiting contests, and boxing matches. A few of them patronized the streetwalkers who were beginning to clog the avenues in increasing numbers, or frequented the Louvre, New York's most lavish brothel. They read Byron and tried to look Byronic. August, with his muttonchop whiskers, his dark, at times almost indolent, eyes, and his continental manners, seemed to them a hero out of *Childe Harold* or *Don Juan*—refined, exotic, brooding, deep, and interestingly wicked.

His guttural accent and occasional use of foreign phrases charmed the New Yorkers who yearned for European polish and chilled those who thought proficiency in two languages cultured but proficiency in four profligate. August kissed ladies' hands, which no one had done in New York since the Revolution, when French officers had come to town. Although—as he told his sister—"American women are rather good-looking," he thought "they lack the youthful freshness of our German women or the English." The extreme and changeable climate caused their "cheeks to lose their rosy color." Like August, other Europeans found New York women pale, almost sickly-looking. One English visitor claimed that the "prominent point of female loveliness which the whole English race so much excel in, is entirely wanting in the American ladies; they are as *flat* as their own horrid seacoast."

"As regards their spiritual education and education of the heart," August wrote Babette, "American women are also inferior to Europeans. However, I believe that in matters of society and knowledge of the world, they display more self-assurance and wisdom than our ladies, which may be the result of the more liberal education and greater independence which is granted to young women here."

The young Knickerbocker girls, attracted by their ideas of sophisticated European society, were adding shadows to their characters, becoming flirtatious. Shifting inflection, they modulated forthrightness into boldness and, already developing an appetite for European titles, were learning to coax romantic curiosity out of the most casual, cool prospects. They practiced a lot.

Flirtations with ladies from good families sparked crises of honor. In the summer of 1839, a year and a half after a federal anti-dueling act had been passed, August, having quarreled in Saratoga with a young Baltimore man named Meredith, challenged him to a duel. Since the new law provided a death sentence for any duelist who killed his opponent and a five-year jail term for anyone who even issued or accepted a challenge, August's and Meredith's seconds patched up and hushed up the dispute. But August was developing a reputation for being touchy and bad-tempered.

He had, in fact, been homesick and depressed.

"Do you realize that it has been three years since I saw you last?" he wrote Babette, who had spent the winter in Mannheim at a private girls' school run by their father's cousin, Dr. Simon Wolff. "Since then you probably have grown into a big, capable, and beautiful girl. I am longing very much for a detailed description of your looks, your activities and daily life."

He sent her a parasol with a rare Chinese handle and begged her to "do everything in your power" to get pictures of herself and their father painted. Wanting accurate representations—as well as showing off his taste in art—he asked her "to see to it that the portraits are not entrusted to a cheap unskilled bungler at Alzey," which to save money his father was likely to do. Simon had gotten so stingy that Babette had complained there wasn't a decent piece of writing paper in the house. August wanted the paintings done "by a good painter at Mannheim or Mainz." Since he knew "that our good father will shun this expense," he offered "to take it upon myself if he should not like to shoulder" the cost. "It will be an extreme comfort to have both your pictures here and I know that you, my good sister, will surely do everything in your power to see this wish of mine fulfilled as soon as possible." It took nine years for Simon to get the portraits painted.

August ran into the daughter of his former schoolmaster, Dr. Hess. Now a married lady, she was visiting New York. Although he found that chance encounter a pleasant interlude, it heightened his nostalgia. "I wish," he wrote Babette, "you or our dear father were here. Then, everything would be all right."

Torn between wanting to visit Germany and fearing that if he did he might lose the position he was creating for himself in America, August kept making and breaking plans to travel to Europe—which depressed him even more. The theaters, filled with dramatizations of Charles Dickens's novels, he thought "rather bad," although an English opera company that toured New York "gave a passable performance." The food was poor, the parties worse. "I feel that my dancing days are over," he complained. And the sleigh rides that, he explained to Babette, "are usually the main amusement during the cold season," were not fun that year. "We went out only once, and the ride was not even nice because the winter was so mild."

He also was struggling in a legal tug-of-war with his father, who refused to send him the 5,000 florins August had inherited from his mother, Frederika. Simon, who was trustee of the bequest, was afraid August would fritter it away on chancy investments or, worse, riotous living. August told the Rothschilds to sue his father if Simon did not release the money within three months. Simon, furious, wailed about "this untender and ruthless behavior" that had "aroused my fatherly indignation." Trying to unite with the Rothschilds behind a generational barricade, Simon wrote to them that he assumed "you would not take on such an unnatural contract, which could only lead to a rupture between a father and a son. Such an unexpected handling I have not earned."

The Rothschilds were unimpressed with Simon's tantrum. They recommended that he pay, which Simon finally—in part—did. He sent the Rothschilds a draft for 1,997.20 florins, explaining that they should add to that the 80.36 florins they owed him. Simon had changed little since August's days at the *Philanthropin,* when he had tried to get August's Uncle Isaac to pay the tuition with money he claimed Isaac owed him. The 1,997.20 florins added to the 80.36 florins made up less than half of August's inheritance. August, usually as stubborn as his father, uncharacteristically accepted the loss and dropped the matter. When Babette complained that Simon was interfering with a romance, August, flourishing his best big-brother manner, wrote, "I think that I can read between your lines that you do not get along with Father in a manner behooving a good daughter." He had learned—and was warning his sister—that the only way to handle Simon was to bow to his superior pigheadedness. "It may be that Father has many peculiarities which, added to his practical experiences in life, do not always harmonize with the poetical illusions of a young girl. Yet I hope that you with your understanding, your kindness, and your sense of duty will give in and that you will sweeten instead of embitter our Father's life."

August sent her a miniature portrait of himself. "Here," he told her, "it is generally considered a good likeness and thus it will serve to bring back to you the memory of your far-away brother." He knew he had changed—he was no longer the clerk in unseasonable trousers or a novice businessman, a mere private secretary. Being proud of the change, he wanted his family to take note.

August, as a result of a business embarrassment, paradoxically became not only successful but triumphant on Wall Street. The international financial situation was unstable. English farmers had had a bad harvest. England, already suffering from a drain on its gold reserves, had to buy £10 million of foreign wheat, corn, rye, and oats. As a result English bankers, unwilling to send any more gold out of the country, were reluctant to honor American notes—especially since the American economy, unsettled by monetary reforms and shaken by a bumper cotton crop that sent the price of cotton plummeting, seemed poised on the brink of another crash.

Because of these shaky transatlantic economics some drafts on the Rothschilds that August had sold to the Bank of Maryland had been returned, unaccepted by the Rothschilds' London branch. The established New York bankers, whose business August had been cutting into, were gleeful. Belmont the swell obviously had more cheek than credit. August, claiming "a mere misunderstanding has occurred," swore that not only would he make the Rothschilds redeem the drafts but they would also give him a 15 percent indemnity—which they did. August had taken on the House of Rothschild and won. His credit never again was doubted in New York.

Three years after arriving in America, August, having made a personal fortune of $100,000, was one of the richest men in New York City and was considered one of the three most important private bankers in the United States. He was so skillful at arbitrage—buying securities in one market only to resell them immediately in another market where their price was higher, a kind of financial legerdemain—that he became known as the King of the Money Changers. He bought "a beautiful horse," which he claimed was "really my only pleasure." He rode to work every warm day along the Bloomingdale Road from a chateau he rented in Bloomingdale, a rural retreat on the northern part of Manhattan Island that was thought to be the loveliest countryside in the area.

Extemporizing on what he had learned from the Rothschilds, he gave banquets so sumptuous that years later people would dismiss the grande cuisine the Delmonico brothers started serving in their restaurant in 1828 and claim that Belmont had introduced the first true gourmet cooking to America. One by one the Knickerbockers were capitulating to pleasure. August, in guiding their surrender, was helping to build the kind of cosmopolitan world that he had left behind in Europe.

On February 27, 1840, August attended New York's first masked ball, which Henry Brevoort, Jr., gave in his house on the recently fashionable Fifth Avenue at Ninth Street. Brevoort probably realized the event was unparalleled—it would later be called "the most splendid social affair of the first half of the nineteenth century"—but it was not for the sake of history that he allowed a *New York Herald* reporter, William H. Attree, to attend. The newspaper had threatened to embarrass Brevoort in its pages if he did not open his doors to Attree, a former sports reporter who came to the party dressed in a suit of armor. Attree, the first newsman ever admitted to a private party in the city's history, wrote New York's first gossip column, which was published under the pen name Ariel in the *Morning Herald* of March 6, 1840. New York Society was born.

Newly hatched, it preened and fluttered its plumage, although— either because of Attree's presence or because at four in the morning Matilda Barclay, daughter of the British consul to New York, eloped, still costumed like a Persian princess, with a young Southerner named Burgwyne—it almost died in infancy. As a result of the scandal and the publicity, masked balls were outlawed for the next fourteen years.

New York society, however, was not prepared to return to a dull round of quiet at-homes. Young Knickerbockers admired August, who seemed to crowd his life with novelty almost effortlessly. But no matter how much they studied him, they could not categorize him. He was unique. He was hot-tempered, always getting into arguments; yet aristocratically aloof and remote. He was arrogant, seemingly uninterested, even disdainful, of New York society; yet he was a hospitable host who gave lavish parties. He was prudent and foolish: a careful businessman who spent unheard-of sums on luxuries.

His success and insouciance made him many enemies. They attended his fetes and soirees and left snickering at his extravagance. His elegance seemed not just flamboyant but sinister. He could—people claimed—sexually arouse a woman simply by staring at her. Men warned each other, "For God's sake, don't introduce that man Belmont to your daughters."

Those who reciprocated his hospitality and invited him home found that he tended to arrive late, after dinner had already been served. But his studied indifference seemed somehow chic, a kind of New York *sprezzatura* that was soon being aped by other less original but equally worldly gentlemen.

The old Knickerbockers wanted to feel complacent, but August made them feel insecure. There was something about him they resisted, something that nevertheless drew them to him.

When he had an accident driving two horses in a tandem on Broadway, the Knickerbockers smirked. Instead of being properly embarrassed, August appeared not too long afterward in a private carriage drawn by four horses, the first four-in-hand New York had ever seen. He invited his friends to ride to Paterson, New Jersey, to visit the falls. On the road over the Jersey Heights one of the four horses fell dead. Everyone had to climb out of the carriage and walk. The Knickerbockers said August was driving either to bankruptcy or the Devil, a remark he enjoyed repeating.

On May 3, 1840, Fanny Elssler, the celebrated European opera dancer, arrived in New York. She worried that the prudish Americans would not tolerate her relatively skimpy costumes. Newspapers warned the public to stay away from her performances. But when she opened at seven o'clock in the evening on May 14, the Park Theater was jammed. Fanny Elssler took her position on the stage; the curtain went up; and as she described it in a letter, "The whole house rose, and such a shout ascended, as stunned my senses, and made me involuntarily recoil. Men waved their hats, and women their handkerchiefs, and all was inexplicable dumb show for several mortal moments. I stood confounded, with tears streaming down my face."

She danced. The audience threw flowers and gave her another standing ovation. She stammered, in broken English, her thanks. The audience erupted again.

Infatuated, August led a band of young men who dragged her carriage through the streets. He invited her to his summer chateau at Bloomingdale. She accepted. He dined her, sat with her tête-à-tête, wandered with her through his gardens, and drove her in his four-in-hand to the Long Island races—inspiring among his contemporaries a jealousy that turned to merriment when, back in New York, Fanny snubbed him. Since most of New York knew she had an illegitimate child stashed in England and believed—as the young banker Sam Ward told his friend Henry Wadsworth Longfellow—that Fanny "has been bought and sold as often as absolution from and by priests," August may have presumed on her reputation as a lover.

Fanny's snub was not the worst social disappointment August would suffer. He was not asked to the City Ball, which was held in the City Hotel on January 24, 1841. One hundred and fifty young Knickerbocker men who were trying to establish Dutch-English dominance of New York's fashionable world had organized the event, which, modeled after the Dancing Assemblies of the previous century, was intended to remind nouveaux riches like August that they could not become true Knicker-bockers merely by accumulating wealth. Society was a matter not of addition but of subtraction. Like good wine a family took years to ma-ture, and only the *premier grand cru* were invited. The eight hundred guests danced in a ballroom lit by two thousand candles and decorated with mirrors, which, multiplying their images, made them feel despite their exclusiveness that they were a majority, an undefeatable army. The hundreds of thousands of dollars' worth of jewels the women wore re-flected the two-thousand-candle flames until the room seemed a holocaust of wealth.

The City Ball was such a success, both as a party for society and as a caution for others, that a series of Assembly Balls was organized at Delmonico's. The Knickerbockers were fortifying themselves behind a wall of light and music. Like the citizens of a city under siege they anxiously surveyed the outside world for any signs of attack and exag-gerated the threats they discovered.

Belmont, furious, they said, that he hadn't been included at the City Ball, had warned the invitation committee, "I have been investigating the accounts of you gentlemen on the Street. I can assure you that either I get an invitation to the Assembly this year, or else the day after the Assembly each of you will be a ruined man." According to legend August got his invitation, but when he arrived at the party he found no one else had come.

At the end of the summer of 1841 August's romantic entanglements again got him into trouble. He was relaxing at Niblo's Garden when Edward Heyward, "the son of a very honorable family," as August explained to his father, "asserted in public and in my presence that I was enjoying the illicit favors of a married lady in whose home I visited very frequently and whose hospitality had been extended to me. I rejected this false and malicious assertion; and, when he repeated it, I told him publicly that it was a lie. Thereupon he hit me on the head with his cane in the presence of witnesses, and thus there was nothing left to me but to demand satisfaction for such a disgraceful and unjustified insult."

The married lady in question was Mrs. Oscar Coles of Saratoga Springs. She was the daughter of the man who ran Brown's restaurant in New York, which, though not as good as Delmonico's, was with its English chophouse atmosphere a favorite of those who distrusted fancier foreign food. Before she married Coles and moved to Saratoga, she had been considered the most beautiful woman in New York City. "She flirts with the gentlemen, married and single," wrote Philip Hone, and was "of course not in the good graces of the ladies, fond of notoriety, and delighted no doubt at the éclat of a duel" being fought over her.

On Wednesday, August 24, August with his second, John T. Purdy, and Heyward with his second, Ned Laight, left New York for Maryland, a traditional refuge for duelists because the authorities there cultivated a chivalrous blindness to affairs of honor. By evening they had reached Elkton, a village just over the border from Delaware. Under assumed names they rented rooms, August's party in one hotel, Heyward's in another.

"Their deportment," according to one Elkton villager, "was exceedingly singular, mysterious."

At dawn on Thursday the two parties headed separately in the same direction, east toward the rising sun. Two locals tried to follow but, afraid to be seen, lagged too far behind and took the wrong fork in the road.

After traveling a mile and a half from town the duelists stopped. Mist rose from the dewy field through the slanting rays of early morning sunlight. Birds chirruped and whistled. The seconds walked out the distance prescribed by the code duello, which was usually between ten and twenty paces, thirty to sixty feet. August and Heyward took their positions. The command to fire was given. The sound of the shots silenced the birds. Heyward's bullet shattered August's hip joint just as August was aiming his pistol. August's bullet went wild, flying past Heyward's head. There was no second shot. August declared honor satisfied.

Valentine Mott, the doctor the duelists had brought along, dug at August's wound, trying unsuccessfully to gouge out the bullet. August had no anesthetic. He lay pale with pain while the doctor worked. Watching the operation, Purdy fainted. Mott dressed the wound. The two parties returned to Elkton.

In New York, while August's and Heyward's friends waited for news of the duel's outcome, the rest of the city reveled in the scandal. Bets were made, rumors exchanged:

—Heyward had shot Belmont in the groin.

—Belmont, hit in the thigh, had hopped comically about the field.

—Belmont's wound was minor.

—Belmont wouldn't recover.

As reports of August's worsening condition reached the city, the gossip turned malicious:

—There was something in Belmont's past he was trying to hide.

—Belmont's real name was Schönberg.

—Belmont's real name was Belmain.

—Belmont was a bastard son of one of the Rothschilds.

Before the duel, people condemned both participants and suggested it would be no loss if they shot each other. "I hope in God," one New Yorker said, "both may get their hot corn." But after the duel public opinion, as usual attracted by success, swung toward the winner. The *New York Herald* accused August of having "abandoned the society of sober, rich, respectable, quiet people" for that of the young and *roué*. It claimed, "We always entertained the opinion that he would end his career in some such way as he bids fair to do."

On Friday night, badly wounded and suffering from blood poisoning, August arrived in Philadelphia. The doctors there examined him and sent to New York for Dr. Detmold, a famous orthopedic surgeon. According to the *Herald,* which betrayed the newly developing anti-semitism of the times, Detmold came with "two famous financiers" who "looked like Jews" and a young Knickerbocker named Livingston, who, possibly because he was August's friend, was described as having "a large nose."

Detmold probed the wound and decided it was, at least for the time being, impossible to remove the bullet. Livingston returned to New York with the news that August would be lame for life. The *Herald,* which had circulated the story that August had been killed, softened its tone. A live banker, after all, could make more trouble than a dead one. Exchanging censure for moral advice, the newspaper said, "During his confinement, we advise Belmont to read the Scriptures."

August recovered quickly. By the end of the month he was able to scribble notes to his office. By the first of September he was well enough to be moved from Philadelphia to eastern New Jersey. In the middle of

September, Heyward, who had been lying low, resurfaced in New York. Because August was out of danger the authorities would wink at the duel and not prosecute—which they might have done if August had died. The *Herald,* whose tone by now was almost avuncular, was denying rumors it previously had published of August's illegitimate birth and protectively explaining that there seemed to be "great hostility to Belmont among certain cliques of young men because he is a foreigner, a financier, and now occupies a position of great responsibility and power in monetary circles." The newspaper limited itself to cautioning, "We hope hereafter he will make a better selection of his associates," and even optimistically reported that "It is expected by his friends—and he has troops of them— that no apparent lameness in walking will ensue." A few days later, when the bullet was at last removed from August's thigh, the *Herald,* indulgent and fatherly, merely said, "Get well, but don't do it again."

The episode transformed August. According to the code duello, gentlemen duel only with other gentlemen. Heyward, one of the Charleston, South Carolina, Heywards, was a gentleman. Therefore, August was now a gentleman.

CHAPTER FIVE

IN SEPTEMBER, August returned to New York. For weeks he lay on his back in bed, able to move only his arms. The end of summer was sultry. To escape the heat New Yorkers traveled to Saratoga; went on day trips to the countryside of Hoboken, Brooklyn, or Staten Island; sailed to Fort Lee; or hid in the shade of the latticed alcoves in the many small gardens of the city. Oystermen blew their horns without enthusiasm. Fruit vendors, chimney sweeps, locksmiths, sang their wares and services spiritlessly. Behind every clattering carriage, dust puffed. Sun burned on the walls of the houses, making the painted red bricks look redder. Official dog-killers roamed the streets, carrying bloodied clubs and wearing blood-soaked, blood-caked clothes, looking for wild dogs that were creating a health hazard. "The poor creatures are knocked down on the pavement and beat to death," wrote a visitor to the city. "Sometimes they are horribly maimed and run howling and limping away."

August, confined to his bed, reviewed the duel, which had upset the Rothschilds so much that they were thinking of taking their American agency away from him—even though, as he wrote his father, "I do not know whether they are justified in their excitement inasmuch as, after all, I first saw to it that their funds were safely protected."

August knew that "it will be very difficult for me to justify my conduct in the eyes of those who are against" dueling; but "any honorable man would have acted the way I did, without taking into consideration any consequences. I have been brought up," he reminded Simon, "in the belief that I would much rather expose myself to death ten thousand times than to swallow the affront of a slap in the face or of being hit." August was no longer in Alzey. This was not the eighteenth century. Jews did not have to bow their heads and suffer abuse. August, like any other gentleman, could demand satisfaction.

"This may be called a false sense of honor," he admitted to his father, who often took principled stands in business matters. "However, everybody has his opinions and principles and I cannot change now."

Knowing he had both a hot temper and a code that would not let him surrender to a slight, August explained that he had tried to avoid any encounter that could lead to a fight. Echoing the *Herald* he promised that "In future, I not only shall be doubly cautious in this respect, but also shall use the greatest care in the selection of my acquaintances and friends"—although he had not been quite as wild and indiscriminate in his associations as the newspapers, which—he said—"contain the most shameless lies," had suggested. "If my character and my behavior were as described by these cheap papers, I most probably should not enjoy the friendship of so many honorable men and families and could not maintain my position in the society in which I have moved."

The duel had in fact made August realize that he was not as isolated as he at times had felt. "During my illness I had an opportunity to find out how many friends and how much support I enjoy among the most respected people here. Therefore even if Messrs. von Rothschild should take the agency away from me, I shall try my luck and will attempt to earn my future living under my own steam."

To Babette, August wrote: "I'm improving daily with God's help and under the constant care and with the assistance of my friends." He minimized the duel so it would not cast a shadow on her engagement to Salomon Feist, a Koblenz wine exporter—who, shortly after he met Babette, began calling himself Stephan. Babette had met Stephan at a neighbor's house and had carried on a romance with him without telling her father. When Simon found out, he at first resisted their marriage. But he liked Stephan and approved of Stephan's family, so eventually he gave his consent and an 11,500-florin dowry.

"I'm very glad," August wrote Simon on hearing the news, "that you did not resist her preference for too long."

The wedding was set for the end of April. Babette begged her father to advance the wedding date. Simon said no but at last gave in. Babette and Stephan were married in Bingen on March 14, 1842. After deciding to settle in Koblenz in the house Stephan shared with his mother and two brothers and their families, the newlyweds left on their honeymoon for England.

Simon felt misused and abandoned. The wedding had been marred by what Simon described to August as "misunderstandings and impatience" and the "needling" of some people in the company. The wedding also had been too expensive. Babette had distributed too many presents to members of the wedding party; and afterward Isaac Mayer, Stephan's brother-in-law, had given Simon a bill for 901 florins 46 kronen for his services as a marriage broker. Simon exploded. Not only had Babette flouted tradition by arranging her own marriage, but the man who had helped her go behind Simon's back and carry on a romance in secrecy was now demanding to be paid for his deviousness. Simon refused to pay. Isaac Mayer sued. Although Simon and Isaac eventually reached a compromise, three and a half months later Simon still was fuming over "the various slanders and mistreatment" he had been forced to put up with on the wedding day, "at a time when I only could think of joy and pleasure."

All during the spring and summer of 1842 Simon brooded over the scattering of his family. His grandfather Isaac Simon's retirement had been disturbed by renewed family obligations: two grandchildren to raise. His own retirement was being disturbed by the absence of family obligations. His children had left Alzey, left him. He was doomed to grow old alone.

The letters he sent to Babette while she was on her honeymoon were bills of grievance. The details he listed so thoroughly and impersonally, as though she knew nothing of the family history, made it sound like he was presenting a defense in a court of law. "After a few happy years," he wrote, "misfortune struck, when on June 9, 1821, I lost my dear, unforgettable wife."

As indignation modulated into anger Simon's defense against the assaults of life changed into an attack on the ingratitude of his children. The defendant became a prosecutor, demanding 5 percent interest on the love he had invested in his children. "I don't want to go into the details of the many sacrifices I made," he wrote.

His letters to August were not so much legal briefs in a civil suit as they were criminal charges. Giving in to his tendency to play the part of a Rhenish Lear, he raged back and forth across the pages that he posted to New York.

"As one says," he wrote his son, "my hairs stand on end. So has it been with me many months. I am almost beside myself with embarrassment" not just because of the duel but because August, feeling distanced from his father, did not keep him well informed. In fact, after the duel August wrote first to his uncle Isaac Hanau; then to Simon—which, if Simon knew of it (and his sensitivity to August's inadequate communication may suggest he did), must have hurt him and angered him even more than the duel had. The angrier he got, the more he ranted at his son. The more he ranted at his son, the less August wanted to write him. The less August wanted to write him, the more Simon felt abandoned. The vicious circle spun faster and faster, throwing August and Simon even farther apart by its centrifugal force.

"How could you not write at all from the 15th of February to the 23rd of May (that means for three and a quarter months)?" Simon complained to August.

Keeping track of postal debts and credits, Simon listed the letters he wrote and the letters he received. Afraid that August was not telling him the truth about the seriousness of the injury, he cross-examined his son.

"In each of your letters you wrote you are better. In the first that the express post brought me out of Philadelphia, you said that, according to the assurances of the doctor, you would be completely recovered. And yet, after a span of nine months, you still need to go on crutches. Even the poor day-laborer and bricklayer in the peaceful circle of his family in his straw hut can enjoy his watery soup, go to bed at nine o'clock in the evening, and, after a restful seven hours of sleep, have his reviving pipe of tobacco and go refreshed to work—while I go around here in Alzey in one undisturbed state of unrest and my son, the agent of the House of Rothschild in New York City, goes around his palace in New York on crutches."

Not only had the duel robbed Simon of sleep and contentment, it also had prevented August from visiting Alzey, a trip that—it seemed to Simon—August was destined never to take. Something was aways making it impossible for his son to return home. But Simon admitted that he found it natural that "both the doctor and you decided you shouldn't travel to Europe while on crutches."

About the Rothschilds' reaction to the duel Simon ventured no opinion, his business caution dampening his anger. But he assured August that whatever might happen he viewed what already had happened as one of the family's "greatest misfortunes. All the ladies and honor in the world are not worth the pain you—and I on account of you—have suffered. My heart bleeds and I get a chill when I think" that August could have been killed, although Simon saw in August's death only a mirror reflecting the loss to the living: ". . . think of your father, sister, and all you would have placed in such great sadness."

After trotting August around and around his rage, Simon finally let him rest. He even tried to soothe his son by explaining his temper away. He did not mean to upset August with his reproaches; he only wanted to get things off his chest. "I could not with the best of will suppress such thoughts; I must give air to my heart." Simon apparently was unaware that his children might have been hurt by his accusations. Why should they be? After all, when he dunned a debtor in court for money owed him, there was nothing personal in his hammering away until he had proved his case. In his letters to his son and daughter Simon was only dunning them for the respect they owed him, which, by their actions, they seemed to have forgotten to pay.

August's appetite improved. Soon he was able to bend his knee and exercise the "limbs which have become stiff by the long rest. Since, thank the Good Lord, I am not losing courage and remain patient, I am confidently hoping that my complete recovery will approach quickly." Ironically he told Simon, "I may say that at this time there is less danger to my health than when I am well"—since he was not out in society where he could get involved in another quarrel. Despite his patience his long convalescence at times depressed him. "If only I could get rid of the crutches," he wrote Simon.

After letting August know of their disapproval of the duel, the Rothschilds were conciliatory. There was no longer any immediate threat to August's tenure as their American agent. The business and social wounds were healing faster than the physical wounds. In 1842 August moved into comfortable rooms in fashionable Murray Street off City Hall Park. By the following year he was exploiting his limp for dramatic effect.

It was a constant reminder of his romantic nature. The duel he had fought to defend one lady's honor left him with an appeal that—gossips claimed —compromised the honor of a number of other ladies, who bragged of having seen the scar on August's thigh.

August enjoyed his role as roué. When Marie Angéline Grymes, whom everyone called Medora, appeared in New York during the 1842–43 social season, August took note of her. She was, after all, the only woman in the city whose beauty was comparable to that of Mrs. Oscar Coles, the woman who had caused the fight between August and Heyward. Medora's father, John Randolph Grymes, was a lawyer who as district attorney of New Orleans had indicted the pirate Jean Lafitte, only to quit his office in order to defend him. He was considered the second most famous gambler in Louisiana and perhaps the most famous duelist.

August met Medora and was charmed enough by her that when she married Sam Ward, the banker and epicure, he parked his grandest carriage and pair in front of the newlyweds' house. In this duel of dollars Ward protected his—and perhaps his wife's—honor by buying a pair of horses that rivalled August's tandem.

By March 1844 August was waltzing. He went to a costume ball dressed, appropriately, as *diable boiteux* (literally, "limping devil" or the "devil on two sticks" from the novel *Le Diable Boiteux,* written more than a century before by Alain René Le Sage, the author of *L'Histoire de Gil Blas de Santillane*). He reported to his sister, who transmitted the news to Simon, that he was—except for the limp he would never lose— completely recovered.

Since August was now healthy, Simon assumed he soon would visit— perhaps even settle in—Alzey. "Little by little, Alzey is growing," Simon wrote. "Opportunities for education and business are increasing, and we have great hopes. Ther are more houses, greater trade, better conditions in general, so, when you come back, you won't recognize your birthplace."

But August, increasingly happy in New York, decided not to return to Germany to settle. In 1844 he became a naturalized American citizen.

CHAPTER SIX

DURING THE NEXT FEW YEARS August settled into the double routines of pleasure and business, a tandem that carried him from New York in the winter to Saratoga Springs in the summer. His parties became even more splendid than they had been, his horses more swift, his wines more rare, his coaches more elaborate, and his servants' livery more ducal. Despite his limp he learned and led the scandalous new dances like the polka that were being imported from Europe.

His business continued to grow. He balanced the larger accounts—investments in new corporations, state bonds, railroads—with small loans to people who had greater social position than wealth. And he followed the smaller loans almost as carefully as he did those involving hundreds of thousands, even millions, of dollars. When, for example, a man named Forsyth promised to pay August a relatively minor debt owed to the Paris branch of the House of Rothschild by giving him a note against the sale of some slaves either to a private party or "at public auction" in a few months, August demurred. Although like most Northerners he did not refuse to do business with slaveowners, he did not approve of slavery and did not want to enter into any affair in which he would be involved directly in the buying or selling of human beings. He told Forsyth he was "very reluctant to exchange real for personal security" and suggested that the money to pay the debt could "be secured by a mortgage on the negroes themselves or by some other tangible security." He was not trying to evade moral responsibility by removing himself from the sale of slaves. He simply thought slavery was as bad business as it was vicious. His decision was economic, not ethical. August paid such attention to small details, because while the large transactions gave him control over the great industries and institutions that ran America, the small transactions gave him control over the men who ran those industries and institutions.

Like the country, August was in an expansionist mood. He wanted to explore new territory. He worked for James K. Polk in the presidential election of 1844, strengthening his ties to the Democratic party and increasing his involvement in American politics. The same year, the government of Austria, acknowledging his growing international reputation, appointed him the provisional Austrian consul general for New York, New Jersey, Pennsylvania, Delaware, Maryland, Virginia, and the District of Columbia—a position made permanent in 1848. While it was not uncommon for a leading merchant or banker of one country to be made consul general of another, it nevertheless was an honor.

August kept his Viennese contacts informed about political developments in the United States—the conflict with Britain over territory in Oregon, the conflict with Mexico over territory in Texas. But the office entailed more business than politics, and it not only gave August an excuse to avoid jury duty—which he joked about—but also strengthened his social position in New York. He was amused that "even though the Americans are Republicans they bestow a great importance on such a position which we could hardly believe."

Being the Austrian consul general also gave August a measure of independence from the Rothschilds. In 1847 the United States government gave August Belmont & Company the right to transfer $3 million to the Mexican government, the down payment on the indemnity that the United States had agreed to pay Mexico in exchange for the land seized during the recent Mexican War. August handled the transaction without taking any commission. He bartered profit for goodwill, hoping that the goodwill would bring him future government contracts and greater profits than he could have made on the single $3 million transfer.

The following year the trade-off seemed to have been a bad risk. The United States let it be known in financial circles that it wanted to borrow $5 million. Bankers interested in making the loan each offered to supply the money at a certain rate of interest. The banker offering the lowest rate of interest would win the contract. August, acting as the agent of the London branch of the Rothschilds and in concert with the American firm of Corcoran & Riggs, bid on and thought he had won all but $75,000 of the $5 million.

Without August's knowledge, however, the United States government two months before already had awarded nearly $2 million of the loan to other bankers. Instead of getting a contract to lend the government $4.25 million, at an annual profit of well over half a million dollars, August and his associates were lending the United States only $2.35 million, at an annual profit of only $296,100, a little more than half of what they thought they were going to make. The Rothschilds could not have been pleased, and they balked shortly thereafter when August suggested bidding on an additional government loan of $16 million.

When in the same year August, again acting as agent of the Rothschilds, loaned the new territory of California—where he kept a branch office—5 million pesos, the Rothschilds were angry enough about the deal to cause rumors that they would publicly disassociate themselves from the transaction, discrediting August. But the price of the loan rose on the stock market, and the Rothschilds' anger declined. August, who knew—as he told his brother-in-law, Stephan Feist—that "the stocks of this government are the safest in the world," took satisfaction from evidence that "The capitalists in Europe are starting to believe it," although he thought they were changing their minds "too late."

The conflict caused by August's faith in the essential soundness of

American investments and the Rothschilds' occasional distrust of them would continue for a number of years. When August tried to get the Paris branch of the House of Rothschild to invest in a United States government loan shortly after Pennsylvania had defaulted on state bonds worth $35 million, which had been bought by—among others—the London branch of the House of Rothschild, Baron James told August to inform his American contacts that "you have seen the man who is at the head of the finances of Europe, and that he has told you that they cannot borrow a dollar. Not a dollar."

Occasionally the Rothschild's instincts about American investments were sound. In 1850 August and the London Rothschilds lost probably as much as £15,000 on the transfer of another installment of the indemnity the United States owed Mexico. But in general it was not August's business decisions to which the Rothschilds objected; it was his autonomy.

One of the Rothschilds said "I am too much of a 'Grand Seigneur' and I have no right to do any business on my own account," August complained to Babette. "Accustomed to flattery and people paying court to them, they cannot forgive me for keeping my independence in spite of my position with them. What provokes them more than my independent manners is that I have made a fortune for myself with which I can live comfortably and happily anywhere I like. These gentlemen want me to be dependent on them and they want to profit from my services and experience as long as it is convenient for them and then they'll show me the door as soon as it suits them."

August was haunted by the way the Rothschilds had severed their business relationships with his uncle Isaac Hanau some years before. He did not want to be in the same vulnerable position: powerful only as a representative of Rothschild wealth. He also wanted to protect his interests in case the Rothschilds suffered reversals—which seemed to be happening as a result of the February revolution in France that drove Louis Philippe to abdicate and the uprisings that followed across the Continent in Germany, Italy, and Austria. "It is true that they [the Rothschilds] have suffered enormous losses," August wrote to Feist in May 1848.

There were rumors that the Rothschilds might even go under, although August told his brother-in-law, "I cannot believe it looks *so* bad and trust that they will remain solvent." Still, in case August was wrong, he had arranged his affairs so that "even in the worst case of a suspension of the Rothschilds, may God prevent it, I am so situated that I can neither be implicated nor will I lose money." August was as cautious and ruthless as the Rothschilds themselves were.

In the fall of 1848 August heard from Baron James de Rothschild, the head of the Paris branch of the House, that he was sending his twenty-one-year-old son, Alphonse, to America. August was outraged. He was convinced that Baron James was "trying to establish his son Alphonse here because there are already too many of this family in Europe." He felt that he was being treated not as a peer, a successful banker with an international reputation, but as a glorified private secretary. He had been keeping the Rothschilds' seat in America warm for their "sons or nephews." He was sure they expected him not only to move aside without objection but to help Alphonse learn the business, an arrangement August refused to consider.

"I have been independent for too long and could not agree to remain in any position which could become in the least bit uncomfortable," he assured Babette.

August had not built up a network of business contacts in America only to hand it over to an inexperienced Rothschild. While he did not "intend to push anything, but to let things come," he promised Babette that, "since I do not need these gentlemen's money, I will hand in my resignation if my anticipations turn out to be true."

Despite his defiant attitude August was depressed. Just when he felt that he had finally consolidated his position in the United States, that he was secure professionally and socially, and that he could accomplish whatever he decided he wanted to do, his world threatened to break apart. He was like an actor who, having learned his lines, runs onto the stage to play his part only to find the scenery being struck.

For the first time since he had become an American citizen four years before, he seriously considered returning to Europe to live, although he told Babette, "At this point I cannot see one place on the whole continent where one can settle down in peace, except for Spain, and this country offers little attraction for permanent residency; and as long as this situation persists, I prefer to stay in America where I enjoy political and personal freedom and where I am able to carry on a profitable business either as an agent or as an independent. However, if things calm down in Germany or France I probably will retire from business and settle near you."

He had enough money to live comfortably for the rest of his life; and while he could continue as a successful banker without the Rothschilds, he now saw no reason to stay in the United States if he lost their American agency.

"With much regret and a heavy heart" he followed closely "the course of happenings in Europe where the rage of political parties and licentiousness increases every day." He waited now for the political and social upheavals to end so he could return to his homeland. But the revolts, which had been triggered by the February revolution in Paris, continued to disrupt life in the capitals and countryside of Europe.

Fighting had broken out on a number of occasions near Alzey, and August repeatedly asked for news of the family as well as for advice. Untypically, he was confused about his future. Incredibly, neither Babette nor Simon answered. At odds with the Rothschilds and apparently at least temporarily abandoned by his father and sister, August again began feeling the loneliness and isolation that had troubled him when he first had arrived in the United States.

"It is now more than three months ago, my dear Sister, that I wrote you last and still I do not have an answer from you to two of my letters," he wrote Babette. "This silence on your and our good father's part is even more astonishing to me as the contents of my last two letters were truly of great importance to me, especially what I told you about the mission of young Rothschild, and it should have been enough to get you interested in my situation. I miss your comment on it with true regret. Away from friends and relatives, in the most difficult epoch of my life, relying solely on my own resources, it would have been of great comfort to me to receive the sympathetic and loving advice of my dear sister which I painfully miss."

Alphonse de Rothschild arrived in New York in the winter of 1848–49. Instead of being treated as August's superior by New Yorkers, he was treated as August's equal "in spite of his name and all my effort," August explained to Babette. "He cannot forgive me for his not being treated with more regard by society than I, who am only his agent."

Such an affirmation of his independent importance must have pleased August as much as it irked Alphonse, who after a stay in the East traveled to New Orleans, the center of the cotton market, where he transacted business for his father and his uncles, as well as for August himself. The kind letters Alphonse sent August masked resentment which August heard about "from a reliable source." This duplicity angered August, who felt that because of it there was no "hope for real communication."

August now was convinced that he had been right about Alphonse's mission in the United States—to replace him as the head of the Rothschilds' American agency. Anger gave way to weariness. August was unable to negotiate the warring interests in his banking affairs and private life. He could not satisfy the Rothschilds: he had written to Feist that they were "very disgruntled because of the events in Europe and the significant losses they suffered, and it is very hard to please them." He could not satisfy his family: If he stayed in New York he was abandoning his sister and father; if he returned to Germany he was abandoning the opportunities his father had sacrificed for to give him.

August's reaction to Alphonse's visit seemed to reflect an inner as much as an outer threat—a hesitation in the face of his own success. He suffered, not from a failure of nerve but from a faltering of aspiration. He had achieved a great deal. He was one of the richest men in America. But he had reached a plateau in his ambition. He was like a climber who, having struggled to what he had thought was the top of a mountain, finds above him another peak that previously had been hidden by clouds.

Unsure what he wanted to do next, shaken by the growing rupture with the Rothschilds, and hurt that they were not being "quite honest with me," as he told Babette, he wanted to withdraw from the life he had created for himself. "As long as I work for them," he wrote, "I will never get away from New York." He missed his sister terribly and looked forward to "the pleasure of holding you in my arms once again after such a long, long separation." He decided to quit his job. In March 1848 he wrote Babette, "When I give up my Agency here, you will see me for sure the coming winter in Koblenz."

By June, however, August had calmed down. Babette had written offering advice and giving him news of political unrest in Germany. Although things still looked bad, August was able to "hope that the good cause will win and that our beautiful Fatherland will not be a victim of the Socialists or Anarchists." He no longer discussed retiring from business and withdrawing to Europe. He still talked about leaving the Rothschilds, but, as he explained to his sister, he had had an opportunity to "evaluate the matter very coolly and prudently, so, if I come to a decision to quit" as the Rothschilds' American agent, "it will be out of important and well-founded motives rather than out of ridiculous vanity."

He was willing to consider working with Alphonse, if the job conformed to the "standard of my current position and is not beneath my dignity."

In a week to a week and a half Alphonse was due to arrive in New York from New Orleans. He would be leaving for Europe in July. August expected him "probably to return here later."

But August was mistaken. Possibly from the very beginning his pride and his anxiety over his future had misled him about the Rothschilds' plans for Alphonse. Alphonse left the United States and did not return to take over the Rothschilds' American agency.

The crisis was over. August's anguish burned itself out; but he was left with the intact remains of a gentle fantasy—like the ash of a match that still holds its shape after the flame has consumed the stick—that he had shared with his sister during the period of his severest worries. His father had asked August about his matrimonial prospects. August, answering in a roundabout route, had written to his sister, "I do not feel like getting married." Playfully and modestly, considering the money he had already made, he added, "Little by little, I will try to make a small fortune for myself, and with God's help years from now I will come back to you as the rich American uncle and will let you and your little ones take care of me. That is, if you can make some room for the lame old grouser."

CHAPTER SEVEN

THROUGHOUT the early and mid-1840s, while August was strengthening his position in America and, later, worrying about his future, he was restless. He moved nearly once a year, as though he were being chased by or were chasing something; and since his homes were extravagant—"palaces," his father had called them—the thing he was trying both to elude and capture may have been the life money could buy. He migrated up Murray Street, over to Jay Street, and on to the newly fashionable Fifth Avenue, where he bought one of the first mansions built in that area, at Fourteenth Street.

In a city where just a few years earlier the first families had lived in modest homes with old Dutch stoops, the mansions on Fifth Avenue were as alien as the slums about a mile away in Five Points. And in the coincidental numerology of the city's growth, Fifth Avenue and Five Points became the poles not just of New York's architecture but of its culture as well. The tenements' Bowery Boys with their flashy costumes were an impoverished reflection of the mansions' swells in their white overcoats with white velvet collars and white silk buttons, their Anglice trousers (black pants checkered by large white stripes), and their red and black satin cravats held in place by diamond pins.

The hostility between the two groups—the poor Irish immigrants who had embraced the American myth of a classless society, and the wealthy, for the most part native-born, Americans who in trying to create an upper class were creating a lower class too—erupted during the spring of 1849.

As the result of a theatrical feud the world August was helping to invent came under attack. For the past year William C. Macready, a British actor, and Edwin Forrest, an American actor, had been quarreling. Macready considered Americans boorish; he played his greatest role, that of an English gentleman, in public. His fans were the young elegants who aped European manners and had aristocratic pretensions. Forrest, a blood-and-thunder actor who first became famous while playing at the Bowery Theater, was a favorite of the working class. Whenever he starred, the Bowery Boys packed the pit. Macready's fans thought Forrest's fans were uncouth. Forrest's fans thought Macready's fans were trying to create a nobility in the United States.

On May 7, 1849, Macready was due to star at the new Astor Place Opera House in *Macbeth,* the farewell engagement of his American tour. The day of the opening, advertisements flooded the city announcing that Forrest would play Macbeth the same night at the Broadway Theater. Thomas S. Hamblin—another favorite of the Bowery Boys; they mimicked the actor's strut and bellow—was New York's third Macbeth. He would be appearing at the Bowery Theater through an arrangement with Macready, who hoped he would distract Forrest's fans. He didn't. When Macready made his entrance at the Astor Place Opera House, the Forresters who had infiltrated the audience threw rotten eggs, lemons, apples, pennies, and chairs at him while they sang and shouted, "Down with the English hog!" Unable to perform, Macready left the stage and the theater and sneaked home to the New York Hotel through dark back streets.

Influential New Yorkers, including Washington Irving and Herman Melville, horrified at the way Macready had been treated, urged him to set another date for his *Macbeth*—which he did: May 10. Hamblin announced he would repeat his *Macbeth* the same evening. Forrest decided to withdraw from the theatrical duel and arranged to appear in *The Gladiator,* a play in which he had received rave reviews three years before when he had visited London and first met Macready.

A rumor spread that the crew of a British steamer had threatened to attack anyone heckling Macready during the show. In response the Forresters, who may have started the rumor themselves, papered the town with anti-Macready handbills. One of them was written by Edward Zane

Carroll Judson, who under the pseudonym Ned Buntline published a sensational magazine. It demanded "Workingmen! Freemen! Stand by your LAWFUL RIGHTS!" and encouraged the Forresters "to express their opinion this night at the English ARISTOCRATIC Opera House!"

The handbill said "We advocate no violence." But as soon as the curtain went up the theater gallery erupted in hoots, hisses, and howls, and outside a mob of between 10,000 and 20,000, including members of the Dead Rabbits and the Bowery Boys, rampaged along Eighth Street, shattering the theater's windows with stones they pried up from the pavement. While the police barricaded the Opera House doors the mob screamed, "Tear it down! Burn the damn den of the aristocracy!"

Macready refused to cut any scenes. By the fifth act the mob outside in Astor Place was throwing stones not at the theater but at the militia, fifty cavalrymen and two hundred infantrymen who had been called in to clear the streets. The soldiers shot over the rioters' heads. The rioters jeered and threw more stones. The soldiers shot into the crowd. Thirty-one people were killed; about one hundred and fifty were injured. The mob dispersed, except for a few angry men who stood in the emptying streets raging at the American aristocrats who had gone to watch Macready play Macbeth.

"You can't go in there without kid gloves on," screamed one man. "I paid for a ticket and they wouldn't let me in because I hadn't kid gloves and a white vest, damn them!"

August was among those who owned kid gloves and a white vest. On Wednesday, May 23, the *Herald,* editorializing on the riot in Astor Place —or, as it was being called, Massacre Place—attacked the rich and fashionable "who style themselves the exclusives of New York society." This new aristocracy, which had developed "within the last few years," was something "not dreamed of in the philosophy of the last generation." The paper objected to "its style and modes of living, . . . its manners, its dress, its lordly dwellings." It deplored the attempt "to introduce the Italian Opera" into New York "on the same offensive system which prevails in the aristocratic capitals of Europe": the private boxes where the elite could drink champagne and recline on "crimson velvet sofas" while listening to the music. It approvingly noted that these new American aristocrats "excite the laughter of Broadway, as they roll along its uneven pavements" in carriages with "heraldic bearings and footmen attired in outlandish livery." And it clucked over how they shocked "our plain American notions of decency and propriety, as they flaunt their finery in the voluptuous movements of some newly imported meretricious dance."

Battle lines separating the classes in America were being drawn. August, who recently had been storming the barricades of old Knickerbocker society, was not just admitted but finally welcomed into the best drawing rooms in the city, a new recruit in what was becoming a war between the rich and the poor.

August joined the Union Club, the mother of clubs, which Philip Hone had founded. And he began spending more and more time with men like Sam Ward, the banker who had married Medora Grymes, and John Slidell, the Democratic politician who had been envoy extraordinary to Mexico before the recent Mexican War. With Ward, August discussed poetry. When Ward's friend Henry Wadsworth Longfellow sent him a copy of his new poem *Evangeline,* Ward wrote, "The metre fills me with apprehension." August, however, liked the poem and, retreating to his home ground, German literature, compared it to Goethe's *Hermann and Dorothea.* With Slidell, August discussed politics.

Slidell's sister Jane was married to Commodore Matthew Calbraith Perry, who had commanded the American fleet in the Gulf of Mexico during the Mexican War. Perry was a dignified, corpulent man with a big fleshy nose, pouchy jowls, and eyes that, dark above and circled below, looked like those of a panda bear. His hair was so thick that Nathaniel Hawthorne thought he wore a wig. His manner was stern; the corners of his mouth pulled down as though his face as it aged were tightening from the chin up. He spoke in a measured, almost ponderous way, and he disapproved of the changing attitudes toward discipline in the United States Navy. He was distressed when flogging was abolished. His brother Oliver Hazard Perry was the hero of the Battle of Lake Erie whose portrait hung in City Hall when August arrived in New York.

The Matthew Calbraith Perrys had a daughter named Caroline, nicknamed Tiny, their eighth child. She was nineteen years old in the spring of 1849 when August met her, probably in the home of her older sister, Mrs. John Hone.

Caroline was a graceful girl with large eyes, eyelids that often seemed slightly droopy, as though she had just awakened from a luxurious afternoon nap, a straight nose, a thin upper lip and a fuller, somewhat pouty, lower one, a round chin, and a slender neck—the beautiful, delicate, unselfconsciously sensuous features of a Botticelli Venus. She was lovely and soft; the slightest pressure—like a fingernail denting gold—could mar her. Throughout her life people would describe her as looking like a fairy-tale princess. August thought she had a "dear angel's face" and was "charmingly built." As he explained to Babette, because she was small they fit together, since he, too, "belongs to the ponies."

Caroline was—he further explained—"just as lovable and good as she is beautiful and well-bred; and, as a result of her simple education in the country, she is very unpretentious and modest in her demands on life." She was so unselfish that when her uncle Alexander Slidell Mackenzie—who had a fatal heart attack while riding his horse in 1848—left her a bequest, she refused to accept it, because she knew that his widow, her aunt Kate, had been forced to sell some property to pay off that and other debts. August, charmed by Caroline's beauty and nature, fell in love with her.

Caroline had three sisters and three brothers. Sarah, eleven years older, had married Robert S. Rodgers, whose father, Commodore John Rodgers, had been in command of the *U.S.S. President* years before when Matthew Calbraith Perry was a midshipman on that ship. Jane, ten years older, had made what was considered to be a brilliant match; her husband, John Hone, was the great-nephew of Philip Hone, and his mother was a De Peyster, so his social bloodlines were irreproachable. Matthew Calbraith Junior, almost eight years older, was a career navy man who had served under his father during the Mexican War. Oliver, four years older, had been in the navy and studied law before being attacked by a fit of romance that carried him to California with the Forty-Niners to search for gold. William Frederick, a year older, was a lieutenant in the Marine Corps, whose greatest battles in his youth were with the bottle. Isabella, nicknamed Belle, was five years younger than Caroline. A brother, John, and two sisters, Susan and Anna, had died when they were babies.

In the summer of 1849 the Perrys went to Saratoga Springs, a resort in upstate New York that boasted medicinal spring waters and that had been attracting a mixed crowd of Western land speculators, Southern planters, New Orleans cotton kings, Washington politicians, and New York bankers ever since Gideon Putnam had built his luxury hotel, the Union Hall, in 1800. During the next few decades other grand hotels opened—Congress Hall, the Pavilion, the United States Hotel—and guests chose their accommodations according to the prevailing fashions. The Whigs stayed at the more conservative Congress Hall; the Democrats stayed at the United States, the largest and most fashionable Saratoga hotel.

The vacationers woke at dawn, drank the medicinal waters, promenaded through the gardens, flirted while wandering along the footpaths in the nearby woods, gossiped while leaning against the pillars of the hotels' colonnades, gorged at indifferently cooked and lavishly presented meals, danced at evening hops and balls, and kissed under the sweet-smelling woodbine festooning the hotels' piazzas.

August arrived and checked into the United States Hotel on July 19, 1849, the week the telegraph line between Saratoga and New York was reopened. It had been out of commission for two years because the telegraph company had been struggling with financial problems. The link provided the resort with direct news of the cholera epidemic that already had killed over 1,200 people in New York City—where, to combat the plague, a law had been passed preventing pigs from being kept below Forty-second Street.

A few days before August arrived in the resort a rumor that someone in Saratoga had died of cholera circulated through the grand hotels, terrifying the vacationers. The holiday threatened to turn into a nightmare like that described in "The Masque of the Red Death," a story written a few years earlier by Edgar Allan Poe. Either the rumor was unfounded or the hotels' managements suppressed the facts. No one could track down the death. By the end of August's first week in Saratoga, whispers about cholera were being replaced by jokes about a sea-serpent hoax in Rhode Island, scoops about the latest sexual and faro scandals, and wonder at how successful the season promised to be.

That year, in fact, Saratoga was so popular the hotels were turning away hundreds of visitors. Nearly 300 people jammed the United States. Congress Hall was so crowded that every day its guests consumed 900 pounds of meat, 600 pounds of poultry, 250 dozen eggs, 3 barrels of flour, 8 bushels of potatoes, 140 loaves of bread, and 3,000 rolls. There was more gambling than in previous years, and for higher stakes. One evening a woman lost an unprecedented $2,000. Young men spent hundreds of dollars on champagne picnics at which everyone, including the servants, got boisterously drunk. Ladies wore gowns cut so low over their bosoms their breasts were virtually exposed. Gentlemen dressed in white trousers, white vests, white hats, lilac shirts, and white, nearly transparent, grass-cloth coats. There were more equipages clattering through Saratoga's streets than ever before; and owners competed by harnessing their teams in startling arrangements to which they gave fanciful names. Those who owned two light- and two dark-colored horses could hitch them up a light and a dark in front, a dark and a light behind and drive them checkered. Those who owned two light and a dark, as August did, could hitch them up the light ones side by side behind the dark one as a unicorn.

August, who kept his horses at Mr. Cook's Stables as did the other residents of the United States Hotel, preferred, however, to drive his sorrel and one of his grays in tandem, which, according to *The Lorgnette*, a short-lived magazine of gossip and fashion, was the most stylish equipage of all. He racketed around town in "a very pretty yellow wheeled . . . buggy, with a seat behind for his servant, who attends him in white top boots."

The mamas considered him an ideal catch for their marriageable daughters because he was romantic. The papas admired him because he was rich; the brothers, because he was stylish; the daughters, because he was all three. His notoriety as a hell-raiser was being replaced by a reputation for "fine tact and taste." He was one of the few middle-aged men—anyone over thirty was considered by the chic young set to be middle-aged—accepted by the smart youths who increasingly dominated society. And he was the only member of that crowd recognized as being above the cliques that formed and re-formed with the rapidity of the changing figures in the cotillions they danced. He was looked up to as an authority on what was in mode. He was invited everywhere.

August attended a dinner for his friend John Slidell in the new dining room of the United States Hotel. A few days later he shared a nonpartisan meal with Henry Clay, the former Whig presidential candidate. He danced the galop, the polka, and the waltz at the hops and balls, which continued into the early morning. The night breezes carried the smell of honeysuckle through the floor-to-ceiling windows; and the lights from the ballrooms cast yellow rectangles on the lawns and lit up the bushes, making the roses look redder than they did during the day. He gambled at faro and monte until dawn, sipped iced brandy and mint before breakfast, and challenged the owners of the fastest horses in Saratoga.

At one of his races Caroline Perry lost a pair of gloves. An admirer found and returned them with a poem, which called her the "Belle of the graceful Polka land" and described how at the balls "every fond adoring glance/ Turns *to her,* in the magic dance/ Enamoured with her matchless grace" and with "The nameless witchery of her smile." She was—according to the poet—the "Enchantress of the social hour." August was not the only man to fall in love with her. If he wanted to win her, he would have to woo her with dispatch.

The two grand costume balls of the season were going to be held at the United States Hotel on Saturday, August 11, and Friday, August 17. Everyone in Saratoga started to prepare for the events weeks in advance. Hairdressers, jewelers, costumers, and dressmakers came to the resort from New York and Philadelphia. In the fitting room of the most popular costumer, an Eskimo discussed dances with a Hottentot while tailors pinned and chalked their sealskin suit and loincloth.

"In one corner is a customer *sans culotte* in preparation to try on a pair of tights," wrote an observer; "at his elbow is another putting on a hump for Richard III, while a cowled monk and a half-dressed clown are discussing the merits of their respective disguises. In the center of the room is a Chinese mandarin, backed by a jockey and a cavalier; a brigand and a Quaker are passing jokes in another corner, and Shylock and Sam Stick are bantering with each other at a counter nearby; Romeo and Napoleon are putting on their clothes before the glass."

On the evening of the eleventh the band struck up a march at nine o'clock, the doors opened, and as though the ballroom were a resort of the dead, characters from every age and place swept onto the floor. August entered dressed as the master of this underworld in his Devil costume, which according to someone at the ball was "composed of the richest red and black velvet, and decorated and trimmed with demons and fantastical figures. It was looked upon as one of the richest dresses in the room, and is said to have cost $200. The character," the writer added in a wry aside, "was well sustained."

The party was raucous. At midnight the guests filed into the dining room to sample the ham glacé, pâté, roast poultry, meat, gelatins, ice creams, and fruits that were piled up to look like pyramids and temples. The banquet was drowned in an unlimited supply of champagne. By one o'clock corks as numerous as mushrooms after a rain littered the floor. After the ladies left at two in the morning, the men danced with each other until the musicians quit.

At the grand ball on the seventeenth August appeared as a less sinister character. He was dressed not in costume but in the uniform of his office as Austrian consul, which was a "red cloth dress coat, trimmed with . . . pure gold, white cashmere pantaloons with a gold braid, and a cocked hat, very rich." Having impressed his station on the assembled company, most of whom—as he had told his sister—were naïvely awed by European titles, he then astonished everyone halfway through the evening by appearing in a second costume, the uniform of an Austrian soldier, which was, according to an observer, "chaste and elegant." Possibly afraid he had frightened Caroline with his diabolical guise, he may have wanted to reassure her with costumes that were irreproachable.

Caroline "was dressed as a bourgeoise of the time of Louis XV, in pink silk trimmed with black and a black velvet bodice trimmed with ribbon. Her powdered hair was adorned with a *toquet*," a cap, "very becoming to her charms and graces."

At eight o'clock in the evening fireworks splashed the sky with color. Hundreds of upturned faces flickered blue, green, yellow, and red as the flares flashed and exploded above them.

After the fireworks the guests wandered through the dewy grass, which soaked the toes of their slippers. Couples sneaked off to court and be courted. The night was warm, the sky was clear. Perfect weather for the grand ball.

At nine o'clock the guests assembled and promenaded the ballroom. The music started. The dancing began. For the first few hours couples swirled about the room in waltzes and polkas and engaged in the musical geometry of the quadrilles. But when August and a number of other experienced dancers started a new dance called the German Cotillion, those who had not practiced the steps objected. The German Cotillion took an hour and a half to complete, they pointed out; it was unfair to introduce it when so many people were unfamiliar with it. Arguments started. People left the room in disgust.

The board of managers, which included both August and John Slidell, negotiated a compromise. The new dances would not be introduced until after the midnight supper. Twelve o'clock came. The guests feasted on a meal even more elaborate than the one given on the night of the eleventh. When the German Cotillion promoters returned to the ballroom, they found the anti–German Cotillion partisans starting a quadrille. August, who was also a floor manager of the ball, stopped the music and ordered the band to play the German Cotillion, which it did. The quadrille dancers abandoned the field to the victorious German Cotillion set.

Just before dawn the music finally stopped. The men and women who had been dallying and dancing all night separated into parties and went on excursions to fields, lakes, and springs around Saratoga. The sky faded from black to purple to blue. When the sun at last rose, the revelers gave three cheers. One group woke the band leader and dragged him off to help them serenade their ladies. Another group sat down to a $500 breakfast. Couples broke off from the larger crowds and disappeared.

Little by little the gatherings grew smaller and smaller. People returned to the hotels. The night of the grand ball became the day after the dance.

During the following weeks people reviewed how much Heidsieck they had guzzled, how much of the select Springfield, Massachusetts, woodcock they had eaten, how late they had stayed up. They traded rumors about whose heart was broken, whose costume had cost more, and who had disgraced himself or herself—and how. One woman, it was claimed, had ridden naked on horseback through the streets.

The end of the month approached. On the twenty-third Caroline celebrated her twentieth birthday. August continued to court her. The weather cooled. Guests made arrangements to return to the city, packed, and left. The hotels emptied. By the twenty-sixth the season was considered over.

Caroline fell in love with August. Commodore Perry was not sure he approved of the match—despite August's reputation as one of the most eligible bachelors in New York. There was, after all, the difference of religion to consider. The Perrys were Episcopalians. August was—well, people were not sure what religion he was.

August told Caroline that he was brought up first in Alzey and then in Frankfurt as a Jew. He wrote Babette that "although she knows my origin and religion, she has not requested any public or even secret apostasy or change in religion of any kind whatsoever." He explained that the same "liberal views" that had led him away from Judaism "would prevent me from being baptised in her religion, and she is completely content to let me keep my views and beliefs. Of course, this is extremely suitable to me. For although I have not had any connection with" Jews in America, whom he disliked (the Sephardim were too snobbish; the Ashkenazim were too ill-bred), "I should not have liked to become a renegade." He promised Babette a picture of Caroline; and he asked his sister to write to his fiancée "in French or even in *English*," since, protective of Caroline and trying to eliminate the slightest discomfort from her life, he knew that her French was poor.

Babette, however, was not inclined to write to Caroline in any language, even though her uncle Isaac Hanau thought Caroline was "an outstanding good choice," and her father, Simon, approved—although he was unhappy because the marriage meant that now August certainly would never return to Germany to settle. She was upset that August was marrying outside the religion and said the thought of it "might destroy

much of my happiness." She was so distraught that the letters about the
match she sent her father were later destroyed, probably by Simon, to
preserve family harmony.

Although August did not have to renounce his religion, it was decided that, since he was content to be married in an Episcopal ceremony,
there was no reason to announce that he was Jewish. Keeping silent about
his faith, August felt, was not quite the same as denying it; and if it would
make things easier he was willing to write to his father, asking Simon to
get a copy of his birth certificate and to have his name on it changed from
Aaron to August. After all, he was August—had been August ever since
he was an infant.

Simon went to Alzey's mayor, who—under the influence of his secretary, Friedrich Ewald, an old friend and former schoolmate of August's
—refused to change the name on August's birth certificate. In fact,
Ewald, apparently jealous of August's success, was unwilling to help
Simon in any way. Simon, who fumed that Ewald was "deluding himself
into thinking he's a big shot" even though he was only "the son of the
shoemaker," went to the district judge. But the judge could not help until
August sent Simon a notarized power of attorney giving his father the
legal authority to ask for the name change. The drawn-out correspondence over the matter frustrated August, who was used to getting his way
quickly and was impatient to wed.

On Friday, September 14, at Christ Church near her parents' home
in Tarrytown, New York, Caroline was confirmed. Her pastor said that in
order to "fulfill the obligations of your baptismal promise and of your
Christian calling," she should remember "to seek those larger supplies of
grace which are promised to the faithful in the blessed sacrament of the
body and blood of our Savior Christ." Although she was marrying outside
her religion, her parents and pastor were armoring her in Episcopal piety.

Two weeks later Commodore Perry announced Caroline's engagement to August, confirming the rumors that—as the *Herald* had said in a
gossip column—August "had popped the question and solicited the hand
of the beautiful daughter of a well-known and gallant naval officer,"
rumors that had "created a buzz in parlor and dining rooms up town" and
that at first had been "hardly credited by wealthy dames with marriageable daughters."

If Commodore Perry had entertained some doubts about the match,
the other family members did not. Thomas Slidell, Caroline's uncle and
her mother's favorite brother, was delighted to hear that his niece was
marrying August and pleased that the Commodore had not stood in the

way. "Caroline would marry no man whom she did not love," he reminded his brother-in-law, "and Belmont is no doubt much devoted to her. To blight a mutual attachment without some grave cause would have been a severe misfortune to both."

The wedding was set for October 31. August did not want to wait longer. He arranged to give Caroline a full city block, the lots bounded by Nineteenth and Twentieth streets and Fifth and Sixth avenues, in the southeast corner of which—Fifth Avenue and Nineteenth Street—he planned to build a house. On October 29, two days before the wedding, August signed the title to the property over to his future wife. But he still did not have his birth certificate from Alzey. The wedding was put off.

Friends were told Caroline was indisposed. Perhaps the postponement was caused because August had to finesse the lack of the birth certificate. Or there may have been some problem with the transfer of the land, since Caroline did not sign the contract until November 5. Possibly Caroline really had become ill and could neither sign the agreement nor say her vows.

New invitations were sent out. The Reverend Francis Vinton, the rector of Grace Church in Brooklyn, and the husband of one of Caroline's cousins, got permission to perform the ceremony at the new Church of the Ascension, four blocks south of August's mansion on Fifth Avenue. On November 7, 1849, a sunny, cloudless, balmy Indian summer day, August and Caroline were married.

PART TWO

❦ *CHAPTER EIGHT* ❦

THE BROADWAY WITS who explained that "The first thing a young [New Yorker] does is to get a horse; the second, to get a wife" felt that August had confirmed their prophecy. To celebrate his marriage he gave a three-day feast for his friends in New York, and he arranged to have a cake sent from Koblenz to his father in Alzey. "It tasted wonderful," said Simon, uncharacteristically enthusiastic. He told August that "it was a big sensation" in the town, which was not used to the kind of elaborate decoration—"this Cake Art," Simon had called it—the bakers had lavished on it. Simon added that "the unexpected news of your marriage" surprised all his neighbors, "because everyone believed you would stay a bachelor." Simon was pleased that they had been wrong.

He tempered his joy, however, with the observation that since the wedding had already taken place, "I see now that you don't need any papers"—even though, he explained, "I could write a whole book about the pains I took." (Five years later, in fact, the request to change August's name on the birth certificate was officially refused.)

Characteristically, Simon told August that although he had not yet bought Caroline a present, he intended to do so shortly. However, he had sent her a letter, which he had composed in German and translated into French, "which is not an easy task for me."

For Christmas the newlyweds visited with Commodore and Mrs. Perry at their farm, The Moorings, on the bank of the Hudson River at Tarrytown, New York. The stone house built a decade before was crowded for the holidays. August and Caroline slept in a downstairs bedroom. The Commodore deployed the rest of the family—Caroline's sister Jane and her husband, John Hone, her cousin Raymond Rodgers and his wife, Julia (who was also Caroline's aunt), her fifteen-year-old sister Belle, and her brother Oliver, who had just arrived from the California gold fields—in the various available bedrooms. The little children and their nurses, the Commodore decided, were to be "colonized in the parlor."

August still assumed that Alphonse de Rothschild intended to return to New York to take over the Rothschilds' American branch, but now he looked forward to the association, which he thought would take some of the pressure of business off him and enable him "to be absent for two or three months, if not longer. Then"—he wrote Babette—"I hope that with God's help I shall be able to come and visit you together with my young bride, and I am convinced that you will open to her your loving sisterly arms. Isn't it strange, my dear little Babette, that I should have a brother-in-law and you a sister-in-law and that we should not have seen them in person?" When Alphonse did not return, August canceled the European trip.

August treated Caroline as though she were not his wife but his daughter. He left notes for her when he went to work in the morning—"You slept so sweetly when I entered your room that I would not wake you"—and he sent letters to her from the office during the day, guiding her personal affairs and instructing her in the management of their home at 82 Fifth Avenue. Like a man launching a new business, which must be nurtured and closely watched, he paid attention to the smallest details of family life from the arrangement of the flowers on the dinner table to Caroline's toilette.

"My dearest Tiny," he jotted in haste one morning, "don't forget to tell" the coiffeur "that he has to come back tomorrow morning in order to dress your hair." He even specified what time the coiffeur should arrive. And although customarily New York women waited a year before they wore their new Parisian dresses, so that they would not seem too ostentatious, too eagerly fashionable, August convinced Caroline to wear her gowns at once, before the styles faded in Paris and London. He wanted his wife to be a modish Continental even though they were living in New York.

Running the household he exhibited the same flair he had shown in his bachelor days. He hired the best cook he could find in New York; and instead of giving him the day off when they were not entertaining, as the Knickerbockers usually did with their cooks, August insisted that he and

Caroline dine as elaborately alone as when they had company, which shocked and titillated New York society. Like an architect instructing a master carpenter, August directed the cook. He oversaw the magnificent meals from the way the dishes were cooked—he once explained that in preparing pâté de foie gras one should "Never lift the lid of the casserole while it's simmering"—to the way they were presented. He even occasionally did some of the marketing.

"I bought for today some fish and wild pigeons, the latter of which please to tell the cook to broil or roast just as you like best," he wrote Caroline. "I have ordered some small seedbirds for tomorrow as a roast. I have bought plenty of vegetables, flour, and groceries."

It was said that August "taught New York the art of giving the perfect dinner," which was not merely a meal but a performance in which the spectators participated. Those who resented his interest in—and envied his gift for—entertaining claimed that he even would go over the maid's dusting himself to prepare for a dinner. They could not fathom why a man would help his wife run the household.

If August seemed unnaturally zealous in his attention to their home, it was because he wanted to relieve Caroline of the burden.

"My dear Caroline," Jane Perry wrote to her recently married daughter, "you have much to learn before you will be sensible of the great blessing of having a husband so devoted to all your comforts and whose chief aim seems to be your pleasure. While surrounded by so much to make life easy and happy, you must always bear in mind, my dear child, that God in his dealings with us poor creatures does not allow life to pass without changes. It often happens that we are many times made to feel sorrows which seem too hard for us to bear. I trust the sorrowful days for you are very far off and would not mention the probability of them, if I were not sure it is the best and wisest plan to feel that our days cannot always be bright."

Jane Perry's pleasure at how much August cared for Caroline was stretched—almost to the breaking point—over a superstructure of disapproval. She objected to August's extravagance not because she thought luxury imprudent, as Simon did, or even because she thought it was ungodly. She objected because luxurious living was, according to her view of the world, unrealistic. Comforts weakened the will, which must be strong to cope with the tragedies every life eventually encountered.

Caroline, however, accepted the comforts as modestly as she would have accepted suffering. As though love were a function of protection,

August, to prove his affection, was trying to create for her an existence without conflict. She became a Sleeping Beauty sheltered in her Fifth Avenue palace by a husband thorny as any enchanted hedge.

In March, Caroline fell ill. To recover her health she went to Washington, D.C., with her father, who, along with his other business and errands, was to dine with the President, Zachary Taylor.

With Caroline away August felt aimless. When he went out to dinner he "talked a good deal" about her; and he judged his companions according to the traditional standard of the lonely husband: "I like her so much," August wrote Caroline about an acquaintance, "because I think she is very fond of you." He went to a stag dinner, which he found "more agreeable than such parties usually are" because all the guests knew one another; there were no strangers at the table. And he took Caroline's sister Jane Hone and her mother-in-law, Mrs. De Peyster, to hear Fanny Kemble the actress give one of her Shakespearean readings, which according to Jane's great-uncle-in-law had "The fashionable world . . . all agog. . . . She reads . . . three evenings in the week, and at noon on Mondays, at the Stuyvesant Institution, in Broadway, a room which will hold six or seven hundred persons, and which is filled when she reads by the *élite*: delicate women, grave gentlemen, belles, beaux, and critics, flock to the doors of the entrance, and rush into such places as they can find, two or three hours before the time of the lady's appearance."

Being able to attend such a chic affair with one of the most respectable Knickerbocker matrons on his arm confirmed August's triumph over New York society. His pleasure at strolling into the reading with Jane Hone and Mrs. De Peyster was heightened by the evening's selection: scenes from *A Midsummer Night's Dream* accompanied by "the large orchestra of the Philharmonic Society playing the music composed for that piece by Mendelssohn," which August thought was "one of the most sublime compositions of the present time."

He wished Caroline had been at the performance. "You cannot imagine, my dear Tiny, how much I miss you," he wrote. "I did not think it possible I could feel so forlorn for so short a separation—it seems to me as if years had elapsed since I saw you and I count the hours until the time when we shall meet again."

He arranged to leave his business for a day, so that he could meet Caroline in Philadelphia. He telegraphed her to find the exact time she would arrive, because he did not want to reach Philadelphia too early and "make my present gloom still gloomier" by having to stay "in a bad hotel all alone."

Caroline's absence developed in August an even deeper love than that which he had felt for his wife before she had gone to Washington. But he was his father's son—the greater his love, the more he worried.

"Please, my own dear wife, remember your promise and not move about too much."

"I beg you to keep yourself *as quiet as possible today*. Pray do not walk up and down stairs. Keep quietly on your sofa, and, if you want to take the fresh air, *take only a very short walk*."

By late spring August's worry had taken on even more urgency. Caroline was pregnant.

Spring was blustery and wet. August clattered around town in a coach pulled by four white horses. Despite Caroline's condition they continued to entertain lavishly. Caroline was becoming "in every sense society's queen."

"When you enter her house," an observer one day would write, "her reassuring smile, her exquisitely gracious and unpretending manner of receiving placed you at your ease and made you feel welcome. She had the power that all women should strive to obtain, the power of attaching men to her, and keeping them attached; calling forth a loyalty of devotion such as one imagines one yields to a sovereign, whose subjects are only too happy to be her subjects."

In April they gave a large dinner, which Commodore Perry, Washington Irving, and Philip Hone attended. The Commodore had become a frequent guest; and August, whose hearty and magisterial manner irked some acquaintances, treated his father-in-law—those acquaintances thought—too familiarly. "There's a good fellow," August said to the Commodore, according to one story, "run down to the cellar and see if there are six more bottles of the *Rapid* Madeira. And try not to shake them on the stairs!"

In the arithmetic of malice August and Caroline had too much; so gossips tried to balance the credits in their life with an equal number of debits. They thought August an upstart and saw in his lack of deference toward the Commodore an overbearing arrogance. They thought because Caroline was so beautiful and amiable she could not also be clever, and they saw in her gentleness a lack of intelligence. Since their marriage seemed such a perfect match—"his worldliness plus her breeding and character proved irresistible," it was said—they saw in August's desire to marry well the calculation of a climber.

In 1850, Babette and Stephan Feist and their new baby, Frederika, came to New York to visit with the Belmonts and to allow Stephan to expand the scope of his business. The meeting between the two families was awkward. Babette's disapproval of August's marriage to Caroline made intimacy difficult.

The Feists visited New York City and Morristown, New Jersey. Jane Perry asked her daughter if they all went to hear a local minister and liked his preaching and wondered if Babette had "learned to eat" corn "as we liked it best," presumably on-the-cob. The visit ended. Babette still did not fully accept the marriage and probably was concerned about the problems which would have to be faced when August and Caroline became parents.

On December 28, a few months after the Feists left New York, Caroline gave birth to a son. She and August named him Perry and agreed he should be raised in the Episcopal Church, a decision that Babette had feared and that could not have pleased her. On New Year's Eve day the pastor of the Church of the Ascension, G. T. Bedell, wrote August that he hoped "the occasion will soon arrive when you can present" the baby "for baptism," adding, "I only wish it might be the offering of hearts which had first given themselves to the Lord." Since August's son was going to be baptised, why, Bedell wondered, wouldn't August join the church as well? "You will not withhold that which you now deem most precious," wrote the pastor. "Why should you not also devote your own soul to Him, a *reasonable* sacrifice." Bedell was a businessman's clergyman; he emphasized the reasonableness of conversion like a salesman justifying the logic of an insurance policy.

But August saw no reason—in business or religion—to commit himself to a contract when he could enjoy the benefits offered without signing any official agreement. To his mind the benefits of the Episcopal Church for him would be mundane rather than spiritual.

Despite August's Episcopal drift, he did not want to reject formally the faith in which he had been raised. But his attempt to navigate between apostasy in one religion and conversion to another failed. When news of his son's baptism became public, the New York Jewish community, which had seen his marriage as defection, disowned him. The occasional contributions he had made and would make to Jewish charities, such as the

Hebrew Assistance Society of New York and the Reform Synagogue in Albany, were not enough to prove he was interested in any continuing tie to American Jewry. He had kept aloof from his fellow Jews ever since he had arrived in the United States; he had married outside the religion; and he was raising his son as a Christian. The Jewish community of New York not only repudiated August but considered his connection to the Rothschilds—who despite their wealth and worldliness had maintained their faith—an affront and his inclusion in any list of American Jews an insult. He was, in the eyes of his Jewish contemporaries, an outcast.

CHAPTER NINE

POLITICS INTERESTED AUGUST more and more—and the exercise of diplomatic power through money. The transfer of funds to Mexico and the loans to the United States government and the territory of California had given him a feel of what it was like to have such power; and he was eager—a little too eager, some thought—to use that power again. Most of the first-class merchants of the time were Whigs. "The Democratic merchants could have easily been stowed in a large Eighth Avenue railroad car," said one contemporary. But August's relatively liberal tendencies inclined him to the Democrats. Because there were fewer powerful merchants in the Democratic party it would be easier for him to rise in the party hierarchy. John Slidell, Caroline's uncle and an influential Democrat, was August's political sponsor. During 1850 Slidell was already at work trying to get the Democratic nomination for the presidential election of 1852 for James Buchanan.

Buchanan was a promising candidate. He had been a congressman, minister to Russia, a senator, and secretary of state under James K. Polk (whom August had supported). He was a bachelor with a terror of train travel and a tragic love affair in his past. He had a high forehead and eyes that stared out from under a ledge of brow with the look of a man watching a street riot from behind a curtain in an upstairs window. A Pennsylvania moderate, he supported what he once called "the constitutional rights of the South in opposition to all projects of the abolitionists and quasi-abolitionists."

Nationally, the Democrats were split: the free-soil Democrats, the States' Rights Democrats, and the moderate Democrats jockeyed for dominance in the party with the controlled hostility of three stubborn men trying to sit down at the same time in the same chair. The primary fight would be difficult. Buchanan's opponents were all experienced and able politicians.

Lewis Cass, the most likely candidate for the Democratic presidential nomination, had been secretary of war under Andrew Jackson, minister to France, a senator, and the Democratic presidential nominee in 1848. According to his enemies he was self-important and sullen; according to his friends he was distinguished and gruff. An inflexible supporter of the Union, Cass adamantly opposed the secessionists. To resolve the difficulties between the North and the South he advocated Popular—or, as its detractors called it, "squatter"—Sovereignty: Each territory could solve the slavery question by itself, without federal interference, and would be admitted into the Union as a state, with or without slavery, depending on what the territorial constitution required. Although he was adept at straddling issues, he was becoming more and more like a man who wants to go for a row but is caught one foot on land and the other in a boat that is slowly drifting away from shore. Cass told Buchanan that he preferred him to the other candidates (even to William O. Butler, a Kentuckian with a free-soil taint who had been Cass's running mate in 1848), and he promised to support Buchanan if his own presidential bid failed.

Stephen A. Douglas, the freshman senator from Illinois, was the least tried and most aggressive of the Democratic candidates. He was supported by the Young America movement, which was nationalistic and expansionistic and which defended the revolutions sweeping Europe. The "Old Fogies" in the Democratic party like Buchanan thought Douglas too young, too brash, and too hungry for office. Although temperamentally Douglas was closer to August's nature than the cautious Buchanan, August—more conservative in entering politics than he had been in entering society—accused Douglas of being a stalking horse for lobbyists who, if Douglas were elected, would indulge in "the wildest schemes for appropriation for Railroads, Public works, distribution of public funds &c." Douglas, however, saw himself as voicing "the sentiment of every Northern man who is not an Abolitionist."

The governor of New York, William Learned Marcy, was the best qualified of the Democratic candidates. A former senator and secretary of war under Polk, he was an honest and effective administrator, respected by all, friends and enemies. But he had been ill and was weary of party politics. Wanting a rest, he was poised on the edge of retirement and had stayed neutral on the slavery question. In 1850, although a presidential presence, he had not yet indicated any intention of running for the Democratic presidential nomination.

If Marcy sat out the race and supported Buchanan, Buchanan would probably win New York, which was a crucial state. And as Slidell told Buchanan, since "you may rely upon almost unanimous support from the Southern states, if you can secure the New York vote, there can be no difficulty" in winning the nomination.

The convention, scheduled to be held in Baltimore, was two years away, which gave Buchanan time to marshal his forces. To prevent Marcy from entering the race Buchanan had to have support in New York that was strong enough and vocal enough to make his nomination seem inevitable, but equivocal enough to allow the party to unify once the nomination was won.

Slidell knew that if Buchanan sent an outsider into the state to run his campaign, the party regulars—or irregulars—would resent the intrusion. To lead his New York fight Buchanan needed a New Yorker who was loyal enough to be trusted, persuasive enough to pull the party together after the nominating convention, influential enough to sway newspapers into his camp, and, if that failed, rich enough to help finance a new paper guaranteed to be pro-Buchanan. Slidell asked August to take the job.

In March 1851 August wrote on Buchanan's behalf to the editors of the *New York Herald* and the *New York National-Democrat,* which like the other Democratic newspapers in the city had not yet indicated whom they would support for the presidential nomination; but his efforts "to make them do partial justice" to Buchanan only partially succeeded.

"It is very difficult at present to get any of our papers to commit themselves in any way for any particular Democratic candidate," August reported to Buchanan; "and besides that I have to be very cautious how I approach them, as they are very unreliable fellows and too much zeal might do you more harm than good."

Ten years before, at the time of August's duel with Heyward, the *Herald* had veered and tacked according to the way the winds of opinion had blown—anti-Belmont and pro-Belmont. August suspected the paper would steer the same kind of irregular course during the next year and a quarter before the nominating convention. Everyone knew the paper's owner, James Gordon Bennett, was a scoundrel. He had, in fact, four months before been beaten with a whip, "cow-skinned," on Broadway "by a Mr. Graham, the unsuccessful Loco-foco candidate for district attorney," who had not liked the way the *Herald* had covered his campaign.

"I should be well pleased to hear of this fellow being punished in this way, and once a week for the remainder of his life, so that new wounds might be inflicted before the old ones were healed, or until he left off lying," wrote Philip Hone.

The *Herald*'s classifieds were filled with advertisements placed by prostitutes, its columns with gossip about the city's leading citizens, and its editorials with intimate revelations about Bennett's private affairs. When he was invited to join the Union Club, Bennett debated in print with his conscience, "Shall I, or shall I not, accept the invitation?" When he decided to get married, he headlined the article announcing his intentions "Declaration of Love—Caught at Last—Going to Be Married— New Movement in Civilization."

Since August did not count on the *Herald* or on any other Democratic paper to give Buchanan the kind of support necessary to keep Marcy out of the race, he and Slidell made plans to start their own newspaper, modeled after the sober London *Times*, that would promote Buchanan's candidacy. "The importance of such an organ," Slidell told Buchanan, "cannot be overstated." August pledged $10,000 to the project, the largest single contribution.

In early summer Slidell left his home in Louisiana and went to New York to help August raise money for their newspaper and to try to convince Marcy that Buchanan deserved his support. Slidell met the governor in Saratoga Springs. As he told Buchanan, "we had several very long conversations" during which Marcy seemed friendly. The field in New York seemed clear for Buchanan to make his move.

But the newspaper foundered even before it was launched.

John W. Forney, a friend of Buchanan's who had been organizing in Pennsylvania, was chosen to be the editor. He was a hard worker at other men's causes. With his prominent nose and insignificant mouth he was a caricature of someone doomed to stand at a banquet smelling, but never tasting, the feast.

"Everything for the establishment of our paper with Forney at the head of it was in as fair a way as we could wish," August wrote Buchanan, "when all at once" Francis B. Cutting, Charles O'Conor, and Theodore Sedgwick, three of the newspaper's leading backers, "urged serious objections to Forney's editorship. This opposition to our scheme and to Forney particularly was decided upon, as I have since heard from undoubted authority, at a meeting between Governor Marcy and the above named gentlemen [Cutting and O'Conor] and it was urged that even if the paper would not openly advocate your cause, yet the very feel of a paper being started with Forney at the head of it would give strong evidence that you had powerful friends in this state and this might interfere with the aspirations and interests of Marcy."

Evidently between the meeting with Slidell and the meeting with Cutting and O'Conor, Marcy had changed his mind about supporting Buchanan because—as Buchanan complained to a friend—"At this propitious moment, the Van Burens [former President Martin Van Buren, who had run for president as the Free-Soil candidate in the last election, and his son, whom everyone called Prince John] began to tickle Marcy with the idea of being President himself. His leading friends . . . who were to support me hauled off; and backed out from the paper, unless it should remain perfectly neutral on the subject of the Presidency."

August told Buchanan "it would have been more than useless to attempt" publishing a newspaper as long as Marcy and his friends remained "not only not with us but in all probability against us." Since Buchanan needed at least a friendly if not a committed newspaper in New York more than he needed Forney as an editor, Forney was sacrificed at Marcy's altar. August told Buchanan, "I have not given up my project and am now active in trying to collect subscriptions for a Democratic Union paper" with someone other than Forney as editor, "which is to direct public sentiment in opposition to the pernicious influence of the *Evening Post*."

Edited by William Cullen Bryant, the *New York Evening Post* was too abolitionist to be counted on to support Buchanan or any of the other moderate candidates August would favor if Buchanan lost the nomination.

"I hope I shall succeed," August told Buchanan, although he admitted that "with the disturbed state of our party in" New York "any effort which requires union and cooperation is almost hopeless."

August felt isolated, visible, and vulnerable as Buchanan's chief supporter in New York. He wanted allies, both for Buchanan and for himself.

His effort to start a pro-Buchanan newspaper had failed. His next project, the Democratic Union newspaper, was not attracting supporters.

And—the most troubling problem—Buchanan would not enter the fight actively in New York until he was assured of the nomination of his home-state convention, which was due to be held in March, three months away. He simply hibernated at his home in Pennsylvania, waiting for his party's call, unable or unwilling to recognize that the party's call is usually an echo of some politician's loud and vigorous claim on the nomination. As long as Buchanan refused to act, August's efforts on his behalf were frustrated.

Very few influential New York politicians were interested in helping Buchanan—at least until Buchanan's candidacy was strong enough for them to gain as much as he would by their support. Their "feelings of indecision and their fear of committing themselves for any particular candidate have paralyzed my best efforts," August wrote Buchanan.

It was not just Buchanan's political future that was stalled in New York but August's own as well. If Buchanan were to win the nomination and the presidency, August could expect to return to Europe as a diplomat. If Buchanan were to lose, even if August were to throw his support to the candidate who won, he would not be among the first to collect the spoils; his chances of returning to Alzey glorified—or justified—by rank as well as by wealth would dim.

Despite his many canceled European trips August wanted to return to Germany. His "wish to visit you and his place of birth becomes stronger with every day," Caroline wrote to Simon, who having just been black-balled from a social club because of anti-semitism must have had ambivalent feelings about August's Gentile wife. "In my case," Caroline added, "I could not think of anything more pleasant. I am very eager to get to know my husband's father and everything concerning him."

The trip to Europe offered Caroline a chance to satisfy the curiosity that drives someone in love to try to solve her lover's past as though it were a mystery—a curiosity that was even more intense than usual in Caroline's case, since the world in which August had lived before he met her, before he had come to America, was so different from the world she knew.

Caroline also wanted to repair the breach with her sister-in-law. She wanted "to see Babette again," she told Simon. "It is quite sad to think of us living so far apart, but I hope the time will come when we all can be together."

But that time seemed to exist in an ever receding future. Trying to intercede on behalf of her husband, whose decision to postpone the European trip surely must have pained Simon, Caroline wrote, "May I ask whether we can hope for your visit one day?"—adding, as though she wanted to assure her father-in-law that the trip had not been delayed because of her reluctance, "I do not have to tell you how happy we would be" if Simon were to come to America. "But I believe you would think that we as dutiful children should make the trip first; and so, with God's will we will do it." August, she explained, "is only awaiting political affairs to be cleared up after which he will travel to Europe immediately —business permitting."

Even if August were to take his family to Europe after the election —business permitting—the ideal arrangement that they all had hoped for the previous year (the travelers reconnoitering on the Continent, the Commodore stationed not far away in the Mediterranean) was no longer possible. In mid-January 1852 the Commodore was ordered to "proceed to Washington and report to the Secretary of the Navy without delay." He had, as August wrote to Simon, "a very honorable and respectable command over the greatest fleet which was ever appointed in peace times to an American commodore. Namely, he is going with 6 battleships to East India, China, and Japan, and, in addition to being the commander of the fleet, also has a diplomatic mission"—to open Japan to Western trade.

Great things were happening, and August was restive because they were not happening to him. He decided to act decisively. When Marcy stopped in New York City in February 1852, August went to call on him late one evening. The governor greeted him genially; after the brief formalities they started to spar. Marcy hinted that Buchanan's health was too fragile for him to run for the presidency. August assured him that Buchanan was as healthy as ever—an honest although not particularly illuminating claim. Marcy boasted of his support in the South. August agreed. Marcy was popular in the South—as popular as Buchanan. In fact, they were the only Northerners the South would support.

To be sure of winning, both men needed the same delegates: the South, New York, and Pennsylvania. Buchanan could not get New York's votes while Marcy was a candidate. Marcy could not get Pennsylvania's votes while Buchanan was a candidate. Each was trying to bully the other into abandoning the race. To get Buchanan to quit, Marcy threatened August with Buchanan's sure defeat at the Baltimore Democratic convention. August, topping Marcy, threatened a split in the party between Buchanan and Marcy, leading to the Democrats' sure defeat in the presidential election. Neither threat budged the other.

Since bullying had not worked, perhaps seduction would. August told the governor that if he would support Buchanan in the convention "fairly and firmly," Buchanan, if he failed to get the nomination, would then support Marcy.

Marcy praised Buchanan "and said that all *his* friends would certainly vote for" Buchanan, "in case they could not succeed in" getting Marcy the nomination.

August had met a threat with a threat; Marcy had met a seduction with a seduction. They were deadlocked.

Early in March, Buchanan won the Pennsylvania state nomination 3 to 1 over his closest rival, Cass. The victory was so unequivocal that it seemed Buchanan's campaign had finally been roused from its torpor. August was elated.

The omens in New York were as hopeful as they were in Pennsylvania. August at last had gained "control of a small but widely circulated morning paper, the *Morning Star*, and"—he told Buchanan—"you will have seen by the different numbers which have been forwarded to you that they advocate your cause and they will continue to do so, being guided as to the manner by myself." August also recently had helped to form the General Buchanan New York Committee.

Now that Buchanan had a newspaper August was cautious about using it too blatantly. A Douglas supporter who had bought a journal called the *Democratic Review* had virtually ruined his candidate by attacking the other candidates so violently that some of the more conservative Douglas men, in disgust, had defected to the opposition. August did not want to make that same mistake. He "thought best to let" the newspaper "for the present come on as moderately as possible so that we may not bring upon us the open hostility of the Cass and Marcy men." He even suggested that the paper might "to a certain extent apparently favor" Marcy's candidacy, which "may contribute toward making" Marcy's supporters "come over to you, when they see (as I have no doubt they will soon) that Marcy has no chance for the nomination."

Perhaps with the Douglas newspaper fiasco in mind August told Buchanan, "You may rely upon my utmost discretion and that nothing can or shall be done by me which could compromise you in the remotest way." For a long time August had been known in New York as a hot-head. He now had to live down that reputation. As though to counteract any hostile rumors about his probity or his loyalty that may have reached Buchanan, August insisted that "[our] *only object* is to render ourselves useful to you."

There was no reason for Buchanan to doubt August's efforts. But August's assurances that he would never do anything that would hurt the candidate's chances appear often enough in his letters to Buchanan to suggest that he may have had a presentiment of the embarrassment his support would cause when Democrats were no longer fighting each other for the nomination but were fighting Whigs for the White House.

CHAPTER TEN

AUGUST FOLLOWED the Democratic National Convention in Baltimore from New York City. He had printed and sent to every delegate a pamphlet praising Buchanan, but the pamphlet worked no magic. In ballot after ballot the various candidates rose and fell like men floating in the swells of the ocean, one head visible on the crest of a wave, another head in a trough, a third head rising to the crest of another wave. They bobbed up and down as the delegates cast their votes first in one direction and then another until, none of the leading candidates having been able to gather enough support to give them the necessary two-thirds of the votes, a black-horse candidate named Franklin Pierce won the nomination.

Pierce was an amiable, reluctant candidate with a doughy face, a mouth as straight and tucked as the crease in the crown of a Parker House roll, and eyes remarkably candid for a politician. He was a political mirror, each faction of the Democratic party seeing in him its own inclinations and foreseeing in him a moldable ally. The party would not split as it had in 1848.

August, proving himself a loyal party member, supported Pierce as vigorously as he had supported Buchanan. When the recently formed Democratic National Committee was unable to raise its goal of $20,000, August, who thought the Democrats "very needy indeed," contributed the amount lacking. He helped organize public meetings, urged Buchanan to risk the train trip from Pennsylvania to New York to appear at an important rally—because his failure to show would have a "chilling effect" on Pierce's campaign—and published a speech Buchanan made defending Pierce. But for all his good intentions, by October, August's backing had become an issue in the campaign.

The Whig candidate, Winfield Scott, had in 1845 urged more stringent laws regulating naturalization; and although he later repudiated that stand, he was not popular with foreign-born—especially Irish and German—voters. To win their support he flattered them; but he sounded condescending and only alienated them more.

Needing to repair the damage Scott had done, the Whigs decided to exploit the Hungarian independence movement in Austria, a popular cause in America at the time. Many naturalized as well as native Americans had been appalled at the brutality with which the Austrian government had tried to suppress the Hungarian nationalists who had rebelled against Vienna's authority. When Louis Kossuth, a leader of the Hungarian movement, arrived in New York at the end of 1851, August watched the crowd give him "a reception the like of which for enthusiasm and warmth was probably never witnessed even from our excitable population." To protest Austria's policies August apparently had resigned officially from his position as Austria's consul general in 1850; however, as late as April 1851 he was still receiving letters from Vienna addressed to him as consul general, and by his own admission he was still functioning in an unofficial capacity as an agent for Austria as late as 1852, the year of the presidential election.

August's connections to the Austrian government made him an ideal target for the Whigs. By attacking him they hoped to ingratiate themselves with the foreign-born voters whom Scott had infuriated. The Whigs pointed out that not only was August linked to the oppressors of the Hungarians, he also was an agent of the Rothschilds—wonderful propaganda. The native Americans hated the Rothschilds because they were foreign capitalists, and the immigrant Irish Catholics and Germans hated the Rothschilds because they were Jews.

On Thursday, October 26, 1852, less than a week before the election, the *New York Tribune* attacked August. The *Tribune* was a Whig newspaper edited by Horace Greeley, an elfin man with a wreath of white hair and tufts of white whiskers that looked like feathers clinging to the cheeks of a man who has fought all night with his pillow. He was, according to one bemused contemporary, "the oracle of his party," a man "apt to be wild, visionary, and abstracted in his notions about politics and the relative duties of social communities."

Under a headline that announced "Austria and the Money-Lenders for Pierce" the *Tribune* described a "circular, which was duly sent to the 'Democratic' magnates of this city," inviting them to a meeting "for the purpose of devising measures to insure the election of General Franklin Pierce and William R. King to the Presidency and Vice-Presidency of the United States." It was signed "August Belmont and others."

"Who is this Mr. Belmont?" the *Tribune* asked.

And the newspaper answered itself:

> He is the acting Chargé d'affaires of Austria and the Agent of the Rothschilds in the United States! Americans! Will you at last understand the influences at work to defeat Winfield Scott! Will you at last open your eyes to the true nature of the party which seeks to rule you. . . . Americans! shall the Chargé of Austria . . . thus impudently dictate to you who shall be your chief magistrate? Workingmen! shall the representative of foreign monopolies be your leader in the path of destruction to American labor? Exiles and friends of European liberty! can you longer be humbugged into supporting a party and a candidate in whose success your hated oppressors and foes take such interest? Democrats! can you hold that to be genuine Democracy which enlists in its behalf the tools of imperial despotism and cosmopolitan usury? We have long known that Mr. Belmont was actively interfering in the election, and that he was hand in glove with the Democratic leaders, but till now we have not had . . . proof. . . . Hitherto he has been notorious as a heavy better on Pierce's election. Now, it appears as a matter of course that he can use the money of Austria and the Rothschilds still more directly to secure that end.

August was "vexed and grieved" at "the absurd attack of Greeley not on my own account, but from fear that this shameful appeal to prejudice and ignorance might injure the party in the election."

The morning the *Tribune* appeared August sat in his office and wrote Greeley:

> I am a *naturalized American citizen;* I own property in this city; my domestic ties are all here; my home is here; my children, if spared [Caroline was pregnant again, and August worried about her condition] will be here after me—in their veins will flow American blood. I should be glad to know why I am to be ostracized and to be prevented from taking such a part in the government of this country as its Constitution allows to every citizen, as my judgement dictates, and my capacity permits. . . .
> The ground of your attack is that I am the *acting chargé* of the Austrian government. You will be pleased to correct this error.

I am not and never have been *acting chargé* &c. of Austria. I am consul for Austria, and no more. The consular office impresses no political character whatever. Of this you cannot be ignorant. . . . The consular office requires not even allegiance to the power by which it is conferred. *I am not and never was an Austrian subject or citizen.* Several consuls of foreign powers in the United States are native born Americans; and a large proportion of our own consuls abroad are citizens of the countries to which they are accredited. . . . Since I have held the office of consul, I have never received one cent in the shape of fees or salary. . . . Your other ground of assault is that I am an agent of the Rothschilds. Since when has it been considered just that private commercial relations should be dragged before the public and made the test of personal abuse for political objects? . . . You have deemed it proper to single my name out for attack. . . . The reason is obvious—it was to make an appeal to an illiberal prejudice against adopted citizens.

In his indignation August allowed his letter to be more heated than he perhaps should have; but his fury remained verbal. He was no longer the young rakehell of a decade before. He threw down no gauntlet, demanded no duel. He would not let the *Tribune* goad him into embarrassing Pierce. And he did not let his anger blunt his shrewdness. Greeley had attacked August as an Austrian sympathizer, a capitalist, and a Jew. August subtly shifted the terms of the attack, making the *Tribune* seem not the defender of foreign-born voters but their antagonist.

Later in the day August went from his new office at 76 Beaver Street the dozen blocks north to the *Tribune*'s offices on Newspaper Row, right across the street from City Hall Park. The *Tribune* building like the other newspaper buildings in the area had, lettered above each row of windows from the ground to top floors, signs advertising the offices housed inside —newspaper, printer, stationery shop, advertising agency—so that the building's façade looked like the front page of the newspaper's daily edition.

August went into the editorial offices and asked to speak with Greeley. Greeley refused to see him. August left the letter he had written. Greeley declined to publish it. August was disgusted.

The Belmont Affair, as people were calling it, was relished by the newspapers—Democratic and Whig, pro- and anti-Belmont—as a scrappy and colorful ending to the presidential campaign. The editors all hurried to attack or defend August. *The New York Times* sided with the *Tribune*. The *Herald*, the *Evening Post,* the *New York Abend-Zeitung,* and the upstate *Albany Argus* sided with August.

The *Herald* and the *Post* attacked the *Tribune* for not publishing August's letter. The *Tribune* claimed the letter was really not a defense of August but a veiled attack on Winfield Scott, the Whig presidential candidate. Therefore they had no moral obligation to print it.

The *Herald* and the *Post* published August's letter to prove that it was not an attack on Scott and that the *Tribune*'s stand was based on prejudice. The *Tribune* defended itself by writing, "we care nothing for the place of his birth, and consider only what he is. That he is no Democrat, in any sense which the dictionary would justify, we know; and we ask, as we have every right to ask, the electors, whether Native or Adopted, to judge how much that Democracy can be worth of which August Belmont is a leader."

The *Herald* defended August's right to back the candidate of his choice and praised his support of Pierce as "a highly creditable position. It smacks of independence and true progressive go-ahead American principles in standing out against the mass of the bulls and bears and stockjobbers for Pierce."

Both the Democrats and the Whigs were running against the capitalists. However, the Whigs were running against foreign capitalists and the Democrats were running against Wall Street capitalists, most of whom —despite Whig rhetoric—were Whigs.

The *Herald* delighted in flaunting August's membership in the Democratic party and his opposition to the "combined powers of Wall Street banks, bank organs, British bankers," as though August were a champion of labor, not a Wall Street banker and an agent of at least one British bank himself.

The *Tribune* accused August of being a member of a secret society that was trying to rig the elections and of spending $2,000 in Richmond County to buy votes for Pierce. The *Herald* published a second letter from August denying the *Tribune*'s charge and accused the *Tribune* of "the grossest disregard . . . of the common decencies of society."

The *Post* claimed the *Tribune* lied. The *Tribune* claimed the *Post* had "lost not only its temper, but its common sense."

The *Herald* called the editors of the *Tribune* "reckless socialists" and "quibbling, equivocating artful dodgers." The *Tribune* called the *Herald* "the Satanic Press."

The *Tribune* attacked the *Herald* for cowardice. The *Herald* attacked the *Tribune*'s editor, Greeley, "in his unwashed filthiness" as being made up of "Dirt and brass."

"The last notable event of the campaign is the *Tribune*'s ferocious onslaught on poor little Belmont for interfering in the election of a Free People and putting his name to some Democratic committee notice or other," wrote George Templeton Strong, a young lawyer who intended to "vote a hybrid ticket." He added, "It seems a very silly business."

The weather on election day was stormy, which everyone agreed was bad for the Whigs, who presumably were less willing to get wet. The wind tore down telegraph wires, delaying news of the returns from other states, especially in the West. When the votes were finally counted, Pierce had carried all but four of the thirty-one states in the Union. The electoral vote was 254 to 42. Pierce had won by a landslide.

"Poor Scott!!!" wrote Strong. "Whether he'll rend his own garments is questionable, but he must be furious, and very like to rend someone else's." And he observed, "General opinion seems to be that the Whig party is dead and will soon decompose into its original elements. Shouldn't wonder."

August was jubilant at the returns. He expected Buchanan—who despite August's support for Pierce was still his main source of patronage —to be named secretary of state. And he hoped through Buchanan to be appointed plenipotentiary at Naples, a city in which he had briefly lived many years before and for which he had great affection. In Naples, the capital of the Kingdom of the Two Sicilies, August had learned to appreciate art and music. And among the diplomatic assignments it was considered a plum. But to get Naples, August needed a bait. He decided the perfect bait was Cuba.

During the campaign everyone expected that if Pierce won, the new administration would try to annex Cuba as Polk's administration seven years before had annexed Texas. In fact, August was so convinced of it he bet Simeon Draper, a Whig merchant, $500 that before Pierce's term was over Cuba would belong to the United States. Spain, suffering too many troubles at home, could not hold the island. It seemed natural that Cuba would become American. The question was how?

"I have no doubt but what if stern necessity should require it, our people would eventually take the Island by force of arms, even against the combined forces of Spain and France," August wrote Buchanan about three weeks after the election.

War, however, was not an appealing policy, August thought. Violence was both a less efficient and a less certain tool of government than was business.

"We must avoid, if possible, the sacrifice of blood and treasure," wrote August, "and must try to obtain this Gem of the Ocean by negotiation and purchase."

August's plan to force Spain into selling Cuba to the United States involved threats and temptations. The United States through intrigue and bluster should maneuver Spain into a position in which it would be suicidal for Spain to keep Cuba. Then the United States should offer to relieve Spain of its troublesome territory for a generous price.

"In order to bring the Caribbean pride to listen to any overture of that kind," August wrote Buchanan, "we ought on the one hand to keep up the present apprehension of invasion, thus compelling Spain to exhaust all the resources of the Island by the maintenance of a large military and naval force"—25,000 soldiers and 35 ships—"while on the other hand the United States must do everything it can in Europe to drain the already impoverished Spanish treasury. To attain this object we must enlist in our favor powerful influences at the Spanish Court and in the financial world of Europe, so that the pressure of public opinion in Spain itself will eventually force the Spanish ministry to come to our terms."

Specifically the plan called for certain American representatives to point out to the major European bankers who owned Spanish securities that Spain's stubborn decision to keep Cuba was threatening to bankrupt Spain. To protect their investments these European bankers should demand payment on any Spanish notes they held. This would further weaken the Spanish economy.

If, however, Spain agreed to sell Cuba to the United States, that would prove to the European bankers that Spain was responding to its financial crisis in a reasonable way. It would create confidence in that government's stability. The European bankers would no longer feel obliged to demand full and immediate payment on any outstanding notes. And Spain's treasury would be enriched by the dollars the United States would pay to buy the island.

It was imperative—according to August's plan—that the United States representatives who would apply this pressure on the European bankers be well placed. The logical choice, the United States minister to Spain, could not be effective. His "official position will impede his movements." But the representatives in England, France, and Naples could be very effective. The representatives in England and France would be in the major financial centers of Europe.

"From Naples a very powerful influence can be brought to bear upon the Queen Mother of Spain," who was the "sister to the reigning King of Naples" and "one of the most influential persons in all Spain," August explained to Buchanan.

So the key to the plan lay in the choice of the representative to Naples.

"Having resided myself at Naples some twenty years ago," August told Buchanan, "I think that by my acquaintance with the place and knowledge of the language I could be of infinitely more use to our government than any other person the coming administration could find, besides which my relations to and intimate acquaintance with most of the leading financiers of London, Paris, and Madrid would also enable me to assist most effectually the efforts of our ministers at these points."

August asked Buchanan's help in getting him the post.

Buchanan pushed August's plan—but not August's appointment—with Pierce. As a former opponent of Pierce's, Buchanan had limited influence with the new administration; and he had political debts to older supporters and closer friends than August. August had done a great deal for Buchanan personally and for the Democratic party, but after all he was a newcomer to politics; this was really his first campaign. He could not expect to take precedence over the Old Guard.

Around Thanksgiving, August heard a rumor that Marcy, who August knew "is very anxious for the State or Treasury Department," was likely to be named secretary of state instead of Buchanan. August already had lobbied for Naples with Buchanan. He now had to see what leverage he could apply on Marcy.

August leaked his plan for Cuba to a Marcy supporter, who told the governor, "It seems one of Belmont's oldest & closest personal friends is in high favor at the Court of Madrid. This friend is said to possess immense wealth and is also endowed with *attractive personal* recommendations and either quite recently or at no remote date held a delicate position of a peculiar nature in relation to a certain exalted personage, as the phrase goes, who is by the way not remarkable for either chastity or patriotism."

If the identity of August's friend is not clearly suggested—although since he possessed "immense wealth" he might well have been a Rothschild—the identity of the lady "who is not remarkable for either chastity or patriotism" was no secret. She was "a member of the Royal Family at

Naples" as well as being part of the court of Madrid, a description that fit the queen mother of Spain, whom August already had described to Buchanan as being both influential and influenceable.

And "as neither purity nor patriotism are supposed to be more in fashion" in Naples "than at Madrid, and as at both points bankruptcy and venality are not terms without meaning," it would be possible to use the relationship between the unnamed gentleman and all-but-named lady to help convince Spain to sell Cuba to the United States. The island, it seems, would be won not only on the stock exchanges but also in the bedrooms of Europe.

The Marcy supporter who transmitted August's plan to the governor pointed out that August did "not lack ability, and his patriotism and zeal may be relied upon, I think. He also suggests that, as the salary attached to the appointment is no object, he might, by the offer of pecuniary inducements, relieve the Administration from another postulant." August wanted the post so much he was willing to buy off the other candidates for the job.

Having planted seeds with both Buchanan and Marcy, August then cultivated them, Marcy indirectly through mutual friends, Buchanan directly through flattery, favors (tips on securities and help in making travel arrangements from New York to California for a friend of Buchanan's), and reminders of how useful he had been in the past, how useful he could be in Naples, and how useful he might be in helping Buchanan in the presidential election of 1856. But Marcy and Buchanan both remained silent about the appointment.

In January 1853 Buchanan stopped in New York on his way back from Washington. August made reservations for him at the Metropolitan Hotel on Broadway at Prince Street, "which," August told Buchanan, "is now considered the headquarters of our friends," a luxurious place with a *sky parlor* from which one could gaze down at the hubbub on Broadway. He hoped that Buchanan's "numerous engagements will admit of your spending some days with us," during which time August expected to learn—or at least get a hint of—what his chances were for the position at Naples. Buchanan, however, was discreet. When he left, August still was in the dark and more anxious than he had been before.

By the end of January, August could stand the suspense no longer. He went to Washington, to petition Pierce as directly as possible, although according to conventional wisdom such a trip could destroy any chance he might have for Naples. One was not supposed to seem too eager for office. Public service was admittedly an honor, but even more—according to a myth that was as transparent as it was long-lived—it was a sacrifice one reluctantly made for the good of the country. Even Slidell, who hoped for an appointment by the new administration, was hesitant to travel to Washington "from fear that his visit might be misconstrued into too great an anxiety for office," although August admitted, "I do not at all share that opinion."

August was honest enough to confess he wanted the Naples post for both personal and patriotic reasons and was confident that he was the ablest candidate. He saw no *reason* to dissemble. One should not act until one was sure one was right. Then one should act in a straightforward and energetic manner. His trip to Washington might lose him the post or clinch it. He had built his life and business on calculated risks and flamboyant actions. He had been successful. There was no reason to think he would not be successful now.

August called on Charles H. Peaslee, a congressman from New Hampshire and one of the half-dozen intimates on whom Pierce depended for advice. Peaslee, apparently pleased with August's Cuban scheme and aware of August's influence among the few Democratic bankers and merchants who supported the party, encouraged him; but, unable or unwilling to make any commitment, he passed the buck back to Buchanan.

"Peaslee urges very strongly that I should get a warm letter to Pierce from you," August wrote Buchanan. "I cannot fail if you ask for my appointment as a *personal favor to yourself*."

August repeated his request six times. There was no way Buchanan could miss his meaning. August was calling in his political IOU's and warning that if those IOU's were not honored he would foreclose on any future help he might be able to give Buchanan.

Buchanan wrote the letter of recommendation to Pierce. August waited for a response from the president-elect. None came.

Pierce was swamped with petitions, demands, and memoranda that had piled up during January—ever since the railroad accident from which he and his wife had emerged uninjured but in which their son Benjamin had been killed as they watched, powerless to save him. Even if August's request—and Buchanan's letter—had required immediate attention, Pierce's answer would have been delayed. But a decision on August's appointment could wait. No foreign posts would be filled until after the secretary of state was chosen.

August's descent upon Washington had not resulted in immediate success. It seemed, in fact, that August had gambled and lost.

In the midst of all the political maneuvering, on February 18, 1853, at 2:30 in the morning, Caroline gave birth to a second son, whom she and August named August, Jr. Distracted by his new son, August allowed political events to move at their own pace. He had done what he could to force the issue of his appointment to Naples. For the moment all he could do was be patient—or at least quietly impatient. He would not have long to wait. The Inauguration, which would be held on March 4, was less than a month away.

The day after the Inauguration, August wrote Buchanan, "Well, the agony is over, and the Cabinet is at last irrevocably known and formed."

Pierce had chosen Marcy as secretary of state. Buchanan had not been given any position in the Cabinet.

"Rumor says that you will be offered the mission to London," August told Buchanan. "I hope sincerely it may be so and that you *will* consent to accept it."

Trying to flatter and console Buchanan, August added that "as matters stand now I consider that more distinction is to be gained and more efficient service to be rendered at that post than by any seat in the Cabinet."

But both men knew the post in London would keep Buchanan out of the country and therefore effectively out of American politics for the next four years. Pierce did not want Buchanan to be in a position to challenge him for the presidential nomination in 1856.

Although August acknowledged Pierce's foresight and shrewdness, he felt that Pierce's attempt to balance the Cabinet with Northerners and Southerners "will not be much calculated to harmonize the party." However, he "rejoiced to see the bold and statesmanlike view the President takes in regard to Cuba," which boded good for August's prospects even though, he admitted, "I have to fight against an immense competition." August estimated there were fifteen applicants for the post of chargé at Naples. He was being optimistic. According to Pierce, "Almost every candidate for the post of chargé selects Naples, and there are one or more candidates from nearly every state." August needed and found reinforcements: Judge James Campbell, the new postmaster general; Theodore

Sedgwick, whom August at one time had suggested as editor for the Democratic Union newspaper he had tried to start; and Daniel E. Sickles —a dashing young hothead who soon would become the secretary of the legation in London and who, a few years later, would shoot and kill his wife's lover in public.

August's letters on Cuba had "made an abiding impression" on Pierce and had pleased him with "their cordial and enthusiastic tone." August felt confident that the new President would not oppose his appointment. But still there was no definite word from Washington. August's enemies were stronger and more numerous than he had thought. He was paying for the times he had flaunted his position as Austria's consul general, wearing the uniform of his office to balls and gilding himself with a foreign title. Remembering August's ducal habits (his liveried servants, his carriage drawn by four white horses), people assumed—wrongly—that his sympathies would be with monarchists, not republicans.

"It seems to be very preposterous that those gentlemen, who are warmly attached to republicanism in Europe, should oppose me," August wrote to George N. Sanders, a former Douglas supporter.

No one could doubt August's ability to help the republican cause in Europe. August's enemies must therefore—August assumed—"doubt my sincerity," which he thought "unreasonable and ridiculous."

"What could I gain by" obstructing republicanism and weakening United States influence in Europe, August wondered. How could anyone suspect him of allegiance to Austria—or any other country—over the United States? "All my interests are here," August wrote to Sanders. "My family ties are here, and it is here where I must leave to my children an untarnished and bright name, which is a better inheritance than all the dollars I might scrape together."

A "sort of monetary crisis" had prevented August from going to Washington to fight for his appointment in person. Stuck in New York City, he lost his temper.

"I do not mean to beg for the support of anybody," he wrote; "the favors of my friends and well-wishers I accept gratefully; those who oppose me have my free consent to do their d——est."

At the end of March the *Tribune* again started attacking August, spreading the old lies about how he had changed his name from Schönberg to the "Frenchified alias of . . . Belmont" and comparing him unfavorably to Pierre Soulé, the former French radical who had become a naturalized

American and who, having been elected senator from Louisiana, was John Slidell's chief rival. Soulé, the newspaper said, was one of the "foreign born citizens who distinguish themselves by their brains," not "by their purses."

August was infuriated by "Saint Greeley's" libels. He realized that they heralded growing opposition to his appointment. If he wanted to succeed, it was "now or never" that he must use all the influence he could muster to support his bid for Naples. He urged Isaac Townsend (a New York merchant with whom he had done business), Prosper Wetmore (who was so close to Marcy that he smuggled snuff, which Mrs. Marcy had forbidden her husband to use, to the governor), and Charles H. Peaslee (Pierce's confidant) to write letters for him to the new secretary of state, who—August had heard—was resisting his appointment. All three agreed to argue August's case with Marcy—even Peaslee, who had taken an oath not to "write a line or sign a petition for any candidate." But none of their arguments moved Marcy.

In his efforts to prove his republican sympathies August may have been too convincing. Marcy distrusted the young radicals in the party. As *The New York Times* explained, "His influence will be exerted directly against any recognition by this Government of the existence of tumult in Europe, except so far as may be necessary to preserve our own immediate material interests."

The new secretary of state also was leery of the wilder expansionist schemes, such as Belmont's plan for forcing Spain to sell Cuba to the United States through bedroom and boardroom plots. He was appalled at the flamboyant, even theatrical, personalities Pierce was choosing for positions abroad. Solon Borland, a senator from Arkansas whom some considered to be no better than a ruffian, was to be appointed minister to Central America. Pierre Soulé, who had been forced to escape fom France because of his republican attempts to overthrow the Bourbon monarchy, was being made minister to Spain; the appointment was almost a provocation to the Spanish royal house. Sanders and Sickles—both too impetuous and hot-tempered to make good diplomats—were to be Buchanan's assistants in London. Even Buchanan himself, although a seasoned diplomat, had once gone on record as favoring the seizure of all Mexico. Pierce seemed to be recruiting for a pirate ship, not a foreign service.

And now Belmont! A canny businessman, no doubt, but one who dueled and flouted tradition, not good recommendations for an aspiring diplomat. Furthermore, he had tied his fortunes to Buchanan and fought

Marcy right up to the nominating convention. There was no reason for Marcy—who was such an avid believer in patronage that he is credited with originating the term "spoils system"—to support August's application for one of the most sought-after foreign posts. And he did not.

Minimizing his disappointment, August told Buchanan, "I am very indifferent about the whole affair; and, if the Governor feels pleasure in defeating me, he is perfectly welcome to do so. I have too much self respect to remain longer in the position of a humble petitioner."

He told Pierce's private secretary that he was withdrawing as a candidate for a foreign appointment.

Buchanan asked August to reconsider. Although weary of lobbying and not very hopeful of success, August agreed. He would continue to seek a chargéship; but on the advice of his friends, including Buchanan, he would be more flexible. Since Naples was such a popular assignment, August told his supporters in the administration to let the President know that "I just as leave go to Brussels if he wants Naples for some nearer political friend." In fact, August decided—or at least claimed—he might "*prefer* Brussels to Naples. Brussels is a central point at short distances from London," where Buchanan would be posted, "Paris, and Amsterdam, the principal money marts of the Old World and the only places upon which Spain relies to bolster up her decayed finances." Brussels would be as good a place as Naples for August to try to pry Cuba free of Spain. But, he told Buchanan, "my arrangements are of such a nature that unless I know soon what the President intends to do I cannot remain longer a candidate."

A few weeks later it became clear that August would not be appointed to Brussels either. August offered to book Buchanan's passage to London, since "the steamers are so full now that it is advisable to engage rooms two months before hand." He intended to make himself as helpful to Buchanan as he could be; if Buchanan won the presidency four years later, August wanted to make sure he would not be passed over for any assignment he might seek in that administration.

And, determined not to repeat the mistake he had made in the past election with Marcy, August wooed at least one other potential presidential candidate. When Stephen A. Douglas passed through New York City on his way to Europe, August wrote him a letter of introduction to Alphonse de Rothschild. He also began flirting with a number of Marcy supporters, such as Charles O'Conor, who had opposed August's plan for a pro-Buchanan newspaper.

August was gathering allies. He never again wanted to be a "humble petitioner."

In the middle of May, possibly reverting to the wild driving habits that had marked his early years in the United States, August spilled his carriage. He hurt his arm so badly that more than a week later, when he heard the news that President Pierce had appointed him chargé at The Hague, he could hardly hold a pen to write a letter thanking Buchanan for his help in getting him the post and letting Buchanan know that he was going to accept the commission.

CHAPTER ELEVEN

AUGUST'S MISSION at The Hague was to negotiate a treaty with the Dutch that would open their ports in the East Indies—as the Commodore was opening ports in Japan—to American ships. The United States and the Netherlands in 1839 had signed a reciprocal trade and navigation agreement and in 1851 had worked out an understanding that in principle allowed Washington to establish consulates in the Dutch colonies, but the Dutch honored the principle more than the practice. In 1853, fourteen years after one agreement and two years after the other, only three ports were open to American ships in the Dutch East Indies, a policy Secretary of State Marcy in his instructions to August called "illiberal in the extreme in a commercial nation which pretends to keep up with the spirit of the age."

"During your residence at the Hague," Marcy also told August, "you may sometimes be applied to, to interpose in behalf of American citizens for the purpose of obtaining satisfaction of claims which they may have upon the Dutch government or the redress of grievances which they may experience in the course of their dealings and transactions." The assignment may have seemed routine at the time. It turned out otherwise.

On Saturday, August 20, at noon, the Belmonts set sail in perfect sunny weather for Europe. Their ship, the *Arctic,* which had been launched three years before, was according to one contemporary "the most stupendous vessel ever constructed in the United States, or the world, since the patriarchal days of Noah."

The public rooms were decorated with Oriental opulence. Expensive carpets covered the tilting floors. Magnificent mirrors reflected the swinging chandeliers. Stained glass, silver, and ornamental gilding glowed in the warm light. The marble of the center tables was as richly veined as halvah. The overstuffed armchairs and sofas were as soft as the pillows in some mythical sheikh's tent. The staterooms were equally luxurious—if somewhat less Eastern.

When August arrived in New York in 1837, the skyline of the city was a stretch of low wood-frame houses, occasionally broken by the spire of a church and only in one place interrupted by the bulk of a six-story building, the Astor House. When he left for The Hague fifteen years later, the relatively few frame houses that remained in the center of the city, and even some of the church spires, were dwarfed or obscured by many newly built six-story stone, brick, and iron-faced buildings.

As a ship approached the Narrows the skyline became a cream, rust, and brown blur marked by the green tip of Battery Park. The banks of Staten Island and Long Island on either side were studded with estates with woods and fields beyond. At the end of the Narrows a ship passed Fort Hamilton on the left and Fort Richmond and Fort Tompkins on the right before following the south coast of Long Island out into the Atlantic.

The voyage across the Atlantic was an exercise in comfortable boredom, punctuated by morning broth, afternoon tea, meals, and games of whist. Some passengers lay on deck chairs, cocooned in coats or blankets, and studied guidebooks. Others leaned on the rail, hoping to see a porpoise, a whale, a stormy petrel, a passing ship, or a stray unseasonable iceberg with its dark caverns and blue-tinted glittering facets.

Only Caroline's sister Belle suffered any seasickness during the trip, and she was ill only for a day or two. The rest—August, Caroline, Perry, August, Jr., and the boys' nurse, Mrs. Egan—did not even have the distraction of nausea to differentiate one day from the next.

Nine days and twenty-two hours after the *Arctic* left New York the Belmonts disembarked at Liverpool, where Buchanan—already at his post in England—had arranged to have them pass through customs speedily.

They reached their hotel in time for dinner and the next morning set out for London.

For ten days they devoted themselves to sightseeing, enjoying Buchanan's company at the legation and visiting with August's old friends. Perhaps because Caroline had been reading so many of Charles Dickens's popular novels, she had expected London to be gloomy and dirty. She was pleasantly surprised. The parts of the city and its suburbs that she saw were cheerful and clean; however, she was entertained not in Fagin's den but in Lionel Rothschild's country seat, where swans glided on the lakes and ladies with swanlike necks glided through the gardens. Caroline found Lionel's wife "very agreeable" and his children "charming." Lunch with the Rothschilds was "the extent of our dissipation" in England.

They had a worse time crossing the English Channel than they'd had crossing the Atlantic. The seas were rough, and virtually everyone on board except Caroline became seasick. They arrived in Paris around midnight. When Caroline woke Perry and August, Jr., from their naps, the children screamed "at the top of their voices" and did not stop until they were tucked into their comfortable beds at the hotel.

Their stay in Paris was hectic. Perry came down with a bad cold; and Caroline felt that it was nearing time to wean August, Jr., who had an enormous appetite and was growing "as fat as a little partridge," but she did not want to stop breast-feeding him until they were settled in The Hague. During the day she was besieged by dressmakers and other tradespeople whose chatter and clatter took her breath away. She was puzzled at first by the difference in money and wearied by the round of sightseeing: the Champs Elysées with its new wooden railway; the summer gardens where people danced on hard-packed earth in the flare of gas lamps; the boisterous cafés; the Punch-and-Judy shows; the narrow cobbled streets that zigzagged away in crazy perspectives. They dined in the finest restaurants, strolled through art galleries, and attended the theater, which Caroline "enjoyed very much, as I found that I understood French much better than I thought I did."

By the end of their two-week stay Caroline was exhausted. She was glad to be leaving. Paris had disappointed her. She felt that by not appreciating what was reputed to be "the center of all pleasure" she had somehow disappointed August.

In Mannheim they planned to stop for a few hours to spend some time with August's uncle, Joseph Florian, a duty visit. August did not like his uncle, and he wasn't sure he "could bring himself to talk to him."

But Joseph Florian was waiting for them at the depot, and Caroline found him "a nice gentlemanly old man, full of fun, and tickled to death with us all." They went home with him to meet his wife, children, and other Mannheim relations of August's. Caroline was surprised to find that they all looked like New Yorkers. She had "expected them to be altogether different."

The afternoon train to Frankfurt arrived about eleven that night. August was happy to be back and pleased to find the city so little changed: the gables overhanging and shading the narrow alleys, the open squares with their whitewashed buildings glowing ghostlike in the moonlight, the streets through which he used to hurry before dawn to reach his lessons. The next morning as August stood at the window of their "splendid" hotel room he recognized a familiar face among the crowd passing by outside. The people as well as the city seemed to have stayed the same. It was he who had changed.

During their three days in Frankfurt, August showed Caroline where he had grown up. Caroline loved the city's many gardens and parks and enjoyed meeting her husband's friends and acquaintances. Old Amschel, the head of the international House of Rothschild for whom August used to sweep out the office, seemed—Caroline thought—"very attentive." He visited them twice and invited them to breakfast at his country estate. As a sign of his favor he gave August and Caroline his box at the opera.

They traveled by Rhine steamer to Koblenz to visit Babette and her family—and Simon. At the last minute August had changed his plans. He had written to his father from London that he would not have time to stop in Alzey; he would meet Simon at his sister's house in Koblenz.

If August had spent one less day in London, Paris, or Frankfurt, he could easily have visited Alzey, but he avoided it for any number of reasons: resentment toward his father; unwillingness to show his family how rustic his birthplace was; distaste for reliving painful memories; or possibly a reluctance to confront a place he may have idealized.

Simon, who in preparing for their arrival had been uncharacteristically extravagant in buying new furnishings and fixing up his house, apparently accepted the news with an equally atypical lack of complaint.

At Koblenz, Babette and Stephan Feist were waiting on the wharf. As they all drove up to the Feists' house August saw Simon watching from a window. While the rest of the party got settled, August went into a separate room, where he embraced his father.

Simon had not seen his son for seventeen years; and, as Caroline said, "Now to have him back again with a wife and two children was certainly a great change." In looking at his son, Simon must have felt a stab of mortality. It was not just in having a family that August had changed. Seventeen years ago he had been only twenty-three. Now he was forty. His hairline was receding; his beard, shaved on his upper lip, made his face look chunky, almost rectangular; there were pouches under his eyes and laugh-lines radiating from the sides. The old dueling wound made him limp; so when he sat he had to perch on the edge of his chair with his lame leg awkwardly out to the side.

For August the shock of change must also have been intense. Simon had grown more wizened, more hawklike. August had seen Babette a few years earlier when she had visited New York; but since then she'd had two more children, boys, the younger of whom was named for August.

They feasted so much "from morning till night" that Caroline and Belle grew plump—or so at least reported Caroline, who, however, was still small and thin enough to deserve her nickname, Tiny.

They visited the local sights, which included a castle Caroline thought looked familiar; Babette had embroidered its likeness on a portfolio that August, instead of using, had kept on the wall of his library in New York. When they took carriage rides into the countryside, all Caroline could think of as she looked at the river below them was the song "On the Banks of the Blue Moselle." About a mile and a half from their house the Feists kept a garden where they spent the afternoons, sipping coffee made in a little gazebo; smelling the ripening grapes that hung above them in the arbors; and watching Perry and his cousins pushing each other on the swing. In the evening, as was the Feists' custom, they played cards. At night Caroline curled up under an eiderdown, which she thought "delicious," pretty and warm and not heavy like a quilt. She was convinced that "the Germans know how to enjoy life."

Caroline was delighted with her father-in-law, whom she found "a very lively and cheerful person, full of fun and jokes." They chattered at each other in their clumsy French and chortled at their mistakes. Simon gave Perry toys. To the merriment of his two American grandchildren and his daughter-in-law, the old man marched around the Feists' house waving a play-sword in one hand and a play-gun in the other as Stephan Feist rapped on a drum. Simon was not at all the cantankerous man August undoubtedly had prepared Caroline to meet. And to have been that jolly

Simon must have been as enchanted by his daughter-in-law as she was by him.

After a week in Koblenz, August and his family boarded a steamer for a day's run down the Rhine past vineyards nearing harvest, terraced fields, castles, ruins, and churches whose spires jutted like the prows of massive stone landships above the brows of the cliffs, until they reached the flat, monotonous countryside of the Netherlands. They got off the steamer at Rotterdam and traveled forty minutes longer past cottages with gardens and brightly painted garden houses, fishponds, fields of grazing cows, and canals that cut the land up into a chessboard. In the foreground, in the middle distance, and on the horizon, everywhere were squat, bulky windmills like chess castles wearing pinwheels.

On Friday evening, October 7, the Belmonts arrived at The Hague.

The following morning the former chargé George Folsom and his wife came to the Belmonts' rooms at the Hotel Doelen to welcome them—and to warn them about the Dutch, who they said were "a very stiff people, jealous of all other countries, and exceedingly averse to receiving strangers." The Folsoms cautioned August and Caroline not to make any forays into society until after they were presented to the royal family, who, however, would be unavailable for the next couple of weeks. Both Mr. and Mrs. Folsom—Caroline thought—seemed "very glad to see someone from home."

Later in the day August and Caroline explored the city where they were to live for the next four years. "The Hague . . . is . . . beautiful . . . a gem of a capital," wrote a visitor in the mid-1850s. "Its principal street—the Voorhout—is a series of palaces, and its great square—the Vyvenberg—is magnificent, with its trees, its basin of water" in which swans paddled, "its palace, and public buildings."

In the fish market storks strutted among fishermen who still wore the traditional balloon breeches. Peasant women knitted on benches outside their houses, their lacy, starched headdresses giving them fluttering haloes and their tight short sleeves making their arms a fashionable pink. Their dresses, Caroline noted, were short; and they wore black stockings and wooden shoes, which she thought looked "very odd, particularly upon the children, who wear them from the time they begin to walk."

In the city dogcarts rattled along the streets, and teams of dogs pulled barges through the canals. On the outskirts of the city was a lovely forest, crisscrossed with shady paths and more canals, where in the evening people gathered in cafés and "music saloons."

"The cleanliness of the Dutch is proverbial," wrote another contemporary visitor. "Their houses are models of neatness and order. The steps and doorways are as bright as porcelain, and every nook and cranny in the interior undergoes incessant processes of washing and dusting. The floors are polished like a table; the walls have not a speck of soil; no spider is suffered to weave his nets in dark corners; and the sweetness of the remotest recesses of cupboards may be confidently relied upon. Yet, with all this care applied to their houses, the Dutch are singularly indifferent to cleanliness in their persons."

Caroline agreed.

"They are very clean in their homes," she observed, "and are scrubbing and washing all the time; but they do not care to wash themselves. I believe there is not a bath to be had in the whole place."

By American standards the Dutch were not attractive, since they tended to be as broad and as stocky as their windmills. If Venus "were to rise again from the foam of the sea and were to select the Zuyder Zee as the place of her birth," an American reported, "the Dutch . . . would drag her ashore in a net, and failing to sell her for a colossal herring, they would shear off . . . her hair, pad her waist, broaden her oval face in a cheesepress, deck her lovely limbs with gallisgaskins [floppy pants], and set her scrubbing floors."

August thought The Hague old-fashioned and "in everything about half a century behind the rest of Europe."

They had trouble finding a house to rent. The only possible place, which was "very large and handsome," had furniture "so old and dirty that it would be impossible to use it." Although she admitted that the city was "very pretty," Caroline expected it to be "so dull that I do not know how we shall manage to pass the winter."

✣ CHAPTER TWELVE ✣

THE BELMONTS' first weeks at The Hague were unhappy and dull. The weather was bad, "generally damp," Caroline found. "We have had but one bright beautiful day since we came here." A local doctor told her the climate was healthy, and an acquaintance predicted she soon would get used to it; but to stay warm she had to wear flannel undershirts. Except for the cheese, butter, and bread, the food was indifferent. The drinking water was so bad they mixed it with claret or instead drank ale, which Caroline liked. The hotel was drab and uncomfortable.

Caroline worried about the filling in a dead tooth, which had turned black. Perry developed a rash on his torso and legs. Caroline treated it with cod-liver oil and oil-and-bran baths. She was afraid August, Jr., also would develop a rash; and she did not want to wean him until he cut his first tooth. But August "made such a fuss" that she weaned him early and hoped "he will not be the worse for it, poor little fellow. I regret it now it is done very much, though he seems to be getting on just as well without me. In fact, I had so little milk for him that I think it will make very little difference."

Trying to run a household from a suite of hotel rooms was unpleasant, and Caroline could not even find distraction by shopping. The stores were "in very little narrow streets, and it is not the fashion for ladies to go to them. The things are brought to your house for you to select." For small items Caroline sent the nanny, Mrs. Egan, who "manages to make the shopkeepers understand by signs what she wants." Caroline enjoyed imagining Mrs. Egan booming at the salespeople "as if they were deaf and flourishing her hands and fingers."

The Belmonts' suite at the Hotel Doelen had no kitchen; and Josephine the cook was—August feared—"beginning to get out of patience not having anything to do." She was, according to Caroline, "crazy to get at her cooking again."

Fortunately, Josephine got along with Mrs. Egan. She helped the nanny care for the children and grew quite fond of Perry and August, Jr., whom she took out for walks every day. During those outings she talked French to Perry, which delighted August even though the boy showed "but little disposition and liking thus far" for the language.

The lack of a kitchen, which had driven Josephine into the nursery, turned out to be a blessing because August was forced to dismiss a nursemaid he had hired in Paris to help with the boys. The girl had cried from the moment they had arrived in The Hague. She was cross with everybody and hated Perry. "You would be surprised to see so young-looking a person get so angry," Caroline wrote her mother; "in fact, she was ready to *burst* with anger at everything Perry would say." One morning she even pinched Perry as she was dressing him. Perry pinched her back.

The weather, the food, the discomfort of living in a hotel, the nursery crises—everything conspired to make the Belmonts' introduction to The Hague a disaster. "To be with wife and children cooped up in a second-rate hotel without any comfort and where everything is fully as dear as in the most expensive hotel of London is no joke," August wrote to Buchanan. It did not "contribute toward making me content with my situation."

The New York newspapers with their gossipy accounts of local events were Caroline's one source of amusement; but even they did not dispel her gloom. The letters from her mother made her homesick. Every day she talked to her sister Belle and Mrs. Egan about how wonderful it would be when Mrs. Perry came to The Hague to visit them. "Even little Perry," August noticed, "scribbles every stray leaf of paper full with letters to his dear Gramma to come over to The Hague." The letters from the Commodore reminded Caroline that her father was half a world away. And he sounded to Caroline "only pretty well."

The Commodore was concerned about what would happen when he sailed into Yeddo (Tokyo) Bay—which, he thought, "will result in no especial advantage, as it will be rather a preliminary demonstration, though I shall have the opportunity of making such observations as will enable me to act more advisedly on my next visit." He fumed at the bureaucrats in Washington who he thought were neglecting him, and he was disgusted at their failure to dispatch "the ships they promised me."

He hoped that the members of his family who were at The Hague "will all enjoy yourselves." But he warned that they "must take good care of Belle, especially in her intercourse with whiskered foreigners. One half the travelers you now meet in Europe are either swindlers, pick-pockets, or coxcombs; and Belle is a little volatile."

Sundays, observed strictly at The Hague, passed very slowly. Caroline went to a church in which the "English service is read"; and although she admitted "we feel ourselves fortunate in having" a church at all, the minister was "rather a tiresome man."

The rest of the week, although livelier than the Sabbath, was still monotonous. Caroline tried to distract herself by having her portrait done in crayons for Babette, and she was pleased that the drawing was turning out to be a good likeness; but posing could not have been very amusing.

Perry also was sitting for a portrait for the Commodore, but the boy was so restless Caroline had to read aloud to keep him quiet.

Because, as August pointed out, "everybody speaks French" at The Hague, Caroline and Belle renewed the French lessons they had started before sailing for Europe. August was happy to see that they worked harder at their studies than "I could have induced them to do when in New York." But Mr. Frincke, their tutor, had—Caroline thought—"a most terrible accent just as one can imagine a Dutchman to have in any foreign language."

At noon every day Caroline and Belle took riding lessons. August—sitting sidesaddle because of his broken hip—occasionally joined them. But the weather was so bad that they rarely ventured outside the academy along the roads of The Hague.

In the afternoon Caroline and August walked about the town or took drives into the countryside. In the evening two or three times a week they went to the opera.

The Folsoms shepherded the Belmonts through the narrow world to which they were limited. Although Caroline appreciated their attention, she found Mr. Folsom "rather tiresome." She wished she could meet people with whom she would be more comfortable.

One evening in the Folsoms' room at the Hotel Doelen, Caroline was introduced to Baroness d'Estoff, "a very intelligent lady of the old school (who makes a curtsy down to the floor)." The baroness liked Caroline. A few days later she called on the Belmonts. Caroline enjoyed the Baroness d'Estoff's company and wanted to return the visit, but could not until after she'd had her audience at court and then "called on the diplomatic corps, everybody in turn according to their rank. If by chance you go out of turn," Caroline explained to her aunt Ann, "they are very much offended. They know all you do in that regard."

There was no privacy in the social world of The Hague and no escape from the rigid etiquette.

CHAPTER THIRTEEN

EARLY IN OCTOBER, August presented his letter of credence to Dutch Minister of Foreign Affairs Floris Adriaan Van Hall, a capable, reasonable man who a decade earlier had stabilized the Dutch economy and who, in 1853, had been asked to head a new cabinet. August requested an audience with King William III. Van Hall explained that the king was at his country seat and that August's audience would be delayed three more weeks. August then brought up the subject of dress.

Secretary of State William Marcy thought the dress uniforms with their gewgaws and gold braid that diplomats traditionally wore at state functions were ridiculous and demeaning to representatives of a democracy. When he took office, Marcy—partly under the influence of Massachusetts Senator Charles Sumner and Assistant Secretary of State A. Dudley Mann—instructed all American diplomats to conform to local custom and wear dress uniforms at court if necessary, but urged them whenever possible, and at their own discretion, to wear "the simple dress of an American citizen: "the current everyday outfit of formal black coat, black trousers, and silk top hat." August decided to follow the spirit of the directive during his audience with the king. He had been conspicuous at formal occasions in America flaunting the uniform of an Austrian consul general; he would now be conspicuous at formal occasions at The Hague wearing civilian dress.

Van Hall told August "the King would much prefer" that August complied "with the established rule of wearing a uniform." Since Marcy's instructions had "left the matter of the uniform at the discretion of each American Minister," Van Hall urged August to change his mind.

August was not inclined to do so. He was surprised that Van Hall objected so strongly, since Folsom "had been received at his farewell audience and dined with the King in a plain dress coat."

Van Hall pointed out that America's new minister at Berlin, the former governor of New Jersey, Peter D. Vroom, had agreed "to wear uniform after having first attempted to be presented in citizen's dress."

August, however, remained adamant. He countered with other examples. Stephen A. Douglas "had been received with much distinction in citizen's dress by the emperors of Russia and France." Henry S. Sanford, acting chargé at Paris, also had worn civilian dress at the court of Saint-Cloud—although as a result the French called him the "Black Cow." And Buchanan, after considering the costume worn by George Washington in a painting by Gilbert Stuart, wore civilian dress when he was presented to Queen Victoria—although, being a prodigy of indecision, he also wore a sword and a three-cornered hat, which August evidently neglected to bring to Van Hall's attention.

August also explained that although Marcy's "instructions were discretionary, the wishes of my government" are "so emphatically expressed and have had since their publication so generally received the approbation of the American people that I cannot disregard them," especially "as they coincide fully with my own views." He requested Van Hall "to ask the King" not *if* but "when he would receive me in citizen's dress."

Van Hall reluctantly agreed to do so.

August left the meeting satisfied that he had acquitted himself well in his first diplomatic trial. He was gambling. Although the Dutch court might ostracize him for his stand, he was nonetheless convinced the odds for success were in his favor.

William III returned to The Hague at the end of October. Van Hall told August that the king had consented to receive him in citizen's dress although, August gathered, "my wearing a uniform would have been better liked." On November 4 at five o'clock in the afternoon August, wearing a black coat, black pants, and a top hat, went to the palace, a three-story marble building with a U-shaped courtyard and rooms that according to another visitor were "plain and neat and very well furnished, but . . . not . . . very royal—not even very stylish." August was ushered into a room where Van Hall and two aides-de-camp, all "attired in gorgeous uniforms," were waiting.

The king, also dressed in uniform, came in. He was a modest man in his mid-thirties with a fleshy nose and a surprisingly pained glance. He had ascended the throne in 1849, the year after Holland had adopted a constitution that guaranteed freedom of assembly, petition, religion, and the press. Politically he was conservative, although he did not seem uncomfortable with the liberal reforms he had inherited with the crown. To help balance the budget he cut the civil list by a third; and he often spent his own money to help finance public projects that would modernize the country.

In his private life the king's behavior was scandalous. He was estranged from Queen Sophia, the daughter of the king of Württemberg, whom he had married fourteen years earlier, and it was August's belief that "the bad understanding existing between them is the cause the court is very dull."

In any case, the king had very little to say and seemed embarrassed, which August was told "is always the case when he speaks to strangers." He was so unassuming, in fact, that some years later one of August's successors as United States minister at The Hague was—according to one report—"entering the palace one evening, on the occasion of some fête,"

when "he encountered a man on the middle of the threshold, blocking . . .
the doorway and obstructing the incoming and outgoing" traffic. Annoyed, the minister "applied his shoulder to the back of the person and
pushed him two or three yards into . . . the hall." The minister then
entered the room only to find that the person he had shoved was the
king.

After August and the king had talked for about half an hour, the
king bowed and left the room. "The *great* business was over. Now," wrote
Caroline, "it is our turn."

Two days after the audience with the king, August was successfully negotiating with a dognapper who had stolen the Belmonts' pet Sam, when
Caroline received a summons to visit the queen the following evening. She
tried to convince herself that the audience was nothing to fear. The queen
spoke excellent English and, from what everyone said, was very kind; she
had liked Mrs. Folsom and used to entertain the Folsoms' children. "I
hope I shall not be as frightened when she speaks to me as I expect to
be," Caroline wrote her mother.

The day Caroline was to meet the queen was also the Belmonts'
fourth wedding anniversary. To celebrate August gave Caroline a bouquet
and a pearl necklace. That evening Caroline and Belle—"looking very
pretty indeed," according to August—were driven alone and terrified in
the Belmonts' carriage to the palace. There they were shown into a reception room. The queen and two ladies-in-waiting entered.

The queen, who seemed straightforward and unaffected, walked
directly to Caroline and Belle and without any undue formalities started
talking easily with them in perfect, unaccented English. She sat on a sofa
and invited Caroline and Belle to sit down on either side of her, framing
herself within their attention. The three of them chatted casually for a
while longer, after which the queen stood, said good evening, and went
out. "Glad that the ceremony was at an end," Caroline told her mother
that she and Belle left "as soon as it was proper."

During the following weeks the Belmonts completed their presentations at
court. When August met the queen he found her "a most charming and
intelligent woman," superior to her husband in everything but authority.
To his authority she provided a counterweight: liberal where he was
conservative, forthright where he was withdrawn, public where he was

private. She evidently found August equally sympathetic, speaking warmly to him about America and her interest in Americans.

The queen mother, the sister of the czar of Russia, was reputedly a formidable woman. But although Caroline was still timid, she was not "flurried or frightened at the prospect of meeting her." She spent several days preparing, practicing her curtsies. On the afternoon before the audience she went out horseback riding and returned to the hotel "in high spirits to dress." She wore a pink silk gown "with three flounces stamped with velvet," pink feathers, lace lappets, diamond pins in her hair, and her new pearl necklace. Belle's dress of white tarlatan was stiff as meringue, "embroidered in white floss," with a bunch "of different colored fruits" at her waist. August again wore civilian clothes.

The queen mother was noted for her "extreme punctiliousness in matters of ceremony" and on occasion was rude to diplomats who out of ignorance or pride violated court etiquette. August—out of neither ignorance nor pride but self-respect—chose not to warn her that he would not be wearing a uniform. The king and queen had accepted his simple black coat. August felt that those audiences were sufficient precedents for all future occasions and that it would not be dignified to appear to be seeking permission to wear what he already had worn at the court.

Madame de Königsmarck, the wife of the Prussian minister, was waiting for August and Caroline at the queen mother's palace. Since she and her husband had been at The Hague longer than any other diplomat, it was her duty to present the Belmonts. Unlike the relatively informal, almost homely introductions to the king and queen, the audience with the queen mother was an elaborate affair, full of pomp, an engine of ceremony with ladies-in-waiting going up and down in curtsies like pistons. The room was crowded with members of the court and diplomats: the ladies all rustling and colorful; the men in uniform, dressed to wage a war of teacups. August was glad his adopted country had not surrendered to "all this tomfoolery." Caroline was tickled by the ostentatious display. She told her mother, "You would have shouted had you been able to look on the scene."

Just before the queen mother entered, a chamberlain arranged the guests in a row, placing August inappropriately to the left of the British chargé d'affaires ad interim. According to court procedure, August as chief officer of his legation should have been given precedence and been placed on the Englishman's right. Etiquette at The Hague was so strictly enforced that every deviation from the rules was charged with meaning. A slight, intended or unintended, would be noted, even magnified; and because power was fed by the myth that one was powerful, any damage to the myth would result in damage to the reality.

August's visible demotion in the diplomatic hierarchy could have been accidental, a petty revenge for his civilian dress or a chronic insult to United States prestige—the latter of which may well have been the case, since August subsequently learned that his predecessor, Folsom, also had been placed to the left of the British chargé ad interim. Whether the slight was personal or political, accidental or not, August, acting for himself and for his government, did not intend to ignore it He would not allow his country to be seated below the salt. And he had come too far from Alzey to allow himself to be personally affronted. But he was not going to cause a scandal; he would wait to call the court to account. He sheathed his anger in his charm and dazzled his way through the evening.

Dressed in black velvet and jewels, the queen mother entered. She spoke to each of the diplomats in turn. August, who was expecting difficulties, was "agreeably disappointed by the very polite and affable manner with which she talked for nearly half an hour with me." Talked and talked. Her conversation was like a passing train, hard to jump onto and impossible to get by; August simply had to wait for the end. She told August that America's extraordinary progress had "attracted the eyes of the whole world," as though recognition of the progress was, in fact, the real accomplishment.

He suspected the queen mother's cordiality toward him was a weapon being wielded against the queen. Everything that happened at one palace was reported at the other, so the queen mother must have heard how warmly the queen had received him and was determined "not to be out-done in politeness" by the daughter-in-law she detested.

When the queen mother approached Caroline, Belle, and Madame de Königsmarck, Caroline watched Madame de Königsmarck curtsy "very slowly two or three times" and, using her as an example, did the same, "bending to the ground." They all sat—at the queen mother's urging—and then the queen mother "talked in a free and easy" manner, interminable and unstoppable. Unlike August, who was impatient with the royal sentences rushing past him, Caroline took advantage of the queen mother's monologue to glance around the room at the curious spectacle of a court in flower.

"The funniest of all," Caroline thought, "was when the Queen rose and bid us good-evening. Of course, you never turn your back to her, but curtsy backward out of the room. As I was sitting the farthest from the door, I had the farthest to go; and I found it very awkward, for my dress was so long behind it *would* get about my feet. And by the time I got to the door, I was ready to burst out with laughter. However, we behaved as if we had seen Queens all our life."

The following morning August wrote to Baron de Tuyll, the Grand Maître, objecting to having been placed on the left of the British chargé ad interim. The baron immediately apologized, and August was never again slighted at the court.

The weather turned cold. Ponds and canals froze over. Skaters crowded the ice, looping and swooping their ways past each other and gracefully avoiding the iceboats with bellying sails that skimmed by, carrying flushed ice-sailors with eyes slitted against the wind. Young men, hanging on to the knobbed ends of wooden poles, formed long chains of skaters who seemed to half-dance and half-march, all the left feet and then all the right feet striking out at the same time in a kind of military choreography so lovely and satisfying to look at, it could make one laugh with joy.

The Belmonts liked to watch the skaters, especially one woman who moved across the ice with such casual grace that she seemed enchanted, drawn forward and backward and spun by a puppet master from one of E. T. A. Hoffman's tales. "It seems so easy," Caroline thought, "that I have been half-tempted several times to learn; but, not being able to find a private pond nearby where we might go alone and where we would not have a number of spectators to laugh at our tumbles, I have given up the idea." August, as a young man in Frankfurt, at first did not have the money and then did not have the time to spend on skating; now he had both the money and the time, but with his broken hip he no longer had the agility. He stood on the sidelines, as he had years before in Frankfurt, and with his wife watched others having fun.

Having finished with the court, Caroline now made the rounds of the diplomatic community. Madame de Königsmarck went with her "so that we can make no mistakes," Caroline explained to her mother, "and, if we do, all the blame will be laid to her door and not to ours," a sacrifice Madame de Königsmarck, cynically at ease in the city, was happy to make for her new friend. Caroline visited by proxy members of Dutch society who never received foreigners. Since both Caroline and Madame de Königsmarck were obliged to call regularly on the Dutch, even though it was always "the same story, *nicht huis,*" Madame de Königsmarck offered to take Caroline's visiting cards around with her and leave them with her own. She assured Caroline that the inhospitality of the Dutch was not personal; after all, the Prussian minister's wife had lived at The Hague for twelve years, and—Caroline told her mother—"two ladies whom she has known intimately during that time have never asked her to go to see them and she has never yet put her foot inside their doors." Caroline thought Dutch social customs were very curious.

As the holiday season approached The Hague became more lively. Horses with red plumes bobbing from their heads drew gilded sleighs through the narrow streets. Caroline's spirits rose.

On December 6, 1853, the Belmonts celebrated the Dutch Christmas, Saint Nicholas's day, by finally moving into a house of their own, a huge place that had been years before a private residence but more recently a small hotel. "The furniture is pretty good in the bedrooms," Caroline told her mother, "but the parlors are not so well" furnished. Still, Caroline thought, with "a little improvement, the rooms can be well arranged."

Early that morning August made sure fires were lit in every room to take the chill out of the air and to get rid of the dusty, unused smell. Josephine attacked the kitchen and started cooking. Until late afternoon Caroline and the children—August, Jr., furiously galloping on a new hobbyhorse and Perry playing with the ball he had been given that morning—waited at the hotel. Then Mrs. Eagan took the boys to their new home, and August and Caroline, after a quiet dinner together, followed.

Two and a half weeks later they celebrated their second and true Christmas. As soon as dusk fell on December 24 they lit their tree. In the darkened room each branch seemed tipped with fire. August, Jr., and Perry were delighted. After Mrs. Eagan put the boys to bed, August and Caroline went to the opera, but Caroline was so exhausted that she could not enjoy the performance.

The next morning Caroline went to church, after which she took a long walk before going home to open her presents. Recently August had given her three diamond stars just like the ones the queen mother was giving to Princess Henry, the daughter of the duke of Saxe-Weimar. On Christmas Day, August gave Caroline another piece of jewelry, a bracelet set with pearls. He obviously wanted her jewels to be the equal of any at The Hague. That night a servant brought Caroline, who was preparing for bed, a message that Madame Doublehoff would be giving an at-home "at which there will be dancing. Good news!" Caroline loved dancing and she admitted "when I hear the delightful music of the polka, the schottische, the waltz, I find it difficult to withstand an invitation" to dance.

In her new bed, in her new house, on Christmas night, Caroline must have gone to sleep happy.

Little by little the world of The Hague was becoming familiar and comfortable—although certain practices continued to seem strange to Caroline. "Tell Mama," she wrote to her aunt Ann, "she would laugh to hear August called *'Son Excellence'* at the beginning and end of every sentence. It is the custom here, but I laugh in my sleeve all the time."

🎵 CHAPTER FOURTEEN 🎵

SHORTLY AFTER ARRIVING at The Hague, August started what he mistakenly assumed would be a routine investigation into the claims of an American ship's captain, Walter M. Gibson, who was suing the Dutch government for $100,000 for "injuries and losses" he had sustained in the Dutch East Indies. The case came close to destroying August's diplomatic mission.

Gibson was a soldier of fortune whose luck was often as bad as his judgment. He tried to smuggle guns to Guatemalan rebels, but the United States government seized them before he set sail. He loaded his schooner, *The Flirt*, with eighty tons of ice to sell in Brazil, but by the time he reached his destination, all but one or two tons had melted.

With an empty hold he headed for the East Indies. His only freight was fantasies about Sumatra, which a seafaring uncle had described to him years before. In Gibson's imagination the island was a spicy garden, planted with flowers that looked like feathers and inhabited by birds that looked like blossoms. In the center of the island slumbered a city that once had been magnificent—legends claimed Alexander the Great was buried there. Now, according to tradition, it waited for another Alexander to resurrect the island empire. Gibson decided he was the warrior the Malays predicted would come to rescue them from the Dutch imperialists.

On Christmas Eve, 1851, when August was making the decision to enter politics that would bring him to The Hague and therefore into

Gibson's life, Gibson reached the Dutch East Indies. He stopped at Banka, a small island across a narrow strait from Sumatra, for supplies. The Dutch colonists asked him why he had come. Gibson grabbed a branch of an overhanging jasmine bush, sniffed it, and said he had come to smell the flowers. On hearing that story, the governor of the island, Dirk François Schaap, became suspicious. Nobody sailed halfway around the world just to sniff jasmine. So, when Gibson asked if Schaap knew of a Malay translator, Schaap recommended Bahdoo Rachman, a police spy. Gibson left Banka, sailed across the narrow strait to Sumatra, and headed up the Musi River toward Palembang, the floating city, the Venice of the East.

On either bank of the river the jungle was dense and dark, with patches of bright green where flecks of sunlight lit up the foliage and flashes of red when birds of paradise momentarily fluttered out of the shadows. Occasionally a low hut on bamboo stilts stood up from the undergrowth like some kind of monstrous wading bird. The sailors on *The Flirt* exchanged rumors about the orangutan, which people said was a kind of monkey-man, and the vampire bat, whose furry body was said to be as large as a child and whose flapping wings sounded just like their ship's sails' snapping when the wind changed.

The third day on the river Gibson set out in a longboat with Bahdoo and a sailor to explore one of the tributaries that fed the Musi. Gibson wanted to survey the kingdom he hoped to win. They rowed upriver close to the bank for the shade of the overhanging tangle of vines and leaves.

Gibson's desire to become the legendary savior of the Malays plunged him into a world that operated with the simplicity and neatness of legend. Three times Bahdoo pleaded with Gibson to turn back; three times Gibson entered a clearing and stopped. The first time, Gibson and the sailor climbed out of the boat "to take a nearer view of some gorgeous flowering trees." As they slogged through the swamp they felt something stinging their ankles. Looking down they found their stockings soaked in blood. Slapping at their legs they stumbled back to Bahdoo, who sat in safety, grinning. In the boat they picked the leeches from their legs. The second time, Gibson had just snapped off a branch from a gutta-percha tree when the air coagulated into a stinging, buzzing cloud of wild bees. The third time, they were surrounded by aborigines, wild men, Bahdoo called them—the Kubu that tradition claimed were the degenerate descendants of Alexander the Great's slaves who had escaped into the jungle more than two thousand years before.

At Palembang the river was crowded with log canoes, praus lined with beautiful carpets in which turbaned men reclined, Chinese junks, and Dutch traders and warships. Children splashed in the muddy water among the boats. Gibson saw one boy dragged under by a crocodile. Blood bubbled up and spread out in a dilating blot on the surface. Elephants, chained to trees, hooked their trunks over the branches above their heads.

Within a short time of arriving, Gibson got into trouble with the three most powerful representatives of the Dutch government on the island. He infuriated Louis Nicolson, the commander of a gun brig, by rescuing two beautiful Malay girls whom Nicolson's men had bought as whores; outraged F. J. P. Storm Van S'Gravesande, a mulatto who was the assistant resident (vice-governor) of the city, by making a racist remark; and provoked Cornelius Albert De Brauw, the military commandant and governor of the city, by flirting with his wife. Gibson started avoiding all Westerners and bragging about how he was a member of a secret organization of Americans that was devoted to overthrowing the colonial governments of European monarchies and that owned twelve warships. De Brauw hesitated to arrest Gibson. If Gibson were boasting so openly about his mission, those twelve warships must be waiting nearby. Neither De Brauw nor anyone else, Westerner or Asian, at Palembang doubted Gibson's claims. Even if someone had told him, it is unlikely that De Brauw would have believed the truth: that Gibson was an unstable and almost broke American with an active imagination who had sailed around the world on a whim and, armed only with one rifle and a revolver so rusted it did not work, was plotting to overthrow the Dutch in the East Indies. No one could be that crazy.

To give his fantasy flesh, Gibson began cultivating the leaders of the three principal anti-Dutch groups at Palembang: the Arabs, Chinese, and Malays. The Arab leader, a tall, vigorous old man in a white turban, a yellow silk vest, a white skirt, a green silk robe, and embroidered sandals, promised to help Gibson. The leading Chinese merchant was less direct. After tea with Gibson he called in a slave girl named Pleasant Night, who, dressed only in a sarong, her breasts bare, performed a dance about an American who sailed into port one day and won the love of a Chinese maiden. The dance was a code. The Chinese would also help. Unlike the Arab, who was candid in private, and the Chinese, who was so discreet he was enigmatic, the Malay leader was so bold that he did not mind advertising his new alliance. In his compound, nailed to the top of a stripped palm tree, flew an American flag.

Gibson had one last alliance to make before starting his rebellion against the Dutch. He had to win over the Sultan of Djambi, who, although he ruled a semi-independent nation on Sumatra, was prevented by the Dutch from trading with any other Western country. Djambi abutted on Palembang, and fighting on that border would draw Dutch attention away from an attack up the Musi. A two-front war could almost guarantee Gibson's triumph.

But Gibson could not simply sail upriver to Djambi, because if the Dutch did not stop him the Sultan of Djambi, ignorant of his intent, might; so Gibson decided to send a message to the sultan explaining his plans. He hired a public scribe, Kiagoos Lenang, to write the letter in Malay.

Kiagoos came on board *The Flirt* at five o'clock in the evening on February 4, 1852. It had taken Gibson only a month to coordinate a revolution. He had plotted efficiently and quickly—and naïvely. Kiagoos —like Bahdoo and Gibson's servant (a friend or relative of Bahdoo, named Moonchwa)—was a member of De Brauw's secret police. All three reported regularly to the governor about Gibson's plans. By the beginning of February, De Brauw must have known that there were no warships waiting for Gibson's call. Gibson's fleet was *The Flirt.*

Gibson left the three spies working on the letter and went to a Chinese wedding feast, where he drank arrack and an intoxicating tea, possibly made from marijuana. Unused to the effects of either the liquor or the drug, he became disoriented. Conversations suddenly had overtones and undertones he had not previously noticed. He found it hard to get his thoughts in order and to judge danger accurately—and all of a sudden everything seemed dangerous.

One of his new Chinese friends warned him about his servants, but Gibson ignored him. He escaped to another room, where some half-naked girls were performing. As though he were in a dream in which the same person kept appearing in different guises, Gibson realized that one of the dancers was one of the Malay girls he had rescued from being sold as a whore to Nicolson's soldiers. When the dance ended she plucked a blossom from her hair and, giving it to Gibson, whispered that he should not trust Bahdoo, Moonchwa, and Kiagoos. The dream was becoming a nightmare in which half the world was plotting against him and the other half knew of the plot. He rushed back to *The Flirt*.

If his servants were spies his only safety lay in starting the revolution before the Dutch arrested him. If they were not spies it was obvious that so many people knew of his scheme the Dutch soon would find out. In either case it was urgent to get the letter to the Sultan of Djambi. Before dawn his first mate, Charles M. Graham, started upriver with the letter. Eight miles from Palembang, Graham was arrested by the Dutch. Nicolson arrested Gibson on *The Flirt;* and drunk, hysterical with glee and anger, he ripped Gibson's American flag from its staff and threw it overboard.

For more than a year Gibson was repeatedly tried, acquitted on technicalities, and shuttled from one prison cell to another. There were rumors that the *Susquehanna*, the flagship of Commodore Perry's Japanese expedition, might sail to his rescue. At last Gibson was found guilty and sentenced to twelve years' imprisonment; but with the help of a Malay princess he escaped and returned to the United States a hero.

✥ CHAPTER FIFTEEN ✥

GIBSON'S FOLLOWERS in the United States organized rallies demanding strong measures to punish Holland for its treatment of Gibson. American newspapers speculated about the possibility of war with the Netherlands. August wrote increasingly stern letters to Dutch Foreign Minister Floris Adriaan Van Hall, demanding reparations for Gibson. And the negotiations over August's principal diplomatic mission, the new consular treaty, stalled. On instructions from his government August refused to give up Gibson's claim of indemnities; and on instructions from his government Van Hall would not negotiate a consular treaty until the United States abandoned Gibson.

Van Hall explained to August that "with the peculiarity and delicacy of [Holland's] position in the East Indies where over five millions of natives" were "governed by a handful of whites," the Dutch government "could not be too cautious of foreign influence and interference." With a nod to Gibson's case Van Hall pointed out that if Holland signed a consular treaty with the United States, American commercial agents who came to the East Indies might take advantage "of their position and inviolability for political purposes which might become dangerous to the welfare of the colony."

Furthermore, Van Hall said, once Holland signed such a treaty with the United States, the Dutch would be pressured to extend equal treatment to other Western nations, in particular to the English; and because the Dutch had already fought the English in the East Indies, Holland did not want to give the English another chance to woo the Asians of the Dutch East Indies into rebellion. Dutch relations with the English were critical enough. As a result of the tensions created by the trouble in the Crimea and the fear of a general European war, some British warships had recently stopped and searched a number of Dutch ships. But Holland resisted turning the issue into a major crisis; it did not want to do anything that might draw them into the universal slaughter that many people, including August, were certain would engulf the world within a year.

If Holland negotiated a consular treaty with the United States it would provoke England; if Holland did not it would provoke the United States. The Dutch—as August noted—"because of their war fear," were as eager to cultivate America's friendship as they were to avoid England's anger. Caught in a bind, Van Hall was using the Gibson case as an excuse to delay making a difficult choice. August, unable to get a satisfactory response to his notes about Gibson or the consular treaty, grew progressively gloomier.

The severity of the winter made travel virtually impossible. August felt trapped at The Hague. He disliked Dutch and diplomatic society. When it was not dull it was mean.

Caroline shied from the social scramble. At balls she tried, as she said, "to keep a little away from royalty where I may enjoy myself and sit down." But it was difficult to hide in the wings. Balls were performances, and the guests were players who were moved about the glittering rooms according to unalterable stage directions. At the palace Caroline was dismayed to find "there is no ladies' dressing room. You are hurried up a long staircase, and on the landing are several men servants who step forward and drag off your things in a great hurry; and before you are half-ready, with your hair tossed and flounces flying, the door is thrown open and you are announced."

Despite her tossed hair and flying flounces and lace that tore as she whirled in a waltz, Caroline with her gentleness, simplicity, and un-affected manner delighted the sober diplomats and staid Dutchmen. When the Belmonts gave a ball at their new house, Caroline so enchanted her guests that they danced until two o'clock in the morning, an unheard-of time for a party to end at The Hague. At another ball when Caroline walked in with two bouquets, one given to her by August and the other by the queen mother's chamberlain, she "created a great sensation" because, she discovered, at The Hague "it is evidently not the custom for gentle-men to send" bouquets. Other women at the ball "eyed them with great curiosity, wondering who they were from and asking if I did not find them inconvenient and heavy to carry."

The clique of women jealous of Caroline resented the special atten-tions she seemed to conjure from her companions wherever she went. Their envy was fed by the admiration their husbands lavished upon her and by the affection the queen had developed for the Belmont children. The first time the queen invited Caroline, Perry, and August, Jr., for an afternoon visit, Caroline was apprehensive. Perry was in a bad temper, and she was afraid he might misbehave. But when they arrived at the palace they were "received without ceremony in the Queen's private apartments. The moment we arrived, the Queen came out in the anteroom and did not give us time to take off the children's things." Evidently in the palaces of The Hague children as well as adults were regularly swept without prep-aration into the presence of royalty. In the queen's drawing room the boys threw off their coats and the queen "threw off all restraint." Caroline and the queen "talked very freely upon all subjects." Perry's mood had passed and the children were amiable. The queen especially liked August, Jr., whom she hugged and kissed repeatedly. Perry and the queen's son, who was two and a half, played together until it was time to leave. When the queen said good-bye, Perry, not impressed by royalty, said, "Good-bye, I'll come again tomorrow." The queen was amused; Caroline's critics, when they heard the story, presumably were not.

Even the king could not resist Caroline. Caroline knew that "some of the ladies of the diplomatic corps are exceedingly jealous," and she "was glad to give them good reason to be."

At one ball Princess Henry came up to Caroline and imperiously asked in English, "Are you an American?" as though her question were an indictment. She seemed to be asking, "Are you uncivilized?" Caroline knew that many people at The Hague thought America was "a poor country, full of strangers and savages," and she found that ignorant assumption "very provoking," particularly when it was held by someone as "haughty and proud" as Princess Henry.

Caroline answered that certainly, she was an American; and then she went off to dance with Princess Henry's husband, who evidently liked Caroline as much as his wife did not.

All during the winter Caroline ignored the social sniping; but early in March, at a supper dance at the king's palace, she found herself the only woman present who was not seated at the highest table with the queen. All the other women in the room were either royalty, nobility, or married to full ministers. August, a chargé, was slightly inferior in rank, and Caroline suffered. The king and queen, who previously had been so friendly to the Belmonts, could not have meant to insult them; thus the arrangements, which were formally correct, must have been plotted by others at the court who disliked Caroline and August.

Furious, August told Caroline to leave the room; but Caroline, a commodore's daughter and the niece of the hero of Lake Erie, would not retreat. She stayed, although, to indicate her displeasure, she sat turned away from the table and ate nothing. "It seemed," she thought, "to create quite a sensation." As the meal progressed, Caroline brooded. Seeing "all those ladies with whom I had been heretofore on equal footing separated from me" made her "republican feelings" rise. She "could hardly," she said, restrain her "tears and mortification. As soon as supper was over, I marched out of the room, past the Queen without looking to the right or left and came home. It is considered proper that the ladies of the diplomatic corps should stay till after the Queen bids good-night. I have always done so before, but this time made an exception. Everyone must have noticed it, and I intended that they should, the Queen particularly. I have not heard anything of the affair since, but I shall never be caught in that situation again."

Within a week the Belmonts left for Paris. August wanted to protect Caroline from any more court functions. Since his diplomatic affairs were caught in a limbo of ceremonious delay, there was nothing to keep them from escaping, at least temporarily, from the claustrophobic circle of acquaintances at The Hague.

Paris was a relief. The weather was warm. The boulevards were crowded. August, as was his custom, enjoyed standing at the window of his hotel and looking down at the colorful mob. The Rothschilds lionized them, which Caroline, recovering from the assaults of Dutch society, enjoyed—although she was disconcerted by Salomon de Rothschild's wife, who she thought was "the most awful looking object I have ever seen. Her face and voice are so disfigured that it is painful and sickening to look at her." But Madame de Rothschild won her over with grace and kindness. By the time the Belmonts returned to The Hague, to another new house and a new start, Caroline, secure in her acceptance by Parisian society, could shrug off any snubs at The Hague.

Gibson arrived at The Hague in the summer of 1854 carrying an official letter from Marcy to August that gave him diplomatic immunity. Although he had escaped from a Dutch prison, the Dutch police made no attempt to arrest him. Holland wanted to avoid a confrontation with the United States.

Before Gibson's arrival August had been his champion. He thought that "even if Gibson were guilty, still his treatment" by the Dutch in the East Indies "was hardly civilized." And therefore August declared himself "*willing* and *ready* to adopt any measure in order to make *Mynheer* pay up." Furthermore, August seemed to think Gibson's attempt to replace Dutch with American rule in the East Indies might even have been a sound idea, since the Dutch—August learned—"receive from their colonies there a yearly income of florins 12 millions for the state beside the immense profits of trade," a sum so great that its loss "could bring about a national bankruptcy within a year." August, his scheme differing from Gibson's only in its scope, had suggested to Marcy that if Commodore Perry sailed into the East Indies with his six warships it would not be too difficult to "revolutionize the whole Dutch archipelago" and receive the rich benefits of its trade. Moreover, since the coal mines in the East Indies could meet the demand of a sizable steam-navy based in Asia and since the iron found there could be used to repair and build ships, the islands could offer the United States a base for further expansion throughout the Pacific and Indian oceans. Also, if the Dutch were weakened by the loss of the East Indies they would not be in a position to help Japan, either directly through military action or indirectly through aid "in the eventuality of a Japanese-American clash."

August's approval of Gibson's imperial designs was modified when August realized Gibson's imperialism was personal, not national; and August's confidence in the soundness of Gibson's case was if not shaken at least ruffled when they finally were introduced. According to Nathaniel Hawthorne, who met Gibson in England, Gibson was a "gentleman of refined manners, handsome figure and remarkable intellectual aspect" with "so quiet a deportment . . . that you would have fancied him moving always along some peaceful and secluded walk of life," although "there was an Oriental fragrance breathing through his talk and an odor of the Spice Islands . . . lingering in his garments." Gibson was too colorful to be convincing, and his stories, Hawthorne fancied, were too convincing to be true. "In fact," Hawthorne said, "they were so admirably done that I could not more than half believe them, because the genuine affairs of life are not apt to transact themselves so artistically." August, who had spent much of his youth suppressing the swashbuckling nature that, for example, had plunged him into his duel, must have mistrusted Gibson, who seemed to have spent much of his youth cultivating the same tendency. And if Gibson told August the same tale he told Hawthorne about his origins—that he really was the son of an English nobleman who accidentally had been switched with the son of a commoner when both were born on a ship crossing the Atlantic—August must have realized that Van Hall was right in his estimate of Gibson's character—that he was a liar and a scoundrel.

Gibson asked to see his file, which included August's letters to and answers from Van Hall. August instructed his assistant to show the documents to Gibson. Gibson urged August to press for the return of the diary he had kept while on board *The Flirt* and of some other personal papers that had been seized when he was arrested. August did, and Van Hall eventually agreed to give them back. Gibson, having been so successful in his demands, asked August for a $500 loan. August politely said no.

Because Gibson's presence was an embarrassment—the Dutch press was demanding his arrest—and because August could not persuade him to leave Holland, August, after assuring himself that Gibson would not be apprehended in his absence, left The Hague—to indicate he disapproved of Gibson's provocative visit to Holland.

Caroline, seven months pregnant with their third child, was happy to get away from the pestilential stink of The Hague's summertime canals. In Germany they took a trip through countryside that Caroline found Eden-like—even to its temptations. From a farmer's orchard August stole handfuls of cherries, the finest they had ever tasted. Leaving his family with Joseph Florian in Mannheim, August made a quick detour to Alzey, where he was greeted as a celebrity. He was a lens through which the

Jews of the town could view the great world beyond. After the social and political trials at The Hague this reception must have refreshed August.

When the Belmonts arrived home at The Hague at the end of August, they found a letter from Marcy announcing that Congress had "authorized the President to raise the Mission of the United States at The Hague." August was no longer a chargé; he was a full minister. At court functions Caroline never again would be banished from the highest table.

Along with Marcy's welcome announcement, however, August also found in New York newspapers that had arrived during their absence accusations that he had not pressed Gibson's claim as vigorously as he should have as well as other attacks on his conduct at The Hague.

The attacks against August had been fed to the newspapers by Gibson. Shortly after the Belmonts left The Hague he had slipped out of Holland, taking with him not only the packet of his papers Van Hall had returned but also August's private file on the case. The theft turned out to be typical. When Gibson had examined his State Department dossier in Washington, he also had stolen a letter of confession he had written to the governor of the Dutch East Indies. "Much of the time, during my stay within the jurisdiction of the Netherlands Indian government," Gibson admitted in the missing letter, "I indulged in bravadoes that I would become a potentate in the East; but I must ever add, in extenuation, that this was after a plentiful indulgence in wine."

Gibson went to Paris, where he told United States Minister John Y. Mason, an amiable but not particularly astute Virginian, that August had made him his special attaché; and he told other people he met in Paris, including the correspondent of the *New York Tribune,* that Mason had made him his first secretary.

At the end of the summer August received an extraordinary letter. In it Gibson addressed him "not in the spirit of a client but as having been authorized by our government to proceed to the seat of your Mission to assist in procuring an indemnity"—an outright lie. He demanded that August give Van Hall ten days to make a definitive response to the claim.

August was outraged. He told Marcy he was "convinced" Gibson "will stop at nothing in order to gain his ends." But smothering pride with duty, August argued Gibson's case with Van Hall at an interview that according to August "assumed a somewhat stormy character." The Gibson affair had completely eclipsed the consular treaty.

August eventually got back his private file on the Gibson affair; but Gibson kept the other papers, the ones Van Hall had returned—within which, it was discovered, some official Dutch documents had mistakenly been included. Van Hall asked for the Dutch government papers back. Gibson refused. August, a harried go-between, was obliged to support Gibson, although he sympathized with Van Hall.

By early fall, like a man who tries to break up a fight only to find himself battling the two antagonists, August was waging a war on two fronts: with Van Hall and with Gibson.

The *New York Tribune* and the *Herald,* acting on invented scoops Gibson leaked to them, charged that August, "this Austrian-born Jew banker," had turned the United States legation at The Hague into a counting house and was loaning the Russian and other European governments the money they needed to carry on the war in the Crimea. To this absurd claim August wrote indignant denials. But the newspapers continued to attack him. August admitted to Marcy that he had learned "to look forward with pain and humiliation to the arrival of the late news from home. Instead of rejoicing at being able to give into the hands of my wife the papers, filled with tidings of all that passed in our distant country, every mail brought abuse and calumnies against me published by a vile but widely circulated press without a single refutation by those who must have been aware of the faithfulness with which I had attended to my duties."

Marcy told August to ignore the press—slanders were the praise of the enemy. Although hurt by Marcy's failure to defend him, August sheepishly said, "I plead guilty to having allowed myself to be too much annoyed by the scurrilous items instigated by Gibson." Both men were ready to compromise with the Dutch government on Gibson's claim or even to abandon him, but the attention the case had received forced them to take a hard line.

August wrote to Van Hall that, because the Dutch had not paid Gibson any indemnities, "It now only remains for my Government to take such measures for the enforcement of Mr. Gibson's claim as it may deem fit and proper."

Van Hall objected to the note but suggested that perhaps because of his imperfect grasp of English he had not understood it correctly. He was not quite sure of the meaning of the word *enforcement.* Was the United States considering armed enforcement?

August circled the word in his dictionary, dog-eared the relevant page, and sent the book to Van Hall with a note asking the foreign minister to make whatever choice among the various definitions seemed most appropriate.

Van Hall did not respond.

On the night of October 3 August was called from his seat at the theater. He found Gibson, surrounded by a mob of policemen and civilians, waiting for him outside. August was thunderstruck.

Why, he wanted to know, had Gibson returned to The Hague?

Gibson explained that people were claiming he had left Holland quickly on his last visit because he had been afraid of being arrested. He had come back to prove they were wrong.

Why then, August wanted to know, had Gibson interrupted him at the theater?

Because, Gibson said, since reentering Holland he had become nervous. At the border the customs guards had held a whispered meeting before passing him through. Outside the customs shed a crowd had gathered to glimpse him. Gibson had had to push his way through the mob to get to his train. At Rotterdam he had been met by a larger crowd and six policemen who silently took the empty seats in his compartment. At The Hague, Gibson had walked from the railroad station to the hotel where he had previously stayed. The police escort had followed. The proprietor of the hotel had refused to give him a room. Gibson had picked up his carpetbag and walked from the hotel to the United States legation. The police escort again had followed, and a small crowd had followed the police. A servant at the legation had told Gibson August was at the theater, and Gibson once more had started off. By the time he reached the theater he was leading a large parade.

No doubt apprehensively glancing around at the policemen and the crowd, Gibson said he wanted August's advice about what he should do.

August told Gibson, "Very frankly, after the disgraceful manner with which my previous words and actions have been belied in the *Herald* and *Tribune*, it could not be expected that I should consider myself safe in giving advice with the same openness and candor I have been in the habit of doing."

Gibson claimed he had nothing to do with the newspaper lies but admitted that perhaps he had said something to the Paris correspondents of the *Herald* and the *Tribune* that they had misinterpreted.

August accepted Gibson's veiled apology and invited him to stay at his own house. Because of Caroline's approaching confinement, August was sleeping in the guest room, and in an act of astonishing generosity offered to let Gibson use his bed. August would sleep on a sofa.

At eight o'clock the following morning August was summoned to the Ministry of Foreign Affairs. Van Hall told August that the Dutch attorney general had signed a warrant for Gibson's arrest and that Gibson would be seized within an hour. He begged August to get him out of town.

August coolly replied that Gibson would be leaving the next day; and if he were arrested before then, August and the entire legation would leave The Hague. Apparently Van Hall countermanded the warrant.

After another comfortable night in August's bed Gibson took August's carriage to the train station. He stopped on the way at the office of a newspaper opposed to Van Hall's administration to drop off more stolen copies of correspondence between Van Hall and August, which he hoped would embarrass them and thereby, in some not-clearly-thought-out way, help his case.

August could hardly believe Gibson's duplicity. With Marcy's consent he allowed the case to die for lack of attention, and he apologized to Van Hall for having so long and so fiercely supported such a scoundrel.

Relieved to be rid of the Gibson matter, which had been weakening his position within the Dutch government, and delighted to have been so triumphantly vindicated, Van Hall agreed to extend the consular treaty with the United States. The new treaty included ports not just in the East Indies but in all of Holland's colonies anywhere in the world, a concession August had not expected Van Hall to make and one that astounded the ambassadors of the other major powers, particularly of England, Austria, and France, all of whom rushed to make similar treaties with the Dutch. Despite the Gibson affair—or perhaps in a roundabout way because of it—August's principal mission succeeded spectacularly.

❧ CHAPTER SIXTEEN ❧

BOTH THE GIBSON AFFAIR and the negotiations over the consular treaty had lured August away from what he originally had expected would be his most important work in Europe: convincing bankers on the Continent to pressure Spain into selling Cuba to the United States. However, August had done what he could to push his plan, even though Marcy did not greet his initiatives with enthusiasm.

"I have incurred and am incurring considerable expense in order to secure the regular communication of well-informed persons in Paris and the other important" European cities, August told Marcy. He learned that the French government would not oppose the American acquisition of Cuba and, in fact, would help influence Spain to sell the island as long as the United States did not try to get its way through force, a condition August applauded since he believed it was more progressive to use money instead of guns to conquer territory. While old-fashioned European states sent their soldiers to the Crimea to slaughter one another, regiments of dollars would advance upon Madrid.

But although August paid for the spies out of his own pocket, and although he was getting information about the general state of politics in Europe as well as about Spain's attitude on Cuba, Marcy remained so unenthusiastic that August finally asked if he should continue to spend the money.

August also consulted with the Spanish minister at The Hague, an old friend who privately was in favor of the sale but doubted that public opinion in Spain would ever allow it to take place. August arranged to have two of his "clever, influential & rich" French friends go to Spain to prepare the way for the sale of Cuba "by bribery & intrigue." August was sure that "if a secret fund of $40,000 to $50,000 could be placed at my disposal," he "could do more with so trifling a sum than the open offer of so many millions."

But Marcy would not go along with August's plan and refused to give August the money. August offered to subsidize a revolution in Cuba with a loan of $5 million, but his generous—or impatient—proposal was never accepted by either rebellious Cubans or obedient State Department officials.

Diplomacy was turning out to be more frustrating than August had anticipated. In his business affairs he was used to making decisions alone.

As a representative of the United States government he was obliged to follow instructions that, like sibylline prophecies, often were vague in content although specific in intent. And he was forced to act in concert with other diplomats who were either opposed to his plans, overly cautious, not cautious enough—or, in the case of Pierre Soulé, wild and irresponsible.

Soulé, the American minister at Madrid, had alienated the Spanish government and many in Madrid's diplomatic corps by laming the French ambassador in a duel over an insulting remark to Soulé's wife, who had worn a sexy, low-cut dress to a ball. Not only had he failed to promote the amicable relations that might prompt the Spanish government to change its mind about the sale of Cuba, but he also was urging the United States to invade the island and foment revolution in Spain.

At various times Pierce's administration endorsed both August's and Soulé's approaches to Cuba—which had the effect of endorsing neither. At first Marcy told Soulé that the United States could not expect Spain—which had turned down a $100 million offer the previous American administration had made for Cuba—to agree to sell the island; and therefore Soulé should not suggest any new deal. Then the Spanish government on Cuba seized an American ship, the *Black Warrior,* when it arrived in the port of Havana. Marcy told Soulé to ask Madrid for a $300,000 indemnity, and Soulé adorned the demand with a forty-eight-hour ultimatum. The Cuban government fined the owners of the *Black Warrior* $6,000 on a minor customs matter; Spain canceled the fine and rejected the American demand for any indemnity; and Marcy, instead of backing up Soulé's threats, told him to offer Madrid $130 million for Cuba. Confusingly, however, he also told Soulé, if Spain still would not sell, to "direct your efforts to the next most desirable object which is to detach that island from the Spanish dominion and from all dependence on any European power." How Soulé should go about detaching Cuba from Spain was not explained.

Soulé, who was plotting with rebels in Spain, told Washington that if the revolution succeeded he could make a deal with the new government to buy Cuba for only $300,000.

During the summer of 1854 the Spanish government was toppled, but the new government was not the one Soulé had supported and was no more eager than its predecessor to sell Cuba. In the United States important backers of August's scheme like the secretary of the treasury had abandoned hope of buying the island and instead were helping to raise money to invade it. This plan was favored by Southerners who wanted

Cuba to enter the Union as a slave state. They feared that if it did not it eventually would become a black republic like Haiti, which by example might encourage their own slaves to revolt. August himself began to think that perhaps the United States should seize Cuba.

A well-financed private army of 50,000 men was planning to attack the island in February 1855. Early in October 1854, a few months before the threatened invasion, the American ministers at Madrid, London, and Paris met in Belgium at Ostend to decide American policy. Soulé represented those who wanted to take Cuba by force. Buchanan, representing those who wanted a peaceful solution to the crisis, urged Pierce to give August a free hand and enough money to carry out his plan. And Mason, who had admitted he had no idea which plan to support and was too embarrassed to reveal his confusion by asking the State Department for information, represented no approach whatsoever.

Seeking greater secrecy they moved to Aix-la-Chapelle. At last they issued a document that reflected more than it illuminated. The three ministers determined that the United States should try to buy Cuba and if that failed would "be justified in wresting it from Spain, if we possess the power."

The only change in strategy seemed to be an amplification of Soulé's growl into a roar: the United States should seize the island regardless of "the cost" or "the odds which Spain might enlist against us." Since France and England, the only two allies that might help Spain in a war with the United States, were otherwise occupied in the Crimea, the noble pose of three ministers, bravely asserting their country's rights no matter what the odds, seemed like mere posturing.

The only fires the document lit were backfires. The American press attacked it. The *New York Tribune* called it a "Manifesto of . . . Brigands." The *New York Evening Post* called it "atrocious." The senators who did not deplore it as Lewis Cass did tended to ignore it. In the elections held the month following the Ostend conference, the Democrats suffered severe defeats. Americans were rejecting Pierce's ineffectual leadership at home and buccaneering diplomacy abroad.

None of the principals at the conference emerged triumphant. Buchanan, who appeared at the end to have been swayed by Soulé, seemed weak. Soulé resigned. And Mason, on hearing that Soulé had written to Marcy explaining that the Ostend Manifesto was really a declaration of war, had a stroke.

Although August had been piqued not to have been included in the Ostend Conference, he was lucky to have been left out. Since most of his plotting to acquire Cuba had been behind the scenes, he escaped the newspaper attacks that no doubt would have come had he played a larger public role. The obstructions that had frustrated him turned out to have been barricades that protected him.

In the midst of the Cuban affair, on September 27, 1854, Frederika Belmont was born. Although the child was big, Caroline's labor was light and the delivery easy. And Caroline's mother, Jane Perry, was present to help.

August was delighted to have a daughter, and he went to Alzey to give his father the news in person. Arriving about noon, he was climbing from his carriage when half a dozen of the town's officials came running from their offices and homes to crowd around him and ask for advice and favors. They followed him into Simon's house and, along with others who joined them in the cramped rooms, stayed until eleven that night.

This visit was even more hectic than the last. Simon had even less of a chance to talk with his son about family matters. He was worried about Babette's health. She did not keep quiet enough. She stayed up at night too late and did not wake in the morning early enough. She wore her corset for too long a time and pulled it too tight. Her food was too fancy. She did not drink enough water or get enough fresh air. She went visiting too often.

He also was worried about August, who he thought was gallivanting around Europe too much. "I prefer to see August at his post at The Hague rather than traveling through Germany," Simon wrote Stephan Feist. "There is nothing more destructive to a person than unrestrained independence, as hard and depressing as dependence can be. The best is to find the middle ground—as is true with so many other things." Simon knew that his opinions might make him sound provincial, but he felt it was his duty to warn August that "moving from place to place—even under the best of circumstances—often leads to exuberance, which has serious consequences, as everybody knows."

August was exuberant. The previous summer when he had visited his father he—like the Stoic youth with a fox concealed within his clothes —had carried the gnawing worries about Gibson and the consular treaty. Now, his troubles resolved, he could feel that his diplomatic career was as successful as the townsfolk of his native village believed it to be. And, swollen with love for his new daughter, he seemed—as new fathers often do—to have continued the gestation that for his wife had ended with the baby's birth; he was pregnant with pride.

At five in the morning, when it was still dark, August and Simon left Alzey by carriage, passing houses in which behind a few windows lights were already being lit as early risers started their day. During the hour-long carriage ride to Bingen, where August would catch a steamer down the Rhine to Holland, Simon talked to his son about the misunderstanding that in the past had blighted August's relations with Babette. They parted at Bingen; and Simon, who would see his son but one more time, finally passed judgment on a question that for him had been open for many years: August, despite his dangerous tendencies toward exuberance, had a good heart.

Commodore Perry arrived at The Hague on November 20 looking, Caroline thought, "uncommonly well," as a hero should look. He would visit a month, he told his family. Then he had to continue on to England to examine British warships and to America to find someone to edit the notes he had kept of his expedition to Japan. (In London, Nathaniel Hawthorne would suggest and the Commodore would reject Herman Melville for the job.)

Caroline was disappointed that her father would miss Christmas at The Hague but was pleased that she had convinced him to let her mother and sister stay until summer. The Commodore told tales of his travels— of how, for example, Seyolo, an African chief, had offered him one of his five wives. The story became a family joke. "Why didn't you accept?" the Perry children would ask their father. "What would you have done if Papa had brought one home?" they would ask Jane Perry.

The Commodore had to get reacquainted with his grandchildren. Perry did not remember him, and the Commodore could hardly have recognized the little boy, who for almost a year now had had his hair cut short, which—his mother observed—made him "perfectly delighted with himself. He says he is just like Papa now."

After her father left, Caroline became despondent. She was cheered somewhat in February by a ball that they gave for Washington's Birthday, to which the king and queen came, a rare honor; "the first time," August thought, "in *any* European *court* a royal family has gone to *the house* of any foreign representative not *holding* the post of Minister Plenipotentiary." But during the rest of the winter, through the spring, and into the summer, Caroline's dejection increased as the day of her mother and sister's departure approached.

In mid-July, Jane Perry and Belle took a valedictory trip to Paris accompanied by August, Caroline, the three children, and four servants. Ten days after they had all returned to The Hague, Jane Perry and Belle started for home.

Caroline spent days on the beach at Scheveningen. The three children played in the sand while their nurses watched and Caroline braved the waves. Sometimes August would go with her. They would picnic and, on horseback, race along the shore. Occasionally they would meet the queen or the Prince and Princess Henry, who had come to stroll along the edge of the ocean. But most of the time the beach was empty and the days were dull.

"I have missed Mamma and Belle so much," Caroline confessed, "that I have for the first time felt homesick."

A trip to a Belgian spa did not dispel her gloom. August bought her a pony-wagon, but the countryside was "so hilly and mountainous" she found "very little use" for it. The morning band concert on the shaded promenade lifted her spirits a little, but the spa became too crowded.

August and Caroline left the Belgian spa for Aix-la-Chapelle. Their coachman was timid and always held the horses back, so August decided to drive the coach himself, letting the horses race for the exercise. Because that pell-mell ride could have been dangerous, Caroline went by train. Her traveling companion, a prince, "turned out to be very troublesome by being too polite."

August and Caroline roamed through Europe for the rest of the summer. But without the presence of Belle and Mrs. Perry, Europe apparently seemed to Caroline like a huge house furnished with religious relics and classics of art—all of which she duly appreciated—but empty of life.

In Mayence, they hurried through a visit with Babette and her family and Simon, whom August would never see again. From Frankfurt, August and Caroline drifted to Hamburg, Baden-Baden, and Paris.

As they wandered through the corridors of the Continent the echo of their footsteps could be heard in Caroline's diary and letters. She wanted to go back to New York.

August also was thinking more and more of home. He wrote with increasing frequency to Charles Christmas and Erhard A. Matthiessen, who had taken over his business affairs for the duration of his service in The Hague. He asked them to "send by the first direct steamer a dozen pair of live partridges to Baron James de Rothschild. Also send to the Baron, when the weather gets cold enough, a dozen Canvasback ducks and a pair of wild turkeys." Like many international bankers, August indulged in a regular exchange of gifts—a barter system supported by a financial order grown far beyond such economic atavism. In his letters, August also fretted about minor matters. His New York newspapers were not arriving regularly. The shipment of apples he had ordered had been ruined; no more than six were fit to eat. His coachman had become a drunkard.

He worried even more about the graver matters of business. The lag in communications prevented him from acting swiftly on information he felt Christmas and Matthiessen ignored or misinterpreted. They should sell his interest in the Pacific Mail Steamship Company. They should lend the Rothschilds 300,000 francs for sixty days and buy about $60,000 worth of French railroad stock and invest in the Panama Canal, despite the troubles surrounding that venture. They should hold on to his interest in the Pacific Railroad because, he figured, "I may play that chance as well as not." "If they can find a responsible purchaser," they should sell the $90,000 worth of Second Avenue Railroad bonds. They must fore-close on the mortgages on the houses he owned on East Twentieth Street. And they should get him completely out of the Illinois Central Railroad, even at a loss, because the business did not seem, at present, sound. But when Christmas and Matthiessen sold ten thousand shares, August worried that "with my usual luck, I suppose that now that I have sold my Illinois Central, the shares and bonds will go up 20% more." When a week later Christmas and Matthiessen sold the remaining shares—which had gone up enough for August to think the transaction was "quite satis-factory"—August, sounding more and more like his father, nevertheless complained that he now supposed "they will soon go to 110 and 120." They did not. Despite August's pessimism, his instincts, as usual, had been right. Shortly after August got rid of his interest in the railroad, Illinois Central declined.

Often instead of dwelling on the specific details of particular deals August would give general suggestions, which were based on a view of the economy that was wider than the one held by many New York bankers. He wrote to Christmas and Matthiessen:

"The news of the death of the Emperor of Russia has sent prices of stocks up in London and Paris [because it promised peace in the Crimea]. It will probably have a corresponding effect in New York. *Please profit of it.*"

"Heavy gold shipments are most welcome in Paris, and I hope you have been and are still able to continue them. The Bank of France is in a very tight fix, and I have no doubt pays pretty well for all the gold on which she can lay her hands."

"I hope that the continued export of grain and the commencement of the cotton season will have put a stop to the drain of gold to Europe."

"I hope that the panic which had taken hold of your money market at the last dates in consequence of the unfavorable accounts of the Bank of France will have subsided and that stocks will have improved again."

Like Tamerlane carving up the map for his heirs, August divided the world for his agents. The old national boundaries were not that important. In reality there were only two nations: the states of Debit and Credit.

Occasionally August's advice became so general it lapsed into financial homilies:

"It seems as if there was something radically wrong in our financial and commercial position—while Europe is at war and has to import food from us, property of all kind on the Continent has not declined half as much as with us Americans who are at peace and who have had most bountiful crops which we are now exporting at most remunerative prices."

"*One* bad loan with the heavy accounts which you have out would swallow up more than all the extra interest of a year."

And—significantly from a man whose father had spent a life in unsuccessful litigation—he warned his representatives to avoid suits. They won't be resolved, he said, until "my youngest boy comes of age."

The most important advice, however, seemed to be: prudence. Over and over in one way or another he told Christmas and Matthiessen, "I do not wish to sell good and interest-paying stocks and bonds, but wish gradually to dispose of the more speculative of my investments." Older and very successful, he was no longer a Wall Street hotspur. In the past he had made his fortune on risks. In the future he would consolidate his fortune and double it and double it again and again on caution.

Caution, however, is not a guarantee against disaster. During his last few years at The Hague, August followed from a distance three crises involving his affairs in New York. One of his copyists embezzled more than $4,000. Although he returned and repaid $1,081, August's confidence in his clerks was shaken. He decided to clean house. He told Christmas and Matthiessen to let a number of his workers go; and he decided that in order to get more reliable men he would have to pay higher wages because of "the increased cost of the necessities of life." Even though the copyist offered to pay back the rest of the stolen money if he were not sent to jail, August, showing a vindictive streak that he thought was a devotion to justice, preferred seeing the man imprisoned. It was not the robbery that upset August, it was the betrayal; he had trusted the man.

More serious than the embezzlement in possible consequences was a doubtful investment Christmas and Matthiessen made. Although August was wary of risky involvements and warned his agents "not to lend more than $50,000 to any one" banking house so long as the economy was shaky, Christmas and Matthiessen loaned $100,000 to a firm called De-Launay & Co., which had suspended payments two years before and which, shortly after it borrowed August's money, suspended payments again. When August heard of the transaction, his letters to Christmas and Matthiessen followed a predictable parabola of anxiety, starting with the apprehensive "I still have not yet received one cent from the suspended firm. This is very much calculated to stagger my belief in the honesty of those people," rising to an almost hysterical "There is an amount of $100,000 at stake, and after eight days I know as much as on the day of suspension," and once the affair had been straightened out dropping to a relieved although incredulous "I really am at a loss to understand how you could so far depart from your customary" prudence "as to give credit of over $100,000 even if only for three or four days to a house like DeLaunay & Co."

The third crisis, however, affected August the most. The warehouse in which his belongings had been stored had burned. August reacted as though his life in America, the world he had built for himself, had gone up in flames.

Inexplicably, since fires were common disasters in New York, where a number of blazes had gutted the city in the past few decades, August had taken out only $5,000 in insurance. Perhaps he was trusting the good fortune that had boosted him to success in America would, like a conscientious agent, look after his affairs while he was gone. Or perhaps he did not want to tempt the fates by investing too heavily in catastrophe.

But even if he had taken out more insurance he could not have covered his losses. Many of his belongings, because they had personal associations or because they were works of art, were priceless. He ticked off the list of what was probably ruined with the resignation of a mourner naming his family's dead: "a Salvatore Rosa worth over $1,000—some very fine Bohemian glass and Saxon porcelain, which I shall lose with a good deal of regret"; "a quantity of Saxon and Sèvres china figures, chairs, tables, etc. of antique and costly workmanship, which was the only reason I kept them"; "some old and rare Madeira and some Johannisberger Kabinett blue seal," one of the greatest wines in the world; "some Steinberger," a wine second only to Johannisberger Kabinett "which cannot now be replaced"; a collection of shells belonging to Commodore Perry; a rocking horse. He kept his sorrow reined in until he came to his library, when he pitifully cried, "Have all my books burnt?"

August, a perfectionist, wanted his damaged belongings replaced with new things. The idea of coming back to New York to a house filled with patched and mended objects was distasteful. He would keep the sets of the complete works of his favorite authors—Voltaire, Buffon, Balzac, Rousseau, Lamartine, and Thiers—and the other selected volumes in his collection only if the binder could "restore to them the quality they had before the fire broke out." If not, the insurance company had to replace or pay for them. "Damaged works will not suit my library."

"As regards to the things which were taken to the dyer to be restored and cleaned," he told Christmas, "I do not believe that blankets, linen, etc. singed by fire and otherwise injured can be made what they were by the dyer, and it would be much more just on the part of the Insurance Company to replace them by new things or refund me the value."

But the insurance company was balky. Why shouldn't August be satisfied with reclaimed goods? The insurance company was concerned with function; August was concerned with form. What use was having a great deal of money if you could not surround yourself with beautiful objects? The insurance company thought August was being unreasonable; August thought the insurance company was being unfair.

"It is disgraceful," he told Christmas, "that the company makes difficulties in paying my loss after having quietly pocketed the premiums for two years."

The insurance company finally settled, although not for as much as August would have liked; but by then, the winter of 1855, August was less preoccupied with what had furnished his former house in New York than with what would furnish his new house there. Starting early in December 1855, almost two years before he would return to the United States, August began shipping to America well-insured cases (eventually there would be more than 250) filled with, among other things, an antique carved wooden mantelpiece, a "mother-of-pearl dish held by two gilt bears," a stag's-horn paper-press, a set of ivory jackstraws, a game of dominoes, a bronze barometer, a carriage, 2 harnesses, 3 saddles, 5 snaffles, 8 tracers, leggings for their postilion, a dogcart, a dog collar, and a dog whip, jardinieres and étagères, bureaus, armoires, dressing cases, pencil cases, penholders, inkstands, lampstands, lampshades, lamp chimneys, lampwicks, oil lamps, candlesticks, candelabra, chandeliers, matchlighters, bundles of tobacco, cigar boxes, snuffboxes, workboxes, card boxes, music boxes, bonbon boxes, sugar boxes, sugar bowls, salt cellars, gravy boats, breadbaskets, fish dishes, toothpick stands, napkin rings, eggboilers, tea caddies, teapots, coffeepots, milk pots, mustard pots, chocolate urns, water jugs, champagne coolers, hamholders, crumbscrapers, 18 tablecloths, 24 towels, 30 pillowcases, 60 sheets, 72 napkins, 80 dishcloths, 90 forks, 109 knives, 150 spoons, Florentine china, Dresden china, French china, Berlin china, 183 cups and as many saucers, breakfast plates, soup plates, salad plates, dinner plates, dessert plates, round plates, oval plates, square plates, made of Majolica, silver, gold, and china (422 plates in all, and 79 dishes), hock glasses, claret glasses, champagne glasses, water glasses, Madeira glasses, liqueur glasses, beer glasses (213 glasses in all), punch bowls, decanters, pitchers, 1 bottle of gin, 7½ bottles of Madeira, 26 bottles of port, 32 bottles of Malaga, 48 bottles of champagne, 81 bottles of sherry, 139 bottles of French wine and 169 bottles of German wine, 110 paintings, 179 books, and dozens of carved figures and pieces of sculpture, glass falcons, Delft cows, a wooden chamois, a bronze bird, a bronze bear, a bronze bull, a bronze Puss-in-Boots. . . .

August set a standard for collecting—in both quantity and quality —that would last for generations.

All of August's newly acquired treasures would need an appropriate setting for their display; so, shortly after shipping the first packing cases to America, August through Christmas and Matthiessen started looking for a site on which to build his new house. He wanted to buy six or seven lots, a large piece of property with plenty of room for a yard and garden, "deep enough to build a stable" in back and wide enough to have a hundred-foot front, which he knew "may appear a little too much, but I cannot do with less." He also considered buying some adjoining lots, which "would give me a certain control over my neighborhood." The social geography of New York City was in flux. The city was expanding northward up the island, and building in the suburbs above Fortieth Street was a gamble. The advantages of space could be offset in a few years by the disadvantages of undesirable neighbors.

When the Commodore suggested that August build near the proposed Central Park, August responded with guarded enthusiasm. If half a dozen families could "purchase a large block together and build at once," they all could be assured of living in an agreeable community. And the park if planned properly would be an undeniable asset. August thought the Central Park corporation "ought to set 30 or 40 acres apart for a zoological and botanical garden. A company might then form, and the entrance would only be for subscribers," who would contribute toward "keeping the grounds in order" and "providing for the animals. A great many much smaller places than New York such as Brussels, Antwerp, etc. have similar establishments without any aid of government, and they succeed very well. If you," August told the Commodore, "and a few of our spirited citizens would place themselves at the head of such an enterprise, I doubt not of its success." By getting involved they could not only promote but also control the project. "Care should also be taken," August noted, "that the corporation pass strict laws forbidding driving and riding in the new park over a certain rate of speed, say 8 or 9 miles per hour at the outside—this will keep the fast-trotting men and other rowdies out. And no licenses for public drinking shops ought to be given in the neighborhood."

If August wanted to have a law against fast-trotting men in Central Park, it was not because he objected to an occasional fast trot or even a gallop. He himself was a fast-trotting man who liked to race horses on and off the racetracks. It was just that he did not think the park would be an appropriate setting for anything that might be dangerous to wives and children who also would be riding, no doubt at a pace slower than a fast trot, or walking along the paths.

August had a passion for protecting his family. Just as he had drawn a magic circle around Caroline after they had married he wanted to draw a larger circle around his children and an even larger circle around the society in which they would grow up. The world was a savage place; like a pioneer August was carving a sanctuary from what he saw as a social wilderness. And like all pioneers he wanted to extend the limits of that sanctuary, civilizing (as he understood it) and making safe greater and greater areas of the untamed world around him.

You tamed a world by controlling not only the behavior of those who lived within it but also the world itself. Streets must be built and kept up, water must be diverted to go where you wanted it to go. So August finally decided against settling as far uptown as the proposed Central Park, because he thought it "will be pretty difficult" to get a group of congenial families to "club together" to build in that area; moreover, he was not sure that the streets were paved so far uptown or that the gas and water pipes were laid there. It might take ten years for that neighborhood to be developed.

Also he was doubtful that such a site was in good relation to the reservoir. He explained to the Commodore, "I do not want any property where the water does not come up into the third story"—which also was why he did not want a house situated too high on Murray Hill. "I have tried the inconvenience" of having water pumped or carried by servants to the upper floors "in the country," he told Christmas and Matthiessen; and as he told the Commodore, "the troubles with servants are already great enough without adding to them by additional duties imposed upon them."

Ideally he wanted a house between Eighteenth and Thirty-fourth streets on the block between Fourth and Fifth avenues, "as the exposure north and south is always better than east and west, but Tiny seems to prefer going to the avenue, and I should always like to please her." Whether the house faced the street or the avenue it should be built— August thought—on good ground, so that he could have a sizable cellar for his wines; it should have "either a porte cochere or a covered gate to drive a carriage under," "good-sized rooms and parlors with a well-lit staircase and plenty of comfortable pantries and closets," and adequate natural light to illuminate his pictures, which he would hang on "very plainly papered" walls in "a picture gallery that would be if possible on the parlor floor."

August eventually bought and renovated a house on Fifth Avenue as Caroline wanted—109 Fifth Avenue on the northeast corner of Eighteenth Street. The picture gallery he built for it was the first in New York to be lit by a skylight. And the house boasted the first private ballroom in the city—although, Edith Wharton later recalled, the room "was left for three hundred and sixty-four days of the year to shuttered darkness, with its gilt chairs stacked in a corner and its chandelier in a bag."

August knew that "the general style of living has become much more expensive since I left New York," and he intended to dazzle when he returned.

CHAPTER SEVENTEEN

THE MORE AUGUST and Caroline planned their return to New York, the duller their life at The Hague seemed to be. The royal family, which set the tone for all social life in Holland, was in no mood for gaiety. King William III of the Netherlands had retreated to his hunting lodge, pointedly not inviting the queen to join him. The queen, after lingering at The Hague, visited her father, the king of Württemberg. A few weeks after the Russians abandoned Sebastopol to the English and the French, the king violated the spirit of a neutral court, the sympathies of many of his subjects, and the family loyalty of his mother (the daughter of Czar Paul I of Russia). He gave a gold cross to Napoleon III, the emperor of France, in recognition of the allied victory. Such an honor was rarely bestowed, and—as August noted—King William's gesture "has astonished everybody. It is true that the King sent the same order at the same time to his cousin, the Emperor of Russia, but this is considered by many as a very lame and poor apology for the unfriendliness of the act of giving so striking a mark of distinction to the French Emperor just when his armies had planted their victorious eagles on the heroically defended walls of Sebastopol. The Queen Mother at all events took it in this sense. She left her son and the Residence in great anger and is now on her way to St. Petersburg where she intends to remain for an extended period."

August's sympathies were with England and France; but although he thought their cause was just, he could not wholeheartedly support their fight. Too much money had been wasted; August's informants told him France and England were each spending about $20 million a year on the Crimean War. And too many lives had been lost.

For what?

August was afraid that whatever the outcome of the battles the outcome of the war would be "a union of the absolute despotisms of France, Austria, and Prussia," which would not hold out much hope for the cause of republicanism in Europe.

"Wars always concentrate power in the hands of the sovereign," August believed; "and, while they enable him to increase his armies, they provide a praetorian spirit among the latter, which estranges them from the masses and makes them willing instruments to be employed against the liberties of the very people from whose ranks they have sprung."

Even though the war was good for the American economy, requiring by August's estimation 400 million francs' worth of grain principally from the United States, he deplored the continued fighting and was happy when, following the fall of Sebastopol, peace seemed near.

His pleasure at this good news was infected, however, by word from Baron Lionel Rothschild. The London *Times* was filled with rumors of plans for an American expedition to Ireland to help the republicans there fight the English. If these rumors were true, England might quit fighting Russia in the Crimea only to start fighting the United States in Ireland or America.

August was appalled at this prospect. "The remotest possibility even of a war between England and the United States is so fearful to contemplate for both parties that everything which could at any future time bring about such a catastrophe should be most carefully avoided and removed," August told the baron, emphasizing that they both must do whatever they could to reduce the possibility of any conflict between the two countries.

Politicians might start wars, but international financiers could abort them. Wars could not be fought without funds. An alliance between August and the Rothschilds could be more powerful than any hostility between their respective nations.

By Christmas the promise of a general peace seemed about to be redeemed. August was in excellent spirits. The King's uncle, Prince Frederick was cultivating him. In the two weeks just before the holiday he had asked August "to three shooting and dinner parties," invitations that were all the more satisfying since they had been extended to only two others in the diplomatic corps.

Caroline too was happy. Pregnant again, she was enjoying a robust appetite, gobbling down dozens of her favorite buttered rolls and feasting on the candy and coconut cakes that Belle had sent and that had arrived with "not a taste of the sea voyage about" them. Belle's treats, Caroline admitted, "reminded me so much of home"; but she did not surrender to homesickness.

With their departure not far in the future she had transformed her distress with life at The Hague into a humorous acceptance and indulgence of those she would leave behind. One of the diplomats who had taken a fancy to Caroline regularly visited her to play chess. "I have played five times with him now and beaten him every game." Caroline was not afraid to seem intelligent or aggressive. She was proud of her chess game and reveled in winning. "He is so excited about it that he says he cannot rest until he has won," she said. "He gets so nervous that it is quite amusing to see him."

Another diplomat whose heart she also had won arrived one evening just after New Year's Day with "an immense bundle under his arm. He said that August had given him permission to offer me a pair of Russian slippers, and he wondered if I would accept them. I thanked him very kindly, and with much curiosity I undid the paper. Inside was roll upon roll of cotton, which made me more anxious still to see the contents. When I got to the end, no slippers were to be found. At first, I thought he was making fun of me, he is such an odd fellow; and then we all shouted and laughed. It seems he had got hold of the wrong package. You can easily imagine how amusing it was—to see him with all his flourishes, making a long speech and a great ado; and after all finding nothing but a quantity of cotton batting."

Shortly after Christmas, August received a vicious letter from W. S. Campbell, the United States consul at Rotterdam. Although August had a policy of not making personal loans to United States diplomats abroad —he had, in fact, turned down such requests from the United States minister resident at Lisbon and the attaché at the United States legation in Brussels—he had made an exception in Campbell's case and the previous summer had loaned him 500 francs, about $200. Campbell promised to repay August by the fall, but did not. August sent him a note to remind him that the loan was overdue. Campbell replied with a nasty attack on August's character.

Through sleight of logic Campbell tried to make his dishonor in trying to avoid paying back the loan August's dishonor in expecting the repayment. Gentlemen—Campbell suggested—do not bother themselves about such mundane matters. If August had the bad manners to want the debt paid off, he was no gentleman; and if he was no gentleman, then Campbell, who was a gentleman, could not recognize August as being worthy of friendship. Evidently Campbell had assumed August would forget about the debt; and his implication was that only a Jew would have bothered to press him over such a trifling sum.

Campbell must have thought himself clever. To avoid Campbell's anti-Semitic slur August would have to forget about the loan. August's contempt for Campbell erupted through his incredulity at Campbell's naïveté. Others had tried and failed to avoid paying debts by hinting that if August would forget about the loans, they would renounce their anti-

Semitism. August was disappointed that Campbell would stoop to such a tactic. He had thought Campbell was more honest or at least more sophisticated than that.

August was further amazed and amused at Campbell's claim that he was owed 100 francs for his expenses in carrying out official duties and an even greater amount for researching in Rotterdam a family matter for a Cincinnati businessman, whose request for help August had forwarded to Campbell as a matter of course. Snidely, Campbell also offered to pay interest on the loan, as though August were concerned only with making money, even a paltry amount, not with the principles involved in a default.

"I have received your note of yesterday and have taken due notice of its contents," August wrote Campbell. "It was indeed a most unwarrantable presumption of mine to remind you by a few friendly lines of a loan, made to you last summer. Having had the hardihood of asking for its repayment at your 'earliest convenience' when you yourself had assured me at the time that it should be paid last October, I must submit to the deserved consequences of the forfeiture of the esteem and friendship of a gentleman whose nice feelings of honor and delicacy I have so grossly outraged. I will not therefore make any further reference to your observations, willing as you find me to acknowledge the enormity of my offense and resigned as I am to bear its doleful punishment."

August was using Campbell's logic against him. If Campbell claimed that August's demand for the 500 francs would cancel their friendship, well, then August, seeing that Campbell had placed a price on his friendship, could not consider such a friendship worth very much—not even 500 francs. He would forfeit the friendship for the money.

As for Campbell's claim that August in his official capacity as minister resident at The Hague owed him money for legation business, August noted that he would be happy to cover the expenses, adding that "as you state that you have made such disbursements, you will, of course, be able to favor me with the necessary vouchers." The claim that August owed Campbell money for the investigation carried out on behalf of the Cincinnati businessman was more problematic. Why hadn't Campbell said something about expenses at the time, August wondered. If he had, August easily could have forwarded the bill to the man in Cincinnati. Why was Campbell bringing it up only now that "I have been guilty of the heinous offense alluded to at the beginning of [Campbell's] letter?" In any case, August told Campbell, all receipts for such expenses should be sent in. August would deduct them from what Campbell owed, since he had "no doubt that the State Department will be able to collect" the money from the Cincinnati businessman and reimburse August.

"Your offer to pay me interest on the loan," August concluded, "though very kind and considerate, I beg to decline. It would be the first time that I accepted such a remuneration for what I, at the time at least, supposed to be a friendly service, and besides that I have in this instance been amply compensated by the considerate and polite tenor of your note."

August was making no effort to be less than heavy-handed in his sarcasm.

Campbell wrote back hemming and hawing, taking offense because August was demanding vouchers and receipts for the expenses he claimed to have incurred. August replied that he thought "there was nothing to wound the most sensitive sensibility in my asking for these vouchers." Campbell sent August the 500 francs to repay the loan as well as the vouchers and receipts. The matter was closed. Within a year Campbell would be making overtures trying to regain if not August's friendship at least his good opinion. August responded civilly, no more. He dismissed Campbell not just for his dishonorableness and ingratitude but also for the shallowness of his intrigue. To make such a fuss—and such a mean-spirited fuss—over a mere 500 francs!

When Jane Pauline Belmont—called Jeannie—was born on April 11, 1856, Caroline decided to nurse her herself. She had not liked using a wet-nurse with Frederika; and she did not feel, as some suggested, that nursing the baby would tire her. She was, in fact, so strong that within a short time she was receiving visits from wives of the diplomats attached to the court at The Hague and, as August noted with satisfaction, from "Dutch ladies as well," a sign that Caroline finally had conquered. Even those ladies who still may have been jealous sued for her favor.

Earlier August and Caroline had traveled to escape the hostility shown to Caroline within Dutch and diplomatic society. Now they traveled because, having overcome that hostility, they no longer had to campaign against it to relieve the boredom of The Hague. August told the Commodore that they would travel to Switzerland that summer and to the south of France and Italy the following winter before returning to the United States in the spring of 1857.

"Under these circumstances," he explained to the Commodore, "I do not think it very advisable that in the letters from home there should be always so much anxiety expressed about our early return. It will not change anything in our plans, which you and Mrs. Perry have yourselves approved, and might make Tiny feel uncomfortable, while at present she is as happy and contented as can be."

And August told Christmas and Matthiessen that "it would really be a great sacrifice to me to have to return without having shown my wife somewhat more of Europe. With a large family it is no joke to travel and cross the ocean, so that when I shall be once home again I mean to settle down quietly."

After a trip to Paris and Switzerland, August returned to The Hague to learn that one of Baron James de Rothschild's railroads, the Chemin de Fer du Nord, had been robbed of between 30 and 32 million francs, more than 15 million dollars. The leader of the gang was Charles Carpentier, a twenty-six-year-old protégé of Baron James who was romantic-looking enough to be described in the popular press during his trial as consumptive. On a trip with Carpentier Baron James was chortling over one deal that had made him 5 million francs and another in the works that would make him an additional 3 million francs: 8 million francs for a day's profit.

Carpentier asked him why he didn't "give me the five; you will still have a neat little sum."

"I am not going to give you five million," said Baron James, laughing at what seemed at the time to be a good joke, "but here is my watch chain as a pleasant memento of the day."

Carpentier put the chain in his pocket and asked for a short leave of absence so he could get married.

Baron James consented.

Carpentier left Paris.

Payday arrived. Carpentier, who had the keys to the safes, was still gone. Baron James, who had a duplicate set of keys, first opened the small safe. It was empty. Then the large safe. It too was empty. All the railroad's cash assets were gone. Later Baron James discovered that the embezzlers had slipped a few hundred shares of stock from each packet of a thousand shares that they had been able to get their hands on. And they had juggled the books to keep the robberies secret.

There were rumors that Carpentier and his accomplices had stolen the railroad's money to cover bad investments in the stock market; that they had bought a steamer for 1,800,000 francs and had sailed from Liverpool; that they had bought a house in New York. Baron James, furious, said he would spend 10 million francs to track down Carpentier; and he asked August to help catch the embezzlers. August told Christmas to cooperate with the detective who was leading the investigation, Henry Goddard of Scotland Yard.

Through his own intelligence system August learned that Carpentier had sailed for America on the steamship *Fulton* and that his accomplices had gone on the steamship *The Atlantic*. Goddard followed up these leads and discovered that, after arriving in New York, Carpentier had lived at the St. Nicholas Hotel, a splendid six-story building that had opened on Broadway between Broome and Spring streets three years earlier.

Carpentier's trail, however, ended there. Goddard was stumped. Christmas offered the next lead. Shortly after Goddard had arrived in New York a Frenchman had come to Christmas with notes for 30,000 francs that he wanted to exchange for gold bullion. Christmas told him to come back the next day. The Frenchman left his card, which said "M. Debud."

Christmas contacted Goddard, who told him to negotiate with "M. Debud." The following day, while Goddard watched Christmas's office from across the street, Christmas arranged to sell "M. Debud" 30,000 francs' worth of gold bullion in thirty days. It would—Christmas explained—take a month to send the notes to Paris to be redeemed. "M. Debud" agreed to the transaction and left. Goddard trailed him to a house on Beekman Street and staked out the place, but saw no signs of Carpentier.

Three or four days later "M. Debud" returned to Christmas's office to say he had changed his mind. He did not want to buy gold bullion after all. He wanted his notes back. Christmas told him that the notes might have been sent to Paris. He would check. If "M. Debud" would come back in twenty-four hours Christmas would be able to tell him.

Goddard and some members of the New York City Police Department were hiding in the room next to Christmas's office the following day when "M. Debud" appeared. The notes were on their way to France, Christmas said. "M. Debud," very upset, dashed out of Christmas's office and, with Goddard and the police close behind, headed for his rooms on Beekman Street.

Once more Goddard staked out the house, this time with success. After a couple of hours two more of Carpentier's accomplices arrived—

and were arrested, as were "M. Debud," who was a former medical student named Auguste Parot, and shortly thereafter Carpentier.

Carpentier and his gang were tried in Paris. His mistress, Georgette Rollet, who—the newspapers reported—appeared in court "in a magnificent toilette" and testified "with considerable impudence," said that Carpentier gave her only 300 to 400 francs a month. Evidently she was outraged that the man who had masterminded what some considered to be the crime of the century had been so stingy.

The jury, of course, was outraged for different reasons. Although Parot was acquitted, the others were found guilty. Carpentier was sentenced to five years' imprisonment.

August suggested to Baron James that he reward Christmas for his help. But his own reward was the satisfaction that the Rothschilds were now in his debt.

⚜ CHAPTER EIGHTEEN ⚜

AS EARLY AS TWO YEARS before the presidential election of 1856, August was predicting that, at the Democratic party's national convention in Cincinnati, Pierce would not be renominated.

Like a chemist measuring out a potentially explosive brew, Pierce carefully had combined in his cabinet free-soil Northerners and proslavery Southerners. But the mix was wrong. Instead of creating a compromise administration that could reduce national tensions, Pierce had committed himself to an administration unable to take a strong position on slavery and therefore incapable of giving direction to the rest of the country. As a result the situation, especially in the West, deteriorated.

Kansas, with two hostile legislatures, one proslavery and one antislavery, had erupted into civil war, each faction fighting to establish how the territory would enter the Union as a state. Pierce had been unable to prevent the violence. He would be repudiated.

At the Democratic convention, after seventeen ballots—and a struggle between Buchanan and Douglas that Douglas ended by releasing his delegates—Buchanan won the nomination. For the first time in American history an incumbent President seeking another term had been rejected by his own party. Pierce was out; Buchanan was the Democratic nominee.

From Europe, August watched his candidate's progress against both the former explorer and former senator John Charles Frémont, who had been nominated by the new Republican party, and the former Whig and former president Millard Fillmore, who had been nominated by the relatively new American party.

The Whig party was moribund, although the Whigs held a funereal convention and, tagging along after the American party, nominated Fillmore. As though the election were seeking historical symmetry, another splinter party, the North American, tagged along after the Republicans and nominated Frémont.

The American party had been called the Know-Nothing party by Horace Greeley, because early in its life, under a different organization, its members had been sworn to secrecy and when questioned had claimed to know nothing about it. In 1856 their platform was proslavery and anti-Catholic. Know-Nothings distrusted foreigners and resented the flood of immigrants who, they thought, were replacing traditional American virtues with odd, exotic, and dangerous customs.

August did not think Fillmore had or deserved to have a chance in a contest with Buchanan. The previous year Fillmore had visited the Belmonts at The Hague. After the visit August invited Buchanan to come to Holland, saying the Dutch "have now seen an American president, but I want them to see an American statesman." August admonished the Commodore, "You must not fail to vote for Old Buck. If Fillmore had any chance, I should not dream of influencing you away from your old friend. He is, however, out of the question." Many people agreed with August. During the campaign one New Yorker jotted in his diary, "Fillmore is in town; nobody cares much."

The Republican party, a haven for antislavery factions from the Whigs, Democrats, and Know-Nothings, was considered, as one contemporary put it, "a sectional Northern party" with one issue. Although everyone admitted Frémont would carry most of the Northern states, those states would not be enough to elect him. Even a Frémont supporter, on hearing cheers from a Frémont rally, thought, "Frémont won't be President, my dear, deceived, enthusiastic, short-sighted brothers. You are bellowing to no purpose, disquieting yourselves in vain. Better for you to go home and to bed. . . . Ten years hence there will be some Frémont who can make it worth one's while to hurrah for him, but *you*, my unknown vociferous friends and fellow-citizens, are premature. You don't perceive that 'the Republican party' is a mere squirm and wriggle of the insulted North, a brief spasm of pain under pressure and nothing more."

August thought Frémont, who years before had eloped with the daughter of a senator (and an antislavery senator from proslavery Missouri, at that), was "a lucky adventurer" whose "appeal to sectional antipathies must, if successful, result in the forcible disunion of the North and South. With that undeniable fact before us, no good citizen can hesitate for a moment in deciding how to vote."

Buchanan tried to maintain a position between these two extremes, the Know-Nothings and Republicans. In doing so, he seemed to some to have no position at all. From England he studiously had kept a diplomatic distance from the troubles in the United States. As usual he had delayed announcing his candidacy so long that John Slidell had to prod him by telling him to "make up your mind that the cup will not be permitted to pass from you."

Buchanan hung on to the cup and drank deeply. He left England, stopped at The Hague to see the Belmonts—of the presidential candidates only Frémont did not feel the need to flatter August with a visit—and returned to the United States like a disinterested but concerned god descending from Olympus. Appropriately, but unfortunately, he was greeted with more respect than enthusiasm.

Although one observer noticed that "the masses take both Frémont and Buchanan rather coolly," he decided that "what little sign there is of life and excitement is for Frémont."

August did what he could to excite the public's interest in Buchanan—and Buchanan's interest in himself. He sent Buchanan a dozen jugs of gin, advice (especially on how at last to win Cuba; August still was obsessed with Cuba), and European political gossip. ("With all his foresight and sagacity, the Emperor Napoleon is very much a creature of impulse. The late Emperor of Russia's refusing to write to him as *mon cher frère* had probably quite as much to do with the Oriental [Crimean] War as the Protectorate of the Christians in Turkey.")

More useful and perhaps more appreciated were the contributions August sent, although they were not necessarily as great as rumor claimed. The *Evening Post* reported that August spent $50,000 in Pennsylvania alone to assure Buchanan of the nomination, but this was probably a Republican fabrication. It is more likely that August made his donation through Slidell directly to the Central Executive Committee of the Democratic party, which is what August told Richard Schell, the secretary of Buchanan's New York organization.

Whatever the amount of August's contribution and however it may have been allocated, it certainly must have been large. August had already invested heavily in Buchanan. He would not alienate the candidate with a miserly donation now that Buchanan was about to win the presidency.

August also did not want to alienate Buchanan by becoming an issue himself in the campaign, as he had four years before. Although he lent his name to a call for an anti-Frémont public meeting as one of "the merchants of the city of New York, and the public generally, who are attached to the Constitution and the Union, and opposed to the organization of parties on a sectional basis," generally he tried to stay out of the eye of the public—or more specifically of the hostile press. And he was scrupulous in trying to make sure nothing he did, even privately, would embarrass Buchanan.

When Schell tried to wheedle money for Buchanan's New York campaign from August by suggesting that August might be named minister resident at the French court, August wrote that "your allusion to my becoming a candidate for the mission to France merits almost that I should not reply to that portion of your letter. It may serve the purposes of that scamp Bennett," the editor of the *New York Herald*, "to fill his columns with such absurd inventions in order to injure Buchanan through me, but I had hoped that you had too favorable an opinion of me to think me capable of enough egotism to have even a thought of such a post."

In fact, the *Herald* had been accusing August of buying the mission to France with his contributions to Buchanan's campaign. The *Herald* had been inaccurate—August thought John Slidell, if he were not made secretary of state, would make an excellent minister to France—although not entirely wrong. August was eager to return home, but he would have stayed in Europe under the right conditions; and while he did not see his contributions as the price of a diplomatic post, he did hope that Buchanan, if elected, would name him minister to Madrid, principally so he could follow up his scheme to buy or steal (he had no intention of begging) Cuba from Spain.

August, watching the campaign from a distance, was confident Buchanan would win, even if John Slidell, closer to the action, was worried enough about the outcome to suffer terribly from diarrhea and to grow old-looking and haggard.

Buchanan did win. Even the Commodore voted for him; and as he told August, "it has been the first time I cast my vote for thirty-five years."

"It is a great blessing for our country that Frémont has not succeeded," August thought; "and every good American ought to offer prayers to God that He has vouchsafed to save the Union from the misery which that election would have brought down upon us."

August's rhetoric tended to become religious when he talked politics—just as it had tended to become political when years before, while judging the effect of his marriage on New York's Jewish community, he had talked religion.

Pleased with the results of the election, August left The Hague for France and Italy. In Paris, Mrs. Egan, the children's nurse, was seized with what members of the family described as a melancholy, during which she evidently suffered from hallucinations. Caroline put Mrs. Egan into a sanatorium, hoping "to find her quite restored to health on my return in the spring," although Jane Perry when she heard of Mrs. Egan's state warned her daughter "against trusting the children with her again. There can be no telling what in her monomania she might do. For though I am well assured that she has received nothing from you and August but the kindest attention, even forbearance in her seeming fits of temper, she may be laboring under some idea in her partial insanity in regard to the children, which would lead her to some act of violence, caused by feelings of jealousy of her control or influence over them."

The children were growing up. Perhaps Mrs. Egan was distressed to see them passing from under her care. About the time Mrs. Egan's melancholy came on, August was discussing the necessity of "looking out for an efficient governess," to replace the nurse, since "the boys are becoming quite unmanageable."

The two girls were cheerful and healthy children. Jeannie—August told the Commodore—"looks as if she was double her age. Her features are really beautiful and resemble very much those of her mother. Frederika walks and talks and promises to be a terrible scamp. She is very dark and looks more in the Belmont style."

They traveled through the south of France and into Italy, not by train but in what Caroline thought was "the most delightful carriage that can be imagined." The daughter of a commodore, she described it nautically as "holding all hands, as the sailors say, namely August and myself, four children, two or three nurses, a dressing maid, and a courier. We are so comfortable in it that it completely spoils me for all other modes of conveyance."

While riding they unpacked from their hampers cold chicken, wine, bread, and pâté de foie gras and ate as they watched the countryside, as though it were a scene in a diorama, through their windows. In the new age of rail the private traveling carriage was becoming an anachronism—and therefore a luxury, which made its use all the more appealing.

August thought "Tiny and the children stood the traveling extremely well." In fact, getting away from The Hague agreed with Caroline so much that August found her "health is excellent; she has not looked so pretty as she does now for some time past."

In Genoa, Perry and August, Jr., got to tour what they called "Grandpa's ship," the *Susquehanna,* which during the last part of his Far East expedition had been the Commodore's flagship; and August gave Caroline a ruby-colored velvet dress. They spent Christmas near Pisa. The children would not go to bed until nearly midnight and woke early the next morning to empty their stockings and open their presents.

In Rome, Caroline and August went to hear a Te Deum. "We had excellent places near the high altar and just behind the Queen of Spain and her two daughters," Caroline later reported. "I pushed on, dragging August after me, and managed to get one of the very best places in the church. I was afraid every moment of being turned back, but we were not, and we had an excellent opportunity of seeing the Pope, who is a fat lazy-looking man."

The boys had less luck in church. The Belmonts' courier, who was evidently Catholic, tried to get them to kiss the toe of a bronze Saint Peter; but they refused, saying that all the beggars who had kissed it had made it too dirty.

During their stay in Rome, August and Caroline went to a few balls. At one Caroline, delighted to be asked, danced with a chamberlain of the Pope. But they both found Roman society stupid and dull; and they preferred spending their time investigating all the beautiful churches and galleries in the city. Occasionally they took Perry and August, Jr., with them. Perry was fascinated. He wanted his parents to explain everything to him and afterward remembered all the pictures he had seen.

On the way home from one of their outings they met the Pope, who, dressed all in white, blessed Caroline as he passed. Caroline in a secular way returned the favor, revising her opinions. "He has," she thought, "a very benevolent and kind expression."

August and Caroline made all the stations of a romantic's tour through Italy with, however, an energy, directness, and curiosity that were anything but romantic. One night, risking "*Roman fever,*" they went to see the Coliseum. Surrounded by servants carrying torches, they climbed to the top of the amphitheater and looked down at the shadowed arena. In February on the first day of Carnival they sat on a balcony overlooking the Corso and watched the merrymaking in the street below. One of their nurses tossed four bouquets into the crowd. A few days later when Caroline returned to the balcony to enjoy more of the milling, confetti-throwing throng—from a safe, aristocratic distance—several men tossed bouquets up to her. That was the difference between being a maid and a lady.

From Rome the Belmonts went to Naples, the city in which August had lived as a young man. They took day trips, into the ruins of Herculaneum and to the lip of Mount Vesuvius. At first Caroline was terrified. But she forced herself to walk to the edge of the crater and peer down. "We were fortunate enough to see two or three small eruptions," she said.

The world was there for them to enjoy. Even volcanoes belched for their pleasure. And pleasing themselves was an obligation. Not to look because of fear was to be derelict in one's duty. "The guides told us that a large eruption was expected next week," Caroline said. "If I were sure of it, I think I would stay to see it."

Caroline found someone to pierce Jeannie's and Frederika's ears. "Poor little Jeannie cried," said Caroline, "but Rickie was so anxious to have earnings like her Mamma that she did not even scream. She was very much pleased with herself when she looked in the glass."

They visited some more ruins—one of which was deserted except for beggars. An urchin covered with sores darted out at August, who in trying to avoid her tripped and fell flat on his back. Caroline found him lying in the street, unhurt but very annoyed. Caroline laughed, and the little beggar girl—"wisely," Caroline thought—ran off.

A sibyl's cave—where they heard no prophecies, unless the silence and feeling of dread Caroline felt there were prophetic—more galleries, more ruins; Florence, Venice, Bologna; uncomfortable rooms, humid nights, damp sheets; Vienna where August took the boys, who were wearing kilts, for a walk; back through Germany. . . .

In April 1857 August returned to The Hague to find a letter from the new secretary of state, Lewis Cass, asking him to stay on in his position for another four years. Buchanan had passed him over for the Madrid post.

August resigned.

"I hope," August wrote to the Commodore, "I may be mistaken in the appreciation which this strange conduct compels me to form most reluctantly of the character of a man I had so much liked and admired."

Caroline spent the spring in Paris, where the weather was pleasanter and the society livelier than in Holland. August stayed at The Hague to complete work on an extradition treaty between the United States and the Netherlands that he had been midwifing for the past two years. It had been a difficult birth, complicated by minor last-minute changes, and every change had to be approved by both governments.

Time was getting too short to keep sending drafts of the treaty back and forth across the Atlantic; and if they missed the deadline for exchanging ratifications, the whole process would have to begin again. "A new treaty will have to be negotiated and signed," August told the secretary of state, "and I must beg leave to remark that such a result would be very mortifying to me."

Finally, on August 22, 1857, two months before the Belmonts sailed for the United States, negotiations on the treaty were completed.

August told Caroline that the new Dutch foreign minister "wants to go out of town himself and that helped me more than anything I could say or do."

By the end of August the last of their belongings had to be packed and sent to the United States; and their horses had to be shipped, which caused difficulties. The steamship lines were balking, claiming they had no means of transporting horses. August told Christmas to talk to Edward Cunard, whose family owned the Cunard Steamship Line, and to "tell him that I will consider it a personal favor if he can help us. I intend certainly to be very much guided in my preference for specie shipments to the line which helps me in this emergency."

Busy with chores and obligations, August could not get away from The Hague. There was a great deal of correspondence to catch up on; he had been receiving letters from New York with increasing frequency, as though his presence there were preceding his arrival and demanding a response from the people he soon would greet. Although most of the matters were routine, some were annoying. Charles Christmas, claiming ill health, wanted to quit before August returned; and Simeon Draper reminded August about their $500 bet that Cuba would belong to the United States before Pierce left office.

August was nettled at Draper's letter, more with the administration's failure to win Cuba than with his own failure to win the bet. And he was disgusted to learn that the *Tribune*—as late as May 7—was still libeling him, declaring that as minister at The Hague he had "managed affairs there to his own immense profit," had "disbursed large sums to secure the election of" Buchanan, and was "claiming urgently the nomination to the Court of Spain."

"I have been shamefully abused by a portion of the New York press," August told Christmas, "and I assure you that it embitters a good deal the pleasure of my return among so many friends. Though I trust that these disgraceful lies and calumnies have not lowered me in the estimations of my personal friends and acquaintances, their effect upon the community at large cannot have been lost. My character and reputation have necessarily suffered among a great many more respectable people among whom my children are to live and who have only had opportunity to judge me by the vile sheets just named."

Even though he tried to avoid making the rounds of the palaces to say his formal farewells, the members of the royal family sought him out.

"The Queen has sent me word that she will receive me this evening at 7:30," August wrote Caroline, who was still in Paris. "This is rather a stretch of politeness as I had not asked for an audience."

August missed the children terribly. They had all been measured, and Perry was distressed that his little sister Frederika had grown twice as much as he had in the past year.

"Tell Perry," August urged his wife, "that little babies and young children always grow more than older ones, and that I am sure, if he only will be good and obedient, he will be in time quite a big man."

Both boys now had a governess—Mrs. Egan had not recovered— and the good reports on their behavior and studies pleased August. Perry gave his parents a present, which he intended as a memento of his lessons in Europe: two addition problems in which the sums added up to billions. He obviously was preparing to follow in his father's footsteps.

"Ricky, I hope, is also a good and sweet girl," August wrote to Caroline. "Kiss them all from their loving father, not to forget my darling Jeannie, who I hope is well and strong."

But most of all he missed Caroline.

"I cannot tell you, my sweet Tiny, how I long after you," he wrote. "Never have I felt so miserable and lonely away from you as I do at this time. This feeling is so strong with me that I cannot bear to go anywhere and have hardly paid any visits. I shall move heaven and earth to be with you by next Wednesday."

At last August was free to leave Holland. He hurried to Paris, where he arranged—as he informed Christmas—"to limit my business upon returning to the United States as heretofore to the agency of the Messrs. Rothschild." August did not get along easily with the older Rothschilds, who remembered when he was just an errand boy; and, in fact, at one point he told Christmas that the Frankfurt branch of the Rothschilds had paid him 2,029 florins, "which you will please credit them, but as I have a great deal of trouble with the business of those gentlemen I do not think it necessary to be too generous in the exchange at which you credit it."

But August was on comfortable and friendly terms with the younger Rothschilds, with whom he continually was trading gifts: five or six thousand Havana cigars for Gustav, four or five dozen bottles of first-rate old Madeira for Alphonse. And, of course, the younger generation were the future.

August and Caroline spent the summer at a spa for August's rheumatism and Caroline's general improvement; she tended to be—or at least both were convinced she was—frail. In the fall August returned to The Hague to give King William III his letter of recall. August's term as a representative of the United States government was over. He was a private citizen again.

PART THREE

CHAPTER NINETEEN

NEW YORK GREETED AUGUST with another financial panic, which people were calling "the Western blizzard." Like Midas the country had starved on gold.

For years ships from California and Australia had sailed into New York carrying $4 million in gold every month. In ten years California alone had produced $555 million worth of gold dust panned out of streams that seemed to flow with money, and nuggets dug from earth that seemed inexhaustible in its riches. The glare of the gold dazzled Easterners, blinded them to the reality; money seemed there for the taking. All you had to do was scoop it out of the ground. It would never run out. You could not spend it fast enough. People went on a speculation rampage, investing in everything: mines, guano, sugar, cotton, real estate, and—especially—railroads.

Hundreds of thousands of prospectors, homesteaders, adventurers, professionals, businessmen, and drifters were heading west. The country needed railroads to help transport them—and to help transport coal (production doubled between 1850 and 1856), pig iron (shipments of pig iron increased in the same six years from 63,000 to 883,000 short tons), and food, lumber, and marble—commodities of all sorts. Rails were the root system of the growing country. During those years—years of extraordinary prosperity and the worst inflation since the nation had declared its independence—the roots spread out across the land. The number of rail miles more than doubled. In those six years more than $700 million was invested in railroads, much of it foreign capital. Business boomed; but the boom was an explosion whose shock waves would shatter the economy.

The European nations—especially England and France—reduced their investments in the United States from $56 million in 1853 to only $12 million, or one-fifth of that amount, three years later. Money got tight, credit short. It became clear that the values of certain railroad stocks—and the stocks of those companies that had invested in the railroads—were inflated.

The *Herald* predicted a crash on "a much grander scale" than the one of 1837, because of "government spoliations, public defaulters, paper bubbles . . . , a general scramble for western lands and town and city sites, millions of dollars, made or borrowed, expended in fine houses and gaudy furniture; hundreds of thousands in the silly rivalries of fashionable parvenues, in silks, laces, diamonds and every variety of costly frippery."

At the end of summer a sugar house in Boston, a bank in Rochester, and the oldest flour and grain firm in New York City, N. H. Wolfe & Company, went bankrupt. People reacted as though they were waiting to hear whether a few cholera cases presaged an epidemic. On August 23 the *Herald* again predicted: "In all human probability, every railroad in the United States will become bankrupt in the course of the next six or eight years."

The smugness and relish with which James Gordon Bennett, editor of the *Herald,* foretold ruin betrayed an undue enjoyment of his role as Jeremiah.

The next day a sign appeared on the door of the New York branch of one of the most respected businesses in the country, which had invested heavily and imprudently in a number of Western railroads:

"Transfer books of the Ohio Life Insurance & Trust Company are closed."

The Ohio Life Insurance & Trust Company, which the day before had been selling at $102 per share, was bankrupt with $7 million in debts.

A crowd gathered in front of the offices of the Ohio Life Insurance & Trust Company. A larger crowd gathered in the new offices of the stock exchange at Lord's Court, 25 William Street, around the corner from Delmonico's. One by one the brokers followed the failures, which over the course of the day were announced. Outside, newsboys running up William Street to Wall Street cried out bulletins about shaky city banks where runs on gold reserves had started.

A week later, as the officers of the Mechanics' Banking Association were trying to forestall failure, they discovered one of their clerks in the process of stealing $70,000. The bank closed. As rumors of default and embezzlement spread, people who rarely visited the Wall Street area descended on the banks to trade their paper currency for gold. The streets, the steps up to the banks, the banks themselves, were jammed. Whenever there was a delay people assumed the bank had gone under, and they shouted and pushed, causing more delays and more panic. As the days passed, the crowds increased, as did the fear that things were going to get worse.

DeLaunay, Iselin & Clark, E. S. Monroe and John Thompson, E. A. Benedict and E. F. Post, even shabby, stooped Jacob Little—called "Little Bear" because he was credited with discovering the advantages of selling short and had made a fortune in the last panic, in 1837—all were ruined in the first days of the crisis.

In the weeks that followed, the list of failed railroads read like the names on boxcars flashing past: the Fond du Lac; the Delaware, Lackawanna & Western; the Pittsburgh, Fort Wayne & Chicago; the Reading; the Erie; the Michigan Central; the Illinois Central. . . .

It looked as though Bennett's dire prophecy were coming true. People estimated that the inflation in paper currency was more than $2,000 million dollars. Was there that much gold even in California? The dream of unlimited wealth faded.

On October 1 frightened, ruined brokers started fighting on the floor of the stock exchange. About two weeks later, on October 13, the bottom dropped out of everything. The stages that clogged Broadway were crammed with passengers who were heading down to the financial district. The crowds that packed Wall Street were worse than at any time during the previous month. The noise was so bad no one could hear the policemen who were trying to calm everyone with angry shouts.

People swarmed from bank to bank—the Ocean, closed; the North River, closed, the Grocers', closed; the Bowery, closed; the East River, closed—looking for someplace to redeem their paper money. Even the Bank of New York, the oldest in the city, was closed. Within twenty-four hours eighteen banks were broken. By the end of the week only one bank in New York, the Chemical, was still paying out gold.

"Wall Street is *dead* for the present . . . ," one New Yorker of the time wrote. "If it don't come to life before long, decomposition will set in."

For the second time in his life August—now with his own as well as the Rothschilds' resources—came to the United States in the midst of a crash to pick up the pieces.

The city had changed in the five years August had been away. Fifth Avenue had indisputably replaced Broadway as the most fashionable area for homes, even though Madame Restell, the notorious and successful abortionist, nicknamed Madame Killer, had built her five-story mansion on the avenue. The wealth of her clientele was enough to keep up her tone and that of the street. What was amazing was not that she had built on Fifth Avenue but that she had built so far up Fifth Avenue: at Fifty-second Street, a dozen blocks beyond the city limits. The city obviously soon would follow.

Broadway had been taken over by businesses. The few old low wooden houses that still had existed when August left New York were gone. The street, lined with towering five- and six-story office buildings, stores, and monster hotels, seemed darker, narrower, busier, so crowded with stages that one visitor complained, "you often have to wait ten minutes before you are able to cross."

As after the earlier crash, building had halted. But because construction had been more extensive before this panic, half-finished structures seemed more prevalent than in 1837.

"Walking down Broadway you pass great $200,000 buildings begun last Spring or Summer that have gone up two stories and stopped . . . ," one New Yorker wrote at the time.

Even though the streets, especially above Thirty-fourth Street, were blocked with bricks, stones, lumber, and other building materials, and even though because of the previous construction the roads were terribly rutted and pocked with potholes, at least during the building lull the air was not always filled with mortar dust, and the explosions uptown of rocks being blown away did not punctuate the day with a drumbeat of progress.

Battery Park had become a wasteland, and Castle Garden, enclosed by a high wooden fence, had become a depot for immigrants, many of whom had settled in New York and, following the crash of 1857, were unemployed and destitute. By the end of 1857 more than 130,000 people, one-seventh of the city's population, were out of work. Fourth Street between Avenues A and B had become Ragpickers' Row. First Avenue between Fortieth and Forty-second streets had become Dutch Hill, where more than a thousand people were crowded together in a few hundred rundown shacks. And along the Hudson River from Fortieth Street far into the countryside up to Eightieth Street was another shantytown.

Altogether there were more than ten thousand squatters living above Forty-second Street in one-room sheds built from discarded timbers and planks and sheets of scrap tin. Even more than within the city limits, where indoor plumbing had reduced some (but not all) of the stench that one New Yorker said smelled "like a solution of bad eggs" in ammonia, these country slums stank of excrement. The animals the squatters owned lived in the shacks like people, and the people lived like animals.

When they could afford it the squatters ate "country pork," pigs fattened on dead horses, dead dogs, dead cats, and dead rats. When they could not afford it they ate the carcasses of the horses, dogs, cats, and rats themselves—if the city had not first cleared the streets of the rotting bodies. If the city had, they ate nothing. Luckily for them the streets were almost never cleared.

Everything was on a larger scale—the crowds, the construction, the poverty, even the number of cattle, which August and Caroline could have heard being driven after dark down Fifth Avenue to the slaughterhouses. So many cattle were killed each night to feed the city's growing population, the smell of blood and decaying offal carried for dozens of blocks.

The city was not the New York that Caroline recalled. It was not just the specific changes—the new statue of George Washington on the recently fashionable Union Square, *The New York Times* building replacing the brick church on Beekman Street—that struck one as different. What was new was the change in proportions, the relationship between the old world, which still existed but in smaller enclaves, and the new, which somehow used to seem temporary as though eventually it would like a fad fade, allowing the Knickerbockers once again to dominate the city.

But the conditions that had been developing when the Belmonts left—the squatters, the increasing presence (and power) of the foreigners, especially the Irish—had flowered while they were gone. New York now was a strange place filled with alien people. After an absence of five years Caroline seemed to find the city in some ways as unfamiliar as it had been to August when he first had arrived in America in 1837.

In an anecdote told about Caroline, her coachman once refused to drive her into one of the impoverished sections of the city. Caroline asked him why. In explaining, the coachman described the miserable conditions under which people lived there. Caroline listened and wept.

It was not just poverty that made certain sections of the city undesirable. What was disagreeable and frightening was the violence poverty bred. Twenty years before, the few murders that had taken place had generally occurred at Five Points. Other areas of the city were safe. Even Five Points, despite its bawdy houses, saloons, and brawls, had been safe enough for a young Knickerbocker to visit. The most he had been likely to lose was a tooth in a fight or his virginity. When August left for The Hague, crime still had seemed an aberration, the shadow cast by the rest of the city.

In the five years of his absence the shadow had lengthened. Even the area around Church Street, where Columbia College used to be, had become so unsafe that most respectable people avoided it.

New York had become savage; 1857 had been an exceptionally bad—or good—year for crimes in both their number and spectacular nature. Every day newspapers reported six or seven murders or attempted murders. The increase in crime was matched by an increase in the public's appreciation of it as a source of entertainment.

Virtually all year the newspapers savored the murder of a dentist, Dr. Harvey Burdell, stabbed fifteen times, his room splattered with blood, even the banister outside his room bloody. People stood in front of his home on Bond Street, gawking as though the very streets of the city had become a theater. If they were waiting for a second act, they were not disappointed. One of the suspects, the woman who ran the boardinghouse in which the murder had taken place, claimed she had married the victim a few months before the crime. There were rumors of illicit liaisons and vicious practices involving not just Burdell and the landlady but other boarders as well. Most people agreed this was the most sensational murder New York had ever witnessed. More gawkers made pilgrimages to Bond Street.

Just as Five Points had grown in both size and influence so the gangs inhabiting the area had become larger and more powerful—and had spawned other large and powerful gangs in other parts of the city. And the gangs—the Empire Club, the Spartan Band, the Dead Rabbits, the Bowery Boys—were becoming New York's shadow government.

The year after August had left for The Hague, certain gangs like the Empire Club and the Dead Rabbits and Tammany Hall (the Democratic machine)—organizations that to a certain extent shared the same membership—supported handsome, soft-spoken, elegant Fernando Wood for mayor. Wood won and shortly after taking office was praised as being "the first mayor, for thirty years at least, who has set himself seriously to the work of giving the civic administration a decent appearance of common honesty."

Beneath the honest appearance was corruption. Although Wood tried with indifferent success to drive the prostitutes off the streets (but not out of the brothels), reduce the sale of pornography, and prevent pickpockets from picking quite so many pockets, he stuffed ballot boxes, took bribes, and did little to discourage people from calling the Board of Aldermen "The Forty Thieves." Nonetheless, in 1856 Wood won again.

A year later, when August returned to New York, the New York State Legislature transferred control of the New York City police force from the Democratic city government to the Republican state government. Wood, however, refused to recognize the legality of the state's newly created Metropolitan Police Force—whose duties, it was widely suspected, would include breaking the power of the city's gangs, which would be tantamount to breaking the power of the city's Democratic machine.

For a few months, as the issue moved into and up through the courts, New York City suffered under the protection of two rival police departments: the state's new Metropolitan and Wood's old Municipal police forces. In the middle of June the two forces fought. A month later the state won in the courts; but the police riot triggered other riots. On July 4 and 5 the Dead Rabbits and Bowery Boys battled. Two weeks later German and Irish immigrants attacked the new Metropolitan Police. And on November 10 the Dead Rabbits seized City Hall for an hour.

The permanently out-of-work and temporarily out-of-work, including the thousands fired as a result of the economic crash and the angry former Municipal policemen, joined forces to complain about conditions. There were regular demonstrations, demanding work and food, in Tompkins Square. And there were rumors that the leaders of the fighting in July had used tactics similar to those used in the streets of Paris during the insurrections of 1848. As had happened after the Panic of 1837, but seemingly with more cause, people worried about or embraced the possibility of revolution.

August responded to the disorder in New York by contributing to a number of charities. Some, like the Five Points House of Industry, attended to the needs of the body, and some attended to the needs of the spirit.

"As I have now a very pretty gallery indeed, containing paintings of most of the first living masters, I have some idea of displaying them to raise money for the benefit of the poor," August had told the Commodore just before he left The Hague. "I think it would answer both for a charitable purpose and help improve the taste of our New York people for the fine arts, so that in the future they will adorn their houses with fine pictures instead of filling them with gaudy furniture."

Soon after August's return his exhibition opened at the National Academy of Design on Tenth Street. It was an immediate success, not only as an instrument to educate both poor and rich but as a social coup. The preview was attended—one newspaper reported—by "the elite of our literary and art circles, with a sprinkling of politicians." Another newspaper proclaimed: "We have never before known on any occasion such a unanimity of opinion, in so large an assemblage, as was expressed in respect to the excellence of this superb collection." Even the hostile newspapers contented themselves with gentle gibes: "One cannot but sympathize with Mr. Belmont on the notoriety which this little affair will give him and which, as everyone knows, will be very distasteful to a man of his retiring and remarkably modest character. But, after all, some of us must be sacrificed now and then for the public good." But even that newspaper admitted the show was "a public treat"; and most people agreed "that the liberality of Mr. Belmont in affording the public an opportunity to examine his collection may induce the owners of other fine collections to follow his example."

The press quickly seized on August as one of its favorite millionaires, one of the "People We Meet . . . Up and Down the Plaza On the Shilling Side":

> Dressed in the English style and with a very English air, this
> short, rather broad-shouldered and full-chested gentleman, brown
> of complexion and with dark side-whiskers modelled on the
> Piccadilly pattern; a broad, rather short nose; large and bright
> brown eyes; dark hair, having a slight tendency to curl and
> growing thin in front; a full, high and capacious forehead . . . ;
> with a small, neatly shaped chin, moreover, and lips capable, by
> the look they wear, of enjoying all the good things of life in
> moderation—such is our good friend August Belmont, Banker,

politician, diplomatist and art patron—for the past twenty years a prominent, if not leading public man of this City.

August and Caroline began entertaining in an even grander manner than they had before leaving for The Hague. When the gallery in their house was completed their guests were overwhelmed by its size and airiness. Its quadrangular dome was made of glass and was set off by four allegorical groups, each of two figures, representing painting, music, architecture, and sculpture. On sunny days the room was drenched in light. The whole effect was modern: the innovation of a private gallery; the paintings themselves, all aggressively contemporary—August's favorite was one by Rosa Bonheur, which he liked for the lifelike rendition of its horses—and the allegorical figures that, one commentator pointed out, were unique: neither erotic angels like those of Boucher or Watteau nor severe classic geniuses, but according to August's wishes, "adolescents which are not definitely of either sex."

August already had a reputation for giving extraordinary dinners; but now, having brought his chef back from Europe, he awed New York. He presided over a table that seated two hundred and was set with gold service. Each guest was attended by his or her own footman, who was dressed in the maroon and scarlet Belmont livery and who soundlessly presented dishes and cleared away the empty plates as skillfully as a magician palming large gold coins.

A typical meal might begin with East River oysters; the soup course that followed might include a consommé de volaille and a green turtle au Madeira. It was a matter of principle and balance to offer a choice. The fish course might be bass à la Normandie and brook trout, both served with potatoes; the entrée, vol-au-vent à la Toulouse, squab, a meat pie, and veal; the roast course, beef in Madeira, capons, Westphalian ham, and simmered tongue with spinach, all served with peas, stuffed tomatoes, corn, and potatoes. (After the roasts, August, Caroline, and their guests might clear their palates with "Roman punch," an ice made of lemon juice, sugar, beaten egg whites, and rum. This course was an interlude, as though the dish were served within parentheses.) The game course would come next: snipe, widgeon (a medium-sized duck), terrapin (an edible turtle), and lobster salad, the dishes following one another in such variety that the dinner turned into a Noah's Ark of a meal. After the game course came the Nesselrode pudding, the gelées au Madeira, the creams, the cakes, and the tarts; then the cheeses would be spread across the table, and the fruit and nuts would be brought. The meal would end with coffee and liqueurs; and each course was presented with an appropriate wine.

Never had New York tasted such excellent food—or seen it served in such a sumptuous manner. Lorenzo Delmonico called August a "Maecenas of gastronomy."

And, even more of a compliment, Jane Perry admitted that although "our cooking is very plain we thank August for our improved taste in the arrangement of the table and have adopted some of his notions in regard to serving a dinner."

When August and Caroline gave a ball, people were astonished by their private ballroom, by the red carpet that was draped down the front steps and out to the street where the carriages stopped, and by the apparent cost—a rumored $15,000 just for one night. Until midnight everyone either flirted or watched the flirting in order to be scandalized; a ball without a scandal was a bore. At the stroke of twelve the doors to the supper room would be thrown open. Then the music would start. August and Caroline, famous for dancing the German, often led their guests in this cotillion, which was thought by some to be reckless and licentious. Under the guise of dancing a man could take liberties that a woman might long for but never tolerate elsewhere. At dawn the party would end; and curious passersby on their way to early jobs would see exhausted, disheveled revelers shambling down the red carpet to their carriages.

Those lucky enough to be invited to the Belmonts' smaller but no less elegant parties found August to be a genial, attentive, sometimes challenging, and occasionally risqué host. It was reported that he once said a woman could learn an accurate foreign accent only from a titled foreign lover. And Caroline was the ideal hostess: Once when a visitor accidentally shattered an Oriental vase, Caroline ignored the disaster and led society to declare that she "was mistress of herself though China fall."

"The best houses were absolutely restful," one observer recalled years later, "and the present generation will never know the charm and tranquillity which was manifest whenever people like Mrs. Schermerhorn, Mrs. William Astor, Mrs. John Jacob Astor, Mrs. August Belmont, and Mrs. Paran Stevens entertained their friends."

August renewed old friendships and bridged old enmities (as with Sam Ward, who was happy to put behind them what he called "all this damnation"). He also made new acquaintances like the young newspaper editor Manton Marble and the young lawyer George Templeton Strong, who thought that August was "quite disposed to be pleasant and free from any offensive millionaire-isms" and that Caroline was "very beautiful."

"As a girl," one woman remembered, "I watched Mrs. Belmont at the opera, ermine and sables slipping from her shoulders, her slender throat wearing a string of pearls, the largest known in this Republic, and every opera-glass in the house turned upon her."

She was so regal that when she sat in one of the six coveted proscenium boxes at the Academy of Music, she reminded one journalist of the lovely Empress Eugénie.

"She was tall and slender," he wrote, "had a queenly bearing, an arching neck and wore her hair brushed back, while her head was adorned with a magnificent gold crown—headdress it could not be called —on which were clusters and flowers of emeralds and rubies, spangled with dew-drops of diamonds."

She was recognized in the press as the Queen of High Life, and became the first of the six grande dames who would rule New York society over the next eighty years. Her whims became fashions. When she started attending the opera on the nights of her balls, she was widely imitated by other women who wanted to show that they could be as nonchalant about having balls as she was—although their studied imperturbability was never as natural as Caroline's.

When the Belmonts would leave the Academy of Music, Isaac Brown, the sexton of Grace Church who played major domo at most of society's affairs, would stand at the door and bow them on their way with, "Good night, Mr. Belmont, Fifth Avenue and Eighteenth Street."

During the day pedestrians—and even riders in other carriages— would turn to watch Caroline passing in her demi-d'Aumont, a calèche pulled by four horses, two of which were ridden by postilions—the first carriage of its kind in America. Most families did not own even one carriage, they rented landaus. In addition to Caroline's demi-d'Aumont, August kept several other carriages, including an $8,000 English brack, also the first of its kind in the States. Almost every afternoon August, his top hat as usual at a 45° angle, could be seen driving it himself, half standing, half leaning over because of his lame hip, giving rides to his children or friends, or racing through the countryside along Harlem Lane.

"Eccentricity, comfort, and health as well as pleasure are said to be the motives that lead him to appear in this unique style," a newspaper reported.

August's flamboyance and colorful past made him a legend among adults, who would wait on the roadside to watch him careering by in his carriage, and among children, especially schoolgirls, who hearing tales of his duel found his limp romantic.

"August Belmont radiated power," recalled a woman who had been a child in the mid-nineteenth century. "Living in a palace and maintaining almost royal state, he was vital, autocratic, as short of temper as he was long of purse. . . . One rebuke of August Belmont to me . . . occurred when I made a snippy, ill-advised criticism of someone, founded on venomous rumor. Mr. Belmont turned to me, saying, 'The private life of any man or woman is none of your affair. If you can manage your own wisely, you will be doing better than most of the human race.' "

August's impatience with bad manners, poor style, fools, and forward strangers made him seem "brusque, . . . anything but amiable to the casual person who met him." And that brusqueness made him seem selfish. "If he cannot have a thing his way," someone else said of him, "he won't touch it at all."

But August was not selfish—although once challenged he did want to bring the world to heel. When he heard that his neighbor across the street, James Lenox, objected to his paintings of nudes by Adolphe William Bouguereau, he hung the most erotic of them in his front hall, where every time the door opened Lenox could see it.

More often, however, if people disliked August it was not for any insult or sleight he may have committed but for what he was and how he lived. In an often recorded but possibly apocryphal tale, Lenox—on hearing that August's monthly wine bill was $20,000—died of a heart attack.

August's success and his obvious enjoyment of the privileges of success infuriated those like Lenox who regretted the passing of the old world and who blamed August for the arrival of the new one with its high spirits and energetic pursuit of pleasure. August—an enemy once said—is "like a man on the back of a donkey holding out, to make the donkey move, a carrot on a stick. He manages to lead the donkey forward and yet, at the same time, the beast is obliged to bear his weight."

Like most public figures he was, in short, admired and despised; and as his fame increased the more passionate the opinions about him became. There emerged over the years two images of the same man, each from a slightly different angle: the honorable, romantic man of the world and the immoral, flashy power broker. But this stereopticon view can be resolved by placing in context the two standpoints from which he was seen.

"He was a great businessman . . . and a financier of marked ability and of conspicuous success throughout his entire career," someone would write of him years later; "among the eminent bankers of his . . . time, he was regarded in many respects as a balance wheel. He embodied all the virtues, as well as the graces, of mankind. He had a brusque, gruff, crisp manner of speech, but his ear bended to every tale of woe, and his heart and purse responded to every story of real distress. He was a lovable man; his courtesy was the courtesy of the heart. Among his business associates he was at all times strictly business, and they learned but one side of his character. Among his friends he was altogether different."

As a businessman he could be brutal, but as a friend he was loyal and generous. Those who knew him only across a balance sheet might well dislike him. And those who knew him outside the office but not as a friend might condemn him not on the basis of his faults but on the basis of what they considered to be their own virtues: If they valued moderation and simplicity in themselves, they censured him for being ostentatious and grand. But ostentation and grandness are not evils, and August indulged in them out of exuberance and inventiveness.

Instead of a man astride a donkey (which in any case damns the society carrying him more than it does him), a more appropriate image for August would have been that of a dancing master who beat time while others danced to his tune—which usually was the latest waltz or schottische.

"His nature is essentially authoritative," wrote one observer; "he does not seek power, but when it is given to him he means to use it at his own discretion. He would probably have been hard to bear as a prime minister of a nation under autocratic rule; but, as a private man or a businessman, he is, like any other human being, at liberty to let his natural dispositions take their free course. Those who don't like him need not have anything to do with him. He won't run after anything or anybody."

August, in fact, did not have to do any running at all. On returning to New York he simply planted himself in the center of the social whirl and let the others revolve around him like planets circling a sun.

CHAPTER TWENTY

ON MARCH 4, 1858, a few months after the Belmonts arrived in New York, Caroline's father died. The Commodore had approached death efficiently. As early as 1856 he had written to August about his will, trying in the distribution of his estate to be fair to both his family and history. He had suggested that he leave to Caroline the silver dinner and tea set given to him by a group of New York merchants in honor of his Japan mission, and the silver salver given to him by the state of Rhode Island for the same reason, since "amongst my children now married Tiny will be the only one probable at my death who can afford to preserve and hand them down to our posterity. From present appearances it is pretty certain that neither of my sons' children will be suitable recipients and that equivalents in other property would be more acceptable and useful to them, and hence this confidential communication to you."

Only August and his children were secure enough in their wealth to resist the temptations of selling the silver in some future straitened time.

The Commodore explained to August that he was "precise in communicating my views" because "in every other case that has come under my notice, similar testimonials have shared the fate of other property," being sold at auction and even occasionally disappearing from sight, thus being lost not only to the family but to the nation as well.

The Commodore believed—and hoped August would agree—that the bequest was important "not in respect to its intrinsic value, but more especially with reference to its historical associations." Caroline—and whichever of their sons they chose to leave the testimonials to (August and Caroline chose their first-born, Perry)—would be caretakers not of silver but of the past.

August was honored "to have such a memorable heirloom preserved in my family." As to Caroline's share of the rest of the Commodore's estate, August said that he and Caroline "feel most gratefully your intention to provide for her equally with your other children and view it as a proof of your love and affection. As God has, however, blessed us with riches, while my sisters- and brothers-in-law are less fortunately situated, I should much prefer if you would make a discrimination in their favor. Poor William [who drank too much] will always be helpless and unable to take care of himself, and I think that Calbraith also might be hereafter placed in circumstances where a certain sum, placed in trust so that he could only touch the interest, would perhaps prevent a good deal of trouble."

The Commodore agreed to rewrite the will in favor of Caroline's siblings; but in denying her a larger portion of his property he gave her a greater token of his love: ". . . the sum of five hundred dollars," the Commodore changed his will to read, "shall be given to my daughter

Caroline Belmont for the purchase of some memento, congenial to her own kind heart and in remembrance of her loving father, and this memento is given to her exclusively as for reason of her abundant means she is not to share in the division of my estate."

Once the Commodore had made peace with the future, he began to fail. Within a year he was complaining about his old malaise, rheumatism, and traveling to Hot Springs, Virginia, to try to find some relief from the pain. Within two years—after an attack of influenza had led to a recurrence of the rheumatism and the rheumatism had climbed like the sap of death from his feet and knees to his heart—he was dead.

New York mourned with his family. Flags all over the city and in the harbor flew at half-mast. On the afternoon of March 6, 1858, the funeral procession, which included national and local dignitaries, a military honor guard, and fifty retired sailors who had sailed with the Commodore to Japan and who had asked to take part in the cortege, moved from the Perry's house on Thirty-second Street down Fifth Avenue, across Fourteenth Street and down Second Avenue to St. Mark's Church on Tenth Street. There, with Jane Perry, Belle, and other members of the family, August and Caroline sat in the front row listening to the funeral service.

Although the Commodore had wanted to be buried in his hometown, Newport, Rhode Island, the terrible weather made it out of the question for the women in the family to travel to the island; so the Commodore was placed in the Slidell family vault in the church's graveyard. August was now the head of the Perry clan.

Shortly after her father's death both James and Alphonse de Rothschild wrote to Caroline urging her to return to Paris: "a change of air and scenery would be most effectual toward the restoration of your depressed spirits" and "we can offer to you every possible consolation." But Caroline preferred to stay at home. She wanted to be close to her mother —and, expecting again, she did not think it advisable to travel so far.

Oliver Hazard Perry Belmont was born at 109 Fifth Avenue just before dawn on November 12, 1858. Caroline had been ill in the months before the birth. Simon, in Alzey, had fretted over her condition and over August's negligence in reporting on her progress.

"Whenever I see the postman," he wrote to August, "I hope he has news, but unfortunately I am always disappointed."

And, as he had for the past thirty years, Simon worried about the postage on the letters that he did receive.

"Although all your letters are marked 'postage paid,' " he told August, "I had to pay postage for them here, because the mail dispatchers here insisted on it and asserted that 'no postage was paid over there.' Inasmuch as I had to pay upon arrival of your last letter 1 fl. 31 kr. again, I am returning herewith your letter with the *repeated request* to let me know whether the person who is taking care of dispatching the mail may have forgotten to take the money out of his pocket or where the mistake may have occurred."

Presumably sending his letters to August's office, Simon also complained that his son had failed to send not only a description of their new house but also its address. Knowing his father's feelings about ostentation and luxury—which were not that different from the feelings of New York's Old-Guard Knickerbockers—August was no doubt reluctant to give Simon something else to lecture him on.

Through Babette and Stephan Feist, Simon nonetheless heard of the house and how much it cost, and he chided August that "one does not need this much money to buy the whole of St. George Street in Alzey."

Along with these characteristic harangues everything with Simon was much the same. His health was not better, but not worse either. He was suffering still from what he described as "the excessive functioning of the kidneys," which sounds as though it may have been incontinence. Although, as he said, "I've never liked fooling with medicines," he intended to discuss his state with his doctor. He wanted to go away for a short time, but he did not want to travel unless the doctor thought he was up to it. He was not sure where he would go, he told August: maybe to Frankfurt to visit the Feists, who had recently moved there from Koblenz.

After the harvest was over Simon did go to Frankfurt, where he attended the Schiller centenary celebration. He returned to Alzey late at night, still exhilarated by the festivities and no doubt exhausted. A few days later, on November 30, either a heart attack or a sudden, severe case of pneumonia killed him. Because of August, New York City newspapers carried his obituary.

August now was head of both his wife's and his own family, and the responsibility touched some patriarchal urge in him. Although, as suggested, he might have been hard to bear as an autocrats' prime minister, he was an attentive, protective, and affectionate tribal chieftain.

🦢 *CHAPTER TWENTY-ONE* 🦢

IN THE FALL OF 1859 Salomon de Rothschild, Baron James's twenty-four-year-old son, visited the United States. He arrived with a retinue of attendants, a reputation for dissolution, a leaded cane and a pair of brass knuckles (presumably to protect himself from the reportedly lawless Americans), and an aristocratic naïveté about how really to look after himself. Shortly after he landed in New York a pickpocket stole his wallet.

Newspapers spread the rumor that he had come, as his older brother Alphonse had come a few years earlier, either to take over the Rothschilds' American agency from August or to establish a branch of the House in the West, possibly in California. It was more likely that, as other rumors claimed, he was in disgrace with his father for having secretly gambled and not so secretly lost a million francs on the Paris stock exchange: the trip to America was part of his punishment.

He stayed at August's house for most of his time in New York, and August introduced him into society with mixed results. One private club in New York pressured August to withdraw Salomon's name from consideration for membership because—as George Templeton Strong (whose amiable feelings for August were cooling) explained—"the Baron, though illustrious and a millionaire, was immoderately given to lewd talk and nude photographs."

August acquainted Salomon with the mysteries of New York politics by taking him to various Democratic rallies, meetings, and dances—also with mixed results, although in these cases it was Salomon who was censorious.

"Introduced into a room where the bosses fortified themselves from a vast punchbowl," Salomon wrote to his brother-in-law and cousin Nathaniel Rothschild about a Tammany ball, "I shook hands right and left with cobblers and corner grocers. Then all of these gentlemen, walking two by two and giving their arms to one another to counterbalance the effects of the rum, came forward, following the band. . . . Caught up in the procession, I advanced triumphantly amidst two columns of ladies—and what ladies!!! Such figures and such clothes! Still, if only they had been pretty! After a lot of speech-making that was required by the occasion, the dancing began . . . This . . . amused me for a time, but as I had forgotten my eau de Cologne I fled."

Salomon, with his patrician disdain for the working class, must have wondered how August could bear to mix with "cobblers and grocers"; but in a democracy "cobblers and grocers" had political power, and as Salomon told his brother-in-law, "Belmont is quite the politician now."

Even though President Buchanan had disappointed August by not naming him minister to Spain, August continued to back him. When Buchanan upheld the questionable legality of the proslavery state constitution in Kansas and, by doing so split the Democratic party, August supported him—even though he inclined to the position of Stephen Douglas, who had come out against the Kansas constitution. When the New York Democratic party fragmented during a power struggle over control of patronage, August, trying to keep above the fray in order to mediate among the various factions, once more supported Buchanan's interests.

After warning the President—through Slidell—not to meddle in a particular patronage case, August explained, "I have only one object in view: the good of the administration and the Democratic Party."

It was becoming clear, however, that what was good for the administration was not necessarily good for the Democratic party and what was good for Buchanan and Slidell was not necessarily good for August.

August learned that the minister at Madrid planned to resign. Once again he talked to Slidell about Spain and Cuba. Slidell promised to speak to the President. August waited. But although the newspapers were considering August for the appointment, evidently the President was not.

To get the mission at The Hague, August had used direct action; perhaps that course would work again. He wrote candidly to Slidell asking for the ministry position and arguing that "my appointment would be a popular one. Almost every Democratic paper throughout the Union has connected my name with the mission, and my availability and fitness have been generally admitted and advocated."

Slidell brought August's letter to Buchanan, who according to *The New York Times* "pressed August's candidacy for the post earnestly until Mr. Robert Toombs the Democratic Senator from Georgia . . . went to him one day and told him in the most positive and unequivocal language that there was no use of talking about sending Mr. Belmont's name into the Senate, for that if it *was* sent in he for one should wage unrelenting war upon it; that it would be bitterly opposed by many other Democrats, and, in short, that it was certain to be repudiated and rejected."

Evidently the South distrusted August. August, after all, was a

Northern banker; and the North was trying—as Jefferson Davis said—to "convert the government into an engine of northern aggrandizement," intending thereby to "grow in power and prosperity upon treasures unjustly taken from the South, like the vampire bloated and gorged with the blood which it has secretly sucked from its victim."

Some Southerners also may have rejected August for the post, fearful that if he got the job he would succeed in pulling off his Cuba scheme. Although most Southerners favored the acquisition of Cuba, which would probably enter the Union as a slave state, many secessionists did not want to win it too quickly. Cuba was, as one Southerner said, "the bait which the Democratic Party holds out to the South" to keep it in the Union. Why should the South wait for the North to tempt them with the island? "It is a mere delusion to suppose that our chances of getting Cuba are less, if we separate, than as a whole," the Southerner continued. *"If separate, we can control the whole commerce—all the shipping. . . . It is better to separate before we take Cuba."*

Nevertheless Buchanan thought the South could be bribed with the island. He supported and Slidell introduced a bill to make $30 million available as a down payment on a $100 million price for Cuba, although why Spain, far more stable than it had been when it had rejected earlier offers, would entertain the idea now Buchanan did not convincingly explain.

The scheme was Buchanan's desperate attempt to find an issue around which North and South could rally. Even seizing the island if a new *Black Warrior* affair turned up offered the hope that the nation might unite to fight the war with Spain, England, and France that could follow. Such a war, one secessionist admitted, was the Democratic Party's one chance left for life.

The New York Times called the Thirty Million Bill "The Little Joker"; although, recognizing that presidential follies—especially presidential follies—can have serious consequences, it predicted:

"Pass it, and in the handling of the Cuban Bonds Mr. Belmont, as a banker, can easily carve out a million of profits, with which to make John Slidell a Louisiana President, who, once elected, would have it in his power to heal August's . . . wounded feelings [over failing to be appointed minister at Madrid] by an application of the highest mission in his gift."

But the *Times* and the other Northerners who distrusted August because of his connection to Slidell were wrong. August was drifting away from Slidell and Buchanan. Once August was passed over a second time for the Madrid mission he was convinced, no matter what he heard about Buchanan's efforts on his behalf, that the President had not really backed him.

August was right. When Slidell brought August's letter asking for the Madrid mission to Buchanan, the President implied that August was out of the running. But neither the President nor Slidell had the grace to write to August to tell him—or to explain why he would not be appointed.

The following winter Slidell came to New York. Infuriated as much with the way he had been rejected as with having been rejected at all, August came to Slidell's hotel rooms to complain. Slidell tried to mollify him. August, flaring, accused Slidell of having been weak in his support. Uncomfortable with August's anger, Slidell soon ended the conversation.

The next day August returned with a letter for Buchanan, which he said he wanted Slidell to deliver in person.

Slidell refused to take the letter. "The tone of it was disrespectful and offensive," Slidell later told the President. He advised August to burn it, and he told Buchanan, "I believe he did." Afterward Slidell added, "I have heard from others that he complains of me. I regret the alienation but shall take no pains to conciliate him."

August with Caroline and their son Perry made at least one social visit to Slidell in Washington the following year. Slidell lived on Lafayette Square across from the White House. While the adults were occupied, Perry, looking out the window, saw the President crossing the square. Buchanan had aged badly in office and occasionally was so ill-looking and unsteady that the newspapers carried rumors he was being slowly poisoned.

The President stopped at Slidell's door. Perhaps, knowing August was there, he had come to make amends. But Buchanan had betrayed him. August would no longer support the President.

"Our friend Belmont," Slidell told Buchanan, "is now a decided Douglas man."

August's respect and friendship for Stephen Douglas had been growing for the past few years. He admired Douglas's directness and his willingness to resist what seemed to be the luxury of wallowing in radical sectional passions. Like Douglas, August wanted to be a peacemaker, wanted to prevent the civil war that threatened. It seemed logical to August that each state should be able to decide for itself whether to allow or outlaw slavery. There was no more reason for one section of the country to impose its beliefs on the other section than for one man to try and run another man's household.

Professionally August maintained the policy he had followed ever since coming to the United States of not recognizing slaves as negotiable property. He refused to accept titles to them in payment or as security for loans. If a slaveowner wanted to do business with August he had to mortgage his slaves in order to get the cash or notes that August would accept—as David Levy Yulee, the Florida senator and railroad speculator, had to do in 1859 when August lent him $15,000.

The abolitionists might claim that by trading with slaveowners at all August indirectly was encouraging slavery; but August believed that, beyond the limits he had placed on his dealings with slaveowners, he had no right to interfere in another man's affairs. He could not prevent someone else from owning slaves any more than someone else could force him to do so. His personal feelings about the institution of slavery would guide only his own actions: he owned no slaves himself.

August's position was vulnerable to attack from both the North and the South; but August would not abandon hope that reason and compromise would succeed in averting secession. Douglas seemed, at least politically, to embody that hope. The rumors that Slidell planned to quarrel with Douglas, challenge him to a duel, and kill him may have confirmed August in his new allegiance. The enemies of enemies—even a newly revealed enemy like Slidell—are said to be friends.

In 1858 August rescued Douglas from financial embarrassment with a substantial loan when virtually no one else in New York would advance him any money. About a year later, in the summer of 1859, after breaking with Buchanan, August joined other New York businessmen in a political fund-raising campaign for Douglas. Then in early October he helped set up the Democratic Vigilant Association, which tried privately to promote Douglas's goal of preserving the Union by upholding the prerogative of each state to make its own policy on slavery.

All fall the Association met regularly in the just opened Fifth Avenue Hotel, a white marble palace that outshone even the St. Nicholas in size and luxury. Because it was so far uptown, at Madison Square between Twenty-third and Twenty-fourth streets, New Yorkers were speculating that it would not be able to attract customers; but August could recall when there had been sheep grazing half a mile south in Union Square where the Everett House, another of the Association's meeting places, now stood.

The city's growth, as natural and surprising as that of a child, was the product of an aggressive economy that could be crippled by a war between the states. August's fear of secession naturally reflected economic as well as political interests. Like the other members of the Association, who also were bankers or merchants, August did not want to lose the valuable Southern trade or the money owed him by Southern businessmen, who would probably default at the start of a civil war.

Altogether the South was $200 million in debt to the North, and Northern businessmen were increasingly nervous about the safety of their various Southern investments. The Association wanted to assure the South that responsible (meaning conservative) Northerners were committed to defend the rights of all states; that the Southern states did not have to rebel to protect their sovereignty; and that it was in the best interests of both sections of the country to preserve the Union, since even more than by a shared history the North and South were bound together by credit.

But these links of credit, which to August seemed the sinews of the country, seemed like fetters to others. Southerners were obsessed with maintaining independence from Northern businessmen. Paradoxically, John Brown's raid on Harpers Ferry, which Brown hoped would inspire slaves in the South to revolt against their masters, seemed instead to Northern businessmen an act that might inspire the South to revolt against the North.

Southerners saw the raid as part of an abolitionist plot to trigger race war in the slave states and were ready to retaliate by withdrawing trade from businesses they suspected were proabolitionist. The founders of the Democratic Vigilant Association, August included, wanted to forestall this economic battle that could serve as a rehearsal for a civil war.

To convince the South that the New York business community deplored the violence of John Brown's raid and the views of the abolitionists, the Association published a tract, passionate in its defense of moderation, rejecting "the doctrine that there is an 'irrepressible conflict' between the North and the South, and that 'slavery must go out in fire, rape, and slaughter.' "

In the weeks after John Brown's raid New Yorkers alternated between disbelief that civil war could occur and fear that it was about to start. City officials worried about the lack of preparedness. Newspapers described possible routes of invasion. The Association sponsored a mass meeting at the Academy of Music on December 19.

An hour before the meeting began the neighborhood was already jammed with spectators standing in the slush, feet numb with cold, listening to the band playing on the theater's balcony, which overlooked Fourteenth Street. On the street corners bonfires blazed, casting tall, wavering shadows on the Academy's façade. Skyrockets shot into the night and sent out colorful tendrils that drifted down over the city. Speakers, their voices lost in the music, the hiss and crack of the rockets, and the booming of the cannon salutes, harangued the crowd from three wooden platforms erected outside for those who could not squeeze into the theater.

Inside, every seat was taken. Standees milled in the aisles looking for friends, trying to get closer to the dais. Onstage, framed by flags and quotes from George Washington, Andrew Jackson, and Daniel Webster, politicians gesticulated and shouted, while below them, making a constant din, people in the audience talked to their neighbors, commented on the speeches, applauded and stamped in approval or hissed in disapproval. Even Republicans admitted that the rally was the largest New York had ever witnessed—an estimated crowd of ten thousand.

That night it seemed that the city supported conciliation, that the North would never elect a radical Republican president, and that the nation did not want war. Stephen Douglas must be, would be, the next president.

August entered the new year, 1860, confident of Douglas's success. In January, a month so bitterly cold and snowy that the steamers bringing news from Europe could not enter New York harbor, August invited leading Democrats to his house. After priming them by donating the first $500 himself, he collected more than $5,000 for Democratic candidates in various important state elections. Throughout the winter and early spring August stumped New Hampshire, where he spent the money he had raised on Wall Street. In March former president Franklin Pierce wrote to thank him for "the substantial interest which you have manifested in a little state with which you have no immediate connection." August also sent an additional $25,000, including another $500 of his own money, to help candidates in Connecticut.

For his efforts August once more was accused of trying to buy an election. Then the Democrats lost heavily in New Hampshire and Connecticut, and businessmen put away their wallets. Douglas's supporters began to suspect that August secretly continued to be pro-Buchanan, that he had joined Douglas only to betray him.

In April three of Douglas's longtime campaign workers grilled August for more than an hour. Still angry at Buchanan and Slidell (who the

month before had tried to woo him back into the administration's fold),
August declared his earlier loyalties were the product of youth and poor
judgment. He supported Douglas, he explained, as a friend and because
Douglas was "the only man in the country we can elect." The informal
court adjourned. August was acquitted. He soon would be accepted as the
principal Douglas supporter in the delegation New York was sending to
the Democratic Convention in Charleston, South Carolina.

Two of the Belmont children were sick, one of them Jeannie, with serious
stomach trouble. As he prepared to leave for the convention August
was so worried that his son, August, Jr., wrote a reassuring note in childish
French, sending his father off on his trip with thousands of kisses, which
in the redundant economics of love he also sent to Jeannie.

At the pier August boarded the *Nashville,* the ship taking the delegates to the convention. While waiting to sail he stood on deck. Some
thugs in the crowd on shore started throwing oranges at the delegates.
August was hit in the groin and stumbled below as the *Nashville* pulled
away from the pier and headed down the Hudson.

The Charleston hotels filled up with delegates. Most of the radical
Southerners, the Fire-eaters as they were called, stayed at the Charleston
House, where the hallways were crowded with house slaves on errands for
their masters. Most of the Douglas supporters—and probably August—
stayed at the Mills House, where the waiters were Irish or German.

In the dining room was a constant clatter of plates, scraping of
chairs, and circulation of delegates who looked like gamblers and gamblers who looked like delegates. Some were just sitting down to eat.
Others, their chairs pushed back from the tables and their coats spread
open to reveal colorful vests and full bellies, flipped through newspapers,
glanced casually around the room while sucking on back teeth, or discussed the latest political rumors. Still others were leaving the room,
singly, slowly, hands in pockets, or in groups, intense, heads bent toward
each other, deep in plots.

Outside, delegates argued in the streets, occasionally throwing
punches. They roamed in packs, raucous, cheerful; lounged on stoops;
and settled in dark taverns out of the glaring sun, where they sipped iced
punches or colorful, exotic mixed drinks. The Northerners, horrified,
curious, or titillated, visited slave markets.

Douglas, ill, had stayed in Washington, as had Buchanan. Although not formally in the race, the President was doing everything in his power through his agent Slidell to destroy Douglas's chance for the nomination. In trying to avoid secession Buchanan had backed into the Southern camp.

The South would never accept Douglas. The North would never accept the proslavery plank that the South insisted on putting in the party's platform.

The radical Southerners wanted the South to leave and set up its own republic.

The more moderate Southerners wanted the South to leave, hold its own convention, and nominate its own candidate—who would split the Democratic vote. As a result neither the Republican, the Northern Democratic, nor the Southern Democratic candidate would be able to win. The election would be thrown into the House of Representatives, which, these moderate Southerners were sure, would pick a Southerner to be president.

The Northerners wanted the more rabid Southerners to leave, because if they stayed they might be able to prevent Douglas from getting the nomination.

But it was easier to flirt with the possibility of a rupture than to face it. When the convention opened, all but the diehard members of each faction were ready to try and keep the party and, by extension, the nation together.

The first three days of the convention seemed to August intolerably slow.

"We do not make much progress," he wrote to Caroline; "an immense deal of time is lost by talk. Though I am glad that I came in order to partake in the interesting work before us, I am passing a most stupid time. Everybody is so taken up with politics that you cannot hear another word spoken. Last evening, I went to a party given to some of the delegates. It was the most stupid of all stupid gatherings I have ever been at. There were about twelve ugly women with about sixty ugly men."

At least the weather had broken, shattered by thunder. Rain cooled off the town—luckily, August thought, because "the intense heat of the last three days had begun to affect the health of our delegates."

Inside the South Carolina Institute where the convention was being held, delegates sat, uncomfortable on the wooden chairs, listening to the predictable speeches. August was sure a vote would not come until the end of the week. His boredom was relieved only by the credentials fight between the New York Tammany Hall delegation he belonged to and a renegade delegation led by Fernando Wood, who had recently been re-elected mayor of New York and had set up a second Democratic organization in the city, called Mozart Hall.

August and the other members of the Democratic Vigilant Association, trying to be impartial, had threatened that neither Tammany Hall nor Mozart Hall would get any contributions unless they stopped fighting. But Wood's Mozart Hall Democrats dismissed the Association as a "kid glove, scented, silk stocking, poodle-headed, degenerate aristocracy." August of course, had gone to Charleston as part of the Tammany Hall regulars; and on the third day of the convention the regulars were officially seated.

That night the street in front of the Mills House erupted in anti-Douglas speeches, but one Douglas supporter was unperturbed. "Never mind, when we get to voting we'll beat them like hell."

The delegates knew that the vote on the platform would be the convention's crisis. If the slave plank was voted down the party would be torn apart.

On Friday the platform committee arrived at the hall late, an hour and a half after everyone else had assembled. They brought with them two reports, a majority report that included a slave plank and a minority report that did not. A debate began that lasted into the evening. The hall got stuffy. The gas lamps hissed. Tempers were short. The Northerners were defending a principle. The Southerners were defending a way of life. The session was adjourned without a vote.

There was no vote the following day either. On Sunday delegates who had run out of money or patience started leaving town. Douglas supporters wandered the streets offering government jobs, foreign missions, trying to recruit new troops. The Ohio and Kentucky delegations had finished their private stock of whiskey; delegates rapped the empty barrel as they passed it. And the New York delegation made one last unsuccessful attempt to keep the party from splitting.

When the convention reconvened on Monday the vote on the platform was finally taken, and the Douglas-minority report won. One after another the delegates from Alabama, Mississippi, Louisiana, South Carolina, Florida, Texas, and Arkansas left the hall. Two delegates from Delaware followed. The next day Georgia joined them. The South was slipping away—from the party, from the nation.

For three days the remaining delegates voted and kept voting; but Douglas was unable to get the two-thirds majority necessary to win the nomination. After fifty-seven ballots the delegates gave up, agreeing to meet again in June in Baltimore.

The delegates rushed back to their hotels to pack and stampeded out of the city. August paused long enough to telegraph the news to Douglas, who later explained that he did not answer right away because he had decided to "send no messages to anybody in Charleston, lest fraudulent dispatches might be sent in my name."

Then August too returned home.

In Charleston, August proved that Douglas had been right in trusting his loyalty. Most of Douglas's supporters now were won over to August.

"In a former article we were led to throw some doubt over the probable action of Mr. August Belmont at the convention," a pro-Douglas newspaper said; "it now gives us pleasure to state in justice to that gentleman, that no member of the delegation behaved better or labored more effectively to promote the interests of Judge Douglas. . . . He may rely upon it that his manly course on this occasion shall not be forgotten, and we tell him that he has established a claim on friends who have tenacious memories—whether for good or evil."

In the weeks between the two conventions August, through business contacts and friends, rallied moderate Southerners to Douglas's support. He hoped a compromise resolution that defended the rights of slave-owners already in the territories might keep the party together, and he was sure, as he told Douglas, that Lincoln's nomination at the Republican convention "must open the eyes of the South to the necessity of adhering to you." Lincoln, August thought, was an extremist and carried with him the threat of war.

August himself rode herd on the wavering New York delegates, helped organize another mass meeting for Douglas at Cooper Union, established a committee of seven that solicited funds for the presidential campaign, and negotiated unsuccessfully to buy *The New York Times* in order to turn it into a secure Douglas newspaper. For him the election was not just a presidential contest but also a grudge match: He was fighting not just for Douglas but against Slidell.

Just before the convention reconvened in Baltimore, Douglas wrote to tell August, "Your conduct toward me has been so honorable that I shall have no political secrets from you in the future."

In Baltimore the convention nominated Douglas—after replacing the bolters with Douglas supporters, which caused four more Southern states to leave. Douglas persuaded the New York delegation to make August its representative on the Democratic National Committee, and when the committe met, August was elected chairman.

Unlike Buchanan, Douglas rewarded loyalty.

✄ CHAPTER TWENTY-TWO ✄

CAROLINE'S FATHER had opened Japan to the West. At the time of the Baltimore Democratic Convention a Japanese delegation opened the United States to Japan. Seventy-two Japanese diplomats and interpreters arrived in New York on June 16, 1860. They paraded up Broadway through crowds that greeted them with curiosity, affection, and delight. In the middle of the procession was an outlandish coach draped with Japanese and American flags, advertising on all four sides in large letters the "Japanese Treaty" that had been ratified in Washington. The treaty was carried in a box on the coach. On top of the box sat the star of the spectacle, a seventeen-year-old assistant interpreter, Tateishi Fujiro Noriyuki, whom the Americans called Tommy.

New Yorkers straining for a look from the sidewalks called out to Tommy as he passed. He grinned and waved his fan at them. Although Salomon de Rothschild, still visiting the Belmonts, thought the Japanese were "all very ugly and effeminate; . . . wrinkled like baked apples," American women were infatuated with Tommy, who had earned a reputation as a ladies' man in the cities the delegation had already visited. It was a reputation he struggled to maintain and a number of his countrymen worked hard to acquire in New York. Within a few days after settling in at the Metropolitan Hotel, the Japanese delegation was well on its way to enriching and exhausting the city's prostitutes.

The delegation members wandered through the city with drawing pads, sketching fashions and fixtures. They bought guns and toys. They were fascinated by the gaslights, which, one of them remarked, "at night makes the street seem as bright as day. . . . The light in the rooms of the houses shining through the glass windows" after dark "is so wonderful and is such a surprise to us that I cannot describe it."

A ball that the city gave to honor the Japanese visitors was a glamorous fiasco jammed with curiosity-seekers. The Metropolitan Hotel, on the corner of Broadway and Prince Street, and Niblo's Theater next door were both elaborately decorated. Guests walked through a tunnel of flowers into a ballroom that, draped with colorful flags, looked itself like the heart of a gigantic flower. The two buildings formed a lovely labyrinth through which nine thousand people milled, hardly able to dance to the music of five orchestras.

The private ball August gave for the Japanese ambassadors the following day was less crowded and more pleasant.

"Splendid house," thought George Templeton Strong, who was one of the guests; "probably the most splendid and showy in the city. The picture gallery is a great feature. Every room fragrant with flowers. Mrs. Belmont (Commodore Perry's daughter) received her guests most graciously and gracefully. She is very beautiful and stately, certainly among the loveliest of our New York duchesses. There was a vast crowd. The first-chop Japanese made their appearance at about four o'clock, looking impassive and insensible, and were duly cultivated and admired by everybody."

August charmed the guests of honor by serving them saki, which the Commodore had brought back from Japan. Everyone except for Salomon, who thought the saki tasted like "perfumed hair tonic," seemed to be content.

Unfortunately the Belmonts' two dogs for some reason would not leave the Japanese guests alone. Wherever they went, from room to room, the dogs followed, sniffing at their clothes. It was awkward and a little embarrassing, although one of the delegation's members thought the harassment amusing and explained it obviously had happened because the pets were Japanese spaniels.

That summer, after traveling through the Northeast and Canada, Salomon rejoined the Belmonts at Newport, Rhode Island. A hundred years earlier the city had been a major port larger than New York, but by 1860 it had become a quiet farming and fishing community where a few Southern planters, New England intellectuals, and staid New Yorkers vacationed casually in modest dwellings. For amusement summer visitors sailed, rode horses, fished, walked along the cliff above the ocean, or swam, with everyone in colorful bathing dresses looking—according to Sam Ward's sister, Julia Ward Howe—like "a ragged rainbow. . . . We eat, we drink, and sleep abundantly . . . and are neither important, influential, witty nor wise." A few large summer hotels had been built in the past decade and a half, but except for one, Ocean House, which someone described as being a "huge, yellow pagoda factory," they could not compare to the splendid palaces found at Saratoga.

It was not a chic resort, but because Caroline's father had been born in Newport the Belmonts decided to vacation there. New York's fashionable society followed—to the regret of the sedate regulars, who deplored the glittering invasion.

August and Caroline introduced the resort to formal ten-course dinners and what seemed to be hedonistically informal dances. Like a prince in a fairy tale August carried Caroline through their gardens in the morning so she could look at the flowers without getting her slippers wet with dew and risking a cold. And their retinue of servants seemed to the Old Guard to be obscenely large.

A maid—who once worked for August and later for Sam Ward's austere aunt Eliza Francis—insisted on comparing the two households.

"Mr. Belmont keeps ten servants," the maid said. "Mr. Belmont keeps twenty horses."

"Mr. Belmont," Eliza Francis retorted dryly, "keeps everything but the Ten Commandments."

The house August rented for that summer was "beautiful," Salomon thought. The fourteen-acre plot next door August bought for a rumored $47,000—extravagant, considering that fifteen years earlier the best land in Newport had sold for seven cents a foot. On this property August built his mansion Bythesea, a magnificent house on the cliff overlooking the water. When it was finished August increased his already large retinue of summer help to include sixteen house servants and at least ten yard-men, a number so far beyond extravagance it verged on theater.

At the resort Salomon was amused by how predatory the unmarried girls were and shocked at how, once married, they became such apparently easy prey.

"A foreigner," Salomon thought, "is entitled to be somewhat astounded when he sees returning at ten in the evening a gentleman and a lady—married or not—who have been out alone together, perhaps walking or in a carriage or horseback riding; or when he hears a girl suggest to a young man not that he take her to the beach, but that he go mixed-bathing with her."

Salomon decided that Americans could be so easygoing because the tempting situations discouraged temptation.

"There is nothing more disillusioning . . . ," Salomon said, "than to see American women in bathing suits."

August had less time than he would have liked to enjoy summer sports. The Southern Democrats who had bolted the conventions had nominated their own candidate for the presidency, Vice-President John C. Breckinridge of Kentucky. As early as 1852 Breckinridge had verbally attacked Douglas and in return had been attacked by one of Douglas's supporters, who accused him of being an Old Fogy. Although Breckinridge believed in the right of the Southern states to secede, he did not believe in the wisdom of secession.

The National Constitutional Union party, a hybrid with a Whig heart and a Know-Nothing head, had nominated former senator John Bell of Tennessee. Bell was a moderate and brave politician who, prompted by his conscience, had been known to vote against prevailing Southern opinion.

And then there was the Republican candidate, Abraham Lincoln.

At this point in a presidential campaign it was usual for Democrats in every congressional district in the country to donate $100 to the National Committee. August sent out the call. A month later not one district had responded.

In New York City, August started a local fund-raising drive by giving $1,000. Five weeks later not another cent had been raised.

August personally asked a number of formerly pro-Douglas businessmen to contribute. They turned him down.

"There is at present an apathy and indifference of which it is difficult to form an idea," August told Douglas. "The opinion has gained ground that nothing can prevent the election of Lincoln and that it is consequently useless to spend any money in a hopeless cause. Others who normally contribute to our funds, are afraid to lose their Southern customers by siding with us."

When Minnesota's national committeeman asked for $10,000 for his state, August told him he doubted there would be $10,000 for the entire nation. When the Democratic candidate for governor in Maine heard that August had no funds for him, he said he "felt as if I could cry."

"Unless we can give our merchants and politicians some appearance of success," August told Douglas, "I fear that it will be impossible to raise the necessary funds for our campaign."

Political logic is circular and vicious. No money, no success. No success, no money. The Democratic party leaders seemed trapped, running around and around that track. They were waiting for someone to rescue them. For August to wave his wand.

With every day that passed August grew more irritated. Did they expect him unaided to raise what it took to run every Democratic campaign in the United States? Did they expect him to foot the entire bill himself? By the end of July he was furious.

"It is impossible for me to go on in this way," August told Congressman Miles Taylor of Louisiana, the head of the Douglas Congressional Campaign Committee. "If the other members of the [National] Committee will not assist me in obtaining funds, *the whole machinery has to stop*."

It seemed improbable to Taylor that August could not raise any money—unless he was, as Taylor suggested to Douglas, either "*unable* or *unwilling* to perform."

The famine in funds fed Taylor's suspicions. Before the conventions August's loyalty had been questioned. Perhaps Douglas had been too quickly convinced. "It will not do to have our chances of success . . . diminished by Belmont's incapacity, inefficiency, or worse," Taylor told Douglas. August's failure to raise even the money traditionally contributed by the districts seemed to prove his "want of attachment."

Douglas refused to believe this. And Taylor after visiting August decided, as he told Douglas, that he had done August "a great injustice by my suspicions. I now believe him to be as sincere in the maintenance of the good cause as I am myself."

Nevertheless, the committee was broke.

Mendicant politicians from Maine descended on Newport and for two days pleaded with August for help. Maine was crucial. The Republican vice-presidential nominee came from Maine and used to be a Democrat. If the Democrats swept the state elections, which were being held two months before the presidential elections, it would signal that the Republicans were being rejected. "As Maine goes, so goes the nation" went the phrase newly minted in 1860 that would stay in circulation for years. A

Maine victory would frighten businessmen, the politicians told August, make them hedge their bets, pay up.

August, convinced, returned to New York and called a meeting of the National Committee. Only two members came.

The next night August invited Douglas's richest and most committed supporters to his house. He argued Maine's case. Halfway convinced, they agreed to put up half the funds—if Douglas's supporters in New England would put up the rest.

August wrote letters, demanded, wheedled, implored; and finally he himself gave most of New England's share—just as he finally covered the cost of printing and distributing pro-Douglas pamphlets and of sending pro-Douglas speakers on campaign tours through New York.

More than Maine, August thought, New York was the key. "This state must be the battleground of the Presidential campaign," he told another Douglas supporter. "If we can carry New York, the defeat of Lincoln is certain."

He still was convinced New York was vulnerable to Douglas. "If we could only demonstrate to all those lukewarm and selfish moneybags that we have a strong probability to carry New York," August wrote him, then they might open if not their hearts at least their wallets.

But as long as Douglas, Breckinridge, and Bell shared the ballot the Democratic vote was bound to split, giving Lincoln an easy victory. If, however, the three condidates could join forces in a fusion ticket, a Union ticket, they could defeat Lincoln and then divide the state's electoral votes.

August proposed the plan to a group of thirty-one of New York's most important, generally pro-Douglas Democrats, who agreed. He recruited some of them into the Volunteer Democratic Association of New York, an organization that threatened to cut off funds to any anti-Republican presidential candidate who did not accept the fusion ticket. By now, because of the complexity of working it all out, it was being called the confusion ticket. Since Douglas was getting almost no contributions, except from August, the threat was aimed at Breckinridge and Bell, who with varying degrees of enthusiasm both consented to the scheme.

Again August picked up the tab, giving $2,500 to help cover the costs of a Committee of Fifteen set up to referee this unlikely three-way marriage. A few other states followed New York's lead. Under this arrangement it was unlikely that Douglas would be elected president; but by now he was running not to win but to keep Lincoln from winning—perhaps ultimately to deprive the Republicans of enough electoral votes to force the choice into the House of Representatives. There Douglas might have a chance.

To stand a chance of winning in the House of Representatives, Douglas would need a substantial popular vote. August urged Douglas to campaign openly. "I know that my suggestion is not in accordance with what has hitherto been customary in Presidential campaigns," August told him, but exceptional circumstances demanded "exceptional exertions."

Douglas agreed and plunged into popular campaigning in which August also participated, even though his public appearances triggered more personal attacks. August was accused of trying to control the presidency and of belonging to a Jewish-capitalist conspiracy that included Salomon (who according to this anti-Semitic myth had come to the United States to help August in his scheme). He and Douglas were lampooned; one newspaper ran an advertisement:

"Boy" Lost

Left Washington, D.C., some time in July, to go home to his mother in New York. He has not yet reached his mother, who is very anxious about him. He has been seen at Philadelphia, New York City, Hartford, Ct., and at a clam-bake in Rhode Island. He has been heard from at Boston, Portland, Augusta, and Bangor, Maine. From some expressions he has dropped, it is feared that he has become insane upon a subject he calls "Popular Sovereignty."

He is about five feet nothing in height and about the same in diameter. . . . Has a red face, short legs, and a large belly. . . . Talks a great deal, and very loud always about himself. Has an idea that he is a candidate for the Presidency. . . .

Any information concerning him will be gratefully received by his afflicted mother. For further particulars, address

August Belmont, New York

Their attacks bothered but did not stop August. In the last months of the campaign he organized rallies and gave speeches in and outside New York City.

One of the largest, most boisterous meetings was held in Jones' Woods beyond the city limits around Sixtieth Street. For days before the rally New York was covered with posters showing a blue eagle with a banner clenched in its beak that said: "Popular *Sovereignty* of the

People"—a tautology, but as a political slogan it had the advantage of an internal echo. The night before the meeting, cooks skewered a 2,200-pound, appropriately Southern ox and started broiling it over a pit sixteen feet long, eight feet wide, and four feet deep. At the bottom of the pit, out of the way of the fire, metal trays caught the dripping grease. The cooks turned and tested the meat with pitchforks. In the firelight they looked like demons. Squatters from the shantytowns stood in the dark and watched.

By morning a sheep, calf, and hog had also been skewered, roasted, and hacked into chunks of meat, which were placed on tables set up in the clearing along with two thousand loaves of bread. At two in the afternoon a ravenous crowd, unable to wait any longer, rushed the policemen and cooks guarding the feast, knocked over the barricades, and, as *The New York Times* later said, "Popular Sovereignty in its most extended significance was . . . exemplified."

One man, a cripple, managed to strap a side of mutton onto his back and hobble off with it.

"The orgy over," Salomon recalled, "everyone gathered around the platforms," where August, the "president of the 'meeting,' gave a 'speech' to the crowd that was nicely done, although improvised."

Salomon hung around Jones' Wood after the rally to watch the famous aerialist Blondin walk a two-thousand-foot rope that had been strung two hundred feet in the air.

"Those who were at the exhibition," Salomon noted, "compared the sensation they experienced with that of seeing a man hanged."

A few days later Blondin carried his agent on his back across a wire strung over Niagara Falls, a demonstration for the Prince of Wales, who was visiting North America. The prince was appalled. Some of the other spectators were also put off by the show, but for a different reason. They had expected Blondin to carry the prince across the falls.

New Yorkers were more easily satisfied. They wanted only to get close to the prince. Girls were setting man-traps, hoping to catch him. Social climbers were setting status-traps, hoping to use him as bait to catch New York's fashionable society. By the time the prince, traveling as Baron Renfrew, a singularly public incognito, finally reached New York, everyone was obsessed with him.

"By Monday next," George Templeton Strong noted shortly after the prince's arrival, "the remotest allusion to His Royal Highness will act like ipecac."

Two hundred thousand people greeted the prince in New York. The city had been charmed by the Japanese delegation; now it was almost worshipful.

When the prince rode through Castle Garden gate on the mare he had borrowed from Caroline, the crowd erupted. Everybody loved him.

"I have never witnessed such a scene in my life," the prince's chaperon, Lord Newcastle, told August, "and never wish to witness any which could diminish the impression this one has made on me."

Presumably the impression was positive.

Like the Japanese ambassadors the prince visited both prostitutes and patricians. What happened at the brothel was not recorded. But at the Academy of Music so many people surged toward the prince as he entered that the floor of the ballroom caved in. Oddly, after the first startled cries the crowd was silent, the only quiet moment of the evening. Everyone caught in the collapse struggled out of the hole. Carpenters were rushed in to repair the floor.

During the crisis Caroline, dressed in rose tulle trimmed with sweet-pea blossoms, watched from the stage, where she sat. She did not have to descend into the crush to talk with the prince. She would talk with him when they danced after dinner.

Caroline's diamonds that night were so extraordinary that one newspaper said they "shone afar even over the glittering crowd." The prince might visit, but August and Caroline reigned over New York. August was even given a title: "From his connection with the Perry family," said a newspaper, soured on the prince's visit and New York's response to it, "August Belmont will be made Earl of Erie and Baron Japan."

"In less than four days you will be called upon to record your votes at an election upon the result of which depends not only the preservation of your property and the prosperity of your native city"—here August was interrupted by cheers—"but also the very existence of this great and vast Republic."

August paused and surveyed the wildly applauding crowd at Cooper Union.

"Whatever the Republican leaders may say to the contrary," he continued, "I fear that the election of Mr. Lincoln to the Presidential chair must prove the forerunner of a dissolution of this Confederacy amid all the horrors of civil strife and bloodshed."

Members of the audience cried, "Yes, yes!"

August made a few more remarks. Soon the meeting was over, the last Democratic rally in New York before the election. Despite the cheers August could not have felt very hopeful. Lincoln seemed certain to be elected.

Election day in New York was clear and cool. Crowds waited outside the newspaper offices for the results. Lincoln won with 180 electoral votes. Douglas came in last with 12, trailing Breckinridge and Bell.

August consoled himself with the popular vote: Douglas was runner-up with 1,376,957 to Lincoln's 1,866,452. He also took consolation in meeting "men who confess the error [of having voted for Lincoln] and almost with tears in their eyes wish they could undo what they helped to do." But the defeat was staggering—and ominous. Lincoln's election was a signal for the South to secede. That night in Charleston, South Carolina, mobs rejoiced, drunk with the dream of a new Southern republic.

The threat of secession triggered a Wall Street panic. If the South defaulted on debts, dozens of merchant bankers would be ruined. As the stock market skidded, many firms closed. *The New York Times* claimed that manipulators were exploiting the political crisis by dumping stocks in order to force their prices down, only to buy them back once they had hit bottom.

"Money is hoarded, cannot be found—it is invisible," Salomon remarked.

To reassure the business community that his credit was good, and to make sure that he had a ready supply of money so that he could take advantage of the depressed prices on the stock market, August had gold shipped from England. He stopped all business transactions with the South, warning at least one Southern merchant that if the South seceded he could not trade with him.

August realized that secession of the Southern states could be in the financial interests of New York businessmen because—as he told another Southerner—"New York, in such a catastrophe, would cut loose from the puritanical East and without linking our fortunes with our kind but somewhat exacting Southern friends, she would open her magnificent port to the commerce of the world." As an independent city-state, New York would become to the Americas—August thought—"what Venice was once on the sluggish lagoons of the small Adriatic."

But however profitable secession might be, August preferred "to leave to my children, instead of the gilded prospects of New York merchant princes, the more enviable title of American citizens, and as long as God spares my life I shall not falter in my efforts to preserve them that heritage."

August used his moral stand as a practical argument: If New York businessmen could put patriotism over profit, Southerners should put patriotism over pride. "The country," August wrote, "disgusted with the misrule of Mr. Buchanan and the corruption which disgraced his administration," had legally elected Lincoln; and the South should accept the results just as Northern Democrats had and work within the Union to solve the problems facing the country. Southerners should not allow themselves to be swayed by demagogues in either the South or the North. The secessionists—August thought—were "short-sighted." And the abolitionists wanted the South to secede so that radical Republicans could take over the federal government, which they could not do as long as the South remained in the Union and helped maintain a Democratic majority in Congress and on the Supreme Court.

"I for one," August told a Southern friend, "would most certainly rather submit to the Constitutional election of an opponent than to the terrorism evoked by a faction whose treasonable designs my best efforts had been exerted to defeat."

Although every day brought depressing news, August could not believe that "the American people will permit their country to be dragged to ruin by a handful of puritan fanatics and selfish politicians." Secession was not inconceivable—August unfortunately could all too easily imagine it—but outrageous. "The idea of separate confederacies living in peace and prosperity on this continent, after a dissolution of the Union, is too preposterous to be entertained by any man of sound sense and the slightest knowledge of history. *Secession means civil war.*"

"The dissolution of the American Union," he wrote, "is the death-knell of human liberty."

Meanwhile, the government seemed paralyzed. Buchanan—it was said—had cracked under the pressure and was wandering through the White House drunk on Monongahela whiskey and muttering to himself. The optimists claimed that he was muttering prayers; the pessimists, that he was just muttering.

Even though, as August wrote, "a *reign of terror* exists in the South which silences the voice of every conservative patriot and renders it impossible for the people to arrive at a correct judgment," and even though "the secession leaders, reckless of patriotic considerations, may succeed in manufacturing packed conventions for the purpose of precipitating secession *without an appeal to the people,*" still August believed that the South would vote to stay in the Union if the question of secession were put to a referendum.

Southerners only needed to be reassured that their rights would be protected, particularly in the territories. That assurance, August thought, Northerners could give them without yielding any of the advantages they had won at the polls. Both Thurlow Weed, the New York Republican political boss, and Kentucky Senator John J. Crittenden, who had helped form the Constitutional Union party, had suggested reaffirming and extending the forty-year-old Missouri Compromise. A line would be drawn from the southern boundary of Missouri, which was at latitude 36°30', to California: Above that line, slavery would be prohibited; below it, slavery would be admitted. This seemed an equitable plan to August. "A most efficacious, if not the only, remedy which can save this great country from ruin and destruction," he wrote to Crittenden—who urged the proposal to keep not only the Union but his family together: One of his sons sided with the North and the other with the South.

To Weed, August wrote, "The wise and conciliatory course which you counsel as the only remedy which can save this great Republic must command, not only the warm support of your friends, but also the unqualified respect and admiration of your opponents. I have fought to the last against the great party, of which you have proved so formidable a leader, but I shall never regret our defeat if your wise counsels prevail."

August, a gracious loser, could recognize an ally even at a political distance. Republicans would be in power for at least the next four years. If August were going to take his own advice, accept the election results, and work for what he believed under the Republican administration, he had to find access to that power. Weed seemed a likely conduit to the White House.

Since August and Weed agreed, particularly on the issue of reaffirming and extending the Missouri Compromise, the temporary truce was easy to negotiate. August, lobbying for Weed and Crittenden's plan with

Douglas, argued that "in my opinion it would not add a foot of slave territory to the Union, except where climate and soil render it more profitable than free labor and *no power on earth can exclude it from there*." In accepting the latitude 36°30′ line, the North would be giving up nothing except that which it had no chance of getting.

Douglas still wanted to let the states enter the Union one by one, with or without slavery as their inhabitants desired. He had fought too long for Popular Sovereignty to abandon it.

"The self-denial and sacrifice of your favored doctrine when the salvation of the Union requires it," August told him, trying to flatter him away from Popular Sovereignty, "would place you higher in the affections of the American people than you have ever been before."

At last Douglas gave in and agreed to support the latitude 36°30′ compromise. But the compromise failed, as did all the other efforts to avoid secession: the peace conferences, the rallies, the petitions. . . .

On December 20 South Carolina seceded from the United States.

On January 9 Mississippi seceded.

On January 10 Florida seceded.

On January 11 Alabama seceded.

On January 19 Georgia seceded.

On January 26 Louisiana seceded.

On February 1 Texas seceded.

And on February 4 representatives from the rebel states met at Montgomery, Alabama, wrote a constitution, and established the Confederate States of America.

Although August admitted that "the seceders are behaving very badly" and it was hard "to put up with their lawless proceedings and their utter disregard of comity and justice," he did not think that the North should try to force them back into the Union. Any "coercion on the part of the federal government" seemed to August "exactly what they want," since "they know full well that it would most assuredly consolidate the whole South under their banner."

Without Virginia and the other border states, August was sure, the Confederacy would not survive. The North should try to conciliate. And wait.

Everything that winter and spring seemed backlit by the fires to come.

Six days after Mississippi seceded August gave a ball that Salomon claimed would "mark an epoch in the annals of New York society. The flowers, the ladies, and the clothes competed in beauty and brilliance, and I confess that the spectacle was charming." Guests circulating among the three separate dinners passed in every room tableaux vivants arranged among the blossoms and candles as part of the decoration.

At the party the wife of a British diplomat—"one of those old English girls," Salomon said, "who is sixty and travels for her education" —told another guest that she had "not seen a single handsome person in America."

Overhearing her, August turned around and to her mortification thanked her for the compliment.

But most of the guests were, like Salomon, charmed by the ball. It seemed far from the world of politics—until the arrival of a Mississippian, a Madame D. who, as a newspaper later pointed out, a few days before had been an American but by the night of the ball had become a foreigner.

That winter even Caroline was not spared from involvement in a public political scandal. When the new president and his wife stopped in New York on the way to Washington, a newspaper erroneously reported that Caroline had visited Mrs. Lincoln at the Astor House. If this were true it would have been a minor, polite betrayal of August's party and her own class. The president was a backwoodsman; and although Mrs. Lincoln came from a good Southern family, it was not necessarily a family the Belmonts socially would know. It was all right for August to attend a breakfast meeting with the president. That was politics. But Caroline was not a politician. She wrote to the newspaper to correct the report.

If Caroline looked down on the Lincolns, others looked down on the Belmonts. An English journalist who visited the Belmonts' house—which, he noted, was only a few hundred yards from the hovels of the shanty-town squatters—found something lacking. Certainly the house was "elegant," and, he said, "I use the word in its real meaning—with pretty statues, rich carpets, and a gallery of charming Meissoniers and *genre* pieces; the saloons admirably lighted . . . filled with the prettiest women in the most delightful toilettes, with a proper fringe of young men, orderly, neat, and well turned-out, fretting against the usual advanced posts of turbaned and jewelled dowagers . . . there was wit, sense, intelligence, vivacity; and yet there was something wanting—not in host or hostess, or company, or house—what was it?"

Trying to get a fix on the lack he felt, the journalist said, "When a man looks at a suit of armor made to order by the first blacksmith in Europe, he observes that the finish . . . is much higher than in the old clothes of the former time. Possibly the metal is better, and the chasings and garniture . . . , but the observer is not for a moment led to imagine that it has stood the proof of blows, or that it smacks of ancient watch-fire."

August's world, the journalist thought, was too unfinished and, paradoxically, in another way too finished. Everything—the society, the city, the country—was too new.

The Englishman, however, was not above devouring political scandal. "I heard it declared," he reported, "that if Monsieur Belmont had not gone to the Charleston Convention, the present crisis would never have occurred."

Carrying this reasoning further, it was August Belmont who had presumably kept the New York delegation from caving in on the platform fight. If August had not been there the New York delegation would have voted for the slave plank, the South would not have bolted, Lincoln would not have been elected, and there would have been no secessions. According to this bizarre logic August's loyalty to Douglas—loyalty that ironically often had been doubted—had destroyed the Union.

On April 12, 1861, Confederate forces attacked Fort Sumter. Soon thereafter Virginia, Arkansas, Tennessee, and North Carolina seceded from the United States.

The Civil War had begun.

CHAPTER TWENTY-THREE

ALTHOUGH AUGUST WAS A FIGHTER, he was not a warrior. Events were shunting him aside. He wanted to be in the center of the action, but the action had moved away from his party, away from peacetime politics. He could play a supporting role, no more than that, backing the President's policies in petitions and at meetings, which he did with energy and enthusiasm because, as he said, the issue had become "a question of national existence and commercial prosperity."

He used what influence he had to get commissions for his friends' sons; permitted one corps of militiamen, the Young America Zouaves, to drill on the top floor of his house in their scarlet fezzes and balloon-leg pants; and helped raise and outfit the Union's first German-American regiment, which before leaving for the front assembled in City Hall Park, where August on behalf of Caroline presented them with a silk American flag.

"It is the flag which for three quarters of a century has been hailed in every quarter of the inhabited globe as the emblem of constitutional liberty and the beacon of hope to the oppressed of all nations," August told the soldiers. "A large number of you have fled from oppression and tyranny in the Old World. You have found on these hospitable shores protection, freedom, and loving hearts, and in offering now the sacrifice of your lives on the altar of your adopted country you pay a debt of gratitude for the blessings vouchsafed to you under our liberal institutions."

August also wanted to pay his debt of gratitude to his adopted country, a debt he felt was not cleared by making speeches or even raising a regiment; but he was not sure how best to do so.

Early in May he found a way.

On May 6, the British government declared that it would recognize as belligerents all Confederate privateers, which were trying to break the Union blockade of Southern ports. August thought this was England's first "step toward recognizing the Southern Confederacy"—which was in fact what the Confederacy was hoping for.

It was in England's interest to help the South, the Confederates argued. First of all, England did not like the tariffs that the North, to protect its own manufacturers, imposed on foreign goods—especially the Morrill tariff that just had been passed by Congress and that increased import duties by 5 to 10 percent. The Confederacy also did not like import duties, since without them the South could buy what it needed from Europe at prices 25 to 40 percent cheaper than those charged by the North; so the Confederate constitution had banned government-imposed protective tariffs, which pleased British manufacturers and inclined them toward the rebels.

Second, England would not want its supply of cotton from the Confederate States cut off or even interrupted. Without cotton, English mills would close down and the economy of Great Britain would suffer serious damage.

Third, the growing international might of the United States would pose less of a threat if the Confederacy survived.

The Confederacy used similar arguments for support from France.

August used all his influence with his English and French friends, particularly the Rothschilds, to discourage a Confederate alliance with the two European nations and to urge them to help the Union, which like the Confederacy needed money to fight the war. "You know that I have never been in favor of the party which is now at the head of our government," August wrote to Lionel Rothschild, "and my convictions on this point have in no way been changed. I am, however, convinced that the whole North, to a man, will stand by the administration in the present struggle and that *come what may* the integrity of the Union and the inviolability of our territory will be maintained to the bitter end."

August may have won the battle with Lionel, but he lost a greater war. The British government soon declared itself neutral—a decision that by treating the North and the South alike raised the Confederacy to an equal footing with the Union and thus implicitly recognized the legitimacy of the Southern republic.

"It would be difficult for me," August wrote in another letter to Lionel, "to convey to you an idea of the general feeling of disappointment and irritation produced in this country" by the British government's decision.

Through business associates, most likely the Rothschilds in France or possibly Salomon, who had been traveling through the South, August heard that French subjects living in New Orleans were with the consent of the French consul forming "a home guard for the protection of property and life in the city."

"It is clear," August thought, "that this gives direct aid to the Rebellion, allowing the Louisiana volunteers to leave the state and meet our troops in Virginia."

August sent this information—as he had been sending his European correspondence—to Washington. Through Thurlow Weed he had made contact with Secretary of State William H. Seward and Secretary of the Treasury Salmon P. Chase. These men represented two poles of the Republican party—Seward tending to favor conciliation, Chase demanding forcible suppression of the rebels. August, taking no chances, was keeping a wide range of administration stock in his political portfolio.

Seward thanked August for the letters and political information. Chase thanked him for his financial advice. August felt somewhat more useful than he had earlier in the year. If he had not repaid his debt of gratitude to the Union, he at least had made a down payment.

Soon, however, he would be able to do more.

On June 3 Douglas died, leaving no political heir. August, as chairman of the National Committee, became head of the Democratic party.

In June, August went to Washington to consult with the administration. The ride from the railroad station to Willard's Hotel went along Pennsylvania Avenue, at one end of which was the unfinished Capitol, its bonewhite marble and the toothlike columns on the portico giving it the appearance of a massive skull that was being dug out of Washington's earth.

"Before the war can be brought to a satisfactory termination," August told Chase, "we shall require from 50 to 60 millions of dollars."

Part of that amount could be raised within the Union—and not just from bankers and professional speculators but also from people who usually did not invest in stocks and bonds.

"A national subscription ought to be opened in all our large cities," August said; "amounts as low as one hundred dollars, or even fifty dollars, should be accepted, and bonds for those fractions be issued. All the subscriptions below five thousand dollars should be filled before the larger amounts are awarded."

By favoring the small investor the government would involve its citizens directly in the fortunes of the Union (and get noninvestors into the habit of investing, which once the war was over would strengthen the American economy).

Although this measure would reduce the Union's dependence on European capital, nonetheless August admitted it still would "be necessary to look to the European money markets for at least a portion of" the money needed.

"It is impossible to say how the capitalists of England and the Continent may be affected toward an American loan," August warned Chase. "There is evidently a belief in the *European cabinets* that by withholding all aid from us, they may force us into a settlement of some kind with the Southern states, and it remains now to be seen whether this delusion is shared by the transatlantic capitalists."

Because a recent transaction in American stocks had been sizable in England, August thought the Union had a fair chance to negotiate such a large loan overseas, especially if by the time negotiations began "our army has in any way been successful in Virginia."

August was guardedly optimistic but cautioned Chase against sending an official government representative to Europe to seek foreign money, because if the mission failed, apprehensive American investors might sell their own securities, afraid that without European support the Union's chances for success would be diminished. An unofficial government representative, however, could secretly explore the situation in the European money markets. If the mission was a failure, "no harm would have been done," August said, "because nobody would know."

August, intending to visit Europe that summer anyway, offered to be that unofficial government representative, "acting," he told Chase, "not as the banker and correspondent of foreign banking firms, but as an American citizen, anxious to do his share in the crisis which has overcome our dear country."

Chase agreed.

August now had a secret mission.

Caroline, Perry, August, Jr., and Belle went to Europe ahead of August, traveling for companionship and protection with Salomon, who was returning home. Frederika, Jeannie, and Oliver stayed in America with their grandmother Jane Perry.

The "voyage from New York was a mess," Salomon said; "it was handled with as much shoving as a maritime cargo ship; it was far too disagreeable. It is called a summer crossing, but you must furnish yourself with the thickest furs, which barely protect you against the cold and the damp. At one point you find yourself surrounded by mountains of ice which have detached themselves from the North Pole and move along toward the south; at another you find yourself surrounded by the densest fog. Further on, a nasty wind rises and makes you dance like a jumping jack, producing the most disastrous effects on your stomach."

Salomon was queasy; but Perry, grandson of the Commodore, was proud that he was not the least bit seasick.

At two o'clock one morning the passengers were awakened by an explosive crack. The engine had broken. The cabins filled with steam. Everyone rushed up on deck, some half-dressed like one of the Belmonts' servants, who to Perry's amusement stumbled from his room "with one shoe and one stocking on, his shirttail sticking out behind, no hat, and no waistcoat, one leg in his breeches and the other out."

A few of the women, sure that the boat was sinking, frantically put on life preservers. One woman, overcome by hysteria or using hysteria to try to snare a Rothschild, threw herself at Salomon. Salomon, evidently too fastidious to be a hero, pushed her into another man's arms.

Order was restored. The motor was repaired. The passengers returned to their cabins.

For Perry, more menacing than the icebergs, the stormy weather, and the midocean accident were all the secessionists on board.

"There was one Englishman who was a secessionist too," he reported to August. "I think Aunt Belle likes him better than any gentleman she knows." With a child's sly humor he added, "It will suit Grandmama better than anything to hear that Aunt Belle likes a secessionist very much."

Just after his family departed, August, according to the jingling phraseology of his military pass, went "over the bridges and within the lines" into Confederate territory with the stipulation that if he "in any way aided the enemies of the United States, the penalty will be death."

Where did he go? Why? How? All histories reserve mysteries. Rumors competed for credence. Did he sneak through rebel lines in the dark? Travel publicly during the day, but disguised? Did he shave off his whiskers so he would not be recognized or wear a fuller, false beard? Some said he went to buy cotton. (Unlikely, since he had told one Southerner just a few months before that he would not trade with secessionists.)

Others said he went to check some of Rothschilds' tobacco, which was stuck in a Southern warehouse because of the blockade. (More likely.) Or did he go to probe the possibility of conciliation? (Also likely, since he would suggest such a scheme later on.) Had he crossed the lines near Harpers Ferry at Point of Rocks, Maryland? Or did he cross the lines at Point of Rocks later in the war on another secret trip into the South?

The few contradictory facts, rumors, and speculations obscure more than they reveal. The evidence suggests a confidential errand but keeps that errand mysterious.

August's trip to Europe, although it had its secret, was not mysterious. He left New York on July 17, 1861, on Cunard's *Persia,* a beautiful ship with embossed paddle-wheel boxes and an iron hull that allowed her a few years later, in a race with the Collins steamship *Pacific,* to crash into an ice field without sinking.

In England, August rejoined his family amid the baying of newshounds who had sniffed a scoop. The *New York Daily News* had spread what August described as a "mischievous rumor" but what was more accurately the mischievous truth: August had gone to Europe to negotiate "a large government loan." And the London newspapers had picked up the cry.

Lionel Rothschild arranged a meeting between August and the British prime minister, Lord Palmerston, in one of the private galleries of the House of Commons. Thinking the meeting might be instructive for his son as well as useful for his country, August took ten-year-old Perry along to the conference.

Lord Palmerston was in his late seventies. Caricaturists always had him strolling about London chewing on a straw—neither of which he did as often as the cartoonists represented. He had a high forehead, which looked from a distance as smooth as polished wood, and deep creases running down from the corners of his mouth, which made his jaw appear hinged like a marionette's.

Both men quickly exhausted the little candor they had brought to the meeting.

The prime minister disingenuously asked "where the United States government expected to get all the money necessary for the prosecution of the war."

August, equally disingenuous, answered, "I suppose we will do like all other borrowers and try to get it where it can be obtained cheapest."

For an hour they fenced, each countering the other's points.

August reminded the prime minister of America's sympathy for Great Britain when India rebelled.

The prime minister reminded August of America's unwillingness to let Great Britain "enlist a few men in the States during the Crimean War."

August—perhaps knowing that Palmerston's wife had been active in international antislavery organizations—referred, as often as chance or craft allowed, to the American troubles as a conflict over slavery.

The prime minister redefined the issue as a conflict between tariff and free trade. After all, they both knew that President Lincoln himself in his inaugural address had said, "I have no purpose, directly or indirectly, to interfere with the institution of slavery in the states where it exists. I believe I have no lawful right to do so, and I have no inclination to do so."

Palmerston left August with the alarming impression that "we have nothing to hope from the sympathy of the English government and people in our struggle" and that England would use any "excuse to break through our blockade" of the Southern ports.

Toward the end of the interview the prime minister summed up his government's position: "We do not like slavery, but we want cotton and we dislike very much your Morrill tariff."

The conversation had been both pointed and blunt; but once it was over the prime minister relaxed and chatted with Perry, who was as impressed by Palmerston's kindness after the meeting as he had been by the toughness of the meeting itself.

Because of the scrutiny of the London newspapers August shortened his stay in England, where his mission and the Civil War seemed in some quarters to weigh equally with the story of how Henry Wadsworth Long-fellow's wife had dropped some sealing wax on her dress, lit up like a human torch, and burned to death while running in panic down the stairs.

His family continued on to a spa while August stopped to confer with bankers and politicians in France. There he learned that "the general feeling is more favorable to us than I had found it in England." In Germany, too, "the sympathies of the whole population are strongly for us." But news of the Union rout at Manassas, the first major battle of the war, had reached Europe and was discouraging bankers from lending money to the North.

Those Europeans who were sympathetic to the North repeatedly emphasized that—as August reported to Washington—it was important for "our blockade to be effective if we expect it to be respected." However, if the blockade was effective it was likely that Union ships would eventually have to stop foreign ships suspected of running contraband—which deepened August's dispiriting conviction that the United States soon would be at war with England and France.

It looked as though any transaction between the Union and England or France would involve not gold but death.

While in Germany, August stopped at Alzey. It was the end of summer. The smell of the ripening grapes was so strong it seemed one could get drunk just by breathing. In the cemetery August plucked a leaf from the roses on his mother's grave and another from the geraniums on his fa-ther's, which he saved and carried with him when he left the town.

CHAPTER TWENTY-FOUR

AUGUST SPENT two miserable and anxious months in a small German village where Caroline suffered from "a dangerous and most painful rheumatic gastric fever."

By mid-October she was well enough to travel to the south of France, where her doctor advised her to winter. She was too ill to risk an Atlantic crossing. So the Belmonts delayed their return to the United States despite August's belief that "this is a time when every good citizen ought to be at home."

The New York newspapers interpreted August's extended absence to mean that he was abandoning his adopted country. Newspapers, in fact, seemed to August more and more like the Furies. In London and New York the press was mobilizing for war between Great Britain and the United States. There was nothing to be done about the English newspapers, but August wondered in a letter to Chase if "the influence of the administration might be profitably exerted toward preventing the publication of hostile articles."

"Your observations on the course of certain presses here are quite just," Chase answered August, "but no one knows better than yourself how difficult, if not impossible, it is to put even moderate restriction upon the press in the United States. In fact, we have hardly yet educated ourselves up to the idea that *printed* correspondence with the enemy in insurrection is unlawful. But," he ominously added, "we are daily growing into the sentiments which the times make needful."

By the end of autumn August did not think there was "the remotest chance" of "negotiating at this moment any portion of our loan either in England or on the Continent." Happily the national subscription in the Union had been successful; and Chase was "confident that, if expenditure can be restricted within reasonable limits, the whole sums needed can be supplied in this country."

August was less optimistic. The government might be able to raise the money it needed if expenditure could be "restricted within reasonable limits," but if war with any European power broke out those reasonable limits would be difficult to maintain. August's fear of a war with Europe grew like a shadow lengthening as the sun sets. He dreaded the night of general conflict that seemed sure to come.

On his way to England to meet the rest of the family, who were joining them in Europe, August stopped in Paris, where he heard from well-placed friends that "the Emperor is very anxious to *recognize at once* the Southern Confederacy and to insist by an armed intervention, if necessary, upon the cessation of hostilities" in order to "stop the derangement of industry and trade which France is feeling." August was certain Louis Napoleon would act soon, unless "a signal success crowns our operations by land or water."

By the time August returned to the south of France he must have had the news of three significant Union naval victories: one near New Orleans, another off North Carolina, and a third off South Carolina. Surely now France and the rest of Europe had to give up the delusion that the North might be pressured to let the South secede.

In the mild Nice weather Caroline improved. When it was sunny she walked through town to look at the sea, which under certain conditions gleamed like polished silver. When it was cloudy, the silver tarnished. (What was happening at home? Was the house all right? Were the servants looking after things conscientiously?) When it rained she stayed inside gazing at the town through weeping windows.

Away from the United States, again out of the center of action, his mission stalled, August fretted about all the Confederate agents and spies crawling the Continent, political lice.

With every newspaper from home August's mood darkened. He could not understand why, "with three times the population of the rebel states, with the command of the sea, and plenty of money, our troops are always outnumbered whenever it comes to a battle." Even worse, he had heard that Caroline's Uncle John Slidell had run the blockade and was coming to Europe to argue the Confederate cause.

August, as devoted an enemy as he was a friend, would not forgive Slidell for not having pressed with Buchanan his request for the mission at Madrid. And even if he had forgiven him, August still would not have been pleased to see him in Europe, since Slidell was a "crafty and clever" politician, someone who would be an effective lobbyist for the Southern states.

"Would it be right for me," August wondered, "to wish my venerable uncle comfortably lodged in prison at Fort Lafayette?"

August's wish, with a slight refraction as it passed from the denser medium of imagination into the purer one of reality, came true: within a month Slidell would be lodged, not as comfortably as August might have hoped, in another Union prison at Fort Warren.

Jefferson Davis had appointed, as representatives to Paris and London, Slidell and James M. Mason, a former senator who combed his long hair back over his ears into wings so that he looked—appropriately, considering his mission—like an aging Mercury. As August had feared, they had run the blockade and reached Cuba. On November 7 they sailed from Havana for Southampton on the British steamer *Trent*. On November 8, around noon the *Trent* was stopped with two shots across her bow by an armed Union sloop, the *San Jacinto*. Slidell and Mason and their secretaries were seized.

"Goodbye, my dear," Slidell said to his wife as he left the *Trent*. "We shall meet in Paris in sixty days."

August had wanted to see Slidell in prison, but he thought it dangerous policy for the Union to seize him from a British ship.

"How enlightened and patriotic men could have for one moment rejoiced at the capture of those men *under such questionable* circumstances is a riddle to me," August wrote one acquaintance.

"Not a dozen battles lost could have damaged our good cause as much as this ill-judged and over-zealous act," he told someone else.

If England used the incident as an excuse to side with the Confederacy she could, as August saw it, "strike a deadly blow at our navy and render complete and permanent the separation of the Union and consequently its ruin and destruction. Is the retention of the rebel commissioners of sufficient importance for us to run the risk of such a calamity?"

England was demanding the return of the secessionists. They had been taken illegally from her ship. August thought the Union should comply. Even if England were not to enter the war, seizing the men that way had been dishonorable. And keeping them was bad politics.

"The retention of the rebel commissioners may and undoubtedly does satisfy a very natural and just feeling of resentment against two of the principal leaders of this unholy conspiracy" of secession, August acknowledged; but "their capture has given to them and their mission an importance in the eyes of Europe which they never would have otherwise acquired, and every day which they are kept in prison will only add to that prestige."

Since the captain of the *San Jacinto* had acted on his own, not on orders from Washington, August thought "the President has every opportunity to get in an honorable and dignified manner out of the difficulty."

Not prepared to war with England if it was not necessary, Lincoln had Secretary of State Seward write not an apology but an explanation that could serve as an apology. The rebel commissioners and their secretaries were released.

Arresting and holding the men had been illegal and politically, diplomatically, and militarily unsound; but August knew that in arguing for their freedom, especially considering his family ties to Slidell, he was giving ammunition to his enemies, who already were beginning to call him a Copperhead, a traitor.

Slidell arrived in Paris only twenty days later than he had promised his wife. August warily followed his movements from Nice.

"On what an errand Slidell has consented to be used by his insatiable ambition!" August exclaimed.

After all, although Slidell had adopted, even conquered, Louisiana (in New Orleans the people called him King John), he had been born in New York. August could not understand how Slidell could use "all the rescources of his ingenuity and cunning to bring a foreign enemy to invade his native soil."

August hoped he would not run into Slidell socially because, he explained to their mutual friend Samuel L. M. Barlow, "I could certainly not extend to him the ordinary civility due among acquaintances."

August enjoyed Nice, but as soon as Caroline was well enough they regularly visited Paris. They went to the Paris season's fashionable ball. The king of Bavaria, princes from Sweden and Norway, the duke of Parma—all of European society was present. Servants dressed as postmen circulated through the rooms delivering flirtatious letters, that the men discreetly pocketed and the women triumphantly shared. At dawn Louis Napoleon danced a cotillion. Everyone stayed until six in the morning.

The Belmonts also attended the more select entertainments given by the Rothschilds, one of which was a sequence of tableaux vivants in which Belle appeared as a serving maid and Caroline appeared first as an angel and then as a nymph.

Occasionally August would stay on in Paris to meet with visiting American politicians like Thurlow Weed; but life that winter was quiet, despite these excursions. And when spring came, August, looking forward to a greater role in the war—and peace—effort, brought his family back to New York.

🜨 *CHAPTER TWENTY-FIVE* 🜨

AUGUST HAD HOPED for a quick war; surgery, not the drawn-out and brutal dismemberment the war had become. It was nightmarish: soldiers slogging through mud, struggling with bogged-down guns, dying under gunned-down horses, blood mixing with mud and soaking into the earth so that in the summer where the soldiers fell plants would grow luxuriantly, a death crop.

"What frightens me more than the disasters in the field," August told Weed, "is the apathy and distrust which, I grieve to say, I meet at every step, even from men of standing, and hitherto of undoubted loyalty to the Union."

One of two things or both should, must, be done, August told Weed:

First, the military must be reformed. The President must "at once establish a system of conscription, by which at least 500,000 *men should be called under arms.* The raw recruits ought to be collected at camps of instruction, in healthy localities, east and west, where under the direction of *West Point graduates,* they should be drilled and disciplined. From thence, as they are fit for active service, they should be furnished to the army to be incorporated into the old regiments, *without reference to states,* and only where they are most needed. This is the only way to create an efficient United States army."

Second, the North must make an effort at reconciliation. "If one or two conservative men, who, without holding any official position, possess influence and weight enough with our people and the government to inspire confidence in their statements to the leading men of the South, could be found to proceed under the authority, or at least with the knowledge of the President, to Richmond, in order to open negotiations, I think success might crown their efforts."

August assumed Weed would show his letter to Lincoln. Little by little August had been insinuating his counsel into the White House, advising the President on economic strategy. The President had responded positively to August's advances, and August was tempted to extend the range of his advice.

To buttress the suggestions he had made in the letter to Weed, August sent to Lincoln an olive branch, a letter he had received from "one of the wealthiest and most influential planters in Louisiana and Mississippi." The Southerner, disillusioned with secession, seemed as eager for a negotiated settlement as August was; and they both represented funds of hidden—and in some cases not so hidden—Union and Confederate feeling.

If the North would "say officially that it wishes for the restoration of the Union as it was," the Southerner believed the Confederacy would stop fighting and would reenter the United States.

Instead of accepting the olive branch, Lincoln shot the dove.

"Broken eggs cannot be mended," Lincoln wrote to August: "Louisiana has nothing to do now but take her place in the Union as it was, barring the already broken eggs. The sooner she does, the smaller will be the amount of that which will be past mending. This government can not much longer play a game in which it stakes all and its enemies stake nothing. Those enemies must understand that they cannot experiment for ten years, trying to destroy the government, and, if they fail, still come back into the Union unhurt."

Others were less vindictive. General George B. McClellan, head of the Union armies, wrote to August that "my profound regret is that the administration could not be induced to act in accordance with your views. Some such policy as that you urged must yet be adopted or we are lost."

When August showed him Lincoln's reply, McClellan added, "I fear that Mr. L. is himself engaged in breaking the rest of the eggs in the basket."

Nevertheless Lincoln ruled the roost, and August tried to repair his relationship with him by writing that of course he supported the President, but it was important not to give the Confederates the feeling that the North was trying to destroy the South.

"While the rebel leaders can hold up to their misguided followers the idea that the North intends their conquest and subjugation, I fear there is very little hope for any Union demonstration in the revolted states, however great the dissatisfaction against the Richmond government might be."

Eventually North and South would have to negotiate; why not now?

After all, August reminded the President, the Union was not fighting *against* the South as much as it was fighting *for* the Union.

"They must become convinced," August emphasized, "that we are fighting only for the Union."

McClellan was thirty-four years old when he was given the command of the Union Armies. He wore his auburn hair cut so short, combed so neatly, and kept so glossy that from a distance it looked as though it were painted on his head. His face seemed too young for his droopy red moustache and his little fox tail of a goatee; but his eyes, piercing and troubled, were old for his face. He was called the Little Napoleon; and with too little humor he accepted the tag, even posing with his hand tucked into his tunic. August thought he was the only man who could save the country.

For a while Lincoln thought so too. The President would hang around McClellan's rooms offering advice, expressing concern, telling anecdotes, until McClellan, beginning to find his commander-in-chief a pest, hid out with his friend Edwin M. Stanton. Stanton, a Democrat, was a chubby man with a long, frizzled beard that was striped down the middle with white like a skunk's tail. In January 1862 Lincoln made Stanton secretary of war; and Stanton, jealous of anyone whose power rivaled his own, turned on his former friend McClellan and began undermining even further Lincoln's failing faith in the general. In March, less than half a year after being made general-in-chief, McClellan was relieved of command of all but the Army of the Potomac, the troops he had been so cautious in advancing.

Stanton had thought that Lincoln, with his long arms and slouch, looked like a gorilla; he had sneered at his "imbicillity"; and he had made fun of a sweat stain on the back of Lincoln's shirt that he claimed looked appropriately like a map of Africa. But once Stanton was made secretary of war his contempt gave way to sycophancy and finally to respect— although his respect, while honest, seemed to be reserved for power. He snarled at inferiors and equals, once flabbergasting Secretary of Navy Gideon Welles with his nastiness and scorn. Not only was Stanton vindictive, dictatorial, and intolerant, but he acted as though those qualities were virtues when exercised in the defense of what he thought was right. He imposed an unprecedented military censorship over the country's newspapers, opened private mail, and took control of the nation's telegraph system in order to screen any message he wanted, including personal communications between husband and wife. Stanton was Lincoln's son of a bitch, a man so mercurial, so seemingly irrational at times—giving orders one day that he angrily would contradict the next—that many were led to believe he was either a madman or a traitor. Or both.

August, who at first had said that the "appointment of Stanton gives me some hope that the President appreciates the necessity of" placing Democrats in high positions in order to create a bipartisan war administration, was appalled at Stanton's excesses. Within a matter of months after Stanton took office, August wrote to Lincoln that "right or wrong, people have lost confidence" in Stanton and urged his replacement.

Lincoln sent Stanton the letter; considering Stanton's character, this was the equivalent of giving an attack dog a sniff of some future victim's blood. The correspondence between August and the President came to an end.

The administration had revealed not the "wisdom and moderation" August had hoped to find but instead a sternness, even vindictiveness, he had not expected. So although he continued to write occasional letters to Weed and Seward, August turned his attention to the off-year elections, working to replace Republicans who seemed determined to humiliate the South with Democrats who would accept the South's return—when it came—with the tolerance due a prodigal son.

To be successful the Democrats would need a reliable newspaper. Samuel Barlow found one that was looking for investors: the *New York World*, a fairly new newspaper run by Manton Marble, a twenty-seven-year-old poet and free-lance writer.

At first August resisted Barlow's suggestion to buy the *World*.

"While I fully agree with you about the importance of securing so influential and able an organ," he told Barlow, "I must confess that I begin to feel that I have done individually as much as my means permit. The sums which I have spent for the last two years in support of the Democratic Party would surprise even you, and what good have they done?"

The initial modest contributions that he did send for the purchase of the *World,* out of a feeling of loyalty to Barlow as much as out of solidarity with the party, August felt were "like all money spent in that direction, a useless sacrifice."

Soon, however, Barlow's arguments won August, who, once converted, enthusiastically supported the plan. During the negotiations over the investment in the *World,* Marble and August courted each other. Marble sent the Belmonts presents like "the charming novel" he gave to Caroline; and August, reminding Marble that "exchange is no robbery," reciprocated with presents like "a bit of Cuban product which I just received." Marble had a passion for Havana cigars.

If they fell out of contact for a few days, one or the other would stop in at the Century Club, to which August had sponsored Marble. If they still did not meet, they would send each other plaintive notes.

"I have been at the club, hoping to see you," August wrote; "but you like the Democratic party nowadays are *nowhere.*"

During the fall of 1862 August worked to rally the Democratic party, to make it somewhere. At the state convention in Albany he helped former governor Horatio Seymour be nominated for governor.

Seymour had been so handsome and gallant as a young man that decades later aging women would remember him with a flutter. In 1862 he was fifty-one years old; his hairline was receding, giving him a high-domed look; his large, heavy-lidded eyes were beginning to be sunken and shadowed, but his chin still had a dimple, as though when his face was being forged the Maker had given it a tap with a small hammer.

"In my youth I valued heads above hearts," Seymour once said; "in my old age I value hearts above heads."

He did not particularly want the nomination August urged him to take. In fact, he had turned his attention from politics to business, jokingly telling a friend that he had given up "ambition for avarice." And he told his sister that he hoped when she heard of his nomination she would not "think me a hopeless vagrant. I did what I could to avoid it but I was forced on, but now that I am in the field, I want a sharp bitter fight. I do not care about my election. . . . But I want the opponents of the bad men who have brought our country into its deplorable condition"—the bad men he was referring to were not just the secessionists but also Lincoln and Stanton, whose actions in the defense of the Union he thought were often unconstitutional—"to be so much aroused as to make themselves felt and respected. If this is done we shall have a strong, compact party that can defy violence and can keep fanatics in check. We live in a fighting world and in times like these they are most safe who take strong grounds and call around them strong friends. I enjoy abuse at this time, for I mean to indulge in it."

August returned from the convention feeling that Seymour's prediction was true. The former governor's nomination had left the New York Democratic party strong and compact. He would find that Seymour's further prediction was also true, although perhaps in a different way than the once-and-future governor had intended. When Seymour had said he would indulge in abuse, he may have meant he expected to enjoy abusing his opponents; but his statement would have described the campaign better if he had meant *indulge* to carry its other meaning. Before the campaign was over he and his backers like August would receive so much abuse, they would have to learn to revel in it.

Barlow and other friends tried to convince August to run for Congress. August admitted that "my nomination would give more strength to our ticket than" that of his competitors; but he wanted to be elected on his merits. He refused to make any deals.

"It would have gratified me to receive the nomination," he told Barlow, "but I do not feel anxious enough for it to make any bargains with my opponent. If our district thinks him a better and more available man, my friends must consider me not to be a candidate."

If August had run he hardly could have been more vilified than he was in any case. August supported Seymour. Seymour was anti-Lincoln. And Republicans confused being anti-Lincoln with being anti-Union.

"Alas for next Tuesday's election!" wailed Republican George Templeton Strong, whose dislike and distrust of August had matured. "There is danger—great and pressing danger—of a disaster more telling than all our Bull Run battles and Peninsular strategy," the former a Union defeat, the latter a strategic failure; "the resurrection to political life and power of the . . . Barlows . . . and Belmonts, who have been dead and buried and working only underground, if at all, for eighteen months, and every one of whom well deserves hanging as an ally of rebellion."

Strong, an ardent supporter of the administration, once apostrophized Lincoln, "O Abraham, *O mon Roi!*"—oddly unrepublican terms. He admitted that the government had been making "irregular arrests" that were "utterly arbitrary" and that "not one of the many hundreds illegally arrested and locked up for months has been publicly charged," but he defended the practice by explaining that the arrests were "demanded by the pressure of an unprecedented national crisis" that "justified any measure, however extreme."

This was the dangerous, tyrannical logic that frightened August and turned him against the administration and its supporters like Strong, who declared that if the arrests were bad policy it was not because they were unconstitutional but because they gave "traitors and Seymourites an apology for opposing the government."

Seymour was elected, as were a good number of other Democrats within and without New York State. August, so far from being anti-Union that he worried about the effect his party's success would have on England and France, wrote to Lionel Rothschild in London and James de Rothschild in Paris to correct any European "misapprehension with regard to the intentions of the conservative Democratic party of the North, which has just carried the elections." The Democrats were Unionists, and the party "will not accept of any compromise which has not the reconstruction of but one government over all the thirty-four states for its basis."

August also tried to keep other Democrats from straying in their loyalties. In fact, knowing that the appearance of disloyalty could have almost as bad an effect as actual disloyalty, he tried to keep other Democrats from even seeming to stray, although since it was a ticklish task he often sheathed his concern in humor.

"Why did you not come to Newport when you were so near to us?" he asked Barlow. "The fact is, I am sorry to say, that you feel more attracted by your old secesh friends than by good Unionists like myself.

"Seriously speaking," August continued, shading the joke but not his meaning, "I think you make a mistake by associating your name with men of that stamp, who are disloyal and unreservedly express their sympathy with the Rebels. I tell you this as a friend, because I know that you do not share their treasonable views, and I trust you will take my advice as kindly as it is given."

However, Republicans like George Templeton Strong ignored August's pro-Union, even proadministration, actions and misinterpreted his attempts at conciliation.

Then, on January 1, 1863, Lincoln formally issued the Emancipation Proclamation, which freed all slaves in areas that were in rebellion against the United States. Although this edict did not affect slaves of loyalists, if effectively destroyed any chance of the Confederate States returning to the Union willingly. The North would have to conquer the South. Conciliators like August were isolated even more, made into even better targets for abuse.

To August everything the administration had done seemed ruinous. Lincoln had interfered with McClellan when he was supreme commander of the armies and had demoted him on the eve of the campaign that Mc-Clellan had been planning ever since getting the command, a campaign that might have ended the war.

The Treasury was hemorrhaging money. August feared the nation might go bankrupt. Even if the country were not ruined, even if the North won the war, the administration's despotic behavior—saving the Union by destroying the Constitution—might make that victory Pyrrhic. It was pointless to free the slaves only to enslave everyone, black and white, by creating a government that used the excuse of national emergency to break fundamental laws. Making illegal arrests violated the Fifth Amendment. Holding prisoners without trial violated the Sixth Amendment. One Union general had even prohibited his men from reading the *New York World,* which may not have violated the letter of the First Amendment—Congress had made no law preventing the distribution of the newspaper—but certainly violated its spirit.

August tried to organize what he described as "a powerful demonstration in our city and state in order to compel the administration to a change of men and measures." Stanton especially had to go. He once told a man who had come to plead the case of a friend in jail on suspicion of treason, "If I tap that little bell, I can send *you* to a place where you will never hear the dogs bark. And by heaven I'll do it if you say another word!" So much for trial by jury. "Individuals," Stanton said another time, "are nothing."

August believed individuals were everything. August did not think Stanton and Lincoln—who kept Stanton at his post—were trying to subvert the Republic; but he feared that their fanatical devotion to the Union had led them astray. Their excesses had to be curbed. But in the climate of fear their high-handed actions had created, people were hesitant to do anything that could be called traitorous—and people were called traitors for very little. Most of those August approached about the mass meeting were sympathetic but afraid to participate, which made it all the more urgent, August believed, to show those who disagreed with the adminstration's policies that there was room in a democratic society, even one that was at war, for honest dissent. August was trying to lead a loyal opposition at a time when any opposition was suspected of being disloyal.

The mass meeting did not succeed. Perhaps a private meeting would. In February, August and others disillusioned with the Lincoln administration met at Delmonico's to set up the Society for the Diffusion of Political Knowledge. Its first director was the famous lawyer Samuel J. Tilden. Like August, Tilden was a wine connoisseur; in photographs he often looks as though he has just been given a sip of vinegary *vin ordinaire:* the wings of his large nostrils flared, upper lip slightly lifted, eyes watery. When he talked politics he tended to put his mouth as close to his companion's ear as possible and whisper. With August and Barlow he controlled the *New York World.*

News of the private meeting leaked to the press, and the *New York Evening Post* immediately accused the society's members of plotting Lincoln's overthrow—which in fact they were doing, although by legal, not sinister, means.

Republican suspicions of August were further fed ten days later. August gave a ball, "one of those stupid, diluted masquerades," reported George Templeton Strong, who heard about it from his cousin Charles Strong; ". . . all the women are masked and all the men exposed, like a fleet of old fashioned line-of-battleships encountering a squadron of ironclads."

At the ball a young English marquis, Spencer Compton Hartington, was approached by a beautiful lady, masked like the other ladies present with an elaborate domino. She asked if he would take her arm. He did willingly. She was fascinating, seductive. But she insisted on an exchange —her company for his wearing her colors. She took out a ribbon. He pinned it to his lapel.

The lady was the notorious secessionist Mrs. Antonio Yznaga; her colors were the colors of the Confederacy; and her ribbon was a small Rebel flag. According to one account, she dared him to wear it when he was introduced to McClellan. Lord Hartington took up the challenge and, Rebel-ribboned, went to meet the general, who, evidently not wishing to dignify the insult with any response, ignored the flag, made small talk, and turned away.

Strong's cousin Charles was appalled and went to find August to object to his foreign guest's behavior; but before August reached Lord

Hartington to tell him to remove the flag, John Heckscher, a young lieutenant who had been wounded in the war, bumped into or grabbed the Englishman.

"It was intentional, sir," Heckscher said, "quite intentional."

"Hee-haw-w-w-what's the matter?" Lord Hartington said and, walking on, added, "It's weally vewy extawawdinawy."

Heckscher followed and jostled the Englishman again, once more repeating that he was acting intentionally.

"I want to insult you, sir," Heckscher said.

Lord Hartington stammered something, excused himself from Mrs. Yznaga, and left the ballroom with Heckscher.

"If you do not instantly take that thing out of your buttonhole," Heckscher said, indicating the Confederate flag, "I'll pull it out."

Lord Hartington took out the little flag, slipped it into his pocket, and according to one report apologized, pleading ignorance of American politics (or at least of American passions) and explaining he had not meant to offend. The apology, given the situation, was dishonest: He had knowingly insulted the country of which he was a guest and compromised August, his host.

Other officers on hearing of the incident were ready to exact a more painful apology. August found Lord Hartington, hustled him out of the house and into the carriage house, and saw him off.

"I have received nothing but the most cordial kindness from every Englishman to whom I had at any time shown even the most trifling attention in America," August later would recall. "There was but one single striking exception, and that was Lord Hartington. He behaved like a hog to me."

Unaware of Mrs. Yznaga's dare, Strong blamed the Englishman's actions on August. Since Lord Hartington "had been consorting with . . . Belmont . . . ," Strong reasoned, "he naturally thought sympathy with rebellion *the thing* in New York. Pity it's wrong and disreputable to put incidents like this into the newspapers. An ingenious operator could use this affair so as to do much good. McClellan's indifference, the ire of the young lieutenant . . . , the bloated British aristocrat flaunting a rebel flag in a gorgeous ballroom, crowded with the millionaires of New York—but snubbed and suppressed and driven to apologize! The subject has immense capabilities."

Another subject with an even greater capability to defame August would appear by spring and would be used by more ingenious operators than Strong.

In February, August had to go to Cuba on business. He decided to take August, Jr., with him. The trip took five days. They were lucky to have good weather for the first few days and wonderful weather for the last two.

"We went to some of the plantations of the wealthiest nabobs of the island," August wrote from Cuba to one English friend; "and it is really difficult to believe that within five days' sail from New York, people of wealth and education should live in such a state of semi-barbarism as I have seen there. All this is the direct consequence of slavery, which exists on the Spanish sugar plantation in the most revolting form. It is exercised with the most inhuman cruelty on the poor black, and degenerates the white both morally and physically."

In writing to Lionel Rothschild, August allowed his indignation freer rein: "Let your statesmen and Southern sympathizers go to Cuba and see the fearful barbarity and misery of slavery there, and I fear they would find it more difficult to satisfy their consciences as easily as they seem to have satisfied their constituents for the course they have pursued toward our people in our hour of trouble." As passionate as he ever became in his letters, he told Lionel that if England had helped the Union "she would have secured forever the abolition of slavery throughout the world, while now instead she is assisting in riveting the fetters on the poor African for another century."

When August returned to New York he found himself the subject of the most vicious rumor spread about him yet. A friend with the Dickensian—and inappropriate—name of Craven had been told by Dr. John Charles Peters that sometime during the previous year August had gone to Richmond to scheme with the enemy. Craven heatedly denied the charge and said he intended to repeat the slander to August.

It had been more than two decades since August had last dueled, but he could not ignore this attack on his honor. Not only was the rumor scurrilous, but for Peters to have spread it when August was out of town, unable to defend himself, was base.

August called on Peters and in his most correct, most icy manner demanded an explanation.

Peters claimed he did not know what August was talking about. He vaguely could recall some conversation with Craven and that Craven had said he would report something to August—what it was had slipped his mind.

August suggested that he try very hard to remember.

Peters wrote to Craven an apparently disingenuous letter asking if Craven happened to recollect their conversation.

Craven did and met with Peters to remind him.

"After the conversation which you have had this morning with Mr. Craven," August told Peters, "your memory has doubtlessly been refreshed. I beg therefore again to ask you whether you mentioned to Mr. Craven 'that I had unlawfully addressed proposals of peace negotiations to the Rebel authorities in Richmond' from your own knowledge of such being the fact or whether you were informed by other parties of such being the case. In that event, I hope you will not hesitate to give me the name of your informant."

If Craven started the rumor he would have to admit it, in which case August could demand satisfaction. If he had not started the rumor he would have to take responsibility for spreading it, in which case August could still demand satisfaction. Or he would have to betray the person who told it to him, and August could demand satisfaction of him.

"The charge conveyed in your conversation with Mr. Craven is of so grave a nature," said August, "that I must claim the right of demanding an early reply to my inquiry."

Peters neither owned up to the rumor nor betrayed a friend. He sidestepped the issue, ducking and weaving and changing his story like a coward.

Peters justified his actions by explaining that "there was a period when the city and the newspapers were very much excited about you and other gentlemen; it was a matter of common conversation that proposals of peace had been made from some persons in the North not connected with the government to some parties in the South. Your name and that of Mr. Barlow were mentioned. I had nothing to do with the origin of this rumor," here Peters caught himself, not wishing to give further offense, "or rather falsehood, as your conversation and note fully convince me that it was. I had nothing to do with the circulation of it. Mr. Craven was probably the first person that I mentioned it to and doubtlessly very nearly, if not quite, the last."

By the end of the explanation Peters became so knotted up in his own contradictions it was obvious to August that he was dealing not with a man of honor but with a moral contortionist.

August pointed out that Peters's "reference to newspaper rumors is unfortunate, because I never knew before nor do I know now that any journal had connected my name with so disgraceful a transaction."

In other words, he was calling Peters a liar.

"I had hoped that you would be able to name your authority for a statement which so seriously affected my character as a gentleman and a citizen," August continued; "and, as you have failed to do so, I am compelled to say to you as I should have done to your informant, if you had fortunately recollected his name"—the sentence almost sneers—"that the whole story is false in every particular."

Peters backed down ever further.

"I honor the indignation with which you repelled the charge," he said, "and have great sympathy for the annoyance you have so forcibly expressed."

But like a man who having scrambled for safety shouts over his shoulder that he will let his attackers off easy this time, Peters added a postscript: "Nothing but a sense of injury could justify the tone of parts of your notes to me, and that alone prevents me from further alluding to it."

August found Peters's behavior beneath contempt, but he was satisfied with the apology. More serious, the charges of disloyalty had continued to spread, becoming embellished as they went. To stop them August wrote directly to Seward.

"In order to substantiate their malignant calumny," August wrote, "they [August's enemies] have stated that there were evidences in the State Department of my having been in confidential communication with the Rebel authorities at Richmond. I have never for one moment wavered in my devotion to the Union, and I have left nothing undone which could strengthen our government in its legitimate efforts to crush the rebellion and restore its supremacy over the revolted states, and I never have had any direct or indirect communication with any of the Rebel leaders in the South or in Europe. If there is therefore any such evidence in the State Department in the matter alluded to above I declare it a forgery, but I suppose that such a thing does not exist."

CHAPTER TWENTY-SIX

THAT SEASON August and Caroline stayed late at Newport.

"When are you coming to New York?" wrote George Bancroft, the historian, former cabinet member, and antislavery Democrat. "You can have no idea of how gloomy the Fifth Avenue has been looking, till now it prepares to smile as the time of your coming draws near."

After staying in town just long enough to give their ball and make the proper obeisance to custom (which this year included sending a wedding present—Caroline chose a set of silver "chaste charms"—to P. T. Barnum's famous midget, Charles Sherwood Stratton, called General Tom Thumb, and his new wife, Lavinia Warren), the Belmonts returned early in the Spring to Newport, where on the evening of July 19, 1863, their last child, Raymond Rodgers, nicknamed Poor Dolly, was born.

The Belmonts were fortunate not to be in New York that summer, because on Monday, July 13, the city exploded in the worst riot in its history. In March, Lincoln had signed a draft law that was put into effect in New York in mid-July when a clerk at the Ninth District draft office at Third Avenue near Forty-sixth Street reached into a drum and pulled out a slip of paper with the first conscript's name: William Jones. Jones was present at the drawing and took his position at the head of the list—and in history—in good spirits.

The drum turned all day. Before the office—one of two in the city— closed for the weekend, 1,236 men were called up. All Sunday resentment brewed. Very few people approved of the draft. It was an alien custom, another example of the increasingly centralized power of Washington. Not only did the law seem peremptory, it was discriminatory. Anyone with $300 could buy a substitute. $300 was fifteen weeks' pay for a lucky laborer with a good job, and less than what a wealthy man might pay at a first-class bordello for a second-class prostitute.

On Monday morning a mob that had been marching and gathering strength since dawn attacked and burned the Ninth District draft office. By noon the rioters, about fifty thousand by now, had torched a number of other buildings. Thick yellowish clouds of smoke billowed from the windows of the burning buildings. Looters broke into stores to steal axes and guns. Bands of rioters cut telegraph wires, tore up railroad tracks, and stormed railroad yards and stage and omnibus depots to close down public transportation. Mobs ransacked and burned the New York State Armory and the Colored Orphan Asylum. They blamed the draft on the war and the war on the blacks, so when they found one little black girl who had failed to escape cowering under a bed, they killed her.

By midafternoon various mobs that had been spread out across the city converged on Broadway and, now an army, marched on police headquarters. Around Bleecker Street the police charged the mob's front line. swinging heavy locustwood clubs. Two other police detachments attacked from the rear. The mob, although outnumbering the police twenty-five to one, was not as organized or as well armed. Boxed in by the buildings on either side of the street, the rioters could not use their superior numbers to their advantage. The police, like farmers scything a field, cut down row after row of rioters. After fifteen minutes the fight was over; the rioters, routed; the police, for the time being, victorious.

The day had been sultry. The night was hot. The air smelled of ashes and scorched flesh. What had started as an antidraft riot was becoming more and more a crusade against blacks. Black neighborhoods were invaded by roving bands of whites. In New Bowery whites chased some blacks to the roof of a building and then set the building on fire; when the blacks jumped to the street, the whites clubbed them to death. Another gang attacked a Water Street brothel and stripped and tortured the prostitutes, because they had hidden a black servant. Even the legendary black madam Sue the Turtle was murdered.

For the next few days the city was under siege. Mobs chased blacks through the streets, hanging those they caught from lampposts and setting fires underneath the dangling victims. But just as the riot had changed character once—from antidraft to antiblack—it changed character again, becoming more and more a looting spree. The first day relatively few stores had been plundered; on subsequent days rioters broke in where they could, sometimes being caught by the police as they were at Brooks Brothers in the process of trying on their stolen duds. Police were backed up by local militia units, which using howitzers breached the rioters' barricades. By the end of the week Union troops, exhausted from their recent battle at Gettysburg, arrived in the city. The riot was over.

The rumors, however, were just starting. The riot had seemed more like a revolt. It had been too organized to have been spontaneous, organized enough for the rioters to have attempted to isolate the city by cutting the telegraph wires. Men on horseback had been spotted rallying the mobs. And one of the leaders of an attack was a young man who, having been impaled on the spike of an iron fence, was discovered to be wearing under his dirty overalls "fine cassemere pants, a handsome rich vest and a fine linen short." Obviously he was not a common laborer; and some thought the riots were the work of the Copperhead conspiracy that had coordinated outbreaks of violence from Massachusetts to Illinois. Since no conspiracy was ever proved, anyone could be suspected.

August had argued for the draft, but he now admitted that enforced conscription was a dangerous policy.

The law had to be upheld; but once "the ringleaders of the late disgraceful scenes" had been punished, August thought it might be judicious of the federal government to avoid enforcing the draft in New York.

"In a city like New York," August told Seward, "with an opposition vote of over 60,000, the desperate character of a portion of whom we have just seen, it would be madness to push matters under a fatal reliance on the bayonet."

If Washington insisted on going through with a New York draft, the city might be faced with something even more serious than a riot; as August confided, "I know large and *powerful organizations,* which had not at all participated in the riots, are prepared to withstand the draft at all hazard."

August thought it more advisable for the President to approach "our different governors" in a "confidential and straightforward" way and ask their help in raising volunteers. He had no doubt the governors would cooperate, because they "themselves must be very anxious to carry out all measures which will save their respective states from the horrors of anarchy and mob-law."

The riots in New York and other cities had been an indication of Northern sentiment not just on the draft but also on the war itself. Furthermore, August's most recent letters from Europe indicated that England and France seemed closer than they had ever been to siding with the Rebels.

Since pro-Confederate sentiment seemed on the rise in the North and Europe just when Union victories were putting the most pressure on the South, August thought "the best and most statesmanlike step to be taken by the President would be the issuing of a proclamation addressed to the *people* of the revolted states, inviting them to return to their allegiance to the United States, to withdraw from the armies of the so-called Confederate government, and to elect members of Congress and Senators to represent them in Washington." Lincoln should also announce a general amnesty and revoke the confiscation and Emancipation acts.

Although August's disgust with slavery had intensified during his recent trip to Cuba, he would have endorsed Lincoln's comment to Horace Greeley: "If I could save the Union without freeing *any* slave, I would do it; and, if I could save it by freeing *all* the slaves, I would do it; and, if I could save it by freeing some and leaving others alone, I would also do that." The survival of the Union—August believed—was more important than the abolition of slavery; and Southerners would not abandon the

Confederacy and return to the United States as long as the Emancipation act was in force.

Seward reportedly had just such a plan in mind. But Lincoln could not withdraw the Emancipation Proclamation. So even though the rabidly anti-Confederate Secretary of the Treasury Chase responded to August's letter (which Seward had showed him) by agreeing that reasonable men certainly would favor leniency to contrite Rebels, August again was frustrated in his attempt to draw the administration into a position of conciliation.

Early in October, August had to go to Europe to discuss the future of his company's relationship with the Rothschilds. Christmas and Matthiessen were leaving the business. It was time to take stock.

Caroline boarded the ship, a Cunarder called the *China*, with August and stayed until just before sailing. After she left, August chatted with the captain and some acquaintances. Then, feeling more despondent than ever before in his life, he went down to his stateroom and wept.

Being away from Caroline and the children, the war, the attacks on his honor he had endured, the change in his business . . . everything oppressed him. Crying relieved him somewhat, but he still felt numb, disoriented, and sick.

He found two other whist players with whom he played tedious three-handed games. He worked on the bottle of excellent brandy a friend had given him as a bon voyage present. He read. His appetite improved, and he took up some of the slack time doing "full justice to breakfast, dinner, and supper, not to forget luncheon, and then passing a good portion of my time in a legitimate manner," presumably—August was not above ribaldry—in the w.c.

The pleasant weather, however, failed to lighten August's spirits and, as though giving in to his dark mood, became stormy. The ship, like all screw-steamers, rolled so terribly that he could not even shave.

Tormented by headaches and insomnia he wandered the decks, sprayed by seas that slapped against the ship's side. In his morbid imagination trivial concerns cast enormous shadows. Although he assumed the children's dancing classes were still profitable, each new step learned a dividend, he fretted about how August, Jr., was doing at school and he hoped that "Perry is more studious with his piano." He had forgotten to tell Caroline to go down to Lafayette Place to examine the just-completed little statue of Oliver, which he had seen before leaving and which he thought was "a much better piece . . . than I expected the poor devil [of an artist] capable of making." He was afraid Caroline would not amuse herself in his absence and wished that she would take the time to go horseback riding in the mornings in the park with one of their servants or Belle if she did not have "a desirable beau" to accompany her. And he worried that things might not go smoothly with the servants. Shortly before he had left, Caroline had let her seamstress and dressing maid go and found a replacement, who might turn out to be as difficult as her predecessor. When a servant was insolent, sullen, or unhappy, Caroline always took it as a personal failure, because—in the nineteenth century's secular interpretation of the Great Chain of Being—she was responsible for the servants just as August was responsible for her. But she took such troubles too much to heart, August thought. In the predatory way that anxiety stalks the world searching for something—anything—to pounce on, August even fussed at length over an insignificant decorating issue. In an attempt to cheer August up, the ship's captain had given him some flowers in square china pots, the kind Caroline had admired on her last trip to London, and August surrendered to the obsession with detail that can be both an escape from and a burrowing into dread. He spent hours figuring out how he would mount them when he got back home. The pots had to be set in boxes made of black walnut. The boxes had to be put on pedestals of a certain height so the pots would "show well over the window frames." And because they could be seen through the window, the pots had to be attached to the boxes and the boxes had to be attached to the pedestals in such a way that when the windows were open, someone could not simply reach in and carry them off. Like a chess player trying to foresee every threat and trap, August followed the combinations his life presented to him as far as he could go, trying to make sure everything was protected.

Suddenly one day August saw bearing down on them a brig that seemed to be out of control and about to crash into them amidships. The brig, much larger than the *China*, miraculously passed right under its bowsprit, escaping collision by minutes. "A fearful sight," said August; and evidently galvanized by the brush with death, he determined to change his life.

He started planning improvements on their country place, vowing— as he wrote to Caroline very soon after the averted accident—"if we live, we shall have a good deal of real pleasure and comfort from it. In fact, I have thought a good deal about the future, and I am coming to all kinds of conclusions, which I think you will approve of and which I trust may insure us a more substantial and real enjoyment of what God has so kindly and mercifully vouchsafed to us, than in some of the ways which we have adopted hitherto."

In confiding his resolutions to Caroline, August used the word *real* twice to help describe a new quality he wanted to cultivate in their lives— "real pleasure and comfort, real enjoyment"—as though he felt that the pleasure, comfort, and enjoyment they previously had experienced was somehow make-believe.

August was too weary to dine with Lionel Rothschild the evening he arrived in London but joined him *en famille* the next night and was encircled by politicians the next.

"I was delighted to see a decided change of opinion in our favor," August told Caroline; although, as he wrote Seward, "we must not shut our eyes to the fact that the taking of Vicksburg and our successes last summer have a good deal to do with the attitude of the British cabinet and that any serious reverses of our armies in Virginia or Tennessee would be followed by pressure on the Ministry for recognition not only by the opposition at home but also by France."

Lionel was personally kind but professionally quarrelsome. He was irritable with August because of the suspicion that, as August told Caroline, "I have realized immense profits by contracts with the United States government and other business, which I might have given to the House of Rothschild. This interferes very much with that confidence which is indispensable for our mutual relations."

The negotiations with Lionel were irksome. Again August was plunged into despair.

"I am more and more convinced that the best thing for me to do is to give up business altogether and to devote my time hereafter to the education of the children and to the management of our own affairs. In a few days I shall go to Paris and then I shall definitely make up my mind what to do. In any event, you may count on my returning by the *Scotia*" —which was due to leave Europe within a month—"if I live."

Paris was cold and foggy, the city dissolving into the mist as though it were a dream from which August was trying to wake. The political climate was worse.

"The place is filled with secessionists," August complained.

"I am making myself bad blood every day," he told Caroline.

August felt increasingly isolated from the generally pro-Southern American community in the city. Many of his French friends were out of town in Rome, which seemed to be the destination of that year's fashionable migration. And the Rothschilds, like their relatives across the Channel, were being both charming and difficult. August certainly could not relax and enjoy himself with them.

The franc fell one percent, making "old James as cross as a bear." Alphonse was "as cold as ever." And Salomon showed a surprising "want of candor and friendliness, which shocked me. The only excuse I can make for him is that he seems to be very much preoccupied, and I fear he is again head over ears engaged in stock gambling. If his father knew or even suspected anything of the scrapes out of which I helped him in America he would disinherit him."

So although the Rothschilds often invited August to dine and took him hunting at their new estate at Ferrières, he spent a great deal of time alone, chosing to nurse his melancholy rather than dispel it.

"I have not been at all well for the past two or three days past," he wrote to Caroline, the awkward repetition of the word *past* betraying his confusion. He usually wrote with pride in his mastery of English and the clarity of his logic. "My old complaint of sleepless nights and horrid dreams has come back again."

August caught a cold, and his eyes swelled so much that he could hardly see. The negotiations with the Rothschilds seemed endless and hopeless. He told James that he was considering retiring. That rumor spread into the American community in Paris and was interpreted to mean that August was abandoning the United States. Belmont always was a foreigner—the expatriate Americans said—and he could not be expected to stand by the Union in its time of trouble: an ironic attack, since most of the attackers, who smugly felt more American than August, had forsaken the Union for the Confederacy.

Caroline's letters, long delayed, finally began to arrive regularly, and for the first time since he had left New York, August's gloom lifted.

Caroline's letters had the casual and familiar tone of bedtime conversation: snatches of the day recapitulated, analyzed, and enjoyed without order, the non sequiturs revealing the mind's dreamy progress through the immediate past. The children were all well. "The baby is off the sick list, but he is looking delicate, which is all owing to his teething." Rickie and Jeannie had a girlfriend staying at the house. "Augy wishes to drop his German, but I think that I will not consent to it; it will be too bad to have him lose all he knows now, and I am sure that he is lazy."

Except for two unavoidable parties Caroline stayed at home, avoiding friends by retiring early. She even cut short her carriage rides in the park "to come home and wait for the mail. I hope, dear August, that by this time you are enjoying Paris and having lovely Spring weather and that you feel well. How lovely everything must look there now, at the Bois, on the Champs Elysées. I know that you will bring me loads of things, but sometimes cheap nouveautés add more to a dress than expensive things." As part of her war effort Caroline had vowed to avoid extravagance as much as possible. She thought that in a time of national crisis everyone should be somewhat austere. "I am afraid," she told August, "you think me foolish on the subject."

August, however, was not in the mood for voluntary austerity. For a few days after hearing from Caroline he was buoyant. If he had shopped in London to furnish the empty spaces in his life, he began shopping in Paris out of a growing—if temporary—exuberance, that dangerous quality his father had deplored.

"Your request not to get you any evening dresses comes too late," August told Caroline; "and I flatter myself that when you see your toilettes you will reconsider your rash resolve not to go out this winter."

He hired half a dozen designers, advised them (suggesting to one some "black lace over white, thin stuff" and some white lace on light pink), made sure they did not duplicate each other's work, and exacted promises from them all "not to send anything to America this Winter, which is at all like Caroline's dresses."

"In fact," he told Caroline, "I think I shall receive your full approbation for my selections, which will be more than a sufficient reward for my trouble"—although, apprehension mingling with pride, he admitted that "if they are not pretty the responsibility rests alone with me, as I did not consult anybody."

August brought as much intensity to his shopping rampage as he did to everything else with which he got involved; and in gathering up clothes for his wife he took so much care that he seemed an American Pygmalion fashioning his Galatea at long distance.

He bought presents for Belle. Bibs for the baby. Frocks for the girls. Hats for the boys. He even found a tiny gun for Perry.

"My room looks like a large ready-made clothes shop," August wrote to Caroline after surveying the stacks of boxes strewn about his suite. "I shall have a nice lot of trunks and fear a good deal of trouble at our customs house."

But reviewing his extravagances, even his most outrageous purchase (a 1,000-franc veil), August sank back into a comfortable and comforting amusement at his excesses. He argued that even the most expensive item cost less in Paris than it would in New York.

"I am like the young Englishman, who, finding that champagne was four shillings cheaper in Paris than in London, drank every day five bottles in order to save a pound daily."

August's romp through the shops of Paris left him spent. His spirits again sagged. His cold got worse. His spasms of longing for Caroline became more and more frequent.

"Oh, how I wish it was the 21st of November," he sighed, "and I was on board the *Scotia* and she was steaming for New York."

The Rothschilds' change of attitude failed to cheer him. James and Alphonse remained "hard customers to deal with," refusing to revise what August thought were their rather odd ideas about American business. But August had found them very solicitous ever since he had told them he was thinking of quitting. In fact, as August wrote to Caroline, "they would not listen to my going out of business. Both the old man and Alphonse behaved very kindly and cordially during all the negotiations, and they expressed repeatedly their gratification at my having come to Europe." Only Salomon, still suffering from his guilty conscience over his American escapades, failed to warm up. August had been right in suspecting that Salomon was preoccupied with risky speculations. When Salomon died within half a year of August's stay in Paris, it would be said that he "died . . . of the excitement of gambling on the stock exchange. . . . Imagine it; a Rothschild dead of a paroxysm of excitement over money."

By the time August left Paris for London, not only had he not retired but, as he wrote to Caroline, he was "afraid that I shall be much more tied down to business hereafter than I have been hitherto, and I am sure that neither you nor I will like that."

From her letters Caroline also seemed to be skidding back into a depression. Her loneliness overwhelmed her memory, and childlike she had begun to read in August's necessary absence rejection and abandonment. August scolded her for her accusations—but scolded gently, knowing that distance can sharpen words written with love.

"I think, my darling," he said, "you do me wrong when you say that I dissuaded you from coming to Europe with me, as on the contrary I was very anxious for you to join me. It is bad enough not to have you with me, without being accused by you that it was *my* fault. So, my dearest little wife, pray don't fret and make yourself ill, be cheerful and content, and we will, if God permits my safe return and that we have health and life, have a jolly time of it for the rest of the Winter."

He closed his letter with a poignant note that proved his love more effectively than all his assurances:

"I feel old as the hills, and it will require all your sweetness, my own darling, to make me feel happy and gay again."

CHAPTER TWENTY-SEVEN

FOR WEEKS after he returned to New York, August was sick, the cold he had brought back from Europe as indestructible as any English tweed. Unable to go to his office, he conducted his business first from his bed and then from his bedside.

He reported to Seward on the tempers of London and Paris. He asked Washington to let the Rothschilds export some tobacco. Lincoln was allowing the Austrian and French governments to pass tobacco shipped from Southern ports through the blockade; the Rothschild shipment had been "*bought and paid for* more than nine months before the Rebellion broke out" and had been sitting in a Southern warehouse for almost three years, enriching the Rebel government with the recently imposed 8 percent per annum tax charged "upon all foreign property within Confederate lines." The request was denied.

August also parried an attack upon his conduct in Paris launched by the Southern sympathizer, sometime business associate, and longtime rival, William W. Corcoran. Corcoran's art collection, his balls (one of which was an annual affair given to both Houses of Congress), dinners, and even wines (especially his Johannisberger) vied with August's. But he lacked August's knack of putting his guests at ease, and so his banquets instead of being festive like August's were as stiff as the meringue on his fabulous desserts.

Corcoran said he had heard that August had accused him of being a traitor.

August replied that the rumor was false, "a malicious calumny invented by some enemy of yours and mine for the purpose of injuring either of us, and I authorize you to brand it as such on my responsibility. I have never said anything of the kind about you here or in Europe."

August granted that their political sympathies diverged. "My own views on our national trouble have never changed," he said. "I have looked upon secession as a great political blunder and crime; but I have studiously endeavored to treat those who differed from me in opinion whenever I have met with them with the courtesy due from one gentleman to another."

As though to prove that August had been guilty of slandering him, Corcoran entered as evidence August's failure to visit him when they both had been in France. August—Corcoran assumed—had avoided the encounter because he had not wanted to face a man he had vilified.

Republicans trying to prove August was a Copperhead often had linked his name with Corcoran's; and August no doubt had been following the advice he had given Barlow—avoid Rebel sympathizers like Corcoran—when he had kept out of Corcoran's way in Paris. But, trying to be discreet, August justified himself by invoking etiquette, the first refuge of a gentleman.

"In my repeated visits to Paris during the past ten years," August told Corcoran, "I have, in common with many of our countrymen, always adhered to the custom of not calling upon American residents until they had left their card upon me. I only make exception in the person of our Minister, and I am sure that most Americans continue to act upon this rule, limiting their first calls to their French acquaintances. This must still be generally considered correct."

Although August was fencing with a tipped foil, he had made a hit. It was a pleasure to counter an attack by taking the attacker to school.

By March 1864 August was fully recovered, his letter to Corcoran of a few weeks earlier no doubt an excellent restorative. The Belmonts were involved in plans for the Metropolitan Fair to be held for the benefit of the United States Sanitary Commission, an organization that raised money for the Union soldiers, particularly the injured and the sick. For a while many Republicans who supported the commission had tried to keep its membership politically pure; but eventually a few of them, George Templeton Strong for one, argued that "we must take in Copperheads . . . like Belmont. . . . They will work the harder for the sick and wounded because they are in a minority of opposition to the war and to government." Although Strong was as usual wrong about August's politics, he was right about August's usefulness to the commission.

As though the commission were plotting sensitive and secret battle strategies, August and Caroline were excluded from its innermost councils and sidelined into humdrum jobs. August was made chairman of "the Committee on Flowers &tc. &tc.," the "&tc. &tc." indicating an absence not a presence of additional duties, while Caroline was asked to give a concert at her house in connection with the fair, which was to be held in Union Square. There was the slight suggestion that she was being politically quarantined; if through any lack of devotion to the Union she muffed the concert, the main event—all the exhibits on Fourteenth Street —would not be affected. And there was more than a slight suggestion that the concert, even if successful, would be merely a sideshow of the circus downtown.

But even if the Belmonts had been rabid Copperheads, their pride would have assured that any effort they made for the commission would be first-class.

August contributed $500 and offered to open his private gallery to the public for a generous admission charge of $1 per person that would go to the commission. The offer was accepted. The press cooed in appreciation.

August's collection was, according to one newspaper, "one of the best in the city, if not the best," and, according to another, "by far the best in the United States"—which must have given him some satisfaction.

"It is a comparatively easy matter for men of wealth to contribute money for a benevolent or patriotic object," a newspaper said. "To volunteer submission to the inconvenience of making strangers free of one's house with the same good end in view, strikes us as liberality of a rarer kind."

Caroline arranged to have appear at her concert a banker's dozen (eleven) of New York's most admired amateur and professional musicians, including the alluring divorcée Fanny Ronalds, who—it was rumored—was accomplished in arts more erotic than the one she would demonstrate that night. The concert would begin with the "Trio in D minor for piano, violin, and violoncello" by August's favorite composer, Mendelssohn, and end with the quartet from *Rigoletto*. Three hundred guests were invited, each one expected to contribute $5 to the commission. Caroline sent out the invitations.

On learning of the arrangements a committee of women from the commission descended on Caroline to inform her that the tickets could not cost more than $2.

Caroline explained that the friends whom she had invited to the concert would be just as happy to give $5 as $2; and since that would increase the contribution to the commission, she could not understand what the committee's objection was based upon.

The committee refused to discuss the matter. Tickets were to cost $2. No more. Otherwise they would withdraw their sanction from the event.

Caroline told them that she was perfectly able to manage her own affairs in her own house in her own way. The committee did not have to feel compromised in the least by her arrangements, since she was happy to dismiss them from any further involvement in the concert—and from her presence.

When August heard what had happened, he took out his wallet, gave Caroline $1,500, and bought all the tickets, which he distributed to everyone on their invitation list.

The concert was a success, the commission was that much richer, and the officious committeewomen were taught, as one newspaper pointed out, that it was unwise to tangle with the combative daughter of a military hero.

The epilogue to the event was less happy.

As a result of either vindictiveness or disorganization Caroline and a few of the other women who had worked for the fair were not given seats of honor on the platform during one of the important commission ceremonies. The insult was so severe that Caroline almost wept when she found out about the slight, and even George Templeton Strong condemned those responsible, although generously chalking it up to ineptness, not malice. Whatever the reason, it was unforgivable. Politics were politics, but gentlemen must always be gentlemen.

For two years August had been squiring General George B. McClellan around New York, taking him to balls and the opera and, with Barlow and Marble, wining and dining him. Clams mignons, truites avec sauce portugaise, terrapine en croustade, poulets de grains truffés. . . . They were fattening him for the political kill.

McClellan was—August, Barlow, and Marble agreed—the best choice for the Democratic presidential nominee in the 1864 election. As early as September 1862 August had been smuggling McClellan into his public speeches, preparing the country to accept him as their leader.

"Out of chaos and confusion," August had told a Newport crowd, "McClellan created one of the finest armies of modern days."

He would be equally successful in bringing order to the nation.

McClellan, however, seemed reluctant to leave the relatively civilized world of warfare for the savagery of politics; and many Democrats objected to him—because he was a Copperhead, because he was *not* a Copperhead, because he was too identified with the Lincoln administration, because he was dangerously identified with antiadministration sentiment. The party was (as usual for the Democratic party in an election year) disrupted—split among the outright pro-Southern Democrats, the Democrats who were not necessarily pro-Southern but who nevertheless wanted "peace-at-any-price," and the Democrats like August who supported the war for the Union but not the present administration. Even its former leaders could not be counted on for support.

"What can be expected," said former president Buchanan, "from a party at the head of which is a speculating German Jew?"

Despite the lack of party unity August was more successful than he had been four years before in raising a quorum of active Democratic National Committee members. At a meeting early in the year at his house, almost all of the committeemen attended. Most of the few who failed to show up sent detailed suggestions for Democratic strategy. The year 1864 seemed likely to be a Democratic year; no one wanted to be left behind.

After all, each of the past eight administrations had lasted for only one term. There was no reason to believe Lincoln would break that pattern: Lincoln was vulnerable within his own party, under increasing pressure from Republican radicals. Even if he were renominated, many people—like Thurlow Weed and Lincoln himself—did not believe he could be reelected. In fact, Lincoln thought McClellan would be the next president.

In order not to distract the Republicans from their interparty strife, the Democrats delayed giving them a target against whom they could rally. At the New York State Democratic Convention no candidate was officially proposed. August, Horatio Seymour, and two others were made delegates-at-large. They would go to the national convention, which was to be held in Chicago (in honor of Stephen Douglas), fairly late in the year on the Fourth of July. By then, many Democrats hoped, the Republicans would have destroyed themselves and McClellan could be nominated during an Independence Day celebration. They would reaffirm the North's dedication to the Union, invite the South to rejoin the United States, and highlight the unconstitutional policies of the Lincoln administration.

The Republicans seemed to be cooperating in making the Democratic strategy a success. The administration's policies were as Draconian as ever, as the pro-McClellan *New York World* pointed out—and as the administration proved by closing the newspaper down in the middle of May. The excuse used to suppress the *World* was that it had published a forged presidential proclamation announcing a day in fasting and prayer (over a military failure) and an increase in the draft. A *World* night editor had failed to check the facts.

When Marble heard about the hoax he recalled all copies of that issue. He himself went down to the docks to make sure none of the newspapers were sent to Europe. The false story could seriously muddle the Union's foreign policy.

The general whom Stanton had sent to silence the paper and arrest its editors was convinced by Marble's frantic scramble to kill the story that the *World* was the dupe not the agent of a conspiracy; but he could not disobey the War Department's direct orders. When soldiers invaded the newspaper's offices, Marble (who was getting married the following day), Samuel Barlow, and another *World* editor went to the general's office to turn themselves in. But the general, Thurlow Weed, and a few others who were trusted by the administration had meanwhile argued their case. The warrants for their arrest were canceled. The *World* was allowed to reopen. And Marble, after a short delay, was wed.

The gagging of the *World* hurt the administration worse than the false story had. Even proadministration newspapers objected. And there were rumors that the forgery had been the work of Republicans who were trying to destroy the opposition press before the presidential campaign.

But the *World* fiasco faded in the glare of much worse publicity for the administration. Radical Republicans met in their own convention and nominated John Charles Frémont. Lincoln split with two powerful

Republican senators. And Lincoln's secretary of the treasury, Salmon P. Chase, resigned.

A faction of Democrats including Seymour "urge postponement of the Convention," as August telegraphed Barlow. They wanted to give the Republicans not the rope to hang themselves—they had plenty of rope—but the time to use the rope. "Leading members of the National Committee are opposed," August further told Barlow. "Myself undecided," although he did not like the idea. It gave the Copperheads and Peace Democrats too much time to plot. "What do you and friends think?"

Barlow and friends—one friend in particular, McClellan—had no objections. The convention was postponed.

"I predict," said Republican George Templeton Strong, "that Belmont and Barlow will manipulate the Chicago convention into nominating McClellan on a non-committal platform; and that, if elected, he will betray the country."

Belle married a longtime suitor and ardent Republican, George Tiffany. August stayed in New York long enough to attend the ceremony and give them a party. Then, taking Perry with him, he left for the Democratic Convention.

In Chicago, August and Perry checked into the Sherman House, a tall building with a colonnaded entryway. Although the Sherman House was the headquarters of one of the most venomous Copperheads, August chose to stay there because it was the most central hotel in the city. At night Copperhead mobs caroled on the street, singing the praises of their leaders, who intended to seize the convention from August's faction and push through a peace platform. August had tried to convince the Democratic National Committee members to prepare positions on the essential issues facing the nation before the convention, hoping thereby to prevent any Copperhead conspiracy from using the convention to undercut the Union war effort. But he had been outvoted. Now he would have to fight the Copperheads at the convention.

Outside the hotel the pro-Southerners massed, demanding peace in a bloodthirsty manner. Inside the hotel the New York delegation met. The situation was volatile, every rumor a spark that could ignite an explosion.

Two arch-Republicans were exploring the possibilities of switching parties. Former secretary of the treasury Chase contacted August to offer himself as the Democratic candidate if the convention would put an abolitionist plank in its platform. And Frémont's agent in Chicago leaked that he had "a pledge from Frémont to declare for an immediate armistice and a peace convention with the Confederates and with this he proposes to secure the Democratic nomination."

There was more danger to McClellan's position from confirmed Democrats than from these roving-eyed Republicans. "Seymour," August told Barlow, "blows hot and cold." It seemed the governor hoped to blight McClellan's chances by withholding support and then offering himself up as a compromise candidate—although he was trying to keep his ambition decently hooded.

"He professes not to be a candidate," August said, "and *will be none if I can help it.*"

August was so sure that McClellan would win the nomination, he disdained using an agreed-upon code when he telegraphed Barlow:

"All going well. Success sure."

One hundred thousand conventioneers jammed into a city with normal population of fewer than two hundred thousand. Those who could not find rooms slept in hotel lobbies or set up tents outside. Brass bands warred with each other. At night fireworks streaked the sky.

A rumor spread about how a band of Confederates was planning to sneak down from Canada and rescue the Rebel prisoners of war who were interned in nearby Camp Douglas. Once freed, they would rampage through the city.

For Perry the political excitement was challenged by more exotic sights like the blacklegs, professional gamblers. Many of them were Rebels, come to Chicago at the start of the war. They lounged about town, conspicuous in their calm amid the hurly-burly.

The gamblers were amusing. But the plainsmen were fascinating with their rifles slung over their shoulders, knives in their belts, pistols in their holsters, and long Spanish spurs glinting in the sun. They rode their horses slowly through the streets, their eyes vacant, as though they could focus only on the great uninterrupted distances of the far West.

August promised Perry that after the convention began he could take off for the Illinois prairie to go game shooting.

On Monday, August 29, the convention opened at noon, which gave plenty of time for a slow morning recovery to any conventioneer who had been up late the previous night scheming, drinking, gambling, or visiting the Chicago brothels.

"Gentlemen of the Convention," August shouted from the platform, calling the meeting to order.

He stood before the murmuring, expectant audience: a short, energetic, impeccably dressed man with a sleek forehead sweeping up to a bald dome. Muttonchops framed his face. His shaved chin was as smooth and round as a child's rubber ball. His skin seemed drawn tight over the bone. As if time had given him a rebate, he appeared to be growing youthful. Only his eyes kept getting older. Their expression often countered the rest of his features, amused when his face was stern, and cold when he was smiling. The pouches below his eyes were darker than ever, larger and softer-looking. The wrinkles around his eyes had ramified, weaving a net within which this increasingly youthful face would at last be caught.

When the audience was quiet, the murmur soft enough to betray an occasional throat-clearing or cough, August continued:

"We are assembled here today at the National Democratic Convention . . . for the purpose of nominating candidates for the Presidency and Vice-Presidency of the United States. This task, at all times an . . . arduous one, has, by the sad events of our civil war, assumed an importance and responsibility of the most fearful nature. Never, since the formation of our government, has there been an assemblage, the proceedings of which were fraught with more momentous and vital results than those which must flow from your actions. Toward you, gentlemen, are directed at this moment the anxious fears and doubts, not only of millions of American citizens, but also of every lover of civil liberty throughout the world."

The convention delegates, those hundreds of upturned faces, a few of which in the anonymous mass August recognized, interrupted him with applause and wild cheering.

"In your hands rests, under the ruling of an all-wise Providence, the future of this Republic," August continued when the uproar had subsided. "Four years of misrule by a sectional, fanatical, and corrupt party have brought our country to the very verge of ruin. The past and present are sufficient warning of the disastrous consequences which would befall us if Mr. Lincoln's re-election should be made possible by our want of patriotism and unity. The inevitable results of such a calamity must be the utter disintegration of our whole political and social system amidst bloodshed and anarchy. . . . Let us, at the very outset of our proceedings, bear in mind that the dissensions of the last Democratic Convention were one of the principal causes which gave the reins of government into the hands of our opponents, and let us beware not to fall again into the same fatal error. . . . We are here, not as War Democrats, nor as Peace Democrats, but as citizens of the great Republic. . . . Let . . . disinterested patriotism . . . preside over our deliberations; and, under the blessings of the Almighty, the sacred cause of the Union, the Constitution, and the laws must prevail against fanaticism and treason."

The roar of approval that drowned the echo of August's voice made Perry even prouder of his father than he had been when he had first seen him stand up to address the convention. August, reaching out to both wings of his party, had united them; and he would hold them together, even if they struggled in his embrace, at least until McClellan was nominated.

The convention did choose McClellan as its presidential nominee, which pleased August, and George H. Pendleton, an Ohio congressman and well-known Peace Democrat, as its vice-presidential nominee, which did not. Even worse, the convention had adopted a peace plank in its platform. The party had not split. Instead it had created a political monstrosity: the former head of all Union armies linked to a pacifist running mate on a peace platform. Although August tried to convince others and perhaps himself that things were not as bad as they could have been if the peace plank had been stronger and therefore more objectionable, he nevertheless listened to the convention's decision with, according to one witness, a "profoundly sad" expression. The party was destroying its chances for the White House once again.

"I have a most horrid time here," August wrote to Barlow.

The newspapers, as usual, were suggesting that August had ulterior motives.

"He supported Mr. Douglas in a similar manner," said *The New York Times*, "and it is said on the same incentive. . . . Mr. Belmont no doubt has an eye to some future contingency, for he is not a man whose tastes, associations, or inclinations would otherwise lead him to adopt politics." The newspaper "supposed that in the event of General McClellan's attaining the Presidency, a foreign mission would be tendered" to August.

Whatever ulterior motives he may have had—and like most politicians August surely had personal as well as patriotic reasons for getting involved in what could be a very unpleasant public experience—he was beginning to wonder if the assets offset the debits. In the gallery of the convention center, for example, the eccentric millionaire George Francis Train, who supported, of all things, women's right to vote, was delighting spectators with his imitation of August. Imagine Train, that oddball, making fun of him!

Why place yourself in the spotlight so jackanapeses could ridicule you and newspapers impugn your honor, when the most you could achieve was a tainted victory? Pendletons and peace planks!

"I don't think you will catch me again on a National Committee," August had told Barlow on the first day of the convention.

But if August gave up his position on the committee it no doubt would be filled by a Peace Democrat—which was the same as turning the party over to the Copperheads; so August stayed on and was reelected chairman. He checked his own personal-political balance sheet and found, with mixed emotions, that he was still in business.

❧ CHAPTER TWENTY-EIGHT ❧

THAT FALL, back in New York, fresh from shooting prairie hens outside of Chicago, Perry, almost fourteen years old, packed a knapsack, took his gun, and with his pal Lloyd Bryce rode a ramshackle train out to Hicksville, Long Island, the last stop, and then headed even farther east, hiking a dozen miles to Babylon. The late afternoon sun cast their shadows longer and longer in front of them. The air got chillier, the sky more overcast. It started flurrying. The flurries turned into a good snow. The snow turned into an early unseasonable storm.

They arrived in Babylon after midnight, convinced that they had reached if not the ends of the earth at least a wild country. They hunted in the dark for Selah Smith's hotel, which they assumed was a small, primitive inn. They found instead a manorial, depressingly comfortable place with lights blazing. Inside was a meeting of the Suffolk County Democratic leaders.

The politicians, startled and amused by the appearance of two wet, shivering, but determined young hunters, decided not to disappoint them with soft, warm beds. They sent the boys back into the storm with Ras Tucker, a market gunner who was a crack shot with a rifle and, even better, an expert with a longbow. Ras rowed them across the Great South Bay to Oak Island, everything ghostly in the dark with the heavy snow falling. Once ashore they took shelter in a hut already filled with market gunners. The three of them flopped down on the floor with the others and slept for a couple of hours. At dawn they woke and, stretching stiff muscles, stepped out into the snowy landscape.

For almost a week the two boys camped in the hut and hunted with Ras and the other market gunners. The men, whose livelihood depended on their marksmanship, at first grudgingly and then generously admitted their respect for the rich city boys who hunted for sport. Perry and Lloyd were patient, disciplined, and, returning the respect, eager to learn from their companions.

On one of their treks Ras as a favor took the boys into an icy Eden, a special tract between Babylon and Deer Park that was teeming with game. Enchanted by the untouched and beautiful land, Perry returned to New York City as enthusiastic as if he had indeed been given a glimpse of Paradise.

August bought the property.

Vacation over, Perry and August, Jr., went off to the Rectory School, a military academy in Hamden, Connecticut, five miles north of New Haven. The school's program prepared boys for West Point or Annapolis. Despite or perhaps because of his maternal grandfather, Perry wanted to go to West Point. August, Jr., was undecided.

The boys had been tutored at home; then for a while had attended day school in New York.

Life at the Rectory School was a shocking change. They woke every morning at five, took cold showers, dressed (in uniforms), studied for an hour before breakfast, went to classes until three (with a noon break for dinner), played in organized sports for two and a half hours, took tea at five-thirty, studied until eight-thirty, and went to bed. They were not permitted to speak while walking to or from classes or at meals. They drilled not with spears as the students there used to do but with muskets. When they climbed trees they scrambled up "five at a time, in regular order, just as on shipboard sailors climb up the yards," Perry said. "Even in swimming, we dove from the diving boards in squads, under orders." The school was a regiment led by three student lieutenants, a student captain, and an adult commander-in-chief—the headmaster, Reverend Charles W. Everest, a severe Episcopalian who was warring against ignorance in the fields of the Lord.

During the occasional recesses the children could break ranks.

"We have splendid games of prisoner's base," Perry told his father in one of the required twice-a-week letters home. "I came pretty near getting two lovely black eyes yesterday. It was not fighting. I ran into another boy or he ran against me, and hit me with his chin right between the eyes. Of course, that gave them a kind of bluish color, but I washed them in cold water, and it showed no mark in the eyes after about a quarter of an hour, but will for some time on the forehead."

All things considered, Perry said in another letter, "I like it pretty well here."

August, Jr., was not having so good a time, although in his letters home he tried to sound brave:

"It has been raining pretty hard," he wrote his mother. "Whenever it stops we run onto the playground and play football and kick each other in the shins and push each other and throw each other over and sometimes get hurt, but that does not make us stop."

More and more his thoughts strayed from his studies to what was happening at home in New York City. The girls were going to dancing classes. Raymond had been weaned from his wet nurse, Ellen. And one of the servants, Robert, had been sacked.

August, Jr., suspected he knew why; and if he was right, then Robert had lost his job unfairly.

"What was Robert sent away for?" August, Jr., asked his mother. "For quarreling with Hippolyte [one of the other servants]? Well, I will tell you the whole thing. The first time they fought was when you were out on a picnic. Ramie Rodgers [a cousin] was staying with us then, and he saw it all. We had spilt a little water on the upstairs hall. And Hippolyte came up to put the light out, and he saw this and he said to us, 'I will make that Irish fellow wipe it up.' So he went downstairs and called Robert."

When Robert appeared Hippolyte handed him a towel and said, " 'Hurry up there,' in a very rough tone," August, Jr., explained. "Robert, you know, does not want to be treated like a dog, so he said, 'No, I won't.' Hippolyte took Robert by the collar to make him, and Robert just turned around and grabbed him by the shoulders and threw him downstairs."

Hippolyte ran back up the stairs, grabbed Robert again, and again Robert threw him down, although this time Hippolyte did not let go of Robert's collar, so they both went tumbling.

"They did that three times," said August, Jr., summing up his case for Robert's defense, "and every time Robert let him up. He did not strike him first once."

Hippolyte was the aggressor, and it was he, not Robert, who should have been fired.

August, Jr., championed Robert not only out of a sense of fair play but also as a way of staying involved in family affairs. He missed his parents and younger siblings terribly. The gifts from home—a Russian leather box from his mother and a bottle of "toothwash" from his father —gave his spirits a boost; but Mr. Everest disapproved of gifts from home, so in the future August, Jr., would be deprived of that little cheer.

He survived on dreams of visits.

"I hear you and Mama were coming to see us," he wrote hopefully to his father.

But even those dreams were dimmed. Mr. Everest disapproved of the boys' taking their parents up into their rooms without permission, and he rarely gave permission. So August, Jr., unable to be alone with his parents when they did come, would have to keep up his gallant public front and not allow himself the luxury, which privacy would have offered, of dissolving into unhappiness, of being not their little soldier but their little boy.

Each day was focused on the mail, and every mail without a letter from home left August, Jr., feeling incredulous. How could they have not written?

"I have not received a letter from you for a week and four days," he wrote to his father. "I counted them one after another, and I tell you I feel very badly about it. I would go every night and see if there was a letter, but I would go back to my seat, hardly being able to keep the tears from my eyes. I hope that you will write to me soon; and, if you don't, I will not write till you have written."

He was so hurt by the silences from home that he would strike out bitterly at his parents; only later, when the letters finally arrived, would he repudiate his anger—an anger that must have been as difficult to deal with as his feelings of rejection.

"I am sure you have nothing to do with the election," he wrote to his mother; "and I think you might write to me, for you have not written to me since you visited here. I have heard Perry's name called for letters not less than three times." He crossed out "three" and wrote in "two"; better not exaggerate, that might weaken his argument. "Ha! Ha! There is my name called. I take all what I said back."

August, however, did have something to do with the election; and although he tried to write to his sons every week, the election was taking up more and more of his time. The peace plank in the Democratic party's platform was alienating War Democrats and anti-Lincoln Republicans who may have considered voting for McClellan. August urged the general to clarify his position on the plank.

"It is absolutely necessary that in your reply of acceptance of the nomination you place yourself squarely and unequivocally on the ground that you will never surrender one foot of soil and that peace can only be based upon the reconstruction of the Union. In other words, cessation of hostilities or an armistice can only be agreed upon after we have sufficient guarantee from the South that they are ready for a peace under the Union."

Trying to keep from sounding as though he were dictating terms to McClellan, August added: "You know best how to express all this."

But August was dictating terms. As head of the Democratic National Committee he was in a better position than McClellan, a newcomer to politics, to judge campaign strategy; and he believed McClellan had to put some distance between himself and the party platform. In fact, he was so sure McClellan would take his advice, he was spreading the word— George Templeton Strong reported—that "McClellan's letter of acceptance will be most satisfactory even to the most resolute 'War Democrats,' and will secure his election."

Strong had feared that "McClellan is in the hands of Belmont and Barlow, and . . . they can manipulate him as they please." Strong was probably right. But McClellan was better off controlled by August than by the Copperheads, one of whose leaders warned him:

"Do not listen to your Eastern friends who in an evil hour may advise you to *insinuate* even a little war into your letter of acceptance."

McClellan did listen to his Eastern friends. Barlow helped him write his letter of acceptance. In it McClellan rejected the notion set forth in the peace plank that the war had been a failure, and although he declared himself ready to welcome back and protect the constitutional rights of any Rebel states that wished to return to the Union, he indicated that there could be no peace until after the Rebel states had returned. McClellan clarified his position so effectively that it became transparent: an obvious attempt to disavow the Democratic party platform—which reassured the War Democrats but now alienated the Peace Democrats, who began demanding a new convention that would change either the platform or the candidate. Running the Democratic party was like managing Chang and Eng, Barnum's famous Siamese twins, when they were having a squabble. The two factions of the party would not stop fighting, but you could not separate them without destroying them both.

"If we carry the election," August said, "it will be owing *entirely* to the stand which the General has taken."

But McClellan confused taking a stand with staying in one place. He seemed to think campaigning meant holding court at his home in New Jersey. He was the general; his lieutenants would report back to him the activity in the field.

Pendleton, the vice-presidential candidate, was also immobile, thinking it improper to campaign actively under the best of circumstances and even more unseemly to campaign when his running mate had just repudiated the party platform.

The only problem August faced more difficult than getting both candidates out on speaking tours was to make sure that if they did go out they never appeared together.

To add to the Democrats' troubles the renegade Republicans, who had held their own convention, had returned to the administration fold. Frémont, to his credit, refused promises of patronage when he withdrew from the presidential race. He knew that his support in the West and the Northeast would draw off enough votes from the regular Republican ticket—Lincoln and Andrew Johnson—to give the election to the Democrats, which he did not want to do. He stepped aside, a true patriot and a disappointed man.

August's fratricidal Democratic party now faced a united opponent. To have a chance in the election the Democrats had to learn a lesson from the Republicans. They had to stand solidly behind their nominees, even if their nominees did not stand solidly together—an admittedly difficult if not impossible feat.

But August worked some minor magic and recruited Democrats representing a wide spectrum of party opinion onto a Central Executive Campaign Committee. August supplemented the committee's fund-raising efforts by contributing additional money when and where needed: $500 for Ohio, $10,000 for Maine, and a rumored $15,000 for New Hampshire.

However much August donated to the Democratic campaign, he was less indiscriminate in his generosity than he had been in previous election years. Certain states he wrote off early: "Boston [a center of abolition sentiment] and Massachusetts are irretrievably lost," he had told Marble long before the campaign began, "and candidly speaking I would not give a farthing to save them."

As the campaign proceeded August was pleased to find Democrats closing ranks, attacking not each other but Republicans. Even Governor Seymour, who had not intended to offer himself for reelection, surrendered to August's argument that because of Seymour's opposition to McClellan in Chicago the governor's retirement would be interpreted as desertion, which would give ammunition to McClellan's detractors. Seymour, weary of politics, gave in; he would run.

Funds were coming into the party treasury. Meetings were crowded and lively. In fact, one rally held in Union Square was, according to *The New York Times,* as large and noisy as the last Fourth of July celebration. Tricolored lanterns were strung over the streets, and boys carrying more lanterns circulated among the mob of people who strolled past the dozen speaker's platforms eating peaches and oranges and treating the gathering more like a carnival than a political event. Cannons on each of the square's corners regularly punctuated the celebration with booms, their noise the aural equivalent of a fireworks display, each explosion seeming to burst into dozens of little explosions as young men, cued by the cannons, shot their guns into the air.

"Indeed if the Peace [Democratic] Party would find as many ball cartridges at the gunnery as they have blank cartridges for the sake of noise," *The New York Times* said, "the war would soon end."

August, introduced on the main speaker's platform, was greeted with cheers.

Temperamentally, August was unsuited to rabble-rousing; but during his years on the stump he had learned how to hold and move an audience. He knew which notes to play, which emotions to twitch:

"We are told that the Democratic Party is the party of disunion and that we are the friends of Jefferson Davis and his rebel government," August said that night. "Hundreds of thousands of brave Democrats who have bled on the field of battle for the sacred cause of the Union and the Constitution have not been sufficient to silence this foul calumny!" August enjoyed mass-speaking more than his aristocratic pose would ever let him admit.

When he completed his speech at the Union Square rally, the crowd cheered and kept cheering.

"Finest possible weather," George Templeton Strong said of that evening. ". . . Strolled about . . . inspecting the outskirts of the great McClellan meeting on Union Square and the tributary streams of banners, lanterns, transparencies, Roman candles, and rabblement that were flowing up Fourth Avenue and Broadway. . . . Meeting very large and showy with its lights and fireworks; its appliances cost a large sum. Belmont must have bled freely."

As the election neared, August grew increasingly concerned about the possibility of voting fraud. The Lincoln administration appeared ready to use any method to win. August heard reports from Maryland that the *Evening Post*, the only Democratic newspaper published in Baltimore, had been closed by the commander of the Union troops in that area the day it printed the electoral ticket of the Democratic party. The chairman of the Democratic State Central Committee in Missouri told August that they were unable to campaign effectively because "soldiers will not allow a Democrat to open his mouth or even declare himself for McClellan, and the reign of terror prevails." In at least one other state such activities were given government sanction.

"Andrew Johnson, a man holding by appointment of the President the office unknown to our laws of military governor of Tennessee and . . . the Republican candidate for the Vice Presidency of the Union," August said in a public letter, "issued a military order . . . prescribing arbitrary qualifications for voters at the election."

The arbitrary qualification was an oath, which had been adopted by a convention in Nashville on August 2.

To be able to vote in Tennessee a citizen had to swear to "oppose all armistices or negotiations for peace with rebels in arms, until the Constitution of the United States and all laws and proclamations made in pursuance thereof shall be established over all the people of every state and territory embraced within the National Union." In other words, if one supported the Democratic party platform, one could not honestly take the oath. August had his own doubts about the Democratic party platform, but such an oath seemed a tyrannical measure. August believed "This oath commands every loyal citizen of Tennessee to vote for the Republican candidate or to abstain from the polls."

Closer to home August learned that voting tickets for his own

Fourth Congressional District, where he was a presidential elector, had been tampered with. His name had been replaced by that of his Republican opponent.

If the Republicans could manipulate the election so blatantly among civilians, August suspected they could do far worse damage within the army. Despite McClellan's popularity, officers might be able to intimidate the troops into voting for Lincoln. August, as chairman of the Democratic party, wrote to Secretary of War Stanton to get some guarantee that the military returns would not be rigged. He was asking the fox to guarantee the safety of the henhouse.

Stanton did not have the courtesy to answer personally.

When August pursued the matter he heard allegations that the fox had locked himself in the henhouse and feathers were flying out the windows.

"Army camps," August wrote in another public letter, "thrown open to the political agents of the administration are sought to be closed to the legal representatives of the Democratic Party. . . . The mails are violated to seize the votes that have been cast against Lincoln and to place his own ballots in their stead; and, when it had been discovered that the votes of the army . . . were cast in great majority for their old commander, a plot was contrived to seize their votes and arrest the agents who had collected them under pretense of punishing frauds."

The two agents to whom August was referring were found guilty by a military commission of forging the names of soldiers on Democratic voting tickets. Although one of the two defendants admitted to his guilt, a number of Democrats continued to feel that there had been something unsavory about the case against them. The confession had been coerced. The man who had confessed had been a Republican agent provocateur. All sorts of wild rumors circulated, some as embellished and complex as a model of a pre-Copernican universe, plots within plots, agents and double agents.

It is probable that the two men were guilty as charged and that a great deal of Democratic hysteria was unfounded. Still, McClellan was sure that he was being—as he put it—"dogged and every person reported who comes to see me." Democratic politicians were in some cases harassed by proadministration officers. McClellan supporters within the army were prevented from voting. And officers and soldiers who campaigned for McClellan were discharged from the service.

When an injustice was brought to Lincoln's attention, he tried to right the wrong; but Lincoln did not dismiss Stanton, who frequently was responsible for the injustices—which Democrats thought Lincoln, if he truly cared about righting wrongs, should have done. And Democrats were not convinced by Lincoln's protestations of evenhandedness.

"Supporting General McClellan for the Presidency is no violation of army regulations," Lincoln said after reinstating one officer Stanton had mustered out of the army, "and as a question of taste of choosing between him and me, well, I'm the longest, but he's better-looking."

The attacks against August were as nasty as ever.

"Let us look at a few undeniable facts," said *The New York Times.* "The notorious undenied leader of the Democratic Party at Chicago was the agent of the Rothschilds. Yes, the great Democratic Party has fallen so low that it has to seek a leader in the agent of foreign Jew bankers."

"The question before the country," said the *Chicago Tribune,* "is— Will we have a dishonorable peace in order to enrich Belmont, the Rothschilds, and the whole tribe of Jews, who have been buying up Confederate bonds" (a lie) "or an honorable peace won by Grant and Sherman at the cannon's mouth?"

McClellan's nomination, said the usually Democratic *Columbus* (Ohio) *Crisis,* was "a sellout to Wall Street and the Rothschild interests."

"Then there is the monied aristocracy," said a pro-Lincoln Democrat at a Cooper Union rally. "I should think the name of Rothschild is a tolerably fair gilt-edged name to represent monied aristocracy, and the agent of the Rothschilds is the chief manager of the Democratic Party of the United States! . . . What a first-rate Secretary of the Treasury he would make if McClellan happened to be elected."

The crowd in Cooper Union laughed.

"There is not a government in Christendom in which the paws or fangs or claws of the Rothschilds are not plunged to the very bottom of the treasury . . . , and they would like to do the same thing here. I have no doubt they have sent out word to their agent that they were willing to lend to the Yankee nation to any extent."

Here the speaker put on a comic Yiddish accent:

"They are an active young people, Mr. Belmont, able to pay shent per shent; and you can lend them any amount."

The crowd again laughed.

"But," he continued, dropping the accent, "it so happened we did not want to borrow, and the Jews have got mad and have been mad ever since. . . . But they and Jeff Davis and the devil are not going to conquer us."

"What a scandal that an election might be carried by the money of a German Jew . . . ," said the statesman Edward Everett.

"McClellan may possibly reach the White House," said a Union general, Henry W. Halleck, "but he will lose the respect of all honest, high-minded patriots by his association with such traitors . . . as Belmont."

". . . Barlow, Belmont, and the like are the rebels' last hope," said George Templeton Strong.

Even a close friend of McClellan's cautioned the general against "Jew-President Belmont's machinations."

And on the morning of October 29 McClellan's aide, Colonel E. H. Wright—according to an entry in his diary—followed up various ominous messages and met in Baltimore with Allan Pinkerton, an old friend of McClellan's and the general's former chief of military intelligence. Pinkerton told Wright that some of McClellan's supporters were scheming to have Lincoln assassinated if the president was reelected. The administration knew who they were, was watching them, and, if they gave any indication of carrying out their plot, was prepared to arrest and hang them.

Who are the conspirators? Wright asked.

You, said Pinkerton. And he named a few others, including August.

People did come to August's defense, challenging the outrageous accusations; but fewer than August could have expected and, when they did, often not as strongly as he could have wished.

After a perfunctory· denial that August and the Rothschilds were in any way supporting the Confederacy, a Jewish newspaper played Pilate and washed its hands of August. According to one report the newspaper explained that August, "though a Jew by birth . . . married out of the faith many years ago, is not connected with a Jewish congregation, and is universally repudiated as a Jew."

August recalled Marcy's advice of many years ago—pay no attention to political smears, fighting them is "lost labor"—and accepted the libels, lies, and laughter as part of the game. The only slur he could not ignore was the *New York Evening Post*'s description of August as a "reputed son . . . of the Rothschilds." August sued. The newspaper apologized. The suit was dropped.

The Democrats were defeated in important state elections in Ohio, Indiana, and even in Pennsylvania, where August had been so sure of victory that he had planned a celebration "in honor of the auspicious results in the Keystone state."

"We commend the prudent foresight of Mr. Belmont," said *The New York Times*. "He might find it awkward to await the official returns from Pennsylvania before celebrating his victory."

A hundred Democratic guns were fired in City Hall Park, but the salute was, according to the newspaper, "spiritless." The returns from Pennsylvania were gloomy. August had asked all Democrats to herald the victory by putting lights in their windows; but there was no victory, and evidently discouraged, he kept his own house dark.

During an intermission at the Academy of Music, August offered to wager $1,000 that McClellan would win. He did bet N. E. Thalmann, another banker, $4,000 on McClellan. And he looked around for other takers.

The *New York Herald* reported that August, who, it claimed, "has hitherto been extremely cautious about risking anything upon the Presidential election"—this at the same time that he was being accused of spending tens of thousands of dollars to buy the White House—*"is now offering to bet heavily upon the election of McClellan."*

August went to the polls early on election day. Despite the wet weather the turnout was large, the wait sometimes as long as two hours.

When August stepped up to vote, an elections inspector told him that he had violated a state law that forbade betting on the outcome of political races; as a result he could not vote.

August had the wit to point out that he had bet only on the presidential election; therefore he should be able to vote for all other offices.

The inspector refused to let him; and according to George Templeton Strong, a little behind August in line, "Belmont went off in a rage. Very few men would have been challenged on that ground," Strong admitted, "but this foreign money-dealer has made himself uncommonly odious, and the bystanders, mostly of the Union persuasion, chuckled over his discomfiture."

Lincoln beat McClellan.

"If only [McClellan's] wife and her mother . . . had not allowed themselves to be talked over by Belmont and Barlow, and brought household influence to bear upon him," said Strong, still sniping, "he would not be in this plight."

During the campaign Republicans like Strong had been against McClellan and Barlow and Belmont. After the election they were against Barlow and Belmont. As August soon learned, those Republicans would be joined by McClellan supporters who were looking for someone on whom to blame McClellan's defeat.

❧ CHAPTER TWENTY-NINE ❧

"IF ONLY THE CONVENTION at Chicago had listened to my advice," August complained to Marble.

If only McClellan had been yoked to another War Democrat, not a Peace Democrat; if only the platform had "declared in favor of the Union and a vigorous prosecution of the war *as I advocated so earnestly in our delegation.*" If only . . .

The Democrats, having thrown away their chance to regain the White House in 1864, now seemed ready to throw away their national chairman too. August was attacked by Peace Democrats as having been too prowar: he had fought against nominating Pendleton as vice-president and had influenced McClellan to make a statement toning down the party platform. And if that were not enough, August was also attacked by the War Democrats as having been too conciliatory toward the South: A rumor, noted by Strong, was circulating that McClellan had "allowed Barlow and Belmont to strike out of his letter of acceptance a vigorous sentence declaring an armistice with armed rebels out of the question."

Anti-Belmont sentiment was apparently concentrated in New York and, as one puzzled newspaper said, "The Democratic world outside of the city of New York does not comprehend what particular axes are to be ground . . . out of the attempt to displace Mr. Belmont from the chairmanship of the National Democratic Committee."

Possibly Horatio Seymour's friends resented August's opposition to Seymour as a presidential candidate at Chicago and his support for Seymour as a gubernatorial candidate in New York. August had virtually browbeaten Seymour into running for reelection, and Seymour had lost.

Whatever the reason for the anti-Belmont movement, it appeared to be a spite-fight. Ousting August made "no rhyme or reason in a national point of view," the newspaper continued. "The functions of the National Committee have ceased, except to arrange for the convocation of the next National Democratic Convention. Its chairman has, therefore, neither patronage to distribute, nor official power, either for good or harm. For the rest, his steady and unflinching Democracy from his youth up and the distinguished services he has performed for the party, should be his shield against any assaults in the *name* of that party, that are merely personal in their ends."

Unfortunately the newspaper that carried this tribute to August came from Mobile, Alabama, still a Confederate stronghold. It could have been worse; Jefferson Davis could have published an encomium.

The stakes involved in this fight over the chairmanship of the Democratic National Committee were higher than the Mobile newspaper had indicated. There was, for example, an effort right after the election to call a national meeting of Democrats to work with the administration in negotiating with the South. August opposed the idea, and it was dropped.

The dissatisfaction with August never developed into a coup. His position was strengthened when McClellan, the apparent leader of the Democratic party, decided to abdicate and go to Europe for an extended visit.

"His departure at this juncture and so *soon* after the election," August warned Barlow just before Christmas, "would be misconstrued by the American people and certainly would be seized upon by the administration press as an excuse for unjust and malignant attacks. In his position, notwithstanding his retirement from the army, he cannot well absent himself from the country on a mere tour of pleasure while the war lasts on the scale with which it does without incurring for himself and the Democratic Party censure and misrepresentations of all kinds. *Noblesse oblige*. And the General has been too highly placed by his own eminent services, ill-requited as they have been, and by the suffrage of two millions of American citizens, not to be obliged to sacrifice his personal wishes. This is a very delicate point."

McClellan could not be swayed. With his family he sailed for Europe on the *China*. August wrote to him; but McClellan's letters back were bizarrely chatty, empty of any political talk.

"You can imagine how difficult it is to find time to write during one's first visit to Rome. We reached here just in time for the two last days of the carnival, which we enjoyed exceedingly, although I confess that I should not care to put myself to any inconvenience for the sake of seeing it again—one is quite enough. We are enjoying our visit. Our only regret is that we cannot remain here months instead of weeks. The weather has not been pleasant here, but at Naples all accounts say that it has been literally infamous. I don't know whether the natives here talk of the weather as we are very apt to do about the mosquitoes at home, but they all say that the Spring has been thus far unusually late and disagreeable. The leaves have not yet commenced to bud."

Have not had time to write. Just in time for the carnival. Weather not pleasant. Mosquitoes at home. Leaves not yet budding.

A letter from a defeated presidential candidate to the chairman of the National Committee of his party just a few months after the election —and, with the exception of one brief reference to a battle Sherman had fought on his march through the Carolinas, all McClellan talked about was sight-seeing and the weather! McClellan seemed to be staging a tactical retreat out of politics, leaving August entrenched as head of the Democratic party.

Like a nightmare that haunts one all the next morning, the election upset August for weeks. Even Perry, seeing how upset his father was, felt obliged to offer comfort:

"You don't know how badly I feel about the election of Lincoln," he wrote to August. "But, as it is over, there is no more use talking about it."

August found it hard to take his son's advice. He had been staggered by the vote. His health suffered.

"I owe you a thousand apologies for having left you all so suddenly last evening," he told Manton Marble, "but I was really so ill that I had to take to my bed. I am afraid my boys' warning that the result of the election could give me dyspepsia is being justified."

Even if he had been able to resign himself to McClellan's defeat, he still was hurt by the wildness and viciousness of personal abuse.

"I have been made the object of the most severe, unjust, and absurd attacks by the Administration press," August, long after the election, wrote to Seward; "and I have reason to know that *even the President* has to a certain extent given credence to the calumnies which have been published against me."

August's distress worried Caroline.

"Poor, pretty, little loyal Mrs. Belmont . . . declares herself made very unhappy by newspaper flings at her husband," said Strong after his wife met Caroline at a concert.

The Christmas holidays would be celebrated under a pall.

After the holiday the short days, the snowdrifts that blocked the school playground, and the aching cold conspired to make life dreary for Perry and August, Jr. The Belmont boys were scolded because their clothes had not been marked with their names at home. And August, Jr., still complained that he was not getting enough mail.

Caroline had explained to her son that she had "talked to Rickie and Jeannie, until I am tired, about writing to you" and that she had "fixed upon Sunday as the day to devote an hour to you, so if you do not hear from them it is not my fault."

But it was not Frederika and Jeannie by whom August, Jr., felt abandoned.

"I will not write to you any more if you do not answer my letters," he impatiently told his mother. "I will get many reports [black marks for bad behavior] and displease you very much, if you do not write. I have more to do than you, but I keep regular at writing one or two letters a week. I can write to Rickie or Jeannie and I am sure they would answer me regularly. Papa is now in Europe"—on a short business trip—"and you do not go out in the evenings so you have enough time to scribble a few lines to your son who is away from home."

When Caroline chided August, Jr., for his tone, he explained that he knew he "should not be impatient about letters. But reason a little, Mother, and try to understand the natural feelings of a son away from home. You know that I have that fault of impatience. Though I am trying to break it, it cannot be done right away. You must know I don't want to make you feel bad, but I feel very disappointed to say I have not had a letter for at least three weeks, except one from Papa, which I think is very kind of him to think of me when he is so far away and has so much to do. I beg you to answer me as soon as you have time."

Despite his final, pathetic plea the letter demonstrated a logic that was remarkably clear and a spirit that was remarkably reasonable for a twelve-year-old boy; and this controlled and understanding view of himself and the world did not desert August, Jr., even in a crisis.

A mid-January thaw followed by a snap freeze glazed the Rectory School sledding hill. The boys could swoop down the slope so fast they could slide all the way across the pond; but, since only the near half of the pond was frozen solid enough to support a swooping schoolboy's weight, the trick was to stop the sled just short of the thin ice. August, Jr., so alert to the danger at the end of the ride, ignored the danger at the beginning.

"I have met with an accident, the marks of which will stay on me all my life," he wrote to his father.

That mid-January thaw, as well as giving the sleds a glassy crust on which to glide, had also exposed a few clumps of grass. August, Jr., had belly flopped on his sled too soon; he hit a patch of exposed grass; and the sled jerked to a stop. August, Jr., pitched over the swan's head on the front of the sled and sprawled facedown on the ice, bashing his chin, which turned black and blue, and snapping a tooth.

When he took tea that afternoon the pain triggered by the exposed nerves made him cry; but all in all he viewed the accident philosophically and, in telling his father about it, seemed as interested in the mechanics of how it had happened as he was in its terrible results. The accident was a problem to solve; the solution: make sure you slammed your sled down on ice, not grass. Within a week he was putting the solution into practice and again careering down the hill.

Each term was divided into quarters; and at the end of each quarter the boys were given report cards that included week-by-week accounts of how many reports (black marks) had been tallied against them. For the week just before and the two weeks just after Christmas vacation, August, Jr., had no reports. On the last week of that quarter he had thirteen. For the four weeks of the next quarter he had twenty. He was becoming a difficult child. And a remorseful one.

"I am sorry that I had so many reports the last quarter," he told his mother. "And I assure you I will try not to get any more. I had none today."

His behavior may have been a manifestation of a growing independence, because in those weeks he also became gradually less homesick than he had been and began showing signs of growing up. He wanted a "private account," some money that he could spend as he wished. And he asked his mother if his name could be removed from the early-bed list so he could go to sleep later with the older boys.

Perhaps sensing that giving him the later bedtime would be an admission that her son was no longer a child but was turning into a young man, Caroline could not bring herself to grant the request; but she also could not bring herself to deny it—which annoyed her impatient son.

"I want a decisive answer," he wrote to her. "If you do not want me to have my early bed removed, say so; but, if you do, say so too." Caroline, hurt that her son was displeased with her, responded to her son's attitude rather than to his petition. And August, Jr., not wanting to pain his mother but wanting the earlier bedtime as evidence of the change he was feeling in himself, desperately tried to make himself understood.

"Mamma," he wrote, "please do not feel so bad. The reason I was a little cross was because you did not write about my early bed. The very next time I do what I have done, don't write to me at all."

By spring August, Jr., evidently had begun to come to terms with the changes through which he was passing. He was down to only four reports for the quarter, and there was a new distance between him and his parents in his letters. He was trying out various poses, experimenting with being grown-up and with using a grown-up's voice.

"Being now at leisure," he wrote to his father, "I seize the epistolary implement to sketch a few lines to you, hoping that the same may find you and Mamma in good health."

And, showing off, he ended the letter by saying—in the tone of a good clubman proving a political point:

"I tell you I can prove that one cat has three tails. To begin with, you will acknowledge, I suppose, that no cat has two tails. And, if no cat has two tails, one will have one more tail . . . than no cat and so he has three tails. That's logic."

"Hang Out Your Banners," The New York Times of April 10, 1865, declared. *"Union. Victory. Peace."*

The day before, General Robert E. Lee, head of the Confederate Army, surrendered at Appomattox Courthouse to General Ulysses S. Grant, head of the Union Army. In the same issue of the newspaper a short item on an inside page described the plans for raising the United States flag—the one that had been flying when the Rebels had first attacked four years earlier—at Fort Sumter.

The Civil War was over.

"Just before the last Presidential election, Mr. A. Belmont . . . made a public offer to bet $10,000 that, if Mr. Lincoln should be reelected, the war would outlast his second term," *The New York Times* later would gloat. "What does Mr. B. think about the matter now?"

Ten hours and fifteen minutes after the flag was raised at Fort Sumter, Lincoln was assassinated by John Wilkes Booth at Ford's Theater in Washington.

Seward, at home in bed, was also attacked.

Rumors of a conspiracy spread, and the incredible story again surfaced that August had been a member of a plot to kill the President. An anonymous letter sent from New York to Stanton claimed that "General McClellan, A. Belmont, Fernando Wood, Charles H. Haswell [the designer of the first steam launch], and Jeremiah Larocque [one of Barlow's law partners], were all cognizant of the conspiracy to murder President Lincoln, yourself, and Secretary Seward. These parties I learn through a servant in Belmont's employ were all together at a supper at Belmont's house with J. Wilkes Booth in November last."

Assassinations breed rumors; and rumors keep ramifying until more and more people fall under suspicion. The obsessed assassination buff finds in evidence that his theory is wrong overwhelming proof that his theory is right and that the conspirators have the power to manipulate the evidence. Innocence becomes proof of cleverly hidden guilt. Such an obsession is religious in nature: it is the negative version of a search for a First Cause.

August, as chairman of the Democratic National Committee, was an obvious target for such rumors. He openly, frequently, and intensely deplored what seemed to be the Republicans' attempt to gut the Constitution: Lincoln's trust in Stanton and Stanton's arbitrary exercise of power. The military censorship. The control of the telegraph wires. The gagging of newspapers. The suppression of honest dissent. The promiscuous accusations of treason and the Draconian policies such accusations justified. The illegal arrests and the prisoners jailed without being charged. The dishonest tactics used in the election. The centralizing of power in Washington and the stranglehold on Washington by the Republicans.

Like many others August believed that the Republicans, having been returned to the White House, would dismantle the Republic and establish a tyranny.

So if August were party to a conspiracy, his motives—although hard to understand with hindsight—would have been patriotic. The situation seemed desperate and required desperate remedies.

But there were competing theories of other conspiracies (one implicating Stanton himself in the assassination). And the evidence against August is meager and inconclusive. The diary entry by McClellan's aide proves nothing; and the person who wrote the anonymous letter to Stanton may have wished merely to make trouble for August. Anonymous accusations can be subtle weapons for revenge, and August had many enemies—some of whom seemed to find in the tragedy of the President's assassination reason to rejoice in the effect it might have on August.

"There are hopeful signs that the community may be ready at last," said Strong a few days after the assassination, "for action against its Barlows, Larocques, Belmonts."

True or not, the rumors branded August. Many people believed that he had led the conspiracy, and this belief forever after shadowed him and affected how he was viewed in public and private life. To some he was a hero, the defender of the Republic; to others he was a traitor. The rumor vested in August a secret and far-reaching power that grew in the public's imagination as the specifics of the rumor were blurred by time— until August seemed to loom over the history of the nation.

PART FOUR

PART FOUR

CHAPTER THIRTY

THE NORTH WAS VICTORIOUS. Peace had come. The country was rich. New fortunes had been made and old fortunes increased during the war. New York banks, which in the early 1860s had only $80 million in deposits, by the mid-1860s had $225 million in deposits. Billions of dollars of securities were now bought and sold on the stock exchange, which had moved to new quarters on Broad Street. The old stables and taverns in the Wall Street area (among the last remains of the quaint Dutch town August had come to in 1837) had been replaced at last by businesses. Messengers lugging canvas bags filled with gold coins heaved their loads from bank to bank. When the bags split and the gold coins spilled, bouncing and rolling in tightening spirals until they fell on their sides and gave a kind of death rattle before lying still, passing bankers and brokers would circle the spill until all the money was gathered up. If someone bent over to grab a coin, whoever was behind him would kick him in the rear—honor enforced by the boot.

There were now more than a hundred millionaires in the city, many of whom had been poor just four or five years before. And many of them seemed as ready to spend their money as they were to make it. Released from the war, New Yorkers acted like children out of school for summer vacation; and the resulting explosion of good spirits was dazzling. The city, dressed in its best, was sitting for its photograph; for illumination the photographer used, instead of magnesium wire, fireworks.

The Flash Age had begun.

Flash: dashing, brilliant, showy, flaunting, splendid, gaudy, smart . . . and of brief duration. But no one believed the end would come quickly. Five years? Ten? The party could go on forever. . . . Flashy houses. Flashy carriages. Flashy clothes.

In the season after the war ended, New Yorkers gave six hundred balls, for which the guests spent about $7 million on dresses (which cost on an average $1,000 each) and jewelry. Assuming the balls themselves cost $15,000 each—which was the estimate for a ball August had given a decade earlier, a much less extravagant time—the bill just for balls, not including other entertainments, could well have been over $9 million. No wonder one New York hostess—it was rumored—psyched herself up for her balls with hashish.

The city was seized by the exuberant style August had pioneered and still set. At the heart of the Flash Age was a band of vivacious and extravagant millionaires who had been circling him for years and who following the war seemed ready to try to surpass all their previous excesses. Addison Cammack, Henry Clews, James Gordon Bennett, Jr., William Travers, and Leonard Jerome. They were called, after their leader, the Belmont Clique.

Cammack, a tall man with a walrus moustache and eyes the color of a slate roof after a rain, was one of the most recent members of the Clique, having come to New York at the end of the war. He was a native of Kentucky who hated the Rebels. He was gruff, candid, and kind. He would squeeze his antagonists on Wall Street but would not bankrupt them.

Clews, who had muttonchops like August and a moustache, was bald. He thought it made him youthful. His pate, smooth and pink, looked more like an egg than a skull.

Bennett, possibly the youngest member of the Clique, had been educated in France and because of this Continental background felt for August an admiration and camaraderie not shared by his father, who owned the *New York Herald*, a newspaper that often had attacked August. To challenge the four admired Thoroughbreds that drew August's coach, Bennett imported four he thought were better; however, one of the two leaders, a horse with a long neck called Kangaroo, would sit down in his harness. August's horses retained their supremacy. Bennett would get drunk and, late at night in his coach, tear through country roads, driving his horses (presumably not including Kangaroo) as fast as he could while he perched on the box, whip in hand, naked in the moonlight—because, he said, "I want to be able to breathe."

The nucleus of the Clique were Travers, Jerome, and August. They were called the Three Musketeers.

Travers, who was Jerome's cousin and sometime business partner, had a nose that stuck out from his face like the gnomon of a sundial. An expert judge of Madeira, he was the Clique's wit. He had a bad stammer, and an acquaintance who had known him in Baltimore, his hometown, claimed Travers stuttered worse since moving to New York.

"W-h-y y-e-s," Travers said; "of course I do. This is a d-d-damned sight b-b-bigger city."

Once, lost in Brooklyn, Travers asked a stranger for directions.

"I desire to r-reach M-montague St-street," he said. "W-will you b-be kik-kind enough to pup-point the way?"

"Y-you are go-going the wrong w-way," the stranger said. "That is M-montague St-street there."

"Are y-you mimick-micking me?" Travers asked.

"Nun-no, I assure you, sir," the stranger said. "I-I am ba-badly afflict-flicted with an imp-impediment in my speech."

"Why d-don't y-you g-get cured?" Travers asked. "G-go to Doctor——. . . . H-he cu-cured me."

Although he could make fun of his stutter, he resented others doing so. When he stopped in a pet store and asked the owner if "th-th-th-that p-p-parrot c-c-can t-t-talk," the owner said, "If it couldn't talk better than you, I'd cut its damned head off."

Travers swore revenge.

Sometime later, because his stable was infested with rats, Travers started looking for a good rat-dog. One of those who showed up with a dog for sale was the pet-store owner.

Travers told the man, "I will g-g-give the dog a tr-tr-trial and, if he p-pr-proves to b-b-be a g-g-good r-rat c-c-catcher, will b-b-buy him."

Travers put the dog in one of the stable stalls where there were three rats. The rats were vicious. The dog, urged on by its owner, killed one rat, then another; but it could not kill the third rat, which hurt the dog as badly as the dog hurt it.

The owner, thinking two out of three was a good score, said to Travers:

"Now you see what a fine dog this is, won't you buy him?"

"I d-d-don't w-w-want t-t-to b-b-buy the d-d-dog," said Travers, "b-b-but I'll b-b-buy the r-rat."

He was not as gentle to others with afflictions as he demanded others to be with him. When he went to see Chang and Eng, Barnum's Siamese twins, he studied at length how they were connected and then innocently said, "B-b-br-brothers, I presume."

Among his own circle his favorite target was Clews—or rather

Clews's shiny dome. After Clews had been profiled in a weekly magazine as one of New York's self-made men, Travers said in a loud voice as Clews entered their club, "Hallo, boys! Here comes Clews, the self-made man. I s-s-say, Cl-cl-clews, as you are a s-s-self-made man, wh-wh-why the d-d-devil didn't you p-put more h-h-hair on the top of your head?"

He liked to present himself as flinty, a hard s.o.b.

"W-w-w-where d-d-did you g-g-g-get th-th-that?" he asked when one of his sons appeared with a shiner.

"In a f-f-fight, sir," said the son, who also stuttered.

"D-d-d-did y-y-you w-w-w-whip the other f-f-fellow?" Travers asked.

"Y-y-yes, sir," said the son.

"Q-q-q-quite r-r-right," said Travers. "H-h-h-here's a d-d-dollar f-f-for y-you. Always w-w-whip the other f-f-fellow."

But Travers did not always take his own advice, and the sparks he struck often were a result less of his flintiness than of his sense of humor. When not in merciless pursuit of a punch line he was kind, helping young men who seemed to have a talent for finance to get a start on Wall Street and discouraging those without talent who would just lose money in speculation.

"I think we can do business together," a well-known gambler once told Travers. "I've got good judgment on horses . . . and you have the same on stocks. . . . I've made $350,000 on horse races in the last two years. Now, you give me points on stocks, and I'll give you points on races. Is it a go?"

"Y-you've made three h-hundred and f-fifty th-thousand dollars on h-horse racing?" Travers asked.

"Yes," said the gambler.

"And you want m-me to g-give you p-points on st-stocks?" Travers asked.

"In exchange for my points on horses," said the gambler. "Yes."

"Well," said Travers, "I'll give you a f-first rate p-point. If you've made that much in two y-years [on the horses], st-stick to . . . [gambling]."

"This genial, benevolent and high spirited man," Clews said of Travers, "has never been known to believe that there was any value in any property."

Despite his success on Wall Street, Travers tended to be cynical about the way in which Wall Street brokers made money handling other people's investments. In Newport he once looked out over a sea of yachts owned by brokers and wondered, "Wh-wh-where are the cu-cu-customers' yachts?"

Leonard Jerome was almost six feet tall and wore an enormous bushy moustache that made the rest of his clean-shaven face seem miniaturized. He had—people said—not a single enemy in the city. He did have some, but perhaps fewer than most men in his position. And he suffered as badly as did August from that terrible disease—which August's father, Simon, had diagnosed—called exuberance.

Like Bennett, Jr., Jerome was determined to outclass August.

"After all," he once said about August, "I'm fond of the fellow, but one can't let him have the pick of everything—he's got the best pictures, the best porcelain, and the best chef in New York as it is."

Jerome built a magnificent coach, which was described in a newspaper: "Gay and laughing ladies in gorgeous costume filled the carriage. Lackeys, carefully gotten up, occupied the coupe behind; Jerome sat on the box and handled the reins. With a huge bouquet of flowers attached to his buttonhole, with white gloves, cracking his whip, and with the shouts of the party, the four horses would rush up Fifth Avenue, on toward the Park, while the populace said, one to the other, 'That is Jerome.' "

But August's coach was even more extravagant.

Because August's house had New York's first private gallery and ballroom, Jerome built a house at Madison Avenue and Twenty-sixth Street with a stable paneled in black walnut and lined with expensive carpets. Because August's parties were decorated with living statues, Jerome for his housewarming ball installed in the great hall on the stable's second floor two fountains, one bubbling champagne, the other, eau de cologne. Because August had given a private concert featuring Fanny Ronalds, Jerome turned the hall over his stable into a six-hundred-seat private theater, Theatre San Jeronimo, where Fanny and other amateur and professional singers and actors could entertain New York society.

Both men wooed Fanny with flowers and stock-market advice, each trying to outdo the other in ardor. The flirtation was a game, and the winner was neither August nor Jerome but Fanny, who flourished in their attention and became for a season or two one of the belles of the city. One spectacular ball she gave became legendary. She presided over her guests, haloed with fire. Her diadem contained gas jets powered by a fuel supply hidden in her massed hair—an appropriate crown for one of the empresses (no matter how unofficial) of an industrial nation.

"August," Jerome said two decades later, "do you remember Fanny's celebrated ball?"

"Indeed, I ought to," said August. "I paid for it."

"Why, how very strange," said Jerome. "So did I."

The artillery of their competition was money; so when they fought each other face to face they exchanged not blows but gifts.

"I chanced to stop in at Tiffany's this morning," Jerome once wrote to August, "and was shown your beautiful present all packed and ready to be sent to me. Tiffany begged so hard to be allowed to retain it a day or two to show to his friends that I consented. Indeed, it is such an exquisite gem that I could not refuse him. I suppose you are aware that it is very much superior to your own. It seems at last you consent to my having one thing better than you . . . only on condition, however, that it comes from you!"

Just once did Jerome get the edge on August. Travers, Jerome, and August decided to see who could give the best dinner. The stage for the contest was the Delmonico's at Fifth Avenue and Fourteenth Street, a four-block walk from August's house. They each told Lorenzo Delmonico to surpass himself—no matter what the cost. Delmonico called them the Silver, Gold, and Diamond dinners. Although the competition was judged a draw, Jerome was recognized as the first among equals. For dessert he had served truffled ice cream; for novelties each lady at the table found hidden within her napkin a gold bracelet.

The rivalry between August and Jerome was an expression of deep affection and loyal friendship. After Jerome—who made and lost fortunes with disconcerting frequency and apparent casualness—took a crippling loss in one unlucky gamble, August was one of the few friends who stood by him. And when some members of a new club evidently objected to Jerome's admission, August interceded—behind the scenes to spare Jerome's feelings; but the curtain was raised accidentally, and Jerome caught August in his role as conciliator.

"I shall accept the invitation to join the new club," Jerome told August, "believing from what you said to me that it is proper for me to do so. I must say to you, however, that I know something of what has taken place and of your action in it, and I assure you that I appreciate your kindness far more that I can express—far more than you imagine. Careless as I seem, no one is more sensitive. My only ambition in life is to be accounted an honorable gentleman and good fellow. Judge then how I must have felt [when his name was first rejected]. Fortunately the wound was too deep for me to say anything. I am therefore left free to accept the rescue your kindness and thoughtfulness has provided."

Jerome and August were similar enough in style and temperament for August to see in Jerome's difficulties problems he himself could have had—and for the two men to be seen by others as equally admirable or deplorable.

"This community is devoid of moral sense," Strong said about the Clique and its imitators. "It has proclaimed an extra Beatitude of greater influence than all the others put together, namely, 'Blessed are the smart.' "

"People like Belmont and Jerome do not enter Society," said another New York critic; "they create it as they go along."

Now that the warm weather had come, August, Jr., was flourishing at school. In the playground he and the other boys turned the playhouse into a fort and staged mock battles. They played baseball, soccer, tag; they rowed, swam, and made kites. Caroline sent a few spools of string, some lathing for the kite frames, and, not wanting her son to use rags even for his kite's tail, some expensive cloth that both pleased and embarrassed him by its richness.

Perry ran footraces, which he liked; fenced, which he liked more; and practiced with broadswords, which he liked most.

"This, the summer session, is the best for all outdoor sports," Perry wrote to his father, who had gone on another short trip abroad; "they make this session pass quickly and pleasantly."

Perry became a corporal and then the captain of the school. Shortly before the end of the term his class was taken on an outing to Yale College, where they were received by a few of the professors; but Perry seemed more impressed by the nearby Colt factory and its guns than by Yale. When he left the Rectory School at the end of the fall term of 1865, Perry—now fifteen and as handsome as his father had been as a young man, with the same heavy-lidded eyes and slightly protuberant lower lip—went to Cambridge, Massachusetts. There, preparing to enter Harvard College the following year, he studied with Francis James Child, the Boylston Professor of English.

"Professor Child is one of the most agreeable, pleasant, and kind men I have ever had to deal with," Perry reported to his father. "I study German, French, Latin, Greek, Algebra, Geometry, Arithmetic."

In his exuberance (Perry was also tainted with exuberance) at being in Cambridge—with its cozy book-lined rooms filled with young men studying hard at being interesting, even eccentric, and its air of possibility, of freedom—Perry tried to reassure his father that this was where he should be, that his time was well spent.

"As to Mr. Child's capacity as a teacher," Perry wrote home, "I will give you some proofs. He has travelled in Europe a great deal; he has a nice family; was one of the candidates for President of Harvard College; is now one of its chief professors; and he wrote the song:

> *The waiter roared it through the hall:*
> *We don't serve bread with one fish baw-haw-hawl!"*

At the Rectory School, Perry had left behind him a reputation that had been magnified by the awe of the underclassmen, including August, Jr., who wanted to emulate his brother in all ways.

"Perry," he wrote soon after his brother had left for Cambridge, "we had the best snow fight this afternoon you've ever seen. A pack of boys got together. I was the captain." August, Jr., was proud that like his big brother, who had been the school's captain, he had been chosen to be the leader on the playground—an unofficial rank but no less meaningful for having been bestowed by his playmates. "We made a fort. Another party came out, and we had a fight. Some had to stop for fatigue, others because they could not use their arms on account of firing so much. Half the boys have their faces banged up. Neither side could whip the other, the sides were so equal."

August, Jr., took fencing and riding. He saved money to buy a tent so he could go camping. On Easter vacation of 1866 he went with Perry on a shooting trip to Oak Island, where he was astonished to see how Perry was accepted by the market gunners whom they met in the little hut. He imitated Perry's flirtations.

"I see you have only just found out that I admired Miss Hatty," August, Jr., grumpily told his mother. "I hope you have not and you are not going to tell everyone or anyone. People are such fools"—he corrected himself; his grumpy tone had carried him away into a severity he did not think he could sustain—"I mean so foolish that they always begin to tease a person about such trifling things."

Emulating Perry in more important ways, August, Jr., apparently decided to behave better and study harder. During the spring term of 1866 he was so virtuous that Mr. Everest chose him to meet a visiting bishop; and although one quarter he received a number of reports, he

August Belmont I, 1854

Caroline Belmont, 1854

Simon Belmont

Caroline Belmont

August Belmont I

The Belmont family, The Hague, about 1854. *(Left to right)* Isabel Perry, August Belmont, Perry Belmont, Caroline Belmont, Frederika Belmont, Jane Perry, August Belmont, Jr., Matthew Calbraith Perry.

August Belmont I's mansion at 109 Fifth Avenue, New York City

Mrs. August Belmont by the sea at Newport, Rhode Island, with August Belmont, Jr.

Perry Belmont

Raymond Rogers Belmont

Oliver Belmont

Jane Pauline Belmont (Jessie)

Bessie Hamilton Morgan

Frederika Belmont

Perry Belmont

August Belmont, Jr.

August Belmont

August Belmont driving his carriage in New York City, groom in rear

"New York City—The Largest Financial Operation of the Period—Fifty Million Dollars of United States Bonds Purchased by a Syndicate of Leading Bankers—A Meeting in the Private Office of August Belmont, Esq." (Caption on 1878 engraving)

August Belmont

explained to his mother that the black marks were not deserved and that he would make certain there would be none in the future.

He stuck to his resolutions. By fall his report card showed not a single report for the quarter; and out of a possible weekly grade of 4 he was regularly getting 3's in reading, spelling, composition, declamation, Latin grammar, music, and Bible.

August still was unable to write to his sons as often as he wanted to. Too much was happening. The election, the war's end, the assassination, the new President, and the new President's break with the Republican radicals over Reconstruction in the South. For two years watching American politics was like looking into a kaleidoscope: The pieces kept rearranging themselves into such surprising patterns.

Andrew Johnson, formerly a Democrat, was a Republican president at war with his own party. Right after Lincoln's murder one of the Republican Fire-Eaters, Senator Ben Wade of Ohio, president pro tempore of the Senate and next in line for the presidency, had greeted Johnson with ". . . I thank God that you are here. Lincoln had too much of the milk of human kindness to deal with these damned rebels. Now they will be dealt with according to their deserts."

But Johnson, like Lincoln, resisted Wade's vengeful policy regarding the South. He granted amnesty to most Rebels who took loyalty oaths, and he worked to get the defeated Confederate States readmitted to the Union as quickly as possible—programs that August supported publicly as chairman of the Democratic National Committee, as well as privately.

"The erring members of our political family should be allowed to resume their wonted places in the social circle," said "An Address of the National Committee to the Democracy of the United States" that August had written. "Let them be welcomed as was the prodigal son in the parable and received back with all their rights and privileges unabridged."

August personally wrote to Johnson "to express my sincere admiration for the patriotic, bold, and statesmanlike course which you have pursued."

Trying to woo Johnson into the Democratic party was only half of the strategy the Democrats had adopted; the other half was trying to make sure there would be a Democratic party left to welcome the President if the courtship succeeded. The Republicans were better organized than the Democrats; they controlled the government; and the government controlled Reconstruction. They were using their advantages to prevent the Democrats from regaining traditional strength in the South and from increasing whittled-away support in the North. To survive, the Democrats would need a party organization that was at least as strong as that of the Republicans.

During the last presidential campaign August had noticed how effective the Republican Union League clubs had been in mobilizing influential citizens; so one of the first steps he took to rebuild the Democratic party was to form a comparable organization, the Manhattan Club, in New York. August contributed $10,000, almost one-fifth of the $55,000 needed to buy the clubhouse, at Fifth Avenue and Fifteenth Street, a convenient three-block walk from his mansion. He could stop in on his way to and from Delmonico's, which was on the next block down.

August also considered holding a Democratic National Convention, which would include representatives from revivified Democratic committees in the former Confederate States, to discuss the party's postwar course. But some pro-Johnson Democrats and Republicans had formed a new party, the National Union, which preempted August's plans by calling for a convention in Philadelphia. Many Democratic politicians whose support would be vital to any Democratic conclave seemed to be switching their loyalties to the National Union. The new movement, August told Samuel Barlow, had "taken the wind out of our own sails." In fact, August felt their ship was more than becalmed; it was scuttled.

To Manton Marble, August started referring to the Democratic National Committee as "defunct." The National Union, although ostensibly organized to bring together like-minded politicians of the two parties in support of the President's program, had ignored August in forming its executive staff. As a result, it undercut the power of the Democratic National Committee and left August feeling that he had been "shabbily treated."

He was disheartened by the personal affront and the stupid politics of the move. Important Democrats were flocking to join a party that was actually run by Democratic foes who were "richly disguised." It would not be long before they woke up to find Republicans in control of both the National Union and the Republican parties; and since their own party would have been bled to death by their desertion, they would have nowhere to turn. August certainly would not be waiting to welcome them home. He contemplated resigning his post in the Democratic party.

But if he did not fight to keep the Democratic party alive he would be as responsible for destroying it as the National Union Democrats were. After all, he could not let himself quit. If he threw the support of the Democratic National Committee behind the Philadelphia convention he might be able to influence the policy of the National Union and keep it from being dominated by Republicans and disloyal Democrats; but that would be tantamount, he told Barlow, to "giving up the *National Democratic organization*," a dangerous sacrifice, since if he was not able to affect National Union decisions after joining, the sacrifice would be suicide. On the other hand, if the loyal Democrats went ahead and held their own convention, the Democratic party and the National Union would split Johnson's support and hand both the 1866 state elections as well as state and national elections of 1868 to the radical Republicans.

"For my own part," August continued, "I *want only to do what* is best for the country and what will most effectively kill the radicals in and out of Congress and really restore the Union."

August decided on a tactical compromise. The Democratic party would support but not submerge itself into the National Union.

"Things seem to shape themselves in a fashion which only can become useful to our party," August told Marble, one of the few people in whom he felt he could confide. "The Philadelphia Convention must bring matters to a crisis." And August was sure any crisis would break the new party. There were too many factions within the National Union, too many fault lines along which the united front could crack.

When Johnson visited New York in the summer of 1866, August attended a dinner in the President's honor at Delmonico's; but instead of sitting at the head table with the President, the mayor of New York, Seward, General Grant, and various other politicians and assorted businessmen, he protected his independence by sitting five tables down. He kept his political distance too at a National Union rally that he officially supported but where he decided he would not speak. He did not want himself or the Democratic party to be too closely associated with the National Union—which was wise, as it turned out.

After his appearance in New York, Johnson left for Chicago and during the trip humiliated himself by arguing with hecklers who interrupted his speeches.

The President "became so aroused," Clews later reported, "that he forgot the dignity of his office and station and condescended to bandy words and exchange terms of ribaldry with people in the crowd. He then became the butt of savage ridicule. . . . My business friends and I were heartily sorry that we had anything to do with this unruly Executive."

Pro-Johnson candidates were defeated in the state elections of 1866. The National Union was dead.

Perhaps as a result of the political strains, August was suffering from debilitating headaches. And Caroline was suffering from the death of her friend Mary Cunard. She clipped the obituary from the newspaper and saved it in a black-bordered mourning envelope along with a lock of Mary's hair and a slip of paper on which she had written, "Forget not the dead/ Forget not the dead who have loved, who have left us."

The season had started so well. August and Caroline had been given a surprise domino party that was a great success. Because of the masks August and Caroline had not known until midnight who many of the guests were; and Caroline had been sent thirty-two of the most beautiful flower baskets August had ever seen.

"We did not go downstairs as we do when you are here," Frederika wrote to August, Jr. The excitement of the event—the laughter and music —filtered up to the children's rooms and left them giddy and longing to take a peek at the festivities.

But after Mary's funeral Caroline did not feel like partying.

Mary's death was not the only reminder of mortality. The family went ahead with plans to disinter Commodore Perry's body and rebury it in Newport near his parents' graves. The war had made death so common that it was a shock when peace once more made death singular.

🪶 *CHAPTER THIRTY-ONE* 🪶

THE BELMONTS WENT to Saratoga to distract themselves from Mary's death in familiar amusements. But Saratoga had changed.

The Union Hotel had been enlarged. The United States Hotel—and a good part of the town—had burned. The Clarendon (where August stayed) was now Sarotaga's most stylish resort. Daring women wore mascara; daring men wooed them. And John Morrissey had arrived.

Morrissey had the build of a bear and almost as much hair. His full beard grew high on his cheeks and covered his mouth and chin in a dense mat that was relieved only by a gaping hole in which his tongue, like a clam in its seaweed-covered shell, occasionally could be seen. He was a former thief, former ballot-box stuffer, former gang-leader, former champion boxer, and former brawler. In a fight over a prostitute named Kate Ridgely he was pressed onto a spilled bed of hot coals by his opponent, Tom McCann, until the room reeked of his burning flesh. His friends threw water over him and the coals, and the steam that shot up around Morrissey blinded and scorched McCann enough for Morrissey to escape—and to beat McCann senseless. Ever since then Morrissey had been called Old Smoke.

Morrissey owned in full or in part sixteen gambling halls in New York City, including one, elegantly adorned with velvet, satin, rosewood, and silver, that was next door to fashionable Grace Church. In 1861 he opened his first casino in Saratoga. Two years later, with backing from Travers, Jerome, and John R. Hunter (a leading horse-breeder), Morrissey opened a racetrack—not the informal kind for trotters that August used to compete on when he visited the town but a formally laid-out stretch with a comfortable grandstand for spectators. The track was so successful that the following year he opened an even better track with a more luxurious grandstand, where August could often be seen in a light top-hat decorated with a silver feather, a hat that for a while became his trademark.

The town in which August had courted Caroline existed only as a memory of an idyllic and quaint resort. Like the country Saratoga was growing up; and partly because of the appeal of the Saratoga track, society was smitten with turf-fever.

In 1865, under the name of the Villa Site Association, Jerome had bought, for $250,000, 250 acres of the old Bathgate farm in Fordham just north of Manhattan. On the property, at the base of a bluff, he laid out a B-shaped racetrack, oddly fashioned because of the terrain. Instead of being level the track had slight undulations that experts thought would benefit the horses; and along the back bar of the B, Jerome built a two-story grandstand 450 feet long with seats for 8,000 spectators. A small stand with private boxes and general seating for 2,500 was reserved for members of the Jockey Club, a group Jerome organized to complement the track. There were also a bandstand; seven stables, each with ten stalls; various outbuildings and sheds; kitchens and rooms for trainers and jockeys; a half-mile exercise track; and opposite the grandstand, on the bluff overlooking the main track, a clubhouse with a ballroom, dining rooms, and bedrooms that often were used by Jockey Club members and their mistresses.

Next to the clubhouse and rising above the rest was a fifty-foot observatory tower that gave a view to the north of villages, farms, orchards, and woods; to the west, the Hudson River and the Palisades; to the east, Long Island Sound; and to the south, New York City, the sun glinting from its roofs. The track—Jerome Park—would hold its first meet at the end of September 1866.

August was determined to have his horses win on Jerome's track. He set out to establish the best racing stud in the country. On the 1,100 to 1,300 acres he had bought in Babylon, Long Island, he built his Nursery Farm where, on a rise in the middle of the property, loomed a twenty-four-room mansion—"a handsome modern structure," as one of the sporting papers reported, "so lofty that we should think the Fire Island Lighthouse and the sea might be seen from the top of it on a clear day." In front of the house a perfectly groomed lawn, as green and smooth as the baize on a cardtable, sloped down to a thirty-acre lake. Across the lake were a trout-stocked hatching pond; a farmhouse; five cottages; two siloes; barns; fields for growing corn, hay, wheat, and rye; pastures for cows, ponies, and workhorses; pens for hogs; runs for chickens. . . . A self-sufficient community.

Behind the main house were the bowling alley, the stables where August kept his carriage horses and gamecocks, the dog kennels, the ice-house, and the greenhouse where, as the sun rose, condensation would bead and streak the inside of the glass. Off to the right was a pine grove, where the horses were put to stud, and five stables with thirteen stalls. The lower branches of the pines were kept pruned; it was a breezy spot. Near the grove were paddocks; in fact, all over the property were paddocks, thirty-six altogether, some of the outlying ones with four-stall stables standing conveniently nearby.

A short distance east of the grove were the main stables, which had twenty-seven stalls; a pair of extra stables with twelve more stalls for any overflow; the trainer's house; a bunkhouse for fifty stableboys; two windmills; a gristmill for the horses' feed; a blacksmithy; and a large square building where the horses were trained and, during the winter, exercised. This training barn was connected to the main stables by covered walkways, so that the horses were protected from bad weather.

South of the main house was a private one-mile-long racetrack with its own grandstand, where August could sit all by himself if he wished and watch his horses race.

August had created a village, an ideal world to which he could retreat; and his retreats were productive. He raided the finest established stables for horses, buying one broodmare with an excellent bloodline from Mayer Rothschild, who told him, "I am glad to hear that you intend forming a racing stud, for I am sure you will derive much pleasure from it and that your energetic and business-like habits will enable you to make it profitable. I have no doubt that you will be a triumph on the Turf"—which August, in fact, was destined to become. After his death he would be recognized by one sporting paper as "probably the most influential man in American racing from 1866 until . . . 1890."

By the time of the first meet at Jerome Park in the fall of 1866, August was ready to challenge Jerome or anyone else on the track. He had already beaten Jerome in the clubhouse.

"When Leonard Jerome got up his park and started the Jockey Club, he was looking for a president," a newspaper later reported. "The name of Mr. Belmont suggested itself quite naturally. Jerome is a man of too broad intelligence to have wished to see a mere figurehead presiding over the club, or to have ever supposed that Belmont was a person of whom a figurehead could be made under any circumstances. But he must naturally enough have expected that he would preserve a kind of complementary influence over the management of an institution upon which he had spent a half-million dollars. Not a bit of it. By the close of the very first season of his presidency, Belmont was the autocratic ruler of the club, while Jerome . . . stood powerless by his side as one of the vice-presidents."

At eleven o'clock on the morning of September 25, 1866, the streets of Manhattan were crowded with hundreds of dogcarts, wagons, hired buggies, old-fashioned coaches, and stylish calèches. Every conveyance in the city except hearses seemed to be on its way uptown to Jerome Park. No doubt as usual "whenever a member of the Belmont clique rode past," as one observer later recalled about those years, "there was no lack of derisive remarks on the part of the Vanderbilt people, and this in turn provoked unprintable answers from those attacked."

The Central Bridge over the Harlem River was jammed with traffic. And at the entrance of the track the crowd was even worse: Carriages three abreast were backed up all the way down the new hundred-foot-wide road Jerome had built. Along either side streamed people who had come up on the Harlem Railroad and were walking from the terminal to the track, stopping on their way to argue about horses, buy beer from the stands set up at the edges of the fields, or sit and watch the carriages moving slowly ahead.

The Jockey Club members had a private entrance. Inside, they parked their coaches close to the fence overlooking the track and, with tablecloths spread on the coach tops or grass, opened their wicker hampers and unpacked picnics. Liveried servants served. Champagne corks popped. The smell of good cigars drifted over the lawn. Every so often another brightly colored parasol would bloom. Pennants snapped in the breeze. Dodsworth's Band played selections from Jacques Offenbach's *Orpheus in Hades.*

People looked for August. Or, if they did not know him, asked that he be pointed out, since word had spread that "while Baron Rothschild is reinforcing his stable and is struggling for supremacy on the English turf, the representative in this country of the great banking house, August Belmont, Esq., is organizing a stable with the hope of eclipsing all rivals. . . . He is now the recognized head of the leading racing association in America."

August had, if not stolen the day from Jerome, at least forced Jerome to share the honors.

From where he sat August could watch the grandstand fill. At first more than nine thousand spectators crammed into the building, some sharing seats, others milling in the aisles. And still people kept pouring onto the grounds. An estimated thirty thousand turned out for the opening day of Jerome Park.

"As a mere popular success, it was complete," said *The New York Times* of the first day; "as a record of turf intelligence, it was most interesting; as an event in the progress of sporting, it opens an era."

On the last day of the four-day meet a special race was arranged between August's Maid of Honor and Jerome's Redwing. Both were well-bred two-year-olds. August had bought Maid of Honor the previous summer in Saratoga for $5,000 and since then had raced her twice, on Morrissey's track and on the second day of the Jerome Park meet. In both races she started fast but was edged out of first place in the homestretch—in Saratoga, by a horse named Ruthless. Redwing had beaten Ruthless, so August figured that if Maid of Honor could beat Redwing, her honor—and his—would be redeemed. He also enjoyed the idea of racing Jerome one on one.

The race was a three-quarter-mile dash for a purse of $1,000. Maid of Honor was the 2 to 1 favorite until just before post time, when the odds dropped to 5 to 4. Then the odds changed again: they were even money. In the last minutes before the race the odds changed once more: Redwing became the favorite. In fact, the last bet placed was for Redwing, $800 to $700.

At the start Redwing took an easy lead. As they passed the grandstand she was a length ahead. But Maid of Honor had the longer stride. At the base of the bluff she started gaining. Slowly Maid of Honor edged up on Redwing until they were neck and neck. At the top of the homestretch Maid of Honor nosed ahead. Redwing fought gamely, but Maid of Honor kept increasing her lead and won by two lengths. August's colors, maroon-and-red, were victorious. He had beaten Jerome on the track.

August, Jerome, and the other members of the Jockey Club had a little more than a week to bask in the success of the park before the storm of criticism broke. The Jockey Club was working a little too hard to make racing respectable, some people thought.

"An attempt has been made within the last fortnight to make horseracing a 'genteel' amusement in this country—something which people belonging to what is called 'good society' will go to see, and, seeing, grow fond of—by the opening of a course called the 'Jerome Park,' " said *The Nation*. "The matter has been taken in hand by the chiefs of what are called 'fashionable circles' in New York. A good course has been laid out, a 'grandstand' provided, the sale of liquors prohibited"—not entirely true; beer was sold and, if *The New York Times* can be trusted, bourbon, too—"and everything done that money or zeal can do to surround the enterprise with an air of respectability, and, above all, to make the course a 'place fit for ladies.' Good horses, too, were entered for the opening races; very fair running was made; the weather was fine; the proceedings were marked by the utmost order, and General Grant was there. And yet we have no hesitation in saying that, regarded as an attempt to naturalize horse-racing amongst us . . . it was a complete failure, and will prove a failure no matter how often repeated. . . . We are anything but an equestrian community. Not one in a thousand of our men knows how to ride or ever gets into a saddle from year's end to year's end. . . . We venture to assert that the principal promoters of this very enterprise—Mr. Jerome himself, for example, or Mr. Belmont—are never seen on horseback and do not particularly enjoy riding." This was also not entirely true: August rode (although because of his lame hip he rode sidesaddle) and enjoyed it.

The Nation's argument was specious. People did not have to ride to enjoy watching others ride. But *The Nation* did not depend on its argument to make its point. It asserted that the turf in America was "abandoned to as thorough a set of sharpers as ever disgraced a moral and religious community."

"Fancy a man in . . . respectable and self-respecting print calling Messrs. . . . Jerome, . . . Travis, and Belmont, &c, 'a thorough set of sharpers,' " said a sporting paper in the Jockey Club's defense, "—not to mention, by the way, General Grant."

Part of the press, aiming for a broader target, accepted August and his friends as representatives of their city and used the occasion to dismiss New York.

"Whenever New York people start any kind of idea," said the *Pittsburgh Daily Commercial*, "it speedily becomes a mania with them. As a general thing they are irrational and absurd over any new sensation, indulge in it to excess, and finally run it into the ground. They have done so with the opera, with different kinds of drama, with every species of literature, with each variety of dissipation, with Princes of Wales and Japanese Tommies. . . . The latest mania there is . . . horse racing. . . . To gratify this irrepressible fancy, a meeting"—extra days of races in November—"is announced to come off at . . . Jerome Park tomorrow. . . . It is almost impossible to imagine anything more ridiculous. Think of spending the half of a bleak, biting . . . day in the open air, waiting by the half hour to see a contest of two or three minutes duration. Imagine the belles' blue noses and the beaus' numbed toes. How pocket handkerchiefs will be in request with the one and whiskey toddies with the other. And the poor animals! Roadsters shivering under the sheds, and racers' lungs strained almost to rupturing by the rarified keen air that will rush through their expanded nostrils. What pleasure can there be in it? . . . When cruelty—which this is—begins, sport ceases."

Another newspaper suggested that one horse, a favorite that was pulled out of a race two days before the meet, had been scratched to manipulate the betting or had been included in the original program only to sucker in spectators.

" . . . Before you could take your vehicle within sight of the course," the newspaper said, "you had to pay a dollar for each of the horses in your wagon, a dollar for the driver, a dollar for yourself, a dollar for your wife, and a dollar for each of the children. Even this complicated tariff only opened the way for you to get a passing glimpse of the course and the racers. After complying with the dues at the outer port, you had to pay another dollar for each of your party to reach the stand from which you could see anything. The whole financial part of the arrangements indeed suggested that the thing was not got up in the interest of horse culture, but like a traveling circus, *to pay*. And the first day did pay. Nearly thirty thousand dollars in all were taken from *paying* visitors."

This newspaper estimated that four days' worth of racing would have brought in about $100,000.

For weeks the sporting papers defended Jerome Park by describing the importance and acceptability of racing in England, France, Germany, Austria, Hungary, Russia, Italy, India, and even Turkey. The accusation that the park—in which Jerome had invested hundreds of thousands of dollars and whose losses he had arranged to cover up to $25,000 a year—had been created primarily to make money was absurd.

Of course Jerome hoped the park would make money; but he had laid out the grounds so that those who could not afford the entrance fee could "do as thousands of others did . . . , witness the contests . . . from public ground where no post of entry must be passed and where no tickets are demanded," as one of the sporting papers explained. "The hills command a splendid view of the course, and these points of observation"— except the Jockey Club's bluff—"are free to all."

The paper further defended the admission charge by saying: "The prestige of Jerome Park only can be preserved by a strict enforcement of the rules which necessitate a grading of classes. Throw the course open to the rabble and in a very brief time it will degenerate and become a synonym for all that is rude and licentious. Unfortunately . . . classes *do exist*, and upon the race course, as elsewhere, we have to deal with this stubborn fact. . . . We do not hope to effect a social reform through the medium of racing."

August's response to such criticism was more terse than that of the sporting paper.

"Racing," he said, "is for the rich."

In the middle of fall that year, the night sky was filled with meteors: shooting stars in a display so vivid and extravagant that it seemed as though the heavens had surrendered to the Flash Age. The highlight of the season was a performance of tableaux vivants given in Jerome's theater, the proceeds of which were to help the Southern poor. Belle portrayed Summer; Caroline, Winter, her icicles diamonds. As though frozen by her jewels she took ill and had to spend the rest of the winter at Hot Springs for the cure.

When she returned August took her to Newport, and there he followed what he called the "ridiculous onslaughts of snobs and demagogues," the anti-horse-racing lobby. His information on their attacks was spotty, since his copies of the *New York World* were not being forwarded properly and, as he told Marble, the *World* was the "only channel through which I derive all my knowledge of politics, finance, and *horse-racing,*" an assertion that sacrificed truth for humor. He was tugging Marble's nose, because the newspaper was having so much trouble getting issues to him.

What August read in the *World* and the other irregularly delivered newspapers was, however, not a joking matter. The complaints about racing had been refined over the winter to include objections to the special privileges given to the nine hundred Jockey Club members.

To counter these charges August gave Marble a simple defense: "You cannot have races without horses, and you cannot have horses without good purses. A large fixed income to provide for these purses can only be secured by a club, and a club can only be established by giving to its members certain privileges."

To prove his point August sponsored a new yearly race.

The Belmont Stakes, originally a race for three-year-olds of a mile and three-quarters, was inaugurated on the first day of Jerome Park's Summer Meet. The weather was perfect. Although Barnum's Bearded Lady and Lightning Calculator (who according to rumor had challenged and been defeated by the Jerome Park master bookmaker, Dr. Underwood) were not present as they had been at the Spring Meet a month earlier, families could still amuse themselves before the races by examining the camel on display and, as one reporter did, watching "the sheep rush . . . headlong through the grass in mad gambols."

Jerome arrived, dashing along in his four-in-hand at more than seven miles an hour, the speed limit in Central Park.

Travers, trotting along more slowly, followed in a calèche.

The stands, as usual, were packed.

The Belmont Stakes, which was run second that day, was won by Ruthless, an excellent horse that some time later was accidentally shot and killed by a hunter poaching on the owner's estate. Maid of Honor had been scratched; and, in fact, she would not have had a chance against Ruthless. But August must have been disappointed not to have had a horse in the race.

It had been a discouraging year. One of August's new colts had won a race in the Jerome Park Spring Meet, but that was an isolated victory among a string of defeats. Maid of Honor was beaten twice during the spring, twice during the summer, and at least once in Saratoga. In one of the races she did so badly that a sporting paper reported she "was now dead as a red herring and ought to have been stopped," which may have been a gentle rebuke to August, who a few months before had joined the executive committee of the just organized American Society for the Prevention of Cruelty to Animals.

The rebuke was uncalled-for. August cared for his horses and had no intention of running any of them into the ground. He accepted the lost races with good grace—and continued buying up the best horses he could find. He had no intention of doing as badly in the future.

❧ CHAPTER THIRTY-TWO ❧

TO FINANCE THE CIVIL WAR the United States government had borrowed gold. After the war a movement developed to repay the gold loans with the paper currency that the government had issued. A paper dollar was worth less than a dollar's worth of gold; so if the loans were repaid in paper, the people who lent the gold would be getting back less than they had given, about fifty or sixty cents on the dollar. Since the public debt was about $2.5 billion, the difference between repayment in gold and paper was substantial. The two positions, progold and progreenback, were held with passions often in direct relation to whether one had lent money or not.

Having lent the government money, August was progold.

The issue, however, involved more than the government and bankers. If the United States paid its debts in gold, a dollar would be worth a full dollar again; and any shopkeeper, small businessman, or farmer who during the war years had borrowed greenbacks worth half a dollar would end up repaying their loans with greenbacks worth twice that much. As a result they wanted the government to repay the loans with paper money; and they accused the bankers of wanting to get gold at the expense of the public good. The controversy dramatized the increasing separation between the classes in the United States, and the geography of this class struggle revealed the growing split between the East and the West, the East tending to be progold and the West tending to be progreenback. For a country that was just staggering away from a conflict between North and South, this East-West friction seemed to be a sign that the nation was drawing and quartering itself.

State governments, too, had borrowed gold and were eager to pay their debts in greenbacks. Acting for the Rothschilds, August had lent Pennsylvania a little under half a million dollars. Early in 1868 the notes came due. August sent the first $190,886.10 note in to be redeemed, along with a letter that said the Rothschilds "again complain of the injustice of the action of the State of Pennsylvania in forcing its creditors to accept payment in a depreciated currency and have instructed us to receive payment only under protest."

Hoping that Pennsylvania might reverse its position, August told the treasurer of the state, William H. Kemble, that he and the Rothschilds would like "to hold the stock, if an arrangement could be made with your state for a continuation of the loan and will only accept payment now, if compelled to do so by a discontinuance of the interest."

"No arrangement can be made by which the Messrs. Rothschild can retain the old loan and continue to draw interest on it," answered Kemble, who added that he had "not the slightest objection" to August's and the Rothschilds' accepting payment under protest, so long as they accepted payment in devalued greenbacks.

With gratuitous cruelty Kemble added, "I have not yet heard of your conscience compelling you to pay your liabilities in gold instead of the legal-tender [greenbacks]. We are willing to give you the pound of flesh, but not one drop of Christian blood."

August was appalled at Kemble's "coarse and impertinent tone," although he was not as surprised as he would have been a decade earlier. In the past few years there had been a noticeable increase in anti-semitism in the country. He had suffered from it in the last election; another election was coming up, and he would suffer from it again. German-American Gentiles composed songs about him telling him to stay out of politics; and at least one German-American club next to an anti-Belmont song in their songbook drew a picture of the three clustered balls signifying a pawn shop. People who during the war had accused August of not investing in the Union and of buying Confederate bonds now attacked him for having invested so heavily in the Union that the United States was in hock to him.

August thought Kemble's "letter deserved a severe rebuke," and in his answer he explained to Kemble that the Rothschilds had bought the Pennsylvania state notes for resale abroad, and that because Pennsylvania was paying off the loan in greenbacks, "hundreds of widows and orphans have been reduced to beggary"—a dramatic if undocumented charge. Not many widows and orphans speculated in state notes. More to the point, August told Kemble that the Pennsylvania loan was "the most disastrous security ever negotiated by" the Rothschilds; and he implied that since the "negotiation had been based principally upon the faith of the State of Pennsylvania," the state's honor had been sullied.

The anti-Semitic gibe August dismissed by saying he regretted that "the State of Pennsylvania should have for its treasurer a person who could so far disgrace the state he assumes to represent and forget the dignity of the office he holds, as to reply to a civil business communication in a manner which must raise the blush of shame on the cheek of every citizen of that great and honored state."

August waited a few days to see if Kemble would send an apology before he gave the correspondence to the press in order, he told the Rothschilds, to "show up the State of Pennsylvania."

"We desire to call the attention of our readers to these letters," said the *Harrisburg* (Pa.) *Patriot and Union*, a Democratic newspaper, "as illustrating one of the many methods by which an unworthy state official may disgrace the Commonwealth he is appointed to serve. . . . Whatever the interests of the state may demand in regard to the proposition made by the London bankers, it would not have been difficult for a *gentleman* to reply in courteous terms. Courtesy, however, not being a Radical virtue, Mr. Kemble does not seem able to manifest it. His answer to Mr. Belmont, even if written as a private individual, would have been ill-bred impertinence; but penned by him as treasurer of the state, it is a gross insult, not more directed to his correspondent than to the citizens of the Commonwealth."

It was to be expected that a Democratic newspaper would champion August's cause; but even a Republican newspaper found August's letters "as usual, gentlemanly, high-toned, courteous, and business-like" and Kemble's letter "boorish, bigoted, and ungentlemanly. We have hitherto entertained quite an exalted opinion of Mr. Kemble as a . . . politician, while in politics we never agreed with Mr. Belmont. Let us hope that our state treasurer was drunk when he wrote that unfortunate letter."

Like the Republicans the Democrats were split over the gold-green-back controversy—just as they were split on most of the other important issues facing them. They had lost the last two elections because of inter-party strife. August wanted to make sure that if they lost the election of 1868 they at least would lose it united.

As early as December 1866 August had called the executive committee of the Democratic National Committee to his house to discuss plans for appointing National Committee members from the former Confederate States. Without state committee chairmen there would be no state committees in the South; without state committees there would be no significant Democratic vote in the South; and without a significant Southern Democratic vote it was unlikely that a Democratic presidential candidate could be elected.

However, it was hard to find politicians to head the Southern state committees. August wanted the Southern state Democratic leaders to be men who had been active and committed Unionists, people who would be able to stand on their records in resisting Republican attacks on their loyalty. But August soon found that many who were willing to serve were suspected of having Republican tendencies; while many who were above suspicion were unwilling to serve. In five Southern states August was unable to get his first choices for the vacancies in the Democratic party machinery. His Georgia candidate was too controversial. And his Florida and North Carolina candidates were too radical. His Virginia candidate declined, as did his candidate from Texas, who said:

"I fear that the principles of government inaugurated by the formers of the Republic are in great jeopardy and that the overthrow to which they have been temporarily subjected by the late war and recent measures of Congress is likely to become permanent."

The lenient programs for Reconstruction that Lincoln and Johnson had supported were overturned by the Radicals in Congress, who wanted the South to be reconstructed Republican. The Radicals' motives were mixed. Some Radicals were idealists; others were demagogues. Whatever their motives, their methods were tyrannical. The South was carved up into five military districts ruled by martial law. These states would not be allowed representation in Congress until they ratified the Fourteenth Amendment, which among other acts gave black men the vote and forbade certain former Confederate leaders to hold office, an incendiary combination. Despite its undeniable humanitarian aims and understandable desire to make sure those who led the Confederacy would not again be in a position to rebel against the United States, Congress was legislating a heritage of hate. Southerners were growing more embittered with every congressional Reconstruction act. In the war the North had defeated its Southern enemies; in the peace it was losing its Southern friends. August's candidate from Texas told him to disband the Democratic Party.

"It can never be reorganized and consolidated sufficiently to save the Constitution," he said. Not, at least, under that name; as a new party perhaps. But the Democratic party, he said, was dead.

In some states August did not even get his second or third choice. One man he approached turned down the offer because, he explained, "the war has reduced me to poverty, and I would be unable to attend the meetings of the Committee if I could accept."

At last August found suitable and trustworthy men for all the vacancies except one—and eventually that vacancy, too, was filled. Now that the Democrats had a truly national National Committee again, it was time for that committee to meet to choose a place and a time for their National Convention.

The meeting was set for Washington's Birthday, February 22, in Washington, D.C.

All through that winter August and Manton Marble plotted policy for politics and society. When Seward increased the already huge national debt by buying Alaska, August told Marble, "I think it will be a good thing to show up Mr. Seward's management of the financial parts of his land speculation," and orchestrated the *New York World*'s editorial attacks on the secretary of state. And when an opera ball threatened to be a fiasco, August and Marble conspired to sell tickets to the dance through puffs in the press. But this year August enjoyed his public activities less than usual because he was frequently ill and family demands were great.

That winter, Perry complained that the cold and high snowdrifts were preventing him from escaping his lessons when he was not prepared by conning Professor Child into the garden to talk about growing roses, Child's hobby, or politics, Perry's growing passion. During the fall Perry had depended on this ruse; he hoped to use it again in the spring.

In the meantime he did his lessons as best he could in between taking music instruction two days a week from the organist at the old South Church; hanging around with the other "subs" who were preparing for Harvard; haunting concert halls and theaters; riding his horse (when the weather allowed); fencing, boxing; being inspired by Longfellow's dignity during frequent teas with the poet and his sister; reading the *New*

York World, which he received as irregularly as his father did in Newport; and generally enjoying himself so much that he usually slept until eight-thirty in the morning, occasionally not appearing for lessons until ten-thirty. Professor Child told August that he wanted "a different arrangement," a mild way of demanding that Perry shape up.

August, Jr., also was having problems. Misunderstandings with his teachers, which had begun the previous year, had matured as quickly as he had. Although he was working harder than ever before, so intently that he let his family correspondence slide, his report cards bristled with black marks—most of which he claimed were unjustly given. His teachers were mean; and he told his mother, "If there is anything I hate, it's meanness. I can't put up with such things like some can." On top of the meanness he felt that the school's quality was "falling off," and he wanted to go home where he could be privately tutored. However, until his parents made a decision, he figured "I will have to make the best of it. I must bear it." He accepted the situation, but he continued to lobby for change.

He tried to distract himself. He wrote affectionate teasing letters to Jeannie, who was unhappy because she thought a valentine he had sent to both sisters had not been meant for her, and Frederika, who had begun calling herself, in French, "Rickie the Wolf." He drew careful pictures with the colored pencils Jeannie had sent him; and because getting sick at school was so unpleasant, he just as carefully played in winter sports. However, even sports were not very amusing this year; the weather was too changeable, heavy snows alternating with unseasonable thaws. When there was good coasting, there was bad skating; when there was good skating, there was bad coasting. You could not have both; there was always a trade-off. The weather was giving August, Jr., a lesson in the economics of reality; and August, Jr., having inherited his father's precise nature, balanced his accounts daily.

"I keep careful track of everything," he told Jeannie—including, no doubt, his treatment at school, each unfair report against him becoming in his reckoning a report against his unfair teachers, so that both he and his teachers were piling up black marks. Life in Hamden was becoming insupportable.

Caroline tried to console him by sending him, when he asked for mittens, an expensive pair made of fur.

"Now it would have been much better," August, Jr., told his mother patiently, "and will still be to send me a common pair of lined buckskin mitts."

When fur mittens get wet, August, Jr., explained, "they get hard and don't keep my hands warm." And they were so delicate that "I would require a new pair almost every two weeks." August, Jr., appreciated the sentiment; but the fur mittens—like the kite-tail material Caroline had sent him—were a thwarted gesture. In being thoughtful she was being thoughtless; in trying to please her son by getting him the best, she displeased him by not being practical.

Anyway, August, Jr., would not be put off by loving gifts, whether they were practical or impractical. He only wanted to leave school. His father looked around for a tutor but delayed making the final arrangements, because once August, Jr., heard that his parents were planning to withdraw him from the school, he stopped writing such desperate letters home.

"It seems as if, since I cooled down in the tone of my letters a month ago," August, Jr., said, "you are now trying to overcome me and make me stay here, to which I don't consent."

Since he evidently had to be frantic to convince his father that he could not remain at school, he became frantic. He wildly promised that he would study as hard, harder, at home than he did at school; that he would not loll around the house wasting time; and that "if I should come home I would be a different boy, pursuing an entirely different course than I heretofore have done."

August, Jr., swore, "I will be prepared by nobody else than a private tutor and at home. I have not been able to study tonight, and I don't believe I will be able till I am out of this nasty hole, which now seems more odious to me than ever. I can't attend to books till I get out of this 'devil's mansion.' "

August wrote to Mr. Everest saying that he wished to withdraw August, Jr. He intended, he said, after having him tutored at home to send him to Rugby in England. Could Mr. Everest suggest a private course of study to prepare August, Jr., for Rugby?

Mr. Everest expressed his disappointment at losing August, Jr., and his distress at hearing where August intended to send his son.

"Rugby is a *noble* school," he wrote August, the frequent underlining in his letter suggesting an inflection in his spoken voice that was Dickensian; "and there is no better. But there are many *usages* in all those *high* schools in England which render it desirable if not *necessary* that a boy who would *succeed* in them should be very *rugged*. I allude to their *sports*, their *games*, their *'fagging,'* and their *'fighting.'* . . . Now Augie is *delicate*. While he is more rugged than he was, he yet is *delicate* and needs tender care and watching. He easily breaks down and requires *humoring*. And I should not *dare* to expose him to so *rough an ordeal*."

August gave up the idea of sending August, Jr., to Rugby. He would find a good American preparatory school for his son. Caroline wrote to August, Jr., telling him to be ready to leave the following week. August, Jr., wanted to bolt immediately.

"It makes me mad and fretful," he told his mother, "to see how much time *I lost* by your obstinacy in opposing my coming home."

Caroline answered that he could come home whenever he was ready, which further irritated him.

"You have not gone about this in the right way," he said. "How can I decide when I am to come home? Mr. Everest would never send me home on the little authority you give in your letter."

It was maddening. Every misunderstanding required an exchange of letters to solve, and every exchange of letters delayed his homecoming. The extent to which August and Caroline trusted their son to make his own decisions was so foreign to the authoritarian spirit of the school that August, Jr., was sure Mr. Everest would use it as an excuse to keep him in Hamden as long as he could.

"Please write by first mail to Mr. E.," August, Jr., pleaded with his mother, "telling him when to send me home. Do not leave anything for him to decide. It will only make trouble."

At last he was freed; but his father was not sure the freedom would be salutary.

"Will you come and see me on your way downtown," August jotted in a note that he sent early one morning by courier to Marble; "I want to see you very much about my child who gives me a great deal of anxiety."

❧ CHAPTER THIRTY-THREE ❧

ALMOST FROM THE BEGINNING of his administration Congress distrusted Johnson's ability and inclination to deal with the former Rebels "according to their deserts," as the congressional Radicals had hoped he would do once he had been sworn into office; so it set out to hobble him. Laws were passed preventing Johnson from naming Supreme Court judges, stripping him of command of the army, and requiring him to get the permission of the Senate before discharging anyone who had been appointed to office with the advice and consent of the Senate. This last, the Tenure of Office Act, was the most galling. Unable to bring his own men into the government, Johnson could not form his own administration. He was a prisoner of Congress.

Johnson tried to break out of his legislative cage by testing the Tenure of Office Act. He dismissed Secretary of War Stanton, whom the act had been designed in particular to protect. The Senate returned Stanton to office. On February 21, 1868, Johnson again dismissed Stanton. That night the Senate again returned him to office. Early the following morning, the same day the Democratic National Committee was meeting in Washington, the man Johnson had nominated to take Stanton's place as secretary of war was arrested for violating the Tenure of Office Act. And if the Radicals dared arrest Johnson's nominee they were obviously ready to take on Johnson himself. By the time the Democratic National Committee was assembled at the Metropolitan Hotel, it was clear that the Radicals thought they finally had gotten what they had been waiting for: grounds to impeach the President.

The Democrats must have felt smug. With the Republicans savaging each other the Democrats had a better chance of winning the presidential election—if they could maintain a united front. After settling on July 4 in New York for the upcoming Democratic National Convention the committee had adjourned to the White House for a dinner given in their honor by Johnson.

During the meal, it was later reported, when Johnson brought up politics August "rather curtly rebuked" him. Politics were not discussed at social occasions. But it is unlikely that August, punctilious in matters of etiquette, would have chided his host even if he felt the President had stepped out of line. It is even more unlikely that if August had said anything he would have been curt. And in any case, given the events of the past day and a half, no one could have pretended that the dinner was not political. The show of fraternity between the Republican President and the Democratic National Committee benefited Johnson by demonstrating that he was not friendless and worked to the advantage of the Democrats by allowing them to combine public duty with partisan ends: they were supporting the President, which might lure some pro-Johnson Republicans into their ranks and would undoubtedly enrage the Radicals, causing further bloodletting in the Republican Party.

Within two days the Republican Radicals plunged in the knives. On February 24 the House impeached Johnson. A month later the Senate tried and failed by one vote to convict him.

While anti-Johnson Republicans were suggesting that Johnson should plead not guilty by virtue of drunkenness or insanity, Democrats were considering the possibility of choosing Johnson as the Democratic party's presidential candidate, thus isolating the Radicals and further tempting Republican conservatives into the Democratic party. August was opposed to that suggestion, although not necessarily for the reasons suggested by Petroleum V. Nasby (the pen name of Republican satirist David R. Locke):

> The President wuz a readin telegrams and letters, and they wuz not uv a carikter to pleeze him. The first wuz from Belmont, and read thus:
> "I hev, ez yoo know, the highest possible regard for yoor Eggslency, and shel regret exceedinly to see yoo deprived uv yoor high offis; but reely, yoo kin scarcely eggspect the Democracy to embasass themselves by espousin yoor coz. The fact iz, no party hevin a fucher before it kin tie itself to a ded past. The teemster draws a sigh over a ded mule, but ez a ded mule can't draw his cart, he natcherly turns his eyes onto them still possest uv vitality. I hope yoo see the pint without my explainin it. Eggscuse me for comparin you to a ded mule."

August, however, preferred other candidates to Johnson. He probed Charles Francis Adams, son of one president, grandson of another, and ambassador to the Court of St. James's, who responded coyly by explaining that while he was not prepared to declare himself a presidential candidate, he would not refuse a draft. August did not urge him—which probably was just as well, since Adams was "a newcomer in the Party, with whom the whole Party will not be satisfied, especially the Democrats in the West," as Perry, now almost as absorbed in politics as his father, observed.

Who else was suitable? August was having almost as much trouble finding a presidential candidate as he'd had finding Southern national committeemen.

A war hero was always a safe bet. But the Republicans obviously had beaten the Democrats to the best choice: Ulysses S. Grant. Even though August and other Democrats had contributed heavily to help him buy a house in New York City, their investments in Grant's favor had not panned out. Republican businessmen had also contributed money, perhaps even more. August still respected McClellan, because he thought McClellan was "cool, firm, and conciliatory," but he was sure McClellan would have "no chance of being confirmed by our Radical Senate." Even if McClellan could be confirmed he would have a hard fight against Grant. As one newspaper pointed out, it would be a race of "the man who didn't take Richmond against the man who did." And even if McClellan could beat Grant it was doubtful that McClellan would agree to run.

"Perhaps," August had told Marble, "we may have to fall back upon some such candidates" as General Winfield Scott Hancock or Admiral David G. Farragut. August, in fact, invited Farragut to attend the races at Jerome Park.

On opening day of the Spring Meet, August arrived, according to one account, "enthroned" on the box of his coach driving "four glossy bays, which moved . . . with the precision of machinery." One of his horses, Fenian, on which August fixed great hopes, placed third in one race, second in another, and again second during the Jerome Park Summer Meet later that year. With a little more training that horse was sure to be a winner.

August was less certain about the championship qualities of Hancock, Farragut, or General William T. Sherman, another possible nominee. If only he could breed presidential candidates as he bred Thoroughbreds. But without a certain winner he had to make do with the mixed lot he had. And if not a military hero, then who?

Certainly not George H. Pendleton. The former vice-presidential candidate was too married to the old Peace Democrat faction, the part of the party that had scuttled the last campaign by insisting on the ill-considered peace plank. Now Pendleton was again causing trouble by championing the greenback scheme. August was determined not to let Pendleton split the party in 1868 as he had done four years earlier.

But who could stop Pendleton?

A distinct possibility was Salmon P. Chase, the former secretary of the treasury and now chief justice of the Supreme Court. Chase, having impartially presided at Johnson's trial, had all the President's advantages and none of his disadvantages as a magnet to draw pro-Johnson Republican votes. He was sound as a gold dollar on the issue of loan repayment; a Hard Money man, he believed gold lent should be paid back in gold. He was sufficiently appalled at the Radicals' Draconian Reconstruction programs. Only his stand on black suffrage might be a problem. Chase believed every man, white or black, should be able to vote.

A large portion of the Democratic Party was opposed to giving blacks the vote. Some Democrats, although committed to universal suffrage, believed that blacks should be gradually incorporated into the electorate as they learned how to read and write and were educated to understand political issues. The majority, confusing the ballot box with the bedroom, were adamantly opposed to letting blacks vote.

"Nor has negro voting ever led to social equality or miscegenation," said one Republican defending universal manhood suffrage. "If my Democratic friends, however, feel in danger of marrying negro women, I am in favor of a law for their protection."

The humor of the suggestion was lost on most of the Democratic party.

The *New York World*, the mouthpiece for August's faction within the Democratic party, zigzagged. At first it told the South "to welcome the negro vote *and control it*," as the Republicans hoped to do; then as the Republicans more and more securely tied up the black vote the *World* came out against black suffrage, using all the venomous and bigoted arguments that were current; and at last it argued for Southern acceptance of limited black suffrage, which in a generation would become universal. The newspaper and its proprietor, Manton Marble, had surrendered to expediency. The moral issue was lost in the political. The question for the *World* did not seem to be whether blacks should vote but whether they should vote if their vote would be controlled as a block by the Republicans.

August thought black suffrage was a smokescreen obscuring the real issue: states' rights. The Republican platform imposed black suffrage in the South and allowed it to remain optional in the North, granted sovereignty to some states and took it away from others. If the Northern states could decide the issue individually, why then could not the Southern states do likewise? August thought all states should be equal, all states should be sovereign. He was less concerned with opposing the black vote than he was with—as the *New York World* put it—"rendering the *white* vote less mischievous than it has been for the last eight years."

Yet whatever his feelings on universal manhood suffrage August intended to make sure that the Democratic platform took a position that Chase would approve.

"In regard to Negro suffrage," he wrote to Chase, "I take for granted that you would be in favor of allowing the states to vote on that question."

Chase's response reiterated his positions: Hard Money, an end to military despotism in the South, and universal manhood suffrage for those Southern whites who were being denied the vote as well as for blacks, North and South.

The *New York World* had been supporting Chase. Soon after August received Chase's letter the *World*, citing Chase's commitment to black suffrage regardless of states' rights, withdrew its support.

"This is equivalent to a pronunciamento by Belmont and Barlow and the other Sagamores of the Manhattan Club," assumed George Templeton Strong, "and it is a sore discouragement to any aspirations the Chief Justice may have been weak enough to cherish."

Possibly Strong was correct, although in analyzing August's politics he rarely was. Probably, Strong was wrong. More than once during the campaign, August and the *World* disagreed. If the *World* had abandoned Chase, it did not mean that August had. In fact, just before the convention opened August said that he supported Chase "with all my heart." August's enemies within and without the Democratic party suggested that his devotion to Chase was founded on color; but the color was not black, it was gold.

On July 4, 1868, New York was sweltering and still. The flags drooped. The arches of greenery and bunting across Fourteenth Street were in the heat as funereal as festive. Inside the new Tammany Hall next to the Academy of Music the magnificent chandelier, the subject of much admiration in the press, seemed with its 320 gas jets not a source of light but a furnace. And the two giant bronze Roman soldiers standing on either side of the podium appeared in this hellish atmosphere to be malignant spirits who, impervious to discomfort, were overseeing the slow roasting of the delegates. Democrats who had wanted the convention to be held somewhere or sometime else had their scapegoat: Belmont.

Belmont had insisted the convention be in New York to make it easier for the Hard Money men to control it.

Belmont had forced the convention to be held in July to let the Pendleton campaign run out of steam.

Belmont was calling the tune. If he wanted Pendleton defeated, Pendleton would be defeated, since, as *The New York Times* said, "pockets are often more potent than friendships and to the former Mr. Belmont holds the key." Another newspaper had put it more boldly months before: Belmont, it said, was "our master, as well as master of the situation."

Belmont was not really for Chase, this newspaper predicted; he would manipulate the convention to get Horatio Seymour nominated.

On the twenty-fifth roll call Seymour was nominated.

Seymour, who up until that day had been presiding over the convention, declined and left the platform.

Two delegates insisted that Seymour could not withdraw his name.

Seymour angrily returned to the platform and again started to decline—this time in favor of Chase—when friends grabbed him and as he wept hustled him off the platform, out a back door, and into a carriage that took off for the Manhattan Club, where he was kept a hostage to others' ambitions while, on the twenty-second ballot, he was made the Democratic candidate for president.

As he was being dragged away Seymour had passed an acquaintance, Peter Harvey, and knowing what was in store for him Seymour had cried:

"Pity me, Harvey, pity me."

Rumors circulated that August had been for Seymour from the beginning; that Chase had been a stalking horse, useful only in knocking Pendleton out of the race; that the convention had been locked up. But it was Seymour, not the convention, who had been locked up. If August had the kind of control the rumors granted him, the convention would not have passed a platform that supported the greenback scheme—which it did.

Seymour was a Hard Money man running on a Soft Money platform. Once again Pendleton had managed to get his plank adopted; once again the presidential candidate was at odds with official party policy.

The vice-presidential candidate, General Francis P. Blair, was too erratic to be comfortable. He was a Democrat who before the war had become a Radical Republican, a Missouri abolitionist in fact. He had opposed slavery because of its unwholesome effect on poor Southern whites. After the war he had broken with the Radical Republicans over their Reconstruction policies and their attacks on Johnson. His stand on the economic issues seemed to August not a stand at all—it was, August thought, supine.

"It is idle to talk of bonds, greenbacks, gold, and the public faith and the public credit," Blair said, until the military "usurpations . . . in the South" were halted and true constitutional government restored.

The convention could have chosen a worse vice-presidential candidate—Pendleton, for one—but it could have chosen better.

So much was at stake. The Radicals, August had told the cheering and applauding delegates, "intend Congressional usurpation"—*usurpation* had become a key word, usurping in that year's political lexicon even *gold, greenbacks*, and *suffrage*—"of all the branches and functions of the government, to be enforced by the bayonets of a military despotism." But the Democrats were helpless to stop them. Seymour and Blair surely were doomed.

Long before the convention, when Marble had asked August for money to help the Democratic cause in the former Confederate States, August had said, "I have spent as much and more money for politics and for the South than I had any business to do. It is never too late to mend, and I have made up my mind not to sin anymore in that direction, even if tempted by so seductive a fellow as you."

Weary of being abused by his enemies and unappreciated by his allies, August had planned to step down as the chairman of the Democratic National Committee. It was time to let someone else support and guide the party.

But—perhaps feeling that others were too ready to rush him into retirement or that his retirement would be misinterpreted as defection from a presidential candidate he did not like and a platform he abhorred—he submitted to another four years of chairing the Democratic National Committee. And, however grudgingly, he opened if not his heart at least his wallet.

He offered $1,000 to Marble to help buy a Southern newspaper. He paid for a political biography of Seymour. He donated $10,000 to the campaign and convinced seven other wealthy Democrats to do the same. Having too little money can tax the generosity of the chairman of a political party's national committee; having too much can tax his ethics. With funds to spare there is a temptation to support schemes that may not be necessary or legal. August often had proved his generosity. Now he proved his honesty. When he was told that he could buy Washington, D.C.'s thirty newspaper correspondents for $3,000 a month, August resisted testing the claim.

Money was cheap; time was dear. Marble had advised August on the opening address to the convention; had even printed the speech, as August had requested, "to give to the reporters . . . and also to help me in case my memory should fail." Now Marble helped August compose an appeal to the voters. August told him to "dwell as little as you can on the financial issue," over which the party was more divided than ever, "but pitch into Negro suffrage, reconstruction outrages, and the disgraceful extravagance" of maintaining martial law in the South. "I would do it myself in my own bungling way," August added, "but I am really thoroughly exhausted and must have a week's rest."

The truth was August did not have the heart to waste time in a campaign he was sure would fail; his health was poor, and he did not wish to be as prominent a target for Republican attacks as he had been previously. Wanting to stay out of sight, he hibernated in Newport.

"Do you think there is any necessity for my coming to New York just now?" he wistfully asked Marble. "I should like to remain here."

Life was pleasant by the sea, where politics seemed to be merely a function of fashion and where the great issues of the daily round were no more serious than whether or not Bachelors' Hall should invite a woman to dinner for the first time in its history. Bachelors' Hall did; the woman was Caroline, whom they greeted with a poem that assured her:

> . . . *as thy* Tiny *boot*
> *Flits o'er our threshold gay,*
> *With timid hand we strike the lute,*
> *Submissive to thy sway,*
> *And with a glowing heartfelt cheer*
> *We greet thy gentle presence here.*
>
> *Naught till to-day had met our ken*
> *Within these graceless halls,*
> *Save the rude forms and sports of men*
> *Who follow Pastime's calls,*
> *And thus with two-fold charm we trace*
> *The advent here of so much Grace. . . .*

They assured her that:

> *We welcome, too, thine* August *lord*
> *To our September feast,*
> *And of the sauces at our board,*
> *Be Friendship not the least.*
> *Once more, most charming guest, we say:*
> *Our thanks and welcome here to-day.*

Why should August trade so much good fellowship in Newport for the knives of New York and national politics?

Marble saw no reason for August to cut short his retreat. August contented himself by playing prompter to the actors, happy to be offstage whispering his advice: McClellan should return from Europe to tour the United States for Seymour; "every effort should be made to carry

Maine"; "our Southern friends are making a sad mistake" by advertising and advocating Blair's belief that the new president should refuse to carry out Congress's Reconstruction acts.

The audience rarely—and the cast never—hisses the prompter. August thought he was safe. He was not. Both those watching and those acting in the political follies attacked him, the Republicans because he was soft on former Rebels, the Democrats because he was Hard on money. The Democrats were louder than the Republicans.

A Democratic journalist in Ohio suspected August had wangled the nomination for Seymour, a weak candidate, to guarantee the defeat of the Democratic party's progreenback platform. August was progold. The Republican party platform was progold. Obviously August wanted the Republicans to win.

This denunciation appeared in the *Cincinnati West and South*, a progreenback Democratic newspaper, although the author of the piece was on the staff of the *Cincinnati Enquirer*, another Democratic newspaper, whose publisher was August's longtime acquaintance.

August expected and ignored libels from the opposition. He neither expected nor ignored them from his own party. He wrote to the publisher of the *Cincinnati Enquirer* to ask why one of that newspaper's reporters was smearing him.

The publisher apologized and fired the journalist, as much for moonlighting as for what he had said about August.

Yet another Democratic newspaper in Ohio, the *Cincinnati Commercial*, picked up the dropped baton and beat August with it. This article claimed that August, who had spent over $10,000 on the campaign, had refused to help finance Seymour's race.

Even Seymour thought that August was if not cool in his support at least no longer the firebrand he had been.

"We have been a long time out of power," he told his campaign manager, Samuel J. Tilden, "and are apt to call upon those who *used to be* efficient without making allowance for the change made by time."

The most widespread attack on August came after Marble suggested in the *New York World* that the Democrats should switch dark horses in midstream. The Republicans were alleging that Seymour was insane and that Blair was a drunk and a declared Rebel who was plotting to overthrow Congress by force if he got into office. The jokes about how Blair's presence on the ticket at least protected Seymour from assassination did not dispel the Democrats' pessimism. Marble argued that the only way the election could be won was by replacing Seymour and Blair with two other candidates—who no doubt would be demonstrably sane, sober, and, in their attacks on Congress, more subtle.

Marble's call roused August from his rest. He thought any attempt to change the ticket would result in a rout—even if were possible or legal to make such a substitution, which it wasn't. Through private and public letters August lobbied against Marble's plan. He saved Seymour but damned himself. Having charged into the limelight he offered himself up to the abuse of Democrats who wanted new candidates and who resented August's defense of the established ticket—and of Democrats who were loyal to Seymour and who claimed that August's lackluster performance as the chairman of the Democratic National Committee had created the conditions under which Seymour's candidacy could be challenged. August, they said, had waited too long (a month) after the convention had ended before meeting with Seymour, and then he had sought him only to make sure Seymour, if he won, would let New York bankers select the secretary of the treasury.

A rumor spread that August was sailing for Europe to escape the recriminations that were sure to follow Seymour's drubbing. August let the rumors travel where they would; he remained in New York and Newport.

Other lies, like flies, buzzed when he did anything, settled when he was inactive, and buzzed again when he moved. Soon the season would be over. The election would be passed. Grant and his running mate, Schuyler Colfax, would be elected. There was nothing to do but wait—and squabble over appointments that would not be made.

Augustus Schell, the brother of the man who before Buchanan's election had tried to tempt August with the mission at Paris, had set his sights on France. August challenged him.

"I want to go abroad and if possible to Paris if we get in," August told Marble. "I wish you could get Tilden committed in my favor. I have done ten times as much for the party as ever Schell did and am certainly better fitted for a diplomatic post than a dried up bachelor like Schell, unfit by education and training for such a thing."

The question was academic.

August put money on some minor races and on whether or not Seymour would carry New York State. He was not going to risk his vote this year by betting on the presidential race. Even if he were willing to risk the vote, he was not willing to risk the money. He was too good a Democrat to back Grant and too good a gambler to back Seymour.

Grant won. And Seymour retired from politics, leaving August once more the head of a party that had been abandoned by its natural leader, the defeated presidential candidate. August was not sure he wanted the job. He considered following Seymour into retirement, leaving the chair of the Democratic National Committee after all—a possibility that pleased Perry.

"I am very glad," Perry said when he heard that August "had finished with politics."

He had seen how badly his father had been treated, how badly he was still being treated by Democrats who blamed the failures of the past three presidential elections on him. The more August was attacked, however, the less willing he was to quit. He would bow out; he would not be forced out.

With Marble's help August launched a defense.

How could anyone accuse him of halfheartedly supporting the party?

"I have spent in these three elections [1860, 1864, and 1868] over $80,000 out of my own pocket," August told Marble. He was not responsible for the Democratic losses.

He would not be made a scapegoat for the party's sins. He would stay in office until he was ready to quit.

✺ CHAPTER THIRTY-FOUR ✺

TWO WEEKS AFTER the election August shifted his attention from the political to the financial battlefield. On November 17, 1868, he sued the Erie Railway Company, Jay Gould, Jim Fisk, and the rest of the Erie board of directors, charging them with malfeasance. He asked the court to replace the railroad's management with a receiver, a caretaker. His action involved him in a legal struggle with roots going back to 1866, a complex web of stock raids and manipulation, charges and counter-charges, threats and deals, that the press had nicknamed the Erie Wars.

The Erie Wars started with a coup d'état engineered by Daniel Drew, who on Wall Street was called Uncle Daniel. Before coming to

New York City, Drew had been a cattle drover. To increase the weight of his stock he fed the animals salt, which made them so thirsty that they drank great quantities of water. Before the cattle had a chance to pass his profits he would sell the swollen animals to the unsuspecting. Once he got to Wall Street he continued to water stock.

"Daniel Drew," said Henry Clews, one of the members of the Belmont Clique, "at one time, could command more ready cash at short notice than any man in Wall Street, or probably than any man in America."

In 1866 he was an elderly man and treasurer of the Erie Railway Company, which connected New York City with the Great Lakes. The company needed money. Drew offered to lend it some in return for Erie stock and Erie bonds that could be converted into stock.

At that time, Cornelius Vanderbilt, who owned the other major railroads leading out of New York City, decided he wanted the Erie too, so that he could govern all traffic from America's prime port to the interior of the country. Vanderbilt started buying Erie stock. Drew, through intermediaries, sold his shares to Vanderbilt. The more Vanderbilt bought, the higher the Erie stock rose, until each share was worth $95. Vanderbilt thought he had bought up most of it and that he controlled the railroad. He did not know that Drew owned the convertible bonds.

Drew converted his bonds into stock and flooded the market with the new shares. Since Erie stock was as a result no longer hard to find, the price plunged from $95 to $50 a share. Vanderbilt lost millions of dollars; and because the new shares reduced Vanderbilt's interest, he also failed to get control of the railroad.

In retaliation Vanderbilt sued Drew. He claimed that the new shares Drew had dumped on the market were illegal; and he plotted with a group of Bostonians who owned a block of Erie stock to oust Drew from his position as company treasurer. The alliance between Vanderbilt and the Bostonians was too strong for Drew. Together they had enough votes to get rid of him. Usually when he was in a tight spot Drew prayed or went home to bed and pulled the covers over his head or pleaded. In this case he pleaded. Weeping, Drew begged Vanderbilt to let him keep his post. Vanderbilt, possibly expecting that he could do better—at least in the immediate future—in league with Drew rather than fighting him, relented. Vanderbilt dropped the suit; but for the sake of appearances Drew was dismissed. The stockholders voted in a new board of directors. The newly elected treasurer resigned. And, as arranged, Vanderbilt reappointed Drew treasurer.

The first Erie War was over.

The second Erie War was about to begin.

With Drew on the new board of directors were two young men in whom Drew had taken an interest: Jim Fisk and Jay Gould. Fisk had been born appropriately on April Fools' Day. During the war he smuggled cotton and sold Confederate bonds to European speculators. He was as fat and sleek as a sea lion. His moustache was waxed into points. His hair was so greased and plastered down that the skin of his scalp showed white in his part. Trying to outdo August and Leonard Jerome, he drove not four-in-hands but six-in-hands with gold-plated tackle. He kept his wife in Boston and his mistress—a divorcée named Helen Josephine Mansfield Lawlor, whom everyone called Josie Mansfield—on Twenty-third Street. Curiously, he himself lived in a modest house with his aging mother and father, a fact ignored by the public. To them he was Jubilee Jim and the Prince of Erie.

If Fisk was the Prince of Erie, Gould was the minister, a Cardinal Richelieu of finance: abstemious, dour, and deadly. He was short and thin, a shadow of a man; and he talked as a shadow might—softly, insinuatingly. He seemed almost timid, as though he were hiding behind his beard. But the timidity was a pose and, if you watched his eyes, you would see flickering behind the meek gaze the watchful stare of a Wall Street carnivore.

He got his start in business selling an excellent mousetrap that had been designed by his grandfather. In later generations that trap snared the imaginations of would-be millionaires. If you want to get rich, they would say, misquoting Ralph Waldo Emerson, build a better mousetrap. The advice became a homily; the homily became a joke. It could not be that easy.

It wasn't.

Gould would go to the stock exchange every morning, deal all day long, and come home late, his bowels wracked with pain as though he found his success hard to stomach.

"The difference between Jay and me," Drew once said, "is, I have more trouble to get my dinner than to digest it, and Jay has more trouble to digest it than to get it."

Gould's only pleasure was flower arranging. The precise ordering of shapes and colors—and perhaps the transience of the order—soothed him. Flowers seemed to be an access back into the familiar world of mortality, an escape from the inanimate, ideal world of figures. Bouquets of bills do not wilt, and the bodilessness of value can reproach creatures with bodies, who age and decay. Money is eternal; flowers and men mercifully die.

Some people thought Gould was too intimate with mortality. He seemed to cast the shadow of a scythe. Ever since one of his partners had committed suicide, people said Gould's touch was death. He became known as the Mephistopheles of Wall Street and the Most Hated Man in America.

Drew, Fisk, and Gould combined forces to edge Vanderbilt out of the Erie Railway Company and gain complete control. A New York State law said that if one railroad company leased another railroad company, the first company could create new stock that could be exchanged for stock in the second. Drew, Fisk, and Gould bought a worthless railroad called the Buffalo, Bradford & Pittsburgh. They leased the B.B. & P. to the Erie. The Erie created new stock to exchange for B.B. & P. stock. And since Drew, Fisk, and Gould owned the B.B. & P., they suddenly—when the stock exchange was made—had a large amount of new Erie stock.

Meanwhile Vanderbilt, realizing that his truce with Drew was unstable and wanting to complete his takeover of the Erie, again started buying Erie stock. The more Vanderbilt bought, the higher Erie rose; but it did not rise as fast as Vanderbilt figured it should have, so he knew that new shares—the shares from the B.B. & P. scam—were spilling into the market. Drew was trying to sucker him again. To protect himself against any more of Drew's surprises, Vanderbilt went to a New York State Supreme Court judge whom it was rumored he owned. The judge ordered that Drew stop selling any Erie stock or bonds that could be converted into stock. Vanderbilt was covering all possibilities. In fact, to make sure his flanks were protected Vanderbilt had his judge suspend Drew as treasurer of the company for malfeasance.

Drew responded by buying his own judge, who stayed Vanderbilt's judge's orders and fired Vanderbilt's man on the Erie's board of directors.

Vanderbilt went to a third judge, who forbade Drew and the other directors of the company from meeting or doing any business.

Drew went to a fourth judge, who stopped all previous suits and put the Erie's directors, with the exception of Vanderbilt's man, back to work.

By this time both Drew's and Vanderbilt's lawyers were so confused that at a hearing neither side knew what to do, so the proceedings were postponed.

While Drew and Vanderbilt were lobbing shots back and forth in the courts, Drew, with the connivance of Fisk and Gould, had the Erie Railway Company issue bonds. These ostensibly would be sold to pay for improvements in the railroad and were immediately bought by Drew's agents. Like the bonds Drew had used once before in a war with Vanderbilt, these could be converted to stock. Drew converted them.

Drew and his associates now had 100,000 shares of new stock that Vanderbilt did not know existed. Vanderbilt, who had been buying every Erie share he could find, again thought he had most of the existing stock and therefore controlled the company; so when Drew's brokers appeared on the floor of the stock exchange with more shares, pandemonium broke loose. Drew's brokers jumped up, offering lots of 1,000 or 5,000 shares of Erie stock. Vanderbilt's brokers jumped after them, buying the lots— at first triumphantly and then, as Drew's brokers seemed to have inexhaustible supplies, with more and more apprehension.

"Hell has broken loose!" they told Vanderbilt.

Keep buying, Vanderbilt said.

Soon Vanderbilt's brokers had bought 50,000 shares—shares that were not supposed to exist. Panic spread through Wall Street.

Then all at once Drew's brokers dumped the second 50,000 shares onto the market.

"The price . . . ," Drew said, "dropped like a dead heifer."

But Vanderbilt's brokers, under his orders, continued to buy. By the end of the day Vanderbilt owned more than 100,000 shares of essentially worthless Erie stock, for which he had paid $7 million.

If the courts upheld the transaction, Drew said, "why, it was good night to the Commodore, because there is no limit to the blank shares a printing press can turn out. White paper is cheap—it is bought by the ream; printer's ink is also dirt cheap; and if we could keep on working that kind of deal—make Vanderbilt pay us fifty or sixty dollars for little pieces of paper that hadn't cost us two cents, we would very soon have all of his cash."

"If this printing press don't break down," Fisk agreed, "I'll be damned if I don't give the old hog all he wants of Erie."

Drew, Fisk, and Gould were stacking and tying the $4 million of Vanderbilt's payment that had been in greenbacks when they were told that they were going to be arrested for contempt of court, for selling the stock in defiance of a judge's order. Rather than fight the contempt charge from jail, they stuffed their pockets and valises with stocks, bonds, and account books, and loaded bales of greenbacks into a hackney coach. Outside their offices they made a dash for the ferry to New Jersey. On the other side of the Hudson they would be outside the jurisdiction of Vanderbilt's judge, who had ordered them arrested.

The day was foggy. The crossing must have been difficult. But all three conspirators reached Jersey City, where they barricaded themselves in Taylor's Hotel. When they heard rumors that Vanderbilt had hired fifty thugs to kidnap them, Drew, Fisk, and Gould arranged with the Jersey City police and the Erie Railway detectives for protection. Under Fisk's direction the waterfront was defended with three twelve-pound cannons and a rowboat navy of forty-eight men. Under Gould's direction the railroad station was guarded. Drew evidently stayed in the hotel, which they had renamed Fort Taylor.

Vanderbilt accused the trio of being criminals whose actions were threatening the stability of the economy. They had millions of dollars literally tied up, which was disrupting Wall Street. They were risking America's well-being for private profit.

Drew, Fisk, and Gould countercharged that Vanderbilt was trying to seize the Erie in order to monopolize the railroads going into and out of New York City. If he controlled the Erie, he could charge whatever he wanted to ship goods. They were fighting Vanderbilt in the public interest.

When he was asked how things would turn out, Fisk said, "Can't tell just yet; but it'll either be inside of marble halls in New York or stone walls in Sing Sing."

Vanderbilt had a judge appoint a receiver for the Erie.

Drew had a judge stay Vanderbilt's judge's order.

Vanderbilt had a judge issue a show cause order asking why Drew's judge's order should not be vacated.

Drew had a judge stop all Vanderbilt's proceedings before the courts, forbid Vanderbilt from starting any new proceedings, and prohibit any other court to name a receiver for the Erie.

Vanderbilt had a judge ignore Drew's judge's previous orders and appoint a receiver for Erie after all.

Drew had a judge set aside Vanderbilt's judge's previous order.

Drew prayed. Fisk partied with Josie Mansfield, who had come to Taylor's Hotel to be with him. Gould packed a valise with $500,000 and went to Albany to call on the legislature.

Gould bought a senator. Vanderbilt paid him more. Gould topped Vanderbilt. Men who one day were ready to jail Drew, Fisk, and Gould the next day were ready to pass a law making their stock manipulations legal. It was a game of musical chairs. Whenever the vote finally came, the side that had paid the most money to the most legislators would win. The music stopped. The New York State Senate passed a bill legalizing what Drew, Fisk, and Gould had done. The New York State Assembly agreed. The governor signed the bill. Drew, Fisk, and Gould had won— apparently.

Or rather Fisk and Gould had won—apparently.

Drew had abandoned his cronies and made a separate deal with Vanderbilt.

One afternoon while Drew was lunching at Taylor's Hotel in Jersey City a waiter handed him a note from Vanderbilt that said, "Drew: I'm sick of the whole damned business. Come and see me."

The following Sunday, Drew slipped into New York and visited Vanderbilt. Drew talked of old times. Vanderbilt, after saying, "This Erie war has taught me that it never pays to kick a skunk," talked of money.

Negotiations continued for the next few days. At last Drew and Vanderbilt settled. Drew agreed that the Erie Railway Company would repay Vanderbilt altogether about $4,550,000, part of it for some worthless Erie stock, and a little less than another $500,000 to two of Vanderbilt's friends for their troubles.

Sometime during this interlude, perhaps while negotiations between Drew and Vanderbilt were going on, Gould visited Vanderbilt to discuss the possibility of peace. They talked for a while. Suddenly Vanderbilt slid off his seat and slumped to the floor. He did not seem to be breathing. Gould ran to the door to get help, but the door was locked and the key was gone. For half an hour Gould was trapped in the room with what he thought was Vanderbilt's corpse. Vanderbilt, who evidently was trying to frighten Gould into coming to terms, finally got up from the floor and resumed the conversation. Despite Vanderbilt's stunt, nothing was settled at that meeting.

When Fisk and Gould finally found out about Drew's betrayal, they had little room for maneuvering. Drew knew too much. If he had gone over to the other side, they would have to settle. Ready to surrender, they surprised Vanderbilt in his bedroom one day.

"The Commodore was sitting on the side of the bed with one shoe off and one shoe on," Fisk later recalled.

Vanderbilt restated his conditions.

Fisk complained and argued and finally gave in—on condition that Drew be removed for good from the Erie board of directors.

Vanderbilt agreed.

The second Erie War was over.

Fisk thought he and Gould had "sold ourselves to the Devil."

Vanderbilt got his money and withdrew his suits against Drew, Fisk, and Gould.

Drew retired.

Gould became president and treasurer of the Erie.

Fisk became vice-president and controller—and he was left with an image that stayed with him: Vanderbilt sitting on the side of his bed like My Son John, one shoe off and one shoe on.

". . . I remember the shoe from its peculiarity," Fisk later recalled. "It had four buckles on it. I had never seen shoes with buckles in that manner before; and I thought, if these sort of men always wear that sort of shoe, I might want a pair."

The money in the settlement of the second Erie War had come not from Gould's or Fisk's pockets but from the railroad's treasury.

"There ain't nothin' in Ary no more, C'neel," Drew told Vanderbilt.

"Don't you believe it," Vanderbilt said.

Gould took over as the leader of the looted company. Fisk settled in as his lieutenant. For their new offices they bought Pike's Opera House on Eighth Avenue and Twenty-third Street, which was connected to Fisk's house by a secret passageway. Up the street was Josie Mansfield's house. It was a convenient location.

The Opera House was a year old. It had been built to compete with the Academy of Music but, unable to attract the lead geese of society, failed. Gould and Fisk installed themselves in offices at the top of the grand staircase. The walls and ceilings were frescoed. Partitions were made of stained glass. Gilt mirrors reflected so many marble statues the rooms seemed inhabited by a race of stone. There were dining rooms and kitchens, and luxurious lounges, where it was rumored orgies took place. The spinal cord of the building was a column of rock topped by a monstrous safe, as though the Opera House were a creature whose brain was money.

At night Fisk, in a red silk-lined cape, would strut downstairs among the crowd that had come to see the naughty musical revues performed on the Opera House's stage. During the day, upstairs, he and Gould plotted the Third Erie War.

To protect themselves Gould and Fisk bought more judges, including one who had been Vanderbilt's key agent. They found a profitable seat on Erie's board of directors for William Marcy Tweed, the acknowledged boss of Tammany Hall. Then, as Drew had taught them, they issued $10 million of Erie bonds that could be converted to stock, converted half of them, and started selling the new shares on the market. The price of a share of Erie dropped from about $70 a share to, at its lowest, about $35 a share.

August, who owned 4,000 shares of Erie, decided to take up where Vanderbilt had left off. He sued Gould and Fisk, not only on all the grounds Vanderbilt had charged but also for using the stockholders' money to settle what had been a private war with Vanderbilt. To guarantee the success of the suit August needed proof of malfeasance. He got his proof from Drew.

The third Erie War had begun.

Bored in retirement, Drew approached Gould and Fisk, who decided to forget their anger at him in order to use his money in a stock manipulation scheme. They would yo-yo the market up and down, buying and selling as appropriate to make a profit.

Gould and Fisk put up $10 million. Drew put up $4 million. The trio deposited the $14 million in banks. The banks, as banks will, lent and invested the money. The trio withdrew the $14 million. The banks, suddenly caught short, had to sell stocks and call in loans. The people who had borrowed money from the banks also had to sell stocks to pay off their loans. All this selling depressed prices on the stock market. Speculators were ruined. Worse, this fiddling with the economy threatened to create a famine. It was harvest time; but since money was tight no one had cash to lend to the farmers so they could pay the shipping charges to send their produce into the cities.

And if the farmers could not ship and sell their produce, they would not have money to pay their debts or buy their necessities. As a result the stores they patronized in their local towns also would not be able to pay their debts. Bankruptcy would spread across the continent like the shadow of a huge cloud.

Gould and Fisk wanted to turn the screws tighter, drive the price of stocks lower. Drew, nervous about the repercussions, argued against it. His two former pupils told him he was no longer teaching the class. If he did not like their methods he could pack up and get out—taking his losses, of course, since he would be leaving prematurely.

Poorer by about $1 million, Drew quit. He decided to do business on his own, taking the advantage but not the risks of Gould and Fisk's ruthlessness. Since he knew their plan was to force stock prices down, he made contracts to sell Erie stock at a certain agreed-upon price and to deliver the stock at a certain future date. He assumed that when the time came to deliver the Erie stock, the price of the shares would be lower than the price at which he agreed to sell it. He could buy as many shares as he needed at that lower price and fulfill his contracts by selling them at the agreed-upon higher price, pocketing the difference.

There was a flaw in his plan. After he had walked out on Gould and Fisk, the United States government, concerned about the effects of the tight-money situation, threatened to release $50 million new dollars into the economy. Gould and Fisk, preferring to keep control of the market, loosened the tourniquet, letting money flow back into circulation; and they and their agents began buying stock—Erie in particular—to push prices up. The more they bought, the fewer shares of Erie were on the market. The fewer shares of Erie on the market, the higher the price of a share of Erie rose. The higher the price of a share of Erie rose, the more frightened Drew became. If he had to meet his contracts by buying Erie stock at the current price, he would lose millions.

Drew asked for religious advice.

He was told to pray.

He prayed.

Erie shares still rose. Not only that, but Drew could not even find for sale at any price, the 30,000 shares of Erie that he needed to buy to fulfill his contracts.

Perhaps he was pleading with the wrong party. He stopped addressing God and turned to Fisk.

He told Fisk that he was short 30,000 shares of Erie.

Fisk, who had been following Drew's activities, corrected him. Drew was 70,000 shares short.

Drew said he knew of certain people who were preparing to sue Gould and Fisk. If Fisk helped him he would tell who those certain people were.

Fisk told Drew to name names. Afterward they could discuss Drew's problem.

Drew waffled and urged Fisk to get Gould.

Fisk did.

When Gould arrived Drew asked if they could issue some more convertible bonds—which Drew presumably could buy, convert to stock, and thereby escape from his awkward situation.

Gould and Fisk played with him. They would not make any promises.

Drew at last told them who was bringing the suit: Belmont.

Gould and Fisk found that interesting.

Drew pressed them about their help; said he would not leave until something was settled.

To get rid of him Gould and Fisk said they would talk again at ten o'clock that evening.

That night Fisk let Drew stew for an hour. He did not show up until eleven o'clock. He told Drew that he and Gould could do nothing to help him.

"Then . . . ," said Drew, "I am a ruined man."

He pleaded. Could he rent some stock? Thirty to forty thousand shares? Just for a couple of weeks? Good rates. Three percent. That's about $100,000 for fifteen days. He employed all the wiles he had used to con Vanderbilt: whinning, despair, invoking memories of old deals.

Fisk was unmoved.

After two hours Drew at last said: "I swear I will do you all the harm I can do if you do not help me in this time of my great need." He left at one o'clock in the morning, ready to sign an affidavit describing everything he knew about Gould's and Fisk's scams, for August to use in court.

The next morning, two hours before August's judge, armed with Drew's affidavit, was going to issue an order preparing the way for Gould and Fisk to be replaced by a receiver, Gould and Fisk had their own judge prohibit any suits against the Erie Railway Company and, incredibly, appoint as receiver—Jay Gould.

Gould had replaced himself as head of the Erie.

August's judge vacated Gould and Fisk's judge's orders and appointed another receiver for the Erie, a former chief justice of the Court of Appeals of the State of New York, Henry E. Davies.

Gould and Fisk struck back by having various judges stay August's judge's orders, reappoint Gould as receiver of the Erie, and open proceedings on suits against—among others—August for $1million for damaging the reputation of Erie, a laughable claim, since the company was known as the Scarlet Woman of Wall Street.

August's judge ignored the stay of Gould and Fisk's judge and officially made Davies receiver of the Erie.

Davies, accompanied by his lawyers, went to Pike's Opera House to take control of the company. The gates were locked. The building was patrolled by Gould and Fisk's hired thugs. One of Davies's lawyers had been a lawyer for the company. He was recognized by a guard, who, not realizing that Davies was there to help depose Gould and Fisk, let the three men in. They climbed the marble stairway to the Erie's offices, where they surprised Gould and Fisk.

Gould, appointed the receiver of the company by one judge, uneasily faced Davies, appointed the receiver by another judge. Fisk left the room. When he returned flanked by his praetorian guard, he ordered Davies to leave.

Davies refused.

Fisk told his thugs to throw Davies out.

A couple of Gould and Fisk's less swashbuckling business associates intervened. The thugs withdrew. Davies gave Gould and Fisk papers that declared him to be the authentic receiver of the Erie. In exchange Gould and Fisk gave Davies papers, issued in yet another court action, staying Davies's appointment as receiver of the Erie. Davies noticed that this order had been signed and dated before he had even been appointed as receiver. Evidently what Gould and Fisk lacked in honesty they made up in promptness.

Having formally taken over the company, Davies bid Gould and Fisk good-day and left. When he returned two days later to start work, Davies again found the gates locked. This time the guards made no mistake. He could not get in.

August and his receiver, Davies, once more returned to the courts seeking a ruling that would remove Gould and ratify Davies as receiver of the Erie.

That night at midnight Fisk slipped into a carriage, rode to the Twenty-third Street pier, and was about to board the ferry to New Jersey when he was stopped by a patient process-server who had followed him from the Grand Opera House. Foiled, Fisk returned to the Erie offices. A short while later another carriage rattled away from Pike's Opera House. Inside the coach someone shouted that he wanted to be taken to the Fifth Avenue Hotel. The detectives who had been staking out the building swarmed across town to the hotel, only to find that they had been tricked. The carriage really had gone back to the ferry. Having eluded his shadows Fisk crossed the Hudson, sneaked into a private Erie Railway car, and headed north.

Newspapers claimed Fisk and Gould had absconded with millions of dollars from the Erie treasury. Safe in Canada, rumor insisted, they were toasting their crime in expensive champagne. August would never trap them in court.

In fact, Fisk had simply gone to visit one more judge, who in his turn appointed one more receiver for the Erie.

After another couple of legal rounds, during which August's judge and Gould and Fisk's judge vacated each other's orders, August's judge— generally recognized as an honest man—tired of the farce. Judges could not keep overturning each other's decisions. For the sake of the dignity of the courts he yielded.

There was still a tangle of cross actions to unravel. One of Gould and Fisk's judges cut that knot of litigation by finding that a railroad company could issue convertible bonds whenever it wanted. Therefore there had been no malfeasance—there was no reason to appoint a receiver.

Gould and Fisk had won the third Erie War.

Drew, who had lost about $1.5 million, never recovered from the humiliation of having been outmaneuvered at his own game.

August, who thought "the aspect of Erie so threatening that I fear the common shares will be worth nothing," sold his stock for about half of what he had paid for it, at $30 to $31 per share, "*making a loss of nearly $130,000.*

"The whole affair," August added, "ends in smoke."

❧ CHAPTER THIRTY-FIVE ❧

THE DEMOCRATS' DISASTER in the presidential election, the Erie struggle, and his chronic dyspepsia left August desperate for a vacation. But a European retreat planned for early in 1869 had to be postponed. During minor medical treatment Frederika had been given nitrous oxide, and the aftereffects had left her too weak to travel.

"It will be three weeks tomorrow since she took the gas and since she has been in bed and unable to hold her head up or to stand," Caroline wrote Perry. "She is the most patient sufferer I ever knew, taking her medicines and doing everything without a murmur that she is told. For three days now, her eyes have hurt her so that she cannot open them. The severe spasms have left her, but she continues to have slighter ones all the time. I never wish you to take laughing gas. It may prove harmless to you, as to many others; but you see what it has done to poor Rickie, and I have a horror of it."

Caroline told Perry not to interrupt his work with Professor Child in order to visit; his presence would excite his sister and bring on new convulsions. Perry sent Frederika books to cheer her up.

Newly bearded, Perry had taken August, Jr., on a trip to Canada before the school year had started—evidently with the hope that he could influence his brother more successfully away from home than he would be able to in New York and Newport. The advantage of having an older brother set an example for a younger brother is that it keeps them both in line.

August, Jr., hoped that in the fall he would be able to study privately with Perry's tutor, Francis James Child. But the professor, perhaps thinking of Perry's galling late-morning habits, said, "I do not wish to take any more pupils. I want to give all my time to study."

Child recommended Phillips Exeter Academy, a short distance north of Boston in Exeter, New Hampshire. August picked up his son in Cambridge and together they went to look at the school: three buildings—classrooms, dormitory, and principal's house—in the center of a small town. The curriculum was classical: Latin, Greek, mathematics, ancient history, and, newly instituted the year before, French. Students also learned composition and theology, both considered more practical than academic subjects. And those who wished could study Spanish and sacred music—frills.

August lodged his son in a private boardinghouse near the school. August, Jr., fixed up his bare quarters with bookshelves, but the place still seemed desolate. He wrote home asking for any ornaments his parents could spare. And for a rug.

Mrs. Means, the landlady, would not give him one; and when he woke in the morning his floor was so cold that, as he told his mother, "I scarcely dare get up to make my fire."

Sometimes the water in the pitcher would be iced over and he would have to break the crust before pouring it into the basin.

The other roomers were a varied lot. One of them—his landlady's son-in-law—was very amusing. He was a jack-of-all-trades, a type August, Jr., never before had had a chance to get to know. He "entertains us with quite witty conversation," August wrote home.

At the Academy, August was learning the classics; at Mrs. Means's he was learning democracy.

At first August, Jr., was content. He was starting over in more promising surroundings. Conscientiously he engaged a private tutor to drill him where he was weak in Greek grammar. He took piano lessons three times a week and played for pleasure at least an hour each day. And in addition to getting Exeter's religious instruction he attended church every Sunday.

About halfway through the school year, though, he began to have troubles. He was sensitive, which made him take too much to heart things others might ignore, and he was strong-willed, which made him stubborn about responding to the slights he felt.

He thought, for example, that his landlady, Mrs. Means, lived up to her name.

"She won't do anything in the way of fixing up my nasty little room," August, Jr., told his parents. "She thinks, if she won't do it, you will; and then, when I go, she will have a room nicely fixed up."

Mrs. Means would give full reports to the Academy on the behavior of the boys in her house. But she would never say anything bad about August, Jr.—which he hated, since it made the other boys resent him. For some reason, perhaps because his father was so rich, she treated August, Jr., specially.

"She is over-kind to me in her way of *talking*," August, Jr., told his mother. "She hypocritically tries to 'soft-soap' me, as we boys call it; and I can't stand it."

He pleaded to be allowed to move into new quarters.

"There is a house very near this in which are two rooms, both larger and higher than this one," he said, "which they let furnished."

August and Caroline disapproved of August, Jr.'s moving in mid-term, but he explained that he did not want to leave Mrs. Means's house immediately, "I only wanted your permission to engage the new rooms for the next term, because there is a great rush for them; and, if I did not take them now I could not get them at all."

August and Caroline understood the situation all too well. They had raised their son to want the best. But these new rooms were not only the best in Exeter; they also were unsupervised. August and Caroline feared the move would encourage an expansion of spirit that might not be appropriate for a young man who was cramming for a college entrance examination. They sent Perry to Exeter to investigate.

"To begin with," Perry told his father, "I will tell you there is nothing serious in the situation. I say serious, because I went to Exeter with the idea that Augy went to bed late, stayed out for the night, and was about to be demoted," information that Perry somehow had gotten from Mrs. Means, who—Perry explained—"like all women in a place like Exeter likes very much to talk and to stick her nose into others' business."

Despite Mrs. Means's tales, Perry, as he told his father, found August, Jr., "in rather good health, a little lazy, and with his natural desire to have fun."

He was doing as well in his studies as he had done the first term, which was well enough; he boxed, rode his bicycle, and went to monthly parties. Perry could find nothing to give rise to the terrible rumors that surrounded his brother.

Obviously, August, Jr.'s wanting to change quarters had loosened Mrs. Means's tongue, which evidently having been triggered moved with the maddening regularity of a metronome; but what had August, Jr., done?

To find out, Perry visited Exeter's principal, Gideon Lane Soule, who received him graciously and "was in the process of telling me that Augy was a good boy when Augy came in. Then, suddenly, Soule took on a cold and haughty manner, which showed that he tried to make the students afraid. From that moment on I asked in vain what report I could make. It was impossible for me to pull a single syllable from him."

Had August, Jr., been caught playing billiards? A capital crime, according to Soule.

Something almost as bad.

Perry eventually discovered that August, Jr.'s disgrace was a result of his entering a public bicycle race. Perry told his father:

"The 'Doctor,' " which is what he ironically called Soule, "with his Puritan ideas doesn't like his students to be publicly associated with the people of the town." August, Jr., was guilty only of not being a snob.

Apparently August was secretly pleased at his son's lack of pretension and flair for good-fellowship, but he felt that August, Jr., could have been more judicious. It would not do to get in trouble at another school. And perhaps August, Jr., to some degree was confusing egalitarian with rebellious behavior. Perhaps he was being led astray.

"You accuse me of forming bad companions," August wrote to his parents. "I have none. I found one who was inclined to be bad, but I dropped him long ago. My circle of friends is small, but I am civil to all whom I meet. You seem to think I am getting to be awfully wicked."

His parents were mollified. So was the school. August, Jr., arranged to live the following year in what he called the clubhouse, which—he hastened to tell his parents—was despite its name "a place where you are under considerable discipline." And he found a member of the faculty who agreed to act as a friendly conscience and make sure he was in his room every night at eight, studying or answering neglected letters from old friends at the Rectory School and family.

Perry had entered Harvard in January 1869. No longer a "sub," he was able to participate fully in the life of the school, especially the camaraderie of intense studying—a bond as firmly fixed as any developed during battle.

He took an informal course in Old French with James Russell Lowell, who conducted his class in the study at his house, where even the most ordinary things seemed to reflect his eminence: the gas lamps flanking the cluttered mantelpiece, the hard couch, the circular table on which books and magazines were stacked in precarious piles. The disorder seemed romantic, evidence of an active mind. Although the students enjoyed reading the *Chanson de Roland* and the *Roman de la Rose*, they did not want to exert themselves. Lowell complied with their wishes. When the weather was good the poet, surrounded by his charges, would wander through the countryside interrupting his discourses on medieval French poetry to point out and name birds. As part of his bargain with his students not to make them study too hard, he got them to agree that he could use their seminar as an excuse to avoid certain disagreeable social obligations.

"He always cautioned us not to give him away," Perry later said.

His favorite teacher was Henry Adams, with whom he studied history in a special honors class. Adams, like Lowell, conducted his course at home, in his apartment, where the atmosphere was informal and the conversation was unbuttoned.

"You know, gentlemen," Adams once said casually—perhaps too casually—about his grandfather, "John Adams was a demagogue."

Perry suggested that in their analysis of a particular subject they should read not just one expert but a number of historians with differing interpretations. Adams readily adopted the scheme. Almost a quarter of a century later Adams classed Perry as one of his two or three best students. The admiration was reciprocal. Perry found Adams wonderful; he worshiped him.

Like his father in New York, Perry in Cambridge was the hub of a circle of the most stylish and vivacious men. When they rode together in the suburbs of Boston, Perry had the best mount, a Thoroughbred named Attraction that August had given him.

The glee club met in his rooms to practice, Perry at the piano leading the songs. Afterward they strolled through the streets of Cambridge serenading the town.

At dinners Perry gave at the Parker House, the toasts grew more extravagant with every new glass raised. Glowing with good-fellowship and good wine he and his guests would often rollick from the restaurant to the theater. They saw Edwin Booth, recently come out of his temporary retirement and seeming exceptionally sinister in his role as bloody Richard III because of the shadow cast over his career by his assassin brother.

In the spring Perry sculled on the Charles in a shell that had been a present from his father. He attended parties and practiced charming the girls he met.

"I am very glad that you go into ladies' society," Caroline told him, since practice makes perfect and she wanted him to be a perfect gentleman.

Just as he had been accepted by the freshmen when he had been only a "sub," now he was accepted by the upperclassmen although he was only a freshman. In fact, he was one of the most sought-after candidates for the best societies. He was ready to join when asked—although in the seignorial manner he was developing he saw membership as not just an honor but an obligation. Anyone "who has passed his years here without belonging to one or two clubs," he told his father, "is very properly regarded as an 'egoist,' in the sense that he takes no part in the general life of the University."

Perry took part in every aspect of "the general life of the University," snowballing and skipping prayers (both of which he was admonished for), socializing (he was developing his reputation as being the Beau Brummell of his generation), studying hard and pretending not to be studying at all.

It seemed to Perry as though he were living in the best, the most energetic, the most hopeful of times. The world was being transformed; and he and his fellow students were being prepared to help advance the transformation.

All spring and through the early part of the summer "my poor Rickie," as August told Barlow, was "perfectly helpless. The nervous spasms continue with more or less violence. Luckily her excellent constitution and cheerfulness keep up her strength and spirits. The physician gives us the most positive assurance of her complete recovery, but I fear it will be a very long and tedious affair. We have been obliged to defer our departure until the 23 of June."

While waiting to sail with his family on their European trip, August allowed an obsession with small debts to occupy him, as though his losses in the Erie Wars had made him sensitive about loans to friends and acquaintances. He seemed to fear that any reneging could indicate a general lessening of faith in his business acumen or, perhaps worse, a contempt for his financial standing. It was an unreasonable fear, but one that drove August to ask Samuel Barlow and Manton Marble for help in collecting one moderate and one trivial amount.

He wanted Barlow to get one man, who came from an old and respectable family, "to fulfill, at last, his promise to pay his share of the indebtedness of his house to me. I should think he would feel too proud to remain, if not legally, certainly in equity and honor indebted to me."

He wanted Marble to intercede in a more ticklish affair. Samuel J. Tilden still owed August $300 for expenses incurred during the meeting of the Democratic National Committee in Washington in February 1868, apparently Tilden's share of a joint dinner he and August gave. Tilden conveniently kept forgetting about the debt, and August was in the uncomfortable position of continually having to remind him about it. The $300 did not matter. But Tilden's failure to pay was an insult—and an indication that Tilden, a canny politician, did not think August had enough political power to warrant staying in his good graces.

About the same time Tilden further demonstrated his scorn by disdaining to help August in a political matter. August had written a defense of his activities in the past election. Through Marble he asked Tilden to sign it. Since Tilden had been Horatio Seymour's campaign manager, his support would disarm August's Democratic enemies, who were still taking potshots at him. Tilden delayed and then refused.

August determined to exact the $300 as tribute—to prove that Tilden's analysis of August's position was wrong. Marble, owner of one of the most influential Democratic newspapers, an organ that Tilden could ill afford to alienate, was the gun at Tilden's head.

Marble wrote a letter to Tilden on August's behalf.

Tilden still did not pay the debt.

August wrote a stronger letter to Tilden and asked Marble to deliver it; but after consideration August changed his mind.

"Pray destroy my letter to Tilden," he asked Marble. "I have taken another course to get my $300, for which he has allowed himself to be dunned thus far without feeling the disgrace of his conduct."

It is not clear what August's other approach was or whether it was successful. It is, however, clear that Tilden was not prepared to give in easily, suggesting that August's political health was even worse than he had feared.

To shore up his deteriorating political position August was preparing a book of his letters and speeches from the Civil War. He had written to William H. Seward and others asking them to return to him copies of his correspondence. He gave what he gathered to Marble, asking him to keep the "manuscripts and scrapbook until my return [from Europe] as I should be sorry to lose them. Next Autumn, I hope to find time to attend to the publication, and hope you will give me your aid."

Marble agreed.

Over the past few years August had begun turning to Marble more and more frequently for advice and support. Marble became August's personal as well as political confessor. While waiting for Frederika to recover enough for the Belmonts to travel, August depended on Marble's company to distract him—during whist games, small dinner parties (August and Caroline were having no large affairs until Frederika was better), and at the races.

Fenian, as August had expected, had become a magnificent horse. And August's stable had another extraordinary colt, Glenelg; he had been so balky the previous year that he had not been run, but this year he seemed ready.

August tried out Glenelg early in June at Jerome Park against Jerome's Rapture. After a false start Rapture broke away with a lead of half a length; but Glenelg overtook the other horse so quickly that some of the spectators thought Glenelg had had the lead from the first. August's jockey, Brock, one of the best in the business, paced Glenelg, staying a comfortable one to two lengths ahead of Rapture until the head of the homestretch, where he let the horse go. Glenelg romped to the finish line, winning by six lengths.

"Nine out of ten who saw Glenelg run," said a sporting newspaper, "think he can win" the Belmont Stakes.

The dissenters were betting on Fenian.

August was taking no chances on losing the Belmont Stakes. He entered both Fenian and Glenelg. Just before the first race the clouds turned to a gray-yellow, the color of smoke from a smoldering fire of damp paper. The rain held off for the first two races, which were run to the accompaniment of distant thunder. It was so dark that from the stands it was hard to make out the shapes of Jockey Club members who were watching the races from the clubhouse grounds on the bluff across the track. The glowing red tips of their cigars moved disembodied through the air.

After the second race a strong wind came up, snapping the pennants and flipping hats off heads. A spattering of drops sent those who had not yet taken shelter into the clubhouse or stands. A gust smacked the grandstand awnings back, cracking the iron braces; and the supports and torn canvas crashed down, blocking the aisles. Ladies screamed; men glanced nervously around. Track workers lashed the ripped canvas and propped up the metal spars, so that spectators could move freely in and out of their seats.

The track was muddy, which August's trainer, Jacob Pincus, thought would be to Fenian's advantage. Fenian was August's choice. There were six other entries: Glenelg, Viola, Onyx, Glengarry, Invercauld, and two horses of no consequence. When the flag was raised, one of the latter two horses skittishly slewed around and had to be brought back into line. The flag again was raised. There was a wait of a heartbeat. The flag fell.

The horses took off, Glenelg in the lead, Viola second, Fenian third. By the first turn Fenian and Glenelg had traded positions. Fenian kept the lead around the bluff, with Viola a close second. At the next turn Fenian still had the lead; Viola, tired, had dropped back; and Glengarry and Onyx, coming on strong, passed Glenelg. At the top of the homestretch it was still Fenian out front; Glengarry and Onyx now fell back; and Glenelg, closely followed by Invercauld, was advancing. Down the home-stretch it was Fenian, Glenelg, and Invercauld. And at the wire it was Fenian, Glenelg, and Invercauld—although Glenelg, who had been held back during the race to give Fenian a chance to win, was at the end running so well that one commentator said, "Glenelg's jockey almost had to pull his head off to let Fenian finish first."

August had won the Belmont Stakes.

CHAPTER THIRTY-SIX

AT THE END OF JUNE the Belmonts—minus the two older boys, who were still at school—sailed for Europe. From there August followed the rest of the American racing season as best he could, given the annoyingly irregular arrival of his issues of the sporting newspaper. The news that did make it across the Atlantic was good.

August's horses were beginning to dominate the American turf, although August was not there to enjoy his triumph.

The Atlantic crossing had, August thought, "done wonders for Frederika and all she wants now is quiet with good air." The family stopped for a few days in London and from there traveled to Paris, which was as hot as the worst summer in New York. Since August's last visit James de Rothschild had died. His son Alphonse, whose reputation as an excellent banker was equaling his reputation for having the most perfect moustache in Europe, had told August that "I trust the business connection, which has existed between our Houses for a long time, will continue to be an agreeable one and that we shall have numerous opportunities of extending it in the future."

In the past August had had his problems with Baron James. But Baron James's death left a tear in the tapestry. August felt old, and Paris seemed a school for mortality. After a short visit the Belmonts escaped to Germany.

On the advice of the Belmonts' doctor August went to one spa for one kind of water and Caroline and the children went to another, twelve miles away, for a different kind of water. When August dropped off his family, he was displeased by what he saw.

"There are," August told Marble, "about a hundred guests, mostly Germans, whom no one ever saw or cares ever to see again. It is really a perfect banishment from society and every comfort. It does, however, a great deal of good to my girls, and so my wife has made up her mind to remain" a full month to let the waters do their work.

Every other day August visited Caroline and the children, traveling by uncomfortable coach, which reminded him of the trip he had taken years before when he left Alzey to live with his grandmother in Frankfurt. Being in Germany conjured up so many ghosts. The past shadows the present; and as a life gets longer the shadows lengthen, as they do toward the end of a day.

August was now almost ten years older than his father had been when August first had arrived in New York.

The spa where August was staying was a lively place crowded with gamblers and courtesans who, August thought, "have not even the merit of good looks." The English were snobbish; the Americans, many of them diplomats on their way to or from assignments, vulgar.

"I hardly know a soul," he complained, "and, as I don't find much amusement in losing my money at the *Rouge* and *Noir*, I pass a pretty doleful time."

He did not even believe that "I shall derive much benefit from the nasty stuff," the waters, "though I am determined to see it out."

He passed the time, writing letters to various friends who were currently in Europe, trying to get up a party to go to see the races at Doncaster in September. But everyone had conflicting schedules; it was hard to pin anyone down. When Marble wrote from New York describing an evidently wild ride in his coach, August thanked him for the "charming letter, which like 'the sun of York made glorious summer of the winter of my discontent.' "

The quote was probably prompted less by Shakespeare than by Edwin Booth, whom August like his son must have recently seen playing Richard III; but the reference was more apposite than August could have suspected.

William Marcy Tweed had seized on the role of Richmond. He would lead his followers into battle to revenge himself on August for his crimes. Tweed's newspapers accused August of having betrayed the Democratic party, of not attending to his job as chairman of the National Committee, of being controlled by the Rothschilds and trying to control the party for them, and of being "foreign born."

The last charge was the oddest, since many of August's most outspoken enemies were also foreign-born, Irish immigrants who believed a false rumor that August had embezzled money that had been raised in America for Irish rebels—who coincidentally were called Fenians. The same year that Fenian, August's horse, won the Belmont Stakes, Fenians were the cause of August's almost losing his position in the Democratic party.

August Belmont "has in no way, except on paper perhaps renounced his attachment, his allegiance, his bias toward European and aristocratic institutions," one of Tweed's newspapers said. "He is not only not a Democrat—he is not even, practically, an American citizen."

Trying to prove that point an irate Irishman ranted to the *New York Herald* that August could not speak or write English correctly.

August, Tammany declared, must be replaced as the chairman of the Democratic National Committee—by Tweed.

Tweed's attack on August was part of a coup de'état by which Tweed hoped to destroy all power in New York's Democratic party that rivaled his own. His followers were vilifying the *New York World*, trying to reduce its influence since Tweed did not control it, and were bent on replacing Samuel J. Tilden with one of Tweed's cronies in the chair of the Democratic State Committee.

Ironically, except for the *New York World*, August's most ardent support came from Republicans. *The New York Times* deplored the attacks on August's origins and warned that "if he should take himself out of Tammany Hall, he will not go alone; that is certain, nor will his following be exclusively of the Hebrew people. Mr. Belmont, whatever else may be said of him, is an able banker and an influential citizen."

Thomas Nast drew a cartoon for *Harper's Weekly* showing a goat with a starched collar and August's head loaded down with bags of guilt that were filled with the "Sins of the Democrats" and the defeats of 1860, 1864, and 1868. Political hooligans were kicking and chasing him past a throne labeled "Democratic National Exec Committee," a chair—and presumably chairmanship—that the cartoon noted was "Reserved . . . for Mr. Tweed," who stood by looking not quite the round-bellied, sunken-eyed polecat Nast would later make him out to be.

Next to the throne was a poster that said:

> A. Belmont is an inefficient, undevoted, unsuccessful, and un-popular chairman. . . . His dearth of capacity, lack of purpose, indifference as to results, and want of acceptability were the chief cause of all our defeats.

The cartoon was captioned *The Democratic Scape-Goat.*

"I have no doubt Dick Schell is behind this movement," August said.

Richard and Augustus Schell seemed to have become August's private furies. Possibly Richard Schell still resented either the condescending way August had chided him in 1856 when Schell had tried to bribe August with the offer of the mission to France or August's contempt at Schell's failure around the same time to pay a debt. Possibly Augustus Schell heard about and resented August's unflattering description of him when the previous year they both were lobbying for the mission at Paris, an assignment neither got because Seymour lost the election. Or possibly —if indeed the Schells were behind Tweed—they were merely making a bid for control of the party organization. It did not matter.

"If Schell only knew how much I care about the position," August said. "Tweed or he or any other damned scoundrel is welcome to it."

Marble sent August clippings about the attacks, which August said did not astonish him.

"In fact," he added, "after Tilden's conduct about our joint bill at Washington"—the $300 Tilden owed August and refused to pay—"I am not astonished at anything dirty from New York politicians."

He repeated to Marble his feeling that "they are welcome to the chairmanship of the National Committee," but he warned that "I shall not resign, nor will I be dragged into a newspaper war."

If the Democratic party was tired of his services, August wrote, "the National Committee can remove me from the chairmanship or the state committee can pass a resolution censuring my conduct and appointing somebody else a member in the National Committee for the State of New York."

He was taking a dangerous stand. If he resigned, he could maintain at least the fiction of dignity and the possibility of political resurrection. If he were censured, he would leave politics in disgrace. He seemed determined to be a martyr.

"It is charming to see myself accused of having caused the defeat of the party in 1864 and 1868," August thought. "Who fought harder against the peace resolution and Pendleton in 1864 and against Seymour and the greenback platform in 1868 and who paid more for the cause?"

The letters and speeches August intended to publish would prove he had been unfairly attacked; but by the time the book was printed and distributed it would be too late for the Democratic party to make amends. Like a sulky child threatening that whoever hurt him would be sorry once he was gone, August swore that the book of his letters and speeches "will be the last act of my political life and the book's expenses will be the last cent I shall spend for a party to which I have been faithful, since the first day I cast a vote."

August's vows were easier to make than to keep. The side of him that welcomed the passion of martyrdom fought with the side that welcomed the chance for a good political brawl. Luckily the strategy for one served equally as well as the strategy for the other. The first law of politics like the first law of motion says, in part, that a body at rest tends to remain at rest. . . . A body in office tends to remain in office. . . . Even if the party wanted to oust him from the chairmanship of the National Committee, it was not likely that August would be censured. That move would be too extreme.

August started marshaling the forces for his defense. He asked Marble for help.

Marble apparently suggested that, since Tilden was also under fire, August and Tilden should form an alliance.

"Your advice is very well meant," August told him; "but I am sorry to say I cannot follow it. Tilden has behaved worse to me than Tweed and his clique. The latter are blackguards and pretend to nothing better. I don't know them, nor they me. They hate every decent man, and they are down upon the Manhattan Club and its dignitaries. Tilden has the pretension to be a gentleman and professes to be a friend of mine, has been the guest of my house over and over, and knows my sacrifice in the cause. He knows also as well as you do that, if my advice had been followed, we would not be where we are now. I have nothing to say to him—nor do I want his friendship."

What August did want was for his "friends, if I have any, to take the matter in hand. It is not for me to come out in my defense. If my friends want really to silence these foul slanders, they have a very good opportunity. They and all those who like fair play ought to unite in offering me a dinner on my return. This would give me an opportunity to make a speech and explain the position which I have held in politics for the last twelve years and more" and would dramatize the support August still had within the party.

"I suggest it to you," August said. "But, of course, you will not mention me in the matter, as it would place me in a false and ridiculous position."

August asked Samuel Barlow to help by "enlisting some of our prominent friends in a suitable demonstration against the disgraceful attacks of the Tammany ring on me."

As with Marble, August warned Barlow to be "discreet and don't tell anybody that I wrote to you about it."

To have it known that he was trying to give himself a testimonial would be an admission of defeat.

The dinner was not necessary. In this case the Tammany tiger seemed to be made of paper. Tweed backed down. The attacks on the *New York World,* Tilden, and August stopped. At the Democratic state convention in September, Tilden was reelected to the chairmanship of the state committee by a landslide. For the moment at least, Tilden had made his peace with Tammany; and he advised Marble to do the same by binding himself to Tammany with as many deals as he could negotiate.

August did not make any peace with Tammany. Or with Tilden. But he retained the chairmanship of the National Committee. Since he had not been in the country to lead his own defense, his victory seemed all the more complete.

"Belmont," the *New York Post* declared, "is revenged on his enemies."

August felt reborn. He had emerged from the fight with Tweed politically renewed. And he had also escaped unscathed from what he called "the storm which just swept over Wall Street." The storm was Jay Gould's attempt to corner the gold market, which climaxed on September 24, "Black Friday," when dozens of August's friends were left bankrupt.

Adding to August's cheer, Frederika—although not fully recovered —was much stronger. And to his surprise the waters he had taken seemed to have alleviated his dyspepsia. August rejoined his family and, meeting up with Perry and August, Jr., who had come from America, went to Frankfurt to visit Babette.

August and Babette surprised each other with how much they had aged; but even more startling must have been the changes in the children —all of them so much bigger, and the older ones like Perry so grown-up. The two families went to see horse races, August making notes on the German interpretation of the sport. On the way back from the track August, Jr., and his father took special notice of a French lady. Perhaps she was very elegant, or very beautiful, or very sad. Whatever else she was, she was memorable.

August had to return for a few days to his spa. While he was gone, Perry and August, Jr., left Frankfurt to go to England and then to the United States and school. As the two older boys said their good-byes the younger children blubbered. Caroline had to stay and calm them, so Perry and August, Jr., went to the railroad station with the Feists, who annoyed August, Jr., by jabbering all the time. August, Jr., thought it was harder to leave than to be left behind, and he resented the intrusion all the talk made on his melancholy.

On the train they shared a compartment with the French lady whom they had seen leaving the races, her maid, and two Prussian officers. The Prussians were bossy and arrogant. They quarreled with the French lady over some hand luggage and, losing their tempers and their honor, threatened to beat her. They apparently ignored any protests from Perry and August, Jr., as much because the Belmont boys were Americans as because they were young. In the midst of this ruckus the train pulled into Mainz.

The Prussians stormed out of the car. The woman began to sob. When the conductor passed, she begged him to give her a private compartment. The conductor was sympathetic and, as there were no empty compartments on the train, added a car, into which the lady and her maid vanished.

The Prussians evidently had thought that, given the hostility between Germany and France (everyone assumed the two countries would soon be at war), their disgusting behavior—humiliating France in the person of a French lady—would be applauded as an act of patriotism. On returning to the compartment and finding that the German railroad officials had taken the French lady's side, the Prussians—submissive to any authority, even railroad authority—became frightened and hid for a good part of the trip in a second-class car.

Perry and August, Jr., arrived in England late in the afternoon. At customs, when the officer asked them, "Have you any tobacco, spirits, or plate?" Perry said "No" so authoritatively that their luggage was passed without being opened—which surprised and pleased the boys.

In London they stayed at a hotel with some other Americans who had also come to England to see the first Harvard-Oxford boat race. The management treated Perry and August, Jr., and everyone else who had any connection to Harvard with exceptional solicitude. The rooms were comfortable, the food excellent. The boys were enjoying traveling on their own.

August felt animated by his old joy in life. He, Caroline, and the younger children returned to Paris, which no longer seemed funereal.

After a dinner party August and Caroline walked through the city, stopping for hours to watch a large fire, which August in his good mood saw not as tragedy but as spectacle.

Even Jeannie's attack of measles—which depressed her since she was not able to go sight-seeing with her sister and their new governess—was not able to upset him. His spirits were higher than they had been for a long time.

On the family's way back to America, August stopped off at Doncaster. He finally had managed to get up a racing party to watch the St. Leger. The course was not enclosed. People wandered through the grounds freely, in both senses of the word; there was no admission charge, and that made the races more casual, more accessible, and, most importantly, more popular than in America.

August returned to the United States with plans for Jerome Park.

"We have a great deal to learn in the way of racing," he thought. "The St. Leger was one of the most beautiful sights I ever witnessed, and for lovers of the sport much finer than the Derby. There were about 15,000 people on the grounds, from the first peers of the realm down to the lowest stable boy, each entering heart and soul into the race and having a good time in general."

August, who once had said, "Racing is for the rich," dedicated himself to drumming up enough support among the upper classes, who could pay for the stands, so that "we can open the field [for free] to the people."

✄ CHAPTER THIRTY-SEVEN ✄

THE EUROPEAN TRIP had intensified August, Jr.'s desire for autonomy. He had liked being more or less on his own and admired—and wanted to emulate—Perry's self-reliance and sophistication, the way he had handled the customs officer, the ease with which he had gotten them seats for the Harvard-Oxford race on the judges' boat, the casual and knowing manner in which he ordered dinner, just like their father. The two boys were far enough apart in age for Perry to seem as though he were living in a world apart, had been inducted into the mysteries of manhood; but close enough in age for August, Jr. to feel that those mysteries were accessible to him if only he could pay the initiation fee. You cannot casually order superior wine with your meals if you are on a limited budget. August, Jr., asked for an increase in his allowance.

His timing was off. His request came just as his father had decided on his own to raise August, Jr.'s allowance to $15 a month. It would be awkward—and would seem ungrateful—to ask for more; but August, Jr., did not think he could get by on less than $20 a month. He asked his mother to intercede. She did, afraid that if her son were strapped for cash he might be tempted to borrow from his friends, which was undignified and could make him unpopular.

August indulged his son and consented to the additional $5 a month. Now Caroline feared that the extra money might tempt August, Jr., to lend to his friends, which also was undignified and could give him a false popularity that was built on resentment.

"I want you to use your judgment in all things," she told him, although it was her and her husband's judgment—how much to let their son have each month—that was at issue.

August, Jr., was not a bad student or a bad boy, but he was irrepressible and increasingly independent, a quality admirable in a man but often troublesome in one who must still bend to the wishes of others. He had matured early, which made him want to be grown-up before his time. In short, he was forever proving himself childish by trying to act like an adult; so he continued to get into trouble at Exeter. The most optimistic prediction he could make for his big brother was to assure him that, "I will certainly be allowed to stay here the term out."

The school year had started depressingly. The squirrels that he had caught the previous spring for Frederika, Jeannie, and Oliver, and that he had left over the summer at school, had died. Then August, Jr., became quite sick, almost developing what he described as an "inflammation of the bone," which he in a sincere although transparent bid for sympathy reminded his parents was "very dangerous." The doctor attending him stopped by every morning, afternoon, and evening; and eventually August, Jr., had to be transferred from the dormitory to a house where he could get better care.

During his illness he fell behind in his studies. By Thanksgiving he was in danger of being kicked out of school. He wrote to Perry asking that they meet and travel to New York together. He did not want to go home alone. Or if he did go home alone he wanted Perry to pave the way first.

"Please," he asked his brother, "do what you can so that I may not have to be scolded so severely and spoil the day for all."

At last the school felt they could do nothing more with him. When the term ended, August, Jr., was let go. Pathetically he again begged for forgiveness and vowed to change his ways.

"I am ashamed of myself," he told his father, "and feel at heart the trouble and disappointment I have caused you, who have always been so kind to me."

"God has granted you intelligence and more than ordinary facility to learn," said August, trying to find a balance between consoling his son, which he wanted to do, and absolving him, which he did not want to do. "If you will only be more steady of purpose, you will have no difficulty in obtaining a good position in College and becoming a useful member of society. You will be seventeen years old in February, and you must give hereafter more time than heretofore to study and less time to fun. Your friends will like and respect you much more if they see there is something more in you than a mere jolly companion."

August, Jr., asked to be allowed to continue his studies in Cambridge under a private tutor.

His father agreed "under the condition that you will be guided by the advice of Perry, who loves you dearly and who knows the place and the people. I want you immediately upon your arrival not only to begin your studies for entering college, but also to resume your lessons in Piano and French."

August, Jr., found rooms near Perry, engaged two tutors, and, experimenting with his new freedom, within a week and a half spent the entire sum his father had sent. He was being extravagant, but he was not being selfish. He bought gifts for his brothers and sisters, as if he wanted to skip being a young man and immediately become an avuncular, even paternal, figure. He wanted not to receive but to give. All his father saw was that his son was living beyond his means. He sent $50 more with the admonition, "You see, my dear boy, it is necessary that you should learn habits of economy," and he asked August, Jr., to be more diligent about sending monthly statements listing his expenses.

August, Jr., thanked his father for the check but balked at sending the statements. It was too much trouble keeping track of how he spent his money. He could not recall specific purchases. Didn't his father trust him? Why did he have to write it all down?

"I cannot tell you how much pain it gives me to see you write to me in so unkind and disrespectful a manner," August told his son. "I do not believe that there is another boy, who pretends to be a gentleman's son, who would think of writing to his father in the tone with which you do. It makes me really sick to see such ingratitude and unkindness. You are angry with me for the trouble which your accounts give you."

Jotting down his daily expenses every night before bed should not take more than five minutes.

"I have had to work all my life," August added, "and yet I have never omitted to keep my accounts carefully."

August loved his son too much simply to chide him. He knew that August, Jr., would read the letter and be consumed with remorse, so he explained that not wanting to bother with accounts could be part of learning to keep accounts.

"Perry was negligent just as you are now in money matters until he went to college," August told his son. "He will tell you so, and also that I have remonstrated with him only last week about the amount of his expenditures."

He wanted August, Jr., to know that he was not alone in his troubles. He should not assume, as he once did, that his parents thought him wicked. It was all part of growing up.

Just as August did not doubt that Perry "will comply with my request," he was sure August, Jr., whatever his objections, would do as he was told.

Because August did not "want to keep it among my papers," he returned August, Jr.'s unpleasant letter, saying: "I shall not mention the receipt of it to anybody," especially Caroline, since "it would give her too much pain." He told his son that "you may destroy it."

Apparently August, Jr., did destroy his own letter; but he saved the one from his father to remind himself that he must improve.

At Christmas, Perry and August, Jr., went to New York. Both boys were handsome and shared the same high brow and heavy-lidded eyes, although Perry's gaze looked amused, indolent, supercilious, and August, Jr.'s looked watchful. Both seemed to be men of the world.

Perry was full of college stories, the hazing of freshmen, which he claimed was more severe this year than it had been for a long time, the clubs (he had been elected to D.K.E.), and the changes at Harvard.

Thirty-five-year-old Charles William Eliot, whose appointment had been vetoed twice by the college's board of overseers, was the school's new president. He was a fine scholar whose body was as muscular as his mind. He had been a varsity oar and still rowed on the Charles. He saw nothing wrong in the students behaving like the adults they were: smoking or riding the horse-drawn bus into Boston to attend the theater. He had taken the fewer than five hundred undergraduates and twenty-one professors who made up the school and was herding them into the modern world. This was, after all, the latter half of the nineteenth century. Harvard had to expand with the country. It could not be content to settle into a role inferior to that of Yale and Columbia, both of which were becoming—as Eliot wanted Harvard to be—national, not merely local, colleges.

Unfortunately the school was not changing fast enough to save Perry from being academically penalized for missing classes and prayers, a policy that eventually would be abolished. And he was letting his German slide. But these were, for the time being, minor matters, nothing to cast a pall over the holiday.

Caroline and Frederika were making presents. Raymond was pestering everyone to write letters to Santa Claus and then was worrying that by doing so he was being naughty and that as a result on Christmas morning his stocking would be empty. Oliver described to Perry and August, Jr., what he was doing at the Charlier Institute, a self-described "English and

French School for Young Gentlemen," which was six blocks up Fifth Avenue and around the corner on Twenty-fourth Street. Jeannie had recovered from—and no doubt was being teased about—her accident; her horse had fallen, throwing her to the earth and pinning down her legs. Since the groom was so far behind that it took him a few minutes to reach and free her, she must have been galloping.

After attending and giving more parties during the vacation, Perry and August, Jr., returned to Cambridge.

New York City quieted down, but only for a short time to let the world digest its Christmas and New Year's dinners and catch its breath before the next round of festivities.

Caroline had a charade party for fourteen of her children's friends.

Frederika and Jeannie continued their dancing lessons at Dodworth's, two blocks up Fifth Avenue from Oliver's school. At three o'clock in the afternoon, the lessons would begin, usually with a march. The students entered two by two, bowed or curtsied to Mr. Dodworth, a thin man with gray hair and moustache, and his wife, who invariably wore a black velvet dress, and walked across the parquet floor, which was the color of honey and as slippery as ice, to their seats along the wall. When one of the boys or girls, tempted beyond control, took a running slide, Dodworth would clap as sharply as a gunshot; the child would jerk as though hit; and Dodworth would insist that the young barbarian walk back to the door and reenter alone, a humiliation worth the thrill that brought it on. Behind the children's seats, raised on platforms, were chairs for the parents, many of whom must have recalled the same temptation to slide on equally glassy floors in earlier years.

Life was settling into a pleasant routine. Assembly balls at Delmonico's, which August organized. A banquet and ball for Prince Arthur of England that August, along with Sam Ward, Samuel Barlow, and thirty-two other men, sponsored, and at which it was discovered that the prince was an awkward dancer.

During the prince's visit there was according to George Templeton Strong "lots of funny gossip about the toadyism and snobbery of our prince-hunters. It's evidently proper that people with fine houses and great wealth, like Belmont . . . and others, should receive and entertain a 'distinguished' stranger. I am glad that there are men in the city who can do it so well. But the amount of envy, hatred, malice, . . . and jealousies which these entertainments generate among those who are invited and those who are not, is appalling."

Even the railing of August's enemies had become so routine that when August heard of it, it did not disrupt his placidity as it had in the past. All the venom he had absorbed had acted as an inoculation against the poison of his critics; he was becoming immune.

He refused to be drawn into a renewed battle Manton Marble was waging against Tweed and Tammany.

"I told you before that I was very sorry that you engaged in that war against Tweed," August told Marble, "and am doubly sorry now as it will deprive me of the pleasure of seeing you tomorrow at dinner. If you have to neglect your friends to fight your enemies, and those enemies such *canaille*, you should leave them alone."

August remained convinced that politics was a waste of time. Only a naïf could believe that anyone ever appreciated one's sacrifice for any political cause.

"Life is too short," August continued; "and I cannot believe that you have illusions enough left to take all this trouble for your unselfish, high-toned, patriotic citizens of Gotham."

As one of the leaders of the anti-Tweed faction, which was calling itself the Young Democracy, Marble tried to bring August back into the fold. Barlow was supporting the Young Democracy. So was John Morrissey. August would be among friends.

Friends? What about Samuel J. Tilden?

Although Tilden kept publicly aloof from the Young Democracy, he privately supported the movement. In seeking August's participation, Marble had evidently dangled the lure that Tilden might win the Democratic nomination and the presidency. If August would forget his anger at Tilden and join Young Democracy's revolt against Tweed, Tilden, who would benefit from the revolt, would remember August's help if he ever got in office.

"I am very much obliged to you for your allusion to Tilden," August said; "but you know me but little if you think that any personal consideration for the future could ever make me forget his more than ungentlemanly conduct toward me. If Mr. Tilden was President tomorrow and offered me any office coveted by me or the aim of all my ambitions, I would spurn it coming from him."

August watched complacently from the sidelines as Tweed outmaneuvered Marble and at least temporarily put down the revolt. He would not get involved. He would allow nothing to shatter his peace of mind.

For a few months, in the late winter and spring of 1870, no major crises—public or private—disturbed the Belmonts' lives.

Unlike Perry, August, Jr., had been unable to return to New York to meet Prince Arthur; but his older brother sent him newspaper clippings about the affair, which when August, Jr. read them must have made him feel virtuous. He had stayed in Cambridge to study.

As a consolation Caroline agreed to buy him what he needed to play cricket in the spring and, for his birthday, a small traveling bag that he wanted, one with "a sort of dressing case" inside.

But even with his mother covering luxuries like those, he still was unable to make ends meet. He was helped a little by a windfall. He won a—probably prohibited—raffle the students at Exeter had gotten up, for which he had bought tickets before leaving the school. His friend Pig, an honest fellow, promised to "send you what has been paid me so far and what I owe you." But that extra money was not enough to pay all of August, Jr.'s bills. He told his father:

"I told you I would fall short with only $100 a month," the allowance agreed upon during the holiday. "I have worked out my accounts to the penny today. I went in town one evening and found I had not enough money with me," he added for his mother's sake, since she had such a horror of his taking loans. "I borrowed a dollar from a classmate."

His father, as he had before, covered the expenses; and, as his son wished, he made sure August, Jr.'s shoes, which had gotten damp and stiff in the snow, were attended to. He could recall when he had to make do with too tight shoes in Frankfurt, when he had so little money he could not spend even a few cents on skating, the old memories of deprivation that would haunt him whenever his children asked for something. He did not want them to lack anything; but if they got everything they desired, would they ever learn to weigh their desires and to discriminate among them? If you can get anything you ask for, how do you learn what you really want? And if you never learn what you really want, how do you develop taste? Raising his son's allowance was not just an economic or disciplinary issue but an aesthetic one.

Prentiss Cummings, August, Jr.'s new tutor, understood that his student would resist any rules except those he made for himself, so he encouraged August, Jr., to be independent and, in being independent, responsible.

"I have not been to the theater or allowed my mind to be taken from my studies," August, Jr., told his mother; "and I am going to see how long I can keep it up."

He studied about six hours a day. When his commitment flagged, he cleverly upped the ante of the challenge by betting a friend $10 that he could keep to his schedule. Like his father he hated to lose a bet, so he continued to work hard, despite the distractions that spring brought.

August sent horses to his sons: Attraction which was lamed on the way to Cambridge for Perry and Lady Love for August, Jr. To make sure the horses had the best equipment (to go with the best breeding) in Cambridge he also sent new blankets, bits, and bridles. August, Jr., was delighted by the tackle and charmed by the animal.

"Lady Love is her name to me," he said.

But because he knew that both riding and rowing every day would interfere with his work, he considered giving up one or the other.

"It is much more important for a gentleman to ride well than to row well," counseled his father, who also was worried that the violent exercise of rowing might develop his son's muscles at the expense of his height.

August, Jr., who had just proudly read an article in *The Spirit of the Times* about his father's stable, complied with his father's wishes. He wanted "to do justice to my name" in work and in play; and since his father was the acknowledged leader of the American turf August, Jr., would school himself in horses as well as in academic studies.

He also had another, just as admirable, tradition to live up to, as a letter from his grandmother Jane Perry reminded him. Since she had decided to go to the Continent with her daughter Belle and her family, she was emptying and selling her house.

"An auction took place yesterday of all the furniture," Caroline told August, Jr. "It makes me feel sad when I pass the street now, but your grandmother bears it all very cheerfully."

Jane Perry seemed to find relief in unencumbering herself of worldly goods. She sent August, Jr., "a pair of Japanese tripods," probably from her husband's Japanese mission, "and a French piece." She told him that "in finding a place for them in your rooms, you will think of me."

August, Jr., must have put the mementoes in positions of honor and, while staring at them, must have thought about not just his grandmother but also his grandfather, the far parts of the world he had visited, the things he had done, what he must have learned. . . .

"Tell Papa," he wrote his mother, "I *will* get into college. Not only that, but I am going to change, for I feel ashamed of my limited knowledge."

He had long talks with Perry about his present and his future. He felt that he was making progress, although the progress was never as dramatic as he wished. It was not a matter of overnight transformations, as he used to think, but of improvement so gradual that it was hard to say when a bad attitude vanished and a good attitude replaced it. To make sure his parents noticed what he knew was not a startling change, he wrote one letter to them (in which he describes how hard he was working) on the back of a geometry homework scratch paper.

Perry reported to his parents that August, Jr., was making a heroic effort to prepare for the Harvard entrance examination. His father felt sorry that August, Jr., had "to shut yourself in a garret," but was, of course, happy that he was doing well—although he found it hard to believe that his son could make up for years of inattention to studies in a few months of intensive work.

"There is no course for you," he told his son, "if you don't succeed in the end."

August, Jr., wanted to change his habits; but "turning over a new leaf," Cummings wrote to August, "for him means drudgery and self-denial, and consequently his good resolutions have seldom lasted till the next day and never longer than that."

He was, not surprisingly, "always gentlemanly and amiable," and his tutor was "glad to do for him everything that can be done; but his own work no other person can do for him. He has more general information than is usual in so young a man," Cummings explained; "but he has no work habits. He *almost* knows a good many things, but does not *quite* know much of anything. He thinks he has improved since he has been with me, and I think so too; but by no means so much as he should. Unless there be a great change for the better in him, and that soon, I can give you little encouragement that he will get into college this summer, still less that he can stay if he should enter. I have sometimes thought it might be the best thing that could happen to him if he should be rejected; for he will be plenty young enough next year, and if he could be thoroughly mortified and feel that he had disappointed the just expectations of his friends it might wake him up."

August, Jr., was rejected. And mortified. And confused. As Cummings had said, "according to his ideas of faithfulness, he had tried to be a faithful student." What more could he do?

Eager to go out to Nursery Farm August put aside unopened a letter from John Hone, his sister-in-law Jane's husband. Probably some business, August thought; it could wait. At the Nursery he read in the newspapers about the death of Alexander Hone, John and Jane's son, news that had been in the letter.

Shortly before the past Christmas his parents had taken Alexander abroad for his health. During the trip to Europe "Alick," as Caroline had reported to August, Jr., "proved to be the best sailor of all. He hoped you would keep your promise of writing to him. He is very fond of you and, sick as he is, he would always make an effort to see you, so I hope you will not forget him."

Because he was occupied with his academic troubles August, Jr., had failed to write to his cousin. He had meant to but had kept putting it off until he was in a better mood and could send a cheery note. No one expected Alexander to die. The worst anyone thought was that the family might have to remain in Europe for several years.

"They say he must have been a great sufferer for a long time," Caroline told August, Jr., not realizing how her words wracked her son with guilt, "but that he bore his pain quietly and patiently and during the last 10 days of his life he was extremely restless, but was kept under the effect of anodynes and died of heart disease very suddenly at the last without a struggle, falling over into his nurse's arms."

Coming at the same time as his failure to get into college, when he was feeling low-spirited and unworthy, the news of his cousin's death tormented August, Jr.

"I blame myself continually for not writing to him," he told his father; "and I don't know how to write Aunt Jane, as Mama wants me to."

But he apparently wrote.

And Jane apparently answered.

August, Jr., learned once more a lesson most people in difficulty find very hard to master: No matter what his faults or failings he was still loved and accepted by those to whom he was closest.

CHAPTER THIRTY-EIGHT

"EVERYBODY THINKS WELL of Perry," Professor Child wrote August that year. In fact, it was Perry's very popularity that was his undoing. By the end of his sophomore year he was a member not only of D.K.E. but also of the Institute of 1770 (a debating club), the Medical Faculty (a secret society), and the Porcellian, to which he had been initiated in March, the first of his class to join. "He is of a very social temper," Child continued, "and has at present no very serious views," which was not true. Child added, "He is having a good time," which was only partly true. By missing recitations and prayers, he was placing himself in jeopardy. His school troubles depressed him.

"Boston, gay Boston is as exciting as ever," he wrote to August, Jr.; "and I am at this moment as blue a mortal as you could wish to see."

The more depressed he became, the more he partied; the more he partied, the worse his grades became.

"I suspect the only means of making him study will be a desire on your part," Child told August, "expressed in such a way as to admit no trifling."

The warnings from school, Child, and his parents did not make Perry more industrious. He was suspended.

August hoped that his two older boys would settle down at the Nursery with a tutor, a young man named Mark Sibley Severance. Perry could stay from June until after Christmas, when he would return to school. August could stay the entire year catching up on his work so that the following fall he could enter Harvard with the sophomore class.

"We shall, of course, see that you have every comfort at the farm," August told August, Jr.; "and, as it is only two hours from New York, you can pass your Sundays in town."

August sent his sons a water filter, since the water at the Nursery was bad; and worrying that they would not use it properly—although the family must have used filters in the past—he gave detailed instructions; his anxiety over his sons' academic performances could be channeled less threateningly into concern over their handling of the water filters. He also shipped to the farm two dozen bottles of good claret for them to drink with the water, a precaution he believed would help keep the water from upsetting their digestion. He discussed other country matters: getting fresh ice, the new pair of ferrets, the health of his fighting cocks, the possibility of trading "our two rams against a good Thoroughbred about 2 or 3 years old"; but he hoped they would not "neglect their studies by looking after the farm."

August, Jr., enjoyed being at the Nursery and, even more, taking care of it. He made suggestions about the farm's operations that his father accepted. But he was impatient with his tutor, who kept him from going into town on Sundays because it would take too much time away from work.

"I'm sorry you have not satisfied Mr. Severance this week," Caroline wrote to August, Jr., when she heard he could not spend the Sabbath with them. "Do try to make up for it, my dear boy, and have some consideration for him. Remember that he is a young man himself, and it must be trying for him to worry over your studies."

Perry was less willing than his brother to be cooped up all summer at the Nursery, with or without a tutor. He had made plans with two college friends, upperclassmen Alfred Rodman and Brooks Adams, the younger brother of Perry's favorite teacher, Henry Adams, to go West—and go West he would.

The trip began in Quincy, Massachusetts, where Perry went to pick up Adams and where he met Adams's father, the former Minister to the Court of St. James's Charles Francis Adams, who had a reputation for being not just cool but arctic. Perry found him warm—not tropical but definitely temperate—and was amused by the way the son mirrored the father's mannerisms. They shared "the same clear, concise way of speaking," he told August, "and the same caustic vein. I know you don't like 'community of goods,'" Perry teased, "but how about 'the aforesaid goods'? 'A community of admirable habits.'?"

Perry also liked the quick interplay of ideas between father and son, a shuttling back and forth of thoughts so rapid and seamlessly connected that the conversation between them seemed to become a monologue, the expression of a single mind that happened to be lodged in two different heads.

They met Rodman in Boston and started their trek: Boston by train to St. Paul, St. Paul by stern-wheeler down the Mississippi River to St. Louis; St. Louis by train to San Francisco. . . . The hills of the East, the plains of the midwest, the Rockies, the Pacific Ocean. . . . The days passed uneventfully. Perry was looking for adventure and finding only local color. They arrived in San Francisco to learn that the Franco-Prussian War had started. They watched French and Prussian sympathizers massing in the streets; but the war was far away and these demonstrations seemed unrelated to what Perry had expected of the West. He had not come to California to learn about European conflicts.

He met Henry R. Rathbone, who had been with Lincoln the night the President was shot. But Rathbone seemed to prefer showing off his trotters to discussing the tragic past. The country was growing too fast, becoming too civilized too soon. Perry wanted the nation to be tamed; he believed in progress—but not yet, not until he had a chance to see and live in the wild.

From San Francisco they went by old-fashioned stagecoach—lurching around inside as the carriage bounced along uneven roads—toward the Yosemite Valley, which was still savage enough for Perry to hope that they would at least be attacked by bandits as a previous party had been.

Instead, what he found was a land that another traveler of the time described as "so gloriously colored and so radiant, it seemed . . . composed of . . . light, like . . . some celestial city."

Perry had found a land beyond civilization; but in it instead of adventure he discovered awe.

After leaving what had seemed a natural celestial city, Perry, Adams, and Rodman headed to a manmade celestial city, the City of the Saints, Salt Lake City, Utah. From the mountains the city, with its straight parallel avenues seeming to converge toward the far end of town, looked like an exercise in perspective. It appeared to one traveler vaguely Oriental or like Athens without the Acropolis. However, on a closer look, instead of a city of light it seemed to be a city of mud.

The streets were laid out at right angles forming a grid, as though the city were built around a great cross, a coordinate and abscissa, so one's movement from place to place on earth would describe a graph of the soul's, as well as the body's progress. But in worldly life one doubles back, changes direction, veers and swerves so often that the graph would be intelligible only to God; and certainly as Perry and his friends wandered through the city their movements, at least to human eyes, seemed aimless enough. The gardens they saw were as orderly as the city, the houses clean and pleasant. They found a hotel and must have luxuriated in the chance to bathe with hot water, dine on linen, and sleep on mattresses.

Because Adams's father while he was minister at London had helped

English Mormons emigrate to the United States, Brigham Young, whose official title was President of the Church of Jesus Christ of Latter-Day Saints all over the World, met with them. As usual they probably were scrutinized by plainclothes guards as they walked along the veranda of Young's house and into his private office.

Although nearly seventy, Young was youthful—and he seemed as angular as the city's streets. Only a slight stoop, a drooping left eyelid, and bad teeth reminded one that he was an old man. Perry came away from the interview thinking that Young was neither the devil some thought nor the saint others thought—meeting a devil or a saint would have been an adventure—but merely "an energetic, capable, successful man of affairs."

In Denver, Perry found the setting of the Wild West for which he was looking: cowboys, cardsharpers, homesteaders. . . . But still no adventure. He had one last chance, a trip into Ute Indian country. The Utes, a nomadic tribe who for a while had conquered other Indians to sell as slaves to the whites, had been put on a reservation two years before. They were still fierce enough to be continually involved in rumors of raids and massacres and, less frequently, in the raids and massacres themselves.

Perry and his friends had trouble hiring guides to lead them into the Ute lands, because the tribe had been harrying local whites recently, in reality not just in rumor. Perry kept raising his offer until one guide could not resist.

"On a beautiful evening just before sunset," Perry recalled, "we rode over the ridge into" the Ute Reservation. "The valley was a carpet of flowers and the grass was up to our stirrups. Just as the Indian camp appeared in view, I saw what I thought was a mink or a beaver in a small stream, well within rifle shot."

Perry shouldered his gun and was about to fire when the creature stood up on its hind legs and, as though charmed, metamorphosed into an Indian boy. Even if Perry had missed the boy the Utes probably would have attacked in retaliation.

A little farther along the trail they came to the tribe's camp.

"The braves were riding around corralling their horses for the night," said Perry, "while the squaws busied themselves preparing food at the newly lighted fires."

Perry, Adams, and Rodman stopped nearby and had just pitched their tent when an Indian rode up. He swung down from his horse. Casually, as though he were a longtime neighbor, he entered the tent and

sat with the guide and three Easterners, who not quite as casually continued what they had been doing. Adams was struggling with a fire. The
Indian reached over and started it for him.

Using the guide as an interpreter, Perry, Adams, and Rodman
chatted with their guest, who since the land they were on belonged to his
tribe was really—and appropriately acted as—their host. He was Colorao, the chief of the Ute, who supposedly hated whites.

They offered him cigarettes.

He accepted, turned them this way and that, and popped one into
his mouth. In exchange he took out a wallet, an Arapaho's wallet, he said;
a dead Arapaho's wallet.

The Arapaho were another tribe, who lived on the other side of the
ridge.

The guide recognized the wallet and said it had belonged to a
prospector who reportedly had been murdered by Indians.

By the Arapaho, Colorao said; that's why it had been found on an
Arapaho's body. The white men should be sure to tell the authorities that
the Arapaho were guilty, he added.

With that settled, at least to Colorao's satisfaction, the chief invited Perry and his friends to attend a scalp dance. An Arapaho's scalp,
he said.

The prospector's scalp, the guide thought; and he told them not to
go.

Perry and his friends declined; but since the chief seemed to want
to do something for them, they asked if he could get them some elk
meat.

Colorao held out his hand.

Either Perry, Adams, or Rodman slowly counted out silver coins
until Colorao closed his hand and bolted.

You won't see him or your money again, the guide said; or any elk
meat.

The next morning a young Indian circled their tent until they
woke; and then, seeing them, he trotted up to the tent flap and dumped
the elk meat at their feet.

It had not been a great adventure, but it had been an adventure,
and it became even more thrilling in retrospect when Perry heard that the
Ute were considered dangerous enough for the United States government a few weeks later to send the 5th Cavalry, led by Perry's cousin
Ranald MacKenzie, onto the reservation to keep order.

Perry, Adams, and Rodman climbed a few more mountains and took the train home.

Around the time Perry left on his Western trip, August and Caroline went to Newport. Frederika, Jeannie, Oliver, and Raymond stayed behind for a few weeks in New York so they could finish their studies and their riding, drawing, and dancing lessons. The nurse, governess, and other servants ostensibly were looking after things; but the two older girls really ran the house. Coming home exhausted from dancing class, Jeannie liked to flop down on her mother's sofa, enjoying Caroline's comforts as well as her responsibilities. When Raymond woke up with a sniffle, "I made him jump into his bath," Jeannie told her mother; "and, when he got out, I gave him a good rubbing."

On occasion Jeannie would wake up early as usual but stay in her nightgown writing letters and planning the day: a trip to the Nursery; a meeting of her archery club, which was called Cupid's Arrow Club, a name that did not satisfy Jeannie, who thought of herself as an excellent shot, having once hit the exact center of the bull's-eye; or tea and dinner with some friends. When their classes ended for the summer, the children joined their parents at Bythesea.

Caroline loved their place in Newport, "where I always feel happy," she said, "even if I am alone." This year she thought the grounds were "looking particularly well. The roses are so handsome that they really look artificial." Any withered, even brown-edged, flower was sacrificed by the gardener as though to banish any evidence of decay or death from this world. August, an American Prospero, was trying to keep this part of the island enchanted; and the magic he used was money.

Caroline rearranged the accommodations, giving Oliver and Raymond their older brothers' rooms and preparing two newly built rooms for Perry and August, Jr., to use when they came to visit. August had given Caroline a new saddle horse, which he had imported from France and which the younger children at once appropriated, taking turns riding it the day it arrived until they got hot and clamored to go for a swim.

August found life at Bythesea a relief from such duties of the city as opening their gallery to raise money for charity or joining the board of the Katy Railroad, both of which he had done in the past year. None of these obligations was onerous—and some of them were quite pleasant—but all together they from time to time could oppress him. Ever since he first had become successful, even when he was still a young man, he had considered retiring and devoting his life to his family, his friends (like Marble, with whom he fished at the Nursery and exchanged cigars), and his hobbies (like racing). There was enough Simon in him to keep him from retiring—although there was not so much Simon in him to keep him from dedicating most of his summers to the turf.

This season was mixed. It started poorly with Telegram, Nellie James, Finesse, and surprisingly Glenelg all being beaten; but it ended with Glenelg being recognized by some as the best older horse—and being accepted by everyone else as one of the two best older horses—of the year. In July, August also bought for the extravagant sum of $15,000 a three-year-old colt named Kingfisher, which, having won both the Belmont and the Travers Stakes, seemed to be a champion. August had great hopes for Kingfisher.

He felt more and more "anxious about my book as the time rolls on," he told Marble. He had wanted to get the volume printed and distributed before everyone left town for the summer; but failing that he wanted to get it out before fall, since he thought "the long warm summer days may induce my friends to bear the book with more patience than they might next Winter." Week after week August heckled Marble. He was as nervous as any new author on the eve of publication, although he pretended that he was not excited, dismissing the book by ironically referring to it as "my great work."

Because he had not been well and probably to escape August's badgering, Marble, who also was spending the summer at Newport, began avoiding the Belmonts' company. August intensified his campaign for Marble's attention.

"You never come to see Mrs. Belmont anymore," he complained.

Why had Marble been making himself scarce? Had he "taken refuge from all the temptations which beset you at" Newport? The place was, as August admitted to Marble, "filled with Circes and Sirens. You probably think that I have fallen victim to the first; at least, I should think so from the tone of your last note and from your keeping away from Bythesea."

Well, Marble has missed his chance for good company. August told him that he was "off to Long Branch (a good place for Circes' victims) and I shall feel at home amongst such noble spirits as Grant and Fisk."

Long Branch, New Jersey, had been a resort for Quakers; but by the summer of 1870 its piety had dimmed. Its huge hotels overlooked the

Atlantic Ocean. On the vast stretch of beach tiny-looking figures could be seen running toward and then away from the breakers. Long Branch had been one of the first seaside vacation spots where swimmers did not use clumsy bathing machines. The ocean breezes flattened the dune grasses, whipping them around so they left arcs in the sand. People strolling along the shore were left with a taste of salt on their lips, and salt crystals caught in their eyelashes, which made the sun reflecting off the sea seem dazzling. Children collected strands of rockweed and popped the air bladders, made Medusa wigs out of mermaid's-hair, and searched for sand dollars, a currency backed not by gold but by whimsey. The sound of the surf, which was pleasantly distracting on the first day, became by the last day unnoticed, like the ticking of a great clock.

President Grant had adopted the resort. Society had followed in his wake. In July a new track, Monmouth Park, opened, which is why August had gone there; but Long Branch was a temporary distraction. August was soon back in Newport sending Marble notes about the book and urging him to visit Bythesea, where "we will treat you with true Arab hospitality, never asking whence you come and whither you are going."

At last August's book, *A Few Letters and Speeches of the Late Civil War*, was published. August sent it out to all his friends and acquaintances. As though waiting for election results, he followed intently the response the book received. Letters began arriving, compliments for the most part, even from Republicans, who, confronted with the evidence of August's devotion to the Union during the Civil War, claimed as one man did that the book was "an ample refutation of that wholesale charge of disloyalty, so often and so recklessly brought against" not just August but "the Democratic Party" itself.

One of the few critics who wrote to August was his son August, Jr. After reading the book several times he confessed that "in some places I cannot agree. . . ." He rehearsed his complaints in a letter to Perry:

"He countenanced, in fact he advocated a peaceable secession of the cotton states, until the taking of Fort Sumter and other war demonstrations in the south. The Constitution provides that this Union should be perpetual; and, right or wrong, a state must abide by it. Besides the peaceable secession of one state means the peaceable secession of any state that wishes. However beneficial the peaceable secession of those cotton states would have been, it would have been the source of everlasting trouble; each state, if dissatisfied with the general administration, would then threaten secession. Therefore, I think that the peaceful secession of any state or states under any circumstances is the beginning of the fall of the republican government in this country and, of course, the dissolution of the Union."

Although not a new idea, the argument was well-reasoned for a teen-ager and demonstrated that, whatever his failings in his regular studies, August, Jr., when he found a subject that engaged him, could think clearly and write effectively.

He hesitated to tell his father about his reaction to the book; but August evidently heard something from Perry and told August, Jr., that "I am rather curious to hear your criticism about some of my letters and should like you to write me what are the points to which you object." So August, Jr., sent his critique to his father, who answered that "your good and loving letter has given me much pleasure, and I hope you will continue sometimes to give me your ideas and views about politics." He apologized for not responding at greater length or in greater detail to his son's thoughts, but he had a terrible headache, so instead of discussing the merits of his son's argument he confined himself to the somewhat deflating observation that "the only thing I have to find fault with and to which you really must pay more attention is your spelling, which is often incorrect."

August, Jr.'s Nursery experiment had failed. He had not gotten much work done. There had been too many distractions and too little supervision. The tutor was let go.

On Professor Child's recommendation August arranged for August, Jr., to spend the year in Haverford, Pennsylvania, not far from Philadelphia, where he would be instructed by Thomas Chase, a professor at Haverford College, a small Quaker school in the town. For his services, Chase charged $1,500, which he admitted was "liberal, but it would not be worth my while to name any lower" figure. Meals and lodging in Chase's house would cost an additional $1,000. Because of the necessity for "constant oversight and the inconvenience unavoidable from having boarders," Chase preferred that August, Jr., "should find rooms somewhere else in the neighborhood. Should you conclude to send him to me," Chase told August, "I should wish to have full instructions from you in regard to the amount of liberality to be granted him in the employment of his leisure time."

The tone of Chase's letters was strict enough to give August confidence in and make his son apprehensive of the man. August lodged his son with Chase.

"If it is possible to prepare him for the sophomore class at Harvard, I will gladly do so," Chase said. "I shall be ready to receive him at any time it may suit you to send him."

August, Jr., left New York City by the 9:30 train, missed the 12:50 connecting train at Philadelphia, caught the one at 2:30, and arrived soon thereafter in Haverford. His rooms, a bedroom and a study, were airy and comfortable; and, despite the severe tone of Chase's letters, he liked the man, who seemed amiably disorganized. Settling in, August Jr. asked his father for a subscription to a New York City newspaper. Everyone he knew was talking about the Franco-Prussian War. August, Jr., wanting to keep up with his friends, determined to stay abreast of the news. Naturally enough, his father got him the *New York World*.

"Pray be good," August told his son, "and don't get yourself into any scrapes; but, if you should have trouble, come to your father. Be sure to remember that you have no truer and more indulgent friend in the world."

Sternness had not worked; perhaps affection would. August often repeated that his son should "remember your father is always your best friend."

The new tactic did not keep August, Jr., from starting his school year with what was becoming a ritual accident. While on an outing he sprained his ankle badly enough to keep him immobilized in the house of the farmer who had rescued him.

August sent the farmer, his wife, and his hired hand checks in appreciation for their hospitality and to pay for August, Jr.'s food. He considered stopping at Haverford on his way to the Baltimore races; but his dyspepsia acted up, he caught a cold, and he canceled his trip, which disappointed August, Jr., who was feeling lonely sitting in the farmer's house all day. Neither he nor the farmer's family had any privacy, and all their lives were disrupted. Caroline wrote to explain that she also could not visit. She and the children were still at Bythesea. August was in New York. If she went away the children would be left in the charge of the governess, whom she no longer trusted.

"Perry is sitting, reading in my room as I write," she added, which must have further depressed August, Jr. His brother, who had been suspended from college, was lounging in their mother's room in Newport while he was trapped in a stranger's house in Pennsylvania, hardly able to hobble, studying at long distance through the mails with his tutor.

But his father's loving and indulgent manner must have given August, Jr., some comfort and apparently did have the desired effect of making him believe in his ability to improve. The arguments about his allowance that had plagued them the previous year vanished. August, Jr., studied harder than he ever had before. He looked around for someone in the freshman class at Harvard who could tell him what was being covered so that he could be sure to keep pace with them.

And he wanted to visit Cambridge to share part of the freshman year he was missing. He was so determined to get into the sophomore class the following fall that he began worrying about Chase's competence as a tutor.

"I have been here three weeks now," he told his father, "and have been trying to find out about my studies. I have written no less than six letters to Chase for information"—August, Jr., wanted to get his curriculum down on paper—"and Professor Chase's answers" were inadequate. In fact, "one thing" Professor Chase said about the course of study being followed by Harvard's freshman class was "absolutely wrong."

"Now is this right?" August, Jr., asked his father. "No, it is a perfect swindle. My work," he said, "ought to be laid out all beforehand for the first term. How does it stand now? I am reading no Greek prose, no book. No algebra, no book. No Greek modes and tenses. All is mixed up. I don't see why Professor Child recommended Chase, unless it was that he wanted to get the thing off his hands as soon as possible. Professor Chase of Haverford College sounds well." But August, Jr., was not impressed, and he became more discouraged once he was on crutches and back living at Chase's house. "He can teach a lesson pretty well," he granted, "but he has no system." The amiable disorganization August, Jr., had liked in Chase now seemed disastrous muddle. "All I have done has been at my instigation," August, Jr., wrote; and he had little faith in his own judgment.

When August told Caroline of their son's intention of going to Cambridge, she at once sat down and wrote that "we think the trip perfectly unnecessary. We *do not* wish you to go; and, if you get this letter in time, you must not think of going. It is madness to travel with a lame foot, and besides you thereby waste a great deal of valuable time. Perry will find out all you want to know; and, when you come home for Thanksgiving, there will be ample time to talk over the matter."

Chase also did not want August, Jr., to go, since, as August, Jr., explained, "it reflects badly upon him." He kept August, Jr., so long at a recitation that August, Jr., missed a train to Cambridge he had planned to take. When he returned to Chase's house he found his mother's letter.

"Which is the best course?" August, Jr., asked, defending his plan.

"To waste three or four weeks going on in a slipshod way or three days in finding out exactly what is to be done," an argument as plausible as his critique of his father's book.

His father explained that their only reason for objecting to his proposed trip was that "we were afraid it would hurt your leg." If he truly felt that he needed to go to Cambridge, he could go during the Thanksgiving vacation, which was only three weeks away. In the meantime "you certainly can study in a profitable manner. I am very sorry that you don't like Mr. Chase, but you have to make up your mind to continue your preparation with him. It is utterly impossible to change now. For my part," August told his son, "I shall be quite satisfied if you get into the freshman class."

And August, Jr., certainly would be prepared for that by the end of the year.

Trying as he always did to end his letter on an encouraging note, August said, "Do take good care of your leg, my darling, so that you may be all right for Thanksgiving and have some shooting with us. I have been out two or three times, but I only have had one fair shot, which I missed."

August, Jr., stayed at Haverford until Thanksgiving, when he arrived home without his crutches. After August, Jr., returned to Haverford, Chase wrote to his parents that he "continues to show commendable diligence, and I am well satisfied."

August had hoped that Perry would also spend the fall at Haverford with Chase; but Perry wanted to pass his one-term exile from Harvard in Newport, which was close enough to Cambridge for him to make frequent trips to his friends at school. August acquiesced, but closed up Bythesea. Perry would have to stay at a boardinghouse. August was not going to encourage his son, who seemed to be getting wild.

Perry had returned from his Western trip with an illness that August found "too painful and too disagreeable" to discuss. When August, Jr., pressed him about it, his father said that "I hope and pray you will strive to preserve your youth from contamination and you will keep your innocence and purity," so it is possible that Perry had contracted a venereal disease.

"I trust that you will day and night watch over yourself and follow strictly the directions of your physician," Caroline wrote to him. "It is your whole future which is now depending upon that."

She recommended bran baths, which were a remedy for rashes. Fill a pillow case with bran, she explained, "tie the end with a string, pour scalding water on it, and let it soak for a quarter of an hour in the bath. Then fill up your bathtub, and stay in the bath at least 15 or 20 minutes. The water ought to look like milk." She also told him to "keep your blood in a cool state, by refreshing drinks of orangeade or lemonade."

Perry found a comfortable boardinghouse and passed his time designing a program for a D.K.E. show (a picture of a ruined Notre Dame with crumbling and cankered walls, perhaps reflecting his concern with his health and musing about his future career).

"Although I would like to take my part in the politics of our country," he told his father, "yet I am far from supposing myself to possess what I conceive the qualities of a successful politician. Time only will show."

He had a mission: "I feel myself impelled to urge upon the citizens of the republic not to allow themselves to be too much governed."

But he was not sure how to turn his vision into reality.

"How is political knowledge to be obtained?" he asked his father. "by careful reading? That's all well enough, but something more is necessary, namely, the practical advice and guidance of an expert. This I ask plainly and plumply of you. Whenever I leave you after my short vacations, I feel that I have lost an opportunity for instruction in things not to be found in books."

Perry, the future politician, was apprenticing himself to his father. And one of the first lessons in practical politics that he could have learned from August was the necessity of making peace with former enemies if you wanted to help your son with his political ambitions.

Tweed was under attack from the Republicans, in particular *The New York Times*, which on September 20, 1870, published the first of a series of editorials that accused Tweed and his minions in the city government of looting New York. Local elections were approaching. To offset the bad publicity Tweed rallied the Democratic party to his support. On the night of October 27 about forty thousand Tweed supporters mustered in Union Square and converged on Tammany Hall. The Republican press claimed that the demonstration, the largest of any meeting except those for presidential candidates, was made up of boys probably hired to swell the numbers and who seemed more interested in the flamboyant fireworks display than in politics.

"Instead of being dragged through the slushy streets," *The New York*

Times said, "the boys ought to have been treated to a good bowl of warm soup and sent to bed."

Inside Tammany Hall, Tweed, fat, happy, and prosperous, sat between Jim Fisk and August—representatives of dangerous speculation and established capital. Also present were former mayor Fernando Wood and former governor Horatio Seymour, ornaments to Tweed and proof of his primacy.

When Tweed nominated August as chairman of the meeting the audience roared "Aye," approval that could not have entirely pleased August, since he was getting it at the price of giving his support to those whom he had a few months before called *canaille*. His speech was short.

"Never before," he said as part of his remarks, "have we been called upon to vote for a ticket which commands so strongly our *hearty* and *affectionate* approval."

Then he gave the floor to Fisk, who like the former circusman he was strutted around the stage clowning. He might be a Republican, he said; but he would vote for this Democratic ticket "three times a day," a promise that those who knew him well could not doubt would be honored, one way or another. Fisk was not one to let legal niceties interfere with his enthusiasms.

August had publicly identified himself with Tweed's corrupt politics and the Erie Ring. The evening could not have changed his opinion about the sometimes ugly demands of politics.

The spectacle of August Belmont, "a man who would not be guilty of any dishonorable deed," sharing the stage with Fisk was, according to *The New York Times*, "sorrowful. . . . How came these two men to be on the same platform, pleading for the same cause, and alike extolling the acts of a clique which is known to be dishonest and is fast covering itself with infamy? Original sin is scarcely sufficient to account for this strange and unnatural coalition."

August had gone to Tammany Hall that night not just for the sake of Perry's future political career—or for the sake of a party he could not, after all, abandon—but to pay a debt of honor. One of Tweed's cronies who was under attack was A. Oakey Hall, the mayor of New York City. The meeting had been designed to boost his chances for reelection. Although August despised most of Tweed's puppets, he would help Hall no matter what the mayor did. In 1864 when the *New York Evening Post* had spread the rumor that August was a Rothschild bastard, Hall had been one of the few friends who had closed ranks with August in fighting the newspaper. And August did not forget loyalty.

CHAPTER THIRTY-NINE

AFTER THREATS OF RIOTS at the polling places, President Grant sent troops and two warships to New York City to ensure an orderly election. The riots never materialized. Tweed's candidates won. Hall was re-elected mayor of New York City. August again retreated from politics.

He and Caroline continued to lead a quiet life. Their few dinners and parties were as elegant as ever. August was still recognized as a leader of fashion; but the very absoluteness of that recognition cast a shadow over his reputation. He had led fashion long enough to have become a symbol of a passing age. The city had moved uptown; and like the other million-aires who maintained their mansions in what was now known as the lower part of Fifth Avenue, August was called by wits as young as his sons "a cave dweller."

During the fall of 1870 August and Oliver went to the Nursery to shoot quail. Oliver came home proudly showing his shoulder bruised from the recoil of the gun. Caroline held more charade parties. And in the absence of August, Jr., who was the best of the Belmonts at charades, Raymond shone. The days grew shorter. The lamplighters began making their pilgrimage from streetlight to streetlight in the late afternoon. By dinnertime it was night.

With the sound of Raymond's music lessons providing a muffled ac-companiment from another part of the house, Caroline waited eagerly every day for the mail, hoping to get letters from her sister Belle and her mother, who were in Italy, and her brother Oliver, who was in Germany, his travels delayed by the shifting of troops, owing to the Franco-Prussian War.

"They are all young, in good spirits, and fine looking men," Oliver wrote, "constantly singing patriotic songs. Their movements are of course secret. The telegraphs are all in the hands of the government, and it is impossible to get from here into France by rail, except by way of Switzerland or the roundabout way of Belgium or Holland. In fact, I hardly know at present how to send this letter so that it will reach you."

He could not read German and could only find old English and Belgian newspapers, so he knew little about what was happening in Eu-rope, probably less than what his relatives in the United States knew. He had been able to visit the area of Germany where August had been born, which he thought beautiful; and despite the evidences of war he would have been quite content, if the Germans had not closed so many museums. The pictures he wanted to see were being boxed, "ready," he said, "for removal in case the French should invade the country."

August must have felt some patriotic stirring for his homeland. He certainly must have been proud to hear that his nephew and namesake, August Feist, Babette's second son, had been awarded an Iron Cross for bravery as a medical orderly. And like Caroline he must have looked forward to further reports from Oliver. But Oliver's letters stopped arriving. He had died in the middle of November. Jane Perry wrote home:

"His nurse says that he died with both his hands in hers, so peacefully and so happy, without a sigh or pain. His last words to her were, 'Write to my dear Mother and say how good and kind she has been and how happy I am—' It is hard for me to write on this subject," Jane Perry said, breaking off her letter.

Since Oliver had left no will, August arranged to make Jane Perry the sole heir. The body was shipped back to the United States, where it was buried in Newport, next to the Commodore's grave.

Oliver's death was followed a few weeks later by the death of Caroline's aunt Matilda, John Slidell's wife. The Slidells, who had been living in Paris, had left France because of the war and gone to Cowes, a resort on the Isle of Wight. One night Matilda went up to bed and an hour later was discovered unconscious on the floor of her room. Her son, Alfred Slidell, was visiting New York. The morning after he had had dinner with the Belmonts, Alfred received a telegram with the sad news.

Christmas was subdued.

Because of the deaths in the family, Caroline did not go to any balls or parties for the rest of the season. Occasionally she accepted an invitation for lunch. One afternoon her host was serving oysters, which were being cooked casually at the table. He decided to experiment by boiling them over a hotter than usual flame. He turned up the wick. The spirit lamp flared. He and another man present went to rescue the dish and in the confusion dropped it, oysters flying, juice splattering. A ball could not have entertained Caroline more than watching everyone trying to maintain his dignity in the hullabaloo.

Perry returned to Harvard more like an explorer come back from some dangerous trek (as though suspension were an unknown land where many perished) than a penitent. He continued to chafe at the custom of deducting academic credit for such nonacademic offenses as missing prayers. As a result he continued to miss prayers and got into trouble academically for doing so.

"I cannot urge you to serious study if your own sense does not do it," August wrote to his son when he heard that Perry again was in trouble. "You are now a man, and you have to act for yourself. If you don't make up your mind to profit of the opportunities given to you *by hard study* and *diligent application, it will be a remorse for you for all the rest of your life.* I contemplate with real fear and suffering the chance of your failing next September in your examination *as a serious calamity.* You know that I rejoice in your having a good time, and I have encouraged everything which could give you pleasure, but I think I have a right to expect that you should give *me* the *satisfaction* and *happiness* of seeing you come up to the standards to which your talents and your opportunities not only entitle, but *imperatively call you.* The great fault is that you belong to too many clubs."

In typical Belmont fashion Perry judged the school rather than submitted to a judgment by it:

"If they wish to make a university of Harvard," he told his father, "they must get rid of the stupid customs of that sort [the policy of academically penalizing students for infractions of the rules, which was causing all his trouble] and allow the examinations themselves to be the test [of how well a student was doing in his studies]."

Perry told his father that if it were not for the deductions his academic standing would be high. He was in fact studying for honors in history and preparing to go to law school when he graduated from Harvard, which in spite of his father's fears was no longer in doubt. By the end of the term, Perry, feeling as though he had won his point, could write home that there had been a change in school policy.

"Deductions no longer count against a man's marks in recitations," he said. "This approaches more nearly my idea of a university."

Harvard would pass Perry; Perry would return the favor.

But August was right. Perry was spending a great deal of time in extracurricular activities; he was being very social. He took up painting, which prompted his grandmother to send him a picture she had bought in Rome. She seemed to understand that Perry was more a connoisseur than an artist and that his painting was more an act of appreciation than creation. He attended plays and afterward dined with the actors. He went to many parties, one week dancing until after four o'clock in the morning three days running. He dropped in on musicales, managed school theatricals, and joined the A.D., which had not yet become a rival to the Porcellian (he could be a member of both), and the Hasty Pudding Club, whose initiation required him to run every step he took for five days, speak with no one, and write three hundred pages of prose and two hundred lines of poetry.

Because Perry's hero-worship of Henry Adams was a foible well-known among his friends, he was conned into believing that the assignment for his Hasty Pudding compositions had come from Adams—which it had, but from Brooks, whose handwriting was very like his brother's, not Henry. It was not a very amusing joke, but the upperclassmen found it uproariously funny.

At the end of the initiation Perry told August, Jr., who he was sure would get into Harvard and be elected to the Hasty Pudding Club, "You have a terrible week of torture before you."

August, Jr., was afraid he would never get to enjoy the torture of being initiated into the Hasty Pudding Club, because he was less sure than ever that he would pass the Harvard entrance examination. But he returned to Haverford after Christmas vacation, resigned to Chase's instruction.

His train arrived at Haverford at night. The station was deserted. August, Jr., bag in hand, trunk beside the tracks, watched the rear lights of the train grow smaller and dimmer and then wink off as the train vanished from sight. After a while the rails stopped singing. It was dark and quiet. He did not want to leave his trunk untended but had no choice. Lugging his bag he started walking the quarter-mile to Chase's house. It was so cold, his fingers got numb. He shifted the bag from hand to hand. The snow was deep and powdery. He had to plow through, making his own path. The moonlight sparkled on the surface of the drifts and made everything, buildings, fences, trees, stand out sharply, but oddly flat, as though they were cardboard cutouts. Above him branches creaked.

At Chase's he warmed himself with tea while one of Chase's servants, a young boy, went off to rescue his trunk. After a while the boy returned to say there was no trunk at the station. The railroad men on a passing slow freight must have stolen it. August, Jr., lost his temper at his bad luck. He decided to go back to the station to see if he could find any traces of his trunk himself. Mrs. Chase sent the servant boy to get a neighboring farmer's horse and wagon. While August, Jr., waited he checked the mail that had arrived in his absence. Engrossed in a letter from the friend at Harvard who was sending him reports of the freshman class, August, Jr., for a few minutes forgot about the boy, the farmer's wagon, and the trunk. He finished the letter and mused about life in Cambridge until he realized that the boy should have returned long ago. August, Jr., checked the windows: no boy, no wagon. He waited a little longer, wandering through the house. When he drifted into the kitchen he found the boy sitting quietly.

"Have you been to the farmer's?" August, Jr., asked him.

"No," said the boy.

"Why?" August, Jr., wanted to know.

"Because I don't like to ask the farmer," the boy said.

August, Jr., looked at the boy. The boy looked at the floor. August, Jr., was sure the boy was lying.

"Are you afraid to go in the dark?" August, Jr., asked.

The boy hung his head and mumbled something August, Jr., could not understand.

August, Jr., realized that the boy, who was afraid of ghosts and refused to leave the house at night, had not gone to the station either. So August, Jr., got the wagon, drove to the station, found the trunk, and, relieved that his father would not have to buy him a new wardrobe, returned to Chase's, where, exhausted, he went to sleep.

Every morning, August, Jr., woke early, pulled on his old slippers—the new slippers Santa Claus had promised at Christmas had not come yet—made a fire to warm the room, which because it had a northern exposure was always below freezing and often below zero, and exercised with ten-pound clubs. He was used to the water in his pitcher icing over; but one morning it was so cold that the bristles of his toothbrush, which he had left wet the night before, froze as hard as the ivory handle.

"When I got up," August, Jr., told Perry, "it being a little late, I hopped around, started my fire, didn't take any bath, dove into my clothes, grabbed my pitcher, emptied some water into my glass, jammed my toothbrush into my mouth. But ho! God, what is the matter with that brush? I went to the looking glass with tears in my eyes, my gums bleeding, and holding my face with my hands." His mouth looked as if he had been chewing glass. "I swore to myself till the pain went away."

Even during the day the room was freezing. Once before dinner, which the Chases ate at midday, August, Jr., as was his custom, went to his room, broke the crust of ice in the pitcher, filled the basin, washed, and went downstairs. Later, "feeling," as he told Perry, "pretty jolly about getting through some Horace," he went to his room to wash for tea.

"I put the lamp on the bureau," he said, "and with a sort of flourish, dove for the basin," which was still filled from his midday wash; "but my hands did not get into the water, for I punched my fist against hard ice."

As though he were in hell, August, Jr., had to suffer ice—and fire. Less than a week later on a particularly cold night he stuffed wood into his stove and crawled under the covers of his bed, shivering. After a while the room warmed and August, Jr., drowsed. The stove grew hotter and hotter, until parts glowed orange and set the fireboard ablaze. August woke, leaped from bed, and grabbed his pitcher, which he emptied and accidentally dropped on the flames.

"As the fire was making head against me," he told Perry, "I went and tore poor Chase from the fond embrace of his bony spouse."

Chase ran into August, Jr.'s room, "a pitcher in one hand and his basin in the other," August, Jr., said. "We watered the room . . . and pulled things around generally." When the fire was out, "Chase and I found ourselves standing in a mixed mess of ashes, water, and chips of wood, here and there dotted with pieces of broken pitcher for the benefit of our bare feet. This is the only excitement I have had in Haverford."

The distant world of his parents and siblings seemed increasingly idyllic to him. As his father had made a myth out of his life in Alzey, August, Jr., made a myth out of his childhood with his family before he went to school.

"It seems to me sometimes as if I'd enjoyed very little of my home since I was eleven years old," he said.

Ever since going to the Rectory School he had been unhappy. He wished that he could start over and do things differently. If so, he would not be paying now for his failures then. He would be with Perry in Cambridge or like Perry on one of many trips to New York. But the past was past. He was in Haverford, not Cambridge; and he could not take time away from cramming to visit his family.

"I suppose," he wrote to his mother, "Rickie still drums her 'Irish melodies.' Jeannie is still idle about her work on her Xmas presents. Oliver still gets good marks sprinkled very frequently with bad ones. Dollie plays bezique when he can. Pop still blows and you still stay at home."

He did not want to upset his parents at all this term. He was good about money, so good that his father offered to pay for any luxuries he might want.

His only major complaint he revealed later in the term to Perry.

"Mama writes so seldom that I've stopped writing to her entirely," he said. "Papa has always been regular in writing to me, and he has tried to smooth over the matter; but, as I cannot forgive Mama and take all the blame myself, nothing has come of it." August, Jr., no longer felt automatically guilty when there was a conflict with his parents. His regime of hard work at Haverford had given him more self-esteem. Perhaps despite the ice and fire he had been not in hell but in Purgatory, clearing his debt of conscience.

He wrote two letters to Caroline, held on to them, and when his mother still did not write, burned them. Caroline thought it was shabby of her son not to write, but she knew she was wrong. Because of her brother's death she had been despondent and listless, and she had let her obligations slip. To mollify her son she sent him an Easter egg, which pleased August, Jr. He dropped his boycott and began writing to his mother again.

Once the problem of getting letters had been solved, August, Jr., had to work on the problem of keeping the letters from prying eyes.

"I would advise you next time to seal your letters to me as tight as the 'gumsticum' will stick 'm," August, Jr., told Perry, "for Mrs. Chase is a great busy-body and from unguarded revelations in her conversation I'm quite certain that she has read letters that I've accidentally left hanging around."

Since Mrs. Chase was not only as nosey but as thin as Mrs. Means, his landlady in Exeter, August, Jr., concluded that a snooping disposition "is rather characteristic of lanky women, along with a very extensive stock of misinformation."

August, Jr.'s parents asked him to burn all their letters to keep Mrs. Chase from seeing them; but since August, Jr., wanted to save the letters he instead locked them in his trunk, an experiment that worked until, climbing a tree one day, he tore his trousers. When he gave the pants to Mrs. Chase to mend he forgot to take the trunk key out of his pocket. When he got the pants back, the key was gone. To frustrate Mrs. Chase's curiosity he stuffed paper and then a leather shoelace into the trunk lock. And he tied up and sealed in neat bundles his collection of letters.

He so persistently asked if anyone in the house had found the trunk key that Mrs. Chase must have known he had guessed the truth.

Nervously she told August, Jr., that she had found it on the floor of his room.

"Nonsense," August, Jr., thought.

He had searched the room thoroughly.

But he thanked her—and made sure he did not lose the key again.

Soon after the incident of the trunk key August, Jr., returned from a fifteen-mile hike to find that Mrs. Chase, possibly as a peace offering, had cooked him a special dinner with ice cream for dessert. After the meal August, Jr., took out one of the Henry Clay cigars that his father had given him and that he had been saving; and, happy, he took two hours to savor it.

Every so often he still felt "like packing my bags and going home," convinced that "this present sort of monastic life is too great a sacrifice for the fruits to be reaped from it," but he admitted, "I generally sleep these feelings off."

He was ahead of the Harvard freshman class in Greek and Latin but felt hopelessly behind in mathematics, in which, it being Chase's weakest subject, he had not had adequate drilling. To make up that deficiency, by the end of spring he was studying ten to twelve hours a day, taking time out only to dream about the future he could have if he were to get into college. He wanted to study international law, and he figured it would take eight years of work before he would be ready to enter public life.

"By the time I get to be thirty or so," he told Perry, "there will probably be a great revolution in politics and a civil service reform will have taken place. In that case, there will be a wide field for really educated men, especially in foreign relations."

At his most optimistic he had a vision of the future in which he and Perry both were politicians exchanging opinions on the great issues of the day—a future that did not seem at all impossible.

"Let us know some time or other about your political views," he asked Perry in what appears to be a dry run for that future. "It won't do you or me any harm."

And he was tickled by the idea that his brother was going to vote in the next presidential election.

But at his most pessimistic he had trouble imagining any future beyond the immediate one of preparing for the Harvard entrance examination. If he failed to get into college he wanted to wait another year and cram so he could enter the junior class with his friends. He did not want to enter a class with students younger than he was.

He stayed with Perry in Cambridge during the three-day examination and returned to Haverford in low spirits. Although he did not have the official results, he was certain he had done as poorly as he had predicted. He wrote home to tell his parents that he had failed.

"He had a depressing feeling," his instructor at Haverford later wrote, "that he was destined always to be 'unlucky.' "

"I am very sorry that you did not get through well," wrote Caroline, who with the rest of the family was in Saratoga for the races; "but, as it is all over, you must cheer up and come among us and enjoy yourself with us all."

By the time August, Jr., reached Saratoga, the examination results were announced. He had passed and been admitted to Harvard's sophomore class.

CHAPTER FORTY

THE DAY BEFORE the races at Saratoga began, the town was almost empty. August woke early and by four o'clock in the morning was at the track to watch Kingfisher work out. A few professional gamblers, each with his own stopwatch, waited to check the horse's time.

"Kingfisher is a high-fly of a horse," said one man who was present that morning, "full of mettle and with eyes red and snapping with passion."

In four days he would be matched for the Saratoga Cup against Longfellow, another four-year-old—an ugly horse that reportedly "starts off like a camel charged with electricity, but, by-and-by, when the electricity is gone, . . . settles into a steady, rolling gait. Then his strides become monstrous, and without apparent effort he shoots by everything on the track." Sporting newspapers were calling the contest "a battle of the giants," and some thought it would be the race of the decade, possibly of the century.

August believed Kingfisher was an exceptional horse. Before bringing him to Saratoga he had run him against Glenelg on the Nursery track; and Kingfisher had won with ease. On the trip up August had been offering to cover all bets from $500 to $5,000, which sobered even those who thought Longfellow the better animal.

Longfellow's owner, John Harper, had $80,000 staked on the race. Harper was an eighty-year-old Kentuckian who, according to one observer, looked like "an animated ghost, with his white hair streaming in the wind. . . . It is a queer sight to see this venerable bachelor . . . tottering along after his only love—a horse!"

Two nights earlier some horse racers had tried to get Harper to estimate Longfellow's chances of winning against Kingfisher; but Harper had dodged the question.

"What is the best he ever did?" one horse racer asked.

"Oh," said Harper, "he's done some right smart trotting down in Kentuck."

Harper had never seen Kingfisher, so the day before the races started he too woke before dawn, and with his stopwatch in hand half-hid behind a post at the track, waiting for Kingfisher to run. He seemed, one person said, "almost breathless," presumably with either anxiety, excitement, or dyspepsia.

"Too much belly on 'the Fisher' today," said someone who stood with Harper when the horse was brought out.

"I'll be dog-on if that little short cuss can beat Longfellow," said another.

"Moves like he could run some," Harper said.

He had no intention of underestimating his competition. He came out from behind the post and wandered down to the track.

"How do you like him, old man?" asked John Hunter, a friend of August's and member of the Jockey Club.

"Putty dog-on full of muscle, Hunter," said Harper as the horse started to run; "and he branches off like he had hell in him, sure, but I guess old Longfellow will have his 'run.' "

Hunter, for August's sake, may have been trying to distract Harper to keep him from getting Kingfisher's time; but Harper would not be distracted. He stopped his watch and checked it. For the mile trial, Kingfisher had done 1 minute and 50 seconds.

"I reckon he kin do 1:41," said Harper.

Longfellow's time for his morning mile trial was 1 minute and 44 seconds.

"You will see a terrible race for that Saratoga Cup on Friday afternoon," Harper said.

"Why?" he was asked.

"Because Longfellow has never had a horse to run with him before," Harper said. "He always comes in on a gallop. . . . If 'the Fisher' beats him this time, he will beat the best horse I ever saw."

"Will 'the Fisher' beat?" he was asked.

Harper shook his head, but it was not an answer; he still refused to reveal his prediction. Instead he said:

"I was offered $60,000 for old 'Long' at the Branch, and if he wins, I can take $100,000 for him; but, if he loses, I will sell him for $25,000. . . ."

"Will you sell Longfellow if he wins?" he was asked.

"No," said Harper, "I shall take him back to Kentucky, put him up, and breed from him. A *mare* with a colt from him would sell for $5,000, and I'd soon get my $100,000 back."

"Would you like a cool day for the race?" he was asked.

"No," said Harper, "the hotter the better. Hosses run better hot days than cool days."

The day of the Saratoga Cup race was in the nineties. For the past week Hudson River steamers like the *St. John* (whose pilot talked aloud to himself during the trip) ferried up from New York City fashionable men and women; young sports using the latest slang words like "swell," "nobby," "spoony," and "jolly"; gamblers; politicians; and Methodist ministers who were headed not to Saratoga but to a camp meeting nearby.

The stands were packed. In the first race of the day one of August's horses with a remarkable burst of speed came up from last place to finish third, a good omen. The second race was the big one, the Saratoga Cup, two and a quarter miles. Longfellow's jockey was Bob Swim, who was considered to be the smartest in the United States, perhaps too smart. He had been known to try to slow a competitor by riding across his path. Currently he was on probation; but he was telling everyone that he intended to win this race even if it was the last he would ever run.

August refused to admit that Swim was the best jockey in the country. When he was asked earlier in the day, "Who is to ride 'the Fisher'?" he said, "Why—Jake, the smartest boy in the world."

"Who's Jake?" he was asked.

"Jake," he said, "is a Long Island boy. I got him pardoned out of the House of Correction. Don't you know Jake?" He seemed almost angry that Jake was not famous. "He has the best whip, the best spurs, and is sure to steal the best place on the track. Last summer he stole two pet chickens from my trainer, and the next day the little rascal presented him with one of *his own chickens all dressed* and ready to cook!"

Anyone that impudent had to be a winner.

August showed up in the grandstand wearing his customary white top-hat and silver feather. Harper stayed on the ground, dressed like a farmer in a simple suit and an old slouch hat. The two horses had scared off competition. They were the only contenders for the Saratoga Cup. Before the race the odds were on Longfellow, two to one, even though Kingfisher had the advantage of starting on the inside of the track.

When the white flag dropped, Longfellow, who had balked and begun the race facing the wrong way, whipped around and shot off at a killing pace. He took the lead and ran the first quarter-mile faster than any horse had ever before. As they passed the stands Longfellow was three lengths ahead; and those who were still betting were so sure Longfellow had the race that they were offering incredible odds: $100 he would win against $8 that Kingfisher would. But Kingfisher closed the gap between them and, for a while, ran as though he were Longfellow's shadow. Every time Longfellow pulled ahead, Kingfisher caught up to him. No one could ever have seen a race like this before. At the top of the homestretch Longfellow again had pulled ahead, this time by an unbelievable six lengths. Swim turned in his saddle and glanced back at Kingfisher, who again was gaining.

August stood, straining forward.

Harper was rigid, betraying no emotion.

Longfellow won by three lengths.

"It was a great disappointment to us that Kingfisher did not win," Caroline admitted; "but both horses made better time than ever was known it seems, so August is consoled."

Longfellow had run the first mile in an amazing 1 minute and 40 seconds and the entire race in 4 minutes and 2¾ seconds, also amazing. If Kingfisher could be beaten, Longfellow was the only horse to do it. August spread a rumor that, since he had expected Kingfisher to be beaten by a hundred yards or more, he was quite pleased by the outcome of the race.

Four days later, Kingfisher and Longfellow were supposed to race again, but Harper refused to let his horse run. At the end of the Saratoga Cup race Longfellow had been winded; but Kingfisher could have gone another mile. Longfellow had more speed. Kingfisher had more stamina. This second race between them was to be three miles. Harper probably correctly feared that Longfellow would lose.

August offered Harper $60,000 for Longfellow, a put-down since everyone knew that Harper considered the horse worth $100,000. But Harper by default had conceded that in some respects Kingfisher was the better animal. August watched, happy, while Kingfisher triumphantly ran the three-mile race alone.

August made some changes at the Nursery: He bought new hens and fighting cocks, killed old ones, made sure there were plenty of partridges and stags on the land for hunting. In the city he anonymously donated $5,000 to the New York Catholic Protectory to help house, feed, and clothe the indigent; gave generously to a relief fund for victims of the Franco-Prussian War; and circulated among wealthy New Yorkers like Fisk an appeal by one of the Rothschilds on behalf of another war-related charity, The Society to Help the French Peasants Ruined by the War. In the evenings he went to one or another of his clubs, where he played whist, engaging Manton Marble in so many games that one of Marble's editors on the *New York World* finally—only half-facetiously—complained.

By the end of summer August's season of calm had ended. There was another family death: John Slidell died in Cowes, where his wife had died the previous year. In 1866 Slidell had written to the President asking permission to visit New Orleans. His letter had been ignored. Slidell resigned himself to never seeing his homeland again. There is no evidence that August ever met or wrote to Slidell after their break many years before, but he must have been affected by the death of one more contemporary, a man to whom he had been bound first by affection and then by anger, the man who had given him his start in American politics.

That bad news was followed by other distressing events. More and more often August's name was being linked to the Erie and the Tweed rings, both of which were composed of people for whom he had little use and no respect. But he like most New York financiers was doing business with them. After all, the Erie Railway Company had proved itself to be at the very least a going concern; and a committee of leading businessmen under John Jacob Astor III had investigated the city's finances and vouched for the probity of the Tweed Ring regime.

Jay Gould, trying to make the Erie Railway Company respectable, had suggested a reorganization that would bring August onto the company's board along with such other reputable businessmen as J. S. Morgan, John Jacob Astor III, and Erastus Corning; but the existing board rejected the proposal. *The New York Times*, however, attacked August for selling Erie Railway bonds in Frankfurt for a profit of at least $192,000 and perhaps double that merely "for the trouble of inclosing . . . the bonds in envelopes and mailing them." The logic was confused. The newspaper seemed upset, first, that he was handling Erie Railway bonds; second, that he was selling them in Europe (which seemed suspicious to them); third, that he was making a great profit (6 to 12 percent); and fourth, that he was making the profit so easily. On the other hand the newspaper did not seem to object to August's making a large, easy profit in Europe on other, less suspect bonds.

But, as August, Jr., had pointed out in another context, newspapers seemed less interested in "cold argument and reason" than in "personal abuse." After all, he said, "writing for the press is generally pursued as a means of livelihood. Thus, the heart not being wholly in the work, the thought is apt to be crude and undigested, the ideas being turned out as a matter of necessity, so many a minute." However unsympathetic this view of journalists who, unlike August, Jr, had no family fortune to fall back on, the criticism was apt. *The New York Times* was attacking his father not just because they thought him wrong in this specific case but because he was a leading Democrat, and *The New York Times*, being a Republican newspaper, was happy for any chance to attack the Democratic party. August's support of A. Oakey Hall and the other Tammany candidates in the last election had made him vulnerable, as had the rumors (which were true) that August had invited Tweed to dinner—as had August's involvement in Tweed's New York Railway Company.

New York City had become enthralled with the idea of a rapid transit system ever since the previous year when Alfred Ely Beach had opened his pneumatic subway. The car, which held twenty-three passengers and was propelled by air, rushed through a tunnel below Broadway along 312 feet of track at ten miles an hour. Even if it did not really get very far, it was a thrilling ride and proved that subways were feasible. Underground tunnels could connect every part of the city. Passengers would wait for the cars in comfortable and elegant saloons like the one Beach had built, which had frescoed walls, a fountain, and a grand piano. The terrible traffic jams on the surface streets would become merely a memory, something not particularly pleasant but over and done with, a quaint story to tell children—like describing how dark the city used to be before the introduction of gas streetlights.

Beach's plan for constructing a privately financed subway from City

Hall all the way up to Central Park was challenged by Tweed's plan for a publicly financed elevated railroad. An elevated railroad had already been tested: a half-mile track from the Battery up Greenwich Street to Cortlandt Street. Its bankruptcy in 1871 did not deter Tweed and his backers. Elevateds were more natural than subways. Instead of traveling underground like moles, people would ride along a track forty feet in the air like birds. The massive stone arches supporting the elevated railroad would add a Roman grandeur to the city. August supported Tweed's project and became one of the elevated railway company's officers. In March 1871 the governor of New York State, John Hoffman, one of the Tweed Ring, predictably chose Tweed's plan over Beach's—to the outrage of many who correctly thought the New York Railway Company was just another device of the Tweed Ring for plundering public funds by giving out fat contracts to friends and getting kickbacks. But by late 1871 the elevated railway plan was in trouble. It would be just one of the casualties of Tweed's political collapse.

Despite August's involvement with Tweed, which was the result of the uneasy alliance among the various factions of the Democratic party, August was prepared to purge the party of Tweed and his followers—except for Hall—as soon as the opportunity presented itself. By the end of summer August and the other reformers had their chance.

The New York Times had gotten hold of and was publishing evidence that the Tweed Ring was bleeding the city of millions of dollars. Together with a number of other businessmen August urged that an open meeting be held to organize an investigation of the newspaper's charges, and he contributed $500 to help finance "the good fight against rogues and corruption." The public mobilized against the ring. Some people wanted to drive them from office. Others wanted to sue, jail, or lynch them.

August wanted the two key members of the ring—Tweed, who was a state senator and the boss of Tammany Hall, and Richard B. ("Slippery Dick") Connolly, the city comptroller—to resign. Peter B. ("Brains") Sweeny, the city chamberlain, who had the reputation of being a good man in a difficult position, the unsuccessful check on Tweed and Connolly's greed, might also have to go. Hall, the mayor, could survive, August thought, "if he will throw himself into the arms of" the reformers.

August wanted to save Hall, not just out of loyalty to a friend but because it was possible that he had been, as he claimed, an innocent dupe of the ring. In any case the Democratic party could not afford to discard him.

"Without a mayor at this juncture, we are lost," August said; "and the Republicans not only get the merit of the present purification, but they will also carry the state" in the upcoming local elections, which would put the Democrats in a poor position for the presidential election the following year. The party had to be purified, but it should not commit suicide.

August met with Hall and Sweeny to plot strategy. If they could get Connolly out, Tweed would follow. But Connolly would not resign. Hall tried to force him and only succeeded in driving him to Samuel J. Tilden, who had his own ideas about how best to clean up the party—and who was keeping those ideas to himself. Tilden did not reveal anything of his activities to August, which, given their mutual distrust, was understandable, or to Marble, which, given their friendship, was not. So August and Marble did not know that Connolly was cooperating with Tilden; and while they were working with Hall and Sweeny to get Connolly out of office, Tilden was working to keep Connolly in office and suggesting that Connolly appoint as deputy comptroller a Tilden man, Andrew H. ("Handy Andy") Green.

Tilden wanted Green in the comptroller's office in order to get access to the records with which to drive Tweed from power. August and Marble wanted Connolly out of the comptroller's office in order to get one of their own reform Democrats appointed for the same reason. August considered trying for the job himself; but, dismissing the idea, he urged the appointment of someone who was above city politics: General George B. McClellan.

Since August would be in Newport during much of the struggle, he arranged a telegraph code with Marble: Tweed = Cane; Connolly = Louise; Sweeny = Night; Hall = Echo; Green = Laura; the office of comptroller = Brick; the office of deputy comptroller = Coal; Tilden = Copper; and—August could not resist leavening the code with humor—Belmont = Mogul, which became one of Marble's nicknames for him. The other more affectionate nickname was Potosi, which may have referred to the city in the Andes, an isolated lonely town but one of the richest sources of silver in history—an appropriate choice.

On September 18 Connolly named Green deputy comptroller. When Hall heard, he went mad—rumors said—and tore his hair out by the fistful. His enemies claimed that he further proved his insanity by refusing to recognize Green's appointment and claiming that Connolly's action was the equivalent of resigning. Since, according to Hall, the comptroller's office was now empty, he appointed McClellan to the post. Connolly supporters gathered near the comptroller's office, ready to fight any police effort to install McClellan in the job. McClellan declined to get involved.

August thought Green was a good choice, and he came into town to urge Hall to accept the move. After their meeting August returned to Newport. Hall thought over the matter and decided against appointing Green.

"I have just called at your mansion," Hall wrote to August; "but you had gone. I called to say what I write and with the greatest personal reluctance, because nothing would give me greater pleasure than to defer to and accept your judgment upon the public interests. But after much anxious reflection I have arrived at the conclusion that I cannot appoint Mr. Green. 1st. Because it would work political disadvantage to the local wing of the party with which I have always acted, from which I have received my breath of public life, and with which, as I have swum, I must sink or subject myself to a charge of gross ingratitude. Mr. Green is fighting my wing of the Democracy; and, if I gave him power, I would give it to an enemy."

Hall thought that Green and his sponsor, Tilden, were interested in destroying the Tweed machine not because Tweed was corrupt, or not just because Tweed was corrupt, but because with Tweed out of the way Tilden and the other silk-stocking Democrats could seize control of the Democratic party in New York.

August was sure he would come around.

"From my knowledge of the Man," he told Marble, "I expect that the advice [August gave him] has not been entirely lost, though he appears now to be stubbornly opposed to it. My advice to you would be not to push the matter any further for the moment, because a man generally becomes more obstinate by being too persistently pressed to do something to which he objects."

Connolly and Green kept their offices. Tilden crusaded against Tweed. And although August met with Tilden, he realized that because of the breach between them his influence in the reform movement was, for the time being, limited—although the following April he would be elected a sachem of the reformed Tammany Hall.

In November, Tweed was returned to the state senate by half the vote he had expected, and much of that vote was apparently fraudulent. Moreover, his reelection was overshadowed by the triumph of the reform candidates at the polls. Tweed was finished. In a rush his cronies abandoned him. Connolly turned state's evidence and, although arrested, was never prosecuted. He left the country—as did Sweeny and a number of other ring members. After a series of arrests and trials and an unsuccessful escape attempt that got him as far as Spain, Tweed died in prison. The ring had milked New York of from $30 million to $75 million. The city recovered about $1 million.

Hall, insisting on his innocence, held on as mayor. August held on as one of his most loyal defenders both in public and in private. Because of the Tweed scandals the Union Club asked Hall to resign. Hall refused. August lobbied in his support.

"Belmont is going about all over the city . . . ," reported *The New York Times*, "telling people in his usual amiable way that they must go to the Union Club and vote for Hall or forever after be deprived of the moral support and encouragement of August Belmont—compared with which death is preferable."

"Belmont fights hard for his friend Oakey Hall," George Templeton Strong said. "Any dirt has a fascination for Belmont."

Because he stood by Hall, August was vilified regularly—twice a week for three weeks—in the press.

". . . The Mayor has found some very good sponsors of late . . . ," said *The New York Times*, "because the Democrats who took part in the recent reform movement . . . begin to think that they have been fighting on the Republican side quite long enough. . . . Among them is Mr. August Belmont . . . a political associate of James Fisk, Jr., the Erie swindler—that is to say, Mr. Belmont has presided at public meetings at which Fisk was a leading speaker and he never offered to quit the chair or in any way to signify his disapproval of Fisk as a political friend."

When August had chaired that meeting the year before, *The New York Times* had described him as "a man who would not be guilty of any dishonorable deed"; and while the newspaper deplored his presence on stage with Fisk, it did not stoop to accusing him of anything more serious than political expediency. Most of the Democratic party regulars of all opinions had turned out. Now, however, through some odd transformation August's sharing the platform with Fisk had become proof of a sinister bond between the two men.

"Now," the newspaper continued, "if Mr. August Belmont has no objection to hold intercourse with Fisk, it is quite natural that he should be in love with Mayor Hall and put himself forward as his principal champion," a non sequitur.

But the newspaper felt no obligation to be logical or consistent or truthful. At various times August was accused of making a deal with Hall, which allowed Hall to stay on as mayor as long as he appointed hand-picked reform Democrats to positions vacated by Tweed's departed—and departing—cronies; of supporting Hall only because of a shady financial operation involving city bonds in which they both were involved (a charge *The New York Times* published, even though the editors said, "We are unable to vouch for . . . its accuracy,"); and of being an intimate friend of Tweed's. In fact, although *The New York Times* knew the facts behind the fight Tweed and August had had over the chairmanship of the Democratic National Committee—and had supported August at the time —it now claimed that the two men were so close that "Belmont and Tweed could not bear the thought of rivalry, so Mr. Tweed magnanimously withdrew."

The attacks against August were vicious, personal, and anti-Semitic—and strayed farther and farther from the political issue at hand, August's defense of Hall.

"Mr. Belmont's ideas on the subject of political morality are a good deal more comprehensive than the ideas of most other men," *The New York Times* said. "He believes in the advice of the Quaker to his son, 'Get money—honestly, if you can; but, at any rate, get it.' . . . The public judges fairly. They see now that Mayor Hall has betrayed them. . . . Why should Mr. Belmont flatter himself that he can change that determination? After all, he rules only in a very limited sphere. Among the blind the one-eyed man is king—and among speculators and bargain-drivers, Mr. Belmont is accounted a great man. But the public is greater than he is as he . . . will find out."

Caroline was outraged.

"I would like to box the writer's ears," she said.

August was fatalistic.

"I don't mind much the miserable article in the *Times,*" he said, "though nobody likes to have dirt thrown at one."

As for the accusation that he was involved in any dishonest dealings, he said, "My transaction with the city bonds is clear and straightforward, and I have nothing to fear from investigation or accusation. Still I hate to let such a hound as the editor of *The New York Times* go about maligning me without having a chance to tell them that they lie."

When August returned from a hunting trip to Virginia—which Caroline thought had done him "much good, as he needed to get away from business and worry"—he defended himself with an open letter that he first showed to Marble to make sure it was not too furious. He did not want to seem personally hurt; he just wanted to set the record straight.

"All the charges, accusations, insinuations, and innuendoes . . . of complicity with corrupt transactions or corrupt men are false and calumnious," he said.

But *The New York Times* dismissed the denial by condemning August of guilt by association.

"Mr. Belmont's . . . complicity with corrupt men may be inferred from his intimacy with them," the newspaper said; after all, he was supporting Hall. And it joked about the " 'Shent per Shent Chairman of the National Democratic Committee' cautioning the public against believing anything that has been said to the detriment of his Imperial Highness."

Ironically the newspaper used as ammunition against August the attack on him that had been published during the fight over the chairmanship of the Democratic National Committee in Tweed's newspaper. In accusing August of being close to Hall, who was close to Tweed, *The New York Times* had aligned itself with Tweed's mouthpiece.

Finally, *The New York Times,* having accused August of virtually every professional, political, and personal sin they could think of, claimed he was not a gentleman.

"Because Mr. August Belmont's name appears so frequently and prominently in the newspaper reports of 'fashionable' society," the newspaper said, "it is not safe to conclude that he is a fair representative of the good breeding of New York."

A few days later it continued:

"To be a 'leader of society' we would naturally suppose rare social tact, liberal culture, elegantly refined tastes, captivating personal presence, fine breeding, and a nice appreciation of the requirements and necessities of particular situations would all be essential. And yet lacking these Mr. Belmont somehow manages to hold his position."

August exploded. He threatened to sue. The newspaper laughed off his fury.

". . . We have been informed that Belmont . . . intends to 'vindicate' himself and Hall at the same time by 'dragging an editor of the *Times*' from his office to jail, and there locking him up on bread and water for an unlimited period," *The New York Times* said. "This is a most alarming threat, and we hope Mr. Belmont will be moved by our supplications for mercy, and spare the unfortunate objects of his resentment."

August's erstwhile enemy, the *New York Herald*, came to his defense, probably because old James Gordon Bennett was failing (he would be dead within a year) and the newspaper was being taken over by James Gordon Bennett, Jr., a member of the Belmont Clique. And, of course, the *New York World* defended August. But those two newspapers were alone in his support. Many people believed August must have been guilty of some wrongdoing with if not the Tweed Ring itself at least Hall. Why else would he remain so loyal to the mayor throughout such an intense assault in the press? One politician usually did not go to such limits to defend another—unless he had to.

August was ready to fight for Hall, no matter how contemptibly the newspapers attacked him and no matter what the effect on his own position in the Union Club.

But Hall could not stand to see August sacrificed.

"It is with feelings of intense pain I have perceived that your advocacy of me in club matters has mixed you up with my unhappy newspaper troubles," Hall wrote to August, "and that malice has been the only crown of your chivalry and devotion to your views of justice. I do not desire to be the unhappy cause of having my friends tarred by my malicious enemies. Let me then as a new favor ask that you no longer peril your own comfort by advocacy of what you see just as regards me."

Hall resigned from the Union Club.

August had been attacked for supporting Hall. Now he was attacked for no longer supporting him.

"Belmont's enthusiasm for Oakey Hall seems to have cooled down a little," sneered Strong, who did not know of Hall's letter asking August to drop the matter.

Hall was tried three times on charges that were brought as a result of the Tweed scandals, but there was no evidence proving he knew of what Tweed and his gang had been up to; and since the largest his bank balance had been in those years was $27,000 or $28,000, there was some evidence that he had not profited from any of Tweed and his gang's crimes. He was found innocent. Hall and August's faith in him were vindicated.

CHAPTER FORTY-ONE

THE PREVIOUS YEAR August had become concerned about the rumors he had been hearing of the Ku Klux Klan. He did not doubt that there was a secret organization that was terrorizing carpetbaggers, blacks, and sympathetic Southern whites. In fact, August, Jr.'s former tutor, Mark Sibley Severance, had written that "the Ku Klux are no myth, and they come even into the heart of the city." But August did not believe that the organization was as large as the Republicans were claiming—or that (as the Republicans also were claiming) it was a terrorist arm of a certain segment of the Democratic party. And he was afraid that such charges would be used by the Republicans to gut the Democratic party in the South.

At a meeting held apparently in February 1871 with Thomas F. Bayard, the Democratic senator from Delaware, and some other politicians, August had offered to finance an independent investigation into the nature and activities of the KKK.

Bayard objected.

August considered the man. His family had been socially prominent for generations; he had been educated by tutors; he had—unfortunately for a politician—the uncommon touch. Nevertheless, he was a good politician; and he had a brilliant legal intelligence, a pure rationality that was saved from being clinical by a nostalgia—the mint in the bourbon—for the simplicity of the prewar world. It was that nostalgia August at first distrusted. It seemed odd that Bayard would object to an independent investigation into the KKK.

Bayard tried to explain his position to August. An investigation would carry more authority if it was sponsored by the government.

August thought the government during a Republican administration was incapable of holding an impartial investigation. Either Bayard wanted to be able to discredit the investigation once it was completed by saying it was a Republican put-up job; or, as August thought, he was caving in to the Republicans who, of course, would want to control the investigation by keeping it in Congress.

"I cannot understand being afraid," August said.

While August and Bayard were arguing a tall, muscular man with a moustache, beard, dark hair, and eyes the color of lead shot stormed into the room: General Nathan Bedford Forrest, the alleged leader of the KKK.

It is unclear where this meeting took place or what Forrest was doing there. It is possible that Bayard or some other politician had him waiting in the wings ready to make a dramatic entrance, since he supported Bayard's position.

"We do want an investigation," said Forrest, the *we* an admission that he was involved in the KKK, although at various times he claimed that he was not a member or that he had tried to disband the group. "We want . . . the investigation, but we want it outside of our own hands," he said, although no one had suggested that the KKK would be asked to investigate itself. "We want the seal of the United States upon it. The Senate should make it. Let Bayard be one of the investigators . . . ," which sounded as though Forrest had Bayard in his pocket.

As for Bayard's being a coward, Forrest shouted, "Oh, hell! he" (meaning August) "doesn't know that you have just been down South, in the very thick of the Carpetbaggers, looking yourself into what on both sides has been going on—risking your life to see and know what's what at first hand."

Since the violence Bayard presumably had investigated was by the KKK against its enemies and since, from Forrest's attitude toward Bayard, it did not seem as though Bayard was an enemy of the KKK, it is hard to say how Bayard had risked his life. But Bayard accepted the compliment.

"Nobody knows it," he said. "Why should they?"

August gave up. Obviously Bayard was committed to a government investigation. Why, August was not sure. August left the meeting with little respect for the senator from Delaware, who seemed to fear the KKK as much as August had thought he'd feared the Republicans.

In 1871 the government did hold an investigation—a travesty. Republicans were so eager to prove what was true—namely that the KKK represented an appalling threat to the security of many Southerners, white and black—they rejected Bayard's proposal that the investigation should be carried out under the rules of evidence appropriate to any legal proceeding. Leading questions, coaching of witnesses, rumors, and hearsay testimony, Bayard thought, should not be allowed. The Republican majority (13 to 8) on the joint Congressional committee thought otherwise. The hearings became a circus: witnesses on both sides substituted lies for truth with the facility of magicians turning water into blood (or, given the brutality of the crimes under discussion and the cynical way the alleged KKK members tried to minimize the KKK's terrorism, blood into water).

By rejecting the rules of evidence Bayard had suggested, the Republicans defeated their own purpose—if in fact their purpose was to discover the truth—because, under the procedures adopted by the committee, witnesses like Forrest could hedge with impunity. Committee members held him personally—but not legally—in contempt.

Unfortunately the Republican committeemen were less interested in learning the truth about the KKK than in damning Democrats, who they wanted to prove made up the entire membership of the group—an absurd charge that of course they could not sustain. The conclusion of the majority report limited itself to observing that "The organizers and managers of the conspiracy, known as the Ku Klux Klan, or Invisible Empire of the South . . . are men of high intelligence, and they must have intended the results they have produced. Their purpose must have been to close the South against Northern men and capital; to hold the freedmen helpless and dependent; to govern the Southern states and finally the country, and thus recover what they value more than all else—property in slaves and political power." A fair statement.

The minority report signed by Bayard and the other Democrats agreed with the Republicans that the KKK was an abomination.

". . . We do not intend to deny," the minority report said, "that bodies of disguised men have, in several of the states of the South, been guilty of the most flagrant crimes, crimes which we neither seek to palliate nor excuse, for the commission of which the wrongdoers should, when ascertained and duly convicted, suffer speedy and condign punishment."

The Democrats, however, did not want to condemn the entire South for the acts of the terrorists and wanted to emphasize that the KKK was not a politically partisan organization.

". . . We deny," the minority report continued,

> that these men have any general organization, or any political significance, or that their conduct is endorsed by any respectable number of the white people in any state; on the contrary, the men and the bands by which such outrages are perpetrated are almost universally regarded by the intelligent people of the several states as the worst enemies of the South, as they furnish the men now in power at Washington the only excuse left to maintain war upon them, and to continue the system of robbery and oppression which they have inaugurated—a system which is destructive not only of their peace and property, but is intended to blacken and malign their character as men before the country and the world. We will show, by testimony incontrovertible, that in no one of the six states of North and South Carolina, Georgia, Alabama, Mississippi, and Florida, has there, at any time, existed combinations of lawless men in one-tenth part of any one of said states.

The KKK was made up of a fraction of the population of Southern whites. They were not representative. The Republicans could not use them as a way of passing judgment on the average white Southerner—or on the Democratic party in the South.

The Report of the Joint Select Committee to Inquire into the Condition of Affairs in the Late Insurrectionary States was made to the two houses of Congress early in February 1872. August was present—and pleased that Bayard and the other Democrats had both condemned the KKK and exculpated the Democratic party. Bayard had stood up to Forrest and the Republicans. August had been wrong about him.

When Bayard came off the floor of Congress, August was waiting.

"Forgive me for hot headedness," August said. "Accept my allegiance. From this time forward my work shall be fixed on the hope of seeing you President of the United States. I dedicate my fortune to it."

Years later another senator would point out that "when . . . August starts out to be a real friend, how he does stand pat. He has spent, maybe, a million dollars rounding out an apology to Tom Bayard—and, when you rally him about it, he just . . . says, 'Oh, hell! It's worth it!' "

By the time August returned from Washington to New York that February, the crisis over Mayor Hall had been all but forgotten. The public was distracted by a more interesting scandal: Jim Fisk had been shot down on the stairway of the Grand Central Hotel at Broadway and Fourth Street, murdered by Edward S. Stokes, who (Fisk had claimed) had embezzled both money from a jointly controlled company and the affections of his mistress, Josie Mansfield. By March partisan tempers, which had flared over the Hall affair, were so cooled that Mrs. George Templeton Strong surprised Caroline with a visit. Her husband had disliked August for so long that her appearance was a source of much amusement.

"You began the business last summer, you see," Caroline wrote to Perry, who was evidently playing Romeo and Juliet with one of Strong's daughters; "and now it is followed up by *Mamma* herself."

Mrs. Strong, no doubt at her daughter's urging, was trying to negotiate a peace between the two families. She invited Caroline to call on her.

Caroline declined but a short time later did go to the Strongs' house to leave her card, after which Mrs. Strong again came to the Belmonts' "with her daughter," Caroline reported to Perry, "so I know them without having taken the least trouble to do it." Caroline thought this was "just as well," since if Perry intended to invite the Strongs' daughter to any parties at the Belmonts' house "matters would get rather complicated" if the parents did not "know" each other.

While Perry played at romance, August, Jr., just played. He let his work slide and then to catch up stayed awake all night, cramming: "a repetition of the old story," his father thought.

But it was not quite the old story. There were some new details. August, Jr., had been caught throwing water out of the window of his room in the new dormitory, Holyoke House, onto a passerby in the street below. He had let his joy at being in Cambridge erupt into happy howling outside Memorial Hall at five o'clock in the morning. And his experience at school plays at Exeter and charades at home had made him a leading force in college theatricals. . . . He had been cooped up with a private tutor for so long, he now wanted to socialize. There was so much to do.

But, having been warned by his parents and professors, he worked hard. And by April, Harvard could write to his father that "all of your son's teachers agreed that his improvement in the latter part of February and March was very marked and that like diligence during the remainder of the year would enable him in all probability to pass his end of the term examination satisfactorily." And he did. His father was pleased. To reward his son he agreed to buy a boat. There was one, twenty-nine feet long, owned by a John B. Herreshoff of Bristol, Rhode Island, which August thought might do; but it was not what August, Jr., had in mind. Although so busy he had to dictate letters, August continued to look for a boat. He knew it was important for him to encourage August, Jr.'s good work.

"I hear that there is a sloop now laying at Providence called the *Ariel*, which I believe would suit you," said August. "There is one laying here too that may be faster, but is not so sea-worthy. You or Perry can run down to Providence some Saturday to inspect the *Ariel*. I suppose the price will be about $1,000, which with $300 for fitting up will somewhat exceed the amount I thought one could be bought for, my opinion being that $800–$900 would purchase such a vessel as you desire. At any rate, do not mention your name if you inspect the *Ariel*, as the owner would probably ask you more on learning it."

Perry at last had gotten serious about his classes. He had become a scholar with a scholar's absorption in his work: French and German history and political economy, about which he asked his father's advice.

"Between the question of paper money and that of free trade," August said, "I should think that the latter would offer a wider scope for research and that you would probably be able to prepare a more able essay on it."

Since August was so involved in the paper-money-versus-gold question in politics, he also may have wanted to steer his son into a field where he would not be so overshadowed by his father's opinions. He did not want his son to shine with a reflected light.

"You ought, however, to study the matter beforehand very carefully," he said, "and bring your own views forward as much as you can."

In the same letter, as though the two thoughts were connected (which they were, the link being Perry's independence, his need to make his own name and not rely on his parents' and grandparents' reputations), August, in discussing how Perry should describe himself in a publication, warned, "You may say about your father and mother's family what you think proper; but I would, if I were you, not enlarge too much on it, as it might be misconstrued with a wish of self-glorification."

The warning was unnecessary. Perry wanted to build his own reputation, and the foundation on which he would build it—he had decided—would be "the development of our Common Law," which he explained in a letter was a study "that will require months to complete," but that "will be of great service to me hereafter" in a legal and political career. With an intensity that disregarded the possibility that his correspondent might be less fascinated by the subject than he was, Perry launched into an explanation of the work.

"The germs of the system are generally supposed to originate after the Norman Conquest," he said; "and the few authors who have traced the matter back to the German institutions of the Anglo-Saxon have differed in so many essential points that all of us, professors and students, are rather in the dark as to the ground we have been over. My task will be to compare these different authors and to form a theory of my own, endeavoring at the same time to found every statement on authority. My general theory is that the contestants personally engaged in 'trials by combat' have been succeeded by the lawyers who today contend for their clients before our courts of justice."

The subject was not so dry after all, saved from pedantry by Perry's vision of lawyers using words as swords and fighting out their cases in courtrooms as their predecessors had done on fields of combat hundreds of years before. Now it was not might and swordsmanship that made right but a different kind of strength and skill: powerful logic and wit. Being a lawyer (Perry believed) was the modern equivalent of being a knight.

His professors thought his subject new and, as a result, attractive; scholarship like fashion finds the novel appealing. They encouraged him.

And August, on hearing the reports, felt that Perry was finally succeeding as he should academically. He was no longer allowing his social life to interfere with his schoolwork. August's only concern was that Perry let his new sense of responsibility lead him astray. Because the previous year's members had not paid their dues, one of Perry's clubs was $500 short. Perry offered to make up the deficit. He asked his father for the money. August gave it to him, "against my better judgement." Perry's club had gotten into trouble because it was too expensive. All of Perry's clubs were too expensive.

"I find it quite out of place that the yearly assessment of a college club should be $175," he told his son. "Why, such a thing would not be admitted in the Union or any other club of grown men here, and it is very wrong in young collegians to launch out in that way. It will kill the club and keep out many most desirable members, as only the sons of very rich men can join. And you know yourself that those are not always the best specimens in college."

This hairline crack had always separated August's life from his sons'. August had been born into modest circumstances; he knew better than to judge a man only by class. His sons had been born wealthy; they would have to keep reminding themselves not to be prejudiced in favor of the rich. The crack might never widen; but throughout their lives as they all grew older it would lengthen. They would never get around it.

Perry's generosity with his clubs had helped boost his expenses to double the amount August thought reasonable.

"I hardly believe that other young men have the permission to make such an expenditure. I am sure that Charlie Russell," one of Perry's friends, whose father August knew, "is not allowed to spend anything like it. I am willing that you should enquire from him, and I am sure you will find that I am right. Charlie's father is fully as rich as I am and has a less expensive household, and you ought not to spend any more money than he does.

"I hope," August told his son in regard to the readiness with which he had bailed out his club, "that another time you won't play Don Quixote."

Frederika and Jeannie looked forward to Perry's graduation, in particular to Class Day with its speeches and poems and the ringing of The Tree next to Holden Chapel with flowers, which the seniors, disreputable in their ragtag rags, fought to grab. The students who had formed close friendships gathered together trying to maintain an intimacy that, with the end of college, seemed fragile. Alternately they felt worldly and innocent. The rakishness they had cultivated for four years seemed, especially in the presence of their parents, artificial. When, while strolling with their families, they met other students also out with their families, they felt a flooding of affection and kinship which for a moment bound them closer than they may ever have been during their college careers; and they would exchange knowing looks, although the knowledge behind the looks was unformed. They could not have explained what they felt. The families, especially the mothers and sisters, seemed so incongruous on the campus, which the students were used to seeing as the dominion of maleness and youth. When they left their families and for an hour or so took refuge in their dormitories or clubs (the ones that were not invaded), they felt an inexplicable relief that, however, made them feel vaguely guilty and uncomfortable. To dispel the edge of embarrassment they joked loudly and regressed to sophomore antics. At night their awkwardness settled; it had been merely some sediment that had billowed up into their lives with the disruption of their habits. Relaxed and happy, and sad too, they danced in the Yard beneath Japanese lanterns and listened to the glee club sing songs that conjured up memories of their first days at college.

A week later the informality of Class Day was replaced by the gravity of Commencement, after which the seniors, feeling as though they had been husked, stepped out of their college years into what seemed a newly made world.

Perry was now a graduate. Within a month after Commencement he joined other Medical Faculty club members at the Somerset Hotel in Boston for a reunion dinner, the intent of which was—according to the invitation that had been addressed to "Illustrissimus Doctor: Belmont"— "to show . . . that there is a heaven beyond the grave of graduation. There will be present an enthusiastic and fighting contingent from the undergraduates, who, however, will be kept under proper control. Some of the noted properties of the Society will embellish the table. The plain, unassuming rough and tough little crockpot will be there. The cellar will be well-stocked. Tales of ancient days will be told with a perfect sense of security. Rejuvenation will be in order."

Perry felt the pleasant melancholy that comes with the clear-cut end of any period in one's life, but he was excited by the prospect of going to the University of Berlin to study law.

"Well, Belmont," a friend said as they walked from Boston to Cambridge one day, discussing the future, "I am not going to leave Boston."

"Why?" Perry asked.

"If I should leave Boston," his friend replied, "I should not think as much of Boston as I do now."

Oliver wanted to go to Annapolis. August wrote to Caroline's cousin, Christopher Raymond Perry Rodgers (who in two years would become the superintendent of the Naval Academy), for advice.

"So many of our family have done good service in the Navy that I rejoice in your determination to send Oliver to Annapolis," Rodgers wrote; "and I need not tell you how earnestly I shall do all that an old officer can to make Oliver's nomination easy and his early career agreeable."

Rodgers thought that St. Paul's, which Oliver currently attended, emphasized the classics at the expense of mathematics and science, which were better preparation for a naval career. But he was sure Oliver would do well, whatever his background; and he confided that "the longer I remain in the Navy, the stronger my faith in it becomes. It does not bring a man wealth, but it is a manly, honorable, and clean profession. It is more than usually free from temptation, and to a well-bred and well-educated officer affords an agreeable access to most that is worth seeing in foreign countries."

At Rodgers's suggestion August delayed sending Oliver to Annapolis; but although he withdrew him from St. Paul's, he made sure Oliver continued to get a good classical background. August did not object to his son's continuing a family tradition in the Navy; but if he did, August wanted him to have a wide enough background so that if he ever left the Navy he could sail other professional seas.

As for August's fourth son, Raymond showed signs of becoming a modern courtier (in the best sense of the word). In a democracy the prince one serves is public opinion; and in public Raymond had *sprezzatura.*

"I had taken Dolly with me to the races," August said; "and he was perfectly delighted; but evidently bent to appear cool." August's horse Victor won; but "the first thing Raymond asked the judges, in whose stand I had him put, was, 'Who is second?' "

🦋 CHAPTER FORTY-TWO 🦋

EIGHTEEN SEVENTY-TWO was a presidential election year, and as usual the Democrats were divided. One of the most serious fissures ran the length of the Ohio border. Ohio was still George H. Pendleton's state; and Pendleton's people were still causing trouble. The previous year in the 1871 Ohio gubernatorial race the Ohio Democrats had reaffirmed the greenback plank that Pendleton had earlier forced into the Democratic party's 1868 presidential platform. It had contributed to Seymour's defeat then. It would, August was sure, contribute to the defeat of the Ohio Democratic gubernatorial candidate, General George W. McCook. If anything, embracing the greenback issue was a worse strategy in 1871 than it had been three years earlier, because in March 1869, Congress had made bond payment in gold a law.

Since the Republicans could not accuse the Democrats of "disloyalty and copperheadism," August explained in a letter to McCook, "they charge us now with revolutionary and disorganizing intentions. This is our great stumbling block and unless we can prove to the American people that we intend to accept the government as it will be handed to us, without disturbing the political and financial situation we can never hope for their votes." August advised McCook to "exert your influence to keep the unfortunate plank in the background. It is made of paper and damned bad paper too, and we are sure to break through if we try to stand on it."

Whenever August advocated any policy, especially economic policy, his motives were called into question; so he assured McCook that his views on the gold-greenback issue were unaffected by any personal interest.

"I have not one dollar at stake," he said. "I am not a 'bloated bondholder,' and I do not have any federal obligation among my worldly goods. All I care for is the success of the Democratic Party."

McCook ignored August's plea and followed Pendleton's lead. Political influence can be in direct proportion to geographical distance. August was in New York. Pendleton was in Ohio.

McCook did lose in Ohio—which gave August hope that the Democratic greenback supporters would be convinced to drop the issue. If the greenback diehards would surrender to gold—and law—it was possible the Democratic party might be able to unite, at last, behind a presidential candidate, since even the Ohio Democrats had agreed that the party should accept the Reconstruction amendments to the Constitution and focus their attention on corruption in the Grant administration, free trade, and civil service reform. The first and last issues struck August as the most important.

For two years August had been arguing that the Democrats should become the anticorruption party. This was why it had been so important to clean up the Democratic party in New York. And why around the same time August had joined with other New York merchants and bankers to complain about extortion practiced by the Republican Custom House Ring. Attacking New York Senator Roscoe Conkling's Republican machine helped balance August's fight against the Democratic Tweed Ring.

"It seems to me," August said, outlining his strategy for Manton Marble, "that the *World* ought to be the reform paper of the country. It should countenance every effort which is meant to be an improvement upon the past, but it should be careful not to repeat the blunders of the *Tribune* by committing itself to any special isms or crude schemes. The *World* should especially give prominence to the labor question, if for no higher motive, for party reasons. The temptation with all newspapers is to take the side of capital for the reason that all great papers must be conducted by capitalists and the social influences which surround the owners are such to keep the labor point of view out of sight."

Since the Civil War the labor movement had been spreading. By 1872 there were in the United States about 300,000 members of more than two dozen trade unions; and a labor party, the National Labor Reform party, had nominated Supreme Court Justice David Davis to be its presidential candidate. August thought Davis was a humbug, and Davis eventually withdrew from the race. The National Labor Reform party—and the labor federation that had been its root—withered. But August believed labor would become an increasingly important factor in national politics. If the Democratic party could support and be supported by workingmen, it had a chance of breaking what was beginning to seem like the Republican monopoly on federal power.

August admitted his strategy had its problems—particularly fighting political corruption through civil service reform. Nevertheless, he told Marble, "Even granting the reforms are illusion as a means of purifying government"—power did not corrupt so much as justify corruption; politics would always be a dirty business—"is it wise to repel from the Democratic Party and drive into the Republican Party the immense numbers of intelligent people who believe that our only safety lies in the adoption of these reforms? What possible hope can the Democratic Party have of getting the support of the best people in the country when its chief organ [the *World*] declares that their pet reforms are 'mere whimsies'?" Marble like August would have to change with the times. Their politics must be responsive to public opinion—even if privately they disagreed with some of the programs they would have to support.

"Personally," August told Marble, "as you know, I am bitterly opposed to women suffrage and yet it seems the part of wisdom for the *World* to give these people a fair show and to get their sympathy and good will."

There were other issues that August thought would affect the outcome of the presidential election—like the claims the United States had made on Great Britain for the damage English-built Confederate raiders— pirate ships, August considered them—had done to the Union merchant marine during the Civil War. Secretary of State Hamilton Fish had negotiated an agreement that stipulated the quarrel would be decided by an international tribunal, a fair way of resolving the problem, August believed. A civilized way.

Still the conciliator, August thought the Democratic party should be the party of peace.

Honesty in government; fair working conditions for laborers; adherence to law, both national and international; and opposition to the military despotism in the South and centralized power in Washington— these were the issues that could win the White House for the Democrats, if only the Democrats could agree to run their candidate on such a platform and in the meantime stay in the background while the Republican party destroyed itself.

Liberal Republicans under the leadership of men like Charles Francis Adams, Horace Greeley (the editor of the *New York Tribune* and August's scourge ever since he first had entered politics), and Carl Schurz (like August a German immigrant and, unlike August, a former avid Lincoln supporter, who was now a senator from Missouri) had broken with President Grant over the administration's corruption and punitive Reconstruction policies. They had worked successfully to get the government to grant amnesty to all except a few hundred former Rebels; and, knowing they would not be able to stop Grant's renomination, they had bolted their party.

August cultivated the Liberal Republican leaders. At a meeting in

November 1871 August significantly had sat between Samuel J. Tilden and Schurz; he wanted to be the link binding the reform Democrats and the renegade Republicans, so that if the two groups fused, either within the Democratic party (which August thought preferable) or within a new party, August would be in a key position. And a fusion party seemed possible.

August promoted collaboration between the two groups in the Connecticut state elections in the spring of 1872. He suggested that the Liberal Republicans should support the Democratic candidates and that the Democrats should support the Liberal Republican senator Orris S. Ferry in his reelection campaign.

"If the Liberal Republicans really mean to cooperate fairly and cordially with us for the overthrow of Grant, now is their time to show it," August said.

If fusion failed in Connecticut, August was sure that "many Republicans now on the fence will certainly fall back into line."

The Connecticut Liberal Republicans did support the Democrats, who won; and the Democrats returned the favor. And it appeared as if the resulting political alloy were strong enough to resist almost any hammering the Grant Republicans might give it. Or so August thought.

Now that the Democrats and the Liberal Republicans had proved that they could cooperate, all they had to do was agree upon a presidential nominee. For the time being, Thomas F. Bayard, who might otherwise have been August's candidate, was out of the question. That debt would have to wait for repayment; but the interest accrued would make the postponement worthwhile. Given the situation, August thought the natural choice was Charles Francis Adams.

In 1868 August had sounded Adams's presidential ambition and found it shallow. Since then it had acquired more depth. Adams had not just a national but an international reputation. His name could be used to conjure up the ideals of the Founding Fathers, whose work, August believed, was being undone by the federal military presence in the South. He was "by far the strongest and least vulnerable candidate," August thought.

But it could be difficult to sell Adams, a Republican, to the Democrats; so August schemed with Schurz to delay the Democratic party's convention until after the Liberal Republicans met. Once the Liberal Republicans had nominated Adams, the Democrats would be compelled to second the nomination—or risk splitting the anti-Grant vote with their own candidate, which would probably allow Grant to win the election. This plan gave the Liberal Republicans enough Democratic support to make their breakaway party viable and gave August and other pro-Adams Democrats a certain amount of control over the selection of the Democratic presidential candidate. If the Democrats held their convention before the Liberal Republicans had nominated Adams, it was possible they would nominate a candidate as lame as Horatio Seymour, as corrupt as Grant, or as wrongheaded as Pendleton; and there were unfortunately many leading Democrats who would fit those specifications. Some Democrats were even suggesting that if the Liberal Republican ticket was acceptable and strong there might be no reason to hold a Democratic convention, a position August deplored. August believed in fusion but not abdication. He hoped the Democratic party would absorb the Liberal Republicans, not vice versa.

The Liberal Republican National Convention was held early in May in Cincinnati, Ohio. August passed through the town a few days before the convention began, on his way to Vincennes, Indiana, and, farther west, Carlyle, Illinois, where he was going snipe-shooting. He passed through the town again on his way back east. Although he must have consulted with various Democrats and Republicans during his travels, the trip was not political. But the press refused to believe that; and as August told Perry, "the papers have made very free with my name and put all kinds of words in my mouth, of which I am perfectly innocent."

Because of his prolabor stand one newspaper claimed that "it is the general belief that Davis [who was running for the Liberal Republican as well as the National Labor Reform party nomination] is Mr. Belmont's first choice." Other newspapers had him more correctly supporting Adams.

"Mr. Adams," a newspaper quoted August as saying, "is a cold man, a man to me personally indifferent and uninteresting in a social respect, but he is *the* man to be at the head of affairs; the man, in short, for President."

"It would be bad policy and worse taste for Democrats to meddle with the Liberal Republican Convention," August told Perry, "though I hope that their platform and candidates will be such as to unite all the opponents of the present corrupt and wicked administration."

Whatever August's reasons for being in Cincinnati, his presence had impact. Even by doing nothing he was doing something. Most newspapers remarked on his influence, which was recognized as an effective passive as well as active instrument, and on the political resiliency on which it was based.

"Times have changed," a newspaper said, "since Bill Tweed had nearly run Belmont off the National Democratic Executive Committee, and Belmont is again a shrewd, cautious, respectable power in politics."

At least one newspaper—perhaps only one newspaper—took August at his word:

"Towards noon," its reporter wrote, "I . . . strolled up to the St. Nicholas Restaurant"—the Cincinnati equivalent of Delmonico's—"for lunch in the dim carpeted parlor where hangs a painting known to Western tourists as the most voluptuous gem in the collection of the late Nicholas Longworth—the portrait of Pauline Bonaparte in all the pomp of her captivating beauty. Here sat a few gentlemen hobnobbing over spotless tablecloths. Sipping his soup alone there was a man whom I scarcely recognized at first. His bronzed face and the brown hand that he extended across the table showed plainly enough that the *Chairman of the Democratic National Committee* had really been snipe-shooting and not, as some correspondents have stated, on a political errand through the West. He had just arrived in town and was to leave at 2 P.M.

" 'There was no other way to get home,' he said."

"My conviction," August told Perry once he had returned to New York, "is that Mr. Adams is the strongest man and that placed upon a national platform he would sweep the country, and I know that the Democratic convention would endorse his nomination. I fear, however, that he is too good a man and that the politicians, knowing that they could not use him, will stand between him and the people."

The Liberal Republican National Convention rejected Adams and instead chose Horace Greeley.

Although Greeley and August were longtime political and personal enemies, August had to convince the Democratic party to nominate him. He had arranged things so that if he did otherwise there would be two anti-Grant candidates, who would split the vote, and Grant would win reelection. August was trapped by his own ploy into supporting a man he despised.

A bellwether is a castrated sheep that wears a bell and leads its flock. August, having been politically gelded by Greeley's nomination by the Liberal Republicans, was a bellwether. Where he led, the Democratic party would follow. Reporters stalked him, trying to see which way he would head.

On the Saturday afternoon after the Liberal Republican Convention, August had just left home for a walk along Fifth Avenue when he was pounced on by someone from the *New York Daily News,* who wanted to know what August thought of Greeley's candidacy.

"Speech is silvern," said August, "but silence is golden."

The reporter hung on.

"If we cannot have what we love," August said, "let us love what we have."

Still the reporter would not release August. Would the Democrats follow the Liberal Republicans? he wanted to know.

"I cannot tell . . . ," said August. "We must wait and see . . . the effect of Greeley's nomination on the press, the people, and, in fact, on many things. . . . It may be policy to adopt the ticket. Mr. Greeley, in my opinion, will run well in the Southern states. But it is too soon to judge yet. I will do most anything to beat this administration."

August had said too much. He backed off. He explained that until the Grant Republicans had their convention he could make no predictions about the Democratic party's course.

"In the meantime," he added, "I judge it better for the party to say or do nothing. That is better. What we might say now would probably be perverted or turned against us when the nominations are made."

A few days following August's alfresco interview, the Democratic National Committee met at his house and, after long debate, accepted August's suggestion that the Democratic party's national convention be held in Baltimore on July 9. For the next two months August kept his personal feelings about Greeley in his pocket; although from time to time he might jingle them, they were, like foreign coins, nothing he used in his daily transactions. Publicly, August was a Greeley supporter.

When a Cincinnati newspaper attacked August, he asked Marble to have the *New York World* print a letter in which he said, "So much am I impressed with the fatal consequences in store for our . . . country by the reelection of Grant, that I would willingly vote for my deadliest enemy in order to prevent such a catastrophe."

"Whatever the letter's merits or demerits," August afterward admitted privately, "it shows one thing clear and that is I don't care a damn for Grant, Greeley, and the New York State Committee."

The New York State Committee's feelings for August were mutual. At the Democratic State Convention, which August did not attend, he was not chosen to be a delegate to the national convention. His longtime foe, Augustus Schell, was given his place.

"I have pretty much made up my mind," August told Marble, "not to go to Baltimore at all."

Even though August's presence at the Democratic convention would remind everyone that he had been rejected by his own state committee, August in the end chose to go to Baltimore. The convention opened on a sweltering day. At noon August called the delegates to order.

"The thinking men of both parties have been alive to the fact that we are now living under a military despotism, overriding the civil authority in many states of the Union," August said;

> that, by the enactment of arbitrary and unconstitutional laws, through a depraved majority in Congress, the rights of those states are infringed and trampled upon, and that Caesarism and centralization are undermining the very foundations of our federal system, and are sweeping away the constitutional bulwarks erected by the wisdom of the fathers of the Republic; that abuses have been so glaring that the wisest and best men of the Republican Party have severed themselves from the Radical Ring which is trying to fasten upon the country another four years reign of corruption, usurpation, and despotism; and whatever individual opinion we may entertain as to the choice of the candidate whom . . . the Liberal Republicans have selected in opposition to General Grant, there cannot be any doubt of the patriotic impulses which dictated their action, nor can any fault be found with the platform of principles upon which they have placed their candidate. The resolutions of the Cincinnati Convention are what the country require, and they must command the hearty support of every patriot throughout the . . . land. In the struggle . . . before us we must look to principles and not to men, and I trust that no personal predilections or prejudices will deter us from doing any duty to the American people.

August's speech was not just a welcome but a nomination. New York's Governor John Thompson Hoffman, who was partly behind August's rejection by the state committee, had wanted to nominate Greeley; but August, much to his own pleasure, as he explained later to Marble, preempted him.

". . . Mr. Greeley," August began—but he was interrupted by a bald man in the center of the convention hall, who shouted "Hurrah for Greeley" and waved a fan over his head as though he were trying to fan his own spark of enthusiasm into a blaze.

August let the bald man have the floor.

For a while he yelled alone; but at last the fire spread. Delegates joined him, at first one by one; then in twos and threes; then by dozens; and finally whole sections of the hall were standing at once, shouting, stomping, hooraying for Greeley.

But sustaining this pumped-up enthusiasm was as hard as trying to blow up a broken balloon with a bellows: one had to keep working at it or it subsided quickly. August waited for the last shouts to die away and continued his speech:

"Mr. Greeley," he said,

> has been heretofore a bitter opponent of the Democratic Party, and the violent attacks against myself individually, which have . . . appeared in his journal certainly do not entitle him to any sympathy or preference at my hands. But Mr. Greeley represents the national and Constitutional principals of the Cincinnati platform, and by his admirable and manly letter of acceptance, he has shown that he is fully alive to their spirit, and that, if elected, he means to carry them out honestly and faithfully. Should you, therefore, in your wisdom, decide to pronounce in favor of the Cincinnati candidate, I shall for one cheerfully bury all past differences, and vote and labor for his election with the same zeal and energy with which I have supported heretofore and mean ever to support the candidate of the Democratic Party.

August's endorsement of Greeley was a handsome gesture. He could have—as he had considered doing—avoided the convention and abstained from championing Greeley. But he had come and dramatized his support and done it honestly. He did not pretend he had no differences with the man he was promoting for the nomination; but he used his overcoming of those differences as an argument with which to convince any Democrats who doubted the wisdom of choosing Greeley. It was therefore a stronger speech than it would have been if it had been all fluff and praise.

At the end of his speech August said:

> And now . . . permit me to detain you one moment longer by a few words of an entirely personal character. With my present action terminates my official function as Chairman of the National Democratic Committee—an office which, by the confidence of my constituents and the courtesy of my colleagues, I have held for twelve consecutive years. During all that time, I have striven . . . to do my duty faithfully to the party and the country. . . . While I was grieved and deeply mortified to see at various times my motives and actions misconstrued by several

Democratic papers and that some even descended to the fabrication of the most absurd falsehoods concerning my social and political conduct, I have the proud and consoling satisfaction that my colleagues on the National Committee and all those who know me did justice to the integrity and purity of my intentions in all the trying situations in which my official position had placed me; and let me tell you, gentlemen, that there is not one among you who bears a warmer and truer affection for our party and our country than I have done or ever shall do. You love this great republic, your native land, as you do the mother who gave you birth; but to me she is the cherished bride and choice of my youth, the faithful and loving companion of my manhood; and . . . I cling to her with all the fond recollections of the manifold blessings received at her hands. I retire from the position which I have held to take my place in the rank and file of that great party whose national, constitutional, and conservative principles have claimed my unwavering allegiance for the last thirty years, and as long as the Almighty will spare my life I shall never falter in my love and devotion to our party and our country.

The rhetoric was sentimental but deeply felt. And like his commitment to Greeley, his farewell was honest. He did not try to hide the past or his hurt with a hearty mask.

His resignation was not a surprise. For days it had been rumored that he would quit or be forced out. A few called, "Good, good"; but for the most part he was warmly applauded—"perhaps," he cynically thought, "because they knew the speech was my last." Still, "half the delegation came up to me to shake hands."

The convention passed a resolution that thanked August for his long and hard labors as chairman of the National Committee and "confidently" looked forward to "his wise counsel and cordial aid."

That afternoon August left Baltimore for Newport.

The convention did nominate Greeley and his Liberal Republican running mate, B. Gratz Brown, which August expected. And August was replaced as chairman of the National Committee by Augustus Schell, which although also expected nevertheless deepened August's political embarrassment.

"The New York delegation, Hoffman at the head, acted like pigs to me," August told Marble. "The selection of Schell in my place was all cooked up before they knew of my intention to retire."

August asked Marble not to defend him.

"I beg you not to say anything or show your teeth in the *World* about it," August said. "I mean to bide my time, and you will see if I don't pay that oily Governor Hoffman back for what he did."

August continued to push for Greeley in a mild way.

"I am glad the *World* is going to support him as the regular nominee of the party," August told Marble, "but still how much better would it have been if you had not been so fearfully ultra in your earlier opposition."

But he did not push very hard or very long. He rapidly lost interest in the race—despite a $10,000 to $1,000 bet he had made that Grant would not be reelected. Even as a gambler he could not bring himself to care. The party seemed to have accepted his resignation as a ticket to oblivion. He was treated not as an elder statesman but as a pariah— worse, as a jinx. He had been associated with too many Democratic defeats. Even Marble disappointed him by not mentioning his name when the *World* was matching leading Democrats with possible jobs.

Renegade Democrats bolted the party, held their own convention, and nominated Charles O'Conor for president and John Quincy Adams, Jr., for vice-president. August, despite his preference for O'Conor over Greeley and despite the shabby way the pro-Greeley Democrats had treated him, nevertheless kept his distance from the renegades. His preference was a moral not a tactical one. He hoped Greeley would win and would do nothing to hurt his chances, but after what had happened he could not vote for him. He would not publicly go back on his promise to the Baltimore convention, but a ballot is a private matter.

Throughout the end of summer August tried to forget his political humiliation in racing and family affairs. He sold Glenelg, who had grown too old to run, because he thought he had another, better stud horse, Kentucky, at the Nursery. It was a mistake. Kentucky's stud record never approached that of Glenelg. But August would not know his error for more than a decade. In the meantime his turf season was almost good enough to distract him. He had the best filly of the year, Woodbine, and two other excellent fillies, Victoria and Medora. His colts Wade Hampton and Silk Stocking did very well. And a colt that had been knocked down the previous year at the start of his only race and again this year by his stablemate just as he was about to take the lead in the Belmont States, went on to win some difficult contests late in the season. Eventually that horse would be injured so badly that his racing career was cut short; he never would fulfill his promise. August had named him appropriately The

Ill Used—which may have reflected August's feelings about how he himself was being treated in politics.

Perry and August, Jr., went off on a cruise to Montauk Point in their new boat. Oliver, whom August was calling "my future naval hero," and Raymond were with August and Caroline at Newport—along with the girls, who, August said, "are growing and learning to try their wings in little archery and fishing parties and looking forward to their flight at Balls and picnics, which is to come next year when my wife and I will have to retire to the background and sit patiently with the old dowagers until the small hours, a charming prospect to look forward to."

Frederika kept August, Jr., up to date on who was dancing and flirting with whom and to whom their crowd was getting married—which Frederika thought ridiculous at their age. She said that one of August, Jr.'s college acquaintances was "a little ass to be engaged while he is studying yet."

Marble, like August, Jr., was absent from Newport that year, recuperating in New York from a general physical collapse. August had offered to send port and Burgundy, which he believed "made blood"—but Marble was resigned to spending the summer in bed.

"Life looks strangely, does it not? to a man on his back," he wrote to August. "As different as the sky to one who is swimming so."

August would have to be Marble's eyes and ears at the resort.

"You will tell me if Newport is dull or delightful this season," Marble said. "I know not for whom you now burn, nor if she is near enough to be a light to your eyes as well as a fire in your heart." Marble enjoyed teasing August about his flirtations, romances that did not affect his love for Caroline any more than did any other sport, like horseracing.

Newport was dull that year. "We are . . . very quiet," August told Marble, "and attend but seldom the many parties, which the new leaders of fashion are giving to Newport society."

August was losing his position not just in politics but also in the beau monde. Life was looking "strangely" to August too. Eight years earlier, even four years, he would have fought for supremacy in both the convention hall and ballroom; but it no longer seemed worth the effort. Although, according to Perry, August voted for O'Conor, there is some evidence that he sat out the election. He wrote to Marble that he planned to leave the country and expected to miss what he assumed would be a Democratic victory; being absent would give him an excuse to avoid voting. With or without August's participation in the election, Greeley and O'Conor lost and Grant was reelected.

August resigned his membership in the managing committee of the Manhattan Club, to the dismay of Marble and other friends, who asked him to reconsider. He put many of his paintings up for auction.

"I felt very badly at seeing them go," said Caroline; "but one or two favorites of mine will not be sold."

He arranged his business affairs so that, as much as possible, they would not need his attention. And, abandoning politics, Fifth Avenue, and Wall Street, he sailed with his family—all but August, Jr.—for an extended visit to Europe.

PART FIVE

CHAPTER FORTY-THREE

THE WEATHER IN LONDON was foul: damp, which made Caroline's neuralgia flare up, and there was so much coal smoke in the air that she and the girls complained they could hardly breathe. Caroline left the hotel only to shop for August, Jr.'s Christmas box and to have dinner with the Rothschilds at Gunnersbury Park. Jeannie, who rarely attended grown-up functions, was delighted with the party. Frederika was less so. She sat between two old men, each at least seventy, she estimated, who talked nothing but politics. One of them asked if Frederika had been for Greeley or Grant and if she had expected Grant to be elected by such a great majority.

"I answered in my grandest style," she told August, Jr.—yes, she had expected Grant to win by such a great majority—"but I spoke very low, for I did not wish Perry or Mamma to hear and laugh at me."

One of the unmarried Rothschilds took a fancy to Frederika, who was flattered but cautious; she felt herself too young for entanglements. Caroline pointed out that the suitor was attractive with his dark hair, dark eyes, stylish beard and moustache, looking altogether "like one of the persuasion, as the Rothschilds call themselves."

The younger children remained in London with their governess. They got a trip to the zoo as compensation. August also stayed in town to dine with some friends whom he enjoyed more than the Rothschilds.

Most of the older Belmonts went on a fox hunt. Oliver was disappointed because he did not go; Frederika was disappointed because she did. August and Perry took day trips to examine schools for Oliver, who finally was enrolled in a suitable place. Perry remained in London. August, Caroline, Raymond, and the girls crossed the Channel to Paris, which despite the French defeat in the Franco-Prussian War, the battle of the Commune, and the new Third Republic did not seem strikingly different from what it had been on their last visit. They settled in their old hotel, the Liverpool. Jane Perry, Belle and George Tiffany, and their family were around the corner on the Rue St.-Honoré. And many of the Belmonts' expatriate friends were in town.

Oliver came to Paris for Christmas. He was concerned that his English education was not preparing him properly in American history, American geography, and American economics. Just before the Belmonts had left the United States Rodgers had told August that the Sixth Congressional District could send a boy to Annapolis after March 1874; and Oliver did not want to miss his opportunity. But he seemed to be doing well enough; and he was enjoying himself at school, on trips to Devon, and on visits to a local squire's estate.

"I wish there was but half the game in the Nursery that there is here," Oliver said.

The squire had invited Oliver to hunt with him. Although Oliver was not on horseback, he was "up at the death and was very much pleased as it was the first time I had ever seen a fox killed. As soon as the dogs had caught the fox, the hunter wound his whip around the fox's tail and pulled it off, as it comes off better when the animal is alive."

The family missed Perry, who chose to stay in England, and August, Jr., who turned down an invitation to pass the holidays in Paris or with relatives in Morristown, New Jersey, preferring both the freedom and the bittersweet sensation of spending Christmas alone.

Nevertheless the family had a good time. Frederika and Jeannie each received pearl necklaces and diamond earrings. The Belmonts visited American friends and admired their tree and had a quiet family dinner at the Tiffanys'. Jane Perry was looking very good for a woman who had spent the last several years preparing for her death.

Jane Perry and the Tiffanys must have remarked on the changes in the Belmont children. Frederika at eighteen was a graceful and lovely Rapunzel: her hair, when not bound, reached her waist. She was waiting for some prince to ask her to let it down. Like her father she had strong features and a long jaw, qualities that combined with her direct gaze gave her a probing, pleasantly challenging look. Jeannie, sixteen and a half now, was softer. Her hair was also long, but her face was rounder, her eyes more Oriental, her cheekbones higher. Like her mother she seemed a little dreamy, as though she spent her life trying to keep from waking.

Oliver at fourteen looked like Perry at the same age and shared with Frederika the clearly defined features of their father. Raymond, who was nine years old, looked like August, Jr., and Caroline. Because she was so used to thinking of him as the baby, Caroline was shocked to see how grown up Raymond seemed compared to her sister's children.

Oliver spent most of his holidays studying French. Jeannie was taking riding in the Bois de Boulogne, which she thought great fun. It consoled her for not being allowed to go to dancing parties like her sister. In Paris, Frederika in her first low-necked gown was as proud as though her flesh were a badge she was showing off. Caroline thought the young ladies in Paris's American community tended to be wild and loud. She was glad when they left for Nice.

Jeannie had not wanted to go south. She liked Paris even though she could not join her sister at the parties. She claimed she did not feel she was missing much because, as she told August, Jr., "hardly anyone dances the Boston here." In Nice life was dull, duller than it had been for Jeannie in Paris. There was a ball (at least what the Americans and British in Nice called a ball) for children to which Raymond was invited. Frederika, whom everyone had teased about feeling grand in her low-necked gown, accused Raymond of feeling grand about sending bouquets to not one but two girls with whom he intended to dance. She was right. Raymond was puffed up with pleasure. He was having a good time in Nice, even if his sisters were not.

The Belmonts visited Cannes and went donkey-back into the mountains. If they had no excursion planned they rode along the Promenade des Anglais. Caroline's horse was so lazy she had to use her spurs just to get it to amble. Jeannie's horse had a broken nose. And Frederika's horse was so weak she described it as "skating on all fours." They did not even have a groom to accompany them, "so," Frederika said, "you may imagine how very fine we look."

Frederika's only pleasures were others' infatuations. She asked August, Jr., if he had sent an anonymous gift to a friend of hers in the United States. She knew he admired her. And she followed the courtship of one of her cousins and a Stuyvesant girl, who was very much in love but "looks so delicate people say she will not live long," the ingredients for a romantic tragedy.

August, too, was ferreting out small pleasures, which he did with the same thoroughness and intensity that he brought to everything. But the stay abroad was less than fulfilling; he rediscovered that traveler's truth: the farther you go from home, the smaller your world becomes. They had many friends and acquaintances in Europe; but away from New York he was not very involved in business, society, or politics—which after all was why they had crossed the Atlantic. To get away. But August seemed to hear in the word *vacation* the echo of the word *vacate*. And behind that an even softer suggestion of the word *vacant*. On vacation, he felt as though he had abandoned something; he felt empty.

Looking at art filled him. He looked at a lot of art. And jewels. And he bought art and jewels for his collections. Although he had arranged his business affairs so he could ignore them while he was in Europe, he could not resist keeping track of the price of gold or agreeing to a few minor speculations, such as investing $84,000 in Hoboken, New Jersey, water bonds, just enough to make the transaction interesting. Socially he received all the courtesy of a noble exile. He was, for example, made an honorary member of the English Jockey Club. And he regularly sent telegrams to leading Democrats; he had nourished himself on politics for so long he found it impossible not to take a taste every so often.

But the taste was often bitter. As on every other extended trip abroad, August was accused of betraying by his absence the country that had given him so much. Typical of the tales current in New York was one that surfaced in a weekly magazine claiming that August, "a wealthy foreigner of Jewish extraction," had returned to Europe to help the Rothschilds make money. Although he had been an American citizen for about two-thirds of his life, he was still "a foreigner" to many of his bitter countrymen. The nation that supposedly claimed his allegiance was not a European state but a transnational, shadow government. August—his enemies claimed—was a loyal subject of Capital. Jewish Capital.

From Nice the Belmonts went to Pau, where Jane Perry and the Tiffanys were staying. From Pau they went back to Paris. Apparently alone, August made a quick trip to Alzey, where, as he had once before, he picked flowers from the graves of his parents. Simon had been seventy years old when he died. August was sixty.

Socially August, Jr., had successfully negotiated his second year at Harvard. He went to an assembly ball at the Atlantic House at Newport, joined the Hasty Pudding Club and the Porcellian, and like his father and older brother drew around himself a group of high-living friends who continually played practical jokes on each other. August, Jr., for example, sent one of them a check for twelve and a half cents.

"I have not cashed it yet," his friend replied, "but am waiting until I get a grudge against some bank and am then going to present it and bust the whole concern."

Academically, he was again in trouble. He had passed enough of his examination at the end of his sophomore year to get promoted, but he had entered the junior class with the understanding that he would finish some work he had left undone. Throughout the fall and early winter he had been too busy to do any of the make-up reading. He missed prayers and recitations and, by the beginning of 1873, was doing poorly in rhetoric and was in danger of failing French.

Fearing the humiliation of failure more than that of quitting, August, Jr., announced that he wanted to withdraw from college.

Since August believed that "a man without profession or occupation in our country has a most miserable existence," he did not approve of his son's withdrawing from school, nor would he allow it.

Perry spent the winter and spring of 1873 in London, riding every day on one of Alfred Rothschild's horses, listening to Prime Minister William Gladstone speak at two in the morning to Parliament, dining with Benjamin Disraeli, who told him, "I do not think we have as many orators as there are in the American Senate and House . . . ," and checking up on the progress of the Belmont Stakes trophy his father had asked him to have made.

"The first thing I noticed," Perry said about the model for the trophy, "was that the two animals were almost on a level and were going in precisely the same direction. This gave the group a rather tame appearance, and the two tails and hind-legs did not look well either from the side or from behind. The horse was much heavier than a mustang. The buffalo's nose was turned up, which gave the head a light appearance. The Indian's profile was very good, but his face was too narrow. He had not the usual high cheekbones."

Perry could bring to his criticism a knowledgeable eye for art and, perhaps more importantly, accurate firsthand observations about life in the western United States.

"The horse was raised a little, and then tipped up behind and turned so that his forelegs are nearer the buffalo than his hindquarters," Perry continued, describing the changes that were made at his suggestion. "His hind-legs have been drawn in, and his fore-legs stretched out, so that he is not exactly in the same stride as the buffalo; before, he was. This makes the horse take part in the hunt, which is perfectly natural, as the horses are trained for such difficult work, and are not guided during the act of using the spear."

Perry was a combination of city sophisticate and outdoorsman. He could talk about Indians and shooting with the same casual authority he brought to discussing fashion, theater, and wine. Understandably he was much in demand at London dinners.

In the summer he went to the races and stayed on James Gordon Bennett, Jr.'s yacht, the *Sappho*, at Cowes. He enjoyed Bennett's wildness and shared with him a passion for pigeon-shooting and an interest in polo, which had been introduced in England in 1869. They decided to make a dash across the Channel for Deauville. Bennett gave the orders to get ready to sail and then, with Perry and some other friends, went to look in on a yacht club ball. By the time they got back to the *Sappho* the crew, angry at having been kept waiting, were mutinous. Bennett handled the situation so well that years later Perry still recalled with admiration his control of the sailors.

Perry admired all exercise of will and intellectual force, which is why he had chosen to attend the University of Berlin. He wanted to discipline his mind the same way that when he went on shooting trips he disciplined his body.

In the fall he arrived in Berlin, almost a month before classes were about to begin. The city struck him, despite its magnificence, as dull. Berliners dined at four or five in the afternoon, which was an odd, in-between hour neither early enough for a decent midday meal nor late enough for a festive evening one. The theaters all closed at nine-thirty at night. Perry went to bed not much later, a change in schedule he did not find unpleasant.

His rooms at 68 Unter den Linden were comfortable, a legacy passed down from one Harvard graduate to another for the past ten years. Perry woke early, walked in the Tiergarten, arranged to take lessons in fencing and in German language, history, and law, the latter two from an ancient professor who in his pedantry and decrepitude seemed a caricature of what Perry had expected a German professor to be like.

Perry decided to travel while waiting for classes to start. In Prague he went to the Thun palace to deliver a letter of introduction his father had written for him to one of the Thuns. Unfortunately Perry did not know which one.

An old one, he awkwardly explained.

The Thun in residence was not old, he was told.

As Perry left the palace he met a young man, Franz Thun (who

Perry did not know was the nephew of the man he sought, a count whom August had met in New York).

Perry explained his predicament.

Thun took the letter but, saying that he did not want to read someone else's mail, did not open it. He invited Perry into the palace for a smoke. Perhaps they could figure out which Thun Perry wanted. His father, Frederick Thun, had been minister to Holland, but that was before the Belmonts had come to The Hague. His uncle Oswald Thun had been in America two years ago, but Perry did not think Oswald was the man he wanted. After climbing among the branches of the Thun family tree, they dropped back to earth.

Why was Perry in Prague? Thun wanted to know.

Perry looked at his host, who obviously had come in from shooting —which is what Perry had come to Prague to do; what in fact August's unopened letter was asking the Thuns to help Perry do. The Thuns, like bird dogs, could point out where game was to be found. But because Thun was dressed for shooting, Perry felt it would seem spur-of-the-moment, not sincere, to admit that was what he had come for.

He was on his way from Berlin, where he was studying, to Vienna, Perry said.

Thun said he was also about to leave Prague. He was going to Moravia to go shooting.

The subject had been broached.

Perry offhandedly mentioned that he enjoyed the same sport.

Thun offered to give Perry letters of introduction to a cousin, Count Bruhl, who lived in Berlin and could help Perry find a horse and introduce him into the right circles there. There was good boar hunting in the Grunewald.

Perry thanked him.

Thun asked if Perry would like to join him at the theater. They parted accidental friends.

Perry reached Vienna in mid-October. As in Prague he had a letter of introduction from his father, this one to American Minister John Jay, who took Perry to the opera, gave him dinner, and, not being a sportsman himself, found someone with whom Perry could go hunting.

Perry thanked him but explained that he wanted to go shooting, which was less formal. To hunt he would need a servant, horse, and outfit, which would involve trouble and expense to obtain.

Perry stayed with a college friend, Frederick Shattuck, who was attending the university in Vienna.

"We dine, eight or ten together," Perry told his father, "very well, cheaply, and in the German fashion," clinking beer steins and singing songs.

At an art exhibition Perry stopped his friend in front of a pair of bronze ducks.

"Shattuck," he said, "there's something I'd like to have."

"Well—you've got it," Shattuck said, showing Perry the card, which noted that the ducks had been sold to a Mr. Belmont.

While passing through Vienna in June, August had bought them. Perry was delighted to discover proof that he and his father shared the same taste in art.

During this short vacation Perry also visited Pau, where he did have a chance not to shoot but to hunt. Since he was the guest of his cousin, hunting was not the trouble it would have been in Vienna. He returned to Berlin with the brush, the fox's tail, a trophy he modestly claimed he did not deserve but of which he was proud.

Bouillon and two eggs for breakfast. From nine to ten o'clock, lectures. Fencing, strolls about town, studying in the afternoon. From four to six o'clock in the evening, four times a week, private tutorials. Pumpernickel, fish, and beer for supper at eight o'clock. An occasional visit to the theater or opera. Early bed.

"I never was more fit," Perry thought. "I like and shall continue to lead this regular life."

"I never go out of my way to find amusement or society," he told his father; "but, when anything turns up, I don't hesitate to accept an invitation, provided I think it worth the time I have to give up. This perfect independence is very pleasant."

With his roommate, a boyhood friend, Neilson Winthrop, he discussed Hegel and Mommsen, philosophy and history, dialectics and Bismarck's policies. Winthrop had Perry read Henry James's "A Passionate Pilgrim," which two years earlier had been published in *The Atlantic* and which would not be available in James's first book of tales for another two years.

"The passion for indulging in such atavistic illusions," Perry later wrote about the story, "often ends in the discovery that the 'pilgrim' does not belong by origin to the ruling class, but, on the contrary, reverts to a situation inferior to that which he holds in his native country. It was difficult for me to imagine that it had been written by the calm, contented personality that very quiet, slight, good-looking man, older than me," whom he knew only as the brother of William James.

Perry was living the somewhat Bohemian life of a student merchant-prince.

Through Count Bruhl, Perry met an officer who was selling all his possessions. Ruined by gambling, drink, women? Perry did not inquire. His intelligence was less interested in cause than effect. Curiosity could lead to compassion; and compassion, like a fire that burns its own flame for fuel, was endless. There were hundreds of ruined men in Berlin.

From the bankrupt officer Perry bought a horse, Sarolta, a three-quarter-bred mare that was, Perry said, "an excellent jumper, very fast, and a very good hunter."

Bruhl became a close friend and invited Perry frequently to regimental dinners (presumably with officers who were not ruined), sponsored him at a private club, the Riding School, and took him to the Royal Hunt, where he introduced Perry to Prince Carl, the emperor's brother. Speaking in English as a courtesy to Perry, the prince asked about both America and Perry's hunting experience, the first question as polite as the second was passionate. When Perry told him he had been on a stag hunt in England, the prince became animated. He wanted to know all the details. He told Perry that having once broken his leg, he now took few risks. And he invited Perry to accompany him on shortcuts, a royal prerogative, through the woods.

"All this time [while the Prince was talking to Perry], the whole Hunt was waiting and looking on," Perry said; "and I felt in rather a conspicuous position."

The count told Perry that he had been favored; he should accept the prince's invitation to ride the shortcuts.

The Grünewald was thickly wooded. As they rode along, often quite fast, sunlight flickered on and off through the branches of the trees. The breeze was sweet with the smell of pines. There was the thudding of the horses' hooves, the baying of the dogs. Ride carefully, Perry was told; two weeks ago someone had been killed in the Hunt. But Perry was used to a good pace; he kept near the prince; and the prince was very careful. After an hour they found the hounds snapping and growling, keeping a boar at bay. The whips cleared off the dogs.

"Two members of the Hunt held the boar by a hind-leg," Perry told his father; "and the Prince dismounted and stuck him with a long hunting knife. Whoever comes in at the death takes off his right glove and receives a small branch of pine-tree, and puts it in his hat. I brought mine home and hung it on my brush."

A few days later, riding in the Tiergarten, Perry met the prince, who was on his way to the Hunt. Perry doffed his hat. The prince beckoned to him and when Perry approached asked if he was again going to join them.

With his permission, Perry said, he would.

They rode together to where the Hunt, about eighty people, were waiting.

"As I was the only person who hadn't a red coat and top boots and came in such a singular way," Perry said, "all these people seemed to think I must be somebody of importance," an impression strengthened when the prince called out as Perry politely was losing himself in the crowd.

Perry, he said, must always ride with them.

Perry thus was made a Member of the Hunt. He was given a copy of the rules. As a result, Perry explained to his father, "I was obliged to go to the tailor to order myself a red coat. Unfortunately, it can only be worn at the Royal Hunt, as it is of a peculiar cut. It has made a rather unexpected hole in my pocket. I had also to buy some white gloves and blue and white cravats. On Friday, I appeared in all my glory."

Until the first frost, every Tuesday and Friday at eleven-thirty in the morning Perry rode the five or six miles from his stable near his rooms through the Tiergarten to the Grünewald and the Hunt. Usually he returned home by four in the afternoon. On one occasion the boar ran into a lake and as the men and dogs circled on shore kept swimming from side to side. After the sun set the boar took refuge in some tall reeds and got away. One of Perry's friends had been thrown from his horse against a tree. Everyone straggled off in the dark.

At a party given by the American secretary of state's son, who was at that time in Berlin, it was quietly proposed that the American minister at Berlin, George Bancroft, present Perry at Court. Perry was surprised by the offer. Bancroft had a reputation of presenting only leading statesmen and generals. But he was an old and close friend of Perry's parents and, in fact, was the one who had suggested that Perry spend a year studying in Berlin. For Perry he would cheerfully break his rule.

Perry asked if his roommate might also be presented. He did not want Winthrop to feel snubbed.

Find out—Perry was told—if Winthrop's father ever held any diplomatic or governmental post.

When Perry got back to his rooms, he probed Winthrop with the delicacy of a diner boning a fish. He found little meat.

Winthrop said his father was innocent of diplomacy or politics.

Nevertheless, as a favor to Perry, Bancroft, perhaps less cheerfully than in Perry's case, broke his rule for a second time. He asked Perry that he wished "nothing said about it as there are a number of Americans here," and he did not want them shoaling around his office demanding introductions at court for themselves, their families, or their friends.

Perry was pleased. If his roommate had not been presented he would have felt obliged to turn down the offer himself. And he wanted to be introduced at court so he could go to the balls to which as a result he would be invited.

"All the diplomatic corps and the strangers were ushered into a long, narrow room," Perry wrote, "where we were arranged in a circle by the Master of Ceremonies. After we had been standing, waiting for about an hour, the Empress came and passed along the whole circle, speaking to everyone in turn; and, as she often had a great deal to say to certain individuals, this lasted a very long time. She only said a few words to me, asking if I did not find many of my countrymen here."

Perry was repelled and attracted by the court. He was not used to feeling outclassed and yet was honored by the attentions paid to him by the imperial family. And he found the diversity and splendor of the uniforms as interesting and enjoyable as if he were wandering through an aviary examining the spectacular plumage.

Soon his regular habits had been subject to so many exceptions (which he excused by saying he deserved the distraction because he was being so regular) that he had fallen into a schedule similar to the one he had been used to in Cambridge: receptions and parties and balls three and four times a week, one week going out to balls six nights in a row.

He was interested to see how different balls were in Berlin and Paris, each reflecting the national temperament. The German version was layered like a parfait, each social level separated from the one above and below it. The French version was mixed like a tutti-frutti, everyone no matter what their rank mingling comparatively freely. Perry thought the Austrian embassy in Berlin gave the most attractive ball, although he was amused by the Austrian ambassador, who trying to act English "stands in the middle of the room," Perry said, "with his hands in his pockets and his legs stretched apart, scarcely speaking to anybody." The French ambassador, who felt uncomfortable in Berlin so soon after the Franco-Prussian War, told Perry he would much rather be a student in Germany than a diplomat and jokingly offered to change places.

At another ball a Prussian whom Perry had met in America two years earlier asked him if there were in his country any houses as magnificent and large as the one they were in—which truly was magnificent and large.

He met Bismarck and Count von Moltke—and so many other great men that he could further justify his social life by viewing it as a lesson in contemporary German history.

What were lost, however, were not just the regular habits that had made Perry feel so intellectually and physically fit but also the exemption from obligations of socializing that had made his first weeks in Berlin so free.

𝒩 *CHAPTER FORTY-FOUR* 𝒩

EVER SINCE JEANNIE had been an infant she had been plagued by stomach troubles, which in 1873 suddenly got worse. The pain ramified, its branches growing inside of her as sharp as thorns. To ease her the doctors prescribed increasing doses of morphine. Because her illness had become so severe August and Caroline took her and the other younger children to Cowes, where during the summer of 1873 they saw Perry while he was living on Bennett's boat. The season was gay. The czarevitch and czarevna were visiting. There were many parties. The Jerome family was there. But balls and friends could not help, and the climate did not help—or did not help enough. In the fall August, Caroline, Frederika, Jeannie, Oliver, and Raymond returned to the United States.

For the third time in his life August stepped off the boat in New York to find the country in a financial panic.

Inflation, scandals (including the Crédit Mobilier frauds, in which Grant's administration had been implicated), a fall in grain prices, heavy indebtedness to European capitalists (foreign investment in American railroads had more than quintupled in the past twenty years), and the shock waves from panics in Berlin and Vienna conspired to shake the American economy. Business was so bad in 1873 that Cornelius Vanderbilt, using a medium, tried to get advice from the ghost of Jim Fisk.

Late in August a few unimportant railroads had been financially derailed. The stock market took a slight, not apparently significant dip as though it were nodding in acknowledgment. On September 8 the New York Warehouse & Security Company went bankrupt as a result, they said, of defaults by a certain railroad to which they had lent money. This was the first serious tremor. Like men who hear of a friend being pick-pocketed and as a result touch their own wallets, bankers all over New York started checking on their own railroad investments. Some, like Daniel Drew, called in loans. The following days were quiet. Then Drew's company suspended operations. The Canada Southern Railroad could not repay the $1 million he had loaned it. The following week the tremors became rumbles and the rumbles became an economic earthquake: Wall Street yawned and swallowed dozens of businesses, including Jay Cooke & Company, one of the most powerful in the country. Before the crisis was over the Street would be transformed, many of the old regulars gone.

"I had been wonderfully blest in making money," Drew said after his bankruptcy. "I got to be a millionaire before I knowed it hardly. I was always pretty lucky till lately. I didn't think I could ever lose money extensively. I was ambitious of making a great fortune, like Vanderbilt, and I tried every way I knew, but got caught at last."

Years later when he died his estate—a watch-and-chain and a seal-skin coat, each worth $150, $100 worth of clothes, and some religious books—would add up to about $500.

The crash even affected the Belmont Clique. Henry Clews went bankrupt. And Leonard Jerome, after a dinner he had given for some friends, excused himself for reading aloud a telegram he had received and read to himself earlier in the evening; "but, gentlemen," he said, "it is a message in which you are all interested. The bottom has fallen out of stocks, and I am a ruined man. But your dinner is paid for, and I didn't want to disturb you while you were eating it."

The guests bolted to look after their own fortunes. Jerome stayed at the table alone with the telegram.

August resigned from the governorship of all his clubs to attend to business.

"I have been more careful and conservative than most of my neighbors," he said; "and the nature of my business does not expose me, in ordinary times, to the risks to which they are subjected. With all this I have met with greater losses, not to count those which I am almost sure to suffer yet, than I have ever known in the many years of my mercantile experience. My money is locked up in a manner, which I never thought it could possibly become; and, while I hope to be able to weather the storm, I find that my safety depends upon my remaining quietly in port, until we have again fine weather, which I fear will not come for a long while. In other words, I have to curtail my business to a point, which renders all profits impossible, hold onto what property I have left, and retrench my expenditure." .

Two weeks later August was even more gloomy.

"Nobody pays," he complained.

If August had not called in so many loans and double-whipped the loose ends of his affairs before going to Europe, he might have been ruined. Instead he was merely inconvenienced. Despite his protestations he—unlike Clews and Jerome—survived the crash quite well, well enough so that within a year he did not feel too pinched to donate $200,000 to an Episcopal church. But had lost enough to make him skittish, and he was afraid the stock market might plunge again. Even once the prices stabilized he did not expect the stock market to be healthy for a long time.

"Everything looks dark," he thought; "and I fear we are entering upon a period of financial embarrassment, both public and private, of a most serious and complicated nature. What we have suffered with the last weeks is only the beginning of the end. The evil has not yet reached the merchants, manufacturers, and mechanics, but their turn must soon come. With it, you will see a still greater shrinking in the value of all kind of personal property."

August was right.

From 1873 to 1878 there were 414 bank suspensions. During those six years business suffered a 32 percent decline. The crisis had ended; the depression had just begun.

The Flash Age was over.

The crash caught Manton Marble short. He turned to August for help. He needed to pay off debts and wanted to expand the *New York World* by getting a new Hoe press that, he explained, "prints *both* sides of *2* sheets at once." It cost only $25,000. He also needed new type. A few other things. The *World* had to expand if it was to compete with *The New York Times, Herald,* and *Tribune* and be effective in supporting the Democratic party in the 1876 presidential election.

August was not prepared to admit he was interested in any more presidential elections. His money was tied up. He told Marble that he even had turned down a relative who had asked for a loan.

Marble tried other approaches.

Friendship: "It would have seemed like ingratitude to you, or at least like infidelity, not to tell my serious needs to you first," he wrote to August. "And that was why I finally asked you, 'What shall I do?' Not to urge what you had declined. I suppose you smile that I put so much emotion into such relations. You're such a cold-blooded and cynical cuss; and it's an everyday affair with you to be on the creditor side, both in the money aspect where you don't care how people feel and in the personal aspect where you can't know how they feel."

Flattery: Marble explained he had written to August about his financial problems, "because my publisher came upon me and said the Devil had swallowed every dollar in town. Naturally, I thought you the most likely to have beaten the tough old fiend."

In a letter that grimly described his current difficulties, August insisted he was not in a position to help.

"I have great confidence in your solvency in spite of your writing me such a beastly blue letter," Marble told August; and as though to prove that he was a good risk, someone who floated when everyone else was sinking, Marble thanked August for a previous loan (perhaps the $25,000 one that August had extended the previous spring) "which enabled me to make my first and last patent speculation at a profit of $11,200. If you don't get money from your present debtors, I suppose you'll take thanks from your past debtors, won't you, my dear crosspatch?"

During this negotiation August sent Marble a scarf pin that he had picked up in Paris and that was meant to rebuke and flatter Marble, to remind him that whatever might happen in their business relations they still were good friends. So as not to embarrass Marble with the sincerity of his affection, August jokingly claimed that he was sending the pin not just as a token of esteem but also "to inspire you with a little editorial pity when you feel most savage" against any enemies.

"It makes life better worth living that such a friend as you are, shares it," Marble told August. "You are so thoughtful in the absence, which makes most men thoughtless, so staunch in all tight places, so persistent in hates, so obstinate in likings, and so damned unreasonable generally. Tennyson's brook, if it hadn't been a babbling thing would have sung:

The men may come, the women may go,
The Belmont stands forever. . . .

Well! it does my heart good like sunshine that you thought of me in Paris, even tho' you brought away this malicious pin to prick the balloon of my pride with. I shall wear it as a saint does a hair-shirt, but it will never mortify the editor so much as it will make proud the friend."

August relented—as he usually did with Marble. He would not give Marble money to buy a press or type; he thought it would be foolish for Marble to extend himself in the current situation. But he would help Marble pay off his debts.

"By the beginning of December," August said, "I have some money of my own, disconnected from the firm, coming in; and, if you can get the bank to wait until then, I have no doubt that I shall be able to assist you by that time."

As a businessman August would not risk lending anyone money in troubled times; as a friend he would come to the rescue with money from his own pocket.

"You cannot imagine the utter prostration of all business," August wrote to August, Jr., who wanted to quit Harvard and enter his father's firm. Things were so bad, August said, that if the economy did not improve, "I am *determined* to give up entirely." So, "why not therefore wait for twelve months to see what events will bring. With the revolution of opinions and politics a good deal of change should occur in that time."

August, Jr., unhappily complied. His year was a disaster. Although the precise nature of his failure is unclear, there is no doubt that he was academically nearly bankrupt. His father talked of suspension, but there is a notation in the school's faculty record that he withdrew in October. However, since the record further reports that in November, supposedly after he had withdrawn, he missed eleven recitations, he evidently had not dropped or been kicked out. It is possible that since August, Jr., would not graduate until 1875, Harvard agreed that he could remain at school if he repeated his junior year—which is evidently what he did.

He must have felt humiliated. From his childhood he had hated being grouped with anyone younger than himself. Years before, he had asked his parents to make sure they invited only children his age or older to a party; and more recently he had said he would rather miss two years of Harvard than enter a class behind his friends. No wonder he wanted to quit school.

As usual when his grades were bearish, his expenses were bullish. Between September and March his monthly expenditure increased from about $300 to $600. In fact, in the last two and a half months of that period he spent three-quarters of a year's allowance. Because his parents had bought him a new wardrobe in Europe, they could not understand where the money was going. Was he gambling? August, Jr., assured them he was not.

He was living luxuriously. He went into Boston at least once a week in a hired coach, treated friends to dinners, haunted theaters, and attended balls not just in Boston and Cambridge (at one of which he danced with Longfellow's daughters), but also in such suburbs as Jamaica Plains. What he lacked in systematic indulgence, he made up in impulsiveness. After a successful interview with the dean of faculty, E. W. Gurney, about his status at Harvard, August, Jr., withdrew "$500 to celebrate the occasion."

Trying to put a brake on his son's prodigality, August pleaded not poverty but reduced circumstances.

"I have written to you for the last five months," he said, "telling you how much money I lost by the panic and how bad and unprofitable my business is; and I can really not understand that you should have, in the face of all this, spent so much money. I cannot leave my children large fortunes," continued August. He was being not honest but true to his apprehensions. As a result he sounded more than ever like Simon used to. "If you *have once got into* habits of extravagance, you will have, when you manage your own fortune and the little which I shall be able to leave you, nothing but trouble and irritation."

During August's school days Simon's harping on how poor he was had seemed to be closefistedness. Now that he had sons of his own, August understood the necessity of deemphasizing wealth. He did not want August, Jr., to relax into indolence from feeling secure about his inheritance. He wanted his son to be a man-of-affairs as well as a man-about-town.

In trying to dramatize the point August went to extremes. One of August, Jr.'s two hunting dogs, Bob, was a flop.

"The best thing you can do is to sell him for whatever he will fetch," August said. "He is not worth the expense of his feed, and we have more dogs already than we want."

But since Bob would not fetch any better on the market—at most $50—than he did in the fields, August suggested that his son might trade him to a dog trainer for lessons for another dog, Guy, an exchange that would save a little, but very little, money.

August was not as good as Simon had been at being tight.

August, Jr., wrote that, because he was badly out of practice in driving a sleigh, "I almost ran into one man, and then almost upset the sleigh," while maneuvering through the heavy traffic. August at once told his son to buy a "reliable horse," one that would not shy, and increased his son's allowance by $100 to cover the expense.

"I pray and entreat you, my darling boy, to be careful," he said.

Soon afterward August again increased his son's allowance, which in seven months had jumped from $2,400 to $3,000 a year. And for August, Jr.'s twenty-first birthday August gave him an expensive stickpin. Often August's pleas for frugality seemed to be heralds of indulgence. All he asked in return was that August, Jr., never go into debt, keep complete accounts (which August, Jr., again had been failing to do), and study hard.

"I can only repeat what I have preached so incessantly," August said; "this is your last chance."

August did not want to order or forbid his son to do things. August, Jr., was too old for that.

"I cannot command," he said, "only advise."

But his advice was emphatic, and he lobbied furiously against what he saw as mistakes in judgment, as when August, Jr., wanted to take some time off to visit New York. Although he was so pressed that he had to dictate a letter to his son, August could not resist adding a postscript longer than the main text, urging August, Jr., not to leave school even for a day.

August, Jr.'s behavior improved. In November he missed eleven recitations. The same in December. By February he was getting to all his classes; although, for consistency, he was tardy eleven times. In March he was not late even once. But his previous record was so poor that he was in danger of being suspended.

"It is of the utmost importance that you should be spared this disgrace a second time," August said. "I *have pledged* myself to Gurney and Child that you will do your best hereafter and merit their indulgence if they will extend it to you."

But giving his word was not enough. His son had to honor it. And hardest of all August, Jr., had to convince Gurney that he would honor it—even if it meant going to him with, as his father suggested, "urgent personal entreaties."

August, Jr., was not suspended. But he felt as bad that people were giving him another chance as he would have if they had written him off. He did not feel he deserved anyone's good opinion. He believed himself to be the Belmont Black Sheep.

"Such ideas are foolish and wicked," August told his son. "You have in your own hands still to retrieve the past; and certainly, whatever your shortcomings have been, we all love you as dearly as ever."

Although August tried to discipline August, Jr., with love, on one occasion anxieties overwhelmed him and he could not hide his pain.

"You will never know the anguish which your mother and I have suffered all this week," he told August, Jr. "I only hope when you will have children that you will never have to undergo what we are suffering, first by the painful and protracted illness of Jeannie and now by your failure."

Jeannie alternated between remissions and relapses so alarming that August and Caroline canceled parties. Soon they did not even plan parties. Caroline and Frederika stayed constantly by her bedside.

"I can hardly get Caroline to take a drive of half an hour to get a little fresh air," August said. "Rica has not been out though she had invitations for dinners and parties everyday. She does not mean to go until Jeannie is decidedly better."

Confined to her bed, Jeannie moped. To cheer her August asked Marble to sign Jeannie's autograph book (he wrote her a poem) and circulate it among "the literary swells of your acquaintance." August, Jr., wrote her funny letters, in one of which he went on at length about how ragged his sheets were. While puffing on a cigar his father had sent him, he sketched a cartoon of a sleeping figure draped with shreds.

Even when something pleased her Jeannie sometimes found it hard to focus on her amusement. She was too drugged to be always lucid. The inflammation in her stomach and intestines hurt her—especially on the right side—as badly as if she had swallowed hundreds of sharpened diamonds. Three times a day the doctors injected her with morphine.

"I feel more uneasy about her than I dare show," August admitted to August, Jr.

The only nourishment she was allowed was milk, four ounces every three hours. Soon she tripled her dose. She was drinking—and keeping down—three quarts a day. Her spasms came less often. She improved, although the morphine shots continued.

As she got better she developed obsessions. August, Jr., wrote a letter to a Mr. Pratt and by mistake sent it home to 109 Fifth Avenue. Jeannie so strongly insisted that her father return it at once to his son that August mailed it without enclosing a note. When August, Jr., got the letter back without any word of explanation from his father, he took it as a reproach; his father—he thought—was damning him with silence for having been careless enough to misaddress a letter. Because of his academic failures August, Jr., felt so bad about himself that he seemed to think he merited the worst punishment for the most innocent lapse. August apologized to his son; he would have jotted something if it had not been for Jeannie, whose "peculiar ways" were "very much increased by her illness."

About the same time Jeannie determined to leave home. She would not be swayed.

"She says the noise of people coming in and going out of the house disturbs her sleep," August told August, Jr. "Poor thing, she is very good and sweet, but her sufferings have made her morbid on some points, so it was necessary to yield to her, as it is the only chance for her recovery. We have taken some rooms for her in a very good boarding house near her doctor, and Aunt Ann is good and kind enough to stay with her."

At last the family convinced Jeannie to go with them to Newport. Instead of "sitting patiently with dowagers" while Jeannie danced, as August had expected they would that year, he and Caroline sat late into the night by Jeannie's bed watching, helpless and heartsick, as spasms of pain furrowed their sleeping daughter's forehead.

Jeannie's pain was intensified by distance. Perry could not see her as she twisted on the bed, but his imagination often provided him with even more horrible images. As for other family news, he indulged in big-brotherly concern for August, Jr., and was proud of Raymond, who ever since his success at Nice, where his bouquets had made a hit, had become a charmer.

"My nieces tell me that Dolly's manners and behavior won their hearts," Marble had written to the family.

Perry increased his hours of work to balance the time he spent at play, but no matter how many lectures he added he always seemed to thumb the scale in favor of parties. He was asked to join a club, which he readily did, since he detested eating at restaurants or being dependent upon invitations for dinner. He often rode with Bancroft, who became voluble on horseback, as though his intellect not his mount were galloping. Rumors that Bancroft would be made secretary of state in Hamilton Fish's place ballooned up through the American community in Berlin and burst. Perry studied harmony, a final assault on music to see "if I have really any talent for it." He battered on the piano as though he were trying to break down a door of sound. He did have talent, and he certainly had enthusiasm. He thought about his future (he had decided to go to Columbia Law School when he reached home) and his politics.

"It really looks as if at last the Western people are showing themselves in their true colors," he told his father. "They believe that the Eastern men and especially those living in large cities are constantly attempting to hinder the growth of the 'Great West,' and whenever anything goes wrong out there all the fault is in other people."

The West was suffering from economic dislocations as a result of the recent crash, but Perry refused to believe what certain Westerners were claiming: that Easterners were alone responsible. The country was too well-knit for anyone to be able to find the seams separating one section from the other. The West was an extension of the East, not autonomous. And since, as Perry believed, Americans were basically an agrarian people, the West was where a new class would develop: educated farmers, who as a group "may do something to improve our social condition," all over the country, even if "in the process we will be obliged to go through a good many disagreeable stages." But if Perry had to take a side in a sectional struggle, he knew without hesitation where his allegiance lay. Despite his romance with the West he would go along with the East.

As the end of the school year approached, Perry became "terribly impatient to begin to live at home, which," he thought, "is the only way of really living at all." He bought two or three chestfuls of books that could not be found in the United States; sold his horse and scouted out others for his father's racing stable; and booked passage on the same steamer on which his grandmother and the Tiffanys were sailing to the United States.

Just before leaving Berlin he received an odd invitation to a court function. Instead of being announced on a card as usual, it was—as Perry told his mother—"lithographed on an ordinary piece of paper." He had no idea to what he was being invited, but he had been hearing rumors that the emperor was intending to give a grand ball. Because of the emperor's recent illness, Perry thought the ball would "probably be the last he will ever give." Perry was wrong about the emperor's health and intentions. The affair was simply a concert. Perry was disappointed. He had wanted to take his leave of Berlin at a spectacular party.

On his way home Perry stopped in Paris, where he was faced with a problem in etiquette. On his last visit, during the Christmas holidays, he had left cards on James and Alphonse de Rothschild. James did not respond. Alphonse sent his card through the post office. Perry was miffed.

He asked his father what he should do.

August apparently told him not to take the slights to heart.

Perry again left cards on the Rothschilds. He would be polite, even if they were not. After all, he was hardly a stranger to them. But the Rothschilds' feelings toward the Belmonts, although usually affable, would always be veined with resentment toward the office boy who had built his own financial empire in the United States and annoyance that the empire had heirs.

In Paris he met a friend of Jeannie's on the street and learned that she was much better. Perry hoped she soon would be well enough to go into society.

"Jeannie is very original," he thought; "and, if her health becomes really good, she will probably have a great success."

Through letters, he discussed farm affairs and racing with his father. At the Nursery chickens were dying. They had to be replaced, or maybe they should give up raising chickens. August was considering selling His Lordship (he decided not to) and Beverly, the latter of which Perry thought could certainly be gotten rid of, since "I never thought much of him, and besides I hope to ride something with more spirit when I get home."

Fiddlesticks, one of August's better horses, had gotten a forefoot tangled in her halter.

"Nobody was near," August told Perry, "and she struggled probably for an hour, when she was found lying down, completely exhausted. It seems that the effort produced a kind of paralysis of the *visionary nerves* (if that is not right, don't laugh)."

For one of the first times in his life August was deferring to one of his children. *If that is not right. . . .*

"She is completely blind now," August continued. "It makes me almost cry to see the poor thing suffer."

August asked Perry's advice and help on important and trivial matters. In these letters he was throwing an arm around his son's shoulders—

not just out of affection but also so Perry could help bear August's weight. Casually August was shifting decisions and obligations onto Perry, beginning the gradual transfer of family leadership to the eldest son. The letters were tentative, loving, relieved, filled with the kind of vulnerability that sometimes is easier to achieve through the intimacy of distance.

He asked Perry to make sure that one of the Belmont's "old and valued" maids, who had stayed in Europe with Jane Perry and the Tiffanys, had a good cabin on the transatlantic voyage, "a better accommodation than usually given to female servants. You know best how to write and flatter the steamship company, so as to get what we want."

And he asked Perry to pick up some things he had forgotten when he was in Europe: "two nice umbrellas from Briggs in St. James's Street. I want them exactly as the one I have. As I am short and lean a good deal on the umbrella in walking, I want the umbrella small in proportion to the whole stick, which must not be over 2 feet 8½ inches high."

It was obvious where August, Jr., got his precise nature.

"I want a good strong stick," August continued, "but not too stout, particularly in the handle."

If the handle were too fat it would be "awkward for a small hand" like August's to grasp it. Of course, the handle had to have August's name burned into it.

August also asked Perry to buy a "half a dozen sets of three buttons each, white mother-of-pearl for shirt bosoms with the outside buttons small in the shape of pearls and the under ones flat and broad, the same as I am in the habit of wearing. I write for so many as I want to give half of them to a certain brother of yours who is in the habit of borrowing mine and forgets to return them."

"The time of your return is fast approaching," August said in a letter written at the end of spring; "and we all look forward to it with great anticipation."

August was willing to let Perry go to law school, if Perry thought it advisable—although, he said, "I should prefer to have you with me. I am getting old, and we have not been much together since you left for school and college."

CHAPTER FORTY-FIVE

AFTER BRUSHING UP AGAINST so much nobility in Europe, Perry returned very polished. The family reunion was happy. August, Jr., had survived his junior year at college; and except for some trouble in physics he had done well enough not to deserve any more warnings. All spring he neither missed nor was late for a class. Oliver was preparing for the Naval Academy, which he would enter in the fall. Raymond continued to charm girls. Frederika was popular. And Jeannie, still on the milk diet, was getting stronger.

Life was returning to normal, inside and outside the house. In the months since the stock market crash the gold dust had settled. The economy, although not healthy, no longer seemed fatally ill. Henry Clews had reorganized his business. Leonard Jerome again was fighting August for control of the Jockey Club; and August, predicting that "if he succeeds, it will be the ruin of racing in New York," as usual was calling on Manton Marble to support him at Jockey Club meetings.

Some things, however, would never be the same. For years whenever August met the banker Joseph Seligman, whom August considered nouveau, August would say, "Hullo, Seligman," and Seligman, deferring, would say, "Hullo, Mr. Belmont."

Now August said, "Hullo, Seligman," and Seligman replied, "Hullo, Belmont." No *Mister*.

August stared.

To admonish Seligman, August for a while purposely misspelled his name—Selligman, Seligmann, Suligman—whenever he wrote to him.

But Seligman's growing importance as a banker was one of the changes August could not forestall. Seligman began working with August and the Rothschilds more and more frequently; and August began spelling Seligman's name correctly.

Because the economy had stabilized, August did not have to spend such long hours at the office; and because, as he told August, Jr., "I have lost my confidence and zeal in racing," he did not go to the track as often as he used to. He was home a great deal, staying close to Jeannie during the day; at night, suffering from chronic insomnia, he played cards at one of his clubs until dawn. Or blinded by headaches, which were becoming more frequent, he lay in bed tracing the affected areas, a geographer of pain.

In fact, for the first half of 1874 August was so out of the public eye that the press blinked and noticed his absence not with expected relief but with nostalgia.

"What has become of the great Mr. Belmont . . . ?" *The New York Times* asked. "Is he dead, socially and politically, or is he only sleeping, as they say on the tombstones? Or is he confining himself to getting up quarrels at the clubs? Surely Mr. Belmont should make himself seen among his party at this moment. He should give some encouragement to the 'boys.' . . . Mr. Belmont may not be a Jefferson, but he is pretty near all the Democrats have left."

August had been so out of touch that when Admiral Rodgers asked him to help get his son out of a scrape in California, August had to admit to Marble that although he was "willing and anxious to do all I can, I don't know how to go to work. Can you give me any hints as to whom in the House of Representatives it would be best for me to address and what influence can I bring to bear upon them?"

By the end of the summer of 1874 August became more visible. The *New York Tribune* conjured him up in order to damn him all over again for his Civil War activities. Horace Greeley's newspaper accused August of advising the Rothschilds not to invest in the Union. The charge was untrue, untimely, and, considering how August had supported Greeley during the last presidential election, ungenerous.

August denied it. In a public letter he described an 1865 meeting at which James de Rothschild showed the then American minister to Belgium account books that proved the Rothschilds were "one of the earliest and largest investors in our security during the war." He assured his critics that "I hold in my possession letters of the lamented Lincoln, as well as of Messrs. Seward and Chase, all written during and after the war, expressive of their appreciation of my devotion to the Union cause and of my exertions for its success, both at home and abroad. Mr. Thurlow Weed, the friend and advisor of these departed patriots, knows the trust which they placed in me. I challenge you to point out one single act or word of mine during the whole period of our national troubles which was not dictated by patriotism and devotion to our beloved Union. It is late in the day for you to try to stir up prejudices against a political opponent."

Marble chaffed August about his kind words for an administration he had fought so hard against.

August responded by inviting Marble to dinner, promising "not to make you miserable by teasing. Nay, I will go further: I will do penance for all my past sins in that line, and moreover repent in sack and ash clothes for having spoken of the lamented Lincoln (whose death was the greatest misfortune that has befallen the South since the war)"—Lincoln's plans for Reconstruction were far less Draconian than those enacted after his assassination—"of Chase, who was your and my candidate for the Presidency in 1868, of Seward, who was always personally very kind to me, and of Weed, who I thought was a great favorite of my cross friend of the *World*. I wrote that letter on the spur of the moment and under strong excitement. My object was to silence these radical bloodhounds effectively, and so I may perhaps have given too much prominence to their own idols. If you had been near me I should have certainly consulted you before giving the letter to the press. I read your kind article, by which you came so effectively to my rescue."

Marble's defense of August was so eager that it attacked those who might have been expected to go after August but who had not.

"When the *World* is short of 'subjects,' and the pedant of the period has failed to send down the usual batch of fudged-up quotations," *The New York Times* said, "it relieves its mind by making mouths at the *Times*. This is doubtless an amusing occupation; but one would have thought it apt to become monotonous. Yesterday the *World* said, 'It will be quite out of Mr. Belmont's power . . . to silence the misrepresentations of journals like the *Tribune* and the *Times*, by stating facts.' Now, considering that we have not even mentioned Mr. Belmont's name for we don't know how many months past, this is rather cool. We thought Mr. Belmont was dead. But, at any rate, dead or alive, we do not want to be dragged into the fight which seems to be going on about him."

August also had to correct another misrepresentation about the Rothschilds, this one promulgated by the *World* itself. One of Marble's correspondents had made a mistake about the activities of the Rothschilds in the United States just before and after August came to New York. Marble defended his reporter. August sent Marble proof that the *World* was wrong.

When Marble stood by what he had published, August blew up.

"I care not one damn about Rothschild," he said, "but I *do* care to see the *World* right."

Marble's mistake—and his stubborn defense of it—was worse, in August's mind, than the *Tribune*'s lies.

In the fall of 1874 August, Jr., began his final year at college. His former class, the Class of '74, had graduated the previous spring. From Cambridge he followed their new careers, envying their independence. With those friends gone Harvard became a foreign country, more alien than Berlin had been to Perry. Everything reminded him that he should not be at school. He should be in Europe, New York, out West, anywhere but Cambridge.

When he was through with school, what would he do? What could he do?

Again he was in danger of suspension.

"I should think that it would be a perfect disgrace to you and to all of us," said his mother in the strongest letter she had ever written to him. "I cannot understand why it is that wherever you go, you fall short of what is required of you."

August, Jr., was as perplexed by his failings as his parents. He tried hard, and people assured him he had the ability; but somehow he could not do the work. Part of the problem was that he had become so convinced he was an academic failure, he could not afford to succeed. Doing well would make him a stranger to himself. This explained his cyclical pattern of being in danger of failing, buckling down to work, making excellent progress, and suddenly again getting into difficulty.

Part of the problem also was that his studies lacked system. And, of course, discipline. He was so eager to know, he did not have the patience to learn. He did not want to woo knowledge but to possess it immediately. This desire for immediate gratification was infantile. It was the soft spot, the fontanel, of his intelligence; and it had never closed.

He was not suspended, but the reprieve felt to him like a renewed sentence. He almost would have preferred being kicked out of school— because then he would not have to worry about studying. He rattled the bars of his cage: his allowance was insufficient; he wanted to begin his adult life. Defensively he presented his complaints as accusations.

His father, who was in Baltimore for the races, received the letters and telegrams August, Jr., sent and bitterly wrote back that they "cut me deeper and harrowed my feelings worse than I can possibly express. I will try to forgive and forget their unkindness, but I feel deeply hurt. How you could write so to your father, even if he had been guilty of the neglect you accuse him of passes my understanding."

August armored himself against his son's attacks by using the third person. *Your father . . . if he had been guilty . . . you accuse him . . .* His son's words were deflected toward an objectified other. However, this ploy could not protect August in a face-to-face confrontation—could not protect either of them.

When August, Jr., went home to argue his points, the meeting was stormy. Caroline was just recovering from a bout of neuralgia that for a while had been so painful she had been unable to open her eyes; but she tried to mediate between her husband and son.

"Your father loves you and means well," she told August, Jr., "but he is irritable and very impatient"—like son, like father—"and you will have to learn to hold your tongue and be considerate towards him."

Nonetheless, August, Jr., renewed his complaints in letters. When his expenses reached almost $700 per month, August wrote him: "I have but a few years left before me and would most gladly reduce the extravagant expenditure under which we live. This is however almost impossible without creating comments and gossip, which in my social and financial position I must avoid. All I can do is to spend nothing on myself personally, which I certainly do most conscientiously, because I think I have no right to bring up my children, as I have done, with luxurious and extravagant habits, without leaving them a competency when I die."

August's continued protestations of straitened circumstances sounded increasingly as though he believed them. Since he was still worth $8 million to $9 million, what he must have been feeling was the pinch not of poverty but of mortality—as though his life were the fortune that was dwindling. Usually when he talked about how poor he was he also mentioned his death.

His obsession with saving small amounts grew. He told August, Jr., to keep all his receipted bills so that tradespeople could not charge him for the same item twice, which he claimed was "a great specialty of the down-East Yankee." He wrote so often about a $15 bill from Dunlop for hats that August, Jr., thought his father indirectly was asking him to pay the charge out of his allowance—which was not what his father had meant at all. When August, Jr., sent his father the $15 check, August could not understand what had prompted his son to do such a thing. He only had been trying to make sure that Dunlop was not double-billing them. Most of all August harped on how they had to get rid of some of their dogs. Bitches were littering all over the Nursery. In some of the outbuildings you had to scuff your way through puppies as though you were walking through piles of fallen leaves. August said August, Jr., had to sell not just Bob (who had survived August's last dog purge) but also Sambo, Skull, and Peter, who August complained was "eating his head off and is of no possible use." Perhaps August's fixation on reducing the size of his kennel (and it was a fixation; virtually every letter mentioned it) was an unconscious reflection of his belief that his world was going to the dogs.

In November, Caroline wrote from Bythesea: "I am perplexed as to how I am to manage to persuade August to let me stay here through the month to please Jeannie," Caroline said. "She is very unhappy at the idea of going to New York."

Being in town would just remind her of all the parties she could not attend, of the life she could not have.

"They tell me," Caroline continued, "that in her state it is important that she should not be thwarted, and her brain kept clear and calm."

It was a raw fall. The sky was strange yellows and yellow-greens. Clouds looking as hard as tumors bulged black on the horizon. When windows were accidentally left open, storms crashed around the house like drunken intruders, knocking pictures off walls and overturning chairs. When the windows were closed, the house seemed preternaturally quiet, as though awaiting some ghostly visitation.

Jeannie's room was a jumble of odds and ends. Medicines. Books read or half-read and discarded. An invalid's clutter. In it Caroline even found a photograph that the gardener had lost. Jeannie lay in bed, feeling like something someone had misplaced.

Caroline despaired of Jeannie's getting better and was grateful she got no worse. She thought about taking her south. But Jeannie did not want to go. August and Caroline were so absorbed in Jeannie's health that they had little time for themselves. Their silver wedding anniversary passed like some splendid, stately steamship that they were watching from shore.

The delicate girl who once had dressed as an eighteenth-century bourgeoise in pink silk and black velvet and the engaging devil who had transformed himself into an Austrian consul and then an Austrian soldier had become a worried middle-aged couple. The young August and Caroline seemed as innocent as figures on a Sèvres plate—and just as brittle; but the old August and Caroline seemed in comparison pliant, as though after being handled so long and so roughly by time they were becoming uncreated. Their old selves were the soft clay from which their young, hard selves were made.

Five and twenty changing years
Have . . . passed, since she a timid bride
Stood first by her husband's side. . . .
Child-wife to a mother grown . . .
She has sweetly learned to be
Queen of our society!

If Caroline felt like a queen, it was the queen in *Sleeping Beauty*. Her child had been cursed at birth with a weakness in her stomach, a sickness that had waited all these years to claim her.

In November August brought his wife and daughter back to New York. He was frantic. He said: "What with paying bills, giving orders to the servants and gardeners looking after the shipping of horses, and above all securing good accommodations for our poor Jeannie, I really don't know what to do or where to turn."

He was terrified that Jeannie might catch a cold on the trip back.

"Altho' "—Caroline admitted—"we cannot have it as gay and jolly as it might be if Jeannie were well," she was looking forward to Thanksgiving. The family would be all together. God willing, Raymond would be over his case of jaundice. Aunt Ann was coming to help; Jeannie had insisted on it. As though her illness had made her old, not sick, Jeannie had adopted Aunt Ann, who seemed in her health younger than Jeannie would ever be again. The house would be so full August, Jr., would have to sleep on the extra bed in Raymond's room; but Caroline assured him, "You will have your dressing room to yourself."

The farther away August got from the humiliation of the Convention of 1872, the more his resolve to stay away from politics wavered. He wanted to be vindicated. In politics that meant regaining power and leading the party to victory. The Grant administration scandals and the stock market crash had made the Republicans vulnerable; 1876 would have to be a Democratic year. August wanted to be in on the hunt; more, he wanted to be in on the kill and, like Perry, come away with the brush.

If he could have truly dropped out of sight, perhaps he would not have been tempted to reenter politics. But the attack by the *Tribune* proved he would not be left alone. You had only two choices: running with the fox or the hounds, being the hunted or the hunter—a lesson he had learned long ago. Since his enemies were going to take potshots at him anyway, he might as well come out of retirement. Even if he did not join the hunt, at least he would be a moving target.

To regain any political power in the Democratic party August had to make his peace with Samuel J. Tilden, who was emerging as the leading Democrat in New York. Tilden had been nominated by the party as its candidate for governor, and Marble threw all his weight behind him— although it seemed to August that instead of pushing, Marble was pulling. Marble was effective in designing the Democratic party's state platform, one that by August's estimation could hoist the Democrats to victory in the presidential election of 1876. Tilden stood for reform. He was, as the slogan went, "the Hercules who slew the Tammany Hydra."

"Not Hercules Tilden," said August. "Hercules Marble, it should be hereafter were it not for the magnificent physical claims"—August was making a cruel joke; he thought Tilden puny—"of Uncle Sammy Tilden to which you cannot aspire."

Nevertheless August supported Tilden. He thought his "nomination the best that could be made under the circumstances; and, though I have not quite forgiven Uncle Sammy for his *unexplained*"—that was a hint: August was willing to forget the past if Tilden offered not an apology but an explanation—"conduct toward me, I am doubly glad at his being our candidate on your account."

If Tilden won, Marble won.

"I hope sincerely that we shall elect him," August told Marble. "If I was younger and possessed of more illusions, I should gladly work for him; as it is, I shall content myself by voting for him."

But August could not resist giving advice.

"I am delighted to see your paper persistently on the offensive," he told Marble. "This is the only way to succeed—*de l'avance et toujours de l'avance*. Tilden ought to cultivate [Charles Anderson] Dana [the editor of the *New York Sun*]. He is certainly a valuable champion and, being a good deal of a free-lance [he was against corruption more than he was for any particular party], it is doubly necessary to secure his sword."

Happy to get August's opinion, Marble sent him copies of pieces he had written and was thinking of publishing.

"You are the most pugnacious of all mortals," August said about one of the articles; "and so I give in and hereby most solemnly declare my absolute faith in the authority of your Democratic faith from the days of the deluge down."

August thought Marble was foolish to even consider not running it.

"As I don't happen to have fifty $1,000 bills about me," August joked (the amount Marble needed for his new press and type), "I must needs beg you to print it."

Although August was well-known by sight in New York, there was a threat that he would be forced to show his naturalization papers to register to vote. People wanted to see him humbled. August was determined not to submit to any such indignity; but to avoid a scene he went to the Nursery and voted with Perry at Babylon, Long Island, where, August proudly told Marble, "Perry cast his first vote for your friend Tilden."

Tilden was elected governor by more than 50,000 votes. All over the state, all over the country, Democrats won. Ten seats in the Senate. Seventy-seven seats in the House. Nearly two-thirds—twenty-three out of thirty-five—of the states went Democratic. For the first time since before the Civil War, Democrats controlled the House of Representatives. The Democratic party had fought hard and succeeded. Democrats rampant had become Democrats triumphant.

The election was a "political revolution," August told August, Jr.; and he hoped that "the conservative spirit of the best leaders of the Democratic Party will prevail, so that we make no mistake in '76, but offer a good man and a good platform to the American people."

To Marble, August said: "If Tilden becomes President, he ought to make you Secretary of State or Ambassador to the Society Islands." The Society Islands August meant were in Manhattan, not in the South Pacific. "The *World* has *done and deserved well*," August said, "old crusty grumbler as I am, I cannot find a fault."

August's description of himself as an old crusty grumbler echoed the letter he had written to his sister three decades earlier, when as a young man he had threatened Babette that he might go to live with her if she could make room for the lame old grouser. What was ironic then was now true. He had become an old crusty grumbler.

"His amiability, when he chooses to be amiable, is still such that it captivates even his enemies and rivals," an acquaintance wrote; "but, when he feels like making himself disagreeable, he can do so more successfully than any other man of his instincts and culture."

He was choosing to make himself agreeable—at least to the Democratic party. He sent a letter of congratulations to a Democratic club in Brooklyn, regretting that he could not accept their invitation to celebrate the Democratic victories and urging them to work even harder for 1876—a speech he had been so careful in writing that when it was printed in the newspaper, he neatly corrected the published mistakes: he had said at one point "nefarious" not "infamous"; at another, "their" not "his."

And he agreed to preside at a Manhattan Club dinner honoring Tilden.

Marble had engineered the dinner, August's position at it, and the truce it implied between August and Tilden, by getting August elected president of the Manhattan Club. If August were club president he could not avoid presiding—and Tilden could not object to it.

Shortly after the election Marble asked if August was going to be at the club on a particular day.

"I shall certainly be at the Manhattan tomorrow," August replied, "and should not fail if it was only to give you a good shaking for your perpetrating the sublime farce of making me *President*. You may count upon the shaking."

August asked that Marble send an invitation to the Tilden dinner to "my young distinguished Democrat, Perry Belmont," because "I want him to learn early with how little wisdom this beautiful world of ours is governed."

And—a kind gesture—he reminded Marble to send an invitation to Charles O'Conor, whose renegade presidential campaign in 1872 had alienated him from many of the Democrats who had supported Greeley.

"If you add a few lines *in your own stupid way*, urging him to come," August told Marble, "it will please him."

At ten o'clock on the night of the dinner August quieted the hubbub; and after introducing and praising the patriotism, sagacity, and integrity of Tilden and William H. Wickham, the new mayor of New York, August jokingly suggested that despite their not inconsiderable qualifications, their successes were actually due to an even greater shared virtue: they both were members of the Manhattan Club.

There was general laughter. Being a member of the Manhattan Club had not, especially in the Democrats' dark days before the recent election, prevented political failure.

August went on to admonish Tilden for not including that essential virtue—Manhattan Club membership—in his recent advice to young men who were aspiring to political careers.

"I desire to remove a slight doubt which seems to exist in the mind of my friend, the President of this club," Tilden began, "by saying that beyond all question he was one of those young men whom I addressed."

More laughter.

"I therefore don't deem it necessary to say that he should belong to the Manhattan Club," Tilden went on, "because he has already fulfilled that pleasing duty."

In both cases their banter had malicious edges. August had implied

Tilden deserved the governorship only as a representative Democrat, not personally. Tilden had implied that August, despite his years as chairman of the Democratic National Committee, was a political neophyte. These were the rough meanings with which their speeches were lined; on the outside, of course, all was as smooth as silk. But August and Tilden were too good enemies to become bad friends.

Despite the undertones August enjoyed himself.

"How is the mighty Earl of Warwick"—August's nickname for Marble ever since the election of Tilden had proved Marble was a king-maker—"after last night's carouse?" August asked. "I think it may be called a legitimate success in the lighter walks of the political stage."

He sent Marble a copy of his speech, which he said could be "put in type with such hurrah's of applause as your kind imagination may lend to it."

You could always tell if a newspaper approved of a speech by where it inserted cheers and laughter.

August, Barlow, and five other Democrats then sent Marble a letter of appreciation for his part in the recent campaign.

The Tilden dinner had celebrated not just Tilden and Wickham's accession to power and Marble's skill as a kingmaker but also August's reemergence, after what had turned out to be a short retirement, into political life.

Caroline was so drained from tending Jeannie that the doctor ordered her South. With Frederika she visited Annapolis and returned to New York only somewhat rested, because she fretted more about Jeannie when she was away than she did when she was with her. Worry is elastic: the farther you are from the object of your concern, the more powerful the tug on your attention.

At Christmas, Jane Perry gave Jeannie a basket, which, hung at her window, cast a shadow in the room. As the basket turned the shadow narrowed like a closing eye. Jeannie also got books from her grandmother and her mother, who gave her William Cowper's works and Oliver Gold-smith's *The Vicar of Wakefield*.

"I am glad your presents to me are books," Jeannie told her grand-mother, "for I am making a collection and have already a very nice little library."

August gave her a bookcase.

Jeannie asked that some mistletoe be pinned over her door—

although, bed-ridden, she would not be kissed beneath it. After the holidays she wrote thank-you notes a few at a time, because it hurt her side to sit up and do so. Aunt Ann read aloud to her from Cowper's "The Task," which became one of her favorite poems.

"I feel about the same," Jeannie said; "but I suppose, when the fine weather comes, I will be getting better."

※ CHAPTER FORTY-SIX ※

AUGUST BEGAN 1875 exasperated. His family was a puzzle he could not solve. Although August, Jr., had begged the dean of faculty not to write to his father, he had sent a letter that was not so much a warning—there had been so many warnings—as a disappointed sigh. Oliver was repeating at the Naval Academy August, Jr.'s performance at Harvard, with appropriate nautical variations. When it had been Oliver's turn to monitor his dormitory, he had—after a riotous night—turned in a report that claimed there had been no delinquencies. And he had been caught in the lie. Perry seemed to be merely dancing his way through law school; if trials were held in ballrooms, Perry was sure to make the Supreme Court.

Perry's frivolousness hurt August the most.

"Nobody knows how terribly I feel this disappointment of my best hope," he said.

On his father's birthday August, Jr., had promised he would pass his upcoming examinations. He hired a tutor named Frederick P. Fish and studied so hard that it took a letter from Jeannie to remind him that his own birthday was approaching. He passed two of the three tests and spent his birthday night studying for the third.

"Late! tired! Sleepy and only 25 minutes more of my 21st year," he wrote to Jeannie in a break from cramming. "It is better I think to be asleep when I begin my 22nd year, for then I am sure of not beginning it badly."

He passed his third test. His graduation was no longer in doubt.

August was overjoyed. A few days after hearing the good news he sent his son two hundred shares of the Bank of the State of New York as a birthday present. The stock was worth about $25,000 and would bring in an annual income of about $1,600. To store those and other stocks August had a special box made with his son's name engraved on it. He hesitated about sending the certificates to Cambridge. The mails were not always safe. And August, Jr., did not have a good record for responsibility in money matters. In fact, when August, Jr., learned of the present he considered using the interest to pay off debts, a course his father could not countenance; but then he asked his father to reinvest the interest for him, sound policy.

Whatever August's initial qualms, he did mail the certificates to August, Jr., "so that you could realize on your birthday," he explained to his son, "the pleasure of seeing yourself as an incipient capitalist."

Filled with renewed vitality, August no longer felt poor. His emotions had caught up with his income. Jeannie had improved enough for the Belmonts to socialize again; and for the sake of Frederika, who was old enough to be wooed, it was time to fill the house with flowers, light the chandelier, and, literally, roll out the red carpet—time for what Jeannie had called "Mamma's and Rickie's winter campaign." Caroline's calling list at that time included the names of 99 single ladies and 127 single men—Appletons, Astors, Coffins, Cunards, Cuttings, Goelets, Iselins, Jays, Perrys, Rodgerses, Schermerhorns, and Whitneys—all neatly alphabetized in a book.

The Belmonts' parties ranged from the casual (which after all was a formal informality) to the grand: from kettledrums to a fancy dress ball. The kettledrum, a more or less ritualized flirtation, was an English custom that Caroline adapted and, as Marble said, "preached" to American society—partly with the aid of the *New York World*, which popularized it. Newspapers from Boston to Baltimore picked up the idea. Throughout the East, families with marriageable daughters imitated the Belmonts, the practices varying slightly from city to city: In Boston written invitations were the rule, while in New York, one newspaper explained, "invitations . . . are always verbal." Gentlemen simply stopped at the house on their way home from work, usually around teatime, no later than five o'clock or five-thirty. It was "considered bad *ton*" in New York, the newspaper continued, "to use engraved cards or notes of any sort. Gimbrede, the card engraver, is naturally of a different opinion."

In some cities where invitations were used a code had developed for indicating the extent of flirtation allowable at the party. And in some cities the host was expected to have a large silver—gold was considered infra dig—bowl in the center of the room. This was the *kettle*, which, if the party were held in a big room, could be six feet in diameter. The *drum* referred both to the crowded party (which in England was called a drum, rout, or hurricane) and to the bowl's function. Unattached men sitting around the bowl would use their spoons to keep up a tattoo. This noise covered conversation in the other parts of the room that if overheard might embarrass those talking—and those listening.

When one of the drummers spotted a young lady with whom he wished to have a tête-à-tête, he would leave the kettledrum and, crossing to where she sat, would offer her a cup of tea, adding, "Do you take it with a spoon?"

If she said "Yes" he would sit beside her and verbally make love to her—possibly the actual origin of the slang meaning of *to spoon*.

The tête-à-têtes would last—for those lucky enough to be so engaged—until the young lady or the young man put down her or his teacup, after which the interview was at an end. At least two newspapers reported—presumably as a joke, since the tone was so whimsical—that such abrupt terminations had, "we regret to say, . . . in several instances been followed by the suicide of the gentleman so dismissed."

The Belmonts' fancy dress ball was set for March 29, 1875. Because of Jeannie, August did not want to have it at 109 Fifth Avenue, so he hired Delmonico's. Frederika took charge of the costumes, making sure August, Jr., in particular knew what he was supposed to wear. Since he was going to be in the quadrille, his outfit had to be coordinated with those of the others.

"I think," Frederika wrote, "the caps ought to be more like this

(O mercy, what a cap). I think the trousers would be more becoming to you frisky animals if you had them below the knees. Don't forget your colors. They are red, black, and yellow or gold. You must write and ask me whatever you do not quite understand, for my scribbles are always vague and muddled, particularly when I am as hurried as I am today."

She told her brother that the partner picked for him was "a very pretty girl and very much in the style you chose when you were rather smaller"; asked him to get his costume made in Boston; reminded him to tell another guest what his colors had to be and to study the dance he would be in, and—oh, yes—let him know "that I should have been happy to dance with him, but I was already engaged. He is to dance with your partner's cousin."

Frederika did not have all the dances planned ahead of time, only the principal ones.

"If you want to engage someone for the cotillion beforehand," she told her brother, "let me know and I will do it for you."

Caroline, however, warned her son about certain girls to avoid—particularly Consuelo Yznaga, the daughter of the woman who years before had caused all the trouble with Lord Hartington. August, Jr., although a future social lion, was now still a lamb, and there would be plenty of predators on the dance floor.

At the last minute August, Jr., announced that he could not go to the ball.

"I cannot consistently with my resolutions about study think of coming," he wrote to Jeannie, who of course also would not be going. Since he told her the news, perhaps he was passing up the ball to make her feel better. She would not be the only one missing out. "The time taken to get up a costume would be more in itself than I can spare."

"You cannot back out of the quadrille now," Frederika wrote; but when August, Jr., insisted, she grumbled, "I think I can arrange so as to fill your place, but I think it would be very very foolish on your part" not to come.

August also urged his son to come.

Having gotten his father's blessing, August, Jr., changed his mind.

The night of the ball all the children's and many of August's and Caroline's friends stopped at 109 Fifth Avenue to show Jeannie their costumes. A few of the visitors, those who for some reason could not go to the ball, showed up at the house *en bourgeois*.

Jeannie, presumably stretched out on a couch downstairs, was surrounded by Cleopatra, a Chinese princess, a Crusader, Queen Elizabeth, Sir Walter Raleigh, a Scotsman, a Hungarian, a Circassian, a shepherdess, a Pierrot, a fairy, Night, and Day. . . . They all could have been figures from some dream she was having as she lay there.

Or she could have been one of them: a girl costumed as an invalid.

But when they went to the ball, she was left alone with the servants.

At Delmonico's carriages rolled up to the door as regularly as if they were part of a huge carousel. Caroline was dressed "in an azure satin, tightly fitting, miraculously lapelled and skirted coat of the great Revolutionary days and wearing . . . a *chapeau* literally blazing with emeralds and other jewels," and August was dressed as "a chevalier of the *Garde Française*," in a coat as white as bone. They caused a sensation when they entered the restaurant.

The following day the press claimed the ball was more splendid than the famous one given the previous year in London by the Prince of Wales or any being given that season in Berlin by the Crown Prince and Princess of Prussia, comparisons that made some Americans as uncomfortable as it made them nationalistically proud.

With the return of such elegant festivities August was feeling so good that his mood was proof against bad news. He was truly sorry to hear that Henry Clews had failed again, but his friend's bankruptcy did not depress him the way similar events had a few months before. He was often in the kind of spirits that Joseph Seligman once described as being too jolly. When he was feeling this cheerful he tended to become impish—a limping, graying, slightly overweight imp—and he unmercifully teased Manton Marble.

"I have a bone to pick with the Warwick, who is not satisfied with making Governors," August said, "but prevents a poor devil like your humble servant from getting a little clerkship for a very deserving young Democrat."

Perry was casting about for a position once he graduated.

However, the abrasive joking that August affected with Marble could rub a sensitive spot sore—particularly since August tended to take Marble for granted. If he wanted company, Marble was there. If he needed a champion in the press, Marble was there. If he needed help getting a job for someone who, as August explained, "married a favorite niece of mine," Marble was there to intercede with the right people. So when Marble suddenly protested about some banter that seemed too close to ridicule, August was taken aback.

"You ought to know me well enough by this time to take my chaff as it is meant," said August in apology, "and to be convinced that *of all men in the world* you would be the last to whom I would say a disagreeable thing or against whom I can harbor any other feeling but that of the warmest friendship."

But because Marble and Samuel J. Tilden were so close, August in his continuing private attacks on Tilden put Marble in awkward positions.

"I was very sorry to have to leave you so early on Tuesday," August wrote to Marble, "but I had a raging headache, which unfitted me entirely from doing justice to your excellent and gay dinner. I could not have even accompanied the Governor had he invited me to join in his erotic wanderings," a mean joke, since Tilden was notoriously cold-blooded and sexless.

Even August's compliments to Marble could be painful.

"You are really a trump," August told him, "and I only wish we could spare you here and send you up to Albany to infuse some of your energy and brains into the being which you placed in such political prominence. I am afraid you will Pygmalion-like, in vain, attempt to give a soul to your handiwork."

Marble may have gotten great political power for Tilden, but that same power flowed back from Tilden into Marble. Politically they were symbiotically bound. To injure one was to hurt the other.

And still, August's friendship for Marble did not stop him from trying to destroy Tilden.

He had been content to see Tilden elected governor. However, he would fight to prevent him from becoming president. All winter and spring of 1875, August was slowly rebuilding his position in the Democratic Party with the aim of getting the party's presidential nomination for his own protegé, Thomas F. Bayard. And in the course of the next year and a half, he often went to Washington to map out their path.

"You must make daily converts to the party of law and justice and insure our victory in 1876," August told Bayard.

August feared George H. Pendleton in the West as much as, if not more than, Tilden in the East. Bayard would have to attract supporters from followers of both, and to do so he would have to choose his issues carefully.

When Grant sent General Philip Henry Sheridan to Louisiana to help maintain, by force, Republican rule in that state, Bayard denounced the decision in what August thought was a "great speech. Your forebodings are certainly very gloomy; and, coming from a man of your sagacity and moderation, I cannot but be very much impressed by them. Still, I cannot believe that the American people will stand quietly by and permit a reckless, sectional party to perpetuate itself at the cost of constitutional and civil liberty."

August's instincts were sounder than Bayard's. The American people did not stand by quietly. Even confirmed Republicans like the journalist and veteran abolitionist Charles Nordhoff and Massachusetts Congressman George Frisbie Hoar were appalled by Republican corruption in Louisiana, where a senator, it was rumored, could be bought for $600.

"What you want to do . . . ," Sheridan said in explaining how he intended to put down the Democratic revolt against Republican misrule, "is to suspend the what-do-you-call-it."

The what-do-you-call-it was the writ of habeas corpus.

August helped organize a public meeting at Cooper Union to protest Sheridan's appointment as military commander of Louisiana. He got the meeting's resolutions into the press and negotiated who the speakers would be. There had to be representatives of the Liberal Republicans, but not so many that they would overshadow the Democrats. And the Democrats had to be picked to give every important faction of the party a voice. August wanted Charles O'Conor to speak, but O'Conor refused, angry that August had asked him to appear on the same platform with so many of his longtime enemies.

August chaired the meeting, which because of the stormy weather was not as packed as he had expected it to be. They had to cancel the outdoor rally, so the evening seemed a bit tame; but indignation at Grant was general enough to make the protest—in New York and other cities— effective. Even members of Grant's Cabinet had threatened to resign.

Another meeting August tried to organize, in March, was less successful. He had arranged for the Manhattan Club to give a dinner celebrating all the Democratic senators currently in office—and one in particular, Bayard, whom August wanted to introduce to important New York Democrats. In the article about the upcoming event that ran in the *New York World*, Marble allowed a slip to get by: the dinner, the newspaper said, was only for freshman senators. Marble could not have more effectively frustrated August's plans for Bayard—Tilden's potential rival —if he had made the mistake on purpose. August assumed he had done it accidentally, which was probably the case. Marble apparently did not yet know of August's commitment to Bayard. In the end it did not matter.

Congress sat late, and the senators were so impatient to go home that, as Bayard explained to August, "there was a general stampede as soon as the end came."

Bayard corralled a few of the strays, but most of them could not make the trip to New York. Bayard told August that he thought "it was better not to put the Manhattan Club to the trouble of entertaining the mere handful of us who would have been able to accept."

August went after useful Democrats, Liberal Republicans, and independents, New Yorkers and out-of-town visitors, anyone whose support Bayard might need in the future. When distinguished foreigners stopped in town, August gave them dinners, using their presence as bait to bring in the more elusive politicians he was trying to catch. Frequently Bayard conveniently happened to be present. August was an impresario grooming his star, and he displayed an impresario's protective jealousy. When Marble went to dinner at someone else's house, August sent him a telegram urging him to eat and run to 109 Fifth Avenue so as not to disappoint Bayard.

In the press August kept up a constant drumbeat, as though he were a young man at a kettledrum, waiting for the Democratic party to come into the room so he could woo it. The noise, not the subject, mattered; he was simply trying to keep himself visible, to maintain his public presence. He wrote about everything from national issues like the election of Indiana Congressman Michael C. Kerr, a Democrat, as Speaker of the House (which August favored) to local issues like snow removal from New York's streets (which he found inadequate), an article that he hoped Marble would edit and publish before "God does for our streets what our authorities do not." And although he told Marble that "I'd be damned before I will go around hat in hand to beg" for contributions to the Democratic party, he damned himself and gave in. You cannot step out of line—as August had when he retired—even for a moment and get your previous place back without a fight. In a way Tilden had been right when he referred to August as one of the young men to whom he had been giving political advice. A number of leading Democrats like Tilden felt they owed nothing to August. An elder statesman if he is not content to be merely a figurehead can be as powerless as a young politician. As though he were paying dues all over again, August had to prove he was a good party man.

August's campaign seemed to be successful. Newspapers again began seeking his views on important subjects like the Hard versus Soft Money controversy. By the end of April 1875 August tested his political influence by urging the appointment of a particular candidate for dock commissioner and, a few weeks later, by lobbying to get Tilden to sign a certain bill into law.

However, in the end he was defeated—not by Republicans or Pendleton or Tilden, but by Jeannie.

The milk diet no longer worked. Jeannie's health and mood became worse.

"She is becoming daily more exacting and more difficult to manage," August said to August, Jr. "Though the doctor tells her that it is very important and necessary for her to begin to walk, she persists to remain lying in bed and makes less effort than she did last year in the worst stage of her illness. All this has a very bad and weakening effect upon the general state of her health and wears your dear mother out."

Jeannie had been sick so long that she had become loyal to her infirmity. To get up and walk would be a betrayal of herself as an invalid. In her weakened state the only way she could fight her feeling of powerlessness was to embrace, not reject, the authority illness conferred upon her—which was why she had become so demanding.

She insisted on visiting her aunt Jane. Although moving her from house to house was, as Caroline admitted, "a great undertaking," she readily complied with her daughter's whim. After three weeks Jeannie returned to 109 Fifth Avenue more despondent than ever.

August and Caroline, discouraged with the diminishing effects of the milk diet, tried open-air rides, a homeopathic physician, and a movement cure for which Jeannie had to spend some time in the spring of 1875 at a clinic on the corner of Sixth Avenue and Fifty-third Street.

"It is a hard trial for her," Caroline said, "and for me to have her leave home, but it is recommended by all the consulting doctors. They say it is the only thing which will get her out of the listless state she now is in. Therefore, I must muster up my courage and take her to the clinic and be content to try this last resort for her benefit."

On May 3 at two o'clock in the afternoon Caroline and Jeannie left home to drive the three dozen blocks uptown. Across the street from the Belmonts' mansion workmen were tearing down the white house that had been there during all the years Jeannie was growing up. There was so much dust in the air from the demolition that Caroline had told the servants to keep the windows shut. The neighborhood was changing, becoming more commercial. Where the white house stood a lecture hall and piano factory would be built.

Jeannie's health forced August to withdraw again from politics. Even Pendleton's activities in Ohio and Tilden's careful consolidation of power in New York failed to rouse him. The Belmonts' few—and casual—dinner parties were nonpolitical.

"Come and dine with us," August told Marble; "we'll make you forget *Tilden* and *Ohio*."

They depended on Marble to keep them company. They could relax with him. When he failed to show up, they chided him.

"Faithless creature," Caroline telegraphed Marble one night. "Waited dinner till eight. Just like you."

The most August could—or would—do was to take a passing and querulous interest in subjects that were pressed on him. He thought the choice of Seligman as a rapid transit commissioner was "damned bad . . . hardly could be worse." As for the factions within the Democratic party or the factiousness of the Democrats and Republicans—August dismissed both sides of all squabbles with what became a litany: "a plague on both your houses . . . ," one of his favorite quotes, perhaps because he felt his own house so plagued.

Marble again came to August for money to expand the *New York World*. He figured he needed $125,000; $50,000 now, $25,000 in the fall of 1875, and the rest later. If after the changes in production and format the newspaper still failed to be profitable—and if the Democratic party lost the presidential election in 1876—then, Marble told August, he would sell the newspaper, "pay my debts, ask you to invest the balance for me in the safest possible way, and live peaceably and comfortably the rest of my days on $20,000 or $30,000 a year and perhaps write three treatises—1. on political economy, 2. metaphysics, and 3. whist! reserving the last for my old age."

August turned Marble down. He could not give him the loan.

"You and I don't agree with regard to the future prospects of the country within the next 2 or 3 years," August said. "You may be correct and I altogether wrong, though the last 18 months have most unfortunately verified my most gloomy forebodings."

Jeannie's poor health and the sad state of the stock market seemed linked in August's mind, as though his private and public world were reflecting each other, the decline in his daughter's condition matched by the slump on Wall Street. And his discouraged feelings about the one reinforced his discouraged feelings about the other. His emotional capital was drained. He would invest only in his love for his daughter.

For August's sake as well as his own Marble kept arguing his plan. August needed to diversify his interests. His dwelling on Jeannie's illness to the exclusion of everything else was morbid. It would do him good to get involved in the newspaper, in politics.

Marble lowered his sights and aimed at only $50,000.

"I wish to the Lord you could and would" put up the whole amount, Marble said; "but I am willing to take some risk myself, so that if you will give me $25,000 I shall go ahead with what other means I can get."

The same day Marble wrote—and presumably August received—the new offer, August telegraphed, "Utterly impossible for me to take share regret deeply."

Marble could not believe August was not coming around as he usually did when Marble asked him for help.

"Your telegram," he told August, "by some blunder of the operator, I suppose, has come to me in an almost unintelligible shape. But I make out the phrase 'impossible to take share,' by which, I sincerely trust, you do not mean to intimate that you must withdraw the hope" of getting at least a $20,000 loan.

The telegraph operator had not defrauded Marble of an investment. The message had not been garbled. For the time being August's relations with Marble would be limited to making sure the calf Marble boarded at the Nursery grew into a healthy bull, asking his advice on a tutor for Oliver, inviting him to dinner, and playing whist. August wanted to liquidate, not add to, his worries. Either professionally or personally.

"It is very good of you to propose returning from the Nursery sooner than you had planned," Jeannie wrote to her father. "However, you must not think of such a thing." The movement cure had been no more successful than any of the other cures. Her illness was like a crystal growing inside of her, sending out lattices, an interior jail. Her mother took her to Saratoga. Perhaps the waters, sunshine, and air would help. They did not. Gradually her health declined.

"My rheumatism is very bad, so I am afraid we are going to have more rain," she said, as though the weather were inside her. Or as though she had turned inside out and were expanding, dissipating into the weather. "The only thing I would like you to bring me would be some very small fresh eggs, the roundest and smallest on the place."

Sometime at the end of summer or the beginning of fall, Jeannie suddenly became much worse. Her parents brought her back from Saratoga to New York. The doctors assured August that "there was no physical defect that would prevent her youth and her good constitution from prevailing in the end," but she continued to fail. She was in constant pain.

Sometime during the afternoon of October 15, the pain stopped. The whole family gathered in Jeannie's room. At 4:20 P.M. she died.

"It was the first deathbed at which I have ever stood," August said, "and it was that of my beloved child!"

※ CHAPTER FORTY-SEVEN ※

"JEANNIE WAS such an endearing, good, lovable child," wrote August, "gifted with uncommon intelligence and with the most charming and attractive manners, beautiful and with all this as innocent, as naïve, and as devoutly pious as a little angel. She knew less about the world and its darker sides than a five-year-old child. Tiny is inconsolable."

Around midnight Manton Marble, who had just heard the news, rushed to the Belmonts' mansion. All the lights were out. Exhausted by the day's events everyone, including August, must have been asleep. Or if August were suffering from his usual insomnia, he must have been sitting or lying in the dark.

"Were there ever such investments as our friendships or our loves?" Marble wrote to August. "It seems as if the high gods held a tender heart in derision and would have it bankrupt in possessions and passions."

There was a funeral at the Church of the Ascension and, after Jeannie's body was shipped to Newport, another service in Kay Chapel. Jeannie was interred in the Island Cemetery in the family vault.

Strangers, business and political associates, acquaintances, friends, and family sent telegrams and letters from all over the world. Some were stilted expressions of grief, some were effusive (at least three poems were written to Jeannie's memory), and some, perhaps the kindest, were blunt in their sorrow and affection.

"We have tasted the same bitterness," wrote one mourner.

"Let me just hold out my hand to you as a friend," wrote another.

The Feists telegraphed their condolences, and then Stephan and August Feist wrote separately to explain that they had not yet told Babette, who had been sick. When she learned her family had kept the news of Jeannie's death from her, Babette was distressed.

"For August's sake," Babette wrote privately to Caroline, "I entreat you to show as much calmness and resignation as you can."

Jeannie's death changed August's emotional economy. He was a tenant whose rent had just been raised beyond what he could pay. But he did not want his family to know about this insolvency. He sent Oliver back to Annapolis with Admiral Rodgers, at whose house the boy stayed for the first day.

"Oliver is very affectionate and tender-hearted," August later said, "and was most warmly attached to our darling Jeannie, whose special favorite he was. When we came to our lonely hour, the dear fellow broke completely down, and it was most heartrending to see him."

Rodgers advised, and August agreed, that Oliver should not be coddled. He should be sent to all his recitations, given no exemption from work.

"At his age," Rodgers said, "the mind is so elastic that, busy with his studies, he will ere long regain his cheerfulness."

August took Caroline, Frederika, and Raymond to the Nursery, their retreat. He tried to attend to affairs but was like a man who, having lost his sense of distance, tries to toss a crumpled paper into a wastebasket. He either overshot or undershot the mark. A telegram to Marble about politics sounded hysterical; a note with a suggestion about newspaper matters was so spiritless that it was hard to understand why August even sent it. He did not involve himself in a coaching club that James Gordon Bennett, Leonard Jerome, and a few other of his cronies were starting, the kind of project he in the past would have dominated. And a letter asking if August Belmont & Company were no longer the Rothschilds' American agents elicited neither the amusement nor anger it probably would have at an earlier time. He puttered about the farm and tried to show his wife the calmness and resignation that Babette had urged Caroline to show him.

Among Jeannie's belongings August found a poem that, although written in English, sounded Germanic and made reference to Jewish lore. It seemed to August to be too worldly-wise—or otherworldly-wise—and skillfully crafted to be something Jeannie had written, but there was no citation. He sent it to one of Marble's editors, William Henry Hurlbert, a brilliant eccentric (he had changed his name from *Hurlbut* to *Hurlbert* because a printer once had misspelled it on his calling cards). Ever since he had been a student at Harvard, Hurlbert had had a reputation for almost unnatural erudition.

Hurlbert did some digging but found nothing in German or any other literature to indicate that Jeannie had copied the lines. Although he granted that "the thought in the second verse about the punishment of the proud usurper by the empty unconsciousness of *Sheol* [the Hebrew word for *underworld*], the blank place of departed spirits, is certainly an astonishing one for a young girl," he was "inclined to believe the verse an outpouring of her own nature, prematurely brought face to face by the discipline of illness with the eternal problem" of death.

Jeannie had known more about certain precincts of the darker side of life than August had suspected.

The Nursery did not calm Caroline. It was a mirror reflecting her past, reminding her continually of her dead child. Perry traveled with Caroline, Frederika, and Raymond to Annapolis, where they stayed with Rodgers and saw Oliver, and to Washington. August and August, Jr., returned to 109 Fifth Avenue.

"The house is very quiet," August wrote to his youngest son. "I miss the gay laugh of my darling Raymond and his playfellows."

His letters to Raymond were gentler than any letters he had ever written to any of his children. He posed riddles; described weekend trips to the Nursery, how a mink that had been after the chickens was killed and how August, Jr., was saving the pelt; asked Raymond and Frederika to think up a name for a new colt, "something having reference to color . . . or something which begins with *M* and sounds, at least in the first syllable, like Maroon," which was the name of his sire; and begged Raymond to get plenty of outdoor exercise to improve his health, which had been poor. August had a horror of any of his surviving children falling ill.

Like his father, August, Jr., tried to jolly Raymond out of his grief with amusing letters; he was a magician using his patter to distract not just the audience but himself. The happy letters were meant to cheer the writer as well as the reader.

"Papa and I have not varied our life very much from mere eating, sleeping, and working," August, Jr., told Raymond, "but in a few instances, such as having a delightful (?) dinner at Aunt Jane's, my occasionally going and getting my head punched at the sparring club, and Papa perhaps going to the club for a little while in the evening, only to come back and feel it was more stupid than staying at home. I was two evenings ago inveigled (I use large words, for I see you like them, such as 'perceptible' & tc) into joining a very quiet whist party of some of my college friends, now all settled into the serious walks of life (as they think) but as that evening proved not to be, for they kept me up till 2 o'clock in the morning and stuffed me with such a good but heavy supper that I have not been able to make many millions here at the office [of August Belmont & Company] ever since."

Raymond's letters had such wide margins, August, Jr., claimed he had thought Raymond had written about his trip to the capital and his impressions of politics in verse.

"This made it my intention to answer you in the same strain," he said, "but I stick to prose. I will, however, if you will try writing me a letter in poetry answer in the same, giving you four lines to one of yours." The hand is quicker than the eye, watch the magic trick, don't think about Jeannie. "Try it once for fun. You must exclude all lines suggested by Rica."

August, Jr., was good at distracting Raymond. It gave him a chance to be the grown-up brother. Finally out of school and working at his father's office, accepted as an adult, he no longer suffered from the frustrations of trying to live a man's life in a boy's world. The letters to Raymond betray none of the self-doubt or self-pity that had oppressed him in prep school and college. He saw himself clearly and with humor.

"I go and play soldier every other night," he wrote Raymond, "and am most unsoldierly in my punctuality; but, as I only play being soldier, I only play being punctual, for which they play being severe on me and for which I play I mind it, which is not such bad amusement for these times."

Thomas F. Bayard was August's protégé. Perry, in an amiable exchange, became Bayard's protégé. Whenever Perry was in Washington he stayed with Bayard and met at Bayard's house many of the leading politicians of the day, both Democrats and Republicans. Every morning Perry and Bayard walked to the Senate; in the afternoon they rode horseback. Shortly before, Perry had written an article for the *New York World* supporting the presidential bid of Speaker of the House Michael C. Kerr; but Kerr fell ill, he could not run. And Perry soon joined his father in support of Bayard's as yet unannounced candidacy.

Bayard was impressed by "The *judicial* temper of Perry's mind and his disposition to look on all sides of a question and to avoid extremes both in expression and opinion." After Perry left Washington, Bayard regularly sent him copies of the *Congressional Record,* which Perry enjoyed as if they were scripts of plays.

"In reading the accounts of the debates in the Senate," Perry told Bayard, "I am now able to picture to myself the whole scene. I can see almost every senator as he rises from his place."

Perry was fair in his observations, nonpartisan in his admiration. He was as ready to compliment one Republican senator about his "clear and incisive" way of orating as he was to damn another who grabbed both horns of a dilemma and, a cowboy fighting a steer, tried to wrestle it to the ground. Such a senator's struggle may have been heroic in its energy but was cowardly in its intent—trying to avoid a decision. Perry had contempt for those who did not stand up for what they believed.

He consulted with Bayard about his studies at Columbia Law School, discussed with him the school's decision to make the examinations tougher than they had been previously, and complained about a speech by representatives of the Society for the Prevention of Cruelty to Animals, whose motives may have been noble but whose activities Perry thought were reprehensible. They were too eager to pass laws about what were private matters.

"The spirit which prompts these men to regulate society until every spontaneous impulse is destroyed and is replaced by rules no matter how benevolent and charitable," Perry thought, "is the same which animates those who would have government destroy all local authority and individual rights."

Perry thought maltreatment of animals immoral, but he resisted the attempt to make it illegal. The more that civil and criminal law replaced moral law, the less force moral law would have. Some statutes were necessary, of course, but the more man looked to courts for guidance, the less he would look to himself and to God.

With youthful energy Perry leapt from the specific—laws that the SPCA was lobbying for—to the general: the widening jurisdiction of the courts. Perry tried out his arguments on Bayard: That was play. He was a wolf cub learning to fight. But he also came to Bayard with more serious matters.

"My father is still very much depressed," he told Bayard; "if he could only interest himself in politics, it would be a great thing."

August was teaching August, Jr., the business, checking his letters and occasionally making suggestions, which dealt with decorum as often as finance.

"As he is a much older man and almost a stranger to you," August said in one case, "I think you had better [address a particular letter] *His Grace*."

August had smashed a finger about the time Jeannie had died. The nail turned black and unsightly: August wore a half-glove to cover it.

Occasionally he glanced up to notice the world beyond his family, but even then it was usually some reference to his family that caught his attention. He cut out and saved an article in the *New York Herald* about a delegation of Japanese officials to San Francisco.

"When Commodore Perry came to Japan, he knocked and no one answered . . . ," a Japanese naval commander said in an after-dinner speech. "He knocked again and *we awoke* and *let him in.*"

The world was now knocking on August's door.

As though Tilden, cold-blooded as he was, were warmed by death, he dropped his quarrel with August when he heard about Jeannie and was surprisingly kind and sympathetic. August was grateful but did not respond to Tilden's overture.

Just before Jeannie's death a progreenback, formerly anti-Belmont newspaper in Missouri surprisingly defended August against the charge that he had "never been a proper representative of democratic sentiment. . . . However much we may dissent from Mr. Belmont's financial views," the *Hannibal* (Mo.) *Clipper* said, "there has not thus far at least been any just ground whatever for assailing his political integrity."

And about the same time William H. Kemble, former treasurer of the State of Pennsylvania, who in 1868 had attacked August with anti-Semitic abuse in an exchange over Pennsylvania State bonds, said: ". . . I wrote . . . Mr. Belmont a foolish and insulting letter, for which I now take occasion to apologize, an apology long delayed, but none the less sincerely given."

Traditional enemies within the Democratic party were seeking peace. Fate is perverse. Now that August had no interest in politics his position seemed potentially never stronger.

But many who would honor August in retirement were prepared to fight if he became active.

Fitz-John Porter was one of August's good friends. In January 1876 his confirmation as New York City Commissioner of Public Works was threatened. Because of the depression he had lowered city workers' daily wages from $2.00 to $1.60, something an interim commissioner of public works should not do if he hopes his position will be made permanent. He came to August for help.

At an evening meeting on January 10, 1876, at the Belmonts' mansion, August told Porter he would go before the Board of Aldermen and plead Porter's case.

The following day the chamber in which the Aldermen convened was crowded. Word was out that members of the Manhattan Club were going to present their views on the matter. It would be a good show. The Manhattan Club against the Aldermen; Democrats against Democrats. When August appeared there was a murmur of surprise—and pleasure. The show would be even better than expected.

August gave the Aldermen a petition, signed by twelve leading New Yorkers favoring Porter's confirmation.

"Can you tell the committee what are the politics of each man who signed that paper?" one of the Aldermen asked.

August read the names aloud and added:

"They are good Democrats—better Democrats than the men who are opposing Fitz-John Porter" like Andrew H. ("Handy Andy") Green, who August said "had assisted the Republicans" in the last election.

No wonder some Democrats were happier to see August in retirement than in action. In a fight he named names, pulled no punches.

"Do you think the confirmation of Fitz-John Porter would injure the Democratic Party?" the Alderman asked.

"I think it would kill it," said another Alderman, playing for laughs, which he got from the audience.

". . . The question is," August said, "whether a Democratic Board of Aldermen will . . . vote for . . . a capable Democrat . . . If I was in Mr. Porter's place, I would have done the same," a statement that surprised some members of the audience, since, as one newspaper said, August was "known to be a friend of the laborers."

"There is no reason why laborers' wages should not be reduced in times of depression," August continued. ". . . I have got a farm, and I employ twenty men on it. I paid them $2 a day for some time, but I told them that I thought of stopping the work, and of their own accord they offered to work at $1.50." Even assuming that "Fitz-John Porter has made a mistake, is that sufficient reason to send him adrift and reject him? We all make mistakes."

The Aldermen harried August during his appearance so viciously that August finally snapped, "Don't catechize me too much."

"It was a gross violation of courtesy to cross-question . . . Mr. Belmont in the brow-beating spirit of a Tombs lawyer toward a slippery witness and ply . . . him with interrogatories that had no proper relation to the question . . . the Aldermen were considering," one newspaper commented.

In returning to politics to defend a friend, August had renewed old hostilities; but the fight, local as it was, had gotten his mind temporarily off Jeannie's death. The door was open; it was just a matter of time before August wandered out. When Bayard, probably in cahoots with Perry, invited August to Washington to discuss the economy, August went.

"My father's trip seems to have done a great deal of good," Perry told Bayard after August returned to New York. "He takes much more interest in public affairs than before."

August made some recommendations on how to settle a Jockey Club dispute, his first truly active involvement in racing in months; and he opened the Nursery to the press, a demonstration that he intended to show more interest in racing than he had recently. The *New York Herald* listed his horses: three stallions for stud, twenty-one brood mares, thirteen yearlings, nine two-year-olds, eight three-year-olds, and two four-year-olds—as though it were giving the census and genealogy of a royal family.

"You will be pleased to hear," August told Raymond around the same time, "that my finger is all right now. The old black nail has dropped off."

In the capital August had surveyed the damage done by the Soft Money Democrats. They were attacking the Resumption Act of 1875, which required the government to start redeeming greenbacks with gold after January 1, 1879. August had worked closely with the author of the bill, John Sherman, and had supported its passage; but that had been a year before. Now the political climate had changed.

"Things look very bad here," August wrote to Marble from Washington, "and I fear that all our Western Hard Money men are getting weak in the knees and that a complete surrender to the Inflationists [Soft Money men] is imminent."

It was possible that the Resumption Act of 1875 would be repealed and replaced by another act that would not set a specific date for the redemption of greenbacks with gold. Or, even worse, it was possible that the Resumption Act of 1875 would be replaced by not a law but merely a declaration that someday the government ought to redeem greenbacks with gold. This, of course, would be an empty gesture.

August believed that it would be disastrous if the Resumption Act of 1875 were repealed. The government could not be allowed to continue printing more and more greenbacks, each of which was worth less and less gold. This was tantamount to what Drew, Gould, and Fisk had done when they watered the Erie stock by printing shares that had no real value.

The only way to save the economy from chaos was for the government to make every dollar equal to a dollar's worth of gold. In the short run this policy could be painful. There would be less money in circulation.

As a result times would temporarily become harder—the walk through the desert to the Promised Land of true prosperity.

"I fear the Democrats in Congress are more disorganized on the Currency Question than ever before," August continued to Marble; "and I fear the crazy demagogues of the West will carry the day."

That prospect left August incredulous.

"How any man can advocate inflation in the face of all the calamities which have crushed trade and *industry as they never have been before* is to me an enigma which passes my understanding. To talk of restoring confidence, reviving trade and raising prices by increasing the volume of an *irredeemable* currency is like trying to build a palace in a morass—the higher the structure is raised, the deeper it sinks into the mire. If our leaders are not able to raise the banner of Hard Money in the next Presidential campaign, we are again doomed to defeat just as we were in 1868, when under the pressure of Western demagogues we adopted the fatal Greenback platform on which we were beaten even in Ohio, the nest where that cuckoo's egg was hatched."

Within a month, however, August's incredulity had surrendered to practicality. With a nod to Livy he told Marble:

"I am afraid that the soul of one of the ganders of the Capitol has in its numerous transmigrations at last descended down upon me. But my great ancestor or rather prototype was able to prevent the impending danger, while I seem to be doomed to do all my cackling without attaining any possible good."

The Soft Money men were too strong; the Hard Money men had to compromise. August still thought the Hard Money Democrats had to "pledge themselves to an early resumption." But he was now calling Sherman's Resumption Act of 1875 "silly" and arguing that the Currency Question should not be allowed to split the Democratic Party. Perhaps the party should table that issue for the duration of the campaign—if that could be done.

"We have battering rams enough to strike down the Republicans— federal and Congressional corruption, maladministration, usurpations, and centralization of power—without Hard Money," August told Marble. "These are only the suggestions of the old gander, who sees again the danger of the barbarians storming the Capitol," the threat of the Republicans gaining back all the seats the Democrats had won in the previous election. "Your paper ought to sound the trumpet of alarm. . . . *cackle, cackle.*"

Within another month August was calling Sherman's Resumption Act of 1875 a "bogus bill" and saying that it ought to be repealed in favor of "a practical substitution for gradual resumption."

Gradual resumption was the compromise, the key that could unlock the door separating the Hard and Soft Money Democrats. August said: "While the Democratic Party should most resolutely hold to the policy of taking steady and progressive steps toward the resumption of Specie Payments, yet the evils of the unsound currency fastened upon us by the party now in power have eaten so much into the very elements of our financial system that great caution must be observed in devising and applying means for restoring us to financial health."

"Then you agree . . . , Mr. Belmont," a reporter asked, "that the anti-resumptionists [a waffling term for Soft Money men] are . . . right in demanding the repeal of the Sherman Resumption Act?"

"I look upon the Sherman Resumption bill as a mere political trick and sham," answered August,

> because it fixes a day for resumption without providing adequate means to meet that day. It is as if an individual who, by extravagance and over-trading has become insolvent and unable to meet his obligations, should promise to pay his indebtedness, say next Christmas, and meanwhile go on recklessly squandering his means and take no pains to husband the resources still within his reach. The fact is that the present generation of active men, say from twenty-five to forty years of age—the life and working force of the nation—have grown up under this abnormal state of our finances, nine in ten of them never having seen any dollar but a paper dollar, so that the very question of resumption has for them not a conservative but a revolutionary aspect. It is not for them a return to sound methods, but a departure from the only methods they know. . . . My firm conviction is that the Administration and the people of this country at the end of the War ought to have honestly and bravely met the situation and said to themselves: 'We have achieved a great victory, and obtained an end of which any people might be proud. We have saved the integrity of the government, but we have done this at the sacrifice of untold millions and of hundreds of thousands of . . . lives. We are infinitely richer in honor and in hope, but we are . . . poorer in material resources. An immense debt has been contracted, and we must set to work like honest people with

economy, . . . retrenchment, . . . discreet laws for regulation of commerce, and . . . resolute endeavor to restore the prostrated industry of our manufacturers and our farmers, so as to accumulate means for meeting this debt and putting the country on its legs again.' Instead of this we allowed the Administration and its party to delude us into the belief that we had carried on a civil war of five years' duration which, in its frightful and wasting effects, is to an ordinary war as an ordinary war is to peace, and yet had actually prospered and grown wealthy in consequence! The evil has become chronic and has now eaten, like a huge tumor, into the vitals of all our interests. . . . The tumor cannot be cut out until the patient has grown strong enough to bear the operation; or, in other words again, the means and the devices for resuming Specie Payment must be preceded by sound fiscal legislation, by rational navigation laws, by a well-devised tariff, and by a sensible and scientific system of general taxation.

The opposition press, like *The New York Times*, scoffed at August's position: "To identify him in the remotest degree with the inflationists and repudiators of his party would seem to be absurd and unjust, and yet we find him pleading for these mischief-makers and for such a modification of the party policy as shall render fellowship with them immediate and lasting."

And at another time saying: "The Hard Money wing of the Democracy represented in New York by Mr. Belmont . . . has surrendered."

It sounded as though August were indulging in paradox: repeal the Resumption Act of 1875 because it hindered resumption. But the position was a well-thought-out and ingenious analysis of the situation. August was right: The government could not simply declare resumption of specie payments without preparing the economy for such a change. August's solution allowed Hard and Soft Money men to join forces; and through Marble's energy it would become the position of the Democratic party in the presidential campaign.

On his trips to Washington, Perry occasionally met with Kerr in the Speaker's room, where Kerr lectured him on the faults in the system of counting the electoral vote in presidential elections. Perry adopted the issue as his hobbyhorse and rode it like Paul Revere out to warn the country. It was good practice for an apprentice politician—more than just practice.

Early in 1876 Perry wrote the first of a series of articles he was preparing on the subject.

"I wish he had asked to have it in the *World*," August told Marble; but Perry did not want to be too associated with a newspaper that was generally accepted as his father's political mouthpiece. Reproached by Marble, Perry promised he would write for the *World* if Marble in return would promise to refuse his pieces "as often as I deserve it." This article, however, Perry submitted to Bennett at the *New York Herald*. Like all young journalists he watched with dismay as the piece was cut. Then anxiously he awaited its publication.

"The article is excellent and effective for its clearness of statement and moderation of tone," Marble told August. "I find in observing a great many young men of Perry's age that nothing is so rare as patience and accuracy in accumulating and appreciating facts. I should be proud of him if he were my boy."

Although the piece created no great stir when it came out, Perry was satisfied. He would graduate from law school in the spring, and he had already begun building his reputation. August would have at least one trustworthy ally in the Democratic party.

August and Perry were both preparing Bayard's campaign for the Democratic nomination. August met with leaders of a growing stop-Tilden movement, some of whom were not convinced that Bayard was the best alternative. But whoever the Democrats chose was certain to win the election. Scandals—the latest one involving bribes the secretary of war had taken for the sale of trading posts in Indian territory—continued to plague Grant.

"This dirty business will help us very much," August thought, "and will counter-balance a good many of our stupidities past and future."

Perry, not yet practiced enough in politics to be quite so cynical, thought "the worst trait in the character of the Republican leaders is the way in which they regard these exposures. They only regret them as hurting the party." He still believed Democrats were different.

Despite his intrigues with the stop-Tilden movement August continued to flirt with Tilden's nomination. His reasons for doing so remain obscure. It is possible that he was willing to be convinced that Tilden was the best, or at least the inexorable, choice. Or his motives may have been less straightforward. In giving Tilden some support he might be in a position to swing Tilden behind Bayard if Tilden were knocked out of the race.

When Marble confided that he was worried about the opposition to Tilden of Sanford E. Church, the former lieutenant governor of New York State, August suggested that he "might be instrumental in bringing about the reconciliation between Tilden and Church or at all events find out whether it is practicable so far as Church is concerned. You know that I was with him in Chicago and here at the National Conventions and that he was, in 1868, my choice after Chase. This he knows, and we are very good friends. I suppose he has given up all hope for himself and I think would gladly go for Tilden if he can see the Treasury or the Attorney Generalship looming up in the distance."

Perhaps August's offer to intercede with Church for Tilden was a Trojan Horse designed to smuggle August into Tilden's confidence. If so, it did not work. Tilden would welcome August's support but was not ready to trust him. In a private meeting with Mayor Wickham, Tilden scratched August's name off a list of secure Tilden men in New York. Wickham told August. August complained to Marble.

"I wish," he said, "if you think proper, you would correct this and remove from Tilden's mind any suspicion to that effect. If Tilden has not full confidence in me I cannot be of much use to him either at Utica," where the state convention was to be held, "or St. Louis," where the national convention was to be held. "I know one thing; that is, having once made up my mind that he is the strongest and most available candidate I will stick longer and more effectively to him than" many others in his retinue.

Whether August was just playing politics or was sincere in his protestations of support for Tilden, by March, Tilden had alienated him. In his letters to Marble, August stopped calling Tilden "our candidate," and along with 120 other leading Democrats signed an anti-Tilden statement —his official break not just with Tilden but politically with Marble. All his efforts were now directed at getting commitments for Bayard.

When August learned that he had been elected a delegate to the state convention and Perry had been excluded, he furiously assumed it was due to Tilden's meddling.

"Of course, I shall have to go," he told Marble; "in fact, I want to go to see whether I can do any good and whether it will be of any use for me with my views to go to St. Louis [the site of the national convention]."

He planned to travel to Utica on the same train as Marble and to room at the same hotel, seeking in physical proximity the political closeness they had lost. Their political differences threatened to damage their friendship, the bruise on a peach that makes the fruit rot as it ripens. August wanted somehow to reinforce their relationship.

But August did not go to Utica. Depression or anger stopped him. The state convention met on April 26. Then August changed his mind again. Two days after the Utica convention started August telegraphed Marble:

"Upon reflection . . . have resolved to go . . . my own opinion of conduct of Albany individual [Tilden] unchanged."

The Utica convention elected August a delegate to the national convention in St. Louis—and endorsed Tilden, although the choice was greeted with no applause. August was not the only New Yorker Tilden had alienated.

⚜

"On returning from Annapolis last evening," August wrote to Marble at the end of May, "I find in the *World* the confirmation of a rumor which had reached me before, but to which I did not give any credence."

Unable to raise enough money to make the necessary improvements on the *New York World* (even Tilden had turned him down), Marble had sold the newspaper.

August congratulated him on a wise move, although he was sure Marble was feeling low-spirited. He invited him to the Nursery. Instead Marble went to Albany to work full-time for Tilden. August and Marble were no longer even in physical proximity. At least for a while there would be no late-night whist games at the club, spontaneous dinners, or urgent meetings to discuss personal or political concerns.

Because he had not been asked to do so, August had never approached Church for Tilden; now he approached Church to stop Tilden. The same week that August learned of the sale of the *World* he received an answer to an exploratory letter he had mailed to Church.

"I have desired to communicate with you for the last year," Church said, "but I was told that you favored Tilden; and, if so, I could not expect to exert any influence over your actions."

Church thought Tilden's nomination would be "fatal to our success in the state and nation and ruinous to the Democratic Party." Although he preferred Thomas A. Hendricks, the governor of Indiana, or General Winfield Scott Hancock, Church admitted that he thought "very highly of Senator Bayard, and I see no reason why he would not make a good candidate."

Church suggested sending "a good man to some of the states [Michigan, Indiana, Illinois, and Missouri] in advance of the convention, quietly to tell the truth about affairs" in New York, the truth according to the stop-Tilden movement; and he knew someone able and willing to spread such stop-Tilden gospel—if his expenses were paid. August agreed to the plan and the man, and in June their agent started on his tour, a modest effort to counteract Tilden's propaganda campaign. Tilden had set up a Newspaper Popularity Bureau to feed stories to the press, and a Literary Bureau to feed stories more directly to the public. He had advertisements printed, Barnum-like handbills, something no presidential candidate ever before had done. August and Church were fighting a Gatling gun with bow and arrow.

A couple of weeks before the convention August and Church decided to send another agent to Baltimore and Washington to promote Bayard with the delegates from Maryland and Virginia. The only two men August felt would be appropriate for the job could not go, so August set off himself, a scout traveling through countryside ravaged by the enemy. Tilden's men had been there earlier and were well organized.

August had hoped to meet Bayard in Washington, but Bayard had to go to Mississippi for some hearings. August sent him a letter that argued the case for nomination so strongly that it sounded as though he were writing to an uncommitted delegate, not the candidate himself. In between listening to witnesses Bayard scribbled a discouraged note back; he was an unconvinced, uncommitted delegate.

The more serious August's political break with Marble became, the more lightly August treated it. After sending Marble a pro-Pendleton letter he had received, August said:

"I am sure it will make you at once a Pendleton man," something neither of them would ever be, even if Tilden and Bayard were to drop out of the race. "Don't tell Sammy that I have been tempting you."

"Your credulity in regard to Tilden is really refreshing," August said at another time. "You are as willfully blind as an infatuated lover who will cling to his illusion in the face of the most damning proofs."

And in discussing their plans for the convention, August feigned fear of Marble's political ruthlessness.

"I shall barricade my room at night," he told Marble, "and shall have your luggage searched, so don't you take any revolver or Prussic acid along."

Marble was not always amused. When he heard that August had bet against Tilden, he upbraided his friend. How could August oppose Tilden? Tilden had worked to get August selected as a delegate to St. Louis. Tilden was going to be the nominee. August was only hurting himself by fighting him.

August denied the bet but defended his anti-Tilden stand.

"I am not aware that any friend of Tilden and particularly not Mr. Tilden did anything to have me on the delegation," August told Marble. "I know that I had your good wishes, but with that exception, I also know that none of the Tilden managers wanted me there. Furthermore, I never shall be able to understand how I can lessen my own position with the party by advocating the nomination of a man like Bayard. As for the friendship of Tilden, I never had it, nor ever expect to have it; and I think I can manage without it even if he should become President."

"I am delighted to know myself misinformed as to your having bet against Tilden," Marble said; and again he tried to convince August that he was wrong about Tilden's feelings for him. August's support was valuable, and Marble was trying to get it for Tilden's sake—and August's. Marble did not want to see his friend deprived of the juicy political plums of victory by backing the wrong candidate in a presidential election the Democrats were bound to win.

August was unconvinced.

"Don't let us discuss the question which divides us," he told Marble. "Let us agree to disagree."

August arranged a special railroad car for the delegates from New York. If they traveled together the trip to St. Louis would be pleasanter than if each went separately. At the very least they could make the time pass quickly by arguing with each other.

Perry, who was invited to ride in the special car, agreed to go reluctantly.

"I confess," he told Bayard, "that, having become acquainted with a number of mean and low tricks which have been resorted to by Mr. Tilden's friends to secure his nomination, I had rather travel alone."

He found it difficult to be amiable to people whose methods he despised. He was taking politics personally, which—by preventing him from being objective—made it difficult to take politics seriously. What made Tilden such an excellent politician was that he did not allow personal emotion to affect his political judgments—because, some people asserted, he had no emotion.

Perry prepared for the convention by reading the proceedings of the Baltimore Convention of 1872, when his father had stepped down as chairman of the National Committee.

". . . I can understand the despair one must feel in the presence of a narrow-minded and unreasoning mob," he said after finishing the transcript. "It is the very thing which I am afraid of now."

Ten days before the Democratic Convention opened, the Republicans, in Cincinnati, nominated Rutherford B. Hayes of Ohio for president and William A. Wheeler of New York for vice-president. Hayes was a large man, almost six feet tall, with eyes like chips of glass. He was a self-indulgent stoic, who years later would brag not to others but to himself, in his diary, that he had had a tooth filled without using any anesthetic. His enemies thought him slow, but he was still too unknown to have very many enemies. When news of his nomination reached Washington, people asked, "Who is Hayes?"

The Republicans had nominated a New Yorker as vice-president to take that state away from Tilden. The Democrats, if they nominated Tilden for president, would have to pick a vice-presidential candidate from Ohio or Indiana to take those states away from Hayes. Since Hendricks was from Indiana, he was the logical choice; but as one senator told August, "That cock won't fight." Hendricks would not be satisfied with the vice-presidency if he thought he had a chance at the presidency.

August and Perry got rooms at the Lindell Hotel. The city was so crowded that some delegates were sleeping on a steamboat, the *Great Republic*, perhaps the best accommodation in town because it was cooled by the Mississippi River breezes. At night the streets were lit by Chinese lanterns and, sporadically, by fireworks. When they had attended the Chicago Convention in 1864, Perry had been too young to participate in the revelry; now August was too old to want to.

On June 27, at twelve-twenty in the afternoon, the chairman of the Democratic National Committee, Augustus Schell, called the convention to order, August's job at the previous four conventions. The St. Louis Chamber of Commerce Hall was sweltering; the weather was sultry, oppressive, the airless feeling that precedes a summer thunderstorm.

August had permission to address the delegates. His speech was lackluster, a general attack on the Republicans, a nod to the country's Centennial celebration with, at the end, a resolution that Perry had written calling on all Americans to let the Civil War end in spirit as well as in fact. He finished, was duly applauded, and sat down. A favor asked and granted. Nothing more.

On the second ballot Tilden was nominated. Hendricks, a cock who would fight after all, took the second place on the ticket. Tilden supported Hard Money; Hendricks supported Soft Money. But instead of dragging in opposite directions, it seemed that, through a compromise platform essentially written by Marble, they would pull together.

After the convention August and Perry went with William C. Whitney, the Democratic corporation counsel for New York City, to Cleveland, Ohio, to visit Whitney's father-in-law. Whitney described a meeting of leading Democrats at Tilden's house on the Hudson River. When Tilden appeared he said, "Come this way, Mr. Whitney."

"The old man is surely going to tell me something important," Whitney thought. Leaving the other politicians behind, the two climbed a winding stairway to the top of a tower. There Tilden confidentially lowered his voice: "You can see Staten Island from here."

Then Tilden turned to go.

Whitney, realizing that was the important secret, felt like pushing Tilden down the stairs.

CHAPTER FORTY-EIGHT

IN THE FALL OF 1876 Perry and his friend Count Louis de Turenne decided to travel from Winnipeg, Manitoba, to Prince Arthur's Landing on Lake Superior, hundreds of looping miles through wilderness and Indian territory. Turenne had hoped to join United States troops in an expedition against Indians, apparently George Armstrong Custer's campaign against the Sioux, which took place at the end of June 1876. But he was discouraged from doing so. An expert on Indian affairs told him he was lucky not to have gone with the troops, since the expedition was a violation of the United States treaty with the Sioux. He was doubly lucky; shortly before he and Perry started off on their own trip they learned the news of the massacre of Custer's soldiers at the Little Big Horn.

While Perry and Turenne were in Washington they had dinner with

Thomas Bayard, Secretary of War James Donald Cameron, and Commander of the Army General William Tecumseh Sherman. Cameron, whose father had been secretary of war under Lincoln, was a gold-plated politician; beneath the elegance and charm he was solid brass. Sherman, whom Bayard described as having "a dashing, attractive style of conversation," told Indian stories. Perry recalled Sherman repeating what Perry considered "the only too-familiar phrase": "The only good Indian is a dead Indian."

Bayard's recollection differed in particulars but not in substance. "In reply to some remark of mine—that he seemed to omit the existence of the Indians in his plans of occupation of the Indian lands, Sherman stated with the most brutal simplicity that his plan was 'to kill them all.' His phrase made me recoil, and Perry heard it and commented upon it when we reached home. Sometimes it seems to me that the red glare of the Civil War and the whirl of excitement and wild excess that followed have destroyed all capacity for calm and just reflection and decision on the part of the successful leaders. The Indian question will have a gloomy, discreditable, and speedy solution I fear, and death in battle will be the easiest exit for the Indians from their woes and persecutions."

If the Indians died fighting for their rights, at least they would die heroes.

Perry was influenced by Bayard's sympathetic attitudes toward the Indians, although he apparently hoped that the extreme Bayard suggested could be avoided and that President Grant's feelings could become the basis of a just resolution.

"The wrong inflicted upon . . . the Indian should be taken into account and the balance placed to his credit," Grant had said in 1873, in his second inaugural address. "Cannot the Indian be made a useful and productive member of society by proper teaching and treatment? If the effort is made in good faith, we will stand the better before the civilized nations of the earth and in our own conscience for having made it."

Perry would remember that passage for decades.

Common wisdom held that American Indians were hostile and treacherous, and the fate of Custer's expedition was embraced as proof. However, Canadian Indians—Perry and Turenne were told—were a milder breed. The risk of traveling through Canada would be less than if their route took them through lands just south of the border in the United States.

Bayard had wondered if "the peace and good order which prevails on the British side of the boundary line, in contrast to the turmoil and bloodshed on the American side" could be explained by "the British inclination to foster trade *in furs* and therefore encourage the Indian occupation of their own lands, while the Americans want *the land* and therefore seek to drive off the Indian occupants." But although Bayard admitted "there may be something in this," he did not think "it accounted for the different condition of affairs." Bayard believed the common wisdom—as did General Sheridan, whom Perry and Turenne met again in Chicago when they bought supplies for their expedition.

And Perry's cousin, Colonel Alexander Slidell Rodgers, had told of how, when traveling through Indian territory in the United States, he had to take a large number of troops for protection, while the Canadian officials he was going to meet had traveled through their own country's Indian territories with an escort of only two Mounted Police.

From Chicago, Perry and Turenne headed northwest through prairies that bored Turenne and forests that seemed to him like Europe, his highest compliment. In foreign lands travelers tend to admire the familiar, as though they travel not to discover how varied the world is but to assure themselves that it is much the same everywhere—which meant they would be strangers nowhere.

After twenty hours of claustrophobic, stinking, sweltering trains they climbed onto a steamboat and gave themselves up to the cool, fresh lake air. From one steamboat to another; from steamboat again to train. . . . Through the windows the prairie was endless enough to be mesmerizing. Occasionally an odd formation in the landscape—a farm, a town, or a band of Chippewas—would approach slowly and then with a nightmarish rush sail toward them, past them, retreating more and more slowly until it vanished. Another boat took them along a narrow river where they frightened away waterfowl and attracted mosquitoes. The sun was intense, the trip slow. This prelude to their expedition wore them out with its monotony.

Early on the morning of August 9, there was a storm. The temperature dropped. In the late afternoon the boat paused and then passed the last outpost in the United States, Pembina, on the extreme northeastern border of the Dakota Territory.

On August 11 Perry and Turenne arrived at Winnipeg. They walked the wooden sidewalks of the town, their hollow footsteps sounding hollower when they passed through an arcade. They took rooms in the best inn and went to the Hudson's Bay Company store to get some more camping gear and enough whiskey and brandy to last the trip. Some of the old-timers in the trading post warned them that the liquor would aggravate the rheumatism they were sure to develop from sleeping on the damp ground.

Take Hudson's Bay Company tea instead, they said.

The tea was excellent and much better for bartering with the Indians, who preferred it to coffee.

That afternoon Perry and Turenne dined with Father Lacombe, a missionary who had worked with the Blackfoot and Cree Indians for about twenty years, one of the few, white or Indian, who could travel between the two tribes when they were at war with each other. Lacombe was a slight man who seemed to Perry quite worldly for a priest. When they visited him again a couple of days later at his mission, they talked about the religions of the various tribes. Perry was struck by the mixture of gentleness and force in Lacombe's character, how each quality paradoxically reinforced the other—and by the respect with which he spoke of the Indians, so unlike the way the Americans talked of them. As Perry and Turenne left Lacombe gave them copies of his Cree dictionary and Cree translation of the Bible.

The Indians called Lacombe *Kamigo Atchakwe*, or Beautiful Soul.

Perry in describing him said, "His remarkable ability and strength of character would have brought him success in any career," the American equivalent of the Indians' high praise.

Before starting their canoe trip to Lake Superior, Perry and Turenne decided to make a short circle west to explore that region. Unable to find a covered wagon, they settled on a small cart in which they packed their supplies. They hired two half-breed Crees, William and Charles Prudent, to be their guides and interpreters. In the middle of August they started off, William and Charles driving the cart, Perry and Turenne walking alongside.

On one of their first nights White Eagle, a Sioux chief Lacombe had mentioned, visited their camp "to satisfy himself," Perry thought, "as to the nature of our expedition." He was unlike any Indian Perry previously had met, with "the unaffected dignity of a man sure of his position and of himself. He wore a deerskin jacket and on his head a single eagle's feather, white with a black tip. His manner and bearing would not have been out of place in the most exacting capitals of the world."

The country through which they were traveling was reportedly filled with elk. Perry was eager to go shooting. Near the Stinking River they came upon an Indian camp: a man about forty or forty-five years old smoking a pipe; two women, one old and ugly, the other young and beautiful, cooking; and six children. Chippewas.

William introduced himself and his companions.

The man replied that he was called The-Deaf-Man. The women were his wives. The children were his sons and daughters.

Would he help them hunt elk? William asked.

My horses are tired, The-Deaf-Man said. They need rest. My provisions are low. I need to hunt for myself and my family.

William offered him money, tobacco, and lard.

The-Deaf-Man ducked into his tent and in a few minutes emerged dressed in what looked like a blue military coat with red facing and Great Britain's coat of arms stamped on the buttons. Outlandishly uniformed, The-Deaf-Man negotiated specific terms. After haggling, he agreed to ride with them for two days.

The-Deaf-Man told his family to break camp. They did. With The-Deaf-Man in his faded blue coat majestically leading the way, the troupe —Perry, Turenne, William, Charles, the undersized cart, The-Deaf-Man's family, and The-Deaf-Man's dogs snuffling along behind—marched across the Stinking River and through the prairie.

Heat defeated vanity. After about an hour's hike The-Deaf-Man stopped, took off his coat, and gave it to one of his wives, who carefully folded and packed it. Then he walked back to the head of the small column and started off again.

They had gone ten miles when suddenly The-Deaf-Man left the trail. Hiking became more difficult. The sky clouded. A storm was coming. After twelve more miles they made camp. For dinner they cooked some ducks that they had shot earlier in the day. Despite the smudge fire they built, the mosquitoes and black flies tormented them, getting into noses and eyes. They built more fires onto which they tossed damp grass and mud until their entire camp was filled with smoke—which kept off the insects but made breathing uncomfortable. A few minutes after sunset it thundered. All night it stormed. They managed to keep the fires burning. Whenever the gusts blew the smoke away the mosquitoes and black flies attacked. At daybreak they packed their gear and left without pausing for breakfast.

The sky cleared. The sun was hot. The colors of the prairie seemed bleached. The flatness was blinding; after a while they stopped noticing the landscape. The prairie became an ache in the eyes.

At last they came to the edge of the prairie and, as though parting a curtain, headed into the woods. Instead of a single all-encompassing horizon there now seemed to be no horizon; instead of endless horizontals that connected everything in sight the world now was broken up into hundreds of separate pictures, each one framed by—interrupted by—tree trunks. In the prairie, no matter how fast they moved they seemed to be standing still; in the woods, because the landscape was so changeable they seemed to be rushing headlong. The prairie demanded patience; the woods demanded attention.

After eight or nine miles they camped at a lake and ate breakfast. The-Deaf-Man inspected the shore and told them that an elk had been there at dawn. Leaving William, Charles, the women, and children behind, Perry, Turenne, and The-Deaf-Man followed the elk's trail. The-Deaf-Man, Turenne thought, glided among the branches, around stumps, over the dried leaves. Perry and Turenne, single-file behind him, trying to step where he had stepped to make less noise, had trouble staying with him. Abruptly he would stop, point right or left, and then slip off in that direction. For two hours he neither quickened nor slackened his pace. It was as though The-Deaf-Man were dreaming himself through the woods while Perry and Turenne, awake, stumbled behind.

They came to the spot where the elk had stopped to rest; but, The-Deaf-Man mimed, bothered by the mosquitoes and black flies it had not stayed long. The-Deaf-Man was ready to head north after the elk, but Turenne thought it was getting late, they should return to camp. Perry agreed.

The mosquitoes and black flies were still terrible. The three men's faces were bitten so badly they were studded with dried blood.

When did the insects' season end? Perry wanted to know.

In the dirt The-Deaf-Man drew a picture of the moon, after which he curled up on the ground, a dead mosquito. In a month they would be gone.

That night it again stormed. The lightning lit up the lake, making it look as black and polished as a lake of oil.

The following day there was a disagreement over the route. The Indian refused to go with Perry and Turenne into another tribe's territory. And his family was tired. They decided to split up. Leaving his wives and children behind, The-Deaf-Man accompanied Perry and Turenne for one mile to help them regain the trail; then, having been paid, he headed back to his family.

That evening as Perry, Turenne, William, and Charles approached a cabin in a clearing near Tobacco Creek a man stepped through the doorway to welcome them. He had heard them coming from quite a distance. They talked for a bit. He was a trapper. Having decided that Perry and Turenne were not hostile, he offered them dinner and a campsite miraculously free of mosquitoes and flies.

In the morning, after sending Charles off to a nearby settlement to buy a fourth horse to relieve their three spent animals, Perry and Turenne went with the trapper to a wood where, the trapper told them, they were bound to find elk. They had tried hunting Indian-style; now they would hunt the white man's way. The trapper positioned Perry and Turenne at one edge of the wood, about half a mile apart; he entered the wood at another point so he could drive the game toward them. When hunting Indian-style you try to sneak up on your prey, convincing it there is nothing to fear, no reason to run. When hunting white man–style you scare your prey into dashing toward its death.

After an hour Turenne heard a shot. After another half hour he went to find out what the shot was.

Perry had killed his elk.

As though Perry and Turenne were pilgrims traveling over a moral landscape, their successes made them feel that they were better men. Conquering the wild conquered something in the self. Perry had started after that elk the first dawn in Newport a decade and a half before, when he had sneaked out of the house to shoot birds at Easton's Pond.

The trapper must have had some charm against mosquitoes; as soon as they left him the swarms returned; dark, buzzing, living haloes. They left the woods and climbed the Pembina Mountains, which disappointed Turenne. They were only hills, three hundred feet high; but, from the top, the panorama was magnificent. Below them the prairie was transformed, no longer a dull expanse to cross but sea of shifting, shadowed colors.

For two days they worked their way toward the United States border and a mission where they could get fresh supplies; about ten miles from the border they approached the greenest, most beautiful prairie they had yet seen. This prairie unfortunately turned out to be a swamp. The horse and cart sank, the horse up to its belly and the cart up to the tops of its wheels.

They freed the horse and cart and camped that night near some Mennonites, who in the morning came from their settlement to welcome them. Since they spoke a kind of German, Perry translated. Turenne thought them shockingly unworldly. One asked if Turenne had come from Paris to Canada by railroad. Another kept demanding to buy Perry's knife. A third wanted to know if Turenne's stockings were made of leather. The Mennonites would not be put off and hovered around, almost as unpleasant as the mosquitoes. Perry and Turenne in vain asked about the trails. They seemed to be as innocent of local geography as they were of transatlantic geography.

Not far from the Mennonite settlement they came to a marsh thick with waterfowl. They wallowed around shooting as many birds as they could. Their blood-thirstiness was infernal. Turenne called the spot a sportsman's Paradise.

A little beyond the Scratching River, Perry realized one of his bags had fallen from the cart. They stopped; and while William retraced their route, Perry, Turenne, and Charles sat by the side of the trail. All around them was an empty plain; no water, no trees. It grew darker and colder. Turenne climbed up on the cart and scanned the horizon, hoping and failing to spot William. They would have to camp in this desolate spot.

Not too far away was a herd of cattle. Perry waited at the cart, guarding it against the void as Turenne and Charles, lassos in hand, went off to capture and milk a cow. When they finally caught the beast and led it back to the cart, William had returned. They got enough milk to make a kind of cream of onion soup. Turenne wrote an explanatory note, which he attached with some money to the cow's horn.

They woke the next morning to a white world. Frost. If they intended to canoe to Lake Superior they would have to hurry back to Winnipeg, get more supplies and boats, and start. It took them two days to reach the village. Just before they arrived they found a bear cub six or seven months old. They named her Françoise, and Perry shipped her to Bennett. As enchanted with her as Perry had been, Bennett took her to the new polo grounds at Newport, where she was penned.

While preparing for their canoe trip to Lake Superior, Perry and Turenne accompanied Lacombe to a prison, where the priest interpreted for two Indians, one a Blackfoot and the other a Cree, who had murdered their wives. The older one, who was about sixty-five, could not understand why the white men had put him in jail. He had learned that his mate had been unfaithful and had acted as his honor demanded. While she was dancing in a circle with others in a large wigwam, he had slit the tent skins and shot her as she passed the hole he had made. In accordance with custom he had given her parents two ponies. He had failed in none of his obligations to himself, his wife (his obligation to her was to punish her for her crime), or her parents. Why then had the white men taken him prisoner?

Interpreting involved more than translating one language into another. Lacombe explained to the Indian why he was in prison and explained to the white men that the Indian had acted in accordance with his tribe's law. Because of Lacombe's testimony the Indian was acquitted.

The fairness of Lacombe and the Canadian government to the Indians continued to impress Perry, as did the unfairness with which the Americans treated the Indians in their territory. He learned that the Indians called Americans "Big Knives." White Eagle, who had treated Perry and Turenne civilly, came from a tribe that recently had massacred settlers in Minnesota.

"We were on the most friendly terms with all the Indians," Perry wrote to his father from Winnipeg, "but had they known that we came from across the line [in the United States] such would not have been the case."

Before leaving for Canada, Perry had been offended by the official contempt toward Indians that he had seen in his own country, but he had thought that the explanation given for such an attitude—that the United States Indians were different from those in Canada—might have been true. Now he was not so ready to believe that; the first part of his trip had shaken his faith in such an easy explanation.

"Our people are very wrong about this Indian question," he continued. "What I heard from Cameron and Sherman in Washington and Sheridan at Chicago, leaves me little hope for any more rational way of dealing with this matter on the part of our present administration. Our Government once tried to make use of a priest's influence. The priest took with him several half-breeds, spoke Sioux himself very well and was, of course, on excellent terms with the Sioux. They told him that they wanted to make peace, and would do so, only they were afraid that the Americans would not hold to the terms of the treaty. On the one hand [in Canada] are those who have adopted peaceful measures [of governing the Indians] and on the other [in the United States] are those who are subduing them by force of arms."

Perry had been witnessing a convincing, living argument for the first course of action.

"Another month among the Indians themselves, the priests, and the officers of the Hudson's Bay Post will give me a still more useful sort of knowledge on this question," Perry wrote.

However, he was not yet completely convinced. As though he were still in Henry Adams's history class, comparing contradictory texts, he wanted to learn what "can be said on the other side of the question and see for myself the practical working of our policy and whether there are reasons which really make a peace policy impossible."

His first semester in the wilderness, studying tolerance, was over; he was ready for the second.

On September 1 Perry, Turenne, and William left Winnipeg. The first day took them through deep woods; the second day, through swamp up to their knees—they could hardly go three miles an hour. That evening they stopped at a mission where they were surrounded by pack-dogs that sniffed and nudged their noses into the supplies. Turenne seemed pleased to note that the dogs spoke only French; to get them moving even Englishmen had to cry, *"Marche donc."*

Nearby was another sportsman's Paradise. The ducks had so little fear of humans that they swooped down and landed just a few feet away from Perry and Turenne, who did better in this second chance at Paradise and resisted the temptation to kill indiscriminately. They shot only what they and the mission could use.

A week later with a crew of four, three Indians and a Scot, Perry and Turenne headed up the Red River in a leaky boat. After a few miles of bailing they put ashore near where an Indian who owned a boat was said to live. Turenne struck off into the woods to find the Indian; he found and negotiated with the Indian's wife, who told him the boat was nine miles farther downriver. Turenne trusted her. Their relations with the Indians so far had given him no reason not to. He paid her. The boat was where she said it would be. And they set off once again. Devil's Creek. Poplar's Point. Broken Head River. Once in a while they passed Indians paddling canoes; but during most of the trip they were alone, six men drifting in silence. Turenne was struck by the "mournful grandeur."

At Fort Alexander at the mouth of the Winnipeg River they traded their boat for a twenty-four-foot bark canoe and their crew of four for a crew of six, all Saulteaux Indians, one of whom, James-Man, was the son of a chief and another of whom was called rather sinisterly Nanengeese, which meant "The Murderer." He had killed his brother-in-law.

Two and a half hours after leaving Fort Alexander they hit their first rapids. Water boiled around them. They slid between sharp spines of rocks; a river of razors. By the time Perry caught his breath enough to be frightened, they had passed the rapids and were gliding through quiet water.

The Indians were reserved. They spoke only occasionally to each other and made no effort to communicate with Perry or Turenne, who at first tried to talk with them using one of the Cree dictionaries Lacombe had given them. Since the Indians were Salteaux, the attempt was useless. After a while Perry and Turenne gave up and contented themselves with studying their companions.

Although Perry and Turenne were dressed in heavy clothes against the cold, the Indians wore very little; and Perry noticed that as they approached rapids they took off their moccasins, not a reassuring measure. If the canoe capsized, the Indians would be prepared to swim. Perry counted on the canoe staying upright.

Later, after a stew the Indians made of everything in their supplies except tea, they all settled down for the night. Made nervous by The Murderer's name, Perry and Turenne agreed to take turns keeping watch. They woke the next morning, less rested than the Indians, but alive.

More rapids, more portaging, more paddling between overhanging crags. Perry was a photographic plate; the wilderness was imprinting itself on him.

"It was simpler to look on such surroundings as the primitive Indians did," Perry would later write, "imagining them peopled by many gods personifying the various forms in which nature expresses herself."

About five-thirty in the afternoon they came to a spot where the cliffs rose up like walls around them, an amphitheater of the gods with whom Perry had been flirting. There they made camp. After supper the Indians curled up by their fire. Perry and Turenne sat by their own fire, smoking their pipes and watching night fall.

"Suddenly," Turenne later recalled, "an hour after sunset, the sky was lit with an extraordinary brightness. . . . Scarlet rays shot out like rockets. Pink bands stretched over a luminous background. The clouds reflected this amazing light, and the river . . . turned red. The light seemed to vibrate. . . . It seemed as if a strange force animated nature."

The aurora borealis.

Perry and Turenne had no idea how long they sat watching the sky. The colors faded. Vanished. If Perry had been looking for some sign from the Indians' gods, they had not disappointed him.

The weather became cold and foggy. Hunting and fishing were poor. They depended more and more on pemmican, made palatable by the

Hudson's Bay Company tea. As the weather grew colder, relations between the white men and the Indians grew warmer. One night, having finished supper, an Indian pulled a deck of cards from his pocket. Perry and Turenne indicated that they had no objection to the guides playing—although there is no indication they themselves joined in the games, which were boisterous. The cards broke the ice. The Indians were no longer reserved. Perry and Turenne no longer alternated keeping watch at night. Since the Indians gambled for clothes, every morning when they set out some were overdressed and the others were in various stages of undress.

A week after Perry and Turenne had seen the aurora borealis they came to the Hudson's Bay Company's outpost at Rat Portage, where they were warned that their intended route was dangerous. It was too late in the season. Temperatures would be going down to twenty and thirty degrees below zero. Perry and Turenne did not consider canceling the trip, although they did modify their route. But their Indian guides would go no farther. The white men might be crazy enough to risk the cold and ice, but they weren't. And they had to return to their traps before the winter set in. After haggling, half of the Indians agreed to continue, and Perry thought only one of the three who refused, The Murderer, had a good reason to stay behind, since they were getting near where he had committed his crime.

The weather worsened. Their supplies, low when they left Rat Portage Fort, were running out. Turenne shot a mink. Aside from that, game was scarce. Twice, the canoe was damaged and they had to stop to repair it. An old Indian they met told them to turn back. Perry and Turenne thanked him, but ignored his advice. A couple of hours later the weather forced them to the shore of the Lake of the Woods.

Carrying his rifle, Perry explored the area. Turenne stayed in camp with the Indians, who played cards. They had no intention of budging until the weather cleared.

The next morning the Indians spotted a government steamboat, which they tried to attract with distress signals; but the boat was too far off. The signals did not carry. Perry and Turenne told them it was time to leave. They objected. Finally, as a compromise, Perry and Turenne agreed to delay departure so the Indians could invoke the aid of the Spirit of the Lake. Using blankets and boughs the Indians built a shelter that they filled with heated stones. The oldest among them stripped off his shirt and, closed up in the shelter, chanted and drummed. When he had finished praying, they set off.

The water was so choppy that by the middle of the lake Perry and

Turenne were ready to give the order to swim for shore; but as a result of luck or the Indians' prayers, a wave lifted the canoe and, as though they were being carried in a huge hand, set them down on the other side of a sandbar in calm water.

More rain. Snow. After four days they reached Fort Francis, their supplies exhausted. They paid their Indian guides and rested for a few days before starting with new guides on the last leg of the journey.

For two more weeks they struggled through snowstorms. In places they had to break through ice to allow their canoe passage. By the time they reached the Lake of a Thousand Lakes, their supplies were again so low that all they could do was grin at the thought of a friend who had envied them their expedition, and dream of luxuries.

"It seemed to us at that moment incredible that in a hotel or club you could order almost anything and have it brought to you," Perry later wrote. They promised themselves that when they got home, if they got home, they would share what Perry modestly described as "a good dinner."

The lake froze solid. Perry and Turenne bought a sled and some dogs from some Indian women they found setting traps along the shore, and trudging on snowshoes they headed for Height of Land, where a wagon was supposed to be waiting for them. It was not. The only vehicle they could find was a cart that was carrying the corpse of an Indian railroad worker. They loaded their baggage next to the body and, led by the dead, walked back to relative civilization, a Canadian Pacific station where they caught a ride on a ballast car to Prince Arthur's Landing.

On Perry's last Western trip he had found, among the Indians, adventure; on this trip he found understanding.

"It has been alleged," he would later write,

> that the Canadian Indians are a different race from those in our country, but this is not the fact. Many of the former came originally from the United States, and almost all belong to tribes which are found in our country. The whole difference, as I found it, was due to the manner in which the Canadian government treated the Indians, who were never regarded as necessarily hostile. Above all, they were treated honestly. A cardinal principal of the Hudson's Bay Company was to keep faith with the Indians. Enormous prices might be charged for articles of trifling value, such as beads or trinkets, but the bargains once made were scrupulously kept. . . . The Indians themselves, whatever may be

said to the contrary, generally lived up to their own code of fair dealing. . . . Once the white man's government had broken a promise or a treaty, the Indian had no further faith in that government. To them, once false is always false. The robbery and oppression of the Indians by many United States Government agents and the unscrupulous breaking of treaties because of white cupidity for Indian lands make an extremely regrettable chapter in our history.

Relations with the Indians were different in Canada and the United States because of a difference in breed of not Indian but white man.

❦ CHAPTER FORTY-NINE ❦

AT PRINCE ARTHUR'S LANDING a letter from August was waiting for Perry.

"I have been in the depths of despondency and anxiety for the last 10 days and more, daily expecting news of your arrival," August wrote. "In the meanwhile, I have read an interesting work by someone who made the same trip in 1870, and the hairbreadth risks of running the canoes up and down rapids worked so upon my imagination that I got almost frantic. I am leading the same solitary life here which I have done all the summer."

Oliver was on a training cruise for the Naval Academy. Caroline, August, Jr., Frederika, and Raymond were in the British Isles. August envied their progress through Ireland, Scotland, and Wales. Or he envied the trip they took in his imagination: a slow journey through peaceful green fields, the exterior calm becoming an interior calm, the alchemy of travel. In reality the magic worked backward. All Caroline saw in the landscape was her own misery. With her children, she rushed from Killarney to Edinburgh to Glasgow, a prisoner frantically circling her cell. August pleaded with August, Jr., to set a slower pace. Caroline and Frederika were "far from being strong," he warned. He feared Jeannie's death was a disease all the women in his family might contract if they became overtired.

But August, Jr., could not quiet his mother's anxiety. She canceled their trip through Wales, and they went to London. August had hoped that Caroline would forget her sorrow in travel, but she did not want to forget. She wanted to be among familiar surroundings that would remind her of her daughter's death, as though Jeannie's memory demanded as much care as Jeannie herself in her last weeks had needed.

"I am more than grieved to infer by your letter that you are not having a nice time," August wrote to his son. "Certainly my lonely and miserable summer does not seem to have brought benefit to anybody."

The tone of August's letters to August, Jr., fluctuated from intensely emotional to offhand, the confusion of feelings that for a long time follows any death—the offhand being the more disturbing, since intense emotion seems predictable and proper. August asked his son to buy a couple of good shot bags, some worsted suspenders, enough of a certain kind of hairbrush for him and all the guest rooms at Bythesea and the Nursery, and some more of his specially made umbrellas.

August, Jr., wanted to get a Gordon Setter bitch, since their present one, Maud, was getting old and probably would never have another litter. August agreed, warning only that his son should make sure of the pedigree. Since the Cunard line did not allow dogs on board, August suggested that the German or English servant Caroline intended to hire could cross the Atlantic with the bitch on another ship.

As for the Southdown ram (a breed that gave fine wool and excellent mutton) that August, Jr., wanted to buy, August was less enthusiastic. It would be complicated to ship it; there were Southdown rams grazing in Central Park, perhaps August could get one, even on loan, from the park commissioner.

When August learned that August, Jr., had left for Europe without paying $17.50 he owed to the Union Club—an oversight into which August read too much meaning—he tried not to chide his son and paid the bill—as he did a $30 initiation fee for the new Polo Club and a $200 fee for the Carroll Island Ducking Club, to both of which August, Jr., had been elected. He offered to give August, Jr., his own number 10 breechloader for duck shooting, although he thought a lighter gun might be better. If August, Jr., wanted to order a gun while he was in London, that could be his early Christmas present.

"I would shoot the gun several times and have it marked with your initials and also have the case marked with your full name and address," August said, "and then perhaps have it so that it does not look too new, so that we can get it in without duties."

August still was feeling poor. Like Simon, who later in his life began thinking of himself more as a farmer than a businessman, August, as though his only income came from produce, worried about the poor yield of crops on his two farms, the one at the Nursery and another, Oakland, that he had bought in Newport. It had been the driest and hottest summer that the oldest residents of Long Island or Newport could remember: 101° in the shade. When August arrived at the Nursery, he tried to get some relief from the heat on the piazza, the breeziest spot around the house, but at six o'clock in the evening it was 98° there. During the next few days August hardly had the energy to tour the grounds to inspect the condition of the farm.

"The grass is all burnt up," August told August, Jr., "so that the lawn and paddocks look worse than they do in January and, in walking on them, it feels as if you walked on broken glass."

Four acres of carrots, parsnips, and beets had failed. August ordered it plowed up and reseeded with Orchard grass, which George Lorillard (whose horse sense and sense of horses August respected) had recommended as being excellent for Thoroughbreds. The experimental planting of different kinds of grasses that August, Jr., had done on the inside of the racetrack also had failed. Bugs had destroyed the potatoes. By the middle of July the corn was less than two feet high; August doubted it would ripen before the frost. The fodder corn was choked by weeds. The hay and rye that was not ruined had been so carelessly harvested that clumps lay scattered throughout the fields. Altogether August doubted that there would be forty tons of hay gathered, less than half of what they should have gotten. The cows were giving only eighteen quarts of milk a day, "so that there is hardly milk and butter enough for my small needs," August said. "Whether all this is the result of bad management or bad luck I am not able to decide but I am very much inclined to believe that it is the former."

Oakland, the farm in Newport, was not as badly off as the farm at the Nursery, although the drought there lasted three weeks longer than the one in Long Island. The cows, poultry, and crops, especially the beets, were all flourishing. And although the farmer, Elliot, had not been able to find any buyers for the bull and cows that August wanted to get rid of (which meant that they would have to be sold to the butcher, something August did not want to do), August was nevertheless pleased with Elliot's stewardship. August thought Elliot was a true farmer, and he respected him for his knowledge and energy enough to forgive him for his family's inclination "to play high life below stairs and usurp the whole house. I have put a stop to that."

Like a general deploying his troops, August sent a horse from the Nursery to Oakland so that Elliot would have transportation to town to sell his dairy products, and a cow from Oakland to Bythesea where the caretaker, Riegel, said he needed one.

Then Riegel tried to sell some of the Belmonts' fruit and flowers on the sly for his own profit. When August stopped that, fruit and flowers continued to disappear. Riegel claimed they were being stolen. August told Riegel to get a watchdog but never heard about the dog or theft of fruit again—which sounds as though Riegel had been using the fruit-thief story as a cover for his own thievery, although August, innocent in his dealings with the farmers, never came to that conclusion.

His reluctance to believe farmers guilty of anything more than incompetence may have been rooted in his idealized view of farming, a fantasy that he had constructed about the agricultural world of Alzey. He was trapped by a syllogism: Innocence is childhood; childhood is life in a simple farming community (that is, Alzey); therefore, innocence is life in a simple farming community—the ideal worlds at the Nursery, Oakland, and even Bythesea, which although not a farm was a garden. August's insistence on transforming the rural into the arcadian was not uncommon. Every New York ball was crowded with elegant shepherds and shepherdesses—Adams and Eves trying to pretend that they were still in Paradise and fooling themselves that even if they were not after all in Eden, Paradise nevertheless existed somewhere, had to exist somewhere: on farms where people lived close to the earth.

More than he doubted Riegel, August distrusted the Newport police. The stables at Bythesea had burned, and they had not been able to learn who was responsible—although August was sure he knew the culprit, someone in town who had a grudge against him. A new stable would cost at least $6,000, but it had to be built.

The upkeep of all his stables and horses was beginning to seem like an expensive duty, which is what luxuries become once they no longer seem like luxuries.

"I think you will soon agree with me that there is a great deal more annoyance and vexation in race horses than real pleasure," August told August, Jr.

Although August had the best and second-best three-year-old fillies of the year, an excellent two-year-old filly, and a two-year-old colt that flabbergasted everyone by coming up from last place to win one of the most important races of the season, most of his horses were unfit to run. One of them had gotten into the habit of throwing his rider; Fiddlesticks, although he had been cupped and leeched, would recover the sight of only one eye; Dauntless was sick. And Olitipa, one of his champions, was injured at Long Branch winning a race for which August was not paid the purse. "So," August said, "I hammered my horse to pieces [on the exceptionally hard track] for nothing."

The management of the racetrack at Long Branch was in financial trouble. August was not the only winner who failed to collect his prize money. The defaults stemmed partly from low attendance and partly from the refusal of horse racers to pay the necessary forfeits when their horses could not start.

"In fact," August said, "most of the racing men" in America were "hard up."

August was having difficulty with his trainer, Jacob Pincus, who did not run a horse August wanted him to and instead ran another that August knew was off its feed. And, although Pincus had managed to unload a bad horse (which died just after its new owner entered it in a race), he had compelled August to sell a good one that now was winning every race it entered. The letters Pincus sent August were "more curt than ever," August complained, "and I have to pump out every word of information about my horses" from him.

August had become embroiled in a controversy over the rules adopted by the principal Eastern tracks increasing the amount of weight the Thoroughbreds had to carry while racing. The horse racers in the South and West objected to the change and accused August and other Easterners of trying to force their system on the racing world. August denied the charge. The Southerners were simply riled at being edged out of prominence on the American turf, and the Westerners, who were angry at the Easterners for all sorts of other, nonturf reasons, were translating their quarrel from one sphere to another. But the failure of the track at Long Branch and the feuding among horse racers, August believed, was giving racing a bad name. That, coupled with his poor season and the increase in racing expenses made August "so sick and tired of the whole concern that I really feel as if I could not go on with it. If we have hereafter plenty of grass and hay, I think I might raise every year from 20 to 25 young ones and sell them at yearly auctions. It would not pay at first, but could not cost over $526,000, while now I spend $20,000–30,000 each year and never make half my expenses."

August regularly sent August, Jr., these reports on how much his horses and other luxuries were costing him and on how little he was making. And to aggravate matters his office was understaffed. August, Jr., was gone. One of August's oldest associates also was traveling. A key worker was so weak from a recent illness that "his hand trembles as if he had the palsy," August told August, Jr. "I told him to take a little longer rest, and I hope that by doing so he will soon be all right again. He is young and leads a very regular life, and so I have hopes for him." To cover these absences August was trapped in the city all summer, his infrequent visits to the country lasting only for a day or two.

"Business is as usual but a sorry show," he told his son, "though we are doing a little better than almost anybody else in the banking line."

"Gold and money cannot be loaned out to advantage," he said at another time, "the first bringing nothing and the latter only 2%."

August ignored the not insignificant detail that unlike many businessmen he had money to lend and with which to speculate. Joining with the Rothschilds and a few other bankers in a syndicate to underwrite a United States bond issue, he nonetheless groused that his company "had to take all the small fry and our share will be small fry indeed. It will hardly pay us for our trouble and the risk."

When he had sold nearly $26 million worth of the bonds in the United States and about the same amount in London, August did admit that such volume in these times was "doing very well"; still, in the same sentence he characterized business as being "terribly dull."

He complained of low spirits and told August, Jr., that he was thinking of closing up his company—which upset August, Jr., who was eager to become his father's partner and eventual successor.

Didn't his father have faith in his ability to carry on the company? August, Jr., wanted to know. Didn't he care about his son's career?

"My darling boy," August wrote to August, Jr., "don't you know that I only live for my wife and children and don't you see the difficulties which surround me in regard to the future course of my business by the terrible times in which we live? When I feel discouraged about remaining in business and letting you continue my House it is not at all a want of confidence in your judgement or fear of your speculating which frightens me. It is the demoralized state of commercial honesty and the bankrupt condition of individuals, corporations, and states. There are other grave reasons of which I will speak to you when you return."

When August, Jr., continued to feel slighted by what he felt was his father's rejection of him, August wrote:

"Now, I want you to do me one favor: don't worry about it while you are in Europe and don't let it become the subject of correspondence between you and me. Only have confidence in my love and affection and in my wish to make you happy by assisting you in the pursuit of your choice for an honorable and useful position in life. When you come here, we will talk the matter over calmly and dispassionately, and I will give you as clear an insight as possible into my position, the nature of my business, and my relations to the Rothschilds, and I have no doubt that you and I shall be able to come to a conclusion what is best to be done. Only, my dear boy, you must have a little patience and forbearance with your old father. My nerves are very much shattered, and I feel very low-spirited indeed all the time. All this has made me excitable and nervous, and I may often say things which had much better been left unsaid; but you ought to know me by this time, and you ought to know that you have no better friend in the world than I am. So be of good heart, amuse yourself as well as you can, and don't take trouble. One hour's conference is better than a dozen letters."

A groom August had hired for one season at Saratoga, "on receiving his wages went with a friend to sacrifice to Bacchus and Eros among some very disreputable partisans of the latter," August wrote to Manton Marble. "His friend was robbed of about $100, and the poor devil was convicted of the theft."

August asked Marble to intercede with the governor in the groom's behalf.

Although August had no idea whether or not the groom had committed the crime of which he had been convicted, he thought "the sentence very severe even if he is guilty."

As August grew older his sympathies broadened. He anonymously gave increasing amounts to charities. And despite his stand on the lowering of workers' wages during the current depression, his reputation as a champion of "the friendless and poor" grew. Although he was gruff and stern, he was fair. He no longer took himself as seriously as he had done even a decade earlier: his sense of honor was tempered by a sense of humor. He found the world amusing to avoid finding it appalling. He was learning to see failings as foibles.

He sent Caroline and Frederika entertaining newspaper clippings and even more entertaining gossip: some girls had tried their hands at polo, "but made a dreadful mess of it"; the widow of Eugene Thorne reportedly married a Mr. Black just twenty-nine days after her husband's death. "Mamma," August told August, Jr., "will be amused by this extraordinary proceeding, which beats Hamlet's mother."

August's letters were more and more frequently filled with Shakespearean references. He found in Shakespeare the kind of satisfaction and comfort his father had found in Schiller. The references were mostly to the histories, as though Shakespeare's clarity about power were a lens through which August could view his own political involvements. Occasionally—as in the nod to Gertrude—these references were to the tragedies. Only rarely were they to the comedies.

Increasingly his letters also included allusions, which had been markedly absent for decades, to Jewish and German culture. As he grew older he was turning away from the present and toward his family's past—and its future.

"I wish Mamma's wish about Augusta Astor might be fulfilled," August wrote to August, Jr. "She cannot wish it any more than I do. If she is a nice and sweet girl, as I hear she is, why not try to win her?"

August wanted a hedge against mortality.

"I am getting very old," he continued; "and I am afraid you will see quite a change in me when you get back. I should like so much to have some grandchildren before I am called away."

After the St. Louis Convention, August was determined to stay out of the presidential campaign. His contribution of $1,000 to the Democratic National Committee was accompanied by an announcement, part threat and part surrender, that once again he was finished with politics. But his exits always were through revolving doors. Marble and other friends in the party successfully urged him to work for Samuel J. Tilden.

Tilden responded to August's letter of congratulations on his nomination with a note that signaled by its length as well as its cordial tone that he sought August's support. He discussed the nomination and spirit of the times and regretted that he had not seen Caroline before she had left for Europe, sentiments exceptionally warm for such an icy intellect— warm enough to suggest that Tilden was trying to build a fire under August.

Not only were people outside the family pressuring August to participate in the campaign but so were Perry and August, Jr.

"Today I had the first opportunity to follow your sage advice to support the ticket liberally," August told his son about a month and a half after the convention. "The National Committee called for contributions, and I gave *$1,000*."

"I could not well give less," he continued, "but I tell you it comes very hard, first because I feel as poor as a churchmouse"—considering

August's expenses, this churchmouse must have lived in a cathedral—
"and secondly because I have no heart in the contest when I foresee what
kind of men will be surrounding Tilden to manage our affairs at home and
abroad."

Around the same time he went on to tell August, Jr., that "I have
already had occasion" to "support the ticket prominently by publicly
and emphatically denying a slander that I had expressed myself very
unfavorably about the honesty and capacity of Tilden."

A speaker at a Republican rally had accused August of once saying:

"Those who claim that Tilden is unassailable do not know him, or, if
they do, then they are quite as dishonest as he is. He has been counsel for
all the broken-down corporations with which New York has been afflicted
for a long term of years, and out of them he has not come with clean
hands."

August told Marble the accusation was "a damned lie, and I am
willing to testify to that." He asked Marble to read over the reply he was
preparing, which Marble did.

"No man of sense in New York ever could have believed such falsehoods concerning Governor Tilden," August said in a public letter. "No
more clean-handed, upright, or sagacious counsellor in my time has belonged to the bar of this city. My first choice, indeed, for President was
Senator Bayard of Delaware. But I concur heartily in the choice of the
St. Louis Convention and in their platform, so direct, explicit, and unequivocal in its every demand for Reform."

"The banker seems to have the advantage . . . in this case," said the
New York Herald about the affair. Not only was the charge ably denied
but—the newspaper said—the denial gave August a chance "to declare
his support of Tilden and express his strong admiration of the St. Louis
platform."

"I think my position is thoroughly understood and appreciated,"
August told August, Jr.; "and nobody in the party doubts my sincerity in
wishing Tilden elected."

As the campaign continued August once again began exchanging urgent
telegrams with Marble and meeting his old friend for strategy sessions—
not just about Tilden's bid for the presidency (August's enthusiasm for
that cause always would be damped by his dislike of the man), but also
about Marble's bid to be governor of New York.

August did not think Marble could win the nomination at the state convention that was meeting in Saratoga at the end of the summer, and he thought Marble in any case was better suited for the Italian mission or the collectorship of the Port of New York. If Marble insisted on being governor August thought he would have to attain the office through indirect means. He should run for lieutenant governor and "exert yourself to get former governor Seymour to accept the nomination for Governor with the understanding of his being sent to England" as minister to the Court of St. James's. Once Horatio Seymour had vacated office and left the United States, Marble would be in control of the state government.

But Marble insisted on a direct dash at the governorship, so August did what he could to help him.

"Command me in any way, which you can think of," August told Marble. "Whatever I can do to make you an Excellency shall be cheerfully done." August wrote letters to leading Democrats, trying to get their support for Marble; but Marble in his work for Tilden had alienated many New York politicians whose help he now needed.

Tilden could have simplified the race by endorsing a candidate; but he never publicly stated his preference.

For Marble's sake August treated lightly a request that he himself run for governor, although it must have been far more gratifying than he let on. He wrote to Marble:

"I forgot to tell you this morning"—what a thing to forget!—"that I was asked whether I would not accept the nomination." August had been informed that a certain faction in the Democratic party "thought a good merchant with a sound record would best suit. Of course, I declined and said that, if the nomination went to the city, nobody would or could be as acceptable to the commercial and financial community as yourself, whose record for hard money and free trade was better and stronger than that of anybody in the state." Better, August was saying, than his own, a compliment indeed.

With August, Jr., however, August was not optimistic about Marble's chances.

"Marble is moving Heaven and Earth to get the nomination," August told August, Jr., "but is very little assisted by Tilden, for whom he has done so much."

August could not fathom Tilden's want of loyalty to the man who had made him governor and placed him in a position to run for the presidency. He knew after talking to dozens of Democrats that the only way Marble could get the nomination was, as he told Marble, "if you could secure a warm support of the convention at the start."

"Albany friend ought come out for you being master of situation," August telegraphed Marble during the convention.

But "Albany friend" abandoned Marble—or at least he let his men throw their support to another candidate. After prowling the hotels of Saratoga, stopping delegates and arguing for his candidacy with extemporary editorials on reform, Marble gave up and withheld his name. The convention, which had to be reconvened in the middle of September, nominated a former Republican. Party loyalty seemed to mean as little as personal loyalty.

Some of Marble's friends suggested that he run for mayor of New York City, but Marble was as disgusted with politics as August, which brought the two men closer together than they had been for many months. However, despite their mutual disillusionment they continued to work to get the presidency for the man who had treated them both so badly.

To keep August, Jr., informed, August sent him all the daily New York newspapers, the weekly *World,* and *The Nation;* and he kept up a commentary on the more significant events. He thought Tilden's and Hendricks's delays in writing their letters of acceptance had hurt the party by implying that, despite the compromise platform, they could not bridge the gap between their stands on the currency question—Hard Money, Soft Money; Republicans rumored the only thing the two men could agree on was that the country was suffering from no money. And when their letters were published, Tilden's rang like tin when it should have sounded like gold. It was evasive—worse than evasive. If Tilden had avoided the issues gracefully, one at least could have taken pleasure in the performance; but the letter was labored. In one particularly unfelicitous sentence he used the legal term *usufruct,* which was an act of rhetorical arrogance. The public pinned him with the word; for the rest of the campaign he was "old usufruct Tilden." Tilden had slipped on his own banana peel.

"Still," August said, "so great is the universal distrust of the Republicans in every branch of trade and industry that the country is panting for a change. I think this feeling will become more intense as we approach the election, because the general stagnation and depreciation must continue. Under such a state of things, the shortcomings or virtues of the respective candidates will be lost sight of and unless some great blunder is made by our party leaders between now and November, I look confidently for a Democratic victory."

Although August told August, Jr., that "my heart is not in the fight, and I really do it now on account of your admonitions," nevertheless he lobbied for Tilden with Democrats who inclined toward Rutherford B. Hayes.

"I did my best and used every argument to appeal to his judgement and his pride, but so far in vain," August wrote Marble after one particularly difficult session with a pro-Hayes Democrat. "I think at the bottom of his stand is his apprehension of the animosity of the Governor to him if once in the Presidential chair. His defection would hurt us in this state, and the Republicans would use it as a strong card. Could not you induce Mr. Tilden to make overtures for a reconciliation? He is strong enough to afford to make concessions now."

August saw strength as a license for generosity; Tilden saw strength as a license to avoid compromise. August was a diplomat; Tilden was a warrior.

August suggested that Tilden ought to establish a "local finance committee" to solicit contributions from New York businessmen, but he declined to serve on it. He was tired of begging for the party; he had done that for too many years with too little success and too little appreciation.

He felt he would be most useful and comfortable simply testifying to his faith in Tilden. With Marble's help he prepared speeches.

"Will you read the enclosed and tell me *cordially* whether any parts of it will do?" he asked about the draft of one speech. "You must *cut, slash,* and *add.*"

August's concern with style was the vanity of the connoisseur. He wanted to furnish his speeches as carefully as he did his houses. More than he wanted Marble's thoughts he wanted his friend's eyes and ear. Like many ghostwriters Marble was less a coauthor than an interior decorator.

Even after Marble's help August thought the speech was "not a very brilliant effort"—although at least it was free of *usufructs.* However, August surrendered to another kind of arrogance. In an atypical and bitter statement August told Marble he thought the speech would "do for my enlightened herds at Babylon."

August felt himself too betrayed by the electorate to have anything but contempt for their political judgment.

His speech at the end of September in the Seventh Congressional District of New York City was better because he was angrier. The ritual election-year attacks on August had begun. The story about August's denunciation of Tilden was reprinted, long after he had denied it, in a Western newspaper. Although August had won a suit against him brought by Irish rebels to recover $25,000 of Fenian funds that the British government had seized when August tried to transport the money to Ireland, the lies about his mishandling of the sum continued to spread. And there were, of course, rumors that through August the Rothschilds had contributed $2 million to ensure the election of Tilden in exchange for—as Hayes was told—"control of United States finances in Europe for the next four years."

"I am boiling over and so I had to open a safety valve," August wrote to Marble. "My wrath is real and deep. If a man gets to threescore, it is rather hard to find *daily* the rubbish that surrounds me. I am really becoming weary and realize what the Germans call *Lebenssatt*," sated with or sick of life.

But, instead of sating him the attacks piqued August's appetite for the fight; and August's reply to the rumor of the Rothschilds' $2 million contribution had the snap his earlier speech lacked.

"It was my custom to read the Republican papers," August told the crowd at the Seventh Congressional District meeting, "but of late they have become so full of vile abuse I had to give them up. They became nauseating. I have read that after the election it is the intention of Mr. Rothschild and myself to buy up the whole United States. Mr. Rothschild has not written to me yet on the subject"—August was interrupted by appreciative laughter from his audience—"but I know that *Uncle Sam will not sell out*. He has different plans for farming out the country, and I'll tell you what they are. He is going to sign a lease of it to his namesake Uncle Samuel J. Tilden with a special covenant of renewal for good behavior."

Tilden was so appreciative of August's efforts in the campaign that he asked to meet. On October 1 August went to Tilden's Gramercy Park house and spent two hours being tempted by the governor, who assumed August wanted to be named Secretary of the Treasury if the Democrats won the election.

"Our friend seems to be under the impression that my specialty and my ambition lay in the financial line," August told Marble the next morning. "They are neither of them in that direction. I would not take an official position in the Treasury and, in regard to the manipulation of loans, that depends entirely upon my continuing in business at all and still more upon my relations with the Rothschilds. On that point, I have not at all made up my mind, and the chances for my giving up the shop altogether, whatever the result of the election may be are very great. If I have any ambition at all it is entirely confined to diplomacy, in which I feel that I could render myself more useful to the administration and to the country than in any other way. If I am not good there, I am certainly not of much good anywhere else. At all events, I don't mean to try to get a diplomatic post"—he would not lobby for himself, as he had done a quarter of a century earlier when he had sought a mission—"and, if it should embarrass our friend to promote my aspirations in that direction then I have to renounce the rest. Of course, I know the difficulties by which he is surrounded, and I most likely place an undue value upon my qualifications and my claims on the party."

If the theme—giving up business—was the same that August had been playing all his adult life, now it was in a minor key. When August had been a younger man, his threat to retire had been a somewhat sulky desire to abandon the world he had made for himself and return to Germany. Now it had more of the quality of total renunciation; he was not going to turn back to another life, he was giving up everything. He would not scramble for either the Treasury Department, a good position if he wanted to control the country's finances as his enemies charged, or a diplomatic post. It was all vanity; whatever you had—position, property, friends, family—you would lose. It was hard to keep playing the game once you realized the game was fixed; but since it was the only game there was, it was just as hard not to play it at all.

August asked Marble to "make my position clear to Tilden, so that there may be no misunderstanding on his part."

The evening after August met with Tilden, Marble asked August for a new contribution to Tilden's campaign. It is possible that Tilden had offered the prize and now Marble was setting the price. August lost his temper and spent the rest of the night "brooding over the conversation." In his mind he tried Marble and found him not guilty of duplicity.

"You must not for one moment think that I impugn your motives when I show impatience at the urgency of your argument," August told Marble the following day. "I assure you I appreciate fully your friendly promptings, and my impatience is caused much more by my utter inability of responding more liberally to your suggestion than anything else."

The same day, August wrote to Tilden: "I send you enclosed $10,000—in 10 notes of 1/m [$1,000 each] as my contribution toward the campaign in Indiana and Ohio where the decisive battle is now being fought. I should have wished to send you a bigger bundle, but I have been fearfully hit since 1873 and am catching it still every day by the continued depreciation of my property."

Because August did not want to feed rumors that the Rothschilds were trying to buy the election, he asked Tilden to keep the contribution confidential.

By giving so much money he was committing himself to the campaign more deeply than he previously had done. The personal element that had been missing was now present. Supporting a candidate is an act of identification; August had looked in the mirror and finally seen Tilden's face.

CHAPTER FIFTY

ON THE ANNIVERSARY of Jeannie's death August went to Newport to visit her grave. There was a bad snowstorm. Except for Oliver, who had spent a short time with him at the Nursery after his cruise and before returning to the Naval Academy, August had not seen his family for months. The falling snow filled in the tracks he made in the cemetery. Although his grief for Jeannie was just as deep as it had been, her death was no longer as vivid; in the end, you lose everything, even your sense of loss.

Once he was committed to the Tilden campaign August's energy and enjoyment in politics increased. He joked more with Marble.

"If *you* don't care about going to the races," August told him, "*I* do, to have you—not so much on your account, as that I want to be seen in company with Warwick."

For the first time since Jeannie's death August began signing his messages to Marble *Augie Mogul. Mogul* was still a code name, but now the code was not political. It was emotional. August was campaigning not just for Tilden but to recapture his former enthusiasm for life. He was campaigning for the sake of the campaign.

Although he still denigrated his speech drafts, he admitted that occasionally "common sense" put in a "little gold." The speeches had so much snap that August was advised—as he told Marble—"that I should rather undertone my statements of attack and indict the corrupt Republican leaders, but not the whole party." August was pleased to believe that the advice was "more for my personal good than on general grounds." It was novel for the Democratic leaders to be so considerate of his feelings.

After the Democrats won the governorship of Indiana, shaved the Republican majority so close in Ohio's only race (for secretary of state) that they drew blood, and got into office in West Virginia—all three traditionally Republican states—August presided over a Cooper Union celebration. Although his speech at one point was interrupted by hecklers (possibly when he spoke in support of Fenians, who still distrusted him) it was well received. The evening meeting with its bunting and band seemed in spirit close to rallies sixteen, twenty, and twenty-four years earlier, when Democrats had plunged into election years hopefully. As August finished speaking the audience loudly applauded.

"Your sound, witty, and eloquent address last night shows that I was right two years ago when I wrote to goad you into taking in national affairs the part you are able to play with so much usefulness and distinction," Sam Ward wrote to August, proof that the speech was a success; his friends were trying to take credit for it.

The *New York Evening Post* reported it had received letters from London, saying that the syndicate that had been formed to handle the new issue of United States government bonds would drop the business if Tilden were elected. Because August was a member of that syndicate he was told by Tilden's managers that it was important for him to make "an emphatic denial of this lie" as soon as possible.

August did not "like much the idea of writing a letter, and I think an interview may be best." A letter was a monologue; August preferred dialogue, a minstrel show in which he could play Mr. Bones to the reporter's Mr. Interlocutor. His preference was sound. In his letters he sometimes seemed ponderous; in interviews he skipped from point to point. Public letters did not allow much room for humor; interviews were susceptible to irony. "But," August told Marble, "I want to be guided by you." Marble thought the situation needed the weight of a written statement, which he apparently drafted for August.

"No such letters from London . . . could have been received either here or in Washington," August wrote in the *New York World*, "else certainly the Messrs. Rothschild, the principal managers of the syndicate in London, as my house is here, would have informed me of the existence of such a state of feeling. The whole story is a miserable partisan canard."

Although August claimed that Tilden was more experienced in financial matters than Hayes, he admitted that "the safety and wisdom of investment in the funded debt of the Government of the United States do not depend upon Presidential elections . . . ," an assertion that was in conflict with his earlier prophecy of economic doom if the Republicans were reelected.

The hostile press attacked.

The *New York Tribune* isolated him: "We have reason to believe that, of all the members of the Syndicate, Mr. Belmont stands absolutely alone in . . . his opinion."

The New York Times went in for the kill: "Mr. August Belmont is in a piteous predicament. His instincts as a Democratic politician conflict with his interests as a financial agent; his duty to Tilden and Tammany is at variance with his obligations to the Rothschilds. . . . In his zeal for Tilden, he has declared that the country is galloping to ruin—that its condition is irredeemable under Republican administration; that nothing less than the triumph of Democracy can save it from bankruptcy and chaos. In behalf of . . . the Rothschilds, he protests that politics have nothing to do with the public faith in United States government bonds— that it is beyond the reach of party, whether Hayes or Tilden be the next President."

A few days later the *Times* elaborated its description of "this curious contest . . . of Belmont versus Belmont. . . . Mr. Belmont, the banker, does not write letters for publication. He is a particularly reticent, cautious, secretive gentleman, who will never be caught explaining to the public his own opinion of any investment. . . . But Mr. Belmont, the politician, does write letters, which, to do him justice, are more gushing and enthusiastic than accurate. The politician knows nothing of the business of the banker, and betrays his singular ignorance at every step. . . . Many persons who do not comprehend the beautiful duality of his character uncharitably hold him guilty of insincerity. . . . If Mr. Belmont could have two votes, the politician would vote for Tilden, and the businessman would vote for Hayes."

In another article, the *Tribune* did not even grant August the benefit of any motive, no matter how dual, for his stand. He was—the paper said—just stubborn:

"He has been the obstinate twelfth juror among businessmen so very long that it would probably cause him a greater sacrifice of pride to agree than to dissent and get beaten again."

For more than a week the newspaper battle continued. Republicans flourished evidence that European capitalists had no confidence in the

Democrats and their Soft Money tendencies and that the Democrats if elected to the White House would pay off the old Confederate debt—accusations that were contradictory in their own right, since enough European capitalists had invested in the Confederacy to make inviting the prospect of the Confederate debt being honored. But both charges were lies. The European capitalists, at least those represented in the syndicate, stood to make too much money selling United States government bonds to stop, and Tilden would not take over the Confederate debt.

When a particularly galling item appeared, August at first was inclined to ignore it; but Perry, who had just returned from his Western trip, told his father it had to be answered and asked permission to reply. August thought Perry's passion "natural on the part of a young man, besides which I fear he has inherited a little of my combativeness." He complied and told Marble "I will see what he will make of it."

But the Democratic leadership told August that neither he nor Perry should take any notice of the piece. They should damn it with silence. Perhaps they felt that what had seemed to be an asset—August's participation in the syndicate, which allowed him to speak with authority—was turning into a liability: the syndicate's natural sympathies were with a Hard Money stand that could alienate the Soft Money Democrats. However, despite the advice of the party leaders the combativeness that Perry had inherited could not be restrained, in either the father or the son. August cast around for a champion, at one point asking Marble to "buckle on your armor." Eventually, backed up by a letter from the Rothschilds, August answered the newspaper himself.

"We do not think the small decline that has occurred here in American stocks is attributable to any fears about your financial credit in case Tilden should be elected," the Rothschilds said.

"Vague rumors and insinuations have indeed been actively put in circulation," August added, "and the authority of the Secretary of the Treasury has even been called in aid, but that distinguished gentleman has too much self-respect to give his endorsement to this electioneering trick, and in his speech of today . . . he does not make the slightest allusion to it."

The Republican press, however, was partly right. August, like most American politicians, was cloven. In the presidential campaign he and the Republican secretary of the treasury might be opponents; but in a larger campaign, the fight to defend American capital, they were allies.

On October 30, 1876, a week before election day, the Manhattan Club hosted a reception for Tilden. Among the three hundred guests were many whom August had known as eager young men. Now, like August, they were old. Even with his opponents within the party, August had this bond, the shared past; their conflicts were familiar, habitual. Friends and enemies. Most of them had arrived by nine o'clock. Milling about in the brightly lit second-floor rooms, they seemed to a cynical eye amusing—as though age makes us into caricatures of our youthful selves. Fernando Wood. John Morrissey. Oakey Hall. William Travers. The old-timers at the meeting were either dim—or so frantic in their attempts to maintain the gaiety of their earlier years that, like kerosene lamps turned so high their chimneys become sooty, they were opaque, their youth hidden by the very blazes with which they were kept alive. There were a few new faces like Joseph Pulitzer and presumably Perry; but for August the reception that night before All Hallow's Eve was a gathering of ghosts. The flowers that decorated the room were funereal.

Tilden arrived fifteen to thirty minutes late, long enough to assure him of a grand entrance. He stood in the center of the room chatting and shaking hands even after August had called the meeting to order. August's speech was interrupted halfway through by the band, which, apparently thinking August was finished, struck up a tune.

"Never since the foundation of this club have we assembled under brighter auspices," said August. "Victory is in the air."

But he spoke so softly that only those who stood near him heard.

Two days after the Manhattan Club meeting August was asked to hold $50,000—$25,000 from each participant—that was at stake in an election bet. Since one of the gamblers was James Gordon Bennett, Jr., and since Bennett had put his money on Tilden, August assumed that in the few days left before the election the *New York Herald,* Bennett's newspaper, could be counted on to come out strongly in favor of the Democratic ticket.

August made a few other last-minute efforts on the part of the party. He paid for the printing of his Manhattan Club speech, made arrangements to get an accurate report of a Republican meeting, wrote another letter to the newspapers, and spent his nights arguing politics at his clubs. The Democrats were afraid that the Republicans were going to vote with bayonets. Federal troops had been sent into South Carolina—to put down riots, the Republicans said; to control the ballot boxes, the Democrats claimed. Federal troops were also stationed in Louisiana and Florida. And in places where troops could not be effective, the Republicans had agents armed with offers of patronage to exchange for votes. However, August believed that unless the Democrats could prove a charge they should say nothing. He thought Tilden's advisers were too zealous, a quality just as dangerous in leaders as the timidity Tilden often demonstrated. And he explored the possibility of staging a coup in Tilden's affections. The day before the election August asked Marble, "Don't you think a triumvirate of *Marcus, Scipio,* and *Brutus* would do better for the next four years to carry Uncle Sammie's administration through all the breakers awaiting it than all the combined wisdom of the Kitchen Cabinet?"

Although August did not make it clear who would play which roles, Tilden had enough enemies among his supporters for Brutus to have many candidates.

"The only fear is we"—August included himself in the triumvirate; possibly he would be Brutus—"might do too well, and the people would insist upon a second and third term."

The suggestion was the track left by an ambition that was long gone. August knew he had no chance of becoming part of the engine that drove Tilden. But the whim betrayed how much August had surrendered himself to the campaign.

"I have taken a more active part in politics that I expected to do," he had said a few weeks earlier. "In fact, I was pushed forward by circumstances and am not sorry for it."

By the day after the election it was apparent that Tilden had at least 184 electoral votes (he needed one more to win) and would have a popular majority (which would turn out to be about 250,000 more votes than Hayes). However, in the three states in which federal troops supported unpopular Radical Republican administrations—South Carolina, Louisiana, and Florida—the election results had been delayed. It was possible that Tilden had lost one (probably South Carolina) or two of these states; but it was unlikely that he had lost three, and all he needed was one in order to be president.

The Republicans sent agents to the disputed states and opened an account in a bank in Philadelphia through which bribe money was channeled. The Democrats also sent agents and money south, although the Democrats in time would claim that, while the Republicans were trying to corrupt the boards of canvassers, they were bribing the boards to keep them honest—which may explain why the Democrats were offering such low bids (in one case $30,000 compared to $200,000, which, at least in Louisiana and Florida, was the going rate for a state's electoral votes). Presumably it was not worth as much to stay honest as it was to become dishonest.

In Oregon the governor, a Democrat who suffered from the excessive zeal that made August uneasy about many of Tilden's closest associates in New York, illegally disqualified a Republican elector in favor of a Democrat. All over the country violence seemed imminent—perhaps a new civil war.

In Florida and South Carolina, where the contest had been close, the Republicans—August feared—would have little trouble in controlling the election results. However, in Louisiana the Democrats had won with about a 10 percent margin, almost 9,000 votes; Republicans would have a harder time manufacturing victory there. Louisiana seemed to August the key.

"If Louisiana can help the Republicans defeat you," August told Tilden, "their returning board will count you out. They are determined to win *at all hazard*."

Two days after the election August asked Abram S. Hewitt, chairman of the National Committee, what the Committee intended to do in the crisis.

Hewitt waffled. The Democrats could do nothing extreme that might compromise the credit of the United States.

"I am as much interested in the credit of the country as any gentleman," August said. But: "I would sooner see every bond I hold sink in the ocean before consenting to the loss of what has been gained by the Democratic Party."

Moreover, Hewitt's fears were unfounded. United States bonds were buoyant.

"Wall Street is evidently not frightened by the Republican bugbear," August had told Tilden.

If August with his combativeness still had been chairman of the Democratic National Committee, he would not have acted as timidly as Hewitt was doing. But Hewitt—who could not have been one of the over-zealous party leaders August distrusted—was a flimsy of Tilden. Both mistook timidity for prudence.

With Tilden, August was no more successful than he had been with Hewitt.

"I suggest a public meeting this afternoon or evening, denouncing this outrage," August told Tilden on November 9, the day he went to see Hewitt. "At the same time, the *World* and *Herald* ought to come out tomorrow against this open violation of our most sacred right. Prompt and vigorous action seems necessary to me."

The idea of mass demonstrations made Tilden uneasy. Couldn't trustworthy Democrats and Republicans investigate the charges of voting fraud and decide which of the two candidates had won in the disputed states? Although Tilden believed this was the way the American people could solve the problem, he was defining *the people* narrowly: a handful of respected public figures. He was throwing away his advantage. However the Republicans manipulated the electoral vote, Tilden clearly was the popular choice. Therefore he should have used people—masses of them in demonstrations—to dramatize his edge. His unwillingness to do so seemed to August fastidiousness.

As for mobilizing the two dependable Democratic newspapers in New York, Tilden seemed not indifferent but hardly like a candidate whose office was being stolen.

"I would advise you to send for Bennett and have a talk with him," August told Tilden. "He is personally fond of you, and it will flatter him to be consulted by you." Knowing Tilden's character, August felt compelled to add, "Should you not wish to do it, please drop me a line; and I will ask him to see me."

Predictably Tilden shied from giving the impression of seeking help; he preferred that August flatter Bennett for him. Although August was sick in bed with a bad cold, he asked Bennett to come to 109 Fifth Avenue between eight-thirty and nine o'clock on the evening of November 10, three days after the election.

"Would you like my proposing to Bennett to come around and see you?" August asked Tilden in another note.

By giving Tilden a second chance to agree to meet with Bennett, August was saying as strongly as he could to a president-elect (which he thought Tilden was) that Tilden was making a mistake by avoiding the newspaperman. Bennett was vain enough to feel insulted at being approached secondhand. Tilden must have understood August's meaning.

He took August's advice and agreed to see Bennett. The crisis was an aperture through which August entered, partway, into Tilden's confidence.

The same day that August met Bennett, Grant sent a group of Republicans to New Orleans to observe—which was interpreted to be active not passive behavior—the canvass. Tilden's scheme for a bipartisan investigative committee was, at least temporarily, dead. The best the Democrats could do was to rush their own "observers" to New Orleans. August discussed such a course with Hewitt, who in this case luckily interpreted prudence to mean suspicion and calculation and who approved of the plan. August immediately telegraphed Thomas Bayard in Washington:

"Can you make it possible to comply with request National Committee to go at once to New Orleans. Situation there very grave. Powerful aid and advice like yours invaluable to protect law and prevent fraud."

Bayard must have realized that the crisis required not statesmen but fixers and, wanting to preserve his reputation as a statesman, declined for reasons of health.

To Marble, another choice for the Democratic delegation to New Orleans, August said:

"Situation becoming serious. Advise strongly your returning from Pennsylvania without delay."

Marble was not able to get back to New York until after the New Orleans group was chosen. He asked instead to be sent to Florida, where he hoped to limit Republican damage. The Democratic National Committee gave him its blessing. Marble prepared to go. His send-off in the press was vicious. The opposition newspapers accused Marble of political skullduggery; and neither of New York's major Democratic newspapers came to his aid.

"The *Tribune* vilifies me daily," Marble told August; "and, the *World* and *Herald* take up no cudgels to defend a friend who is unjustly aspersed, even tho' it be a friend whom the editors have known for 20 years. I do not think therefore that they would take up the cudgels at my request. But, if my request would induce them so to do, Hell will freeze over before I will make the request."

In Florida, Marble would make honorable men of the *Tribune*'s editors: he was indeed guilty of political skullduggery. The election in Florida would be decided by a mere 100 votes (which both parties were claiming as their margins of victory). To guarantee that the votes would be counted fairly—which Marble believed would give the Democrats the state—he apparently offered bribes to Florida's secretary of state (although at that point he had no authority to do so) and to Florida's board of canvassers (with, evidently, some authority—although not necessarily Tilden's). But the second bribe was either too little or too late. Florida's board of canvassers decided the state had gone Republican; the Democrats rejected the decision. Similar scenarios were enacted in the other disputed states. On December 6, Louisiana, Florida, South Carolina, and Oregon each sent Congress dual returns, one Democratic claiming victory for Tilden and the other Republican claiming victory for Hayes. Congress had to decide which returns were valid. The Democrats controlled the House of Representatives; the Republicans controlled the Senate. If the House of Representatives counted the votes, Tilden would win; if the Senate counted the votes, Hayes would. The two parties, of course, could not agree on which branch of Congress should do the counting.

During Marble's visit to Florida, August was in constant, often mysterious, contact with him. Unsigned coded telegrams passed back and forth; and, like a shaman reading messages in seemingly random scratchings, August interpreted the telegrams for Tilden, whom he continually assured of victory.

"No other solution but your election can end the agony of the country and prevent the most disastrous consequences," August told him.

August developed an intelligence network through which he learned of secret Republican meetings; current vote-counts (sometimes incorrect; at one point he thought, "The agony is over. Florida has gone Democratic"); who was in town; what could be even more important, who had left town suddenly; and, very important, who wrote a damaging, unsigned article in the *New York Sun* that offered as a solution to the current controversy Tilden's giving the election to Hayes and running again in four years—an unacceptable notion.

The author of the piece was a good Democrat, the respected lawyer and writer and old acquaintance of August's, George Ticknor Curtis. August visited him and, as he later told Tilden, "made it all right. Without entering into the discussion of the merits of his argument, I told him that all our friends viewed the question differently. *He will keep quiet I am sure.*"

While August worked behind the scenes, Perry was onstage writing articles for the *New York Herald* in which he discussed his pet subject: the counting of presidential votes. He had sounded the warning before the election, earlier in the year, and he was unhappy to have been so quickly vindicated. After the election, he thought, the Democrats in Congress, particularly in the House of Representatives, should have pushed the Republicans for an agreement on how the votes would be counted long before "the critical moment for counting arrives. It is to be hoped," he thought, "that the Democratic House would take the initiative in this matter so the *onus* of refusing to promote a fair count should rest upon the Senate."

But the new Speaker of the House, Samuel J. Randall of Pennsylvania, tended to be more sanguine in this matter than his predecessor, Michael C. Kerr, had been. All the Democrats had to do was wait—he thought; the election would naturally be thrown into the House and then, Randall told Perry, "We'll vote the Democratic President in!"

Randall had reason to be optimistic, for precedent seemed to be on the side of the Democrats—which Tilden, John Bigelow (one of Tilden's intimates), and Marble, back from Florida, were in the process of proving in a history of presidential vote-counts.

Democratic strategy was to have the contested returns invalidated; as a result neither candidate would have a majority and the election would be decided, as the Constitution stipulated, in the House of Representatives.

August thought this tack possible, although he believed that in following it the Democrats had to make a "clear distinction between the counting (enumerating or adding)" of votes, which would undoubtedly be done by the president of the Senate, "and the verifying or determining the votes to be counted," which would be done by the House and therefore give the Democrats the advantage—a point Tilden did not seem to be taking into consideration.

"It may be presumption on my part to make suggestions on such a question," August told Marble after they had left a meeting with Tilden and other Democratic leaders. "In any case, if you deem them of any value, don't give them to the Governor as mine, because I don't want him to think that I pronounced a criticism upon his very able arguments."

Because of the crisis everyone was touchy. When Marble failed to show up at an agreed-upon time, August uncharacteristically lost his temper with his friend, went home, and scribbled a note, his anger flattening his handwriting.

"With telegraphs and messenger boys," August wrote, "a gentleman has no right not to keep an appointment, *a solicited one in the bargain*, without a word of warning; *much less has a friend*. I say this, not in anger"—the denial advertising what was denied—"but all in sorrow, for I feel deeply mortified, more than I can express and infinitely more than you ever will give me credit for."

The flash used up the powder. August's anger did not last.

Within the circle of Tilden's trust August was nonetheless uneasy. He was used to being the pivot around which policy swung. With Tilden his advice too often was ignored. He became a major domo as much as a counselor, arranging meetings at his and Tilden's houses. At one gathering just before Christmas, August brought Tilden and his advisers together with leading Democrats in Congress in order to coordinate Democratic actions. Bayard had recently complained, "My wings feel so clipped, and my want of power so plain." But he showed up and soared above most of the others present. Everyone who attended denied to the press knowing anything about such a meeting. They were in town—they all said—on personal matters.

Power is personal.

August thought that Tilden "made a very favorable" but not very deep impression on the visitors from Washington.

"I should like him to be more explicit *to his friends* in the affirmation of his determination to *stand the test at all hazard* if the Republicans intend to carry out their treasonable scheme of robbery and usurpation. Such an assurance on his part will give the additional incentive of personal fealty to the patriotic courage of such men as Randall and Bayard and will inspire confidence to the more prudent and hesitating ones."

August again pressed Tilden to agree to a program of mass meetings to "*frighten* the *traitors*," which Tilden again rejected. Mass meetings could become mobs and mobs could turn to violence. In fact, rumors of planned Democratic violence had become common.

"I don't see why it is so difficult to distinguish between a firm opposition which would prevent the accomplishment of wrong and a revolutionary resistance to an established authority," Perry said.

When August once more advocated mass meetings, which he was sure would make Tilden president, Tilden, still afraid of being responsible for violence, once more rejected the idea. Turning down a crown three times does not make a man a Caesar. Tilden was more like Caesar's wife: he wanted his actions to be above suspicion.

At the meeting in August's house Tilden had stressed the need for the crisis to be resolved through arbitration. Perhaps, misunderstanding him, Bayard and Hewitt thought Tilden was not committed to the plan of getting the disputed votes thrown out and sending the election into the House of Representatives. As a result they supported the creation of a bipartisan electoral commission that would decide the issue. Fifteen men: five from the House of Representatives, five from the Senate, and five from the Supreme Court. The delegation from Congress would be split between Democrats and Republicans; the Supreme Court justices would be chosen by chance.

August, Marble, and Tilden met and agreed that none of them liked the plan. August thought that "having the whole right and three-quarters of the People on our side, we give away too much under the desire to compromise." After he composed a telegram to Bayard saying that, he offered to let Tilden add a note. Tilden, who was particularly disgusted by the provision of choosing the justices by lot, said:

"Mr. Belmont, individually I do not care the snap of my fingers for the Presidency and will not consent to raffle for it."

The plan was slightly changed. The justices would not be randomly chosen. The Supreme Court delegation would be evenly balanced; two of the judges would be pro-Democratic, two would be pro-Republican. The fifth judge and fifteenth commissioner would be David Davis, who was believed to be nonpartisan. By a lucky accident of history, one man's reputation would allow the country an honorable solution to the electoral crisis.

"Have no fear that 'dangerous departures' from the Constitution will be sanctioned by me," Bayard telegraphed August. "I seek justice under the law. Mere party advantage I neither give nor take, but stand firmly"— he crossed out *firmly*, which may have sounded too inflexible, and added —"steadily by what I believe the honor and welfare of my country require."

His editing also implied that he knew he was writing for posterity; he wanted to choose his words carefully. The audience was the future, which one day would perform its own play—a play including a retelling of the story of the crisis of 1876—for an even more distant future.

August, receiving the telegram, was only the first of many who would read Bayard's words; because of that he read them with the most innocent eyes.

"I am afraid the mischief is done," he told Marble.

But it was too late to change course. The measure had too much support, so August tried to take comfort in whatever reassurances he could find.

"I begin to think that the opposition of some of my friends as well as my own is based upon erroneous grounds from the very fact that the ultra politicians on both sides denounce the bill," August told Bayard.

And he sent Marble an encouraging telegram from Sam Ward, who August admitted "is, of course, personally of little weight, but he has the ear of everybody in Washington and stands particularly well with Bayard and some other of our friends. The measure, in his opinion, is sure to elect and inaugurate Tilden and the latter would make a great mistake to oppose the bill."

Although a few Democrats—perhaps August among them—were, as Perry told Bayard, "allowing themselves to become excited," the bill to form an electoral commission was popular. Most of the people in New York, Perry continued, "are only too willing that some agreement should be reached. I don't believe that even the party press, which has already come out against the plan, will succeed in doing away with the general feeling of relief."

"I do not in the least wonder that the electoral vote bill should have startled you and other friends, simply by reason of its suddenness and apparent novelty," Bayard wrote to August, "and yet the whole scheme seemed safe and valuable." It was, Bayard claimed, "a bridge over threatened disaster" and "practically speaking, I believe Mr. Tilden's induction to office is by this bill made not only possible but probable." Bayard had only one reservation. "Within a few hours, the bill has gone to the President for his approval—in regard to which it is said there exists no cause for doubt. I shall, however, breathe more freely when I know that the matter has passed beyond his reach. It is a fearful thing to reflect such great consequences lie within the measure of alcohol he may happen to swallow in a given time."

Grant signed the bill.

"It will be a struggle of life and death before that tribunal," August thought; "and we must go there armed 'cap à pied,' otherwise we shall be outwitted at the very moment of our expected triumph."

During the last half of January 1877 August was relaxed, cautiously confident, and cheerful. Now when Marble failed to show up at a meeting, August became not angry but jocular.

"I certainly thought the summonses of the Great Mogul were to be respected," he wrote to Marble; "and so I confidently counted upon seeing you. But you have neither the fear of man or God before you."

He was in one of his frisky moods—and when he became angry, this time at Tilden, his anger seemed almost joyful, a release of pent-up emotion, the confusion of resentment and pleasure a man can feel when let out of prison. Tilden, although a multimillionaire himself, had asked August to help cover the Democratic National Committee's postelection debts. August lambasted Tilden for letting the expenses get out of hand.

He long had been losing patience with Tilden, who with every day the crisis lasted seemed to withdraw farther and farther from the struggle, as though he were involved in an indirect way in the fight: the chained maiden watching the knight battle the dragon. It mattered to him who won, but he was not in a position to help.

"What is going on at Headquarters?" August wanted to know.

The answer was: nothing much—although, as August pointed out, "the Republican radicals are getting bolder and more reckless every day and are made so by the silence and inaction of our people."

August did what he could, including organizing a defense of Hendricks's record, which must have been a distasteful task (since August was a Hard Money man and Hendricks a Soft Money one); but the Democrats would drift until Tilden took some strong action—almost any strong action. A leader had to lead, not hide.

Perry went to Washington as secretary to Bayard, who was one of the three Democratic senators on the Electoral Commission. The old chamber of the Supreme Court in which the hearings were held was crowded. Perry examined the faces of the commissioners. Justice Joseph P. Bradley had replaced David Davis, who—perhaps to escape the burden history tried to put on him—had resigned from the Supreme Court to accept the position of United States senator from Illinois. Assuming an equal split along party lines within the rest of the commission, Bradley would decide who became president. Bradley was a Republican appointee.

Perry thought Bradley, who had small and not particularly strong features, looked like a priest, and he assumed he was "probably a great student. His son tells me," Perry wrote to August, "that, during the last three or four nights, his father has scarcely slept at all. The night before last he went to bed at eleven and got up at three. The only question in my mind is whether he is susceptible to the pressure which the Republicans have been exerting upon all their people."

The commissioners voted party loyalty. In the first case they examined, Florida, the eight Republicans including Bradley carried the state for Hayes.

Since the Democrats were certain to lose South Carolina (where Hayes may have won honestly) and Oregon (where the Democrats, in throwing out the Republican elector had acted illegally), August invested his hope in the Democrats' strongest case: Louisiana. When it looked as though the Louisiana Democrats were about to sell out Tilden in exchange for control of the state, August told him, "Best be in advance of them and denounce it in Congress and in the press as a got-up job of the radicals [Republicans] to influence [the Electoral] Commission at this juncture. I would advise your telegraphing your agents and friends in Washington at once. . . . The whole thing looks fishy. All our friends at the South have too much at stake for any one of them to attempt so wicked and useless a crime."

But it seemed as though their friends in the South were, in fact, attempting such a wicked crime, which infuriated August.

"If the Democratic party is to exist hereafter as a national party," he said, "such bargains as the one contemplated in Louisiana ought to be frowned down by every honest man."

The only chance for success Tilden had was for him to rally his forces and make it clear that the Democrats would not accept any decision based on fraud.

"Vigor and firmness can alone save us now," August told Marble; "and our leader must give the signal and take the management of affairs in Washington into his own hands."

The Democrats—August asserted—had been "hoodwinked in the formation of this Commission, because it does not carry out either the letter or the spirit of the law which created it. The House of Representatives should take what action it can to abolish the Commission. Could it not pass a resolution instructing its members to withdraw?" Then, because the vote could not be counted, the country could "have a new election next autumn. This may be considered revolutionary, but it is better to fight now than to lie down and have our liberties trampled upon. It is all very well to talk of principles and country, and denounce Party, but we have to deal with perjurers and highway robbers, and Party alone can save us. Party at this juncture means country and all that we hold dear."

As for the hope that Bradley might see reason, August thought, "As well might you now expect the wolf to let the lamb escape unharmed from its clutches as for a rightful decision from the radical majority which has got us at the throat. If we had shown only half the courage in our good cause which our opponents have evinced with the wicked overthrow of our institutions, we should not be where we are now."

But Tilden still temporized. August had no more patience. In his contempt for the governor, he capitalized and abbreviated *our leader* to an ironic *O.L.,* which is what he called Tilden from then on—when he had to talk *of* him. He would not talk *to* him. Giving Tilden advice was a waste of time.

Bayard and the other Democratic commissioners remained at the hearings, which August began referring to as "the infamous play of the 'Righteous Judges' "; and the Republican majority, which he began referring to as "the eight thieves," gave all four contested states to Hayes.

"From all I can see and hear around me," August told Bayard, "I am sure that the Republicans are by no means triumphant over their success. They are like robbers who have secured their booty, but are dreadfully afraid of the consequences of their crime."

"Hayes will come into office crippled in advance," Bayard told August, who found such speculation irrelevant. It did not make what had occurred any more acceptable. In fact, by weakening the government Hayes's election was doubly disastrous.

The Electoral Commission's decision was, August thought, an "unprecedented wrong done by the most ruffianly set of unhung rascals which ever degraded the halls of the Capitol." It was all "simply revolting. Woe to the country whose rulers dare thus defy public opinion and trample under foot everything which is true and honest." August raged like an Old Testament prophet, too furious to be depressed.

The very bargain that gave Hayes the White House this year—the Democrats would acquiesce in the Electoral Commission's decision if the Republican administration would withdraw federal troops from the South —promised to give the Democratic candidate the White House in four years. And August intended the Democratic candidate to be Bayard.

"You were the leader of my choice in our last campaign against corruption and sectionalism," August told Bayard. "You are still so to me."

"I only wish," he told Perry, "I were ten years younger, so as to be able to consecrate a longer period of my life to the cause of my country."

CHAPTER FIFTY-ONE

EARLY IN JANUARY 1877, Cornelius Vanderbilt, as though he were touching another man's corpse, lifted his hand, fumbled his own eyelids closed, and died. The people who had dominated American finance when August first came to New York were almost all gone. Although it seemed he just recently had been a young man building his fortune, fighting duels, leading balls, careering in his carriage along the Bloomingdale Road, August was now one of the old men of Wall Street. His friends and acquaintances, even some younger than himself, were dying. Others were retiring from active life. The Belmont Clique was dissolving. Even James Gordon Bennett, Jr., one of the youngest of August's cronies, would no longer be around.

August had always thought Bennett was "reckless and wild," which was one of the reasons he had liked him. But he seemed to be getting more reckless, and August was attracted less and less to recklessness. A few months earlier in a polo game Bennett had ridden right over a fallen player, his horse kicking the man in the head. The man lived, but August predicted disaster on the playing field. Disaster struck, but in a different game.

On New Year's Day 1877, Bennett arrived at his fiancée's house so drunk that the other guests who had been celebrating the holiday began to leave. Bennett stumbled around the room and—reports do not agree— finally either vomited on his future father-in-law or urinated in the piano or fireplace. His fiancée asked her brother to throw Bennett out. Bennett hid for a couple of days and then went to the Union Club, whose members greeted him normally. He was not a pariah, not yet.

After lunch he was attacked outside the club by his future brother-in-law, who started to horsewhip him. Bennett fought back. They rolled around in the street until friends separated them. New York newspapers, although not the *Herald*, reported that Bennett's engagement was off.

On January 7, the day Vanderbilt was buried, Bennett and his former future brother-in-law went south, as August had years before, to duel. Death or injury could have conferred dignity upon the affair, but both men shot wildly (though apparently not on purpose, which might have solemnized the event). The whole business, especially Bennett's part in it, began to seem so comic that Bennett's reputation suffered the mortal wound his body escaped. Ridicule, not rudeness, made Bennett a pariah. He went into exile in France.

According to legend the duel was the last fought in the United States. Vanderbilt's death was not the only sign that an era was ending.

"Why don't you come see us and congratulate us on Rica's engagement?" August telegraphed Manton Marble on February 23, 1877.

Frederika's fiancé, Samuel Shaw Howland, was known publicly as S. S. Howland, as though he were a steamship—a thoroughly modern, self-contained, solidly constructed, and tastefully appointed ship, the product of wealth and sensibility. His family had been whalers from New London, Connecticut, who had come to New York at the end of the eighteenth century, looking for bigger game. They heaved their harpoons into a shoal of Knickerbockers; and while they never conquered, they remained connected to good families like the Wolcotts and Roosevelts for so long that they became indistinguishable from them. They made money in the East and West Indies and Pacific trades, invested wisely, and lived well. Samuel was one of Perry's few rivals for best-dressed man of their generation; but although a high-spirited sporting man like Bennett, interested in racing and polo, he was not wild nor given to unconventional excess. Bennett was more interesting, but Samuel made a better son-in-law.

During the spring Caroline and Frederika prepared for the wedding, which would be in the fall. August was thankful to have his family at home and spent as much time as possible with them. He was picking up the loose ends of his life and, shuttling back and forth between New York, the Nursery, and Newport, wove a pleasing pattern: politics, business, recreation.

He was still bitter over the decision of the Electoral Commission and, in fact, thought that the men who were being rewarded for their part in it by being given Cabinet appointments should be uncompromisingly opposed by the Democrats; but his desire for vengeance cooled enough for him to tell Marble, "I don't see why I should put myself forward at this moment" to argue against confirmation of—especially—William Maxwell Evarts, who had been the Republican counsel before the Electoral Commission and whom Hayes wanted as secretary of state. "Nobody else" was willing to carry on the fight; and August suspected that if he gave such advice to "our senators" they would "probably laugh at my presumption."

In this matter August surrendered to the Republicans. There were plenty of other battles to fight.

For August politics began to seem fun again, no longer an apocalyptic struggle between the forces of good and evil. The country seemed to be withdrawing from the brink of a terrible calamity.

A suit Samuel Barlow was handling for August was progressing relatively well; and although August described leaving work as flight from "annoyances," the company prospered, August, Jr., was learning fast, and August no longer talked about retiring.

Pincus had left August's stables. The new trainer was not as good, but he was easier to get along with—which August valued. Racing no longer seemed a chore. Though he won less often, he enjoyed it more, the dinners at Jerome Park as important to him as the horses circling the track.

August entered enthusiastically into the Coaching Club, to which he, Perry, and August, Jr., had been elected on December 1 of the previous year. In a little over a month after joining, August took charge. He became, with Leonard Jerome, a member of the two-man executive committee. When the club held its second annual parade on May 27, he lent Perry his dark brown drag with the brown and red undercarriage and four of his best bays. August, Jr., Samuel Howland, and Jerome were among Perry's passengers. A cold evidently kept August at home. The eleven coaches in the parade left Madison Square at four o'clock, drove up Fifth Avenue to and through Central Park and back down Fifth Avenue, arriving by six-thirty—a balmy spring twilight—at the Brunswick Hotel. The Brunswick, a six-story building at Fifth Avenue and Twenty-sixth Street, was not political like the Fifth Avenue Hotel, which was a Republican headquarters, or the Hoffman House, which was a Democratic headquarters (and which would achieve fame for its cigars, the invention of the Manhattan cocktail, and the Bouguereau nude that hung over the bar); it was neutral territory, which was probably one of the reasons why it had become the meeting place of the politically varied but socially uniform horsey set. After a well-planned dinner they had an impromptu ball.

August gave a public exhibition of his paintings; threw many informal but extravagant dinners—he called them potlucks; attended the first Westminster Kennel Club Show at the Hippodrome, on Madison Avenue at Twenty-third Street; participated in a Narragansett Gun Club pigeon-shooting match that Perry won; and played whist until three in the morning so regularly that an absence from the table was the occasion for an apology.

"I had barely energy enough left to drag my weary legs home," August told Marble after one early night; "and before eleven struck I was in the arms of *Orpheus*, as a poetical friend of mine once wrote to his inamorata. So please excuse if I did not keep my midnight engagement with you. Besides that, what was the point of meeting you to be plundered again (you have got into that bad habit of late)."

August was losing at cards so often that, in unconscious burlesque of his father's niggardly habits with writing paper (which had so annoyed Babette), he wrote to Marble on scraps, claiming that the poor stationery proved how unconscionably Marble was bleeding him. Even in defeat August found an advantage, however; he used Marble's success to draw him out to the Nursery for short stays—to play more whist.

"I have contributed so much to your pleasure this week," August told him, "being the real dummie, that you must do this much for me."

August's good spirits and energy once more propelled him to the forefront of New York's society. The newspapers, honoring his survival as much as his presence, began running eulogies—those obituaries for the living—for him.

"He delights in everything which embellishes life and makes it pleasant, a princely establishment. . . . fine pictures, well-appointed equipages, and polished society," said the *New York Sun*. "No one in this city entertains more elegantly and more grandly than Mr. Belmont. He specially understands the art of gathering around him the more attractive portion of the social element. He is a great believer in youth and beauty." In renewing his dominance of New York, August drew to his company men and women half his age. Power was not youth but youthfulness. . . . No one, the newspaper said, would believe, without knowing it, that he was in his sixties. "He does not ride on horseback any more, but he walks much, and thinks nothing of remaining for ten or twelve hours out in the field during the shooting season. It is only on winter mornings that he looks somewhat faded . . . ," after staying up half the night playing cards and then "getting up at eight, as if he had enjoyed his full allowance of rest. . . . In business transactions, he is very strict. . . . Yet when, a couple of years ago, the failure of a large banking firm involved him in a loss of some $250,000, he appears to have been very lenient and to have even tried to help the concern. . . . His establishment at Newport, his breeding farm at Babylon on Long Island, and his farm in Rhode Island, ought to be the objects of study to a good many of our rich men. They would then understand that, if it is easy enough to spend money, to do it tastefully is an art by itself."

On April 20, August received a cable from Stephan Feist that said:

"Poor beloved Babette expired softly, painlessly this morning."

His little sister, whom once he had been afraid of startling with the news that the Rothschilds were sending him across the Atlantic, was dead.

Oliver had done so poorly at the Naval Academy that he was being dropped from his class. August, who had been educated in disappointment by his two older sons, particularly August, Jr., tried to maintain a stern paternal attitude with Oliver, but he smiled behind the mask and treated the news not as a crisis but a problem to be solved.

"My prodigal will return at the end of the month," he told Marble, "and I am very anxious that he should at once be placed into *good* and *strict* hands."

As usual, Marble helped. He lined up three prospective tutors who seemed to come out of The Three Bears' house: one was too young, one too expensive, and one—Mr. Moore—just right. By the end of the negotiations August, Jr.—who, his father said, "has got his notions about his own way of managing the matter"—was in charge.

August had expected Perry, as eldest son, to take over as head of the family, but Perry did not seem inclined to do so. Much to his family's surprise August, Jr., filled the role—and filled it well. All through his childhood he had been impatient with his youth as though he had been in a race with his older brother and by growing up fast could beat him to the finish. But Perry, disinterested in the contest, had years earlier dropped out of the race. Perhaps he had never been in it and August, Jr., had all the while been running against himself.

While August, Jr., handled the tutor August worked on the secretary of the navy, who had the power to reinstate Oliver. With Marble's help he mobilized admirers of Commodore Perry, friends, and political associates.

"I should think that with all their influence," August said, "we might succeed, if *we only go right to work.* Would Sam Ward be of any use? Have you written to Carl Schurz [who was now Secretary of the Interior]? The great difficulty is in Admiral Rodgers, who plays the Brutus with my boy. I hope he never be called to show his Spartan virtue when his own flesh and blood is to be judged."

August's campaign was successful. Oliver was readmitted to the Naval Academy. But still August's demands on Marble in the matter did not end.

"Would you advise me to write to the Secretary of the Navy to thank him," he asked his friend, "or would you wait until an opportunity offers to thank him personally?"

August, to whom New York looked as an arbiter of etiquette, looked to Marble; and he so often asked Marble such trivial questions that the questions themselves could not have been the point. The more removed August became from his past, the more he needed someone who could remind him of the social distance he had come. August did not want advice as much as he wanted reassurance. He wrote to Marble the way a man might glance in a mirror while passing to check the tilt of his hat or the plumpness of his cravat.

Babette's legacy to August was a feeling that his own death was imminent, and like all inheritances it took a while for August to collect. Soon after Oliver's trouble was settled, August began complaining that "I am really more troubled in mind and shaken in body than anyone around me believes. They will find it out, however, but too soon."

His self-pity was a way of mourning his death in advance; but, as mourners discover, life overtakes grief. Within two weeks he was again racketing cheerfully around the city, preparing for the season at Newport.

"I am crazy to see you," he telegraphed Marble, "Won't you be at the Union Club this evening at eleven?" And he signed the message *Great Mogul*, proof of his improved spirits.

When Marble failed to stop at August's office or 109 Fifth Avenue to say good-bye before the Belmonts left New York, August told him that "this is so grave an offence that no written apology in prose or verse, even from your pen, can make amends. You can only do penance by coming here as an humble pilgrim and craving forgiveness at the shrine of the fair ones," Caroline and Frederika. "It may be granted, but it will take all your eloquence at least one week to obtain it, so you had better prepare yourself to stay."

August's demands for the companionship of his friends intensified as he grew older. The manner—making it sound as if someone's company is a favor to the host—was rooted in a polite convention; but August took it to such an extreme that it began to betray a pathetic gregariousness, as though his friends' presence had more symbolic than real value, their visits demonstrations of their loyalty. August at sixty-three was closer than he had ever been to the lonely young boy in Alzey and Frankfurt who used to watch other children at play. His insistence on bringing his friends to his houses, even when he could not be around to entertain and be entertained by them, revealed an acquisitiveness behind the companionability—and the fear that unless he continually surrounded himself with friends, he would spend the end of his life as alone as he had spent the beginning.

Marble, who sent a supply of good wine ahead, William Travers, and Bayard arrived in Newport; but August, although he had urged them all to come, had temporarily left.

The season was better than it had been for years.

"I have never seen Newport so bright and blooming," August said. "The lawn and flowers are fresh and fragrant."

"Newport," Perry agreed, "is gayer than ever."

Frederika spent so much time with her fiancé that when she developed a slight case of rheumatism a cousin teased her by suggesting it was the result of being "imprudent at night. Look out."

It stormed late on September 17. The morning of September 18 was foggy. Sexton Springer of Newport's Trinity Church woke before dawn and walked to the church in a drizzle.

He would have to rig up some awnings outside the doors, he decided.

But the wind changed. The drizzle stopped; and when the sun rose the fog burned away. By the time most of the wedding party and their guests woke the weather was magnificent, balmy, "one of the loveliest September days," a newspaper reported, "ever seen in old Newport."

All morning as people dressed, Bellevue Avenue was deserted. About eleven-thirty the first carriages rolled down the long drives from the cottages and into the street. Within fifteen minutes the avenue was backed up for a mile with dogcarts, phaetons, clarences, coupes, landaus, and drags; open, closed, two-wheel, four-wheel, two-seater, four-seater vehicles drawn by one, two, four, and six horses. At noon the town hall bell rang. The stragglers cracked their whips and hurried.

The nine carriages carrying the bridal party arrived at the church.

Inside, the two high-backed pews on either side of the altar were enveloped by flowers; roses, fuchsia, and pond lilies spilled in tiers to the floor. The walls at the front of the chapel were draped with roses and japonica. The altar rail had become a blossoming hedge of pond lilies and dahlias. Above was a canopy of smilax.

The church bell rang. Perry's former music teacher, J. B. Lang, improvised a fanfare; and after a few false alarms the doors of the vestibule opened and the procession began. August, Jr., Oliver, and Raymond were among the five ushers. Perry was one of the groomsmen. The best man—whom an etiquette book of about that time described as being similar to "a second in a peaceful duel"—was Samuel's brother-in-law, James Roosevelt (whose son Theodore, although still a student at Harvard, intended like Perry to go into politics). The bridesmaids were all cousins, assorted Hones and a Rodgers. Samuel, dressed in the English manner in a blue frock coat with light trousers and vest, accompanied Caroline, who wore white silk covered with lace, traditional in its design but startling in its beauty. She looked like a frosted window on which someone had drawn flowers with his thumbnail.

Frederika came in on August's arm, in white silk with bands of gold. In her hair she wore a single sprig of orange blossom, "which," one newspaper said, "was a very noticeable feature, orange blossoms being usually more profuse." From the orange blossom dangled seven diamond stars, which, set on springs, flashed as she moved. Her earrings were diamonds. Her veil, about fifteen feet long, was fastened with a pin that spelled out her name in diamonds. At her throat she wore another diamond pin that was in the shape of a tree, in the center of which a gemmed dove swayed like the diamond stars of her crown. Her lace was a family heirloom.

One account said that the groom seemed nervous, although another claimed that "his friends remarked . . . they had seen him look more apprehensive while playing an exciting game of polo."

The ceremony was performed by R. S. Howland, Samuel's brother, who was Rector of the Church of the Heavenly Rest in New York, John Cotton Smith, Rector of the Church of the Ascension in New York, and G. J. Magill, Rector of Trinity Church. Lang played themes from Beethoven's "Mount of Olives" and one of August's favorite compositions, Mendelssohn's *Italian Symphony*. After the vows, he played the "Wedding March" from another of August's favorites, Mendelssohn's *A Midsummer Night's Dream*. When Frederika and Samuel left the church they were greeted by a crowd of children who had collected around the red carpet out of curiosity and who cheered them as they hurried to their carriage.

The guests followed the couple to Bythesea for a reception. They streamed through the tessellated vestibule into the wide hall, then turned right, passing through the blue parlor and the drawing room into the blue and gold ballroom, which was festooned with smilax, and the dining room, where flower arrangements spelled out *B H* and *Congratulations*.

Telegrams from all over the world kept interrupting the banquet. Revelers danced the German, drank too much champagne, and gossiped about the extravagance of some of the gifts: an aigrette, which with its spray of diamonds and rubies resembled a heron's crest, from Baroness Rothschild; a diamond and ruby necklace from Bennett, who, of course, was not present; the wedding crown, earrings, and dove brooch from Caroline; the wedding dress, which the newspapers valued at $25,000, from August; and "a gift . . . of a very substantial nature," according to a newspaper, to Samuel, also from August. Less opulent but just as treasured were a family Bible; Gustave Doré's *Christian Martyrs* from John Hone (which he admitted was "not a very appropriate subject on such an occasion"); a lace fan and handkerchief from Raymond; a lace and pearl fan from Oliver; the lace handkerchief that Frederika had carried in church from August, Jr.; and black lace flounces, a shawl, and—appropriate to the outdoorsman reputation of the giver—a moosehair tablecloth from Perry.

At five-thirty in the evening Frederika—after making sure a piece of wedding cake was sent to a servant who had hurt his back closing a window for her—and Samuel left for Boston. Within the month they would sail for Europe, where they would spend a short time before going for the winter to Egypt.

The house emptied. The last few guests smoked in the billiard room or library, strolled along the piazza that circled the house, or wandered through the gardens and grounds, past the peach house, greenhouses, and grape arbors, down below the sunken wall to the beach and the sea.

⚜ CHAPTER FIFTY-TWO ⚜

THE SUMMER HAD BEEN TROUBLED by strikes and violence. A protest over wage cuts on the B & O Railroad spread West along the rails:

Baltimore, Pittsburgh, Chicago, St. Louis. . . . Mobs rioted and fought the militia. August, Jr., returned to New York. His playing at soldier, which he had thought not bad amusement after Jeannie had died, threatened to become serious. His militia regiment was kept in readiness. August told his son that he hoped "the authorities will have the good sense not to send the regiments away from the city, since we have probably the worst population in the U. S. and want at least 2 good reliable regiments besides the whole police force to prevent riot, pillage, and bloodshed." The militia could certainly help suppress riots and stop pillage, but to do so they probably could not avoid bloodshed. The people who were killed in the battles between strikers and soldiers were not playing at being dead.

To August the strikes were a violation of social order; to Perry they were a violation of divine order. August wished politics would become what it had seemed to be when he was younger: an elaborate high-stakes game. Perry, who had grown up during the Civil War, felt that unless politics reflected a battle between good and evil, each election playing out in miniature the future conflict at Armageddon, the contest was trivial. For August politics was the pursuit of policy; for Perry it was the pursuit of morality.

"I have often heard it said," Perry told Bayard, "that no people, and certainly not our people, had reached that state of goodness that their better impulses may be trusted to prevail in the great contest between good and evil, which accompanies every struggle for political power. I never believed that was true, and I never will, so long as there are men who know how to call upon their better impulses. In commercial life even the most depraved have discovered that honesty is the best policy, and I never could see why in political life the same thing is not true. Just as we attract or repel people according to the manner in which we approach them, so we arouse all the bad that is in their natures if we take it for granted that nothing else is there, or we call out the good if we only recognize its existence."

Perry was an idealist. He wanted Congress to be an Arthurian Round Table, Congressmen to be knights. He thought misguided the people who "are so beset with the idea of doing away with 'parties and politicians.' " The way to improve public life, Perry thought, was to eliminate from it the "contemptible class of 'statesmen,' who while pretending to despise politics and politicians take all that can be got from both parties." They were opportunists who exploited their antipolitical stand to indulge in the basest kind of politics, out only for their own good. The best candidates for public office were the professional politicians,

"party men," who like knights were trained for their jobs, under obligation to act according to a code, and whose work was to right wrongs
and protect the powerless. Beyond that, the true—that is, the Democratic
—knight's mission was to unite the country.

"The very fact that the Democratic Party is divided sectionally
proves that it is and always will be the party which most truly represents
the interests and wishes of the people in their respective sections," said
Perry in an ingenious argument: a divided country can be represented
only by a divided party. "And we cannot be a Union until the Democratic
Party is united," a miracle Perry expected could be accomplished "within
the next two or three years."

Bayard was amused by Perry's idealism. He sent August one of
Perry's fervent letters.

"As his father," Bayard said, "you will be glad to see his lofty
suggestions for the conduct of men in daily life."

Despite his quixotic notions about politics, Perry chose his windmills
with a practical eye. He worried that "there is not a more pronounced
Democratic paper" in New York and conferred with party leaders about
what could be done to correct that lack. He lobbied for the introduction
of a bill that "would require our cabinet officers to come before the House
at stated times" to answer Congressional inquiries about executive policy.
In one case he argued a point so well a leading Democratic politician
admitted that until listening to Perry, he had not understood the issue.

While investigating the possibility of fraud in Louisiana and Florida
during the electoral crisis, Congress asked for copies of certain relevant
telegrams from the Western Union Company, which at first was inclined
to resist on the grounds that the government had no right to force the
company to release them. Perry had joined the law firm of Porter, Lowrey
and Stone, which was the Western Union Company's counsel; and he was
given the task of researching precedents. An English judge had ruled that
telegrams, like letters, could be demanded by the government. Perry
based his opinion on that case. And his firm recommended that the Western Union Company comply with Congress's request, which it did. In a
second case involving the telegraph company Perry argued that telegraphing fell under the laws ruling interstate commerce, a position the courts
upheld. Both cases were landmarks. Perry may have been an idealistic
knight, but he was an effective one.

August may have been less idealistic than his son, but he was equally ready to tilt at windmills. He plunged into a controversy that had been heating up for almost a year.

Just before the previous Christmas the House had taken time out from its discussion of the electoral crisis to pass a bill that would legalize the coinage of silver—a blunder, thought August. Because the bill had been introduced by a Democrat, Richard P. ("Silver Dick") Bland of Missouri, and got most of its support from Democrats, it was bound to lose the Democratic party "the sympathy of the commercial and financial classes," which were passionately against the measure. The Bland bill set the value of silver compared to gold at 16 to 1, but the discovery of new silver mines in the West contributed to making silver worth less than 16 to 1 on the marketplace. As a result, if the bill eventually became a law people would tend to pay with silver (which was really worth less than the government was saying it was), driving gold out of circulation—similar to how paper money had begun to replace gold. August was convinced such a policy would make the American economy unstable.

It was the old story. A farmer borrowed $1,000 in greenbacks when the greenbacks were worth only $500. If the Hard Money men won and a paper dollar was worth a gold dollar, then the $1,000 the farmer paid back would be worth not $500 but a full $1,000. The farmer would lose $500. If the Soft Money men won and silver was legalized as currency, there could be worse inflation and the $1,000 the farmer paid back could be worth not $500 but even less. The farmer would gain $500 or more.

August thought it was dishonest of farmers and planters to take advantage of increasing inflation to pay debts with money worth less than it was when it was borrowed—just as farmers and planters thought it was dishonest for bankers to take advantage of the coming resumption of specie payment to be paid with money worth more than it was when it was borrowed.

Also, if the coinage of silver were legalized, other nations would pay their debts to the United States in silver, while the United States would have to pay its debts to other nations in gold. As a result, "every dollar of gold would be taken from us," August said, "and we would be flooded with the silver other nations did not want." And capitalists both at home and abroad would hesitate to invest gold in the United States if they thought they might be repaid in silver.

The effects of legalizing silver could be traced along a spiral that led from a farmer paying his debts to a local bank to a national gold drain.

"The disastrous consequences which this Silver Bill would bring upon our country, its resources, its industry, and its commerce," August said, "can be summed up in two words: *Disgrace . . . Ruin.*"

The Senate, taking the side of Hard Money, sat on the Bland bill. But popular demand for it—especially in the West and South—continued. Early in November 1877 the House of Representatives once more passed the bill, which was then sent to the Senate Finance Committee, where Bayard tried to scuttle it. He asked August to come to Washington to testify before the committee, but August declined the invitation.

"I should have liked very much to have a quiet and dispassionate talk with our . . . political friends from the South and West, who have caught the Silver Epidemic," August told Bayard; "but the experience I had some 18 months ago when I conferred with the Chairman of the Committee of Ways and Means was too discouraging for me to make another attempt."

In the year and a half since his talk with the chairman of the House of Representatives Ways and Means Committee, August had become—at least, among certain politicians—even less welcome. The syndicate that had been formed to sell government bonds was negotiating the handling of a new bond issue of $260 million. Critics were complaining that the syndicate's profits—members would eventually make about $25 million on the deal—would be excessive. Also, because investors would hesitate to buy the bonds if the country might redeem them in silver, the syndicate became one of the major forces fighting the Bland bill; and as a result August, who was the best known of the American syndicate members (the press called the group the Belmont Syndicate) was anathema to prosilver politicians.

"It is rather a sad commentary on the liberality and intelligence of our Western legislators that it is best for me not to appear in Washington to state my views and convictions on a financial question deeply affecting the credit and welfare of our country, though my position and experience would seem to entitle my opinions on such a subject to some considera-tion," August said. "But I am a 'Bondholder' and have the misfortune to represent large 'foreign bondholders,' who, trusting in the good faith of this great republic, paid their gold for its low-interest-bearing obligations; and this disqualifies me from being heard. My political friends forget that I have been a faithful and unwavering Democrat for forty years, during all of which time not even my worst enemies have been able to successfully accuse me of allowing selfish and pecuniary considerations to sway my judgement and influence my actions on public affairs. All this talk of 'Bondholders' is the merest bosh."

However, Bayard had to agree that "it was just as well you should not have come just then."

A week later Bayard told August, "I comprehend perfectly that you should chafe at the petty imputations" about August's motives "when you really take the views of a statesman, enlightened by a practical knowledge of the workings of finance. But politics is an *inexact* science, and you can well afford to smile at the ignorance and prejudice that fail to comprehend your *real* relations to the proposed legislation of Congress and to forgive the ingratitude of unthinking men."

Despite the attacks, August continued to lobby against the bill—mostly behind the scenes, making secret trips to Washington, arguing his position with William Henry Hurlbert when the editor heard "about some intrigues of the syndicate," huddling with Bayard on his Christmas trip to New York, and writing long letters to John Sherman, the new secretary of the treasury, an unlikely ally.

Sherman, the former senator from Ohio, had been—August thought —one of the worst culprits in the electoral crisis, "the staunchest defender of the rascalities of the Louisiana Returning Board and the most bitter assailant and defamer of the downtrodden people of that state." However, in the negotiations over the government bond issue, Sherman "treated me so kindly," August said; "and showed so much candor and straightforwardness" that August did not feel too uncomfortable joining forces with him to defeat the Bland bill—although to Marble August admitted that his correspondence with Sherman was a "literary curiosity" and that he thought Sherman was "timid and undecided."

To give Sherman the courage of desperation August warned him that "the threatening position of the silver question will check completely any demand for the bonds here and in Europe. The damage which the passage of this measure will do to our public credit abroad *cannot be overestimated.* All my letters from abroad and conversations with persons familiar with the English and continental money markets confirm my convictions on that point." The administration had to demonstrate "the most uncompromising hostility to the *blind and dishonest* frenzy, which has taken hold of Congress."

The Bland bill was watered down in the Senate. Coinage of silver would not be unlimited; the government could issue no more than $4 million worth of silver money each month. The amended bill was now called the Bland-Allison bill in recognition of the change, which had been proposed by Senator William B. Allison of Iowa, a Republican. It went to the Senate floor for debate. August still thought the bill "iniquitous." A sin was no less sinful for being indulged in moderately; if it was wrong to coin silver, coining less was no virtue. The Senate's sin was in fact compounded when another senator proposed that all bondholders should be paid their interest in silver.

August, a missionary for gold out to save the souls of those tempted by the Silver Calf, contacted key politicians who seemed ripe for conversion. When he went to Washington in January 1878 to guide one straying senator back on the path, the *Washington Telegram*, a prosilver Democratic newspaper, found something sinister in August's visit to the Senate gallery; he was obviously there on behalf of the "European Shylocks—the Rothschild Jews." Judas betrayed his Savior for silver; August—the newspaper implied—was betraying his country for gold.

The Senate approved the resolution that the government should pay the interest on the bonds with silver—and by such a large majority that it was clear the Bland-Allison bill would pass. Now that the cause seemed lost, August fought harder. He gave $150 to General James A. Garfield, the Republican congressman from Ohio who had been one of Hayes's most active supporters on the Electoral Commission, to print an antisilver speech that would—August thought—convince "the Western farmer" unless he had "become entirely crazed by the teachings of reckless or ignorant demagogues." And although he was warned by one antisilver senator that "memorials from bankers and Eastern interests are misunderstood in the present heated state of public opinion," August wrote an open letter refuting a prosilver speech by the former Democratic vice-presidential candidate, Thomas A. Hendricks, that called on Democrats to rally behind the bill.

"I am not at all a blind and stubborn opponent of silver," August would say at another time. "On the contrary, I should be sorry to see hasty legislation excluding it altogether, but national faith and honor must not be jeopardized."

Conciliatory as usual, August was trying to find some compromise that could link the less dogmatic opponents of the Bland-Allison bill and "the intelligent and well-meaning portion of the silver advocates (who intend a bimetallic circulation on sound and honest principles)." Such an alliance would protect those who, having paid gold for the United States government bonds, naturally wanted the bonds redeemed in gold and those who wanted, through the monetizing of silver, to increase the supply of money. Together the moderates of both positions would "secure the passage of a bill for the appointment of half a dozen or a dozen scientists and practical men to meet an equal number of experts from other nations in conference." Once an international policy on silver had been developed, August said, "I will go as far as anybody toward protection of our large silver production and toward trying to secure a sound medium of circulation of sufficient volume to restore prosperity and activity of industry and commerce."

The responses to August's letter—and the conciliatory principles it implied—were predictably good among New York's business community. The criticism in the press was double-edged.

Although the *New York Commercial Advertiser* granted that August "nails Hendricks to the counter like a base coin," the newspaper did not think, as some people were saying, that "Mr. Belmont ends Hendricks for the Presidency. Not so fast, gentlemen; not so fast, if you please. Mr. Belmont is an eminent banker, an illustrious citizen, an honorable man, and a leader in the Democratic Party, but his influence and power are limited." He had not been able to stop Tilden's presidential nomination; he might not be able to stop Hendricks's nomination. And if Hendricks were nominated, the newspaper, recognizing August's loyalty even when his loyalty was to a bad cause, predicted that August would "support Hendricks just as . . . he did Tilden. . . . Mr. Belmont will stand by the Democratic Party, no matter what happens. When August Belmont turns his back on the Democratic Party, flowers will lose their odor and trees will shed no leaves, beasts will laugh, the new Pope will join the Mormon Church, and the Czar will accept a Democratic nomination for Congress in the Fourth Congressional District and be elected. Look for the millennium, but never expect to see August Belmont anything but a reliable Democrat—silver or no silver, greenbacks and repudiation, and all other evils counted in."

August was loyal to some memory of the party, the party as it had been two decades earlier. In a speech he gave early in 1878 he said that only once in the past eighteen years had the Democratic party fought its presidential campaign on its traditional principles. As a result the party had become "disorganized and disaffected to an extent which threatens its existence as a national party." The Manhattan Club had "barely 250 members." And as *The New York Times* said in reporting August's speech, "instead of battling with the Republican enemy and inculcating honest principles, . . . the Democratic Party's zeal is expended in family recrimination."

The newspaper chided August for having allowed the growth of Soft Money power in the Democratic party.

"The best time for resisting the doctrines denounced by Mr. Belmont," it said, "was when they were originally promulgated. That gentleman and other Democratic friends of sound finance played with the movement when they should have crushed it, courted demagogues who should have been proscribed, and actually went through a Presidential campaign hand in hand with the very men who now brand them as Shylocks. . . . Does Mr. Belmont believe that his idols, Jefferson and Jackson, would have remained in fellowship with an organization which belied their convictions or that they would have tolerated for an instant the threats now hurled at the Bayards . . . and the Belmonts for no other reason than their fidelity to honest hard money? The time is coming when it will be necessary to choose between the obligation to a party whose traditions are trampled under foot by its present rulers and the obligation to principles whose ascendancy is essential to the peace and prosperity of the country."

The newspaper in effect was offering August an entry into the Republican party. After all, August was fighting Democratic leaders and allying himself to Republican leaders. It seemed natural that he should recognize a change of loyalties that apparently had already occurred.

But agreement on one issue does not constitute a conversion. August still thought the Republican administration of Hayes was guilty of "bad taste" and "arrogance." He distrusted Sherman's brother, the head of the army, so much that later in the year, when the general rattled his soldiers' sabers in defense of the administration, August said, "Oh, for a Richelieu to order his arrest. With the selfish daring of the general and the slimy adroitness of the Secretary of the Treasury—purse and sword in the hands of such men—the future is really dark. Unfortunately, one cannot oppose Hayes and his infernal crew of scoundrels without being suspected of Tildenism, which, right or wrong, emasculates every effort."

No, August was not ready to switch parties. Beasts would not laugh.

But he also was not ready to admit that by staying loyal to the Democratic party he had in a different way already switched parties, the Democratic party itself having changed so much since he had first joined. When August became a Democrat the party—or at least his faction of it—had been the Young America movement. Aggressive. Expansionist.

The territory they had wanted to colonize had been not just outside the boundaries of the United States but within themselves, within the part of themselves that was just discovering what it meant to be leaders of a young and strong nation. August and the others in the Young America movement had called the conservative members of the party Old Fogies.

Now the aggressive members of the party, still expansionist, wanted to expand not the boundaries of the country but the supply of money. They were colonizing new economic territory that, built up, would become a kingdom of deficit spending, an illusion like Tennyson's Camelot where Merlin saw " 'solid turrets topsy-turvy in air' " and where " 'there is nothing in it as it seems. . . . The city is built/To music, therefore never built at all/ And therefore built for ever.' " As long as the music played the city would stand; August was afraid that someday the music would stop. Politically, he had become an Old Fogy.

August did not believe, as one antisilver senator did, that the prosilver public was "simple-minded," but he did think that they were misled. Why they let themselves be misled was to August a mystery. Perhaps, as one of his correspondents suggested, it could not be adequately explained.

"Old Sir Thomas Browne had a theory that occasionally nations go mad," he told August. "It seems the American people are insane on this money question, and dearly will they pay for the delusion."

August's opposition to the bill, his attempt to fight delusion with facts, was more admired than effective. The Senate passed the bill, and the House of Representatives approved the Senate's amendments.

President Hayes noted in his diary, in dialogue with himself and monologue with history, that "Belmont . . . fears the effect of a veto—prefers the bill should be approved, *bad* as he thinks it is."

Although earlier August had told Sherman that the only way the syndicate could continue to sell United States government bonds would be if "we had the assurance that the President will veto any bill which contemplates payment in silver," August now thought the country could stand the bill becoming law better than it could a crisis over the veto; and he agreed with a Republican congressman from New Hampshire that the law could be temporary, that once the people "understood the principles of honest [hard] money, you may be entirely sure of an upright verdict." It might take awhile to educate them, and so the ultimate success of Hard Money "may not come for some years—not in season to arrest all the impending evils; but, when there is so much beyond immediate business interests at stake, we can afford to begin at the beginning and wait."

Like the Republican congressman from New Hampshire, August was afraid that the passage of the bill—after Hayes had vetoed it and Congress had overridden his veto—was "a wedge driven by those who contemplate much greater evils for our country later," that America might be slipping down a silver slide toward socialism and anarchism, which in the past five years had developed a growing following in the United States. The Socialist-Labor party had begun infiltrating trade unions, and the public generally had sympathized with the strikers of the previous summer.

To August's despair, politics refused to be civilized conflict between honorable men who disagreed with each other; it continued to be a matter of national survival. Now the country was being divided not between North and South as in the Civil War, or even between East and West, although the East-West split over bimetallism was still serious, but between rich and poor, between classes. In the echo of the strikes and violence of the summer could be heard the cry of the man who three decades earlier had stood outside the Astor Place Opera House during the riots:

"You can't go in there without kid gloves on. I paid for a ticket and they wouldn't let me in because I hadn't kid gloves and a white vest, damn them!"

🪶 *CHAPTER FIFTY-THREE* 🪶

FOR THE TIME BEING, however, labor unrest was a "brimstone" match: more spark than flame. Capitalists did not lose faith in the stability of the country. In fact, starting in the spring of 1878 the Belmont Syndicate handled $50 million of United States government bonds. August went to his office just long enough to take care of the matters his son and associates could not handle. He spent long weekends at the Nursery, trying to get the farm there to run as smoothly as the one at Oakland, where even the farmer's pneumonia did not interfere with the work. Once in a while at Oakland August discovered a serious blunder, as when a horse was put out to graze in a lot that was full of rusting iron scraps, rags, and stones; "it is a wonder," August thought, "the horse was not lamed for life."

But in general Oakland functioned like a clockwork mechanism, geared to the turning of the seasons.

The Nursery farm was a shambles. When August stayed there he became "so miserable and bedevilled by a thousand things" that he could not remember to whom he had and had not written letters. The kennels were not kept properly. The dogs were in an appalling condition. Two of his favorites, Robin and Sandy, were "actual skeletons." August found some bread and meat and fed them by hand—which the dogs never would have tolerated if they had not been famished. It upset August terribly to see some fox terrier pups covered with an ugly skin disease. A dog he had promised to send to one of Samuel Barlow's daughters was missing. Oliver, who was visiting the farm, asked about it and was told it had wandered away somewhere; but when August asked he was told it had died. He was sure he was being lied to and, as he told August, Jr., "felt very badly about it, but not trusting myself, I kept perfectly silent."

August did not believe in abusing his employees. Nor did he like firing them unless he absolutely had to; so he contented himself with rearranging the pieces on the board, giving the woman who had been in charge of the dogs other duties, putting one of August, Jr.'s servants in her place. . . .

He reorganized the use of the paddocks, looked for a new cook for the stable cookhouse, and rearranged the dormitory for the stableboys according to August, Jr.'s plans. August, Jr., did not think his father went far enough with the changes and asked if he was offended by his suggestions.

"Believe me," August told his son, "I am not at all displeased at the candid advice which you give me; and, so far as I can, will follow it."

But August, Jr., young and energetic, wanted to change the stable by revivifying and expanding it, while August wanted to cut back and simplify.

"There is some deviltry in my stable behind which I cannot get," he said. "Everything which gets there is sure to come to grief."

He no longer wanted the grief or the expense.

"I have such an awful number of horses," he said, "that they eat me out of house and home. My bills for the racing stable and farm"—in 1878 they ran about $50,000—"are larger than they have ever been, and I have not yet received the bills for the windmill and racetrack. (I tremble when I think of them.) It is really *a heap of money,* the return of which I fear we shall never see."

August, who needed recreation, sought in amusement profit. It would have profited him more to accept the loss as the cost of play. But August had helped transform racing from a casual afternoon contest on Harlem Lane and the Bloomingdale Road into a professional sport. And in a professional sport it is impossible to untangle competition from cash. It would have been mad to race in order to lose; but in racing to win he made the sport into a business, into what for him had become a bad business. When Midas turns the world into gold, it is tragic; when he turns the world into brass, it is pathetic.

"I have come to the firm conclusion," he told August, Jr., "it would be cheaper and better if I gave away all my blooded stock, mares, foals, and stallions. You and Perry don't think so, and I only hold on to please you both: but the day is not far when I am sure you will say that I was right."

If he was going to keep the stable, it would at least have to be weeded, but it seemed harder to get rid of bad Thoroughbreds than to maintain them. He sent some to be sold at auction for whatever they would bring and one not particularly bad one to Bayard—which August thought was "a good way to get rid of him."

Bayard, who wanted the horse to stud, was delighted with the animal.

"At first he was utterly inexperienced in the mysteries of copulation," Bayard reported, "but since then has given proofs of his virility."

Although August spent so much time in the Augean task of cleaning up his stables and also worked hard to reorganize the racetrack at Monmouth Park, his bet on the comparative quality of two wines, Rauenthaler and Johannisberger, interested him more that year than any gambling on the horses. Bayard Taylor, who had been appointed United States minister to Germany principally for his recent translation of Goethe's *Faust* (as though an intimate knowledge of Faust's bargain with the Devil might help Taylor in his diplomatic negotiations with the Germans), took the conventional view that Johannisberger was the better wine; August said Rauenthaler was. The bet was informal, the stakes merely the judgment of each bettor. Before Taylor left for the Continent, August gave him two bottles of Johannisberger.

"In strict conformity with your instructions," Taylor later told August, "one bottle was opened just after we passed the Narrows; and not only myself, but at least twenty of my near relatives and friends enjoyed the odor and the flavor of *true wine*. . . . Never before, I think, did one bottle give more delight or do more efficient service. I waited until I reached Berlin; and then (also as you commanded), . . . on the 20th of

May—the anniversary of my betrothal with my wife—I invited my . . . secretaries to dine with us; and we drained the second bottle. Now, if you had any expectation of proving to me by your most generous and poetic gift that *Johannisberger* is inferior to *Rauenthaler*, you have failed! I have never found a more superb and celestial vinous aroma than in those two bottles; and, if any Rauenthaler can surpass it, I can only expect to find such in another and better life. I do not mean to question your experienced taste in fine wines; but, when you deliberately strengthen me in my own opinion, what is to be done?"

By losing the bet, August won. His generosity conquered his judgment.

At six o'clock in the morning on May 4, 1878, eleven members of the Coaching Club gathered at the Brunswick Hotel. They all wore the club's costume, green cutaway jackets, which made them look like upright beetles. All but one, Perry, wore white top-hats; Perry's hat was black. As servants carried the hampers of food from the hotel hall to the coach waiting outside, the club members drank toddies, discussed the weather and the condition of the roads, and greeted friends and relatives who were arriving to see them off on their expedition. Just before six-thirty the horn sounded; the club members left the hotel and took their places on the top of the coach; Joe Mora, the society photographer, snapped their picture; and, the coach's lanterns glowing pale yellow in the gray morning light, the Coaching Club set off on its first long (twelve-hour, ninety-mile) trip: New York to Philadelphia.

Fifth Avenue to Sixteenth Street, which was so rutted everyone had to hold onto his seat to keep from being jolted off, down Broadway, where early morning risers on their way to work stopped to cheer, onto Canal Street, then along Desbrosses Street to the ferry, where a crowd gathered as the coach waited to cross to New Jersey. By the time they left Jersey City and got to the old Post Road, the sun had risen and, low in the sky to their left, was casting slanting rays, which seemed because of the mist to be tubes of cloudy light. A marsh with whiffs of decay, tree roots arching above ground, and slimy ponds as dark green as their coats stretched for miles on both sides of the road. They shivered as the coach hit pockets of chilly air, handed around a flask, and fell silent. When they approached Newark the mist was gone. Houses sat on the edges of their shadows, as though the shadows were abysses. A crowd was waiting for them at Newark's Grace Church, where they stopped four minutes ahead of schedule.

After a five-minute rest they changed horses and drivers. Each club member had been assigned by lot a particular stretch of road. In Rahway spectators remarked on how dusty the club members looked. Perry took the reins, cracked the whip, and racketed out of town. Beyond Rahway was the worst stretch yet. The red dust billowed, and much of the road was uphill. One of the lead horses hurt a leg. But Perry drove skillfully, and they made good time. Farm families who had somehow heard in advance about the coach's passage waited at the side of the road. One girl waved with more urgency than usual in a simple greeting. Perry slowed the horses as a servant hopped out of the moving coach and received from her a basket of flowers in which Perry found a card that said, "For Mr. Belmont." At Menlo Park the townsfolk had built an old-fashioned tollgate, which was raised by an old-fashioned tollgate keeper, who more than half a century before had been assigned to the road through Murderers' Hollow at Uniontown. Among the crowd at Menlo Park was Thomas Alva Edison (who that year patented the phonograph and the following year would perfect the incandescent light). In New Brunswick, Perry gave up the reins.

They stopped for lunch at the University Hotel in Princeton and just before six-thirty in the evening, thirty seconds ahead of schedule, arrived in Philadelphia at the St. George Hotel, where they were met by a crowd estimated to be the largest that had gathered in that city since the Fourth of July of 1776.

That evening, having been joined by August, Jr., Leonard Jerome, and six other coaching enthusiasts, they had their monthly dinner-meeting at a house on Rittenhouse Square. The following day, Sunday, it rained. They dined at the Rabbit Club and kept as much as possible out of sight of celebrity hunters. Monday morning ten of the eleven club members woke at five o'clock, breakfasted, and by six were ready for the return trip. They waited for a tardy companion, the oldest among them, whom they twitted when he appeared. He explained: "I sleep very slowly."

Down Nicetown Lane into Powder Mill Lane, through Frankfort, past the Forrest Home for Aged Actors. . . . Princeton, where the president of the college told them that the day was marked by "the transit of Mercury and the transit of the Coaching Club" and where some stranger frightened the horses with an explosion that sent them into a wild gallop. . . . Kingston, where schoolgirls in sunbonnets greeted them. . . . Along the Woodbridge Pike, where it rained. . . .

In Rahway, the coach picked up an escort of carts, wagons, and carriages that swelled as they passed from town to town. In Newark the vehicles were four-deep along the road. In New York City the streets were so crowded that the coach could hardly move. On Fifth Avenue the club members again took out their watches. They reached the Brunswick Hotel at five forty-nine in the afternoon, eleven minutes ahead of schedule. They congratulated each other and decided that some such long excursion would have to be an annual affair.

Three weeks later August, driving his best coach, the most elegant in New York, joined the club in its spring parade. The excitement generated by the New York–Philadelphia trip was still so intense that by the time the coaches returned to the Hotel Brunswick from their circle through Central Park, a mob of thousands jammed the streets. The popularity of coaching as a pastime for the rich and spectator sport for the poor spread to other cities. What had begun as a private fancy, when August in the late 1830s had introduced New York to its first four-in-hand, became in this more elaborate form a national craze.

August, Jr., nurtured other crazes that year. His fighting cocks, called stags by the aficionados of the sport, were among the best bred in the country. Some of them traced their lineage back to the 1730s. His hens regularly won prizes. He also bred dogs, especially fox terriers, which became a particular passion, and when some of his best were disqualified from a show because their pedigrees had vanished, he went into a rage and on circumstantial evidence accused one of the judges of suppressing the pedigrees out of spite.

"I give you fair warning, sir," he wrote to the judge, "that, if you do not return me those pedigrees, you will regret it more than the whole thing is worth."

Since one of his dogs was stolen after the show, it was possible the pedigrees had been kept so the dog could be illegally sold.

What fascinated August, Jr., so about fighting cocks, show dogs, and Thoroughbred horses was the breeding. He spent hours tracing the genealogy of a particular bird or writing a treatise on how a certain trait had been refined through a number of generations of dogs. This interest in bloodlines was a working out, in small, of society's obsession with ancestry and family—which itself was not just snobbery but a confused and misapplied notion of progress.

The illusion of universal progress—the belief that with the proper guidance anything, everything from pets to progeny to society would get better and better—became one of August, Jr.'s driving forces. If August had turned his recreation into business, August, Jr., turned his recreation into demonstrations of life's itch for improvement. Even polo was not just a thrilling game, it was an advance on the games the previous generation played.

It was also dangerous.

"Pray do what you can to prevent Augie playing in the match next Saturday," August wrote to one of August, Jr.'s friends. "He is entirely unfit for it, not only by an accident to his wrist, but by his general health. Don't, for Heaven's sake, mention that I have written to you. This dreadful polo drives me to my grave."

Almost every year since it had opened a quarter of a century before, the New York Academy of Music had lost money. The board of directors, charged with mismanagement and nepotism, had never been able to arrange for a successful, permanent opera company. "Spasm opera," one music critic called it. In the early part of 1878 the stockholders were assessed a total of $17,500 to cover the Academy's deficit. Outraged, they gathered on April 29 and voted more than 2 to 1—140 to 60—to oust the directors and elect a new board. August, one of the most prominent stockholders, was chosen to be the new president.

He was such an obvious candidate it is surprising that he had not been asked to reorganize the Academy sooner. Ever since, as a young man he had led the infatuated mob dragging Fanny Elssler's carriage through the streets of New York, he had supported, financially and emotionally, many of the major dancers, actresses, and—especially—singers of his time: among them, Fanny Ronalds, whose favors he apparently shared with Leonard Jerome; Minnie Hauk, who was rumored to be Jerome's illegitimate daughter and whose musical training he and Jerome underwrote; and Emma Abbott, who one rainy night walked to August's house and showed up drenched and muddy. Although his butler was offended by Emma's appearance, August was not. He welcomed her, made sure she dried off, and had her sing. The guests who were not charmed by her voice were intimidated by—and imitated—August's unconcern with Emma's unconventional arrival.

August accepted the presidency of the board of the Academy with, as he said, "the distinct understanding that I shall be allowed to resign as soon as we shall have been able to get the machine going."

He began negotiations to bring to the Academy a first-class company including "one or two of the great stars like Adelina Patti or Christine Nilsson. With Patti alone a manager would make a fortune and Patti herself would have a people of sovereigns at her feet instead of only the czar. And the three parties—Gold, Silver, and Greenbacks—would vie to see who could offer the largest amount of its special panacea for all financial ailings."

But eighteen years earlier, after Patti had sung triumphantly at the Academy, complications over the rental of the hall had deprived her of her fee and her share of the profits. As a result Patti never again went on stage anywhere until after she had been paid. Even with the promise of payment in advance she distrusted American tours—as did most other performers. The financial situation in the United States was so unsettled that, as one of August's European friends told him, "no decent artist or impresario wants to have anything to do with America." The partisans of gold, silver, and greenbacks might vie for her services and favor, but Patti was content to sing for royalty. A single czar applauded louder than a hall full of Americans.

To lure Patti or any other star across the Atlantic, August needed an opera house manager with special qualities: more snob appeal than Max Maretzek (who had ruled the Astor Place Opera House when it developed its kid-glove reputation); more impudence than William Niblo (who once hired the Astor Place Opera House to present a trained dog act); more flair than P. T. Barnum (who promoted Jenny Lind as though she were a sideshow act); more stubbornness than Carl Rosa (a tiny man married to the huge "Incomparable" Euphrosyne Parepa, whose high notes were rumored to have pierced one man's deafness); more extravagance than Max Strakosch (who first brought Nilsson to America by offering her $1,500 per performance); more craftiness than Max's brother Maurice Strakosch and Bernard Ullman (the two impresarios who once promoted a singer by claiming he was the lineal descendant of Charlemagne); and more class than Frederick Gye (who ran Covent Garden and who Ullman, a former rival, admitted was "a great manager").

These qualities combined in only one person, an Englishman: Colonel James Henry Mapleson.

Mapleson had a high forehead, bushy eyebrows, moustaches that curled like bass clefs, and a chin as round and prominent as the bulb on the bottom of an English horn. He was the most colorful impresario of his era: pathologically optimistic, flamboyant, impulsive, ready to spend money he did not have, and often able to escape the consequences of such irresponsible generosity. To the fury of other, less prodigal impresarios he once paid Patti $5,000 for one night's concert, a sum she thereafter demanded for every performance.

"He is a good-natured fellow," said Bernard Ullman, "but slippery and not to be trusted. His word is as bad as his bond, not from perversity, but from the embarrassed state of his position, from the very first day he became manager fifteen years ago. He will promise anything very boldly, very well knowing all the time that he cannot keep the promise."

Although he might promise what he did not have, he also might deliver more than he promised. Whether he would disappoint or delight, he always surprised.

In planning his courtship of Mapleson, August sought the advice of Ullman, an old friend, who years before in one of the few successful seasons at the Academy had raised the value of a share in the opera house from $200 to $800. Ullman apparently misunderstood August's letters. Thinking August wanted him to take over the Academy, he grandly explained that the past was irretrievable, unrepeatable. Someone else might rescue the Academy. He could not.

But since Ullman still took an interest in the Academy, he offered to help August in any other way he could.

"Being the official representative of Gye at Covent Garden for the entire Continent," Ullman said, "I am always in contact with artists and impresarios and thus know everything that is going on both before and behind the curtain. All this information is at your disposal."

He agreed with August, who thought Maretzek and Max Strakosch during their terms at the Academy had "served up" the "second class (using a very mild term) leavings of European opera." In fact, Ullman was more candid than August; he thought Strakosch was "a conceited ass, unfit to manage opera in Peoria. No wonder opera at the Academy went down with him." Ullman said Strakosch "frequently" went to Mapleson's operas at Her Majesty's Theatre in London "to study him." Gye, Ullman thought, would be August's ideal manager, but—as Ullman told August —"I, myself, tried to persuade him in his own interest to go to America two years ago and even consented to accompany him. It was nearly settled but at the last moment he backed out."

August, however, did not want Gye. Or Gye's son, Ernest. Or Strakosch. Or Maretzek. Or even Ullman. He wanted Mapleson, whom he had tried to bring to the United States in 1868.

Mapleson, Ullman warned, was penniless and crippled with debts "amounting to a larger sum than ever was lost in New York during the last twenty years. There are twenty-seven actions against him pending in court." His costumes and music had been repossessed.

All of which proved his ingenuity. If he could survive in such a position, he had to be clever.

"Mapleson is *smart*," Ullman admitted to August, "but with all his smartness, activity, and *savoir faire* I do not see that he will be able to come up to half your expectations." He would not be able to hire a decent company. "All good artists," according to Ullman, "are engaged for the winter in Europe."

But the *all* was more emphatic than inclusive. There were half a dozen excellent singers available. However, Ullman said, one was worn out from a love affair, another's voice had fallen off, a third's voice was still good, but the public seemed bored with her. A fourth, Etelka Gerster, the Hungarian soprano, who had Carmen's eyes in Brunhilde's body, was possible, although Ullman thought she was "nothing great," merely "a Berlin reputation" who had the advantage of being unable to get "good engagements next winter." As for Nilsson, "to whom Mapleson offered $2,000 a night," according to Ullman, "she refuses to have anything to do with Mapleson." And Patti? So far, Ullman said, she had turned down all Mapleson's offers.

Still, Ullman told August, Mapleson was the Academy's "best" and "last chance." He "is at all events a real director of opera." August should be wary of him but should also "aid him all you can" and "give him a fair start. Should he gain the day, so much the better for you and him. Should he fail, I will ponder and try to find what may set the machine going."

The negotiations with Mapleson that followed threatened to become as complicated as any discussion over the syndicate's handling of United States government bonds. Strakosch, the previous manager-director, had paid $600 a week rental for the Academy, but August thought Mapleson should pay "$250 a night and the same for the matinee, which would be $1,000 a week." If the season ran for thirty nights and if, as August believed was necessary, the Academy's stockholders could be induced to give up at least some of their unprofitable privileges, which included free admission, then even with the increase in rent Mapleson should be able to make enough money to tempt him. However, August was willing to charge less rent for the Academy if that would help Mapleson bring a big enough star to make the season brilliant.

Mapleson was interested in the deal, but according to one of August's European agents, "His desire seems to be to secure a lease of the Academy without binding himself to furnish any *particular* stars."

August insisted on a star, particularly Patti or Nilsson.

Patti would not even consider an American tour, no matter what the financial arrangements were, unless she could come with Ernest Nicolini, her favorite tenor and paramour, whom—James Gordon Bennett, Jr., said—"she either *loves* or *fears*. I think there is some of both, but *most* of the latter."

Although August did not particularly want Nicolini, he would accept him to get Patti.

Mapleson still could not make any promises. "I have been running about trying to get . . . artists," he said, "but find it very difficult in the absence of an absolute contract to be able to clinch matters." Without a contract he could not get the stars; without the stars he could not get a contract. "And the longer I am negotiating with them," Mapleson complained, "the higher their prices become."

August would not budge. Patti, Nilsson, or nothing.

Mapleson changed his tactics. He began dangling Patti before August. She "has been in London for some time," he told August, "and she has asked me to go and see her."

"I had breakfast with Patti yesterday morning," he said a few days later, "and discussed the matter fully with her."

There were rumors that Mapleson had groveled at her feet and wept. He was doing everything, anything to sign her up. She was virtually under contract. If only the directors of the Academy could make Mapleson's appointment definite. On his terms.

Mapleson's terms were outrageous: for the Academy's rent he would not consider paying more than $300 per week, less than a third of what August wanted and half of what Strakosch had paid the previous season. If Mapleson got the theater for that price it would be a triumph over his predecessor and rival, proof that the Academy's directors valued Mapleson so much that to get him they were willing to make a sacrifice they had not even considered when hiring Strakosch. The change in the Academy's administration was irrelevant; a status war is fought on appearances, not substance.

August, indifferent to the jockeying for position between the former and future manager of the Academy, was willing to agree to Mapleson's terms—if Mapleson brought Patti or Nilsson.

Cables shot back and forth across the Atlantic, August trying to get a contractual assurance of a star, Mapleson trying to panic August into signing a contract without such an assurance. *"There is not a moment to be lost,"* Mapleson told August, "and it must be settled without fail this week."

"Authorize contract at 300," August answered. "Have contract worded carefully."

The day the contract was signed, August's London agent wrote to August, saying, "Gerster is a very great favorite here, and has now an offer at a very high price for an engagement in Russia, an answer to which she is obliged to give this week," an ominous message.

During the negotiations, while Mapleson was baiting August with Patti he was also denigrating the bait.

"Her attractive powers have considerably diminished," he had said.

She will cost too much and, as a result, will "ruin all the other nights," he added a week later.

At the same time, he was raving about Gerster, "a most admirable singer and a charming woman into the bargain and in addition a most attractive artist and easy to manage." She was, according to Mapleson's promiscuous enthusiasm, "equal to either Patti or Nilsson and certainly superior to the latter." In fact, he said, she was "the principal Prima Donna of the present day."

And just in case August did not consider her enough of a star, Mapleson lectured the Academy directors on the dangers of putting too much stock in personality: "I may add that the cause of failure hitherto of Italian opera in America I believe to be solely attributable to the *star* system, as the large sums demanded by the stars have prevented the manager from bringing a complete company."

Mapleson promised to bring a complete company. The logical conclusion was not elaborated.

"I know by experience what he, Strakosch, and Maratzek call a good stock company for an American audience," August told his London agent.

Trying not to sound too displeased at what seemed like a quick shuffle, Gerster for Patti, August wrote to Mapleson that a good stock company "will work well under two conditions, *viz.*: when you have to deal with a really artistic audience like that of yore which filled the parterre of the *'Italiens'* in Paris or when you have a permanent opera, established year by year for four or five months; neither of these conditions exist here. We have a very music-loving and enthusiastic audience, but not yet of sufficient culture to do without the additional stimulant of some European celebrity or some native phenomenon (a combination of both as in the case of Patti, of course, most desirable)."

August reminded Mapleson that he had gotten the opera house "at a much lower price than it has ever been given to any of your predecessors, in fact, at what may be called a nominal rent. The directors"—by which August meant he himself, since the decision to give Mapleson the contract had been his alone—"have thus assumed a great responsibility toward the stockholders and the public at large, and we can only be justified in their eyes and escape their censure if you will give us a brilliant," which meant stars, "and complete troupe for next Winter." Angry Academy board members were good conductors for censure; any shocks August felt would be passed on to Mapleson. If Mapleson hoped his three-year lease would be renewed, his first season had to be a great success.

Mapleson tried to distract August with a tale of the fireworks display in the shape of the Academy that he intended to sponsor in London, but August refused to be dazzled. He still wanted to know whom Mapleson was engaging as prima donna.

Mapleson tried another dodge.

"Strakosch has suddenly cropped up in London," Mapleson said, "and is busy all over the town, offering four times the terms to everybody for the sake of spoiling my business as he has no intention of making any on his own account."

Max Strakosch, tall and angular, looked like a sinister marionette who could be folded up and packed in a small case. He could not bear to see Mapleson succeed where he had failed and was willing to risk the fury of singers—tempting them with fat contracts that did not exist—in order to ruin his rival. Mapleson used the threat, inflating it in his letters, to justify the difficulty he was having in getting artists.

But even the Strakosch story failed to deflect August's insistent curiosity about who would be prima donna, so Mapleson said that Patti "is most desirous of coming, but she has a law suit pending with one of the Strakosches and also a divorce case, and she is consequently afraid to move."

Mapleson was a magician, displaying Patti and then cloaking her in mystery. Finally he had used all but his last trick: the vanishing act. The trapdoor in the stage opened; Patti dropped out of sight (the truth was, said Ullman, she was afraid to cross the Atlantic); and up popped Gerster. The switch August had suspected was done. August, one of the greatest businessmen in the world, had been bested by a bohemian who had the reputation of being no businessman at all.

"I see that it was *you* who gave authority to close the lease for $300," Royal Phelps, the treasurer of the Academy, wrote to August. "I am not aware of any resolution of the Executive Committee authorizing you to make a lease at so low a rate."

August did not get along with Phelps, who was allied to the pride of snobs that circled Caroline Astor and her prim prime minister, Ward McAllister. Mrs. Astor ran her increasingly large portion of society while McAllister—who looked with his sweeping moustaches and tuft of beard like a gelded satyr—ran Mrs. Astor. He organized her parties and picnics and decided who was and was not acceptable. Mrs. Astor and McAllister worked so hard and so seriously at their amusements and they seemed so much more concerned with making others feel excluded than with enjoying themselves that August thought them silly. August and his crowd had been extravagant out of high spirits; the Mrs. Astor–McAllister crowd were extravagant as a demonstration of their position in society.

August may have exceeded his authority in agreeing to Mapleson's demand for such a low rent for the Academy, but Phelps's anger at August for doing so seemed fueled by his pleasure at being able to take August to task.

Phelps pointed out that the contract the executive committee had discussed "required a rental of $600 per week. I wonder how you could have offered the Academy *the next day* for $300." The rent "will barely pay the city license, lighting, heating, and cleaning of the house." He thought August was "too good a businessman to do a thing of this kind."

Phelps became the Academy's memory: whenever anything went wrong with the arrangement with Mapleson, he recalled that August had rented the theater so cheaply.

Many things went wrong.

At the end of August, Mapleson's painter, Charles Fox, arrived in New York, aggrieved and indigent. Mapleson had sent him across the Atlantic—with, as Fox said, the "stroke of a Harlequin's bat" and not a cent for expenses—to examine and repair the Academy's scenery, which was in a poor state. The rocks for *Il Trovatore* were ripped. The tomb for *Lucia di Lammermoor* would set Edgardo brooding over not Lucia but the set designer. The bridge for *Rigoletto* would not support even the most generous imagination. *Don Giovanni* and *Il Trovatore* had to be rebuilt from the ground cloth up. To get everything in order Fox figured it would take him six weeks at $50 per week plus $7 per week for a paintboy, and the cost of some carpenters, canvas, lumber, paints, brushes, and other supplies.

The contract with Mapleson did not give him or his painter the right to repaint, repair, or build scenery. He could make recommendations, but the Academy's directors reserved the decision for themselves. The expense of any work that the directors agreed was necessary was split fifty-fifty between the Academy and Mapleson.

August inquired around the city and learned that Fox's charge, although high, was not out of line with what New York painters were asking. August told Phelps that he thought Fox's "terms are reasonable; and, if you will give your consent, the other members of the Executive Committee will do so. And the work will be done at once, as there is no time to be lost."

Not only was Mapleson arriving in about a month, but Fox had nothing to live on until the matter was settled. To tide Fox over the secretary of the Academy, Daniel Kingsland, lent the painter $10 and, as he told August, "furnished him with civility and tobacco."

But Phelps delayed. He thought "the message from Mr. Fox is simple insolence—what authority has he to call on the Academy of Music for money? Where did we ever agree to advance money?"

"In fact," Phelps told August in another letter, "we do not even know that Mapleson has sent him. He may be one of his hangers-on and comes over here on his own hook to get some work. Though," Phelps added with the afterthought of a man who has just realized he has been raving, "this is not probable."

Lastly, Phelps did not like the form of Fox's estimate. It was unbusinesslike, and he wanted Fox to "see that he has to deal with businessmen."

At last Phelps gave in to August's calm sense. Two and a half weeks after arriving in New York, Fox started work.

By then, Phelps had other reasons to complain. News reached New York that two tenors who had been signed suddenly no longer were on the bill. The bass turned out to be, in Ullman's words, "a mere utility." Mapleson kept announcing that he had engaged artists who were already committed to other companies; and when his lies were discovered, he bragged that even better singers would join his troupe halfway through the season.

"But such is the man," said Ullman. "He cannot tell the truth were it to save his life. Out of ten facts as represented by him, nine are—politely speaking—inventions. I would bet an old hat that, on his arrival, he will assure you that his new opera house will be ready next year, he has bought Covent Garden, and engaged Patti."

However, a rumor also was circulating that Mapleson would not even reach New York, that he would have no opportunity to demonstrate in person his wonderful imagination. Ullman suspected this rumor was a ploy to squeeze the Academy.

"You must be prepared," he told August, "that a short time before starting, Mapleson may telegraph that he cannot start unless you advance him a certain sum. This is a matter for *your* consideration, not mine. But should you be willing to assist him, you must take great care that the money shall not be used to pay European creditors or London arrears."

"I hope for the sake of all of us," Phelps told August, "that Mr. Ullman's estimate of the financial condition and reliability of Mr. Mapleson may be exaggerated."

Mapleson's valid expenses included about $15,000 to get his costumes out of hock and whatever it cost to bring his troupe to New York. Except for Gerster, who wanted some guarantee against her 4,000-francs-a-night's fee—which Ullman thought was twice what she was worth—all the artists had for the moment waived the customary advances. Ullman was impressed.

"What he, broken in credit, has done, is wonderful," Ullman said. "Even I, in whom artists always had great confidence, could not have done that business for under $50,000 in cash capital."

The miracle was partial. Ullman's surprise at what Mapleson had done with so little money was less pertinent than his prophecy of what Mapleson would do to get more.

"The preparation of an entire wardrobe for some fifteen or twenty operas, the musical library, properties, etc.—to say nothing of the traveling expenses—has entirely exceeded my expectations," Mapleson wrote to August. "Under these circumstances, it will be necessary for me to solicit your kind aid in obtaining an advance for at least £2,000."

"There is not a ghost of a chance of Mapleson getting £2,000 or 2,000 cents advanced to him," said Phelps when August transmitted the request.

August warned Mapleson that "I fear it will be difficult if not impossible to obtain" the advance, but he was willing to consider the question. Like Ullman, Ferdinand Rothschild had cautioned August about trusting Mapleson with money. There was also a rumor current that Mapleson did not really need the money, that he had a sleeping partner who was investing in the troupe for a share of Mapleson's profits. And even if there were no sleeping partner, Mapleson's was playing Ireland on his way to the United States; he should in those concerts make enough to cover his expenses. August could marshal plenty of arguments against giving Mapleson an advance.

But Mapleson's arguments for getting the advance were stronger. The Irish tour had bombed. The artists, panicking, were demanding salaries before setting foot on any transatlantic ship. And—the key argument—if August did not send the advance, Mapleson simply would not, could not, come to the United States.

August presented Mapleson's case to the Academy of Music's directors; and in spite of Phelps's displeasure the executive committee voted to lend Mapleson the money, which would be raised by asking the stockholders to contribute $50 for each share they owned.

Phelps, who owned four shares, sent his $200 to August; but he told him not to use it unless all the other stockholders paid too.

The contributions came in slowly; August advanced out of his own pocket half of the entire sun. Mapleson received the loan the morning the troupe was to sail. But his artists did not trust him any more than Phelps did; they would not board the ship until they were paid, not in pounds or greenbacks or silver but in gold. Like many of their future fans in New York, the singers believed in Hard Money.

Although Mapleson's company was the best that ever had come to New York, without a star it was doomed. The Academy's hope was Gerster. Mapleson had to make her a celebrity.

"Upon her," Ullman told August, "rests the *fate* of the *season*."

Two days before the company's debut Gerster was quarantined with typhoid fever. Minnie Hauk was chosen to replace her, but the lead baritone refused to appear with what he considered to be a less than first-class talent. Luckily the baritone who took his place was a hit—as was Gerster, when she recovered.

"The people are perfectly wild with enthusiasm about Gerster," said August. "She is at this moment actually a greater favorite than Nilsson ever was." Mapleson, the Academy, and New York had their star. Gerster would shine for three years and for a while would rival Patti.

August no longer had to write flattering letters to the editors of New York's newspapers urging them to support the opera. There was, August told August, Jr., an "overflowing house every night." But the Academy's troubles were not over. The treat of the season was *Carmen;* and although August and much of New York liked it, *The New York Times*, which thought it coarse and vulgar, panned it. Then around Thanksgiving, E. Fellows Jenkins, the superintendent of the society for the Prevention of Cruelty to Children, threatened to have Mapleson arrested if he allowed the underage girls who danced in *Lucia di Lammermoor* to perform.

Three hundred girls had applied for the parts, Mapleson said. Only twenty-five were good enough to join the troupe. This was no cheap theater where the girls were mistreated. They were "trained to dance under my personal supervision. I insist that they attend school and see to it that their engagement in no way interferes with their avocations. I am training them to be artists. And here comes this fellow and tells me it is all contrary to law and I must obtain girls over sixteen years of age, who have lost their suppleness and cannot make first-class dancers. They will perform, and Mr. Jenkins or Jennings—I really don't recall the name—can arrest."

The opera went on as usual. Agents for the Society for the Prevention of Cruelty to Children shadowed the girls on their way home from the show and got their names and ages from their parents. In the morning when Mapleson arrived at the theater, he was arrested. After he was released on $300 bail, the Society for the Prevention of Cruelty to Children told him that if the girls appeared again he again would be arrested, along with all the girls' parents.

That night the backstage was crowded with agents of the Society for the Prevention of Cruelty to Children, members of the Academy's executive committee, reporters, angry parents who wanted their children to be stars, and the girls. Although they were in costume, Mapleson had decided they would not perform; but excitement at being the cause of such a disturbance had overpowered their disappointment. They hung around the reporters, recounting their professional credits and, to prove their studies had not been slighted, offering to read. The curtain came down. No one was arrested. The Society for the Prevention of Cruelty to Children had won. The girls were permanently cut from the production.

Two weeks later the Academy once more suffered bad publicity. At the end of his term as manager of the Academy, Strakosch had stolen the sets for *Lohengrin, Aida,* and other operas. As well as repairing the scenery that was at the theater, Mapleson had to replace the missing drops and flats. When he presented the bill for half the cost to the Academy, Phelps, as treasurer, delayed payment while he verified the cost of every item. Mapleson, insulted, threatened to move to another theater, probably Booth's, or return to England.

By itself Mapleson's bluster and the disagreement within the executive committee over paying for the Academy's share of the scenery would not have created a crisis; but it became the focus of a more serious conflict. Only thirteen stockholders had attended a meeting August had held at his house to discuss ways of reducing the Academy's debt. Fourteen others sent proxies. Thirty-six were unrepresented. August claimed the unrepresented stockholders were indifferent. Phelps claimed they had been ignored, that August was trying to railroad through some pet plan. He demanded another meeting, at which he was either forced out of office or gave his resignation.

The executive committee tried to keep the commotion out of the press, but a reporter for *The New York Times* ferreted them out at a fourth meeting, held late one December night in a Wall Street area office.

"Several of the directors . . . appeared to be in bad humor," *The New York Times* said the next day. "August Belmont was in a particularly unhappy mood and refused emphatically to say anything about the rumored bickerings between directors and the causes of Mr. Royal Phelps's resignation."

However, an unnamed spokesman for the opera company—probably Mapleson himself—was less discreet.

". . . Mr. Phelps had resigned," the newspaper explained, "because he could not familiarize himself with the manifold duties of operatic management. Coming from a successful career in ordinary business life, he had found it difficult to learn . . . how to estimate the cost of painting a scene or making a 'drop.' He had endeavored to apply to his labors as Treasurer of the Board of Directors the rules of commercial business and in doing so had caused inconvenience to the management of the opera."

This unnamed source also said that "Colonel Mapleson . . . would be glad if Mr. August Belmont should obtain control of the Academy, as he is a liberal man, who sees that the best interests of its owners are served."

The day after the secret meeting of the executive committee, another meeting, which was not so secret, was held in August's offices. Mapleson's bill for scenery was officially presented and accepted, and it was announced that the Academy's current $10,000 debt would be covered by taking out a new $25,000 mortgage on the building, which would give the Academy $15,000 to cover the cost of running and improving the theater.

In an effort to wrest the theater from August, Phelps offered to put up the entire $25,000; but his financing was rejected. August had no intention of releasing his grip. The Academy was not just an entertainment; it had become a symbol. He who controlled the Academy decided who could buy the prestigious boxes and therefore controlled to a great extent the pecking order in New York society. Caroline Astor and Ward McAllister could make up their lists of who was acceptable, but August decided where they sat at the opera.

☙ CHAPTER FIFTY-FOUR ☙

DURING THE SUMMER August had drifted into the reverie of a busy man at a concert. The rhythms of the negotiations with Mapleson had lulled him, distracted him from politics. The worrisome Hard–Soft Money split, which a little over a year earlier he had warned was diverting the Democrats from their proper fight against the Republicans, now became the meat of a joke.

Why didn't Thomas Bayard come to Newport to plan political strategy? "Hendricks and Pendleton are here," August wrote to Bayard, "and you will have a chance to be instructed in sound principles of finance. Having theoretically and practically studied that question for nearly half a century, I thought I knew something about it, but thanks to the Soft Money men I find now in my old days that in order to come up to their requirements I must first unlearn all I know."

Having gotten what good he could out of the joke, August spat out the indigestible part.

"I cannot become a neophyte to the new Gospel of American finance," he said.

In the music world the jealousies and treacheries were grand. In politics and business they seemed constricted, the joyless struggle for an increasingly vague prize. Power in the theater was the ability to control what happened onstage. Political and financial power seemed paradoxical: the more you had, the less efficiently you were able to use it, as though it were a weapon grown too heavy, too unwieldy to handle.

August intervened with James Gordon Bennett, Jr., for Manton Marble, who was hoping to take over management of the *New York Herald:* Such intervention depended on influence, not power. Influence was manageable, understandable, quantifiable; you could gauge, if you were attentive, how much you had and how much you needed to accomplish a particular end. Power was clumsy; if you had it and used it, it often seemed too much—what was meant to be a tap would become, uncontrollably, a crushing blow. Influence seemed modern, scientific, civilized; power seemed primitive, rude, a savage god as liable to destroy the one who used it as the one against whom it was used. Although he occasionally used it—as he did in his capacity as president of the Academy of Music—August had a growing distrust of power.

However, influence even when carefully applied could be resisted more easily than power. If August had owned the *Herald* he could have guaranteed Marble the job. But August did not own the *Herald*, and his influence with Bennett was insufficient to help Marble get what he wanted.

"Bennett would be very glad to give you a prominent place on the editorial staff," August told Marble, "but he will not entertain the idea of giving up the management of his paper for a moment. He spoke very kindly of you and appreciates your talents, but you might as well move Mount Atlas than try to overcome his Scotch stubbornness and cunning."

Perhaps if politically August and Marble had been working for the same goal August might have pressed Bennett harder; but under Bennett the *Herald* was safe, not helpful but not particularly harmful. Under Marble it would amplify Samuel J. Tilden's voice, which August, committed to get Bayard the presidential nomination in 1880, did not want. He told Marble what he had been saying for years, that he was "utterly disgusted with the downward course of the Democratic Party" and that "I have lost all interest in the game—it was worse than whist with Edward Cooper," who apparently was an atrocious player. But August, a good player of whist and politics, was bluffing. He was hoping to goad Marble into showing his cards—or abandoning Tilden.

"You are really not only 'crazy,' but 'stark mad' on the question, not on the Louisiana and Florida frauds, but of that worst of all frauds of Gramercy Park," August told Marble, who was as obsessed with how Tilden lost the last election as he was with how he would win the next one. "Your own good nature and the intensity of your feelings lead you astray. Any movement connected with Tilden is doomed to defeat as surely as anything can be sure in this world."

During the electoral crisis of 1876 Tilden had seemed fatally weak to many Democrats. To get the presidential nomination in 1880 Tilden would have to prove that the Republicans had been able to steal the last election, not because he had been indecisive but because he had been betrayed. Privately he accused Bayard and other allies of selling him out, although publicly he made no charges. When one Tilden supporter attacked Bayard and the other alleged traitors, Tilden and Marble, like pedestrians avoiding a raving lunatic, crossed the political street. They did not want to split the party openly—or more accurately they did not want to seem responsible for the party's split. To counteract any talk that Tilden held a grudge against any former supporters and to dispel the suspicion that Tilden had been ineffectual in the crisis of 1876, Marble wrote a long article that August read "with the greatest attention and pleasure. If anything could save the desperate fortunes of your candidate, your clear and adroit defence ought to do it. I fear, however, that it is all in vain, and I am only sorry that you will pursue this phantom."

Perry was chasing his own phantom. With a distant relative, Dudley Vinton, the son of the rector of New York's Trinity Church, and a friend, George Frelinghuysen, the son of the senator from New Jersey, he had formed a law firm. Vinton, Belmont, and Frelinghuysen was housed in the same building on Nassau Street as August Belmont & Company. Perry intended to use the law firm as a base of operations from which he would make his assault on Washington.

If his office on Nassau Street was his general headquarters, his beachhead was in the First District (comprising Richmond, Suffolk, and Queen's counties), where he decided to run for Congress. He began shuttling back and forth from the capital, conferring with politicians like Bayard, newspapermen like Charles Nordhoff (who four years earlier had become the Washington correspondent for Bennett's *New York Herald* and who recently had published an account of his visit to the utopian communes that were flourishing in the United States), and old friends like Henry Adams (who the previous year had moved to Washington).

He found Adams changed, discontented and pessimistic, at odds with what Perry felt was the spirit of the age. Adams insisted on playing Banquo's ghost and disturbing the feast, which Perry thought a fault in him—all the more since he to a lesser extent shared the fault.

August hoped that Perry would be serious about his run for the nomination and said, "I shall, of course, assist, but the thing is by no means certain, because Perry is, of course, the Hard Money candidate and will have all the ragamuffins against him."

Toward the end of September August wrote August, Jr., that "Perry finds the nomination is difficult (in my opinion almost impossible). . . . It makes him very cross and I have to curb my temper more than I ever thought I could be capable of doing." August, who had often chided August, Jr., for being impatient and grouchy with his parents, was seeking approval from his son for his restraint. With Marble he talked about not Perry's ill-humor but his pain:

"Poor fellow, he is entirely at a loss and perfectly bewildered and, with that *amour-propre* so natural at his age, does not wish to acknowledge his ignorance." And he added, "I am fully as out of my element as he is—only I confess it," an odd statement from a man who had run presidential campaigns. Perhaps he was puzzled by the change in scale. Perry certainly seemed to be; he kept talking about national issues—the necessity to reduce the size of the army (which he thought the Republicans might be tempted to use to stay in power) and to stop the murders of whites and blacks in the South—instead of addressing local concerns.

August sent out an agent to learn who were against Perry, called in as many political IOU's as he could, and advertised through Marble that "I have this matter *very much* at heart. If the party will seat Perry, I will not only say *quits* to politics, but I will put a good large balance against me as due to its future success." August was offering a good deal to his enemies in the party who were blocking Perry's path: if Perry got the nomination they would be rid of August forever in politics and August would contribute generously to the upcoming campaigns.

Perry was defeated for the nomination.

"I was afraid it would prove a hopeless case," August said, "but, as he had his heart set on it, I did not want to discourage him. He feels badly, but tries to put a bold face on. The worst is that he feels discouraged and cast down for the future."

At least, since the attempt to get the nomination had been "a very expensive job," August hoped "it will prove to him that I have done and am willing to do all I can to further his views, which I have, of late, to my deep sorrow, had often occasion to believe that he doubted."

A distrust of power does not necessarily prevent one from seeking it— either for a son or a protégé. During the fall campaign August advised Bayard to make a major address on the financial question, to become the principal spokesman for Hard Money, the obvious future presidential candidate for Hard Money Democrats.

"I see too plainly the enervating, not to say demoralizing influence of Presidential ambitions upon other men not to feel intent upon keeping myself free from them," Bayard told August; but he did what August suggested. At the end of the summer of 1878 Bayard gave what was unofficially the opening speech of his campaign for the Democratic presidential nomination: an attack on Soft Money. August thought it good, but it was not particularly effective. The Soft Money men in the Democratic, Republican, and new Greenback Labor parties continued to gain strength.

In the off-year elections the Democrats gained a majority in the Senate for the first time in two decades. To August, however, some of the victories were defeats because the Democrats who won were Soft Money men. And fourteen members of the Greenback Labor Party were elected to the House of Representatives.

Bayard alternated between optimism and alarm.

"It is a great mistake to suppose there is not a strong Hard Money sentiment at the West," he said at one point. The Hard Money men, made fearful by the clamor for Soft Money, were merely silent and so gave the appearance of swelling the Soft Money chorus.

At another point he brooded that politics was changing so quickly and there were so many splinter groups active that "the parties organized two years hence can scarcely be conjectured."

August's analysis was more bitter.

"What has become of the astute intelligence and the common sense of our people!?" he asked Bayard. "Don't they see that distrust and want of confidence are now the only obstacle to our return to prosperity?"

As long as the silver dollar—which really was worth only about eighty-eight cents in gold—continued to be legally valued at one hundred cents in gold, capital would be scarce; and investors would avoid risking their money.

"In the face of all this," August said, "even real estate," traditionally one of the safest investments in New York, "declines, because sellers *cannot* find purchasers, who are frightened away by the uncertainty of the future."

August himself had been nervous enough to sell one large parcel of land, thirty lots around Eighth Avenue and Seventy-second Street.

"Will a dishonest and fluctuating currency render the future more certain and encourage capital to come out from its hiding place?!" August asked. "The man who asserts this is either a fool or a knave."

Congress—August thought—was filled with fools and knaves. One of the worst was Senator Roscoe Conkling, the boss of the Republican machine in New York, an arrogantly intelligent man so ornate in his eloquence he invited ridicule and so dignified he invited self-parody. An enemy once described him as walking with a turkey-gobbler strut. Although he was a good target for humor, he was a formidable opponent. In an effective speech he attacked the Democrats for being inflationists, a charge August had predicted.

Because of the power of the Soft Money Democrats—especially in the West where, August thought, "the Democratic Party is more tainted with the Greenback and Socialist heresies than our opponents"—the Democrats "shall again be placed on the defensive." He feared a "reaction against Soft Money will come before we enter upon the next Presidential campaign," and the Soft Money stigma "will cost us the election in 1880."

August's anger at Conkling was spiced with contempt. Conkling had become infatuated with Kate Chase Sprague, who a decade earlier had tried to make a president of her father, Salmon Chase. Conkling was so in love that he did not get angry when she once finished a Latin quotation he had faltered over, which he would have taken as an affront from anyone else. Kate's drunken husband, William, ascended into jealous rages over the flirtation (and in fact within a year would threaten to shoot Conkling while the New York senator was staying at his house). August thought the whole affair was ludicrous. Kate was a social python; she had swallowed Conkling whole, and all society watched the bulge his passage made along her coils.

In October 1878 the *New York Tribune* uncovered a series of coded telegrams that the newspaper claimed proved the Democrats had tried to buy the presidential election of 1876. Trying to piece together the story the telegrams told and working on alternate interpretations of the code became passions in New York.

"One could hear quotations from the dispatches . . . on street corners," said the *Tribune* in a follow-up article. In the horse-drawn streetcars, "lawyers and merchants discussed the . . . discovery of the telegrams and speculated on the influence it would have on politics. . . ." Interest in them "transcended all limits of politics and pursuits. It embraces all classes and was the staple of conversation at all tables. Even gossip was forced to give way to this all-absorbing topic, and ladies might be found patiently wading through the mass of details that they might be able to understand intelligently what was said."

A reporter for the *Tribune* hunted August down at the Manhattan Club and sent in his card.

August, a gentleman even in anger—that is, a true gentleman—did not keep the man from the *Tribune* waiting. He excused himself from dinner and went to the club office to meet the reporter.

"What do you want of me?" August asked.

"The editor of the *Tribune* sent me to say he would be glad to obtain your views on the . . . cipher dispatches," said the reporter.

"The editor sent you, did he?" said August. "He couldn't have sent you. He knows better than to send anybody to me. That paper has told too many lies about me for him to send anybody to interview me. That's all I have to say. Good evening."

August started to walk away.

When the reporter said "Good evening" in return, August glanced angrily back, suspecting the reporter of mocking him—which may have been the case.

"Belmont," the newspaper said, "should at least learn to put a restraint upon his natural propensities and imitate, as well as he can, the manners of a gentleman."

Marble, whose code name was Moses, was implicated. The press, delighted at a chance to turn on one of their own, ridiculed him. One story described him as hiding out, frantically trying to construct a defense, having "his food handed to him through the cat hole at the bottom of the door"; another suggested that "somebody should write Marble's obituary before he is forgotten. Of course, it will be in cipher."

Marble denied writing certain of the telegrams and disputed the translations of others. Although Tilden's nephew, Colonel William T. Pelton, admitted his own and Marble's guilt before a congressional committee, Marble insisted on his innocence. He had not recommended that the Democrats bribe any officials; he merely had been warning that certain officials were for sale. When confronted with one of the most damaging telegrams—in which Pelton agreed to a certain proposition, presumably to trade $200,000 or $250,000 for the electoral votes of Florida—Marble said:

". . . I never mentioned it to a human being. . . . I put the dispatch into the fire, lit a cigar, smoked it, and went to bed," dismissing the matter as casually as he might have waved away smoke from his cigar that night.

While the evidence against him was inconclusive, Marble's reputation was nonetheless marred. As Moses he did not lead Tilden to the Promised Land in 1876; nor would he in 1880. His career as a president-maker was ended.

Tilden escaped into an innocence that damned him. He told the committee that he had no knowledge of the coded telegrams, which indicated to some that he was not a strong enough leader to control his subordinates' actions. August did not think he would be a threat to Bayard in the coming fight for the Democratic presidential nomination.

At the end of 1878 August took stock of his life. In a chart he described the increase in his expenses; in his correspondence he described the decrease in his vitality. He had always talked in his letters about doing this or that *if he lived;* but in the past the phrase seemed a way of tapping wood or a recognition of the possibility of accident. With the passage of time his age gave the phrase a new context. Now when he said, ". . . next Summer, if we live . . . ," he meant it. He had begun living his life in the subjunctive. "I am dreadfully tired, used up, and miserable," he told August, Jr. "Three nights ago at Newport, I thought I should never see you again, being taken with the most fearful stomach cramps, which were only relieved by copious mustard plasters all over me."

Business was "such a strain upon my energy and health," he told Bayard, "that I fear I shall have to give it up," an often repeated threat that he was beginning to act on. He was spending less and less time in the office, and he admitted that "I have been so long out of harness that I am not fit for the daily routine."

The Rothschilds had declined to join August in handling a $6.9 million New York City loan, although they had made over $2.5 million during the past three years in August's syndicate. Why were they backing out now? They offered no adequate explanation, merely that the business outlook was discouraging. August, who had committed himself to putting up half the money, had to back down and take only a quarter share, about $1 million. And he had to join with Drexel, Morgan & Company, who—he told August, Jr.—"were so afraid that others would bid higher" that they agreed to buy the bonds from the city for much more than August would have paid if he had been in control of the negotiations.

"We shall not lose anything by it," he thought, "but it will be a long-winded operation with a small profit and will keep the money locked up in it at a great inconvenience for a long time."

But the amount of profit and the inconvenience were secondary to the humiliation. Since most of August's capital was invested in various other ways and since the Rothschilds would not come in on the deal, for "the first time for more than twenty-five years," August said, "I have had to go to a New York bank for money."

On top of that the Rothschilds refused a consignment of bonds August had sent as a matter of course.

"There is not a house in Europe, even utter strangers to me, which would not have accepted it with our name as security," August told August, Jr., the *our* including his son in the business more than any formal arrangement could.

The Rothschilds seemed to August to be "systematically determined to refuse every offer for business from me." Perhaps they were just flexing their muscles, trying to remind August where he had gotten his start.

August did not need to be reminded—and thought because of the long connection he deserved to be better treated.

"On the 8 of September last," he told August, Jr., "it was 50 years that I have been connected with them, entering as a mere boy in their office at Frankfurt. For nearly 42 of those years have I represented their interests in America, and this is the thanks I get."

August sounded like Simon complaining about August's ingratitude.

"I cannot refrain from saying that I felt deeply how small my hold on your good will and confidence is," August told the Rothschilds.

Under such conditions the "continuation of business seems an impossibility and I really don't see why I should make a slave of myself and pass the few years which I have still to live in this strain upon my system and health," August told August, Jr. He wanted to retire. "You don't know how I long for that," he said.

August sent August, Jr., who had just returned from a business trip to New Orleans, to London to talk to the Rothschilds. He could not retire under these conditions with honor—and would not, unless he had no choice.

"I will give it a trial during the next three or four months," he told August, Jr., "and, in the meanwhile, expect to hear what impressions you have received at their house and what is your advice."

He cautioned his son against being discouraged if the meetings were not productive and told him "if they are kind and courteous, as I trust they will be, meet them in the same spirit." He knew his son had inherited his impulsiveness and quick temper.

As August had predicted, August, Jr., had trouble pinning the Rothschilds down.

"You were quite right not to force an issue or even push for a decided expression of opinion the moment you saw that the Rothschilds wanted to avoid talking about business with you," August said.

August, Jr., felt that he had been undercut. August had told the Rothschilds that his son's health had been poor, and August, Jr., was sure that was why they would not negotiate with him.

August explained that the Rothschilds would have used anything for an excuse not to talk business.

"Their peculiar reticence on all such questions is a *parti pris* with them," he said, "and I don't think I could get any more out of them if I was there daily from morning until night."

Christmas neared. The country received an early present. On December 17, anticipating the resumption of specie payments that was to start on the first of the next year, each greenback dollar for the first time since 1862 equaled a dollar's worth of gold. The two sides of that equation balanced without the thumb of government adjusting the scale. Economics once more held out the hope that the country could be run as a large family business, subject to the same essential rules that all families, all businesses, had to follow to stay solvent. The discomforting sense that the government could make up its own rules, could referee and play at the same time, receded.

But August's pleasure at the financial news was diluted by his moodiness over his family.

Oliver and Raymond both had gotten into trouble at their schools; and while Raymond shrugged his scrape off, Oliver took his to heart. He was getting disenchanted with the navy, which seemed more discipline than glory.

With all the children gone the house at 109 Fifth Avenue seemed empty. August felt unbearably lonely and desolate—and was made more so by August, Jr.'s letters. After leaving England he had continued on to the Continent where August hoped he would visit either the north of Italy, which was "very interesting and beautiful," or Spain, which being "more out of the beaten track would," August admitted to his son, "attract me more."

August, Jr. spent some time with Frederika, who was looking well, although she and her husband used her health, which they claimed was fragile, as an excuse to stay in Europe another year. Once more unconsciously repeating Simon, August objected to their gadding about so much; and he could not understand why they did not intend to winter in the south of France instead of going off to Florence, which he considered a social "Botany Bay." Apparently August wished for August, Jr., an adventurousness and curiosity he thought improper—or at least eccentric —in his daughter.

By the holiday Perry, Oliver, and Raymond had come home; and August, Jr., arrived either Christmas Eve or the next morning.

🦢 CHAPTER FIFTY-FIVE 🦢

HAVING OBSERVED the local elections of the past fall, August told Marble, "If self-government can stand all this, it must be really the best of all modes to manage the great beast!"

The beast August meant was presumably the public, which he saw increasingly not only as a mob but as something struggling to be born, something alien to him. What he feared was not just socialism—in fact, he hoped the Socialists would get control of one state, California, so they could show how incompetent they were, thereby disillusioning people about that utopian solution—but an inchoate power that had less to do with politics than culture, a new quality of mind, a new way of looking at experience, which promised a world as different from August's as August's was from the old Knickerbocker New York that existed when he first had come to the United States. However this new beast expressed itself politically, August would oppose it; but perhaps politics was not where it would develop its fullest expression.

In the meanwhile there were purely political battles to be fought. In the previous fall elections the Democrats had lost their state majority "foolishly," August thought, "by our own mismanagement and the corrupt bargains Tilden's friends [made with New York's Republican machine]."

The Democrats in New York had been drawn into a fight between two factions within the Republican party. President Hayes, who was supported by one wing of the party, called the Half-Breeds, was attacking Roscoe Conkling, the leader of the other wing, called the Stalwarts. Conkling was too powerful and too independent for Hayes to be comfortable with him; at one point, in the electoral crisis of 1876, Conkling had in fact inclined toward Tilden. And he was conveniently a symbol of the corrupt system of patronage that Hayes had promised to destroy. Hayes was Saint George; Conkling was the dragon.

Tilden's cronies, hoping to undermine Hayes, sided with Conkling. August, hoping to undermine Tilden, sided with Hayes.

"Conkling deserves nothing at our hands," August said, "and is as bitter and unscrupulous a partisan as there exists in the Republican ranks."

August knew that even if Hayes won he would be defeated by his victory: The Republican followers of Conkling were conjugating their rejection of Hayes. They would turn, were turning, had turned, against him. New York was the arena in which the Republicans were playing out the coming presidential election year struggles—as it was for the Democrats.

In New York, August and the other anti-Tilden Democrats were faced with a dilemma. If either Tilden or his hand-picked successor, the current governor of New York, Lucius Robinson, ran for and won the governorship in 1879, Tilden would control the powerful New York delegation to the Democratic National Convention. This would give him a strong purchase on the presidential nomination. To stop Tilden and Robinson the anti-Tildenites could let the Republicans win the gubernatorial election—a move, however, that would reduce the national influence of New York's Democrats; virtually give the Democratic presidential nomination to a Soft Money Westerner; and in turn guarantee by August's reckoning that the Democratic candidate would lose the White House. Not an acceptable alternative, since, August thought, "this is the crisis not only of the destiny of our party, but of our country. With another defeat [in the presidential election], the Democratic Party, so far at least as its principles and aims are concerned, ceases to exist. And should Grant, as I fear [be chosen as the Republican nominee over Hayes and win the White House], republican institutions will hereafter *exist* only *in name* in the United States." August and Perry agreed that the Democrats had to win the governorship of New York to win the presidency.

The only way to stop Tilden and Robinson without throwing away the governorship was for the New York Democrats to find an alternate candidate who was acceptable to both the Tilden and anti-Tilden men.

However, such a compromise governor would be either too weak to be useful or, more seriously, too strong (one more potential presidential nominee) to be safe.

Only one man would be both a strong and safe governor: former governor Horatio Seymour. He still had great influence but no longer any presidential ambition. If August could get Seymour to run for his old office and Bayard to announce officially his entry into the presidential race, Tilden could be squeezed out of action.

A number of Democrats argued that Bayard's declaration at this time would be too early. It would put anti-Tilden men on the spot, forcing them to choose prematurely between Bayard and other candidates rather than uniting against Tilden. Others were afraid that it would turn the gubernatorial race in New York into a test not of Tilden's but of Bayard's strength; and as one Bayard supporter said, "our failure in this contest might be visited upon you." Still others disliked it, August suspected, because it did not fit in with their own ambitions; those men, August told Bayard, "would even be willing to let the Presidency slide to secure the control of the state." And a few thought that it would make Bayard the target of so much abuse that his campaign would be crippled in its infancy.

But Bayard would be attacked anyway as a candidate or potential candidate and as August said, "not only by the Republican press, but also by the Tilden organs." August even warned Bayard "not to be astonished if the *World* gives you a hit now and then. I like Hurlbert for his marvelous cleverness and he has always been nice to me, but as the editor of a leading Democratic paper he is not *sound*."

Since Bayard could not avoid abuse no matter what, he would be in a stronger position to counter it if he announced his intentions. As a noncandidate he would have to ignore his critics; as a declared candidate he could answer them.

Beyond all this it simply did not seem right for Bayard to wait.

"You are too young," said August, "and have too high a destiny before you either in the Senate or the White House to have this equivocal position of a *would-be* candidate."

Bayard's strong speeches had made him the second choice of almost everyone, and as August said, "This is a strong position to hold"—which he could not do by being politically coy.

Charles Nordhoff of the *New York Herald* agreed. The Democratic party was drifting, he told August; and "it will go with any leader who has courage to assume command. But nobody offers to lead; and the conclusion of a few men with whom I have talked is that no one can so well take the lead as Senator Bayard."

Bayard allowed himself to be convinced.

"I can see nothing to be gained by a suppression of an avowed intention and desire to nominate me in 1880," he said. "Of course I am aware that the open fact of my being an intended nominee will draw upon me the fire from all sides in all the forms of misrepresentation and defamation, but if I really possess the confidence and good will of the American people," he added, "such attacks, if unjust, will not weaken me; and, if they shall show me to be really assailable, then it will be better I should be gotten out of the way—for, if I cannot stand the *trial* gallops successfully, how could I be relied upon for the race itself?"

Within a month August was able to tell Bayard, "We are moving quietly, but surely in the right direction." Important New York Democrats were "coming to the conclusion that early action and organization are necessary if we mean to carry the state this autumn in the gubernatorial race and counteract the intrigues of Gramercy Park at the Democratic Nominating Convention later on." Nevertheless August still found "at every step the miserable selfishness and petty jealousies of New York politicians."

August's persuasion was less successful with Seymour than it had been with Bayard. Seymour agreed to meet August to discuss New York politics, but he ultimately explained in a letter that his failing health prevented him from even considering coming out of retirement.

"You will see how little we can expect that Seymour will join in any energetic movement," August said when he forwarded Seymour's letter to Bayard. "His friends all unite in assuring me that he is very much opposed to Tilden and that he will, when the time comes, aid us; but I have little confidence and don't share these hopes."

He continued wistfully: "If he would consent to run for Governor, we could undoubtedly carry the state and assure a delegation hostile to Tilden in which I am confident we would have a majority for you."

Wistfulness made August as uncomfortable as the wearing of pajamas, which some eccentrics, most of them members of the Knickerbocker Club, had begun preferring to nightshirts. Rather than hope, he acted. On April 5, 1879, he held a secret meeting for all important New

York Democrats, pro-and anti-Tilden. Only Tilden and Robinson were not invited. The two factions discussed Seymour's candidacy.

Tilden's friends did not want to foreclose on Tilden's or Robinson's chances for the governorship. And, they added, Seymour had no intention of returning to politics.

If he thought only he could save the Democratic party, August said, Seymour would not refuse.

On the contrary, he would; he had, said someone who happened to have a letter from Seymour in which the former governor wrote:

"I cannot be a candidate for any office nor can I accept any nomination if made."

To find out if the letter was accurate and, if accurate, whether Seymour could be swayed, a committee of seven headed by August was organized.

"The reasons which lead your personal and political friends to ask you to reenter public life are obvious," the committee wrote to Seymour.

Seymour did not doubt that their motives were obvious, but he thought it was equally obvious that the "matter *was disposed of*."

August insisted.

Only Seymour could unite the Democrats and carry the state. Without a victory in the fall of 1879, August said, "we cannot possibly hope to elect the President in 1880." And if the Democrats failed to elect the president in 1880, then "the party in power, emboldened by the successful fraud in the last Presidential election, reckless, corrupt, and unprincipled by an almost uncontrolled sway of twenty years," would effectively destroy democracy in the United States. August was applying the most effective pressure he could: Only Seymour, by running for the governorship of New York in 1879, could save the country.

Seymour declined the honor.

August's plan and his unwillingness to give it up began to seem amusing and fanatical, and the press—as usual—took note.

"The public is becoming anxious about the fate of Mr. August Belmont and his gallant companions who started out, ten days ago, in search of a Democratic candidate . . . , and have not been heard of since," said the *New York Tribune*. "It was reported . . . that they were going first to Utica to make a desperate attempt upon the Hon. Horatio Seymour; but Mr. Seymour as soon as he heard of it warned them off his farm. . . . There is a wild and little travelled country back of the Catskills where a delegation of prominent statesmen . . . might lose themselves. . . . And there is a disquieting rumor that they carried no supplies beyond a delicate portable lunch put up at the Manhattan Club and a few bottles of champagne."

August did in fact suffer a mishap, but not in the wilds of the Catskills. Most mornings that he was in town he was in the habit of taking one of his light two-seater carriages out for a drive. From his house at Eighteenth Street August would go up Fifth Avenue past the Union Club, the Fifth Avenue Hotel, the Brunswick Hotel, the Dutch Reformed Church (which, because of the weathercock on its spire, was called the Church of the Holy Rooster), some of the recently built mansions (gaudy, August thought), the massive sloping walls of the old reservoir, and all the way up to Fifty-ninth Street, where he entered Central Park. After a circuit through the park August exited at Eighth Avenue and Fifty-ninth Street, turned east, and drove the two blocks to Sixth Avenue, where he gave the reins to the groom and left his carriage to catch the elevated railroad downtown to his office.

On April 22, August stopped as usual on the corner of Sixth Avenue and Fifty-ninth Street and was climbing down from the driver's seat when a heavy grocer's wagon, which had been following ever since August had left the park, hit and locked wheels with August's carriage. August lost his footing. He and his groom yelled for the grocer's wagon to stop; but it kept going, overturning August's carriage. August was thrown against one of the carriage poles, slipped under the wheels, and, when his horses bolted, was dragged thirty feet.

The driver of a W. & J. Sloane wagon jumped down and helped August, who was gashed over one eye, bruised, breathless from pain in his hip and groin—and furious at the driver of the grocer's wagon, who he was sure had collided with him on purpose.

After the accident the grocer's wagon continued along the street but was flagged down by a park policeman, who arrested the driver, a man named Hugh L. Slavin. August was taken to his house; Slavin, to the police station, where he said that he had not meant to run into August, that he kept on going because he did not realize anyone had been hurt, and that he was an honest man on the first day of a new job with a family to support.

That afternoon Perry and August, Jr., appeared in court when Slavin was arraigned. The park policeman who had arrested Slavin charged that he had willfully crashed into August's carriage.

Slavin had no money for bail. As he was taken away to a cell for the night, he wept. He was later tried, found guilty, sentenced to ten days in jail, and fined $100.

August, "more shaken than I first supposed," assured Bayard that "I expect to be all right again, though my beauty will be marred for a little while by all the colors of the rainbow, sadly out of place around my eyes and forehead."

During the spring of 1879 August convalesced. He worried about the insects—those "terrible carpetbaggers," he called them—that were destroying his grapevines; felt little interest in the plans that Leonard Jerome—who felt August had cheated him out of the racetrack at Jerome Park—had for a new racetrack in Brooklyn that would be run by a new organization, the Coney Island Jockey Club; and avoided politics. Bayard went to Europe for his wife's health, so August was not even tempted to conspire about the presidential nomination. The most August involved himself in Bayard's affairs was to send slips of paper Bayard had signed to various bankers on the Continent so Bayard could identify himself and draw money as he needed to.

August, Jr., was taking on more responsibility at the office. August allowed him to decide whether or not to fire an employee and asked him to go on a business trip to San Antonio, Texas, which, August told him, will "give you an opportunity to see what the West claims as the commercial rival of New York."

By the end of May, August was well enough to participate in the Coaching Club parade.

About the time August, Jr., went west, Perry went east, "to Europe," he told Marble, "on business for my father; and, although I hope to be back in a matter of weeks, it is pretty hard to pull up stakes, much harder than I imagined when I consented to go."

Perry's law firm was doing well; he was widening and improving his reputation with newspaper articles, one of the best of which was wisely on a local issue, taxation of city bonds; and his political future seemed more promising. He was afraid to lose his momentum; but as August told August, Jr., August Belmont & Company was having troubles with the Rothschilds, "the usual song."

The Rothschilds had turned down a $10 million bond deal, which, had they accepted it, "would have made a pretty profit," August told

Perry. The syndicate that had formed to handle the business "offered me in the most pressing manner an interest of $5,000,000, guaranteeing me even against loss, and though there is now a profit of $50,000"—August later revised the estimate upwards to $75,000—"I declined it, as I could not afford to place myself under obligation to them, nor did I wish to have anything more to do with these syndicates after the Rothschilds are out of it," a scruple that was rooted in "a pure feeling of loyalty to the London House of Rothschild, which I hardly think they will appreciate."

"Whatever the future may bring," August said, "I shall never falter in my attachment to their family."

This loyalty—although it was based in part on self-interest, a belief that the two businesses reinforced each other in a unique and beneficial way—was also surprisingly sentimental. Not only were August's financial operations interwoven with the Rothschilds', so was his past, his childhood. This loyalty, practical and sentimental, was not reciprocated: August wanted Perry to have a "plain talk" with the Rothschilds to find out what lay behind the current breach.

"The whole course of the Houses of Rothschild in London and Paris for the last five or six years has shown an unwillingness to put American business on the footing upon which it ought to be placed and which alone can render it worth my while in the future to continue my business relations with them," August told Perry.

This reluctance on the part of the Rothschilds offended not just August's professional and personal, but also his national, pride. His desire to overcome the resistance sprang from a defense both of the past he shared with their family and of the present, of the country that he had adopted.

The Rothschilds seemed as perplexed by August's sentimental allegiance to his country as they were by his loyalty to their family. How could he allow feelings to interfere with business?

"Why does your father take such an active part in politics?" they asked Perry, who later in his life would attribute the troubles in those years between the Rothschilds and his father to August's "very strong and outspoken political convictions, which he maintained in opposition to the party then in power."

August was, as he told Bayard, "very glad Perry went on this mission. He had not been very well and wanted a change of air and scene, though you must never tell him that I said so, as he is particularly sensitive on the subject of his health."

In London, Perry had such a good time with "everybody from the

Prince of Wales on down" that he extended his visit before crossing to Paris. The negotiations with the Rothschilds, "though only partially successful," August said, "were fully more so than I expected." He said Perry had done "as well as I could have, and probably better."

Some points of disagreement still existed, but August felt he could live with them; and he thought the Rothschilds wanted to accommodate him. But as generous as he was in his assessment of their motives, he was harsh in his judgment of their business acumen.

"Your lack of complete success is only owing to the utter want of appreciation of the importance of American business on the part of the Rothschilds and a disregard of the changes produced by cables and by the great competition of bankers, banks, and syndicates," August wrote Perry.

If August had been honest he would have admitted that he was as set in his ways as he accused the Rothschilds of being. And although he did not recognize it, he did make such an admission when, in explaining to Perry why he did not want to agree to a certain business proposition, he said:

"This would be a complete departure from my whole manner of doing business for the last forty-two years, and so contrary to the principles and traditions of my House that I could under no consideration consent to it at this late date."

Like the rest of the world the business community was changing. Financiers with methods as different from August's as August's had been from the bankers who used to keep their banknotes baled in their office windows were beginning to dominate Wall Street. August frequently began joining other bankers as a supporting, not leading, partner in transactions—as he did that year with Drexel, Morgan & Company, J. S. Morgan & Company, Morton, Bliss and Company, and Jay Gould in buying an interest in the New York Central. August was stable, and he no longer took the risks he had as a younger man.

"The house he built was like a lighthouse on a rock," a newspaper would say of him years later. "It stood unmoved amid the rush and roar of Wall Street's troubled sea. The waves that lapped its feet have often beaten high . . . , engulfing in their violence many more pretentious structures, yet never had the house of August Belmont trembled. It was a financial fortress built, if not for all time, at least for many generations. Had he been as bold in business as he was outside it . . . , he might have been the richest banker in America."

Lighthouses rarely sink, but neither do they sail to the Orient.

PART SIX

CHAPTER FIFTY-SIX

FOR THE PAST YEAR Caroline had been, according to August, "better than I have seen her for many a day." Although she preferred opera to balls and in fact had been happily foregoing grand entertainments since Jeannie's death, she began to feel, also according to August, "a desire to mix more with the outer world than she has done for the last five years." Frederika and Samuel's return from Europe in the summer of 1879 was going to be her excuse to start partying.

But in the middle of May her plans were disrupted. Jane Perry, now eighty-three years old, fell ill; and Caroline hurried to Newport where her mother was staying with Belle and George Tiffany. August soon followed. Contrary to everyone's expectations Mrs. Perry recovered. And by early June, she was as alert and energetic as ever. She took carriage rides with Caroline in the afternoons and no doubt returned to her daily habit of visiting her husband's grave.

On June 14 she seemed to August "particularly cheerful" and was looking forward to a drive later in the day. She "relished" her midday meal and before leaving the table apparently fell asleep in her chair while watched over by her three daughters, Caroline, Belle, and Jane. As though death were a dream from which she could not wake, she died peacefully in her sleep that afternoon.

She had so surprised everyone, including herself, by living so long that when her life finally came to an end, she left them stunned.

August, Caroline, Belle, and George retreated to Saratoga, which was not yet crowded. They walked out their grief along pleasant paths and avoided the few other people who had come early to the resort. When

Saratoga filled they returned to Newport. Caroline was irritable and would not ride in the afternoon alone; August urged Perry and August, Jr., to accompany her. She lost—and then found—herself in preparations for Frederika and Samuel's arrival.

"When we are all congregated together again," she said, "it will be a happy day for me. The house is all ready for my large family, and the place itself and grounds never looked lovelier than they do now."

Since Oliver's ship, the *Constellation*, would be stationed in Newport, even he would be on hand to welcome his sister and brother-in-law.

August continued to reduce the operations of his racing stable; and he occupied himself less with farm problems than he had in previous years, concerning himself only with the poor tarring job that had been done on the buildings at the Nursery and a lawsuit that had been brought against him as a result of a flogging one of his employees had given to a stableboy. August did not approve of the flogging; but after a visit from the boy's mother, who apparently tried to blackmail him, he determined to see the affair through the courts. The stableboy and his mother must have felt their case was weak, for the matter seems to have been dropped.

From the end of June through July and August the Academy of Music demanded attention. The secretary of the Academy let Wallack's Theater borrow half a dozen pieces of scenery, and August was caught in a cross fire between Academy officials who wanted the secretary dismissed and the secretary, who claimed that it was customary for theaters to lend each other scenery and that what he had done, even if it had been wrong, was too trivial an offense to cost him his job. Obviously a cabal in the Academy was out to get him. Then, Etelka Gerster, having been made a star, was unwilling, at first, to sign up for another season. And Mapleson still had not paid back last summer's loan.

To compound August's frustrations, the New York Democratic party, unable in the early fall to find a compromise candidate for governor, split. The Tilden forces nominated Lucius Robinson for another term. The anti-Tilden forces chose their own man. And in the three-way race that resulted, the Republicans, of course, won.

The troubles seemed endless.

After the election Marble sent August a present, which he claimed was to pay off a bet they had on the results. August did not recall any bet and jokingly accused Marble of having invented it "to give you a chance to heap burning coals upon my devoted head and make me ashamed of having voted against *Sammil's* candidate." If August had not abandoned the regular Democratic nominee, even if he had been Tilden's choice, the Republicans would not have won—or so, at least, Marble facetiously implied.

Their wit was barbed: they wanted not to hurt but to hook each other so securely that during the strain of the coming presidential contest they would not drift apart as they had in 1876. They watched each other for signs of disaffection and were quick to apologize when they were in bad tempers. August sent Marble a magnificent ceramic vase as a Christmas present to make up after one outburst. But in anticipating avoiding a breach they were too ready to spot offense when none was meant.

One misunderstanding almost caused a rupture. On the stairs of one of their clubs August snubbed Marble. As a result Marble was furious— at least according to the rumor that August heard. As far as August knew he had never ignored Marble; but the chilly tone of a note from his friend seemed to confirm part if not all of the story: Clearly Marble was angry about something.

"How you could imagine such a thing passes my comprehension," August told Marble. "Why you must be crazy, and I really ought to be offended at your suspicion. When an old lame fellow goes down the steep staircase of the club at 2 A.M., he has to look at his feet and steps; and so, if I passed you without speaking, the natural and only conclusion was *that I did not see you.* And a much less clever man than you would have guessed that. Now, my dear old fellow, hide your face and your blushes; and, if you have a photograph of mine, make an humble apology to it."

Marble explained—truthfully, perhaps—that the mutual friend who had passed the rumor to August must have had a "mind affected by his defeat at billiards." Marble never had accused August of snubbing him.

"Besides, if I had met you anywhere on the face of the earth when you were preoccupied," Marble said, "I should have spoken to you. You were quite right to think me crazy if I could so behave after all these years."

In their misunderstanding, however, August and Marble understood a great deal. Their political differences were irreconcilable and undoubtedly would come between them during the election year. August's accident and subsequent withdrawal from the campaign for the governorship had not altered his commitment to get Bayard the White House. He, Perry, and Charles Nordhoff had pressured James Gordon Bennett, Jr., into placing the *New York Herald* behind Bayard; and William Henry Hurlbert, although fickle, would eventually come around and give Bayard the support of the *New York World*—a buttress that Tilden, who had the backing of the *New York Sun*, also wanted.

As the backstage crews for each candidate prepared for the campaign, August participated in a curtain raiser: a little social whirl. There were the Coaching Club's regular and not so regular activities. The Belmonts enjoyed two visits from Arthur Sullivan, whose new play, *The Pirates of Penzance*, was opening in the United States—perhaps too soon, since his collaborator, William Gilbert, was having difficulty getting the pirates to seize the ladies properly. But the climax of the winter season was the revival of the opera ball, a custom that had long been ignored in New York.

"Nothing quite so gorgeous in scenery, decorations and flowers has ever before been displayed in the Academy of Music," a newspaper reported. "Nothing so expensive has ever been seen at a public ball in New York."

The lobby had been turned into a cave of flowers, giant ferns, orange trees, and vines. The auditorium was a hanging garden so luxuriant that those in the boxes could not see the stage—and, more significantly, could not be seen from anywhere else in the theater. Almost everyone was masked or in costume; and, although the Academy directors had promised that they would keep secret who had bought which boxes for the night, many women—who were, as a society column said, mischievous but not wicked—traded boxes once they had arrived, to further assure themselves of anonymity in their flirtations.

One side of the stage had been transformed into a Moorish pavilion with wood carved like lace. The other side had become a Renaissance pavilion with multicolored pennants. An arched bridge connected the two. Behind all a painted moon lit up a painted sky and was reflected in a painted lake.

August was the magician-on-call in charge of sustaining the illusions. When a man who was not properly dressed paused before entering the auditorium to get a program from an usher, August stopped him and said in a voice that the hostile *New York Tribune* claimed could be heard "half way across the Academy":

"What are you doing here?"

"I am here," said the man, "because I have a right to be."

"In what capacity?" August asked.

"As a gentleman who has paid for his ticket," said the man.

"You have no business on the floor without a dress suit," said August.

"When I go upon the floor, you may speak to me," said the man; "but now you are impertinent."

The interloper wore no evening dress, no mask, no costume. . . . It is hard to keep reality from intruding on even the most extravagantly created fantasy.

In the fall when Bayard had returned from Europe he and August had greeted each other with mutual apologies. August's was less personal but more serious.

"You find our poor party anything but improved for the present," he said. "At this moment, we have lost nearly every northern state. Radicalism is more rampant than ever."

Still, August said, simply out of an "instinct of self-preservation," the Democratic Party leaders would have to "rally around you."

Bayard's apology was for surrendering to the demands of the campaign—for the "numerous, stupid, and out of taste" interviews that had appeared after his arrival.

"But I am rather to be pitied than blamed," he said, "for I was tied to the stake and surrounded by the baying hounds of the press, and I had to say something to avoid a report drawn from the inner consciousness of a reporter! Fortunately, I have no political secrets and no opinions I am afraid to admit."

Not only was Bayard not afraid to admit his controversial opinions, he advertised them at inopportune moments. Just when he should have been courting the Soft Money wing of the Democratic Party, he introduced legislation that would stop greenbacks from being used as legal tender. The Soft Money Democrats' howling was joined by that of others whose positions were not as rigid but who thought that Bayard was going too far. Bayard was unfazed. People who professed a hybrid economics, a little Soft Money, a little Hard Money, made Bayard feel, he told August, like "a French country girl" he once saw "inspecting with a very puzzled look the sleeping figure of *Hermaphroditus* in the Louvre. She paused between a recognition of the woman's breasts and the masculine organs of generation in amusing bewilderment."

August and Perry circulated a petition among New York Democrats and tried to organize a mass meeting in support of Bayard's resolution. But the anti-Tilden Democrats of Tammany Hall would not support any measure the Tilden Democrats did; and vice versa. And the petition and mass meeting would be damned by the backing of only half the party.

"It has been very difficult to bring about a union of the two factions here," Perry told Bayard. An understatement.

Perry was not inclined to give up. Nordhoff did what he could from Washington. After all, pressure from Washington often worked in New York; the lever was long enough, all you needed was a proper fulcrum. But the *Herald*'s Washington office was unfortunately not as good a fulcrum as, say, Capitol Hill would have been. And in Congress the resolution did not have great support. In the end, Nordhoff's efforts to help were largely ineffective.

Perry meanwhile concentrated his lobbying on the Tammany boss and bitter enemy of Tilden, "Honest John" Kelly, who formerly had been a street-brawler (like many Tammany leaders), office boy for Bennett, congressman, and sheriff of New York. Although he was suspected of being for the former vice-presidential nominee, Thomas A. Hendricks, Kelly kept telling Perry that he would be happy to help Bayard's resolution, if. . . .

"If" proved elusive. Trying to bring Tammany and Tilden together was as hard as touching two magnets, north pole to north pole. Perry delayed sending the petition to Bayard, hoping to convince the resisters to sign. But he could not hold on to it forever. And in the end Bayard's resolution was defeated.

Bayard had hoped the resolution would be a call to arms for all Hard Money Democrats, but he was like a general who fights guerrillas by marching into the woods and sounding trumpets: he was not rousing his troops to fight as much as he was giving his enemy an obvious target for attack. And the Soft Money Democrats were ready for battle, capably led in the West by Hendricks and Senator Allen Granberry Thurman of Ohio. Thurman was short with a large head that he would sway with dignified slowness from side to side as he observed a crowd—leonine, observers called him; but that implied an exotic nature he lacked. He was, with his

American heartland ways and attitudes, more like a buffalo. His hair and beard were long and shaggy; his eyes were watery from the snuff to which he was addicted. He carried a red bandanna and used it often, as though he were trying to flag down history: a wonderful prop. People began calling him the Knight of the Red Bandanna. He quoted the Constitution and Balzac with equal ease; and although he traced his party lineage back to Stephen Douglas, as though his short stature implied a political as well as physical comparison with the Little Giant, nonetheless he and August, who also had been a Douglas Democrat two decades earlier, were as politically different as Esau and Jacob.

"Thurman is undoubtedly developing strength," August told Bayard. "His *unsound* financial votes and speeches for the last two years were bids for the Southern and Western votes too tempting to be resisted. Still, I think it very desirable that you and your friends should keep on good terms with Thurman and his followers. Your personal relations with him having always been so friendly, I am sure that he would prefer you to Hendricks or Tilden."

Don't fight, August was telling Bayard; don't lose your position of being everyone else's second choice. In the South, as in the West, Bayard should alienate no other candidate in the course of building a base for himself. Since Bayard was from Delaware, August hoped that he would have the advantage of regional sympathy. If he could go to the Democratic National Convention with the South solidly behind him, he would be irresistible.

But "the South in the last ten years has become timid and fearful of responsibility," a Virginia politician told August. "Inexperience and repeated failures have made her distrust and even have deprived her of political sagacity and forecast."

It would not be easy for Bayard to win the South. August decided to reconnoiter. In February 1880 he followed the Atlantic Coast—Baltimore, Washington, Richmond, Wilmington (North Carolina), Savannah —to Florida. The weather was uncomfortably hot. The political climate was no better. August's activities were limited. In Washington, he told Bayard, "I waited for you at the hotel until the last moment, as I did not like to go to the Capitol to have my doings heralded and misrepresented." And other candidates—Tilden, Major General Winfield Scott Hancock (whom August liked no better in 1880 than he had in 1876), and Samuel Jackson Randall, the Speaker of the House—had already organized the area so well that Bayard's hopes for uniting the South behind him quickly wilted.

Major General Winfield Scott Hancock was a good soldier and a limited politician. He thought, or at least spoke, in platitudes, and—unnervingly—seemed to believe them. If Thurman was a buffalo, Hancock was a buffalo, tamed and barbered; the buffalo equivalent of a show poodle. His hair was trimmed; his cheeks were so clean-shaven they appeared naked, innocent; and his mustache, a very proper brush, looked like one more decoration conferred upon him, a badge of maturity. For those who recalled his gallant figure in the Civil War, he seemed disguised, as though getting older was a process of going undercover on some secret assignment. He was slow, a tortoise in a race of rabbits.

Samuel Jackson Randall was so swift he had outrun his origins. He represented a poor and tough district in Philadelphia. As elegant as his constituents were rough, he was a gilt mirror in a waterfront dive: his polish allowed him to reflect all the better his voters' wishes. But he felt his scope was too narrow. If mirrors had desires, they would want to be placed in an uninterrupted landscape so they could embrace everything up to and including the horizon. Randall wanted to be president.

"Randall is making a canvass for himself," Perry told Bayard. "This ought not to be an agreeable occupation for one who thinks himself worthy of such a high place."

Perry, the son of the man responsible for setting presidential candidates unashamedly on the stump, was fastidiously censuring a politician for stumping.

August, in his old age, agreed more with Perry than he did with his younger self. When the New York Chamber of Commerce asked Bayard to speak on his financial views at a dinner that also would be addressed by the Secretary of the Treasury, John Sherman, August advised him to decline.

"Your record on this question is so well-known that it is neither necessary nor politic to enlarge on it at this time," August said.

And another of Bayard's friends reported:

"Belmont says, 'that he don't believe in prominent candidates traveling about.' "

Why should Bayard risk a debate with Sherman, when he could maintain a statesmanlike superiority that made him no enemies?

Just as August thought Bayard was Thurman's choice over Tilden and Hendricks, he thought Bayard was Tilden's choice over Seymour, Randall, Hendricks, and Thurman. Once Tilden saw "he cannot get the nomination himself," August thought, "Bayard could certainly be the most available and in fact the *only* choice left for him." So August did not want Bayard to do anything to antagonize Tilden—like joining forces with Kelly, which one of Bayard's advisers had suggested. It was one thing to woo Kelly to support Bayard (as Perry had when trying to drum up support for Bayard's proposed antigreenback legislation); it was another thing for Bayard to come out in support of Kelly in his fight with Tilden over control of New York's Democratic party.

"It would be worse than folly to attempt that proposed organization now," August told Perry. "It would not only be money thrown away and time and labor wasted, but it would render it impossible for Tilden's friends to support Bayard. Bayard may be nominated without Tilden's assistance, but he *cannot* be nominated against Tilden's pronounced opposition, which would surely follow any alliance with Kelly."

Perry passed his father's dictum on to the faithful.

"Our only chance for Bayard lies in a united delegation," he told the man who had suggested the pact with Kelly, "and that unfortunately I fear we can only get through the help of such friends of Tilden as are convinced that he cannot be elected. This, of course, is a dangerous and delicate game."

A game that did not work.

The pro-Tilden *New York Sun* attacked Bayard for a speech he had given two decades before in which he had said that the South should be allowed to secede from the Union. Since Tilden, whose views on Hard Money were similar to Bayard's, could not attack him on the currency question, he was—through the *Sun*—attacking him the only way he could: on a position he had taken at the start of the Civil War.

Some of Bayard's "political rivals may try to make a bundle of it in the nominating convention, but"—August told Bayard—"with the people it will not hurt you or in any event only with a few blind fanatics who would never vote the Democratic ticket anyhow."

On Tilden's part it showed desperation.

"The Tilden people seem to be more alarmed now than ever before; that is, as far as I have been able to judge," Perry told Bayard a short time later. "The surest sign which I have always noticed about them whenever their candidate gets a fresh setback is an attempt to get the Democratic press to let up on the old man. They"—Marble, for example, who had come to see Perry—"say the poor old man may die, and besides that his friendship is necessary. You have heard of this sort of thing before."

Bayard would not be sucker-baited. Tilden's timing had been off; if he had waited until closer to the convention to attack Bayard, Bayard might have been seriously injured by the *Sun*'s revelation. But Bayard's timing also was off. No longer concerned with alienating Tilden, Bayard let Kelly know that he now was ready to form an alliance. Kelly, however, was no longer interested.

As usual, the anti-Tilden Democrats of New York were unable to present a united front. At the state convention in Syracuse, Tilden triumphed and the New York delegation to the national convention was bound by the unit rule: all delegates—including August and Perry—no matter what their preference, would have to cast their first ballot for Tilden.

During the weeks before the convention August with Perry's help did all the things a backer must do for his candidate. He knew the route by rote. Raise a $50,000 campaign fund, $10,000 of which he guaranteed. Give $1,500 to produce a campaign biography, more money to save a failing pro-Bayard newspaper in Delaware, and even more money to print and distribute literature that tried to explain away Tilden's capture of the New York delegation. Gather information. Make lists: who was for, against, undecided. Lean on the undecideds.

But Tilden was strong enough to frighten into silence those who might oppose him. The Long Island delegation, of which Perry was a member, "went away from Syracuse holding the same opinions as to the impossibility of electing Tilden, and yet every one of them was afraid to do anything which might appear to be owing to Tammany influence." Even if Tilden did not become the presidential nominee, he would still be a power in New York; and many New York politicians were not prepared to lose his goodwill—or his indifference.

August and Perry began to feel themselves drifting from the center of power. Perry worried about the influence of railroad money on the Democratic party, which he thought would be a greater evil than another Republican administration, even Grant's reelection—which, since Hayes had pledged not to run for a second term, was a possibility frequently discussed. August worried that "our party leaders will make the mistake of forcing a Western man upon the convention, arguing that New York cannot possibly be carried for a Democrat." If only the Democratic Party would realize that "thousands and thousands of independent voters and equal numbers of intelligent Republicans would support Bayard, if the political wire-pullers who control . . . the convention would give them a chance to do so."

August did not seem to recognize that he, too, was a wire-puller; in this convention he just had to pull his particular wires a little harder than he was used to.

The Republicans chose as their presidential nominee not Grant but James Abram Garfield, the tall, bearded senator from Ohio. In one of the most famous photographs of him, taken that year, he is standing in a standard pose that nevertheless seems typical of him: His back is to the camera but his head is turned to show his profile, as if he were caught between desires for privacy and publicity. He was born poor and achieved much; and like many such men, like August, in fact, he had created a self-contained world of his own on a farm in Mentor, Ohio, a place to which he could return when his welcome in or his tolerance of the outside world of power wore out. Although he spoke often about his distaste for the unpleasantness of politics, he was unable to give it up; and he knew, as he told his wife, that if he did retire to his farm he would miss all the things he had tried to escape.

He was a conciliator. If he did not have a great many intimate friends, neither did he have many passionate enemies. Unlike the abstemious Hayes, Garfield indulged in enough minor vices—drinking, smoking—to make people feel comfortable with him; and, unlike Grant, he indulged moderately enough not to let them feel contemptuous. He was a good listener. He was, in short, an ideal dinner guest—and the Republicans had invited him to sit at the head of the table.

The Republicans' vice-presidential candidate, Chester Alan Arthur, was a crony of Conkling's. As collector of the Port of New York he had been one of Hayes's targets when the President was trying to break Conkling's power over patronage in that state; as a result, although he was honest, he became the focus of an attack on corruption. The quality of not being quite appropriate for the role he was called to play was characteristic of Arthur. He was a party man who held himself aloof; a behind-the-scenes worker who was caught with the curtain up; a politician who did not seem to like people. When Garfield sat at the head of the Republican table Arthur was surprised to be seated above the salt. After being offered the second place on the ticket he said:

"The office of the Vice-Presidency is a greater honor than I ever dreamed of attaining."

After the Republican Convention the Greenback Labor and Prohibition parties nominated presidential and vice-presidential candidates. August took note of them the way he might check out, in whist, low cards in a nontrump suit.

The Democratic Convention was held in Cincinnati with the usual hysteria, as though politicians were shamans who had to whip themselves into a frenzy in order to seek divine guidance on important matters. Fireworks, bands, speeches—August hardly noticed them. All that commotion was like the weather, bad weather, and August just wanted to come in out of it.

He and Perry arrived early with Charles O'Conor's blessing, a pro-Bayard letter that August hoped would sway delegates who respected O'Conor: Some were swayed; others swayed—and swayed back to their original anti-Bayard stance. In politicking August followed too well O'Conor's parting admonition to "strain every nerve and put forth all your strength." On the day after the convention officially opened August wrote to August, Jr., "I am quite used up and cannot go out, suffering perfect torture of headache and general prostration."

Tilden withdrew his name from consideration on the grounds that his health was not good. August, trying to get Tilden's support for Bayard, begged Marble in a telegram:

"Cannot you induce leader telegraph transfer his forces to mine. Insure victory nomination election. . . . Proper acknowledgement hereafter"—the bait for Tilden—"Delay or hesitation places nomination beyond control."

August never found out if Marble could or would have helped him.

"Your telegram came too late," Marble telegraphed back. "The whole thing was settled last night."

The wires that August pulled broke. Hancock was nominated for president "under the pressure of an organized mob in the galleries and on the floor," August told Bayard. Governor William H. English of Indiana was nominated for vice-president—principally to assure the Democratic Party victory in his home state.

"These conventions, as at present managed, are a severe stain upon popular institutions and make self-government a tragical farce," August added. "It is lucky that the result is not worse and that we were not doomed to be called upon to support a legatee of [Tilden] the arch intriguer of Gramercy Park. You know the intellectual capacities of our candidate, and I need not dwell upon them. However, everything is better than Tildenism or Republican misrule, and so we must give our hearty support to Hancock, hoping that when elected he will surround himself with statesmen possessing all the qualifications which he so sadly needs."

Although Bayard must have felt a "momentary disappointment at the folly and ingratitude of a party you have served so well and faithfully, I cannot but express to you my firm conviction that you are a gainer not a loser by the unsucccessful result of the efforts of your friends," said August, struggling for an optimism that seemed proper, although undeserved. "You are today the foremost statesman, not only of your party, but of the country at large; and, at a comparatively early age, you have already secured for yourself a name in American History along with that illustrious trio: Calhoun, Webster, and Clay. Your position for the next four years as the leader of a great party in the United States Senate is a prouder and more enviable one than that of the President."

August's letter, written in gold-watch rhetoric, sounded more like a testimonial at a retirement than encouragement for the future. But it was August's exhaustion as much as Bayard's political setback that influenced the tone.

August avoided the campaign all summer, although uncharacteristically he did not fling himself into any other activity to get his mind off politics. He further reduced the size of his stables, sending one horse off to England for the Rothschilds to run and, in America, entering fewer races than he had done since the founding of the Jockey Club. Even if he had been eager to race this year, he felt his staff was not up to it. One of his promising horses died after being so badly treated that August claimed it had beeen as good as murdered; and when August, Jr., tried to cheer him up by giving him encouraging reports on the horse's brother, a new colt, August dismissed the attempt by saying: "Two years to wait for that colt to be ready to race is long for an old man like me."

In exchange for August, Jr.'s hopeful platitudes August gave gloomy ones. When August, Jr., complained about having been disappointed by someone in a business deal, August said: "As you grow older, you will find that this is the way in 99 cases out of 100 and that people shirk responsibilities and labors, which is the cause of the many failures and defalcations in private and public enterprises and positions of trust—" which, in later years, August, Jr., would recast as a phrase that became one of his most quoted statements:

"If you want a thing done, go; if you don't, send."

In the middle of July, at Bythesea, August came out of the house to investigate a ruckus on the back lawn. Three of August's hunting dogs— Sandy, Toby, and Moor—were tormenting a small stray Scotch terrier. Afraid the three larger dogs would kill the stray, August called for his servants; none were around. He called for his sons; they were gone too. So to break up the fight, August—an old man, dwarfed by the house behind him—went running down the lawn hollering and waving his arms, dancing around the animals.

❧ CHAPTER FIFTY-SEVEN ❦

IF HANCOCK WON, August figured Bayard would become secretary of state. That was worth fighting for; and August fought, although not as energetically as he had in past campaigns. He accepted an invitation to become a member of the Hancock-controlled Democratic Congressional Campaign Committee, which—he was told—hoped to offset the power of the Tilden-controlled Democratic National Committee.

"The especial friends of General Hancock recognize that they must look for aid (of every character) in this campaign from other sources as well as from those who have fastened their grasp upon the National Committee," Hancock's campaign manager wrote to August. "General Hancock is *utterly and absolutely uncommitted to anyone* and it shall be my earnest effort to prevent any influence so deadly as that of the old regime from fastening itself upon him in any way."

The repetition of *fasten* to describe the influence of Tilden on Hancock could have been evoked by a cartoon in a *Harper's Weekly* of the previous year, in which Tilden, his face looking as desiccated and finely webbed as dried orange skin, was shown sucking the life's blood out of a prospective candidate; but seeing Tilden as a vampire gave him a dignity, no matter how sinister, that August was reluctant to grant. *Fasten* also suggests the action of a tick; and like a tick, Tilden was hard to pick off.

The anti-Tilden Democrats scratched and dug at Tilden and in the end drew more blood out of themselves than Tilden did.

August occasionally stopped at the national headquarters; kept in touch with Bayard and offered him advice on where and how he should campaign for Hancock; unsuccessfully urged McClellan to stump for the ticket; and gave a few speeches. At one rally he became furious when John Kelly through "stupidity or want of consideration" failed to introduce him as chairman. After the meeting August went to Bayard's hotel to exercise his anger; but Bayard did not appear, and at eleven-thirty, too impatient to wait any longer, August left.

The next morning August told Bayard: "Kelly will not have another chance in a hurry to place me in so awkward a position."

August over-dramatically called one of his speeches, which he asked Marble to fix, his swan song. He was not retiring; he merely was withdrawing farther into the background, which he told Marble he "preferred particularly now that Perry [who again was running for the First Congressional District] is on the field. These powerful millionaires"—August's half-ironic and half-serious reference to his political enemies like Tilden —"might wish to visit the sins of the father upon the son. For this reason, I have also concluded not to notice the filth" being spread, as usual, about August.

He asked Marble to check a speech of Perry's and told him that "I shall be personally very grateful for everything you can do to help him, but pray don't tell him that I spoke to you."

Wisely, August wanted Perry to feel that he was getting the nomination for himself.

Perry, however, misunderstood his father's intentions. He thought, as he had two years earlier, that his father was unwilling to support him properly. Marble, Perry's confidant, became an intermediary between father and son—or more precisely a translator of gestures, interpreting each one's actions for the other.

However little Perry thought his father was helping, the public was convinced that August was buying the nomination and election for him.

"The 'barrel' has been tapped already in the preliminary canvass," reported *The New York Times,* "and good Democratic judges say that young Mr. Belmont or his father will want to spend from $1,000 to $20,000 before November 2, if they expect to succeed. An idea of the

money that has already been expended may be gathered from the trustworthy statement that $500 was used to carry the primary in Riverhead
alone and proportionate amounts in every one of the ten other towns of
the county. . . . The old-time Democrats and yeomanry . . . are . . .
indignant at . . . their candidate being shoved aside to make way for
young Mr. Perry, whom, they say, they have never heard of before, except
as a polo player and not a particularly brilliant one at that."

A brazen lie, Perry thought, although it was not clear to what he was
referring: the allegations of money spent, the charge that he was a political unknown (he had run for office two years earlier), or the slur on his
polo playing.

Perry countercharged that a fixer known as "Dublin Tricks" Hastings was offering $100 bribes to anyone who would vote for one of the
other candidates.

In response, rumors now said that Perry was spending not $1,000 to
$20,000 but $25,000 to win just the nomination—and that he would
spend at least as much again for the election.

After the meeting at which Perry finally was nominated, one old-
time Democrat who was not particularly happy with the "polo-ticket," as
it was called, said:

"Well, we'll bust the staves off old Belmont's barrel for this night's
work; see if we don't. We'll find out what that Babylon barrel's made of,
you bet."

If three decades of supporting presidential candidates had not emptied August's barrel, one congressional election—no matter how lavishly
run—was hardly enough to break the barrel up. Perry traveled his district
in a special train. He gave speeches at county fairs to farmers, who
squinted up at him as though he were emitting a harsh, unfamiliar light.
He met local leaders, some so fat they seemed bloated by power and
others so thin they seemed seared by it. And he tried to change his
clubman's heartiness (which struck these strangers as condescension)
into a promiscuous amiability (which, although truly condescending,
made him appear a comradely fellow).

On the last day of the campaign bonfires burned along all the roads
leading into the center of Babylon. People bundled against the fall cold
paraded with torches and banners, their chants and cheers swelled by the
barking of dogs and shouts of children. Dry leaves drifted down from
trees like confetti.

In the flares from the flames Perry's face was a mask: the highlights on forehead, cheeks, and chin so bright they looked painted on, the shadow making his eyes and mouth dark holes. He gave a long speech, which the crowd frequently interrupted with roars of pleasure—the political equivalent of responsive reading in a church service. The election results temporarily seemed secondary to the joy of the campaign. Temporarily.

Hancock lost the presidential race to Garfield.

Perry won his seat in Congress.

August's complaints during the campaign—about the Democratic wire-pullers and the millionaires who might oppose Perry's election and Perry's concern over the influence of railroad money on the Democratic party— betrayed not merely an eccentric illusion father and son may have shared about the family's function in society but also a position August was taking and was prepared to defend: He was an antimonopolist international banker, a curiosity as amusingly bewildering as any hybrid Hard–Soft Money economist or Bayard's *Hermaphroditus* in the Louvre.

Soon after the election August told Bayard that a protective tariff was an "unsound policy" that acted principally "for the benefit of Eastern monopolists."

Then he lectured the senator, his long letter having some of the poignancy of a talk an unpopular professor might give to his one loyal student in an otherwise empty hall:

"This policy might have had some excuse when our national debt was nearly all held abroad and the interest on it increased the balance of trade against us. Now, with the exception of perhaps $150,000,000 at the outside, our whole national debt is owned at home. About $300,000,000 are used as the basis of the national bank circulation, which gives us as sound and stable a paper currency as human ingenuity can make it, while the other $1,200,000 are in the hands of banks, savings institutions, insurance companies, trust funds, capitalists, and small investors spread over the whole extent of the country. Our federal government has thus become a great savings bank for our people, where the poor and the rich are willing to be satisfied with a low rate of interest for the sake of undoubted security. Such a debt, if not excessive, is a bond of strength and union to a people, as it interests the voters in the stability of government, the capacity of its legislators and administrators, and the soundness of its financial policy."

Like any business a country can raise money by borrowing. The

IOU that it gives the person from whom it borrows is called a bond. If someone buys a government bond, he is lending that country a certain amount of money; in return the country pays him interest every year— until, after an agreed upon time, the bondholder sells the bond back to the country for the amount of money he originally lent it. Many of the syndicates August had been involved in were groups of capitalists who bought bonds from the United States and resold them to people who either would hold onto them and collect the interest until it was time to redeem them or would sell them, in turn, to others.

Previously the United States had sold most of its bonds to Europe; so it had to pay the interest on those bonds to foreigners—which added to the flow of money out of the country. The government could not stop paying interest on its bonds; but it could try to keep other money from crossing the Atlantic by discouraging Americans from buying foreign goods—through the use of tariffs, which were financial dams built of import taxes.

However, August argued, now most of the government bonds were owned by Americans. The government was paying the interest on those bonds to its own citizens. Money was not draining out of the country—so the government did not have to discourage the buying of foreign goods. Tariffs were unnecessary. In fact, tariffs were only "for the benefit of Eastern monopolists," since by raising the price of European commodities the tariffs made it difficult for them to compete with American products. And the American manufacturers, not having to compete with their European counterparts, could charge an artificially high price for their products.

That was why the "Eastern monopolists" wanted tariffs and why August was against the Eastern monopolists—one of the reasons why he was against them.

Another reason had to do not with the relationship between the bond market and tariffs but with the bond market itself.

Whoever owns a government's bonds is naturally concerned with that government's solvency and survival. When a government's own citizens hold the bonds they are concerned, as August said, "in the stability of the government, the capacity of its legislators and administrators, and the soundness of its financial policy." The more citizens who own government bonds, the wider the government's base of support—just as the greater the distribution of the country's general wealth, the greater the interest the citizens will have in their government's welfare.

During the Civil War, August had wanted to sell government bonds to Northerners to keep them loyal to the Union cause. Now with labor unrest and socialist agitation August thought the government should keep the country's wealth widely enough distributed—through bonds and other means—to keep Americans loyal to the economic system. Rightly or wrongly August saw his function as a distributor of wealth—through, among other ways, the buying and selling of government bonds.

August did get involved in monopolistic schemes like being part of a syndicate that paid $40 million for Northern Pacific Railroad mortgage bonds, a transaction a contemporary described as "then unparalleled in its magnitude" and the purpose of which was to preserve the dominance of the Northern Pacific Railroad over its territory. Nevertheless he saw himself as an antagonist to the monopolists, because monopolists by concentrating the country's wealth in a small number of hands reduced the government's base of support among its citizens. Monopoly capital, August thought, upset the harmony of the system—as though all the other instruments in an orchestra were slowly crowded out and replaced by tubas.

This odd position, so apparently contradictory to everything August had done in his life, served to set him, at least in his own mind, apart from others in his class. It was a way of sentimentally connecting himself to his youth when he always felt that he was an outsider. But since he was so responsible for helping to create the financial and social world in which he lived, to feel an outsider in it he had to be an emotional and intellectual contortionist. His position could be explained, but it was so convoluted it seemed impossible that it would not crack under the strain.

Perry had picked up his father's beliefs; and even before he was seated in the House of Representatives he—according to a newspaper report—had "rendered valuable service at Washington in destroying a contemplated monopoly" that would have threatened the existence of a number of independent breweries.

Under the influence of their father and older brother, August, Jr., and Oliver also came to think of themselves as antimonopolists. For August, Jr., being antimonopolist seems to have been simply a matter of social balance. The question of right or wrong affected him no more than the color of the plates he is juggling affects a juggler. The system existed; it was the way things were; and one had to make it work because, right or wrong, if it were upset all would go smash.

Oliver's tendencies were more toward being a crusader; and, although he was not yet actively recruited, he was beginning to form the opinions that in two decades would prompt him to start a magazine called *The Verdict*, the purpose of which was to fight "trusts, monopolies, and the money power on behalf of the common people."

The noblesse oblige that rings in the phrase "the common people" reflects what was both admirable and despicable about such warriors in such a fight. In a way the Belmont brothers were becoming like the knights Perry thought politicians should model themselves on: They were out to defend the people who were suffering from the system that gave the knights their very power. The final dragons they would have to fight were themselves.

The apparent change in August's position on the national debt had been gradual; but it is clear that he now thought that a national debt—if modest and if the government were in hock to its own citizens—was not a bad thing. In fact, a modest national debt was a philosopher's stone that turned want into prosperity.

Acting from this belief he supported that winter the proposed passage of a new long-term government bond issue, although he admitted to Bayard that the "House and particularly the Democrats there have shown so much ignorance and prejudice in handling this question that I have almost despaired of any practical measure being passed. The cry of the demagogues is reduction of the national debt."

Bayard could offer little hope. Washington was awash with office seekers making deals.

"The incoming administration will be in a sea of political trading and bargaining," he said, "and there are no indications that the tone of administration will be raised."

And contrary to any illusions August may have had about his lack of power as one of the leaders of Wall Street, Bayard said a certain member of the Cabinet would be so inhibited by "the keen eyes of 'Wall Street' that he would fear" to do anything of which "Wall Street" disapproved.

August helped pay off the debt that Hancock's Democratic Congressional Campaign Committee had run up. And he urged Bayard to support the appointment of an anti-Conkling man to the job of collector of the Port of New York. The appointment went through. Conkling and the other senator from New York, who was one of his lieutenants, quit their offices in protest. Conkling's power was finally shaken, and he was never reelected.

🐉 *CHAPTER FIFTY-EIGHT* 🦚

PERRY WENT TO WASHINGTON. Caroline, August, Jr., and Raymond went to Europe. The Belmonts' house in Manhattan seemed so empty that August spent as much time as he could at the Nursery; but, because he had been reducing the size of his racing stable, the farm also seemed desolate. He had an eye operation that did not turn out as well as he had hoped it would. Cold, wind, and light hurt his eye so much that he was forced to stay inside in darkened rooms. His doctor suggested that he join Caroline in Europe later in the year for his health, perhaps even going to Marienbad for his dyspepsia. August made a reservation for June 18 on the *Celtic*, one of the White Star Line's extraordinary new ships, which was heated by steam and wired so a passenger could call a steward with an electric bell. He previously had trusted only Cunard ships, which were supposed to be the safest, but he was willing to experiment with one of these huge, luxurious floating hotels, the first of the true ocean liners—if he went.

August was not eager to cross the Atlantic. First of all, he continued to have difficulties with the Rothschilds, who balked at keeping a permanent fund of $300,000 to $500,000 in the United States for August to draw on when speed was necessary to close a deal. They would not even keep $10,000 in the country; and as August told August, Jr., "I want you to tell Nathaniel that, if N. M. Rothschild and Sons cannot spare *$100,000* for our joint account, *August Belmont & Company certainly cannot*. If he can do without the American business, so can I do without his." August had heard about another banker, who had much less money than the Rothschilds, putting $400,000 in a special fund in a small German bank, *"none of the partners of which is worth my income,"* so he felt it was not unreasonable to expect "the first and richest house in the world" to treat a longtime associate in a comparable manner, particularly when such an arrangement was "in the *common* interest. Are you astonished," he asked August, Jr., "that considering all this I don't want to go to Europe?!"

As for Marienbad, August told his son that he had "but little faith in the efficacy of mineral springs against a chronic disease such as my dyspepsia, particularly adding to it *my incurable trouble of old age*."

Although he told Caroline that he tried to ease his heartburn by making himself agreeable to an amiable lady he met at a dinner party, apparently that cure did not work, because he did not go into society much that spring. He did get involved in a "somewhat stormy" battle over the control of the Knickerbocker Club; his faction, "the old regime," he told August, Jr., "carried the day." Once in a while he went to the opera; but usually he gave up his box to friends or to Frederika and Samuel, with whom he frequently and quietly dined. He was trying to convince them to settle next to his house on a lot on Eighteenth Street; but they were flighty and already were talking of returning to Europe.

"A short visit [to the Continent] is what we must expect her to want to do every now and then, like everyone else," Caroline wrote to console August. "As the years go on, she will become tired of great excitements and will, I hope, be much more with me and want to come oftener to see us."

August sent his carriage, flowers from Bythesea, and fresh eggs from the Nursery to his sister-in-law Jane Hone, who was very ill. When he visited her he was shocked to see how emaciated she was. Her body was devouring itself and in that effort to live was killing her. Jane Hone was only ten years older than Caroline; but Caroline at fifty-two seemed to August "too young and too pretty" to bury herself in mourning.

She had just been recovering from Jeannie's death when Jane Perry had died, and this trip abroad like her previous one was supposed to be a journey back into society, into life. But now because of Jane Hone's illness Caroline wanted to return home and retreat into the security of grief. Society, instead of seducing her into forgetting her troubles, seemed repellent. So many of her former friends and acquaintances—those who were not dead—were becoming decrepit, feeble, or senile. In London she visited with Lionel Rothschild's wife, Charlotte, whose hair, she told August, "has grown quite gray." Other than that she looked well, and she "asked me as usual a world of questions. She sat in her little salon on the lower floor, where we were always received, embroidering; and she had her books, etc., about her. I should never have known that she was out of her mind, and indeed from all accounts she is much better. They say that she used to imagine herself a grain of sand."

Society increasingly appeared to be a sanitarium.

August urged her to stay in Europe and enjoy herself; to buy herself pretty dresses and "to go about a good deal and accept every invitation from pleasant people."

"Many thanks for giving me *carte blanche*," Caroline wrote to August. "I think I am naturally economical, for it comes hard with me to spend money, and I do not like paying large bills. I suppose it is because I have never before been quite so independent."

She sought refuge from the giddiness of this freedom in the familiar search for fine furniture, art, and bibelots—August's pastime when he traveled through Europe. But she knew she did not have his eye. So although she bought some large things—a rug, a chair that had to be refinished—mostly she confined herself to a specialty she felt she could learn to master: old embroideries. They had become very popular, especially among Americans abroad; and Caroline, unwilling to pay the exorbitant prices for what were in some cases mere scraps, found a satisfying challenge in trying to find bargains.

"I am a perfect fool about it all," she told August.

She went to Worth's twelve times a day for fittings to have an entirely new wardrobe made.

"Although I wear black," she said, "I am having my dresses made without crepe. Worth is very expensive, but he has always worked for me, and is extremely anxious to make me pretty things. He would have me look gayer than I am willing he should, so I will let him mix some white with the black."

The spring weather was chilly but clear. The trees along the Champs Elysées were beginning to be misted with green, as though their leaves were formed through condensation of colored air. Caroline's spirits improved; her headaches vanished. The city was comfortingly familiar— even with its new republican street names, which on this trip no longer startled; even with the new electric lights that blazed in the recently built opera house and that seemed to make Paris simply more of what it always had been: gay and bright.

The Rothschilds gave Caroline their opera box and invited her to dinners. She spent a formal evening with the king of Naples and an informal one with the Princess Hohenlohe. She raised her eyebrows questioningly at the Frenchmen who ranted against the Germans and censoriously at the Frenchwomen who affected an extreme Grecian bend: head up, back swayed, buttocks jutting out. She approved of the passionate attempts of one old friend to stop some terrible stories that were being spread about him. And she disapproved of the even more passionate attempts of another old friend (James Gordon Bennett, Jr., who was then in Paris) to start some terrible stories about himself—or at least to keep the gossipmongers well supplied with scandals.

Caroline declined all his invitations, since, as she told August, she made it a practice "never to go to bachelor's entertainments without you." Bennett then sent her a gold bracelet ornamented with an owl's head, which she at first decided to refuse. But when she learned that it was not a sign of any particular favor (he in fact had had a dozen made to give to all his lady friends), she figured that keeping it could not be misconstrued as a promise of any particular reciprocal favor. And since she thought "Bennett would get angry" if she sent it back, she kept it, she told August, "on your account and Perry's with his newspaper. Do write and tell me if I was right not to return it."

Caroline's good mood soon vanished with the good weather. The spring turned colder. It rained all the time. The days were dark. She felt as though she were living in a permanent night.

"I cannot get warm in the apartment," she told August, "although I have two fires burning."

Her servants, Agnes and John, were inexperienced and spoke only English, which meant Caroline had to handle most of the problems that arose. For example, her coachman was not punctual and kept forgetting addresses.

"This may seem a trifle," she told August, "but I am not accustomed to take care of myself."

Her new independence at first made her feel incompetent.

"The fact is," she told August, "I miss you and don't like to decide about important things."

"I would rather have someone take care of bills for me," she said at another time, "and look after me."

But she kept her finances straight and not only got a new coachman but also changed stables. She was learning to assert herself and apparently enjoyed doing so. Shortly after she coped with the problem of the coachman, she told August: "You must not worry about me now. I get along very well."

And in time she began to fear that things were getting more out of hand at 109 Fifth Avenue than they were in Paris.

"I hope," she said, "the servants are not having too good a time in my absence."

Caroline's transformation was not dramatic. Transformations rarely are. And she would never like taking care of matters for herself. But she was learning that she did not need to depend on someone else. She would always be a fairy-tale princess; but in some small way she was reinterpreting her role.

Her new and growing confidence must have come in part from her handling of two crises that spring: a minor one involving Raymond and a major one involving Oliver, both of which August refused to deal with.

"I have done my duty and *more than* my duty to these boys," August said. "One of them is a man now and ought to act as a man, and I am determined not to be tormented to death in my old age." He vowed, "*I cannot and will not* be placed into a position of arguing and fighting. It will simply kill me, and I feel now in regard to Oliver and Raymond as if I would rather die than have to contend against them. I want to be left alone. If they come to me for a decision, *I shall simply run away.*"

Before leaving England for the Continent, Caroline had found a tutor, William C. Lawton, for Raymond; and she had established them in Chertsey, a quiet, too quiet, town on the Thames in Surrey. After a short and studious stay they were supposed to follow her to Paris. But August, Jr., who had been in London, and Oliver, whose ship had stopped for a while in Nice, both had appeared at Caroline's hotel. And not wanting to invite more confusion Caroline asked Raymond and Lawton to delay leaving Chertsey. In fact, she began to think that it would be better if they stayed there for the spring and summer while she traveled.

Neither Raymond nor Lawton liked that arrangement.

"I shall regret losing the pleasure of traveling with you," Lawton wrote to Caroline, "and must frankly acknowledge that I should be very unhappy over my wasted time, 'if pocketed' for the rest of the year in an English country house."

Raymond, who was equally bored in Chertsey, wanted to disregard his mother's desires and leave immediately for Paris.

Lawton telegraphed Caroline for instructions—which infuriated Raymond, who (according to Lawton) "called my action an unwarrantable interference in his relations with his mother, a very nasty thing to do, etc. He assured me that where he went was no concern of mine and that he did not care in the least whether I stayed in Chertsey or went with him." Raymond then took the next train to London.

"You will doubtless agree that this brings our relations to a crisis," Lawton wrote to Caroline. "Either he is utterly wrong, or I am. The least I can accept is an acknowledgement from him that I am right and an explicit apology for his most unwarrantable expressions. I shall remain here until I hear from you."

Caroline thought that "Raymond has been wrong to speak as Lawton says he did to him." But it seemed clear to her that Lawton was more interested in traveling with Raymond than in educating him; and as soon as the trip seemed doubtful he "took the first excuse to retire" from his job.

"I do not wish to shield Raymond in anything he has done," she told August, "but Lawton had no business to break off in this abrupt manner without first bringing Raymond here and having an interview with me. I am glad he did not come, but such should have been his action under the circumstances."

She also disliked the "curt and disrespectful" tone of Lawton's letters. She wrote him a businesslike note, accepting his resignation, in which she practiced her new forceful manner.

"I regret extremely," she said, "the cause and tenor of your correspondence and will endeavor to rectify that which may be necessary in this case."

When Raymond arrived in Paris he announced to Caroline that he was not going to Harvard in the fall. He would enter the year after and in the meanwhile would travel—with or without his mother.

"He has a most extraordinary bulldog tenacity in sticking to his opinion or any plan he may make for himself," Caroline told August, Jr.

"Raymond can stay away from Harvard for a year if he chooses," August told August, Jr.; "but he cannot remain in Europe *alone* and only if Mama prefers to spend the Winter with him in Italy or on the Nile. I *shall not* permit him the money to remain alone or to go around the world." And, annoyed that he had been drawn into the discussion even this much, August added, "They must settle all this between themselves."

Caroline was content to have Raymond's company, although she fretted about how much she could control him "in this gay and dissipated place." At first, intimidated by Parisian society, Raymond stayed close to his mother.

"He feels out of place, awkward, and sensitive at not looking his age," Caroline said.

Raymond was a baby-faced eighteen.

"At the same time," Caroline added, "he is willing to go with me to various amusements, and I think it will be of much service to him to see the best people here and brush up his French, dress, and manners. He has difficulty about his white ties, their length and breadth, also as to whether he shall wear gloves, etc. And we go off into arguments on these important subjects."

Very quickly, however, Raymond fell in with a group of wild young American boys, learning as much from them as from Caroline's friends about fashion (scarf pins in the shape of insects and odd animals were all the rage) and French society.

"He *will* go to the theaters," Caroline told August, "which as you know are running pieces of the most immoral tendencies; and they finish so late that it causes me great uneasiness until he comes home. It makes me feel as if I must decline all dinner engagements to stay at home with him to keep him out of trouble; but, then, he dines with me and goes out, leaving me to spend my evenings alone. I had enough of that sort of thing at home, which finally became unbearable and was one of the reasons why I came away. I have a raging headache."

They finally came to enough of an understanding so that Caroline was able tell August that "Raymond is good and affectionate and takes my reprimands when necessary very sweetly and, what is better, minds what I say. I feel less uneasy about him."

Oliver's problems would not be solved so readily. Like his younger brother he arrived in Paris with an announcement: He wanted to quit the navy—immediately, before his current tour was up.

"If you knew how unhappy this sort of life is to me," he wrote to his father, "you wouldn't care about my staying in the service. I never can get myself to like it."

"His first visit to me was full of complaints as usual," Caroline told August, "and I dread his second one. With Raymond and him together, I shall have my hands full. The fact is, Oliver is luxurious in his tastes and habits as far as he can be under the circumstances, more so than any of the other children, which is saying a good deal, and I am too weak in mind and body to battle with them, now that they consider themselves men."

With suggestions from August (who wanted Oliver to study farming, mining, or engineering), Caroline negotiated the terms of Oliver's resignation from the navy: since he wanted to go into business, he would take a clerkship in a Bremen bank for two years. August gave his consent.

"I hope now he will, at least, be satisfied with life in general," Caroline said, "for he is by nature the most dissatisfied young man one can imagine."

The true source of Oliver's dissatisfaction soon became apparent.

"I sometimes think he fancies Sallie [Sara Swan] Whiting," Caroline said; "then again, I don't."

Oliver not only fancied Sara Swan Whiting, he was passionately in love with her.

"Among the faces that look out from the shadowy land of yesterday," Sam Ward's niece once recalled, "none is brighter than that of Sallie Whiting—a slim girl, the very spirit of the dance, always the center of a large group of admirers in the ballroom."

Her father, August Whiting, was a solid clubman and coaching enthusiast, who according to a coachman of the era "could crack a whip with the best of 'em." He owned Swanhurst, one of the magnificent cottages on Bellevue Avenue in Newport. Caroline was afraid that Sallie had inherited too much of her father's sporting blood.

Caroline did not deny that Sallie "is amiable and good-hearted like the rest of her family." She did not mean to suggest that she was "a bad or fast girl." But she did think that Sallie suffered from "a want of refinement and good training" and that "she has flirted with a number of young men."

"She would be a bitter pill to swallow as a daughter-in-law," Caroline told August. "I shall do what I can to get Sallie out of his mind."

Oliver had arrived in Paris about the same time as Sallie and her family. Caroline tried to keep the two lovers apart but did not succeed. Oliver evidently asked Sallie to marry him. They were, as he described it, "half-engaged." Now all they needed was to get their parents to agree to what they considered a fait accompli.

Oliver worked on Caroline, whom he called "my dear little Mo," a nickname that had become as automatic as affectionate. And Caroline said she would "stand by" him and "help him through." But she delayed giving her consent and told August that she hoped Oliver's infatuation would pass.

When Sallie's parents wrote to Oliver asking him what his intentions were, a decision could no longer be avoided.

"I don't ask now for a final arrangement," Oliver told Caroline. "I perfectly understand that this, at present, cannot be done. What I ask from you and Papa is your consent to the engagement. This I must have, please I cannot put the girl in a false position. It would make me a blackguard. I have committed myself, as you know, beyond any retraction, even if I wished a retraction, which, you know, is altogether out of my mind. I want Papa's consent. I beg you to do what you can. If you only try, you can do it, little woman, you know. It's impossible to explain myself properly."

Oliver's letters, rambling and at times nearly incoherent, convinced August and Caroline to agree conditionally to the engagement. For the two years that Oliver was at the Bremen bank he and Sallie could not see each other.

"If at the end of that time," August said, "you and Miss Whiting entertain the same feelings for each other, which you do now, we both will be happy to have her for a daughter-in-law. And she must divest her mind of any idea that we have any personal objection to her. Only you must first learn how to support a wife and family before you have a right to marry, and you are both too young for so serious a step now. At all events, you are both young enough to wait."

Oliver felt like one of the bulls with rubber-capped horns that had fought the previous summer in Harlem: No matter how violently he charged around his small arena he was helpless. His parents were patronizing him. Because marriage was such a serious matter they were not taking him seriously. As his older brother August, Jr., had been, he was in a rush to grow up; and perhaps because of that affinity August, Jr., was the only sibling in whom Oliver confided.

August, Jr., in fact, had become the confessor for everyone in the family except Perry. His father especially turned to him for solace and advice. When August, Jr., was younger and having trouble in his schools, they had grappled so frequently it had become a habit; and the grappling, stripped of struggle once the school troubles vanished, had become an embrace.

August still worried enough about his son's potential extravagance to keep August, Jr., up to date on the bankruptcies within their set, as though he were a minister describing hellfire to confirm a former sinner's repentance.

"These young men all live beyond their means," he told August, Jr., after Frank Iselin, one of August, Jr.'s friends and a businessman from a good family, suffered a dramatic smashup that seemed as much a failure of virtue as of banking. Virtue may be its own reward, but a lack of virtue often is not its own punishment. August added, "I shall be very glad if Iselin's example will open the eyes of some of them."

But for the most part August trusted August, Jr., who drew substance from that trust. In the two and a half years since he last had been in Europe to talk to the Rothschilds, August, Jr., had developed authority. On this trip to Europe they were unable to put him off; and he represented his father's interests forcefully. At his father's request he also placated another business ally, who was "unscrupulous" but who, August said, "has me entirely at his mercy" in a particular deal. And August, Jr., made amends to a lady who, August told his son, "has been very good and kind to me. I am very fond of her as a *sympathetic* and intelligent woman. She was for some reason or other badly treated in our house some years back. She has now, without rhyme or reason, been persecuted by malignant, annoying letters on my account, and I thought and still think that your mother owes it to herself as well as to the injured woman to extend to her the courtesies to which she is in every way entitled and *which she did not receive when she was our guest.*"

Caroline's apparent and surprising hostility to a guest suggests that August and the woman either had or were suspected of having a compromising relationship. If so, August's request that his son patch things up indicates that he trusted August, Jr., to carry out even the most sensitive of missions.

Before leaving for Europe, August, Jr., had helped organize a Bachelors' Ball at the Metropolitan Concert Hall, a building with a two-story-high, arched entry way and a rooftop garden, which had been built the year before at Broadway and Forty-first Street. The festivities were intended, according to the press, "to repay in a measure the favors . . . the bachelors have received throughout the season from their lady friends." Innocent favors.

Nearly a thousand people wandered through the building: supper on one floor, dancing on another. The decorations, green and scarlet silk and more than $10,000 worth of flowers, flashed back and forth among the many mirrors, as though the mirrors were playing catch with the colors. All was artfully arranged to confuse the natural and the artificial: The broad-leaved ferns seemed as carefully wrought as the ladies' laces, and the laces seemed as effortlessly elaborated as ferns.

After returning to the United States, August, Jr., found a more eloquent way of expressing his affection for one particular lady friend, Bessie Hamilton Morgan. He asked her to marry him. She accepted.

Their decision was not a surprise to August and Caroline, since the courtship had been long and obvious. Bessie had ridden with August and

August, Jr., in the Coaching Club's spring parade; and August, Jr., had asked Caroline if Bessie could use her horse, Geneva—which, of course, she could. In fact, Caroline said, "I would give her the horse if your father did not object. I think that, by the time I get home, I shall have given up riding altogether."

Bessie came from a good family. Her father, Edward, a banker, and her mother, Elizabeth, were people with whom August and Caroline could feel comfortable. Bessie was modest and quiet; and although not pretty she was not unattractive. Her plainness seemed a kind of simplicity, and the simplicity was pleasing. Her one or two touches of real beauty —her clear eyes and wonderfully shaped upper lip—both accentuated and adorned the regularity of her other features the way, among the Pennsylvania Dutch, painted flowers and vines ornament a simple piece of furniture. Caroline was as delighted to have her as a prospective daughter-in-law as she was unhappy about Oliver's Sallie. During August, Jr.'s final days of doubt, she had chided him for hesitating:

"You are a very long time at settling this affair," she said. "I am afraid that you are exacting and a little hard to deal with; but I hope it will be all for the best and that in the end you will be sure of each other. I shall look daily for a cable."

All summer Caroline waited. Finally, while escaping the heat of Paris at Trouville, she heard that the engagement was definite.

"I am so pleased, my dear boy, that you are to become a married man," she told August, Jr.; "and I hope that you will be happy in your choice. What I saw of the young lady I liked very much, and I shall welcome her into our family with great pleasure."

Caroline was writing to her son with her stationery propped on her knees, because her room was so small there was no space for a desk. The hotel management had promised to find her a suite as soon as possible; but the resort was so jammed that days passed before she was released from her cell.

August, who had come to France, knew how crowded Trouville would be and refused to budge from their comfortable apartment in Paris.

"Besides," Caroline said, "he does not wish to mix himself up with the races here which I perfectly understand."

That year August acted on his frequent promises to get out of racing. After inviting the Coaching Club out to the Nursery for a weekend to look at his stables and the horses that he was selling, he made his decision public. The *New York Herald* reported, "He hereafter will raise, not run race horses, although he still continues to be president of the American Jockey Club."

August's retirement from the track "was received with regret by hundreds of the habitués of Jerome, Monmouth, Saratoga, and Sheepshead Bay," said the *New York World*; "for, as one of the heaviest backers of horses remarked . . . : 'I may not back Mr. Belmont's horses, but I do like to see the maroon and red in a race—it helps.' "

Still, the newspaper admitted, August was not "really popular," because, "having . . . assisted in the framing of the laws now governing the American turf, . . . Mr. Belmont . . . cannot be induced under any consideration to willfully violate any one section of them; and, when . . . he is in the judges' stand, the rules are carried out to the letter without regard to the feelings of friends or the opinion of the crowd as to the decision rendered."

August still had eighty-one Thoroughbreds at the Nursery and a few running out of the Rothschilds' stables in England; but now that he was no longer actively involved in the turf, he would have been pained to hear the racing gossip at Trouville. The past should stay past.

But it did not. Memories—not just of racing—continually bobbed to the surface of his mind: other visits to Paris, his children when they were younger, Caroline when she also was younger.

The memories made him melancholy with nostalgia. He tried to dim them by brightening his present. Ignoring his doctor's advice, he partied in Paris, eating his favorite dishes at his favorite restaurants, drinking too much champagne, and staying up late. During the day he poked about jewelers' shops looking for a good diamond for August, Jr., to give to Bessie.

Before making a final choice, however, August waited for Caroline to return from Trouville. Then, happy to be on a quest together, they spent three days examining and comparing stones, until they found one old diamond from India that Caroline thought was a "beauty."

August's reprieve from melancholy was brief. His joy at his son's engagement was shadowed by a misunderstanding. August, Jr., did not object to his father's leaking the secret to Alphonse de Rothschild—which August did, he explained, "knowing his discretion and wishing to show him my confidence," a gross mixing of business and family. But he did take exception to an innocent insensitivity on his father's part: At the end of the cable he had sent to congratulate August, Jr., August had added a short business note—an economy that August, Jr., thought was so crass he felt compelled to upbraid his father in a letter that apparently was unmercifully didactic.

"Your strictures on so natural a circumstance as that of combining in a cable the things I wished to communicate rather than sending two cables are neither kind nor just and have hurt me very much," August replied. "However, let that pass."

It was an inopportune time for them to quarrel. August, Jr., accepted his father's defense as an apology. By bending toward each other, they relieved the tension between them.

August and Caroline wrote to "dear Bessie," and August hoped that "she won't be angry for our calling her so already."

But the trouble between father and son was not the only shadow on the summer of 1881. President Garfield had been shot two days before the Fourth of July; he lingered on until mid-September. When he died, Chester A. Arthur, whom August thought a most unpresidential man, became President.

Lorenzo Delmonico was killed at about the same time by a more subtle assassin: old age. The restaurants would be taken over by his nephew Charles, with whom August once had had a run-in. Delmonico's had a rule that a man and a woman, no matter what their relationship, could not dine in one of the private rooms with the door closed. One night the people whom August and Caroline had invited to join them did not show up. When the Belmonts prepared to go ahead with the dinner by themselves, Charles explained that he could not break the rule even for a married couple: They would have to leave the door to their private room open. Furious, August left the restaurant saying he would never return. He subsequently forgave Charles. But in August's eyes Charles could never replace his uncle, whose death August mourned. It was the passing of not just a man but also a part of August's New York.

Jane Hone continued to fail.

"I am very glad that Caroline is away from all the worry and anxiety, which she would have had by being present at this sad ending of her sister," August said, "particularly as this cancer disease works such terrors upon her imagination."

And word came from Germany that August's namesake, Babette's second son, August Feist, had committed suicide.

"He had just returned to Frankfurt from Switzerland," said August. "It is a sad fate for so young a man; but, as he had been laboring for some time past under a heavy melancholy, which took even the character of monomania, it is perhaps a blessing for him though very hard for his family."

This suicide, the first of a rash of them that the Belmonts would hear about during the next year, apparently affected Raymond profoundly—although at the time he did not seem unnaturally upset.

August, however, was very upset. Like streetlamps that are lit all day but only become noticeable as twilight falls, those memories that he had been trying to escape were revealed once the present became darkened by death. Faced with tragedies, August now seemed even grateful for the memories. No matter how melancholy memories made him feel, they at least cheered him. If August had resisted their appeal before, it was only because to surrender to them was to give up ground, to be edged toward death, something others also felt. Just before August left Paris, Bennett wrote to him: "It was a real pleasure for me to see old friends like you and Mrs. Belmont again. It brought me back to those happy days long ago when we were all much younger and full of illusions. I haven't many now."

August prepared to return to the United States, and Caroline considered going with him. Although he had asked August, Jr., to delay the wedding until spring so Caroline and Raymond would have a chance to winter on the Nile, August, Jr., was impatient. He wanted to get married as soon as possible. Caroline did not want to miss the ceremony, but she also did not want to go back and forth across the Atlantic Ocean. One crossing on the rough fall seas would be quite enough.

Frederika and Samuel had decided to join her on the trip to Egypt. Perhaps—Caroline thought—she could go home and Raymond could travel with his sister and brother-in-law.

"I think it is absolutely necessary for Raymond's health and morals to be away from New York, where he has many friends who would encourage him to keep late hours, etc.," Caroline told August, Jr., adding, however, that he should drop no hint of her possible homecoming to Frederika, "for she might give up her plans; and now that they have no house, it would be inconvenient for them to stay. At any rate, I don't want my movements to influence them."

She had just booked passage to New York when she received a cable from August, Jr., in which he suggested that he and Bessie also go up the Nile with Caroline.

"I shall have more of your society by staying and having you come and join me than if I went home for the wedding," Caroline told her son. "I would see little of you before and probably nothing of you after the wedding day were I to be in New York."

So Caroline agreed to August, Jr.'s proposal. Traveling together would also "be a very pleasant way of becoming intimate with my future daughter-in-law," Caroline told her son—although to assure him that she would not intrude on their privacy, she said, "You know that I am not of the meddling kind. I want everyone to do as they like, and a little attention is all I ask from my children. I should like to feel that they want to be with me sometimes, and I shall always endeavor to be myself amiable and kind, so as not to be considered only in the light of a mother-in-law."

"I hope I shall find Bessie affectionate by nature and that she will be a comfort to me," she later said to him. "But, as she has her own mother, she will never probably devote much time to me. I shall expect little so as not to be disappointed."

As for August, Jr., she told her husband:

"I will be glad to have him married and hope he will make a good and constant husband. He has frolicked so much that there is every reason that he would settle down completely."

"What a pity," she thought, "they could not be married on the 7th [of November]," August and Caroline's thirty-second anniversary. But she was glad that the ceremony would be held at the Church of the Ascension, and she reminded August "to give [the rector] John Cotton a handsome fee."

Her long-distance help with the wedding arrangements principally consisted of making suggestions for the guest list. August was having an impossible time working with Caroline's visiting book, which had been left in chaos in New York.

"I have tried to keep it well," she apologized, "but the fact is there are so many changes by people's deaths, marriages, and moving that it is most difficult to be *au courant* of it all, especially if one does not go into society."

Also, since she would not be home to act as a sometimes necessary bridge between August and August, Jr., she warned her son:

"We have been very busy selecting some presents, which I hope you will approve of. Your father has taken great pains about everything, and I want you to let him see that you are pleased. I would advise you to let him know by writing all you want to say to him in regard to your trip and money matters, as conversation always excites him; and then comes misunderstanding on both sides. Deference to his opinions and judgment, he likes to have; and, by showing a due amount of that, you will please him and get along much better than by opposition. I tell you all this so that your marriage may go off pleasantly and satisfactorily all around. It is only a mother's advice."

She also had some advice for her husband, who had returned to the United States and was suffering from his intemperate behavior in Paris.

"If you could only deny yourself champagne and only drink one kind of wine, even when you dine out, I am sure you would enjoy yourself and feel well the next day," she said in one letter.

"The trouble you have in your kidneys proceeds from cold," she added in another, "so I hope you will wear warm shoes and stockings and thick drawers."

Although it would have been natural for Oliver to be jealous of his brother's engagement, he took it in good grace.

"I have never seen Miss Morgan," he told August, Jr., "but I have no doubt I shall learn to be very fond of her and hope we shall become great friends when I know her."

And he wished August, Jr., "all the success and good luck which it is possible to have" and which he himself, in his romantic affairs, lacked. In fact, August, Jr., secure in his own engagement, attacked Oliver's relationship with Sara, which made Oliver more sad than angry.

"I think we have always been a little closer together than the rest of the family," he wrote, "and it would be a great pity if we could not be friends. I received your first letter objecting to Sara and did not answer it for two reasons. First, I had nothing to say, and second it was too disagreeable. You are very much mistaken if you think I am going to blackguard you for saying what you did about Sara. It would be different if I did not know that you wrote from a kind feeling toward me. You have always looked out for me as long as I can remember, and I fully appreciate it. I am sorry you feel as you do about it, but hope you will learn to change your ideas."

In his Bremen exile Oliver worked from nine o'clock to one and from four to seven. His only pleasure was in going to a rathskeller where German wines, some as old as 1624, consoled him in his loneliness.

"The people are awfully stuffy and cocky and fearfully serious," he told August, Jr. "My great friend here is my black poodle, and"—he added dolefully—"he is down with the distemper at present."

August, Jr.'s marriage to Bessie was, according to the press, "the most largely-attended" and "the most brilliant wedding of the season," so socially important that one newspaper claimed it meant "the old-fashioned" Church of the Ascension in which it was held was "getting ahead of" the chic Grace Church.

"... The bridal carriage, ... drivers ..., footmen, and horses were adorned with ... marriage favors [white ribbons and flowers]," it was reported. "This is the ... latest-imported English custom; and, as it is both pretty and appropriate, we trust it may be adopted here."

Bessie's dress, very simple white brocade and satin, popularized not a new but a very old style, which a newspaper presciently hoped "will be generally followed by future brides." From her diamond necklace hung a brooch in which was set a diamond another newspaper said was "the largest and most valuable in America," a gift of one of the Rothschilds.

The church was decorated with tropical flowers as vividly colored as brightly lit stained-glass windows. Rising from this lush undergrowth were fifty African palm trees, some twenty to twenty-five feet high—perhaps in honor of the honeymoon in Egypt.

The ceremony, it was reported, "was performed without the slightest hitch." August, Jr., and Bessie said their vows in loud, clear voices. Afterward it took over an hour for the crowd, which had lingered to gossip and wonder at the interior jungle, to disperse. The reception at the Morgans' house, 328 Fifth Avenue, was also held in a jungle: Palm trees filled the rooms. In the front hall, above where August, Jr., and Bessie stood greeting the guests, was a large bridal bell made of camellias, lilies of the valley, and white roses. Cornucopias made of roses and lilies of the valley spilled blossoms as though they were turning themselves inside out. The newlyweds spent the night in New York and left the next day for Europe and then the Nile.

❧ *CHAPTER FIFTY-NINE* ❧

IN MIDAUTUMN Caroline, Raymond, Frederika, and Sam (the latter two recently arrived in Europe) left Paris in a new luxury railroad car, the only one of its kind (it even had its own water closet), which Gustave de Rothschild had made available to them.

If the trip through Europe and Egypt was intended to be for Caroline a journey back into society, it was for Raymond a journey into maturity. He had left New York a boy and would return a man. When denied entrance into a gambling hall in Monte Carlo, he was reminded that he still was just starting his admittedly comfortable rite of passage. In a young man's Grand Tour each city offered the possibility of challenge; and the initiate's success required not just overcoming but often discovering the challenge.

Sometimes the challenge was simply learning to cope with frustration. On the way to the railroad station to catch the train for Genoa, Raymond noticed that people standing alongside the road were shouting and pointing at their omnibus. They stopped and found that one of the wheels was about to fall off.

"In a few more turns," said Raymond, "we would have been over with our enormous lot of luggage about our ears."

An accident would have been terrible but exciting; avoiding the accident was a bore. They had to wait either for their omnibus to be repaired or for another one to pick them up. By the time they got to the station they had missed their train. They had to spend another night in Nice. Still, any interruption in their itinerary seemed more than simply a delay, as though their trip were a great machine producing pleasure and any breakdown meant lost profit.

For Raymond, Italy was a lesson in anatomy. In churches he examined statues, the way the marble muscles appeared to strain against the stone out of which they were fashioned. In museums he studied faces: the expression of a Saint Sebastian that, torn between pain and pleasure, seemed about to rip open to reveal a peaceful indifference to both; and the Madonna in Titian's "Assumption," so vulnerable in the presence of some inconceivable and awful force.

In a circus, he was fascinated by "two beautifully made men who did tours de force" and a "tightrope dancer" who, wavering from side to side, seemed to be trying to balance a number of interior sliding weights.

Raymond's interest in bodies masked a surreptitious fascination with death, which had been either sparked or fed by the news of his cousin August Feist's suicide. At Genoa's great cemetery, the Campo Santo, he wandered all afternoon until the "miniature street lights" that illuminated the graves were lit. And in Milan at the Ambrosian Library he was spellbound by a lock of Lucretia Borgia's hair, still, after three and a half centuries, "beautiful . . . golden."

In Venice he heard of the death of James de Rothschild. Since there were rumors that James had lost heavily at the Bourse gambling in volatile stocks, it was suspected that he had committed suicide. Coming so soon after Feist's death, the news must have affected Raymond.

August believed that committing suicide was an act not of brutal sanity but of an unbalanced mind; but Raymond on his tour was learning how common both suicide and craziness were. At the Grand Hotel, where they at first stayed in Venice, Raymond with his open and cheerful manner stumbled into the confidence and therefore delusions of a Mrs. H. C. Paul of Philadelphia, the mother-in-law of William B. Astor, Jr. Mrs. Paul apparently was suffering from a paranoid belief that she was being taken advantage of by everyone—except Raymond, whom she looked on as her savior. Because he gave her some advice—to contact a family connection about her troubles—she began writing him frequent rambling letters.

"It is evident, I think, that she is deranged and quite incapable of controlling her movements intelligently," said someone who had seen the letters; "and there is good reason to fear that she may fall or has fallen into bad hands." Her paranoia had become either self-fulfilling or convincing. "She appeals to Belmont for advice, which she repeatedly promises to follow implicitly. His influence over her is so great that it may be the easiest way to control her."

"I am sorry to have got myself at all mixed up in their affair," said Raymond. And although he was afraid he "might be making an ass of myself," he said, "I shall try and get Mrs. Paul to go to" a distant relative of hers in Paris who could help her.

Even if Mrs. Paul had not made the Grand Hotel uncomfortable for Raymond, Caroline would have wanted to move. The rooms were too large and drafty. After changing suites twice, Caroline, Raymond, Frederika, and Sam switched to the Hotel Britannia, where they met a New York acquaintance, Dick Peters, who Raymond thought "confirmed the story that he is cracked, for he rambled in the most insane way about his experiences, speculations, etc., saying such queer, senseless things that Rica thought he was a little tight."

About a week and a half after they moved into the Britannia, they discovered that it was the model for Wilkie Collins's mystery *The Haunted Hotel*—the plot of which turns on a chamber hidden beneath the hearthstones of a massive and ugly fireplace. The severed decomposing head, the foul vapors and uncanny emanations in room 14, and the betrayals—all the props and machinery of a mediocre gothic tale—added to the burden of death and insanity that Raymond was lugging.

Deepening the already morbid atmosphere was the Church of Santa Maria della Salute, which stood across the street from the hotel and had been built as a memorial to the great plague of 1630. On its fete day Raymond watched on its steps hundreds of diseased and crippled supplicants who looked as if they had been disgorged from tombs.

The days were damp and foggy. Gondolas slid out of and disappeared into the mists. Raymond in his own gondola let the city flow past him in fragments: the curve of a dome, the arch of a window, the face of a carved saint appearing when the air momentarily cleared. He found the women of Venice were "awfully handsome; even the poor girls with simple shawls thrown over their heads look like madonnas."

Often he saw on one canal or another a beautiful girl riding in a gondola with what he assumed was her little sister. She always wore a black sailor dress with a red sash; and she became for him the embodiment of all the romance of Venice. Day after day he glided through the maze of the city's canals, hoping to catch sight of her.

After mornings out exploring he would return to his hotel room chilled and spend the afternoon bundled up, smoking. Under the influence of all the art around him, and perhaps in anticipation of the trip up the Nile, he sketched profiles of androgynous figures who wore vaguely Egyptian headdresses. He read Homer, Cicero, and Herodotus. And on one page slipped into his diary he wrote—the only exercise in Latin conjugation he saved—a pathetic admonition to himself:

> *If I am good, it is well.*
> *If I was good, it was well.*
> *If I was good, it would be well.*
> *If I had been good, it would have been well.*
> *If I am good, it will be well.*
> *If I should be good, it would be well.*

Caroline was pleased when Raymond took a solitary side trip to visit

Verona—unaware that while there he spent his time examining tombs. She had no hint of his dark thoughts on suicide and madness and in fact found him "more loving and affectionate to me every day. He pets and kisses me and makes me feel happy and contented."

Venice struck her not as uncanny but as simply inconvenient. Its fogs reminded her of Newport; and as she told August, "I can't say that I would like to live in a place where one has to go about continually in a boat. I live in my fur-lined cloak and visit the shops in overshoes stuffed with silk to protect my feet from the cold stone floors."

The day after Raymond returned from Verona they left Venice on the S.S. *Bokhara*. From the deck, the city—the whole sweep of buildings with such familiar sights as the campanile of the church of Santa Maria della Salute—dissolved in the fog. At the public gardens the ship turned out to sea.

Caroline sulked because she had not received any letters describing August, Jr.'s wedding before having left Venice, which meant she would have to wait until the mail caught up to her in Cairo before learning the details.

They all lolled about on deck, watching porpoises leaping. Brindisi. The Albanian coast. They passed Corfu while Raymond played whist. The sea was smooth. At night the moon was brilliant. The world that they had left behind seeemed in retrospect like a large room, the walls of which had been painted with outdoor scenes. Here the walls were down. Nature was not painted but real. Raymond got drunk on the spaciousness.

"It is just nine months today since I left home, little thinking that I would stay away so long and make such a journey," Caroline wrote to August the day after arriving in Cairo.

She shared few of Raymond's romantic feelings about the trip. The voyage across the Mediterranean was "like steaming down the Hudson." And Egypt was not so much a world into which she had plunged but a distant pageant on the other side of a proscenium.

Raymond found everything absorbingly exotic: the women dressed entirely in black, with only their eyes and hands uncovered; the girls draped in white, who looked as though they were ready for "a sheet and pillowcase party"; the women in "long dresses of filthy silk," some of whom had bare faces and wore studs in their noses and made up their eyes with kohl so they looked intense and dissipated.

When a carriage carrying women from some wealthy man's harem clattered through the streets preceded by runners in colorfully embroidered jackets and accompanied by a huge man who—Raymond was told—was a eunuch, Raymond was thrilled by the spectacle. Caroline was simply curious about the customs. Raymond was awed by the pyramids. Caroline tolerated them.

"The guidebook had prepared me to be disappointed with the size of the pyramids," Raymond said, "but I was less so than I expected to be; and, when I reached the top, their overwhelming height exceeded my most extravagant ideas." As he turned, the desert wheeled around him: sand "rolling as far as the eye can reach"; small towns, "some without any vegetation and presenting with their dark walls a very dingy appearance and others situated in fresh green oases; Cairo. . . ." At the summit one could feel like the axis of the earth.

This giddy sensation was intensified by the descent. His guide tied a long sash around Raymond's waist and belayed him, so that Raymond, feeling as though he were defying gravity in seven-league boots, could leap down the pyramid from stone to stone, leaning out almost perpendicular to its side. Raymond also was impressed by the Sphinx. Caroline thought it "more interesting to read about than see." Caroline kept translating the exotic into familiar terms. Raymond kept trying to escape the familiar and enter into the exotic.

When they went to see the whirling dervishes, Raymond thought it "a most extraordinary performance. They first grunted, then howled, then panted, each of these phases lasting about three minutes and being enough to tire out any ordinary man. All the time they swayed their bodies to and fro and were accompanied by a head man who trilled and sang in falsetto. One man acted so violently that he foamed at the mouth. They howled, panted, shrieked, groaned, beat drums, blew horns, and made a terrible din."

It was certainly unlike anything Raymond had ever seen before. Caroline, on the other hand, although she admitted the sight was extraordinary, focused on "one old man, who," she told August, "had long gray hair, which reminded me of Aunt Ann's."

Sometimes with Caroline, more often without her, Raymond explored the city. He bought a gun, an amber pipe, and some curios with which to decorate his room when he went to college; but mostly he just absorbed the strange sights, delighting in how comic he appeared in this alien world. In the morning he would start out in the ridiculous position of being a prize over which the donkey boys fought; but he would wait for a bit, letting them quarrel, before making his choice. Then, he would set off, straddling the donkey, his feet almost touching the ground.

"No man," he said, "looks very stately on an ass."

In a mosque he "could not help laughing," he said, "as I shuffled about in my straw overshoes," which one had to put on before entering holy ground. In some of the mosques he came upon schools, which he found intriguing. He began going especially to watch.

In one mosque there were "many courts, where the pupils lolled about in every position, studying or not as they pleased, some reading attentively, others buzzing in groups over some lesson. There is a special place reserved for the blind. These, I understand, are fanatics and have at times created sensations by parading the streets in a riotous manner, when they have felt themselves injured. Generally the cause has been bad food. Today, there was only one pupil there. He evidently asked who I was. On being told, he strongly expressed his contempt for me."

His curiosity drew him deeper and deeper into the maze of court-yards until he came to one that "was more crowded than any other. The sun, even at this season, poured down upon it with great heat and peddlers walked about shouting their wares, making a frightful noise. The ground was covered with reclining students; and I created quite a sensation as I skated in and out between them. They all looked at me and whispered and seemed much amused."

Raymond created as great a sensation, although for a slightly different reason, at the railroad station, when he went to take a train for the necropolis of Sakkara.

"I arrived rather late," he said. "A first-class compartment was opened especially for me. Judging by the dust in it, it was not often used; and the occasion attracted a small crowd who stood around the carriage and stared at me with curious but pleasant looks. The European animal always excites the Arab's curiosity, but a young one seems to amuse and please them better, just as we are more interested in young monkeys than in old ones."

Some sensitivity or humility allowed Raymond to realize that he— not any of the Egyptians around him—was the curiosity; he was a sight as odd to the Egyptians as they were to him, as funny to them as he found the snake charmer whose cobra kept trying to bite everyone, or as alarming to them as he found the juggler who was—he said—"going through what was probably the invocation of the demon, banging on a banjo and uttering low howls, whilst four boys were dancing and wriggling around him, joining his chant at intervals with the most fearful yells." Unlike his mother, who from her first trip to Europe with August many years earlier saw the world as a show put on for her pleasure, Raymond knew that he was the performer.

Opium dens, "houses of ill repute, before which squatted hideous hags with eyes done up with kohl and hands with henna"; a museum where they got a private tour and Frederika found and was given a stray scarab; a Persian juggler who entertained in the parlor of Caroline's suite. . . . Raymond took it all in and tried to open himself to the transformations that the exotic world promised.

The morning of his last day in Cairo he put on a tarboosh and took a long walk through the town.

"My headgear was a great success," he reported, "as it effectually protected me from the donkey boys and beggars."

Raymond finally had entered this new world enough so that he was not taken by the Egyptians to be a stranger.

For their trip up the Nile, Caroline hired one of the largest dahabeahs, the *Ida;* one of the best cooks; "an excellent man servant"; a good crew; and the best dragoman in Cairo.

"Our dahabeah . . . is painted . . . bright green and is about sixty yards long," said a traveler who went up the Nile a few years earlier in a similar boat.

> The after-part is covered by a wooden house with eleven windows on each side and one story high above deck. . . . We each . . . have a bedroom, . . . bathing-room, and dressing-room; and we share . . . a large square saloon, lighted by eight windows and a small glass cupola. This saloon, which we use also as a dining-room, is furnished with a table, mirrors, book-cases, curtains, and hooks for guns. The wainscots are painted white with red borders, and sofas are ranged along the walls. Everything is small, but neat, convenient, and even elegant. The roof of the house, to which you ascend by a small outside staircase, is flat, and forms our terrace. It is furnished with chairs and tables, is surrounded by a balustrade, and protected from the sun by a tent.

Just before leaving Cairo they had lunch on board the *Ida* and were plagued by flies, which they incorrectly assumed would blow away once the boat began to move. At one forty-five in the afternoon they started. A light breeze bellied out the sails. They watched Cairo grow smaller and smaller until it looked like a toy city. Then they arranged their quarters.

"Raymond has already made his room look very pretty," Caroline said. "I am so glad that he is not valeted, because he will learn to help himself. Sam also does all his own unpacking and attends to Rica's wraps, cushions, etc."

Having gotten settled, Raymond and Sam spent the rest of the after-noon loading shot into two hundred and fifty cartridges so that they would have a good supply of ammunition for hunting. After four hours of sailing they stopped at Badrasheen, which by train was only three quar-ters of an hour from Cairo. The trip would be slow but, if every day was as peaceful as this one, restful. After dinner Caroline and Sam took turns reading aloud, then they all went outside in the dark along the deck to their rooms and bed.

Raymond usually woke early and in the chilly fog of daybreak went out in the canoe Sam had brought or walked along the shore hunting birds. At the beginning of the trip he was selective about his prey.

"I shot a poor little ibis," he said, "not knowing what it was."

But soon the quantity of game made him greedy. As Perry had been at the beginning of his Canadian trip, Raymond became kill-happy. He went after everything: pelicans, sandgrouse, ducks, sparrow hawks, plover, doves, owls, hoopoes. . . . Unlike his brother he did not learn any lesson about restraint. The more he shot, the more he wanted to shoot. And, as though this shooting-fever carried its own curse, the more he wanted to shoot, the less game he bagged. Time after time he described how he went out and "banged away hopelessly." When failure did not temper him, he hit a stretch of land almost empty of birds.

"I went on shore before breakfast and walked through some very promising looking grass, but saw nothing and did not fire a single cartridge," he said. "I got my feet all wet and did not enjoy myself, but Pinch, the dog I took with me, had a fine time, pointing at larks and gallopading about generally. . . . He suddenly made a bolt at three large buffaloes, guarded by an urchin of about three years old at most, putting the whole party into tumultuous flight. The urchin, as he stretched his little legs to their utmost under his long white robe and rushed stumbling over the uneven ground, reminded me of a child galloping in his night-gown over the tossed bed clothes of a huge bed."

Raymond's passion for shooting seems to have been the cover under which he retreated from his emotional plunge into the foreign world. He began more frequently than before to see, as his mother did, the strange in terms of the familiar. And his observations increasingly had the bemused and cynical ring of the sophisticated Harvard student he would become. Living on the *Ida,* which was a protected world, encouraged his return to the habits of his country and class, to the arrogant distance from which they viewed everything beyond their limited circle.

Then once he no longer felt the pull of the exotic he became less passionate about shooting, more comfortable about sight-seeing.

"I went ashore at one village with my gun," he said, "but as the inhabitants did not like to have their pigeons shot, there was nothing left to kill; and I quickly returned to leave my gun and take a walk with Mama and Rica. We were followed about by a small band of wandering boys; and, when we returned on board, these sat themselves down closely huddled together on the bank above us and strongly resembled a bunch of owls as they gazed stolidly down upon us from their perch."

He had changed from a seeker into a tourist; but perhaps that change indicated that he had found what he had been looking for. The trip was supposed to help him grow up. Becoming a tourist meant identifying with the values of the world he had left at home; meant therefore that in the terms of his society he had grown up. In a way he had gone on this Grand Tour not to find but to lose something. He lost his childhood.

About forty miles from Cairo the *Ida* ran aground on a sandbank, and for three days they sat waiting for a favorable wind to carry them free. The crew, struggling along the shore, tried pulling the boat; but since the screaming that accompanied their efforts gave Caroline a headache, she preferred waiting in peace—and the delay would give August, Jr., and Bessie a better chance of catching up to them.

Life on board the *Ida* was, Caroline thought, "monotonous." She entertained herself by fishing. Once after she had abandoned her line Raymond pulled it up to find an eel on the end; another time "I caught Mama's line from the cabin window," Raymond said, "and put a little fish, which had been caught before, upon it. It took me a long time to get the hook in the beast's mouth, as during all that time I had to hold the line tight with Mama tugging away and thinking she had a whale. She never found out about the joke."

In fact, in her letters home she bragged about her catches.

"Tea is being served," she told August, "and Rica and Sam are fishing. *As yet,* we have got between us about four fish in two weeks, two of which were caught by me, so I still keep up my reputation as a fisherwoman."

On the morning of December 24, 1881, the Christmas presents August had sent from New York reached the *Ida.*

"How well you timed it," Raymond wrote to his father.

They put the presents aside to open the next morning but did not wait to read the letters from the United States that also had arrived. Caroline devoured particularly those that described the wedding, the first accounts of it she had seen.

"Aunt Julia wrote that she thought of me on the wedding day and how I looked myself over thirty years ago as a bride at the Ascension Church," Caroline told August. "I hope you did not forget me then either. I don't believe you did."

But reading about the wedding "made me feel very homesick," Caroline said, "and excited me so much that I had a return of one of my bad headaches."

She collapsed onto the sofa in her bedroom and moped there all day. Frederika, perhaps in sympathy or competition, developed a headache too, so Raymond and Sam ate lunch and dinner alone, which, Raymond complained, "was not very lively."

Raymond spent part of the day on the upper deck, watching the river sights.

"We passed a merchant dahabeah," Raymond said, "and saw on board a lovely little tame gazelle, which they refused to sell."

However, since August later mentioned in a letter to his son that Caroline had told him "you have given her a nice little gazelle for a pet," Raymond apparently was able to change the merchant's mind or to find another gazelle for sale. Since he already had a pet monkey named Moses aboard, and since the cook kept livestock, the *Ida* must have looked like a floating menagerie.

By Christmas Eve, Frederika had recovered; and she, Raymond, and Sam had a hilarious time filling stockings for each other and Caroline.

"Rica's will be tremendously overloaded," Raymond said, "as Sam has been picking up things for her everywhere."

Because Caroline still felt ill, they put off the fireworks display that they had been saving for a special occasion.

Raymond woke before daybreak. As a joke he blew up a bladder and sent it flying into Sam's room to rouse him. By seven-thirty they had rousted Frederika from her room and were all sitting on Caroline's bed emptying their stockings.

In Paris, Raymond had bought a mechanical hopping pig, which, the night before he had wound up, weighted with a towel, and hidden under Frederika's bed. After opening their presents they all went into Frederika's room to see the surprise. Raymond yanked off the towel and the pig, its spring mechanism released, went, as Raymond said, "skipping very successfully across the cabin."

In the afternoon on the upper deck Caroline and Sam wrote letters as Raymond dozed on a sofa and Frederika fished. Suddenly Frederika, getting a bite, yanked up her line; and an eel went flying past Caroline's head. When the shrieking and laughing were over and everyone had settled down again, a Cooks steamer decorated in greens for Christmas puffed by and saluted. Because the wind had dropped, eighteen of the *Ida*'s crewmen trudged along the shore dragging the boat up the river. But after a while they stopped. It was hot; it was a holiday; they were tired; and—as Caroline indignantly reported—"a large buffalo is in the water and will not get out of our way."

"It is now sunset," Caroline wrote, "and our steersman and other men on shore are saying their prayers. It is a most interesting sight to see them so devout; and it would do Aunt Ann's heart good and perhaps make her think as I do that their religion is quite good enough for their needs and the missionaries sent to this part of the world had better stay at home."

For dinner, Raymond said, "Mama and Rica decked themselves out in their presents with lace fichus, etc., etc.; and, seeing them so gaudy, I determined not to be left out in the cold and accordingly dressed myself up in my Eastern dressing gown, tarboosh, turban, sash, and slippers. I created quite a sensation and incited Sam to emulation, so that he frisked out and returned with a shawl, hat, parasol, and *chest protector* of Rica's."

The crew gawked at them through the windows. If Raymond was now parodying his earlier attempt at blending into Egyptian life, Caroline and Frederika, bedizening themselves as they had, were parodying the small New York world to which he in spirit had returned. And Sam was parodying all their attempts at parody.

Turkey, plum pudding, sugared doves and cupids. . . . Their dinner was a feast, thanks to their cook, whose success everyone agreed was due to his being Maltese. They toasted August in his absence and also, no doubt, Perry, August, Jr., and Bessie. After dinner the cook, dragoman, and one of the manservants sat around singing to a guitar.

"Some of their songs were gay," Raymond said, "and they were tremendously merry. I think the champagne had gone to their heads."

The next morning a dahabeah flying an English flag sailed into sight and started to race the *Ida,* whose crew began poling vigorously to stay ahead. But the other boat, which was called the *Estelle,* was smaller and therefore faster than the *Ida;* and soon it drew close enough for Raymond to get a good look at its passengers, a man and two women, who he thought were "queer looking." All afternoon the boats fought for the lead, their crews hooting and yelling insults at each other. If the wind had held, the *Estelle* would have won; but at about four o'clock in the afternoon it died down. The *Estelle* fell back and the *Ida* pulled into shore. According to custom the *Estelle* could not pass once the other boat had stopped for the night.

For four days the two boats raced, the *Estelle*, with the advantage of speed, eventually getting so far ahead that Raymond figured the *Ida* had no chance of regaining the lead. But the wind dropped; the *Estelle*'s small crew was unable to pole very fast; and on the afternoon of December 30 the *Ida* closed the gap, caught up, and was just about to slip ahead when one of its small boats got loose. By the time the *Ida* retrieved it the *Estelle* was out of sight.

The day before New Year's the *Ida* received a cable telling of Jane Hone's death. Raymond, Frederika, and Sam conspired to keep the news from Caroline until after the holiday. On New Year's Eve they sailed by moonlight until eleven o'clock. After stopping they sat on the bank and watched their fireworks display spangle and streak the sky and turn the boat, river, and desert blue, red, green. . . .

On New Year's Day they visited the garden of a small town, where they were presented with armfuls of flowers, which they brought back to the *Ida*. They filled the saloon with blossoms. Stretched out on a sofa within all this color and fragrance, Caroline looked like Persephone.

The day after New Year's, "after I had taken my early breakfast of tea and toast and got comfortably settled in my chair on deck, Raymond and Frederika told me the news about Jane," Caroline wrote.

Having expected Jane's death she was at first able to bear up bravely; but then she began worrying that August might have caught a cold at the funeral and become seriously ill. As the days passed, her fear for August's health increased, particularly since his letters included alarming accounts of renewed dyspepsia, "my old enemy," as he called it when he wrote to Raymond. He was suffering from "about as severe an onslaught as I can remember," he said. "Such bursts of wind and blowing storms as would frighten the most timid; and, if I ever had to change my name, I would call myself Mr. Blower."

He could keep no food down and because of the pain could not sleep. For ten days he took nothing but milk. Then his appetite began to improve; and he vowed to avoid wine and smoking, "and for that purpose mean, as far as I can, not to go out to any dinner. When I am among people, I talk and talk, and get excited, forget my good resolutions, eat and drink, and up I go! This must not happen again. I have come to the years of discretion, and the last ten days have shown me that an old fellow does not recuperate as quickly as a young one."

August's complaints were as chronic as his dyspepsia. He always had worried about his health, so it is difficult to judge how serious his infirmities were. However, Caroline thought them severe. She did not want to return to New York a widow. The older she got, the more health seemed a greased pole.

But the depression into which such thoughts would have plunged her at home never materialized; instead she became lazy, as though by being careless in one sense of the word (taking no care) she could, through some sort of sympathetic magic, become careless in the other sense too (having no care).

"Our clothes are washed and ironed by the sailors," she said, "so, of course, I economize in the luxury of frequent changes. I live in a dressing gown, seated in a sea chair on deck. Sometimes I don't have my hair put up, only well brushed."

It seemed Jane's death had triggered in Caroline an interest in bodies similar to that which had animated Raymond after he heard of the suicides of August Feist and James de Rothschild. Caroline, lounging in her chair, would spend hours scanning the shore for glimpses of poor Egyptians, the fellahin.

"Mama takes great interest in all the queer people we see here, being especially delighted when she sees nude figures. She peers at them with her little glasses and says they look like bronze. She has a book, which tells all about the private life of these people, and she never gets tired of reading how they marry, how many children they have, how much they wash, what kind of drawers they wear. It is just the book she wants, for before she began it, she was continually wondering about these things."

Caroline's interest in the customs of the Egyptians had intensified during the trip up the Nile. In a way she and Raymond had reversed the roles they had played earlier. Now that Raymond had become the tourist, Caroline had become the seeker—although she had no desire to identify with any foreign culture, as Raymond temporarily had; but she did have a need for a reference point outside her limited world from which she could examine her own life. She seems to have had intimations of something beyond what she had experienced, something that under other circumstances might have satisfied her more, perhaps a hint of the way her world was changing, of the way her grandchildren would live—if she ever had any grandchildren. Her hopes rested on August, Jr., and Bessie. She correctly suspected that Frederika and Sam would remain childless.

The flies grew worse.

"Nothing short of killing them will drive them out," Caroline said. "The natives allow flies to settle on their faces and around their eyes." Their faces crawling with flies, the crew looked like corpses; the *Ida* seemed to be sailed by deadmen. ". . . They don't seem to perceive the nuisance," Caroline said. She had to eat her meals holding a flyswatter in her left hand and wearing a handkerchief over her head. Once, Raymond was forced to stop writing a letter because the flies swarmed into his ears, up his nose, and into his eyes.

They stopped so the sailors could bake bread in the public ovens of one of the riverside towns and made a brief visit to a village where their steersman's family lived. Caroline, Raymond, Frederika, and Sam—as Raymond said—"all got the artistic craze."

They had Frederika's houseboy, Achmet, whom Raymond called "Rica's little slavey," pose cross-legged as they sketched him. "The poor boy," Raymond said, "looked as though he would like to sink through the ground."

Days blended together. Boredom had become transformed into a kind of indifference. The river seemed so long; the desert on either side of the river seemed so vast. Humans and all that pertained to human life appeared insignificant. Once, while gazing into the distance at a town of mud huts, Raymond was shocked to realize that, as he said, "I could not find out whether everything looked larger than it was and nearer or smaller and farther." Emotional as well as physical perspective seemed distorted.

At Luxor they again stopped. Caroline, Raymond, Frederika, and Sam explored the temples of Luxor and Karnak, the Valley of the Kings, all the sites in the vast ancient city of the dead. In one of the tombs Raymond saw scenes of boys fishing "as boys do in America" and hunting for birds. In another he saw sketches of hieroglyphs that had never been finished. "Even the corrections are distinctly seen," he said.

These scenes were so natural, so recognizable, and seemed so recently done that they bridged the vast gap of time separating him from the past. "The colors are as fresh as though they were laid on yesterday," he wrote.

Raymond's sense of the expansiveness of time collapsed under touch of a painter's brush.

Then he slipped in a tomb and fell, cracking his head hard enough to get a black eye. Another tomb, he told his father, "was infested with bats. As you passed from one chamber to the other, you saw the ceiling perfectly covered with them. As soon as you entered, they would dart down and fly about you with a rush of wings, often coming in your face. By merely flourishing my stick over my head, I knocked them over two and three at a time, killing a great many."

There were no more revelations.

Raymond began spending more of his time thinking about college. In one letter he thanked August for "the very *liberal* margin you left me for furnishing my rooms at Harvard"; and in another he said, "I must study with a tutor before trying my exams. I hope you will have engaged one for me, so that I may go straight up to Cambridge and begin work as soon as I get home. It would be well to have inquiries made as to when my rooms should be engaged. To get good ones, it may be necessary to bespeak them early."

He was eager to get back to the United States. The wonders of Egypt now seemed grotesque, like something out of Barnum's show.

Caroline, who had sprained her ankle and was confined to the boat, was also weary of this adventure.

"I wish that I was already on my return," she wrote. "In the future, I shall do very little, visit only what I can comfortably see without much exertion. We go along a quiet, stupid river; and, after the novelty of looking at antiquity and seeing the half-clothed Arabs wears off, everything becomes monotonous. I shall be more than happy when I find myself back in Venice, after having made the nasty crossing of the Mediterranean. Then, I shall be in a land where I can hear regularly from home and work my way towards it. I must not say yet how glad I will be when I am once more under my own roof with you to talk to and dear old Betsy, Jacob, and my other servants to look after my comforts."

Like Raymond, Caroline was gazing at Egypt and seeing New York behind it, as though the desert were painted on a backlit scrim.

August's health was improved. He had recovered from what Raymond called the jimjams. Every day he took sulphur baths and had a servant give him massages. And, filling in for Caroline, he was attending services at the Church of the Ascension every Sunday.

"You are a good old boy to go to church," Caroline said. "I only hope you will not get out of the habit of it, when I go home, and convince yourself that I can do it all for you, whilst you take the Sunday *pill*."

She went over matters of family policy in her letters to August, approving of the generous settlement he had given August, Jr., since she felt "it is just as well to make the children a liberal allowance. The boys I mean. Rica has everything she wants. She and Sam spend money very freely, so Sam must have a larger income than when he married. They deny themselves nothing." To avoid any bad feelings over money between Frederika and August, Jr., Caroline told August that, "I shall say nothing of the allowance to Augie, and I hope he will not mention it."

Although she was not particularly looking forward to mixing in society when she returned to New York, she admitted that "it delights me to hear that my friends miss me and that the poor blind man inquires after me." The blind man was one of many beggars who hung around the Belmonts' Fifth Avenue house because August never turned away anyone who was broke or hungry without giving money or food.

Although much would be the same, Caroline feared everything would be different, as though the city and not she had gone away and been subjected to alien influences. When she heard that their rector, John Cotton, had died, one more death to add to the growing obituary list she and Raymond carried in their heads from continent to continent, she said:

"Ah me! what changes I shall find at home! But I pray God that our family circle will be spared and that we shall all meet in health and happiness when the time comes for me to return, which I long to do."

Caroline had not heard from August, Jr., since she had reached Egypt; and the silence kept her vibrating between being angry with him and figuring that "he may want to give me a pleasant surprise [by showing up unexpectedly]." Just before heading up the First Cataract she received a telegram saying he and Bessie were "pushing on as fast as possible." Caroline assumed that he was in the dahabeah she had rented and left for him in Cairo and that they would meet him on their way down the river.

For three days the *Ida* struggled up the First Cataract, a distance on land of about five miles. The sun was hot, and the noise of the two to three hundred men who were dragging the boat was terrible. This was the start of the last leg of their journey. Just when their minds had turned most attentively toward home they reached Abu Simbel, the farthest point away from civilization that they would go.

"You must not be surprised if you do not hear from me very regularly now," Caroline wrote to August, "as the mail is carried by runners."

The first day of the *Ida*'s trip back down the Nile, a cigarette butt that had been snapped over the boat's side caught in an awning and started a fire. Caroline, who had just finished lunch and was lounging on the upper deck, sprang up and as quickly as she could hobbled to safety. The strong winds blowing that day fanned the flames until one side of the boat was blazing. Raymond feared their supply of gunpowder would catch and blow them up. As the frightened sailors tumbled over each other splashing water on the fire, the *Ida,* no longer being steered, scraped aground on a sandbar. At last the fire was doused and the boat was freed. As soon as it was clear that the damage was minor, Raymond's alarm turned into annoyance. The accident had delayed them so much that the other boats they had been racing from Abu Simbel down the Nile were out of sight. Raymond sulked, playing with Leon, his pet chameleon, and scanning the river for crocodiles all the way to Aswan, where Caroline hoped August, Jr., and Bessie would be waiting for them.

🏵 *CHAPTER SIXTY* 🏵

EARLY IN FEBRUARY 1882, August, Jr., and Bessie reached Aswan, where they found a letter from Caroline that asked them to stay there until the *Ida* arrived. August was outraged.

"We are thus done out of 10 days of our 60, waiting for them," he complained. "I am sorry we came to have been exposed to such treatment. We shall start back down the Nile when the *Ida* gets here. I am so sore on the subject, the name sticks in my mouth."

Caroline and Raymond were as responsible as Frederika and Sam for the *Ida*'s schedule and for August, Jr., and Bessie's having to waste days in what they found to be a not very interesting town. But August, Jr., blamed only Frederika and Sam.

"Poor Mama was tied hand and foot by Sam and Rickie," he told his father, "and it is to the former's double dealing and crooked disposition that anything went wrong."

They "have been selfish and unfeeling from the beginning," he said at another time, "and have learned to live but for themselves." They "will have to always carry the grudge which I cannot help feeling."

Anger twisted his logic. He, not his sister or brother-in-law, was the one who would carry the grudge. Or perhaps since he was unused to bearing his own burdens, a grudge like a suitcase was something he expected others to carry for him.

"Sam has his weaknesses, having been spoiled by his mother and having a too big opinion of himself," August wrote to his son; "but he is kindhearted and means well and, above all, as far as I can make out is an excellent husband to Rica. You know we are all somewhat selfish, and we must not be too hard if others sin in the same direction."

While waiting in Aswan, August, Jr., did some shooting with both gun and camera. Since the simple box camera and roll film would not be available for another decade, few people took photographs as they traveled. August, Jr., was a pioneer snapshot-shooting tourist; and like many who would follow his lead in subsequent years, he photographed everything indiscriminately, taking 220 pictures often with undistinguished results. But he had unflagging optimism—in which faith in the camera's technology compensated for any doubt in his own talent. He also had a hunger for trophies. He thought of the photographs very much as he did the birdskins he dried for his collection or the hawk he shot and had stuffed. After all, the key to successful photography and shooting seemed to be the same: simply a matter of aim.

"I cannot point the camera yet properly," he said; "but the negatives are good, and ultimate success is a mere matter of time."

They took camel rides, which surprised August, Jr., by being comfortable. He built a flat-bottomed boat; and with Bessie, perhaps in that boat, he shot the rapids of the First Cataract.

"It is not often done in such a small craft," he said, "and is a very exciting feat."

Around them as they flew downriver were young Egyptians who, sitting bolt upright on logs, flashed by going even faster than August, Jr., and Bessie. To show off, possibly spurred on by the unusual bravery of not just an American but also an American woman, two of the crew of August, Jr., and Bessie's dahabeah took the rapids swimming.

August, Jr., discovered in himself a surprising affection and sympathy for the Egyptians, particularly the poor. His reaction was free of the romantic admiration that Raymond at first had felt and the curiosity that had consumed Caroline. It was not quite respect. August, Jr., suffered too much from the cultural smugness of his times for that. But it was something very close to it.

Once when he was in town he came upon some soldiers who were beating some "citizens." (Unlike many of his compatriots who were visiting Egypt, August, Jr., did not call poor Egyptians *natives*.) Made invulnerable by his commanding attitude and appearance of wealth and importance, August, Jr., ordered the soldiers to stop, which they did.

Examining one of the victims who was badly hurt, August learned that the six civilians whom the soldiers had attacked were brothers. Although he did not find out what had caused the trouble, he assured himself that peace had been restored and went on his way. As soon as he disappeared from view the soldiers attacked the brothers again, nearly killing one and severely injuring two others.

When August, Jr., heard about what had happened he went to the governor, a bore whom he and Bessie had entertained on their boat a few days earlier. The governor apologized for the soldiers' behavior but explained that there was nothing he could do. August, Jr., kept after him. The soldiers' arrogant and brutal treatment of the people of Aswan was—August thought—"a shameful and inhuman outrage. They fear no one in the town and care for nothing." He was determined to get them recalled. Or to do something that would improve the situation. At last he got the governor to telegraph the Ministry of the Interior in Cairo and to close the town. By the time Raymond (who had come down the Nile ahead of the *Ida* to look for his brother and new sister-in-law) arrived, August was in the process of trying to reform the administration of Aswan.

At last the *Ida* met up with August, Jr.'s dahabeah; and the rest of the way down the Nile, the two boats sailed together. In the morning Caroline and Bessie would signal to each other from deck to deck with little flags. The two women got along wonderfully.

"She is very sweet," Caroline said, "just a girl after my liking. Ladylike, amiable, neat in her dress, and has so much intelligence and good sense. She will have a very happy influence over Augie."

In fact, August, Jr., seemed a changed man: strong-willed, responsible, secure.

"We may feel very happy that Augie has wound up his youthful follies in such a brilliant manner," Caroline told August. "I wish the rest would do as well."

Raymond fell a little in love with his brother's wife. "I think she is very sweet," he said, "and Augie is a very lucky fellow."

And he worshiped August, Jr., who returned the compliment by finding his younger brother to be "nice, manly, and clever."

Raymond hung around on August, Jr., and Bessie's dahabeah, fiddling with the photography equipment, lounging in the sun, studying. Sometimes he would go out just to drift with his brother, sister-in-law, and his pet monkey, Moses, in the little flat-bottomed boat August, Jr., had built. Or he, August, Jr., and Sam would go shooting. Sam went after quail, Frederika's favorite food, and he would bag as many as eighteen a day. August, Jr., and Raymond went after more exotic birds. August, Jr., got a rare black stork; Raymond, an Egyptian eagle. Together the brothers skinned and stuffed the best specimens. Once the bird they were working on was so rotten that when they cut into it, it released such a stink everyone else on board begged them to heave it over the side. They refused and for the rest of the operation joked about its disgusting condition.

"I am having a much better time," Raymond said, "now that Augie is here."

On the way up the Nile, Raymond had felt rushed. Frederika and Sam, who had been in Egypt once before, had been bored with seeing the same old sights; and Caroline wanted to get through the tour and get home. Now although Frederika and Sam sometimes argued with August, Jr., and Raymond about where they should stop for the night, "they acknowledge," Raymond said, "that it is natural for us on our first trip to wish to see and do everything." And "Augie has shown Mama how foolish it would be to come all these miles simply to race up the river and back without getting any enjoyment out of it."

August, Jr., insisted on having fun.

"I have done nothing but amuse myself and remain selfishly oblivious of all things," he said.

His enjoyment of Egypt made the country more vivid to the others. Everything they did—even buying two mummified heads and a mummified ibis—seemed charged with humor and excitement. Because of August, Jr.'s presence, Raymond found his "second visit to Thebes more interesting than my first."

With August, Jr., and Bessie's joyous encouragement, Caroline did things on the way down the Nile that she had not even considered doing on the way up, such as going to see dancing girls.

"This dance is very ugly and vulgar," Caroline said, "and can only be seen by foreigners at the Consul's, where he takes pains to control the dancers' movements, so that they will not outrage decency."

No matter how much she claimed she went only "to please" the children, she could not stop talking about the dance and dancers.

"Their principal effect," she said in another letter, "is to shake their stomachs and contort themselves until you would think they had a wire frame underneath their clothes to make the movements."

Trying to sound offhand, she told August: "You need not mention to anyone my having gone."

Sam apparently went back to see the show a third time and stayed so late that Frederika in a jealous fit locked him out of her room. Somehow —possibly through Sam's joking about it, which he did to disarm his wife—the story traveled to the other boats that were moored near them, and, as Caroline said, "I am told there was some talk and laughter about it among the Americans visiting here."

Caroline, egged on by August, Jr., and Bessie, went into a temple and even crawled into a pyramid that had been opened for the first time eight months earlier and that after their specially arranged visit would be closed to the public.

"We had to scramble down very far to reach the opening, which was scarcely large enough to admit me," Caroline told August, "so you can imagine how small it was."

Caroline got stuck—evidently mentally, not physically—in the opening and refused to go on. August, Jr., Bessie, Frederika, Sam, Raymond, and their guide, Brügseh Bey (the head of the museum in Cairo, who had given Frederika the scarab) all urged her to continue, telling her about what interesting things she would see and how she would regret it if she did not go.

"So," she said, "I went in, feeling suffocated and as if I never would get out again, on my hands and knees."

She was not impressed enough with the interesting things inside the pyramid to tell August what she saw; but what she saw was not what was important. What was important was overcoming her fear.

"I wish you could have seen us emerge," she told August. "It must have been as good as a play. Our hats knocked to the side. Clothes loaded with dust. Faces scarlet from the exertion. I am glad I went in."

She came out of the tomb as animated as a girl. What she had found inside was a memory of their first trip to Europe.

"It reminded me of the sibyl's cave near Naples," she said. "Do you remember when I insisted upon going into it because poor Mary Cunard had said no lady should go?"

For a short while she became again the young woman who had forced herself to walk to the lip of Mount Vesuvius and peer into the volcano's mouth.

The last days aboard the *Ida* were unpleasant. The wind blew sand into the rooms, the heat of the sun had become intolerable, there were extraordinary fogs, and the boat kept running aground on sandbanks. The flies, fleas, and "other more disgusting insects," Caroline wrote, were everywhere. "I saw our steersman the other day take off his turban and the linen scull cap, which the men always wear under it, and pick off *lice*. He scratched his head well, his beard, and then he attacked his breast from which he also picked a quantity. Often these nasty things are found on our linen, when it comes from the wash. Mercifully, I am nearsighted enough not to notice them."

They reached Cairo at the end of March, had a last lunch on board, and left the *Ida*. Caroline, having settled alone in a suite in Shepheard's, the city's most fashionable hotel, thought it "a comfort to be independent once more. I have had some contretemps with Frederika and Sam during the trip, but it is over now. I shall never place myself in quite the same position again. People who have lived as I have and to my age are better off in their own establishments, where they are sole mistress of the situation."

Yet on reconsidering, she later wrote that she would prefer to have the children "lean upon us a little. Then I would feel as if I was of some use still to them. Sam and Rica have such independent spirits that I never can do them any good. They don't even want my help or care to consult me."

Frederika and Sam started for Constantinople. August, Jr., and Bessie, taking advantage of their last week in Egypt, went off on day trips. Raymond, who was—Caroline thought—"crazy on the subject" of shooting a pelican, left Cairo for one more try. Caroline found herself taking care not of her children but of Moses, the pet monkey. It was easier for her to give up being dependent on others than it was to give up having others dependent on her. Giving up the former made her feel capable; giving up the latter made her feel impotent. Both made her a stranger to herself and therefore to her world. The trip—instead of preparing her to reenter society, as it was supposed to—left her distanced from it.

"I don't feel as if I ever could go to a ball again," she told August when he suggested that she pick up some new gowns on her way back through Paris. "I would not enjoy it. As for hobnobbing with Mrs. Rives, Mrs. Astor, and any [of the other ladies in their circle] at that late hour of the night, I don't think it would pay me for the trouble of dressing and sitting up blinking around with sleepy eyes, wishing myself in bed. My continued headaches have really made me deaf, so that peering about with an eyeglass and not hearing quickly all that is said around me would prevent me from entering into the amusements of large gatherings. I feel as if I looked not only old, but ugly; and I am sure that nobody would wish to talk to me." Still, she thought "it is very sweet of you to want me to shine once more in society."

🌿 *CHAPTER SIXTY-ONE* 🌿

DURING THE TIME August, Jr., and Bessie had been in Paris en route to Egypt, they had tried to talk Oliver out of his infatuation with Sallie. Oliver refused to listen. He began spending less time with his brother and sister-in-law and more with the Whitings, who were also in Paris. When August, Jr., and Bessie left to join Caroline on the Nile, Oliver, instead of going back to Bremen as he had promised his parents, stayed in Paris for two months. Since August and Caroline had agreed to consider the engagement on the condition that Oliver would avoid Sallie during his two years at the Bremen bank, they now, according to August, Jr., had "the right to withdraw consent." August, Jr., drafted a letter he thought his father should send to Oliver:

"I charge you with informing Miss Whiting that because of your violation of our agreement, I have withdrawn my conditional consent to your engagement. I allow you one month to inform Miss Whiting of my decision. Should you fail to do so I shall write directly to her mother. Should you persist in direct opposition to my wishes, I should under no circumstances allow you any more money than the amount you were receiving at the time of your placing yourself in opposition to me on this subject."

"To all this," August, Jr., added, "he will fail to answer, of course."

But August, Jr., did not think his brother would give up his patrimony for Sallie, since he believed "Oliver doesn't really love her." Bessie agreed: "He will drop off," she said, "if only kept away from Sallie."

Even if they were wrong and Oliver did love her, they were sure she did not love him. She was being urged on too aggressively by her mother, who apparently had considered stalking Caroline in Egypt, hoping to trap her into giving her blessing. True love is not so premeditated.

If the Belmonts could not get Oliver to break off the match, perhaps they could get Sallie to do so.

"Now," August, Jr., wrote to his father, "the question is how can Oliver's prospects be made to appear hopeless to the Whitings in the event of his marriage."

When August, Jr., heard that Sallie's mother was trying to force the issue by saying that she would not give her consent until "the time of the engagement was shorter," he told his father that this was a "weak spot," which "can be worked for what it is worth." Whatever strategy August and Caroline decided on, they had to act decisively. Their stand "must not have the faintest trace of being a half-way measure. If you take one step in direct opposition to the marriage, it must be followed by a firm and uncompromising attitude." In the meantime August, Jr., promised that he would do whatever he could "to influence Oliver in good directions. On intimate acquaintance with him, you will find more that is good and worthy in him than you imagine." And he told his father to "cheer up, we will soon be home, Oliver will be saved, and things will improve."

While August, Jr., was advocating a hard line, Caroline was suggesting accommodation.

"If Oliver was made very unhappy by not being able to marry Sallie," Caroline told August, "he might become dissipated," take to drink, "and make a far worse match, marry some foreign adventuress or a still more objectionable American." So since they might "have to accept Sallie," Caroline added that "we will do well not to say too much against her." In any case, before making a final decision on the matter Caroline wanted to wait until she got back to Paris, where she would not be disoriented by strange surroundings. "It is impossible under the circumstances to form an opinion, although by the time I reach Paris, things will have developed into such a state as will require immediate action."

By telegram August ordered Oliver back to Bremen. Oliver went, explaining that "I had intended to do so anyhow. I am very sorry that you are so provoked at me." He admitted that he was wrong to have stayed so long in Paris, but defended his having done so, since—he said—"it is the custom at the Bremen bank to give employees permission to take leaves of absence. I also asked for the extension, which was granted; and I only looked upon it as taking a Christmas holiday, the first in eight years. In your telegram, you say my conduct justifies your withdrawing your consent. I don't know if you mean by that you have withdrawn it."

Oliver, more clever than wise, had found a loophole: August had said he would be justified in withdrawing consent; but he did not say he was acting upon that justification.

"I beg you not to," Oliver said. "If you are so displeased and wish me to be punished, do so, please, in some other way. By withdrawing consent, you punish both Sallie and me." And, Oliver said, Sallie had done nothing to deserve punishment. "Can't you forgive me once more?"

Oliver was pleading with August to open his heart—which August did. Out spilled resentment.

"At last, after nearly four months of the most unpardonable silence," he wrote back, "I receive your letter, full of excuses and promises, as usual, that you will do better hereafter. You have made these promises over and over again for many years; and they have invariably been broken. I managed by my personal influence to get you into the Naval Academy, offering you thereby the chance of a most honorable profession in which your grandfather, great-uncle, and so many of your other relatives had gained, not only most enviable distinctions, but bright and lasting fame in the history of our country. You entered the Academy under the most favorable auspices with your friend and kinsman Admiral Raymond Rodgers at its head, and yet what was the result?! It took you six years instead of four to pass and during that time it was only by my personal and political influence that I could manage to keep you from being dropped. In the face of all this, you insisted on resigning the first year after you had received your commission. All the entreaties of your loving mother and myself were of no avail, and at last we were perfectly heart-broken and almost made desperate by your obstinancy."

Then, "your dear Mama was fortunate enough to place you with one of the most respectable banking houses of Germany to learn the rudiments of business as you have a determination to become a business-man, much to my regret. And yet, before you have been five months at your post, you absent yourself *without my permission*. There is no possible excuse for such a scandal."

Forgetting, or at last choosing to ignore, the painful times he had gone through with August, Jr., he continued:

"None of my children have given me as much anxiety and trouble as you and *to none have I been kinder and more indulgent*. What is my reward? Disobedience."

Once again August explained that Oliver's exile in Bremen was not punishment—no matter what Oliver thought—but prudence. Before getting married, Oliver had to have a profession.

"Suppose, for an instant, that I should lose my fortune," August said. "Richer people than I have been hurled by financial panics from affluence to poverty. How would you support a wife and family? You would find it pretty difficult to tell me how."

"I appeal to your good sense," he wrote at another time. "Miss Whiting has been brought up in luxury; and, as the youngest child in her family, she has been indulged and petted. *Is she capable to struggle*

against privation and cares of life when"—August did not say *if*—
"*adversity comes?* I think not."

After ranting, August pleaded:

"Why not quietly wait the two years without any formal engagement? This is certainly not asking too much and is all for your own good."

"I know very well that you are acting only for my good," Oliver told August. But further delay would only "make a break, which would be anything but pleasant later on. You think that there is not much affection lost between us. I can assure you that such is not the case. I am very much in love with Miss Whiting and can say as much for her. She knows that I never will be rich"—August's message about limiting Oliver's patrimony had gotten through—"and besides is ready to make any sacrifices. You are naturally of the opinion that she is a worldly thoughtless girl, which is what you hear. If you knew her, you would quickly change your mind, and I am sure you would learn to be fond of her. I am more sorry than I can tell that you feel my neglect as you do. I can only say that it is not from want of affection that I fail to write and seek your advice. I cannot explain it to myself. I am sure I am as fond of you as any of your children; and, if I have not shown you as much attention as the others, it only comes from my not knowing how."

August gave in.

If from this point on Oliver kept his promise and worked hard at the Bremen bank, August said, "You will find me always, not only just and liberal, but also indulgent and affectionate, willing to do everything in my power for your future happiness and welfare."

But—August warned Oliver—the final decision was up to Caroline.

"She will soon be back in Paris and will write to you on the subject," August said; "and, oh, my own dear boy, listen to her and trust to her loving heart. *You don't know what a blessing you have that so loving and good a mother has been spared to you until you became a man!* If I had not lost my poor mother when I was a mere infant, how many troubles and miseries would I have been saved in my early youth."

On April 25 a carriage carrying Caroline, August, Jr., Bessie, and Raymond clattered up to the Hotel Westminster in Paris. Since Sallie and her mother, Milly, were nearby at the Hotel Bristol, Caroline was certain to run into them somewhere in the city. They would want to call. And

Caroline would have to decide whether or not to receive Sallie as a future daughter-in-law.

The day after arriving in Paris Caroline, as she told August, "caught a glimpse" of Sallie's mother at the dressmakers.

"I dodged her," she said, "but she must have seen me." Returning to the Westminster and waiting for the visit she knew the Whitings would make, she worried about what to tell them.

Sallie and her mother arrived after lunch "before I could prevent it," Caroline said. "Fortunately, some other friends came at the same time and the conversation was general," sparing Caroline from having to commit herself. The question of the engagement would not be broached in front of a third party. Caroline could be gracious without being evasive.

"Sallie looked quite pretty and lady-like," Caroline admitted, "and she was very quiet."

As the Whitings left, Caroline casually said to Sallie:

"I will come to see you."

"Oh," Sallie answered, "that will be very sweet of you."

Her sprightliness grated.

"I have made up my mind," Caroline told August, "after much thought and worry, which brings back my headaches and buzzing in my head, to write to Oliver and say that I cannot consent at present to an announcement of his engagement. I wish to be at home and with you when I have to go through the formality of accepting Sallie as our future daughter-in-law. I do not feel in the mood to accept her now, but I think we must do so. We are both very much prejudiced against the family— and you are more than I am, for I have always liked [Sallie's mother] Milly, and I don't know any young woman who has more friends than she has and all amongst our Newport set. And tho' Sallie has very bad manners, she is liked, and said to be very amiable, and has money, which will be absolutely necessary for Oliver with his extravagant tastes. I rather think the Whitings are good managers in money matters, and make it go far. Altogether Oliver might go further and face worse. The great objection in my eyes is that he is too young and does not yet know how to take care of himself, but I don't believe he ever will. My children are all good, but they are desperately spoilt."

Although Caroline was ready to give in once she returned to the United States, she wanted to hold the line in Paris, which became more and more difficult every day. The Whitings had laid siege to her. They showed up for visits unexpectedly. They urged mutual friends like Count

Louis de Turenne to bring them all together for dinner, invitations that Caroline regularly refused. And incredibly Mrs. Whiting gave the impression that it was she, not August and Caroline, who was delaying the match.

As Caroline felt her defenses crumbling the Whitings called up reinforcements. Oliver wrote that he was about to leave Bremen for Paris; and Caroline was afraid that he would torment her until she made an immediate decision.

She could not prevent him from coming, but she tried to delay his arrival until her last day in the city.

"I am so hurried that I could not devote my time to you," she wrote to Oliver, "and besides your father will be very angry with you if you stay too long in Paris."

Anyway, there was no point in his coming for an extended visit, since "I will not decide upon this important question [of the engagement] until I get home. I could not receive with any grace or amiability Miss Sallie as my future daughter-in-law in the mood I am now in, and I tell you plainly I *will not do it*. When I get home, I promise you that I will decide at Newport; and, if the thing is to be, I will prepare myself to do all that is required of me in regard to receiving the Whiting family into ours."

Despite Caroline's protestations Oliver sweet-talked her by letter into letting him come sooner than she had wanted. When he arrived, Frederika (who with Sam had also come to Paris) was amazed at how much he had changed.

"He has become very strong and handsome," she said.

Caroline was amazed at how little he had changed.

"He is the same easy-going fellow. I don't think he will ever make a businessman. He tells me that he and Sallie have a perfect understanding with each other and that he will wait for an announcement of the engagement, that even if it were broken now he would renew it when he got home."

When Caroline said that Sallie seemed less than committed, since she was receiving visitors just as though she were still unspoken for, Oliver explained that "Sallie accepted the attentions of young men purposely, so as to avoid any comment. If she were to retire from society and shut herself up," she would give life to the very rumors of a secret engagement to Oliver that Caroline wanted scotched. When Caroline brought up how Sallie had once stayed at the Brunswick Hotel in New

York under questionable circumstances, Oliver said he knew all about it and furthermore—Caroline told August—"he approves of all she does. So you see there is no help for us."

Oliver told Caroline of how beautifully Sallie sang and how that made the Whitings' evenings at home "pleasant for visitors." He cajoled and pleaded and wooed, as though he were courting Caroline, not Sallie. Although he may have seemed to Caroline not to have the makings of a successful businessman, he assuredly knew how to make a sale.

"There is no use in bluffing in this affair any longer," Caroline said. "The girl will be of age next Spring and will have $15,000 a year of her own."

Then she and Oliver would not need August and Caroline's permission to marry.

Anyway, Oliver's "main idea," Caroline thought, "is to get home and enjoy himself, and he had better do that with a wife than bothering us." Otherwise "he will only be lounging idly around at home, worrying both you and me with his easy, lazy ways, and smoking all over the place from morning until night. I have had more than my share of that sort of thing, and I am tired of the confusion. He had better have Sallie keep him in order than me. I get very tired of correcting and advising when there is a more influential personage than I am in the background." So Caroline capitulated; she agreed to an immediate engagement. In fact, she decided "they had better be married at once."

Caroline's last days in Paris were occupied with chores. She had to replace her dressing maid, who had gotten pregnant; and she hired a man to help with the luggage on the trip back and to take over an old servant's duties when they got home: but she rejected the suggestion that she look for a seamstress, and wanted three slovenly, lazy New York servants sacked.

"You don't see such servants here," Caroline said.

If they were going to have servants it was better to have proper butlers, and fewer of them. Too large a staff made her feel claustrophobic. Perhaps she recalled how comfortably her parents had gotten along with far less help or perhaps her taste of independence had made her impatient with depending on servants.

"If I had only the strength to exert myself in waiting upon myself," she said, "I would do it."

But she had sprained her arm and was having trouble packing one-handed—a convenient excuse. Even if her arm were well she would not have given up all her servants. She was trapped by convention and habit, doomed to being coddled. A revolution in custom is as hard to start from the top as it is from the bottom.

She had to change her travel plans, because August had learned that the ship she had intended to sail on was unsafe. She had to do last-minute shopping for August. And, also for August, get her portrait painted.

She was too "fagged and worn out," she complained; the picture would make her look like a hag. But because August insisted she made arrangements with the painter whom he suggested—although she abhorred the thought of daily sittings—"dressing and undressing with a new maid, getting my hair arranged."

The painter was annoyed because her portrait was going to be a companion piece to one of August, and Caroline was unable to describe adequately August's pose to him. But she thought him "a nice little man," so she kept her temper and submitted to his outbursts.

Frederika told her father that she was "delighted" he had at last "prevailed" upon Caroline to agree to a portrait, since, as August, Jr., said, all her other pictures failed to communicate her "petite appearance." And this painter, August, Jr., thought, "has struck exactly that cocky little attitude Mama has, which at the same time is dignified and graceful."

The portrait completed, Caroline left at last for London, where, hoping to avoid socializing, she left her cards at a few houses only. She did, however, have to make some duty calls, one of which was to Ferdinand Rothschild to meet the Duke of Edinburgh. They all ate a quick, informal luncheon and then listened to a woman "play the piano with *one* hand wonderfully well," Caroline said sarcastically, "and a Frenchman sing equally badly."

Ferdinand asked Caroline what she thought of the concert.

Caroline said she was appalled at the man's voice.

Ferdinand promised he would never have him sing again.

Caroline left early, pleased at Ferdinand's attentions but bored by his entertainment.

"At first," she told August, "I intended to refuse the invitation; but, after reading your letter to Augie, relating to the business troubles you are having with the Rothschilds, I thought the more we mix in a social way with the family, the better."

Business relations had continued to deteriorate. The London branch of the House of Rothschild was still rejecting virtually all American ventures, and August had begun getting "nagging" letters about "imaginary losses of interest on paltry sums. It looks as if the Rothschilds had all at once become as poor as rats," August told August, Jr., "or as if they suspected us of trying to swindle them out of ten or twenty dollars because that has been the amount at issue several times!"

Often the London Rothschilds cabled August about trivial matters and then charged the cables to August's account, which made him livid; however, he refused to stoop to such pettiness.

"I shall pay for my cables myself," he said, no matter what the Rothschilds did.

There was "no possible excuse or cause" for the Rothschilds' behavior. "They would not treat even the smallest banking house with which they have business" this way, August told August, Jr. "It is now *45 years* that I have represented them in this country and *54 years* since I entered their office in Frankfurt." Whenever he felt aggrieved at the Rothschilds, he computed how long he had been associated with them, as though in the face of their bad behavior that length of time were a measure of their malice and his martyrdom. "I have more faith in and consideration for Jacob [his long-time servant] than they have for me. All this is hard to bear."

The only explanation August was able to offer was that "they want to exasperate me so that I will throw up the business"—which, as usual, he was ready to consider until he learned that one of Nathaniel's assistants, a man named Lorent, was "undoubtedly at the bottom of all this."

"Lorent is an 'intrigant' who evidently dislikes me, though I don't know why," August told August, Jr. "He has got on the right side of Nathaniel, who is selfish, suspicious, and not very clever and who has not the slightest attachment or regard for me."

However, Nathaniel must have restrained Lorent a little, because when Nathaniel left London for a trip to the Continent "there was," August said, "more fault-finding and recrimination than ever." Lorent's hostility was strategic; he wanted to replace August as the Rothschilds' agent in the United States. August fought.

"I don't mean to play into Lorent's hands," he said, "and will stick at all hazard." No matter how much Lorent "may wish to vex and exasperate me, he will never see it again from the letters or cables of August Belmont & Company."

As for Nathaniel, August wrote to tell him that "this state of things breaks my heart, and I am really just about as miserable as a man can be." And to his son he swore that this "is the last private letter I shall ever write to Nathaniel about my personal feelings and wishes in our business relations unless matters should take a very different turn, which I don't think they will." If Nathaniel was not loyal to August, August would no longer be loyal to Nathaniel.

"I shall put aside all feeling," he said to August, Jr., "and only look after my own interests, which will also be those of yours and my other children."

August, Jr., wanted to repair the breakdown in trust between the two companies. His father, at the end of his business career, might be willing to settle for an armed truce; but he, at the beginning of his business career, wanted an ally.

At first August—unsure of his son's ability to handle the Rothschilds —tried to control August, Jr.'s behavior.

"I want you to make believe that you don't know a word about all this," August told him.

August, Jr., should stay away from Nathaniel, "from whom I fear very little is to be got," and Lorent. The Rothschilds' weak link was Leopold, who—August said—"does not know or care anything about business." August, Jr., should "get him alone, as he is awfully afraid of Nathaniel." Join him at the track, August told August, Jr., and pump him for information.

When August, Jr., insisted on approaching Nathaniel, August said: "You will have to play your cards very nicely."

And although August no longer urged his son to pretend ignorance of the state of affairs, he still thought it would be "best not to say much of my having written to you."

By the end of August, Jr.'s stay in London, he apparently had convinced his father that he was ready to take on Nathaniel, because now August merely was suggesting: "Nathaniel will like much better if you say to him direct all you have to say" and "you must do according to your own judgment and wishes."

Raymond was to sail from Europe before the others. Just before he left he heard that two more of their family's acquaintances—Philip Van Rensselaer and Cornelius Jeremiah Vanderbilt—had committed suicide. Every time he heard of another suicide Raymond added layers to the shell inside of which he hid like a periwinkle within its whorls; he hid so deeply that eventually he would get lost.

While Raymond had spent the trip building a shell, Caroline had spent the trip escaping from hers. She had begun the Grand Tour learning how to be free and was ending it resolved to consolidate and extend the freedom—especially the freedom from accommodating others—that she had gained.

"As long as Raymond belongs to me and no woman monopolizes him," she said, "I am glad and willing to entertain for him and let him have the run of the house; but, when marriage steps in, then he like the other children had better live by himself, for I like my way in my own house."

When Frederika and Sam decided to stay in Europe for a little longer, Caroline willingly gave her consent, "because I see so little of Rickie anyway in New York. Friends and society take up so much of her time and what is left is generally devoted to resting herself, so I would only have to run 'round to her house and fatigue and worry myself over her."

Of all her children August, Jr., and his wife, Bessie, gave her the least trouble. Bessie would spend hours sitting with her and entertaining her. But even they would be a strain to have around all the time. Their very youth oppressed her.

"It is hard to recognize the fact that our children are grown into men and women and that they *will* consult their own tastes and wishes and only laugh when we try to get them to take *our* way in anything for their own good," Caroline told August. "They don't and won't see it in that light, and I must say that I find it hard work to battle with the opposition and only find relief when I am in the society of congenial friends of my own age. The *younger set tire me out* and consider me an old fogy. I entirely lose my identity among them and feel like a psalm-singing old governess."

Her identity was not just lost but stolen.

"It is quite strange to me to hear my name made use of so often," she told August, "and half the time it is for Bessie. Parcels come for *Mme. Belmont jeune.* The few that I have are for *Mme. Belmont mère.* So you see I have tumbled at last into an old woman."

When she was again by herself in her own home, she would not be *Old Mrs. Belmont;* she would be *Mrs. Belmont.*

But at the last minute August, Jr., and Bessie decided that they wanted to stay at 109 Fifth Avenue for a while. Caroline told August to close the picture gallery, the large drawing room, and the red room, so the servants would have a head start on the spring cleaning when they arrived and would have time to indulge August, Jr., and Bessie.

"I shall want the chambermaid to pay great attention to them and their rooms," she told August, "especially the *water closets,* which I hope are in clean working order."

Everything must be cheerful and sanitary and designed to make Bessie comfortable. She was pregnant. And her pregnancy was a family secret.

"I pray," she told August just before leaving Europe, "that you will not *blab.*"

CHAPTER SIXTY-TWO

NOT LONG AFTER PERRY was elected to Congress, he had dined at Delmonico's with James Gillespie Blaine of Maine. Blaine was considered to be one of the handsomest politicians in Washington. His long, narrow face was made even longer by his white beard; and his arching eyebrows gave him an alert, expectant expression, like a marten sniffing the air for the scent of squirrel. He had a genius for familiarity; while calling a stranger by his first name he made him feel like an old friend. But he was impatient with and inattentive to the details of public policy. He would stuff important documents into his pockets and forget they were there. His casualness was almost studied. When he was Speaker of the House he once called the representatives to order with his eight-year-old son hidden under his desk. Yet, eccentricities aside, he extended his influence as a senator until he was arguably the most powerful man in the United States government. He led the Half-Breed faction of the Republican Party; and one of the few politicians who could challenge him was Roscoe Conkling, the leader of the rival Republican Stalwart faction. They clashed directly and fought through their puppets. Blaine controlled President Garfield; Conkling controlled Vice-President Arthur. Blaine, who was dubbed the Plumed Knight, perhaps had the edge over Conkling in charisma, which in the nineteenth century was called magnetism. He almost certainly would be the Republican nominee for the presidency in 1884.

At the dinner with Perry, Blaine confided that Garfield had just asked him to be secretary of state.

"They want to shelve me," Blaine complained.

Nonetheless he accepted the job. And when Garfield was shot and Conkling's protégé Arthur became President, Blaine resigned. Frederick T. Frelinghuysen, the father of Perry's law partner, replaced him. Frelinghuysen was so dull that when he died—according to one anecdote of the time—he went to Heaven where, to his surprise, he was not recognized.

Who are you? asked Saint Peter.

Frederick T. Frelinghuysen of Newark, New Jersey, said Frelinghuysen.

Sorry, said Saint Peter, turning him away; but you're not on my list.

Frelinghuysen, growing a little nervous, then went to Hell, but he was not recognized there either.

Who are you? asked Satan.

Frederick T. Frelinghuysen of Newark, New Jersey, said Frelinghuysen.

Sorry, said Satan, turning him away; but you're not on my list.

Good Lord, said Frelinghuysen, now in a panic; that means I'll have to spend eternity in Newark!

At the time of Blaine's resignation and Frelinghuysen's appointment as secretary of state, Perry wanted to be on the Committee on Commerce where, because it had "jurisdiction over questions of vital interest" to the Port of New York, he could work for the voters in his district, many of whom earned their livings in occupations related to the port. Perry knew that "my political strength depends upon my service to my constituency, as I have no political organization supporting me."

The Republicans, however, wanted to keep Perry from building a political base in his district, in order to block his reelection. Since they controlled committee appointments, they tucked him away at the bottom of the Committee on Foreign Affairs, where they thought he would be powerless. He was not.

The Peruvian minister at Washington slipped him a document that seemed to prove corruption in the State Department. The United States minister at Paris, the banker Levi P. Morton, allegedly had tried to manipulate American foreign policy for the benefit of a French business that wanted to control Peru's nitrate deposits. In exchange for his efforts

Morton—or rather his firm, Morton, Bliss and Company—would get a monopoly on the sale of Peruvian nitrates in the United States.

Perry leaked the document to Charles Nordhoff of the *New York Herald* and Charles A. Dana of the *New York Sun*. The day the newspapers published it and the uproar over the scandal broke, Perry met the chairman of the Senate Committee on Foreign Relations on the New York to Washington train.

"There will have to be an investigation," the chairman said.

Perry, wanting to finish what he had begun, asked if the Senate would defer to the House and let the House Committee on Foreign Affairs hold the hearings.

The chairman said yes, if Perry promised to "go the whole length."

The whole length eventually led to Blaine—who during his brief tenure as secretary of state seemed to have supported the scheme until it conflicted with another shady deal uncovered during the investigation that involved another Frenchman and Peruvian guano. The Frenchman, Jean Théophile Landreau, insisted that Peru owed him between $7 million and $125 million—the figure was never clear—for discovering guano deposits. The Peruvian government rejected the claim. Landreau appealed to the French government, which also rejected the claim. He then appealed to the United States government on the grounds that his brother was a partner in the guano venture and an American citizen. Therefore Washington had a right to get involved. Although it was never proved that Landreau's brother was either his partner or an American citizen, Washington mysteriously did not reject the claim. As the facts came to light it appeared that Blaine, as secretary of state, had tried to force Peru, then involved in a war with Chile over nitrate and guano deposits, to accept Landreau's claim by tying it to peace between the two countries.

"You will take special care to notify both the Chilean and Peruvian authorities of the character and status of the claim," Blaine told the United States minister to Peru, "in order that no definitive treaty of peace shall be made in disregard of the rights which Landreau may be found to possess."

There were even rumors that Blaine was ready to defend the claim with force. Perry said, "Instead of acting as impartial arbiter," which he thought the United States could and should have done, "our government became . . . a speculator upon the helplessness of Peru."

He suspected Blaine had a financial interest in the success of Landreau's suit and perhaps at one time in the Morton deal; but it was hard to prove since certain key documents had mysteriously vanished from the

State Department's files. Perry introduced a resolution in Congress that the House Committee on Foreign Affairs look into all these questions. Playing at David, Perry had found his Goliath.

August thought the whole business seemed "pretty fishy," but he predicted that Perry's committee "will not get anything out of the witnesses, who will wriggle out of it by hook or crook. They are all a precious lot of intriguers and the country might have been plunged into a war with Peru if poor Garfield had not been assassinated," precipitating Blaine's resignation. "Blaine is about the most unscrupulous politician we ever had since Aaron Burr."

The night before he was scheduled to testify, Blaine told friends, "I intend to give that young Belmont a lesson tomorrow morning."

The lesson came at the end of the first day, which up to then had gone smoothly, since the Republicans who had been asking the questions had no interest in discovering anything that might compromise their party's potential presidential nominee. Perry was the only member of the committee who was committed to the investigation, but few expected he would have any success. The spectators—more than a hundred of them—were mostly Blaine supporters. They all were waiting to see their hero swat Perry down.

Just before the committee adjourned Blaine tried to provoke Perry, who kept repeating that he wanted to avoid any discussion until the following day, when it would be his turn to question the witness. Blaine kept needling him until they exchanged sharp words.

"First blood for you," Marble telegraphed Perry that afternoon. "Keep perfect temper tomorrow at all hazard. Blaine's art is irritation."

"I fear my boy lost his temper a little," said August, "and it is clear that Blaine means to go for his scalp. Perry has done so well until now that it would be a pity if he were to slip up against this arch-trickster, who had the double advantage of being more skilled in such a situation and having the majority of the committee with him."

"I hope Perry will get the better of the old schemer," said Caroline.

The next day Perry focused his inquiry on Blaine's instructions to the United States minister to Peru. Blaine said that he merely was urging that Peru judge Landreau's claim, not necessarily accept it. Perry disagreed and said that Blaine seemed in fact to be throwing the weight of the United States' prestige behind the claim by saying in one dispatch to the United States minister:

". . . While you cannot . . . make an official demand for the settlement of this claim, you will employ your good offices to procure its prompt and just consideration."

Blaine said he had meant *unofficial* good offices. They argued about whether or not *unofficial* should be understood when not said explicitly.

"Why," said Blaine finally, "nine Secretaries out of ten, in writing that, would . . . [do] it exactly in the same way. . . . It is the most intense effort of hypercriticism to dwell upon the understanding of that word 'unofficially.' You might as well say that here in one of my letters I used the phrase, 'I am, very respectfully, your obedient servant,' and in another of my letters I used the phrase, 'I am your obedient servant'; and then some fellow comes along and asks me why did you leave out the words 'very respectfully.' It is of no more consequence than that."

Perry said he found it hard to believe there was no difference in diplomacy between *official* and *unofficial* good offices.

For two days they niggled over such seemingly insubstantial but actually significant questions, Blaine playing for the press, Perry trying to be conscientious. Every time Blaine gave an evasive answer, Perry repeated the question—and he intended to keep repeating the questions until Blaine responded adequately. At one point when Blaine grew theatrically irate, Perry said:

"I am sorry that the question seemed to excite the witness."

"What question?" asked Blaine.

"Various questions which have been asked," said Perry.

"Oh," said Blaine, "not at all."

"Then I am very glad," said Perry ironically, "to have pleased the witness. . . . Now, Mr. Blaine, without any more nonsense—"

"Well," interrupted Blaine, just as ironic, "I am very glad to hear that, Mr. Belmont; I am very glad to hear it, indeed."

"Now," Perry continued, "will you answer that question?"

"If you state it again," said Blaine, "I will."

When Blaine still danced around a question, Perry said:

"That is not an answer."

"That is the one I want to give," said Blaine; "it is not the one you want, perhaps."

"But you do not answer the question," said Perry.

"Yes," said Blaine; "I answer it as I want it answered, not as you want it answered. . . ."

"I will repeat the question," said Perry, "and see if I can get a more definite answer."

When Blaine accused Perry of misquoting a dispatch to prove his point, Perry seethed and said that Blaine's attitude "relieves me of all considerations . . . which I intended to observe toward a man who has held the position of Secretary of State. You have now placed yourself on a level with any witness who might appear before this committee, and I shall examine you in just that spirit."

"What do you mean, sir?" Blaine interrupted.

"I mean this," said Perry, "that you have been before committees before this time, that you have endeavored to threaten, and that—"

. . .

"Why, Mr. Chairman, this is intolerable," Blaine complained; "it is intolerable. The insolence of this young man is intolerable."

"You have brought it on yourself," said Perry.

"Brought it on myself!" said Blaine. "Why I have no more regard for his insults than I would have for those of a garbage boy on the streets—not a particle more."

. . .

"Mr. Blaine has had experience before in committees," said Perry, "and has done the same thing before. He has done it for the last time. He will not do it with me."

When Perry doggedly continued to press for an answer, Blaine complained that "when you have a . . . session in a close room with bad air, it is a little trying upon . . . human patience, when great matters of moment and consequence are to be examined . . . , to have a ceaseless iteration of the same question."

". . . I know the room is close and the air is bad," said the committee chairman, "but the committee spends most of its time in a bad atmosphere . . ."

At the end of Perry's examination Blaine, holding a book of dispatches in each hand, said:

"Mr. Belmont . . . has, during two days, . . . tried, by tortuous questions . . . to establish his original misrepresentation of me—that I had stated that no treaty of peace should be made in which the Landreau claim should not be recognized. Now, I have always heretofore regarded Mr. Belmont as a gentleman; but, if he leave this committee without acknowledging that that was an error, I shall be compelled to change my judgement of him. All I ask of him is to say that he made a mistake; that he misread my language; that, instead of saying what he avers I said, . . . I said directly the opposite . . . ; that I gave a mere direction of what should be done in pursuance of the laws of justice. . . . And yet Mr. Belmont . . . insists upon saying that I declared, in my last instruction . . . , that no treaty of peace should be made that did not recognize the Landreau claim. That has been the slogan of the dirty Democratic press throughout the United States. It is the slogan of the press that stands as prompter and mentor behind Mr. Belmont—"

"Now," interrupted Perry, "don't you see that the aggressiveness is on your part?"

"I am very aggressive on that point," snapped Blaine, letting the books drop to the table before him. "I am very aggressive against a statement which is not true; and although I do not want to say a word which is not perfectly parliamentary, . . . I say that Mr. Belmont speaks there that which is not the truth"—Blaine slammed his fists on the books with each word—"absolutely not the truth, and without any semblance of truth, and that up to this time, being advised of it . . . and having for two days an opportunity, as a gentleman, to correct it as a mistake, he has persistently refused to do so. That is what I state."

Blaine sat, made a great show of arranging his papers, and squinting around the room at the audience said in a loud aside:

"*Untruth* is not unparliamentary."

The crowd laughed.

Twice Perry started to say something; twice he was interrupted. At last he, too, lost his temper.

"Wait a moment, now, until I speak," he said, standing up and pointing his pen at Blaine. "The construction which I put upon your dispatches is a correct one, and I leave it to those who choose to read your dispatches carefully enough to decide between us. As to your statement about my apologizing . . . I do not propose that this committee-room or that the press or that the country in any way shall undertake to judge my method of replying to your assertions. That I will convey to you in private. . . . I do not propose to make any scene here with you or to make any political capital one way or the other. You may do that, if you please. I think it is your method. I think that is what you are usually guilty of. I think you are a bully and a coward."

The room erupted.

"This must not be allowed," said the committee chairman; "it cannot be allowed."

". . . This man [Belmont] has disgraced his place," shouted Blaine;

"he is the organ of men who are behind him. He was put here to insult me; his mission was to do it. I beg to say that he cannot do it. It is not in Mr. Belmont's power to insult me!"

Trying to get back on the offensive Blaine as he sat again said, louder than before:

"*Untruth* is not an unparliamentary word."

This time no one laughed. Perry, according to *The New York Times*, "stroked his mustache, leaned languidly against the table with his face to . . . Blaine, and answered very deliberately, 'But it is a very dangerous word, Mr. Blaine. You shall very soon learn my method of dealing with this question and with you.' "

Blaine grunted.

The crowd laughed—this time not at Perry. Within an hour after the hearing ended it was rumored that Perry would challenge Blaine to a duel.

"Cannot you come to see me this morning?" August wrote to Manton Marble the following day. "I have just received the enclosed letter from Perry. He seems to have lost his senses, and I really cannot advise him in such a state of things."

The letter from Perry must have indicated that he was going either to duel with or to apologize to Blaine, because August was distraught.

"I may ransack my brain ever so much," he said to Marble, "but cannot see a possible way out of the dilemma. What can Perry in the name of Heaven write to Blaine now and what kind of retraction can he ask after what passed in the closing scene yesterday. Any communication to Blaine, verbal or in writing, would be received with scorn and given to the public."

Considering Perry's temperament and August's regret that "even the idea of a challenge has got into the papers," it is probable that Perry was leaning more toward fighting Blaine than making up with him. Although August snapped at Marble because he felt "so utterly wretched and help-less" about the affair, Marble patiently explained his plan: Perry should write a conciliatory letter to the committee. "A very bright idea," thought August, who apparently insisted that Perry do so.

"In the examination of yesterday and the days immediately preced-ing," Perry said among other things in the letter, "provocation so gross and persistent was offered to me by the witness testifying before the committee that I was led to use language, which, although unparliamentary, did properly describe his conduct and my appreciation of his character."

He was apologizing to his colleagues, not Blaine.

August thought "it is excellent so far as Blaine is concerned," although "a little too aggressive."

Public reaction to the affair was mixed.

"Mr. Belmont's movements today have been fraught with mystery," said the *New York Daily Tribune*.

> He was absent from his seat in the House, and the fact that he had been seen last night in the railroad depot just before the departure of the New York train led to a rumor that he had gone there to throw himself under the wheels of the engine. This report, however, proved to have given him credit for a keener appreciation of his position than he really has. It was also reported that he proposed to resign his place on the committee, on the grounds that the committee did not support him properly. There is every reason to believe that such a conclusion would have been received with satisfaction in the . . . committee, one of whose members was led by his natural disgust to say in the hearing of several persons, as the committee broke up . . . , that Mr. Belmont was an "ass." . . . Mr. Belmont's manner, from the moment Mr. Blaine appeared upon the stand was disrespectful and vulgar and often positively insolent. He had evidently been inspired by others with a boy's lack of self-restraint and a native want of courtesy.

He was described as having

> an unfortunate manner: perhaps he does not know how unfortunate it is. His face runs somewhat to a point, and from a protruding upper lip there stands out a stiff mustache, giving as a whole an expression of habitual pertness, not to say impertinence. . . . To see this young man, who only by the grace of a large bank account has been made a member of Congress. . . . , sitting in his chair with his head thrown back and trying to . . . browbeat a man who has been twenty years in . . . public life and who is probably the most popular man of either party in America today, was a spectacle that was sometimes ludicrous and sometimes unpleasant.

He was accused of reading questions that others had prepared for him and that he did not understand. And he was dismissed as "a very stupid man animated by a malignant purpose."

However, others thought that Perry exercised remarkable self-control while Blaine "kept up a rattle of rhetoric and stump speech oratory that might easily have broken down a man whose training in politics was obtained in Washington rather than in the Union Club"; that Blaine's "persistent and clumsy evasion of some of Mr. Belmont's questions" was obvious to "those who were not blinded by . . . Blaine's verbal fireworks"; that "while Mr. Blaine was extremely sensitive to interruption by Mr. Belmont, he allowed scarcely one question to be completed by the examiner without an interruption"; that Perry's tone was "respectful, not to say deferential" until Blaine "pounced upon him"; and that Perry should be "complimented" for having the "nerve to encounter such an antagonist."

And even his enemies admitted that "there is a general belief in . . . Mr. Belmont's sincerity in his line of investigation. It seems to be a common opinion that he really believes there is a great conspiracy and fraud somewhere behind this Peruvian business."

It is impossible now to say whether Blaine was innocent or guilty. But his behavior before the committee was not candid; and the whole affair was uncomfortably similar to an earlier scandal when Blaine was accused of misusing his influence as Speaker of the House on behalf of a railroad company. The alleged proof in that case were letters that Blaine got hold of and refused to place in full on the record.

In the Peruvian matter the committee nonetheless exonerated Blaine; and although Perry gave a long speech in the House explaining his position and filed a minority report on the Landreau claim, he signed the committee's report to make it unanimous. But because of the investigation the Landreau claim was dropped. Thereafter the State Department adopted a code that would outlaw any repetition of the Morgan scheme, and the United States' policy toward South America—which Perry condemned because it reflected a "Big Brother" attitude, Blaine's legacy—was revamped. For their own sakes (and Blaine's presidential ambitions), the Republicans probably should have given Perry the assignment he originally had wanted on the Committee on Commerce.

"I should like myself to pull Blaine's nose for behaving toward Perry in such a bullying manner," said Caroline.

Fredericka supposed that Perry "is as tough a political opponent as Blaine has had to deal with." August, Jr., assumed Perry's political "success is now assured, which is a great thing at his age, for he has plenty of time to climb the upper rounds."

Others also recognized that Perry's political stock was rising.

"The sons of our wealthy men go into the professions or into business . . . ," said one newspaper; "but few . . . of them are deliberately trained from childhood to become . . . Congressmen, Senators, Governors, or ambassadors. The Adams family in Massachusetts is an exception. . . . We find another exception in Perry Belmont."

A reporter for another newspaper was buttonholed in City Hall Park by a prominent Democrat, who said ". . . It's about time for a new deal in politics." It was necessary "to invent a new Democratic Party" in New York.

"How many young men have joined the Democratic Party of late years?" the politician asked the reporter. Pulling the reporter close, he whispered into his ear, "None." Rearing back, he bellowed, "Why?" Again he leaned close: "Because the old-time cliques have their hands on the lever. What we want is blood, new blood, fresh blood."

"But," interrupted the reporter, who later on claimed that this howl for blood was beginning to make him apprehensive, "where can you find . . . this Democratic savior?"

The politician pointed East.

"On Long Island," he said.

"What's his name?" asked the reporter.

"Perry Belmont," said the politician.

The reporter thought the voters he believed Perry had bought would agree—at least partly.

"We know he has blood!" they would say. "We've bled him."

By the fall elections Perry was being mentioned as the Democratic candidate for governor of New York—a boom he wisely discouraged. Such a move would be premature. First, he had to consolidate his position. He had to win renomination and reelection as congressman of his home district.

Blaine, determined to punish Perry, led the fight against him. It was rumored that Blaine was willing to pay $50,000 to $60,000 to any Democrat who would enter the race. Put on the defensive, Blaine's supporters ridiculed the accusation, claiming that they doubted "whether Perry is of sufficient consequence to be conspired against" and ironically predicting that as "soon as it becomes generally known that Blaine is hunting up and down Long Island for a . . . candidate, not a Democratic clam-digger on the island will venture out at low tide for fear of being corruptly approached."

Blaine's supporters also spread the old stories that Perry had bought the last election, adding that he had paid his predecessor $7,000 not to run. They made fun of how proud he was to be a graduate of Harvard College.

"This fact was stated several thousand times when he entered politics," one newspaper said; "and we are not certain but that photographs of his diploma were circulated through the district to convince the incredulous."

They caricaturized his pose: he was indeed a knight but armed only with the pen he had pointed at Blaine.

Not content to attack Perry, they went after August, resurrecting the story of his duel years earlier—presumably to show that Perry's readiness to challenge Blaine was hereditary. And in a scurrilous effort to lose Perry the Irish vote, they renewed the charges that August, in 1865, had mishandled some Fenian funds.

"If Perry did not inherit his father's dishonesty," one newspaper reported, "he certainly enjoyed his share of its fruits."

"As one who has looked at political life from both the inside and . . . outside of a newspaper office," Marble felt that Perry should be cool toward the press. He should ignore attacks and even with friendly reporters "affect, if you cannot contrive to feel, an absolute indifference to their speech or silence concerning your doings and you. If you cannot sympathize with Milton's austere view that 'Fame is no plant that grows on mortal soil,' be assured at least it cannot be made to thrive by the seeker's digging and dunging."

Perry did not take the advice. Although August was afraid any action before the election might hurt Perry's chances, Perry insisted that no matter what the consequences his father should sue for libel John Devoy, the publisher of the *Irish Nation*, a newspaper that had repeated the Fenian fund lies; and he sought support for the suit in the friendly press.

During the trial August said about the affair: "I have done all that an honest banker could do."

"We'll leave out the honest banker," said Devoy's lawyer in cross-examining August.

"We will not leave out the honest banker," said August angrily.

Devoy's lawyer let August rant about how his reputation had been attacked and how he did not intend "to leave to my children the name of a rogue and a thief!" Then the lawyer abruptly asked:

"What is your name?"

"August Belmont," August said, calming down and evidently puzzled by this odd direction in the questioning.

"Where were you born?" asked the lawyer.

When the judge objected to what seemed an irrelevancy, the lawyer explained:

"Your Honor, we are in a position to show that this man's name is not Belmont, or at least that he has used another name—"

"You lie, sir," shouted August, banging a fist on the arm of the witness chair and springing up. His face was flushed and his eyes bulged from his head. Controlling himself, he sank back into the chair and said:

"I beg your Honor's pardon. I don't mean to be in contempt of court, but this is beyond human endurance."

"Let Mr. Belmont swear that he never went by any other name," said Devoy's lawyer.

August's lawyer objected. Devoy's lawyer tried to talk over him. The judge tried to talk over both of them. And the spectators jabbered at August, the judge, the lawyers, and each other. Finally August quieted the room by shouting:

"I will swear. . . . Years and years ago . . . from the moment that I took an interest in politics, the opposition pounced upon me with the most infamous lies; one of them, this one, was spread by a man who is dead now. . . . I had befriended him and . . . he came to me afterward and went upon his knees and begged my pardon for defaming my poor mother." August's voice cracked, and he almost broke down into sobs. "I bear the name of my father and my grandfather, and I am known by that name where I was born—honorably born—I swear it! I wish I were twenty years younger and not holding a position of trust. No man should then say anything different to me."

Devoy was convicted and sentenced to sixty days in prison. The whole unpleasant incident was thrown into ironic relief by a rumor in London that August was supporting the Irish rebels. A member of the British cabinet, who believed the rumor, told Nathaniel Rothschild he also had heard August hoped to be the United States minister to the Court of St. James's if the Democrats won the presidency in 1884.

"I leave it to you," he said, "to judge if Her Majesty could receive such an apostle of murder and crime."

August wrote to Nathaniel that "your zealous minister was nursing" a "cock and bull story," and he tried to find amusement in how "a local district episode" had turned into a "tragical tableau in which I figure as the 'apostle of murder and crime.' " He told Nathaniel that "I am out of politics absolutely and irrevocably. All my political friends have been, prior to and since the election of 1880, assured that no office at home or abroad can induce me to leave the quiet walks of private life."

One day "a slender military-looking man in a frock coat" marched into Perry's campaign headquarters at the Battery and announced:

"Mr. Belmont, I belong to an Irish organization."

Perry did not answer. Given the anti-Belmont feelings among the local Irish, the man could have been an assassin.

"I belong to an Irish organization," the man repeated, this time in a voice loud enough to attract the attention of everyone in the room. "In that Irish organization there is complete agreement; and I am the only member, sir!"

After this cryptic utterance he bowed in what Perry thought was "the most friendly manner" and left.

Perry learned that the apparition was Jeremiah O'Donovan Rossa, an Irish revolutionary in exile and "a mysterious, but influential figure." Despite Rossa's claim that he was the only member of his Irish organization, he had a large following; and as Perry said, "his visit to my headquarters meant . . . that he favored my election" and his speech was "a hint to his followers to act together" on Perry's behalf.

Charles O'Conor, one of the most respected Irish politicians in New York, also came to Perry's defense on the Fenian question—although he thought that August had been wrong to sue since Devoy was beneath contempt; and libel suits, like duels, were governed by a code that said adversaries should be of equal station. And Perry was backed by Roscoe Conkling, who must have been delighted to do anything that might upset Blaine, even if it meant helping the Democrats.

Perry had a solid record. Along with the Peruvian investigation he had fought for legislation that supported shipping, the creation of an international prime meridian, the relief of local oystermen (whose oyster-beds had been damaged by a federal dredging project), and that opposed polygamy—all popular causes in his district. To further offset the Devoy attacks he came out strongly in favor of home rule in Ireland. And he traveled widely in his district, working as hard as, if not harder than, he had in the previous election.

He won so easily that he called it "a walkover." Now he confidently could look forward to higher office. August, who was proud of how well Perry had held his own against a man most politicians of both parties went out of their way to avoid antagonizing, could dream that one day his son might be president.

❧ CHAPTER SIXTY-THREE ❧

WHILE PERRY WAS CAMPAIGNING and August was suing Devoy, the rest of the family drifted home. First came Raymond, who before going to Cambridge spent a few weeks at Newport. After a swim he was walking naked out of the surf when he noticed a young man strolling along the beach. As nonchalant as if he had been dressed in a bathing outfit, Raymond introduced himself and learned that the stranger was Bessie's brother. Raymond was tickled by the encounter. With his family's imperiousness he left it up to his companion to feel awkward.

Soon thereafter Caroline, August, Jr., and Bessie returned to the United States in a ship that got stuck on a sandbar while entering New York harbor. Caroline went to Bythesea, where she found the grounds looking so bad that, as she told August, "friends remark on it." She asked to have a dozen palm trees brought from the hothouse at the Nursery and planted for the summer on her Newport lawn. Their fruit trees also had done poorly. The peaches and nectarines, their prizes, were barely edible. August hired a new gardener.

Throughout the summer and into the early fall Caroline entertained lavishly, every week giving a couple of large dinner parties and a few elaborate picnics. When she sponsored an appeal on behalf of Emile Brügseh Bey (the museum director who had been so hospitable to her in Cairo and who since then had been driven penniless to Constantinople by the revolution in Egypt), she was able to attract a number of prominent subscribers. Despite her forebodings about how old she had become and how out of the swim she was, she easily regained her social throne; and surrounded by her souvenirs of Egypt, with her new pet cat on her lap, she seemed to be the wife of a pharaoh.

"I don't know what sex the cat is and shall defer the christening until you come to Newport," Caroline wrote to August, Jr., and Bessie, who had gone to the Nursery.

"I long for home and family life," August, Jr., said. "It seems to be a so much better base from which to face the serious side and difficulties of life."

It is a young man's illusion that family life is not as serious as business.

In order not to feel that his father was doing him a favor by letting him live at the Nursery, August, Jr., decided he was doing his father a favor. He had gone to the Nursery, he said, "to straighten the place out." And he did.

He conducted a scientific survey of the farm; dredged the pond; surpervised the breeding of the dogs (experimenting with crossing Gordon and Irish setters to give the pups the Irish setter's courage); exiled most of the dozens of cats that were forever getting into fights with the dogs; killed the dog that attacked one of the hands and made sure the injured man was well cared for; arranged to pay another hand, a superior worker, an extra $10 a month (in secret, so the others, who were agitating for higher wages, would not demand similar treatment); and generally oversaw the running of the Nursery. It was an idyllic time. As Bessie's belly swelled he watched with wonder. By working so hard on the farm August, Jr., was trying magically to put the rest of the world—into which his child would be born—in order.

August thought that August, Jr., should make the Nursery his home, staying there every year from May to November. The other five months, when he would want to be in New York City, he should let "furnished apartments in one of the handsomer new flats." But August added, "I suppose this is a foolish notion."

More and more August deferred to his son's judgment. When Elliot, the farmer at Oakland, quit because August had upbraided him about something, August wrote a frantic letter to August, Jr., asking for advice. Elliot was obliged to give a month's notice, August, Jr., said. When Elliot agreed to stay on until his replacement could be found, August wrote another frantic letter explaining that he was afraid the farmer might "do as much damage to the place between now and the day of his leaving as possible" and pleading with August, Jr., to come to Oakland to take inventory to guard against theft.

He sought August, Jr.'s advice on what to do with the horses that he had sent to England and that, to his dismay, Leopold Rothschild had ruined by running too early in the season. And he let August, Jr., handle the yearly sale of horses at the Nursery—an event that was important enough for the Long Island Railroad to schedule a special train to Babylon.

He still was prodigal with advice (like explaining that J. P. Morgan "is brusque but fair"); but he left most of the day-to-day trading at August Belmont & Company in August, Jr.'s hands—and even in matters of basic policy August, Jr.'s opinion swayed him. Although August was as uninterested in doing business with the Paris Rothschilds as the London Rothschilds were in doing business with him, August, Jr., convinced him to bend—if for no other reason than to play on the jealousies between the two branches of that family. Business with the Paris branch might spur the London branch to greater activity. For his joint account with the Paris Rothschilds, August agreed to invest heavily in the Illinois Central Railroad, a transaction he was sure would not be particularly profitable and would entail a lot of work since, as he told August, Jr., "we have to wait until others sell and can only pick up very gradually what is offered. If we were to appear in the market as bidders, even for 1,000 shares," the prestige and power of August Belmont & Company was so great that "we would put the market up 1 or 2% without finding much stock." If August were buying, others would immediately follow; prices would jump; and there would be fewer shares available.

With August, Jr., taking over the routine affairs of the firm, August's attention skidded into the past. He remembered and called in a debt that had been incurred more than a quarter of a century earlier—an action so sudden, arbitrary, and eccentric that the debtor (a longtime friend who was under the impression the matter had been settled in the 1850s) attacked him in public. August was so puzzled and hurt by this reaction that when the friend wrote to explain that "a long and serious illness has made me nervous and irritable," August at first drafted a note rejecting the apology. In the end he had a change of heart or mind—it's not clear whether his emotion or common sense was aroused—and wrote that "I most heartily forgive and will try to forget everything connected with the painful scene. Don't let its recollection worry you."

When August did surface from the past and squinted into the future, it was simply to rewrite his will, trying to control the disposition of his fortune far into the twentieth century. He feared disorder more than death and accepted mortality as long as it was logical. He had a horror of any more children dying before he did. When August, Jr.'s horse bolted and smashed his cart August felt responsible, because, as he told his son, "if you had not gone to the Nursery, all this would not have happened." He pointed out that August, Jr.'s horse "has done this now twice to you." And he said that "in the present condition of your wife, you ought to be careful," although he was quick to back off.

"I only make this suggestion," he said, "as I don't want to fall into my old failing of giving advice."

Because his children resented his aggressive concern, August was loath to show any concern. The previous year he had abdicated responsibility for dealing with the children's crises; now he was withdrawing from the sidelines. He decided to "say nothing" about August, Jr.'s renewed interest in polo, retreating into prayer that his son again would tire of the game. Although he did not want Raymond "on any account to ride His Lordship to the hounds, as the horse is too hot, and Raymond would be sure to come to grief," he said, "I do not wish to interfere with his sport." He disapproved as much as ever of Frederika and Sam's flighty ways; but when they returned to the United States and immediately began planning another European trip, he kept quiet. And when Oliver came home he did not argue with him about Sallie; he limited his meddling to wondering if he should give Oakland to Oliver "for him to live there after his marriage." It would cost only $4,000 to $5,000 to put the house in "good order." If Oliver did not take it, he was inclined to sell the place. But he warned August, Jr., "Don't mention this to anybody, if you think it is a stupid arrangement as you no doubt will."

In Christmas week of 1882 Bessie gave birth to August Belmont III— and Oliver married Sallie. After the wedding, which was held in Newport at Swanhurst, the newlyweds left for Paris, where they soon were joined by Sallie's mother and two unmarried sisters. The five of them lived together in an apartment on the Champs Elysées. The honeymoon, which had begun with Sallie telling Caroline, "My dearest petite-mère, Oliver and I are writing to you side-by-side in the most romantic manner," soon ended. Oliver wanted Sallie for himself; he said they had to get a place of their own. Sallie refused; she would not leave her family. Oliver insisted. Sallie apparently exiled Oliver from her bed. Oliver went wild.

"The great personal abuse," Sallie told Oliver, "the disgraceful scenes before others, the personal violence to which you subjected me, the condition you were in a great deal of the time, the manner in which you repeated I was no longer your wife, besides going day and night to places where a man in your position should not have gone made my life perfectly wretched."

"I can do absolutely nothing with him," Sallie told Caroline, "and have tried my very best." But he was "past listening to reason."

Sallie fell ill. She missed her friends.

"I wish I were home," she wrote to Frederika.

New York was having one of the gayest seasons of the past decade. William Kissam Vanderbilt and his wife Alva had hosted the first fancy dress ball given in the city in years.

To cheer Sallie up Caroline sent her an Easter card.

"You don't know how much it touched me," said Sallie.

It was a sign of solidarity. Oliver—she thought—could expect no sympathy from his family. In fact, his family might be able to force him to capitulate—to accept marriage on her somewhat crowded terms. When he threatened to make a public scandal by demanding a separation or divorce, Mrs. Whiting begged him to tell his father of his intentions. Oliver, feeling ganged up on, left Paris for "a few days" to think things over.

"I hope he will remain away a little while," Sallie told Caroline, "for I have borne already all that I have strength and courage to bear."

Oliver's trip grew from a few days to six weeks. Sallie got reports that he was in Bordeaux, Spain, and Tangier.

"I hope the change of scene has been of service to you," Mrs. Whiting wrote to him. He replied it hadn't. She wrote that she was "sorry to hear that you are still suffering."

Abandoned by her husband on her honeymoon, Sallie must have felt humiliated. She sought solace in the church (she was confirmed in Paris); in activity ("flying around trying to get good clothes; I never want to look at a shop again"); and in the company of her friend Edith Newbold "Pussy" Jones, whose engagement to Henry Stevens recently had been postponed indefinitely by her fiancé's mother. A sympathetic companion in misery, Edith sent Sallie a silver basket filled with roses. (Years later Edith would marry Edward Wharton and begin writing novels—one of which, *The Age of Innocence,* features a character named Julius Beaufort, which is a cruel and unfair portrait of August.)

Early in spring Sallie learned that she was pregnant. She also learned —if she could believe the gossip—that Oliver's traveling companion was a disreputable French dancer.

Oliver, presumably on hearing of Sallie's condition, wanted a reconciliation; but now Sallie—or at least Mrs. Whiting, who seemed to have taken charge of her daughter's life—wanted a separation or divorce. Sallie, Mrs. Whiting wrote to Oliver, has "forgotten nothing of what happened to her." Mrs. Whiting could afford to take a hard line; the pregnancy was a trump card.

Feeling acutely how little she could say or do, "three thousand miles away" and "in utter ignorance of the causes which could have led Oliver to act in such a dreadful manner," Caroline nevertheless tried to patch things up. She told Oliver that "Sallie's letters to me lately, while very affectionate and sweet, seem to evince restlessness and unhappiness." She explained that she knew Sallie was pregnant and that Oliver had to "take into consideration the fact that women, particularly those of a nervous nature, are sometimes subject to serious misgivings in the most unaccountable ways; and the fear of the unknown and possibly terrible results of a first confinement preys upon the mind. This is a time when a husband's gentle and forbearing treatment and devoted attention is put to the test and above all things alleviates a wife's restlessness and gives her the peace of mind necessary to a proper development of her child and its safe delivery. You would never forgive yourself, if you were to do anything in ignorance which could cause your wife or child's ruin."

To Sallie, Caroline wrote:

"Have patience and forbearance with my poor boy, when he should be at fault. He is your loving husband and the father of your yet unborn child, and he ought to be nearer and dearer to you than all the world."

The letter contained the slightest ring—like that caused by the rim of a crystal goblet rubbed by a wet finger—of reproach. Caroline was implying that Sallie had erred in making her mother and sisters nearer and dearer than Oliver. She suggested that when Sallie and Oliver returned to the United States they find "a small cottage in the country," where they could live—by themselves. "Young people always get along best alone when they have their own snug home."

As for Oliver's alleged brutishness, Caroline said that Oliver never before had shown any sign of an ugly temper. If he had "sadly changed," it must have been the result of something that happened since the wedding, something—she implied—Sallie may have done.

But reproach was overwhelmed by sorrow.

"My misgivings at your engagement and marriage," Caroline told Sallie, "have given way to sincere affection for you." Both she and August were "ready to love and cherish you as one of our own children."

The rupture between Oliver and Sallie "almost breaks my heart. What is to become of you, when on the very threshold of your wedded life, such things can happen?" Caroline implored Sallie "to do *all* that a loving wife and true woman can do to guard against calamity."

In a letter addressed to not "My dearest petite-mère" but "My dear Mrs. Belmont," Sallie defended herself. The doctor said that the change in Oliver, which astonished and horrified her, "Can be accounted for in no other way than alcoholism, probably absinthe of which Oliver took a great deal in Bremen" long before the wedding; she had not driven him to drink. As for her mother and sisters meddling in the marriage, they "knew absolutely nothing of what I was enduring until my life became utterly unbearable, and I went to my mother for protection. This speaks for itself." So much for Oliver's fabled sweet temper. Finally, "the plan you suggest of taking a cottage next Summer and being alone under ordinary circumstances would certainly be the best; but, as it is, nothing on earth would induce me to be alone with him for an hour, as I am in perfect terror of what he may do."

When Oliver rushed back to Paris he found an empty apartment. Sallie, her mother, and her sisters were gone. He must have spent a desperate time before getting a note from Mrs. Whiting that said they were at Claridge's in London and were sailing soon for America.

"I leave for London tonight," Oliver cabled Sallie.

"Do not come for the present," Sallie cabled back. "Cannot see you now. Will write."

Then, possibly at her mother's insistence, she cabled again:

"Everything at an end."

Sallie, her mother, and sisters arrived in New York on May 15, 1883, spent the night at the Hotel Brunswick, and, avoiding the Belmonts, left the next morning for Newport, where they holed up in a house on Catherine Street while Swanhurst was being readied for them. They were preparing for a long war. Sallie's last letter before the fighting began betrayed a nostalgia for the few happy weeks of her marriage:

"I never can forget," she told Caroline, "how sweet you have been to me."

It also betrayed a clear understanding that the marriage was over.

From Newport the Whitings evidently launched a propaganda blitz, making their side of the story public to mobilize sympathy for Sallie— although Sallie, in a possibly disingenuous letter to Caroline, claimed to be "overcome with horror and distress" at "finding all my efforts to keep things quiet have been unsuccessful." Ironically the first press item about the affair appeared in the *New York World*, the newspaper August so often had used for his own propaganda.

"You cannot be more horrified and distressed than I am at the reports which your sudden return without your husband have called forth," Caroline said. Her position was beginning to harden: the scandal was Sallie's fault, not Oliver's. But she still hoped for a rapprochement. "Things cannot and must not remain as they are now and an early solution is demanded by every law of decency and propriety."

Left to their own, Oliver and Sallie might have made up. But their families did not want to lose face and could not afford the indignity of allowing either of them to make any passionate plea or loving apology. Like two exhausted fighters egged on by their trainers, Oliver and Sallie could not surrender or call it a draw. They had to slug it out to the end.

When Oliver arrived in New York his parents apparently told him to stay in the city. If he went to Newport, to Sallie, it would be an admission of guilt. She, the straying wife, had to come to him. Since he had sprained his ankle and was hobbling on crutches, he could claim he was unable to travel—a weak excuse, especially if he had hurt himself in Europe and crossed the Atlantic with the injury. Still, it had to do.

Caroline drafted a letter for him to send to Sallie in which he expressed his "surprise and deep regret that you should have come to this country with your family in my absence and without my knowledge." But he was willing to forget that injury and "do what I can to save us both from scandal and from steps which will affect us all our lives." He demanded "as your husband by all the ties that bind us that you return to me at once."

Sallie said that she had been compelled to leave and would not, could not, return.

"In my present condition," she said, "if you had continued your conduct, it would have been almost certain death for me. I need scarcely add that it was by the doctor's advice that I sailed for home *and you know that this is all true.*"

Oliver said that the accusations against him—"which I pronounce once and for all false, untrue, and unfounded in every particular"—were inventions of "those around you who have ever since their arrival in Europe stood between you and me and who have aided you in wrecking our married life."

Society chose sides. Of the two, Oliver's position was the shakiest.

He may have been provoked, but he had abandoned his wife to travel around the Continent for a month and a half. During that time it is possible he was accompanied by another woman—although two years later Sallie said she did not believe that any more than she believed the story of Oliver having been married secretly to someone else before their wedding. Still, enough people did believe Oliver had gone to Spain with a French dancer that August and Caroline had to lobby to save their son's reputation.

Caroline gave dinners, at which Oliver presided, for the older, influential members of their set. She and August wrote letters to keep the sympathetic in line and to woo or worry the disloyal. Slowly the number of Oliver's partisans grew until by summer the two camps were about equal and the two families were at a standoff.

To prove Sallie had not won Newport, Oliver settled at Oakland. He did not call on the Whitings; they did not call on him. When Sallie went to start divorce proceedings, her lawyer in a curious coincidence was discussing erecting a statue of the man for whom Oliver had been named: Commodore Oliver Hazard Perry. After Sallie gave birth Oliver was not allowed to see the baby, a daughter named Natica Caroline—the *Caroline* for Caroline Astor, not Caroline Belmont. For the rest of his life he never recognized the child as his daughter.

During the time Oliver's marriage was dissolving, Perry lost his balance in a flirtation and fell in love with a woman in his set, Marion Langdon.

"Such great changes have taken place with me," he wrote when he thought Marion had accepted his proposal of marriage. "It has been possible so completely to obliterate the past [which did not include Marion]. I have no thought but for the present and the future, and it certainly appears as if I did not deserve this happiness, which has come to me. Deserve it or not, it *has* come."

But it hadn't. Alarmed by the violence with which Perry had landed at her feet, Marion changed her mind about the engagement. She wanted time to reconsider.

Disconsolate, Perry wandered the streets of New York, looking so wretched that a friend stopped to ask what was the matter. Perry explained—in too much detail.

"He does not seem to be able to keep from talking about himself," one of Marion's connections said. "If he will only keep possession of himself, I think much can be done to convince Marion to agree to the engagement."

Marion refused to be convinced. She rejected Perry.

"I know how much it has cost her to give you pain," another of Marion's connections wrote to Perry. "And yet she has done what was right in being so true to you and to herself. She could not have acted otherwise."

Marion apparently had the good sense to know that the marriage would not have worked out.

"I am told," Caroline said afterward, "that Marion is very intimate with a fast Englishwoman who dresses very much like a man, wears short hair, a high hat, and smokes cigarettes."

Oliver's divorce and Perry's failure with Marion put August, Jr., in a foul mood. He felt responsible for his siblings or, perhaps more accurately, responsible for the family name. And he was made even more out of sorts by feeling rootless. He was not content to live in his father's place at the Nursery, where he, Bessie, and August III had spent a year so dull that even the servants rebelled against staying another winter. He wanted his own home. August offered his son the house next door to 109 Fifth Avenue that he had offered Frederika and Sam, but August, Jr., turned it down. He did not want to be quite so literally in his father's shadow, and he wanted to settle in Hempstead so he could be near the Meadowbrook Hunt Club kennels. When his father resisted buying a house there, August, Jr., complained.

"What more can you wish?" Caroline asked him.

August, Jr., apologized, but his mother was not easily placated.

"You say you grumbled because you felt out of sorts," she said, "and because you like to, *I add*. Perhaps, if you had a piece of the moon, it would be all the same."

August, Jr., and his family moved to Hempstead. It was lucky that he had not asked for a piece of the moon. His father could not deny him anything.

Toward the end of Summer one of August, Jr.'s polo ponies escaped from a groom and while galloping through Hempstead kicked a twelve year-old boy in the face with a hoof; the boy lay unconscious for two or three days—or so said his father, J. C. Tower, a traveling salesman for a cracker company, who arrived at August, Jr.'s house to demand that August, Jr., pay the doctor's bill of $25. August, Jr., told Tower he would look into the matter. He questioned his groom, who had visited Tower's house the day after the accident to pay his respects and found the boy, in good health, running around the family's yard. August, Jr., assumed Tower was trying to bilk him.

A few days later August, Jr., and Bessie were standing on the platform of the Hempstead railroad station, waiting for the train into New York City, when Tower walked up and asked:

"Mr. Belmont, will you settle that bill you owe me?"

"I have nothing to say to you," said August, Jr., turning away.

"Well," said Tower, flushing, "I have something to say to you, sir!"

August, Jr., faced Tower, looked at him for a long time, and then said: "I owe you nothing, and I desire to have no talk with you."

Shaking his fist in August, Jr.'s face, Tower said: "You are a deadbeat and a fraud."

August, Jr., cracked him on the head with his cane. Tower clawed at August, Jr.'s throat and started to throttle him. A bystander separated them. As August, Jr., was being led away he shouted to Tower: "If you were not so old a man, I would smash you to pieces."

Tower examined his hat, which had been ripped by the cane, and telegraphed ahead to the police, who, however, did not arrest August, Jr., because they did not have a warrant.

Tower sued August, Jr., for $10,000 for his son's injuries and another $10,000 for his own but lost both cases. Now that August, Jr., was vindicated he covered the $25 doctor's bill, which he apparently had decided was authentic after all. However, feeling either modest or foolish he dropped a note to Joseph Pulitzer, the new owner of the *New York World*, asking him, "Please do not allude to my having paid."

The emotional shocks of the past year drove August and Caroline into hibernation. Caroline hated meeting "that horrible family," the Whitings, so she shied from society, a withdrawal from which she never would recover. August, too, avoided people. The new breed led by the Vanderbilts was taking over. Even the recently built Metropolitan Opera, which one of the Vanderbilts had created when his wife had been unable to rent a box at the Academy of Music, had recovered from a disastrous first year and was threatening to become the principal opera house in the city. For years August had wanted to placate the Vanderbilt crowd by adding twenty-six additional boxes to the Academy; but the representaives of the old-money Knickerbockers—the Barclays, Barlows, Beekmans, Livingstons, and Schuylers—resented the mob of new-money millionaires and refused to compromise. Loyal to the theater he had rescued from ruin, August publicly sided with the Academy; but privately, to show his disapproval of the Knickerbockers' arrogance—which years before had been directed at him—he resigned from the presidency of the Academy's board of directors. And he defended the Vanderbilts, the progeny of his former rival, when they were attacked by Caroline Astor, Ward McAllister, and the other self-proclaimed guardians of what August called "our misnamed best society," which, he added, "was interested only in scandal."

He wanted to resign from other boards of directors and wished he could drop everything to return to Naples, where the Rothschilds had sent him at the beginning of his business career and where he recalled seeing Charlotte Rothschild, Lionel's wife, in 1836 when she was a young "beautiful bride." Now she was dead.

The past was a stain spreading through the present. He received a letter from C. Louis Heck, who had grown up in Alzey and was now living in Maryland. While leafing through a hymnbook from 1831 Heck had found a slip of paper with August's name on it; and he remembered when, fifty years before at the time of the village fair, August, dressed in a "black velvet jacket, buckskin riding pantaloons, and hightop boots," had ridden into town "on a dashing fine horse."

How unfamiliar that younger, vital self must have seemed to August, who was increasingly bedridden. Age seemed to be a form of gravity dragging him down; but the only way to resist the pull of death—casting off the flesh that like ballast kept him sinking—was to invite death. The lucid invalid's paradox: the clear mind cannot live without the corrupt body. From a newspaper he copied a poem about death:

> *If we could know*
> *Which of us, darling, would be the first to go. . . .*
> *I only wish the space may not be long*
> *Between the parting and the greeting. . . .*

His eyes had gotten so bad he could no longer read, one of his favoirte recreations. His hand shook when he wrote. As he told August, Jr., "my nervousness has become quite alarming. The misfortune of all this is that while I am often right in principle in an argument I put myself in nine cases out of ten wrong by my temper and worse than all that every one of these incidents is a nail in my coffin. Kiss the baby from his poor old grandfather, who is having a pretty hard time of it."

Age brings, with the shortness of life left to live, a corresponding shortness of temper. One can condemn in a moment, but it takes time to let wounds heal, to forgive; and old men do not have time. August became peevish, misanthropic, and he kept to a small, increasingly vicious, circle of friends.

Early in 1884, during or after a card game at August's house, Manton Marble played a joke—worse than tasteless: bitter—on another guest, James V. Parker, who became furious and apparently violent, although his raging, like the thrashing of a snared rabbit in a bush, is hidden behind a tangle of letters sent back and forth among the others who were present at the disagreeable performance. The next day Marble sent August his "sincere regrets" that "I should have been the unwitting occasion of any unpleasantness in your house."

"If anything could add to my regret at the painful scene of last evening," August told Marble, "it is that you should have thought it necessary to express to the gentlemen present and to myself an apology of your share in the occasion. I have no blame to find with you. I am truly sorry that a harmless joke should have been so incredibly misapprehended."

August mediated.

Marble told him, "I will follow your advice. Nor is it difficult. I am a very hard man to break a friendship with."

And at August's prodding Parker left a note at Marble's office:

"I came for atonement. But unhappy me. I find the altar closed, the priest abroad, and no chance of shedding blood." Sacrificial, not angry, blood. "Pray dream that I have sacrificed and allow me to remain as ever your friend."

Although this episode had a happy resolution, it revealed the strains within August's crowd. The bonds that linked them had become fetters; and, a social chain gang, they toiled away at having fun, all the while dreaming of freedom from one another. Even August and Marble tugged at their tie and finally broke it.

For months they saw less and less of each other—and blamed each other for the cooling of their mutual affection. Their letters became demanding and at last accusatory. August, who said that he had "been fool enough to wear my heart upon my sleeve all my life" and that in friendships was no "wiser at 71 than I was at 20," complained that Marble was ignoring his invitations.

"I suppose," he said, "that in your charitable amiability you preferred silence, thinking that it would be less lacerating to my feelings than
a refusal."

To prove that Marble had been slighting him August sent his friend
copies of his last few letters, "marked from 1 to 5." Marble could read in
them the sad story of his inattention.

"One must forget a quarrel with a friend, they say," answered Marble. "But how?" He protested that "my feelings toward you have always
been colored by the fact that you gave me your confidence when I was
young and scarcely could have earned it; you staked something of your
established reputation and your known high character upon me when my
character was unknown and perhaps was in the making—namely your
good word everywhere and your friendship at home. So far am I from
having deserved your reproach, never in any single instance, any where,
at any time to any human being, have I failed toward you in sincerity, in
loyalty, in devotion." He insisted that any breach between them was
August's fault—or at least his invention.

August replied that Marble's letter was "not what I expected or what
I thought I have a right to expect at your hands. It would be useless and
probably painful to both of us, certainly so to me, if I were to attempt the
refutation of your charges and innuendoes by which you try to prove and
certainly seem to prove to your own satisfaction that I have been and am
unjust and ungrateful to you. You are happy in the conviction that I
am entirely in the wrong and that I have now as well as in the past 'failed
in the offices or the implied obligations of an avowed personal friendship,'
and so I must abide by your decision though I am not aware of having
been guilty of any such failure at any time from the first day of our
meeting until this hour."

Marble stuck August's letter in his trunk, left for Europe, and did
not answer it for more than two months, eventually explaining to August
that he "looked for it in vain and feared it had been left at home by
error." Finally, once it had slipped out from "between some white waistcoats to my great relief," Marble wrote that after "25 years of happy
friendship" they should be able to resolve their differences. "It should be
enough that neither of us ever wished to be less than generous to the
other; and, since you have the luck to be my senior, let me take a junior's
privilege or duty and propose to you to forget and cancel all else than
that." Marble was offering a solution to their discord. Neither of them
would have to apologize. Both could save face.

Perhaps August would have accepted Marble's peace terms if Marble had not had the lack of grace to make fun of August's righteous indignation by ending the letter with "Come! my dear Belmont, you shall not have a monopoly of the virtues. Will you 'divide the blame fair . . .?' "

They remained companions out of habit; but the forms, empty of feeling, became merely polite ritual masking rancor. Former friends are resented more than former lovers, because a friendship has less reason to end than a love affair.

August's alienation from Marble left him not cross but "deeply mortified and disappointed. I have been taught many a hard lesson in my long and checkered life; but it was reserved to you," he told Marble, "to rob me of the last illusion by teaching me how foolish and Don Quixotic I was when I believed that sincerity, loyalty, and devotion such as I gave to you freely and without stint, would find an echo in the world in which we live."

August, who had gone from signing his letters *Great Mogul* to *Pseudo Great Mogul,* finally became for Marble merely *August Belmont.* The name he had made into an institution had become a refuge; but, having retreated, he found that the refuge, with its doors locked and windows barred for protection, had become a lonely prison.

❧ *CHAPTER SIXTY-FOUR* ❧

THE WALL STREET PANIC of 1884 bankrupted Bessie's family.

"It must be sad indeed to see your father-in-law so broken down," Caroline told August, Jr. "It is a bitter trial for them who have always been so successful in business and accustomed to every luxury and comfort."

The Morgans' fall from wealth was a fall from grace. They became quarrelsome. August, Jr., tried to referee their panicky family squabbles, and he took in his sister-in-law to ease the shock of poverty for her. But the more he helped, the more the Morgans resented him for not sharing their bad luck. Among them August, Jr., felt anachronistic, as though they had moved into a future that he luckily had escaped. Money can buy the illusion of stopped time; poverty like illness sharpens the sense of mortality. And like illness it can seem contagious. August advised his son to avoid infection.

"You must not let it worry you beyond where you can be of any good," August told him. August, Jr., should treat "the erratic conduct of your father-in-law" with "patience and tact" and not let any bad blood lead to "an open rupture" that would cause "suffering in the family" and give "to a malicious and heartless world food for scandal. Keep aloof from any interference and advice, direct or indirect, about the business arrangements of Mr. Morgan; and, if it should become necessary, say politely but firmly that you decline discussing the question."

Perhaps to protect August III from Bessie's distress at her parents' troubles, August, Jr., sent his son to Bythesea for the summer. Accompanied by his nurse, Ada, the boy arrived—according to his grandparents—"bright and lively and did not seem to mind the jounrey at all." August, because he had a cold, had to eat in his study; and as though he were a spy he moused around the house and grounds watching his grandson from a distance.

When he was better he romped with August III—and cheerfully worried about him. The boy needed a new pram, lots of fresh air and sun, and "strong lace boots, stiff at the ankles," so he could learn to walk. By the end of summer August III was calling August "Banpa" and was toddling, a stunt August wanted to surprise August, Jr., and Bessie with. But Caroline blabbed the news in a letter. August sulked.

The economic slump finally drove August away from his grandchild and back to New York. The city was muggy. Soot from the elevated trains fell, black summer snow. On the packed streets women swooned or, nearly swooning, fortified themselves with smelling salts. Marble fountains in drugstores, sticky with spilled sweet drinks—lime the green of a blowfly's body; cherry the pink of a cat's palate—collected crowds. In theaters blocks of ice were used to build barricades against the heat; the breezes blowing over them cooled the jammed auditoriums where people went for relief and only incidentally to watch the shows. At night stoops were dense with men in shirtsleeves without their collars and women in dresses that looked cool but were not; on sidewalks children raced, a fast-boil in the heat. At his house on Fifth Avenue, August sat behind drawn curtains and ate nectarines and grapes sent from Bythesea.

At the office August was more critical of his son than he had been in a long time. He absorbed with a dry cynicism August, Jr.'s enthusiasm for the West. And he warned August, Jr., that *"extreme caution, patience, and a firm determination not to depart from the legitimate nature of business* are the only safeguards against failure, and *any departures from these principles are sure to bring loss and ruin.*"

The crisis was a convenient excuse to climb back up on the box and take the reins from August, Jr., who had been replacing his father not only in business but in civic affairs (lobbying for an extension of public parklands in New York City) and in society (hosting the Coaching Club at Hempstead). When August, Jr., balked at his father's reassertion of authority, August said, "I will not touch upon your remarks about my want of confidence in you as they are undeserved and out of place."

August was looking for his youth in the shambles of Wall Street. As a young man he had made fortunes in economic crises; he could not resist a last chance to work the old alchemy and once more turn panic into profit. August, Jr., would be free of his interference soon enough.

"The time will come," August told August, Jr., "when my children will do me better justice than they do now; but by then I shall be far away on that road from which no traveler returns."

Like an inhabitant of a plague-ridden medieval city August was hesitant to head into the unknown; but he was repelled by where he was. His opinion of humanity was summed up by an incident that infuriated and disgusted him. While being shipped in a small box, two of his favorite dogs suffocated, "simply butchered by the stupidity of the men" responsible. The image of the dogs' pathetic death stayed with him: two panicky creatures trapped in the dark, gnawing at each other and themselves in an effort to escape.

August blunted Caroline. When he was away, she felt honed, able to cut cleanly, more decisively, through life. Alone at Newport with her grandson and the servants, she indulged her will. Her life was regular—strolls with the boy at the same hour every day, meals on time. She ran a tight ship. Age was making her—a commodore's daughter—into a commodore. One night while she was dining out someone smashed a dining-room window at Bythesea; and the servants, afraid to frighten her, did not tell Caroline about the break-in until the next morning. Unfazed, Caroline considered the possible suspects and decided the thief was the gardener. Even if she were wrong, she was not intimidated, and as though to prove it she sent the old dog that had been sleeping on her bed to the stables. She could handle any intruder. She was less upset by the threat of someone breaking into her life than by the prospect of someone slipping out of it. When August III returned to his parents, Caroline wrote to her son:

"Don't let him forget me."

Raymond spent the summer visiting the dives of Europe. On a typical day in Paris he woke midmorning and passed the afternoon with "a very pretty girl," after which he shared a cab with another girl, much younger, poorly dressed, but "nice-looking." She spoke English surprisingly well; and they had such a pleasant conversation that when Raymond reached his destination at a restaurant, he had the cab wait and he sent her out a sandwich, which a friend he had met—Bud Appleton—wanted to deliver.

"I had all the trouble in the world," Raymond said, "keeping Bud from going home with her."

After dinner Raymond and Bud picked up Mike Peters, another friend who was in Paris; and the three of them went to explore a bordello where Raymond "singled out a Turkish girl and Bud a French one. We started on the grand tour of the rooms." Although they had come to satisfy their curiosity, not their lust, the people who ran the bordello "tried to stick us for the girls, saying that we had a chance to be naughty, but we made believe we could not talk French."

Drinking bets and bouts, wallets lost in cabs, cabs lost in the maze of streets, rides to his hotel room under skies spinning with stars. . . . The summer ended too soon.

On the trip back to the United States the ship's steering mechanism broke the second night out and they almost collided with another transatlantic liner in the fog. The next morning the seas were so rough that Raymond was the only passenger at breakfast—which made him cocky. Later when his friends, as disoriented as owls in daylight, straggled into the public rooms, Raymond organized a betting pool on how much progress the ship would make each day. The third night out the seas were rougher. Waves crashing against the hull made Bud feel as if he were sleeping inside a drum. His room flooded. Frightened, he asked Raymond to sleep in his cabin—which Raymond did on the fourth night out, although since he had "to tramp through steerage to get a bath," he abandoned his friend. Bud would have to deal with his night terrors by himself. The fifth night out the weather got worse. Waves were so high that even Raymond's room, one of the best on the ship, was flooded. His bed was soaked. He was awakened before dawn by a horrible grinding, which convinced him that "we ran into another ship or else the barber's hair brushing machine got out of order." Raymond was jaunty with fear. The seventh night out a frayed electrical wire set fire to a bench in one of the companionways—not too serious, just "enough of a mishap to give the ladies a chance to exercise their lungs. We have now had every sort of divertissement," Raymond said, "excepting the breaking of the shaft." The next morning the bad weather—not the shaft—broke. It was so lovely that Raymond and his no-longer-seasick friends stayed on deck all day. Bud initiated a tug-of-war: Americans against English. The Americans won. An Englishman, sore about losing, said that the Americans had all the shit on their side.

"But why did we have all the shit on our side?" Bud asked.

"I don't know," said the Englishman.

"Because," said Bud, "we pulled it over the line."

Raymond discovered scatological humor as though he were uncovering ancient occult lore.

Back in New York he hailed a cab that on the way to 109 Fifth Avenue lost a wheel. The driver was thrown into the street and knocked senseless. Raymond climbed out of the tilting carriage, not at all shaken. Given his transatlantic voyage it was a fitting homecoming.

He was "delighted to get back" to his "old Harvard club," and he and his friends at once began plotting their fall campaign. One of their first forays was to Bud's family farm at Ipswich, Massachusetts, where they had a horse race for five and a half miles under an afternoon sun so hot that Raymond almost was sick at the end. They idled for hours at a kennel drinking and gossiping and started back at night under the moonlight through fields of burning brush. Jumping a deep and muddy ditch, Raymonds' mare stumbled and landed on her knees. Raymond hung on; the horse recovered and scrambled up the bank. One of his friends was not as lucky and, tossed from his horse, plopped into the deepest part of the ooze. He was dragged out unhurt but coated hat-to-boot in muck. They did not reach the house until ten o'clock and then stayed up with some local girls telling ghost stories.

After an interlude at Newport, where he walked along the cliffs with the Heckscher girls and was entertained by a friend, Ray Miller, who sang a duet with a dog, Raymond took advantage of his parents' temporary absence from 109 Fifth Avenue to move his revels to New York City. On his first night in town Revvie Travers bragged so intolerably about how good Racquet Court champagne was that Raymond challenged him to prove his case. Revvie, joyously confusing quality and quantity, offered a trial by endurance: he would buy all the champagne the four of them—he, Raymond, and their two companions—could drink.

"I gulped it very quickly and greedily," said Raymond, "for I wanted to make it as expensive as possible for Revvie."

In half an hour they had finished three bottles. The others were too looped to force down another swallow, but Raymond, determined to outdrink them, killed one more half-bottle. He figured that, including his earlier glasses of claret and liqueur, he had over two and a half quarts of alcohol sloshing inside him.

While they weaved their way along the streets, their party lost one member—who (Raymond later discovered) was robbed by a woman he met. At another night spot a girl from Boston recognized Raymond, who, having drunk more, was too muzzy to place her—probably to her relief, since he vomited over the back of a sofa and was asked to leave. Revvie took off for an establishment called Rosa Bell's, and Raymond staggered to the nearest refuge, the Fifth Avenue Hotel; but the management, afraid he would foul the room, refused him admission. Just before passing out he made it to the Hoffman House, which took him in.

The next morning he woke covered with a crust of dried vomit. He went home; bathed; and in the midst of getting dressed fell asleep across his bed. At eight-thirty in the evening he roused himself, finished dressing, and, on going downstairs, found Revvie passed out on a couch. At Demonico's they had an evening breakfast, which Revvie flamboyantly topped with a Rosa Perfecta cigar. Then Revvie calmly walked outside and puked in the gutter.

Instead of going to Long Island as they were supposed to, they spent the following day at Jerome Park, where on the first two races Raymond won $55. Revvie, who trusted a twenty-five-cent tip-sheet called *Lucky Uncle Al*, did not do as well. In a later race Berry Wall, another member of their clique, put $2,000 on Wallflower—which stampeded Raymond and Revvie into betting heavily on the horse. Wallflower came in last. Blaming each other for their losses the three separated. Raymond returned to the city, had dinner, and afterward stopped at a night spot called the Adonis, where he met Revvie, drunk again.

"I treated him coldly," said Raymond, "but accepted his drinks."

Back in Cambridge, Raymond rollicked on more drunken club trips, one of which ended with a friend's galloping into a house and posing before the front parlor fireplace astride his horse.

"We jumped fences, investigated a haunted house, rode through gar-

dens and on piazzas, and finally started for Boston on the train track."
Riding the rails on a noniron horse.

In a race Raymond's mount bolted. "The damned brute," Raymond
complained, took him a mile and a half beyond the finish line. Three
extra times around the track. His stirrup had gotten fouled. He felt helpless. The only way to stop the horse was to head for the stable. At the
stable gate Raymond fell. The horse galloped to its stall. Raymond painfully stood; and holding himself carefully, as if his body were a cracked
mirror he was carrying to the trash, he climbed the stairs of the house
where he was staying and, in his room, lay down. A "very pretty house-
keeper" plumped his pillow and took "the best care of me. I felt like a
fool, especially when she offered to take my spurs off. I tried to take them
off myself, but I was so tired that I could not and had to let her do it."

Later that night Raymond, one of the few who had survived the
champagne cocktails, wandered among the bodies of his friends who were
passed out "all over the hall." A battlefield after combat. Their fall campaign had been successful. They had lost the war against excess.

August doubted that Perry could get reelected to Congress in 1884. Perry
had made too many enemies in politics. Wanting to match his triumph
over Blaine he had scoured Washington for comparable scandals. "Mr.
Perry Belmont has his weaknesses as a statesman," a hostile newspaper
said, "but want of courage is not one of them." He sniffed out a possible
fraud in the Treasury Department; accused an elderly colleague on the
House Committee on Foreign Affairs of cravenly apologizing to the British minister for a congressional resolution that had an anti-English whiff
to it; and led the fight against the proposed Nicaragua Canal, which he
feared would invite European belligerence rather than protect against it.
These crusades had made him as unpopular with certain Democratic
leaders as he was with the Republicans. Also, he had made the tactical
mistake of standing aloof from all factions within his party; thus, he could
not herd together with one group to discourage the other group from
attacking him. His moderate—and often misunderstood—stand on the
increasingly important tariff question, for example, left him isolated; a
conciliator like his father, he tried to find a middle, perhaps linking,
position between the free traders and the protectionists—and ended by
alienating both.

He was too independent of the old machines—local and national—
which is not to say he was politically pure. By distributing patronage to

his own cronies he was creating his own machine. This, combined with the frequency with which he was being mentioned as a potential senatorial candidate, frightened the old-line Democrats. The power of the machine Perry was putting together on Long Island at least would be limited by his district's narrow geographical boundaries. But as a senator he could build throughout the state a machine that would have a tremendous national impact. To run for reelection Perry would have to fight his own as well as the rival party.

Perry was vulnerable. Although his policies were popular, he lacked the common touch, that reverse Midas quality that transforms aristocrats when they shake hands with laborers into plain folks. The previous year, he had organized a political fund-raiser at the Argyle Hotel in Babylon.

"The price of liberty is eternal vigilance," said a newspaper, "but the price of the Belmont dinner was $12 per head. It was too much."

"Such things might do in New York City," said a local Democrat, "but Belmont must not bring them down into the country."

A few days before the dinner it was clear that virtually no one was going to come. Twelve dollars a plate—or even $10, as another newspaper reported—was so steep that the Long Island politicians, fishermen, farmers, and shopkeepers thought it betrayed Perry's arrogance when it merely revealed his ignorance. Among his rich New York City friends $12 was a paltry sum; he had no idea his constituents might not be able to afford it.

Two Long Island Democratic politicans called on August to warn him about his son's impending fiasco and apparently to guarantee a full dining room the night of the dinner—for a price. August threw them out.

To avoid certain humiliation Perry at the last minute canceled the fund-raiser. The hotel sued him for $750, which the manager claimed he had spent on preparations. He thought Perry would settle the bill rather than risk the bad publicity. On principle Perry refused to pay. The publicity wounded his pride more than his position. He was renominated for an unprecedented third term. After three debates with the Republican candidate, which also were unprecedented in the district, Perry won the election, becoming the first congressman from that area to serve three consecutive terms, an extraordinary victory that reflected the success of the national ticket.

⚅

"In selecting the 1884 Democratic presidential candidate . . . ," one observer said, "August Belmont will have, perhaps, much less influence than.ever before, because . . . among other reasons he has willingly ceded his place to his son, the popular young Member of Congress, who is clearly marked out as one of the statesmen of the future. Nevertheless, Mr. Belmont's long and intimate experience in politics, his great wealth, and public spirit, his relations with the most famous of European capitalists, his position in society, and his life-long devotion to Democratic tenets, in spite of his personal aristocratic tastes, give to him, even in his voluntary retirement, a special importance which can hardly be overestimated. He is, in effect, a financial ambassador, and to overlook or neglect his advice about the Presidency would be to ignore one of the great Powers not only of this country, but of the world."

As expected, the Republicans nominated Blaine for president and, not so expected, the fierce former Union general, Senator John A. Logan of Illinois, for vice-president. Tandem tempers. The Plumped Knight and the Black Eagle. The ticket sounded like a sideshow bill. August was certain they would be defeated.

But by whom?

Among the Democrats, Winfield Scott Hancock and Samuel J. Randall were too weak; Allen G. Thurman (unfortunately, thought August) was a possibility; and Samuel J. Tilden (luckily, thought August) was too sick—although many in the party were still fascinated by Tilden, who had the charm of a former aging mistress. Benjamin Franklin Butler, the governor of Massachusetts, attracted the poor, the greenback supporters, the Irish, and the suffragettes. Rumors spread that if Butler were the presidential nominee Perry would be his choice for the vice-presidency. August remained loyal to Thomas Bayard, who was perceived by many as being "too clean and too cold." By the spring before the election it became clear that the favorite was the governor of New York, Grover Cleveland, a good-natured upstate lawyer whose ponderous honesty seemed to his enemies to be a lack of imagination. Probably it was more a matter of inertia: His moral sense bulked so large that its momentum kept him going on the right road. Like many men who are sure of themselves, he seemed to have fattened on certainty. Under his eyes, on his cheeks, and under his chin, the flesh was tucked so tightly into creases that his face looked quilted. In the past he had preferred Bayard over Tilden; now he preferred himself over Bayard.

The previous year Cleveland had tested August's support by asking him to intervene about a certain matter with the boss of Tammany, John

Kelly. Although August had inclined toward Cleveland's view in this affair, he was at the time seeking Tammany's backing for Bayard and did not want to side with Cleveland against Kelly; so he had begged off, explaining to Cleveland that he had retired from politics. He had bet on the wrong horse: At the Democratic National Convention in Chicago, Cleveland was nominated on the second ballot. To offset Cleveland's Hard Money stand the Democrats as usual balanced—or, as August thought, unbalanced—the ticket with a Soft Money vice-presidential candidate: Thomas A. Hendricks again.

During the convention August and Perry grew gloomier day by day. The press reported that Perry predicted Cleveland would not even carry his own state—an opinion Perry publicly denied, although August (and probably Perry too) thought that the Democrats were mad to run Cleveland, since "the Irish were so deeply opposed to him." They left Chicago before the convention ended. August, feeling "terribly gloomy about politics," thought:

"How lucky our predecessors . . . and successors have been or will be not to have lived in 1884!"

Neither Cleveland nor the Democratic National Committee approached August for help. After years of threatening to quit politics, August felt left out. No Mohammed, he refused to go to the mountain. Although he told August, Jr., that he "will do my best and my duty to the party and the country" and that he had "given the National Committee my services even without being asked for in a quarter where I have some influence and have also contributed some money," he had not come out for Cleveland publicly, despite the fact that virtually all his former political allies had done so. And his private services and contributions must have been negligible.

August, Jr., and Perry urged him to get involved actively in the campaign. The Democrats were going to win. By staying silent August would lose influence with the new administration.

"I thank you for your kind advice about my own action, which you evidently don't approve," August told August, Jr. He asked his son to forgive him for not "entering into a lengthy discussion of the question as I am not well"; and then he launched into three pages of defense.

"The conduct of the men, who have the campaign in charge, toward me has been and is as absurd as it would be humiliating to me if I cared at all for what comes from that quarter. I have been for 40 years an active and for more than 30 years a prominent man in the party, have been 12 years Chairman of the National Committee, and have spent $500,000—if I have spent one dollar—in the service of the party; and what do I get in return? Because I was in favor of the nomination of the foremost man in the party and in the country, I have not even had the recognition of being asked to speak or to preside at any meeting (a thing which has not happened in more than a quarter of a century)." As for his son's suggestion that he should make a substantial contribution to Cleveland's campaign in the hope of being appointed minister somewhere, August snapped:

"Am I now *to buy* the good graces of the men in control of the party!! I would not and I could not at my age and with my infirmities accept any office even if it was offered to me and were I fool enough at this late day to have any such ambition. The pecuniary sacrifice which you wish me to make would only be thrown away and carry with it further disappointment. Tilden and his friends will rule the next administration should Cleveland be elected; and they have friends enough, Heaven knows, to provide for."

August, Jr., tried to goad his father into action by repeating a rumor, spread by a Wall Street broker, that August secretly was backing Butler, who was running for president on the National Greenback Labor party ticket. After all, hadn't August attacked Cleveland at Chicago?

"I never was hard or harsh on Cleveland at Chicago," August told August, Jr., "and *never uttered a disparaging word against him*." As for Butler, "I don't think that anything I ever said or wrote can possibly be twisted into an approval of his course." Butler was "unscrupulous and selfish." And the man who spread the rumor that August was supporting him is "an ass and I wish you would tell him so in my name. The idea of some ignorant fool, probably a new fledged neophyte from the Republican ranks daring to sit up in judgment over a man who has served unswervingly and zealously the Democratic Party for more than 40 years and has made *heavier pecuniary sacrifices for it, during its darkest hours than any man living in the United States.* I wish you had not written me this. It makes my very blood boil and has spoiled this quiet bright Sunday for me."

August knew his son's advice was "well meant," but he said "I think I know what I am about and what I ought to do" and "you must let me paddle my own canoe in that line at least."

Both Cleveland's lieutenant, Smith M. Weed, and the most influential member of the Democratic National Committee, Senator Arthur P.

Gorman of Maryland, contacted August—Weed through Marble; Gorman directly, when Perry told him how depressed and ignored his father felt. Their attention soothed August's hurt pride. He no longer held himself aloof from the party. He recommended to Gorman that the pro-Cleveland press stop antagonizing the Irish.

"Of course," August said, "certain of these elements are bad, pernicious, and loathsome"—no doubt he was thinking of John Devoy and his band—"but you have to take things as they are and not as they ought to be," advice he himself did not often follow.

Instead of alienating the Irish, Cleveland's supporters should be seeking their votes by reminding them of Blaine's long anti-Irish and anti-Catholic record, which Blaine now was trying to hide.

"This ought to be taken hold of and repeated every day by every anti-Blaine paper throughout the land," August said.

August sent Gorman $3,500 for the Democratic National Committee and Kelly $2,800 for New York City's campaign. He committed himself to Cleveland.

Even when he had been chairman of the Democratic National Committee, August had felt like an outsider; but his children felt like insiders—even when they were excluded from the inner councils of the party.

Despite his initial doubts Perry regularly interrupted his own campaign to stump for the Democratic ticket, speaking at rallies in Babylon, Flushing, Newark, Providence, Rhode Island, and Newport, where August proudly watched his performance.

"It is the first time I ever heard him speak," August told August, Jr., "and I was astonished at his quick self-possession."

"The ticket suits me to death," said August, Jr. "I am and have been for Cleveland from the start and intend to shake things up for him where I live at Hempstead. I think Cleveland and Hendricks are going to sweep the deck."

He organized a Cleveland-Hendricks club in Hempstead, where he recruited Perry to speak, while in Cambridge, Raymond participated in "a flag-raising in honor of Cleveland and Hendricks. There were several good speeches, a band, fireworks, and a strong punch so the evening went off very well." Afterward he joined fifty of his classmates. They went to a skating rink; and, woozy with punch, went careening over the ice.

"I had the pleasure of tripping up one of the spangle-capped professors who was there and bringing him and his girlfriend down like two ducks flying 90 miles an hour."

The climax of the campaign for Harvard was a torchlight parade in which the four classes were arrayed in different uniforms: seniors in red gowns, juniors like Raymond in blue and white swallowtail coats, sophomores in black and yellow gowns, and freshmen in red and white Eton jackets.

The other classes "went in for dignity," said Raymond; only the juniors were "disreputable." Most of them carried at least one flask. Raymond had two of rum and ginger, "but they did not last long. I had to borrow, switching off on every drink from sherry to gin and back again." By the end of the parade the juniors were so drunk that they all marched off in different directions, and "many even took little siestas on the pavement."

Raymond had a bunch of Roman candles that, he explained, he was going to fire at Blaine, who was scheduled to address the students; "but somebody set the whole dozen off in my pockets, and they nearly blew off the heads of my nearest neighbors. However, I consoled myself with throwing an apple at Blaine."

Raymond was conked on the head with a torch and set on fire. On the way home he got into some fights. Back at his club he found that one of his friends had collected more than fifty handkerchiefs that had been tossed at the students by the women and girls lining the route of the parade. Their combined perfumes made the room reek. Raymond went to sleep convinced that virtually everyone was "booming for Cleveland."

The election was close. New York was the key. August feared the Republicans intended to steal the White House as they had in 1876.

"A generally well informed politician just tells me that the Republican managers are *confident to count their man in,*" August told Gorman. "Vast sums of money have been spent and are being spent all over the state in order to falsify the returns, and my friend thinks it has been done so successfully as to insure Blaine's victory by a small majority." He suspected that Jay Gould was "at work" in "criminal intrigues" on behalf of Blaine. "I need not urge you and your colleagues to the utmost watchfulness. The *people, rich and poor, merchant and mechanic, are with us.* A firm and decided stand and no possible compromise of unconstitutional tribunals must be our watchword."

August assured Cleveland, who felt betrayed by John Kelly and Tammany, that Kelly and Tammany were loyal.

"The falling off in our vote was, in my opinion, due to a large portion of the Butler vote being transferred to Blaine," said August—and to dissension within Democratic ranks in New York over local candidates.

Not only was Tammany "staunch and true to you," but even the chairman of the Board of Canvassers, *"though a Republican,"* is *"for you."*

Unlike Tilden in 1876, Cleveland did not hesitate to announce that he believed he had won and he would not permit any fraud to deny him the presidency.

He carried New York by 1,149 votes, a feather tipping the balance.

"Thank God, you are elected," August told him, "and nothing can or shall be done by Blaine and his fellow conspirators to rob you and the Democracy."

Cleveland was the first Democratic president since Buchanan.

August was "delighted to have lived long enough to see Democracy once more triumphant."

August presided at a rally at the Academy of Music. The era of corrupt and swollen federal bureaucracy was ended, August predicted; "the rich and powerful monopolies" and the "unscrupulous leaders" they placed in power would no longer control Washington.

In the past August had looked out at so many crowds, and so few of the gatherings had been victory celebrations.

The Cleveland clique may have been willing to display August; but they were not ready to trust him, which August realized and accepted. When Nathaniel Rothschild raised, as he had a number of times in the last few years, the possibility of August's being named minister to the Court of St. James's, August dismissed the notion. Once before he had admitted to Nathaniel that "some eight or ten years back" such an honor "would have been the height of my ambition" and that "nothing would give me a greater pleasure and gladden my old days more than residence of a couple of years in good old England." But he knew "these are fairy visions." He told Nathaniel that Cleveland "will have twenty applicants for every office within his gift" and will not "step out of his way to tempt me. Even in the most improbable event of his doing so, my resolution to pass the rest of my days in private life will remain unchangeable." Any "ambition there might yet have lingered within me has been crushed by the sad disappointment caused by the unhappy marriage of my son Oliver."

Although he had no desire to take any appointed office, August did expect his counsel would be sought. It was not, although Perry's was.

Through an intermediary Cleveland asked Perry if Bayard would accept a cabinet post.

Perry said yes.

Cleveland considered giving Bayard the Treasury Department, but Tilden and others argued against that appointment. They thought it would give Bayard too much control over patronage and would give August, through Bayard, too much control over the Treasury.

Again through an intermediary Cleveland asked Perry if Bayard would be satisfied with the State Department.

Perry said: Ask Bayard.

Cleveland did.

Bayard accepted, although his appointment would not be announced —and August would not learn of it—until Inauguration Day.

During his discussions with the president-elect, Bayard had passed through New York City twice without calling on August.

"I am sure you did not lose anything by being spared visiting an old fossil like myself," August wrote to Bayard. "People, when they get to my age are very apt to offer advice, when they are not asked to do so, and generally have a high appreciation of such advice which is not shared by others."

Although he directed his irony at Bayard, he aimed his wrath at the party, to which—he told Bayard—he had sacrificed his "health, time, and money. Having, however, in my obtuse judgment preferred since 1876 at each recurring national convention the foremost man of the Democracy as my candidate for the Presidency and having again done so last Summer at Chicago against the choice of the machine politicians of my own state, I am placed in such antagonism to them that I am virtually laid on the shelf."

By not including Bayard among those who were treating him badly (even though he felt that Bayard had done so by neglecting him), August indicated that he assumed Bayard would start treating him better—specifically, that Bayard would take him into his confidence as he used to.

While August insisted that *"I do not wish to know before it is announced to the public whether you take the State Department or not,"* it was obvious that he wanted to know just that. And more. He wanted to know who else Cleveland was considering for his Cabinet. He wanted "to see whether I cannot through you prevent a great mistake, which I fear from the papers Mr. Cleveland is likely to make . . ."; Thurman and any other Soft Money men must be kept out of the Cabinet.

Bayard was discreet—and more loyal to his new boss than to his old patron. In a pleasant letter to August he betrayed no secrets.

"You know the counsel with Cleveland was *his* rather than mine," Bayard said, "and there was nothing else than absolute reticence to enable me to leave him in sole control of his own affairs. Even now he must be allowed to take his own way and time to announce his determinations."

Bayard was—perhaps correctly—a better public servant than friend.

Soon after Cleveland took office August said, "If I don't agree with the present tendency of the administration in many of its appointments, the fault may probably lie with my old-fashioned notions of party discipline and policy."

During the next few years August would write letters of recommendation for people he knew who were seeking federal appointments; but his influence in the administration was limited. And except for an alleged interview in the *New York Tribune* that claimed August had scorned the leaders of the party (which August told Cleveland was merely "another instance of the newspaper's unscrupulous recklessness and disregard of truth"), the press left August alone. He was no longer an important enough Democrat to attack. Not only was he on the shelf, but the shelf was in some back storeroom and the door had been closed. August's political career was over.

⚜ *CHAPTER SIXTY-FIVE* ⚜

NOTHING INTERESTED AUGUST very deeply anymore. He skimmed over his life as effortlessly as the skaters he used to watch in Frankfurt sailed over the ice. His health grew worse. His eyesight continued to fail; as a result he moved in a world of shadows, as though everyone around him were turning into ghosts.

He reminisced and wrote letters to the shrinking number of old friends with whom he had not quarreled—and then quarreled with them.

He spent days, weeks, even months, trying to discover the identity of someone who three years before had spread an indiscreet tale about him and an Englishwoman.

"The miscreant's attempt to injure me failed," August said, "but his fiendish attack against the character and reputation of a most estimable lady had brought shame and misery upon her, undermining her health and destroying her happiness to such an extent that the few friends who stood by her in all these troubles have been and are still seriously alarmed about her. She has been the principal, nay the only person who has really suffered and as my name had been used in all those foul anonymous calumnies, every principal of honor and manhood made it imperative upon me to hunt down the wretch."

He was reenacting in a minor mode the defense of a lady's honor that had led to a duel four decades before. But now he was too old to fight; and even if he wanted to issue a challenge, no one dueled anymore.

He considered going to Europe; but Frederika was so ill that she had to be carried to and from her carriage for her daily ride through the park, and he was afraid that if he were to leave, his daughter would die. His depression deepened. Even Bayard's attempt to mollify him by saying that he wanted "to have a long and confidential talk" about "public affairs" did not cheer him. His unhappiness affected those who loved him.

"The stones are dropping out one by one from our whole family structure," said August, Jr.

"I really don't know what you mean," said August.

But he must have understood. When the foundation weakens, the house comes down; August was the foundation. He had to do something to shore up the family's confidence, something to prove he had faith in the future. In the late fall of 1884 he decided to buy a new stud farm two and a half miles outside of Lexington, Kentucky, and to reenter racing.

Wise madness.

He felt too old and poor "to indulge in this expensive luxury of farming and horse-breeding." It was almost impossible to find a good trainer. And since it took three or four years to develop a stable, by the time the stud was successful he might be dead.

But the decision heartened his sons, and the activity quickened him. He bought the best horses he could find, including St. Blaise, an English Derby winner that was so famous its arrival in America was greeted by headlines in the national press. Once he had lured Jacob Pincus back to again be his trainer, August almost could feel that time was an illusion and that one could re-create the past.

Farming, Oliver thought, in upstate New York. No, not farming; viticulture. But not in upstate New York, in Maryland. And not viticulture, but farming after all. He would enjoy farming more.

Oliver in casting about for an occupation snagged his attention on the new Lexington stud. That's where he would settle.

August was happy that Oliver wanted to farm and would have been delighted to have him take over the Nursery; but he refused to consent to Oliver's running the Lexington stud, because, as he told August, Jr., "the people all around Lexington are mostly a rough and hard-drinking set, lounging about in the towns and on race tracks, gambling and betting on races; and I fear the influence upon Oliver *would be fatal.*"

Like Oliver, Raymond seemed disinclined to treat life seriously. He continued to drink too much, roister, and have bad luck with horses, both the ones on which he bet and the ones on which he rode. In one cross-country race his horse refused to jump, rearing and dumping Raymond at every fence and wall. The more Raymond tried to control the animal, the wilder it became. At last it clubbed its head against Raymond's nose, which started bleeding. Again Raymond hoisted himself onto the horse. The saddle slipped. Again Raymond tumbled, this time "almost breaking" his back. For fifteen minutes he lay on the ground, numb, unable to move. When he stood, he could barely walk. All night his back ached and his nose bled. The next morning the bleeding had stopped, but he still was hobbling.

When he recovered enough to carouse, he went with his pals to the Park Theater bar, where while getting drunk he watched an Irishman and a Jew playing pool. When the game ended, the Irishman, who was named Dave Barry, challenged any or all of the Harvard men. One of Raymond's friends beat Barry and won a bottle of champagne, which was shared all around. They drank toasts to each other; and almost everyone, including Raymond, by blood half-Jewish, made anti-Semitic jokes, which the Jew, who was named Osman, met with impassive—to the point where it began to seem sinister—good humor. Osman was not a burlesque Jew, no stage Shylock or lisping ragman. And although he had claimed to be a shoemaker, he admitted after they all went out to dinner that he was a jeweler, pimp, robber, and smuggler. He bragged that he could not pass through any customs in the world without being stripped and "very closely searched." However, "they never take off the underclothes"—which Raymond thought "strange." Osman described his various adventures and told about how his brother-in-law, who also was a smuggler, had been stopped at the Canadian border and caught with $1,200 worth of gold chains around his waist. Raymond's contempt turned into fascination and then respect. By confessing to wickedness so uncommon as to be romantic, Osman proved his common humanity.

The pleasant fall weather passed. Winter set in. Raymond and his friends bundled up and clattered into Boston in a crowded carriage, leaning from the windows to shout taunts at any diehard Blaine supporters they might pass. But they were so unable to pick a fight that Raymond said everyone must think "John L. Sullivan was in the cab." Before their surprise could set into smugness, someone who had been walking along the side of the road took up their general challenge. The Harvard boys stopped the carriage and clambered out. One of them squared off with the stranger and knocked him down. The stranger cracked his head open on the pavement, and Raymond and his friends had to rush him to a doctor to get the messy wound stitched.

One of their clique became a one-hour champ when he went off to spend an evening "in 'fragrant delight' with a lady on the wharf of the Brighton Bridge, which," Raymond said, "was at least an original experience, considering that the thermometer was way below freezing." Another became a one-hour chump when, disgusted with his friends' debauchery, he hid their bottle of absinthe and would not return it until Raymond threatened to toss all the club's champagne out the window. Raymond and the few others who dared riddle their brains with the wormwood in the absinthe drank so much that one of them was "seized with a frenzy, was morbid for a few minutes after this, but soon chippered up and began getting off 'gaglets.' " While their friend suffered they made up a song that made fun of their classmates from Boston.

> *I'm a pretty little Boston boy.*
> *Every Sunday I go home,*
> *Eating baked beans all day long. . . .*

It did not rhyme, but it satisfied the hostility they as New Yorkers felt for the locals.

That night most of the club members went home early, leaving, Raymond said, "Brothers Winthrop, Curtis, Parker, Clark, and myself," the serious boozers, who "passed the loving cup around many times, drinking to all the pretty girls from Boston to Kamtchatka." Then they "worshipped with all due form Winthrop. Indeed, he was almost worshipped out of the club." They ate a riotous late dinner of eggs and beer, after which Clark was seized by a desire to explore the attic. He stumbled up the stairs and moments later clattered down in drunken terror, because he was being chased—he said—by "the Brown Man," a hobgoblin that when the others went up to investigate turned out to be a coal scuttle.

"His imagination now fully aroused," Raymond said, "Clark showed great bravado, fiercely attacking and demolishing some half dozen ghosts, which we fixed up in different parts of the club."

Raymond went barhopping in New Haven, which he thought—with a Harvard man's antagonism to Yale—"is a Hell of a hole." On the way back to Cambridge in the train he told stories in German to the immigrant cooks in the dining car, who in return gave him a whole cooked duck. He took it—a warm, fragrant bundle—to Locke-Ober, a Boston restaurant frequented by Harvard men, where he "enacted a miracle and multiplied the number of ducks and champagne bottles." On his way home he stopped at a friend's place for a nightcap of very old, brown-as-mahogany rum.

He was so hung over the next morning that he stayed in bed and did not stir even when someone crashed into his room to tell him that the nearby horsecar barn was on fire and all Cambridge was in danger of going up in flames.

A quick trip to New York during which he was almost tossed off the train because he had no ticket (he placated the conductor by giving him some good cigars, which, however, turned out to be broken); a pageant celebration of George Washington's farewell to the troops, in which Raymond played Ethan Allen; boxing matches in Boston; a party at the opening of a new bordello, which Raymond almost missed by getting the address wrong (he repeatedly rang the bell until the door opened and disclosed a man and woman in their nightclothes; he apologized and finally found the right house). . . .

Weary of the work of maintaining such a high standard of debauchery, Raymond studied for rest and relaxation. He began spending nights alone, reading; wrote a paper on the effect on the working class of the introduction of machinery; and the week before Christmas stayed "quite straight," no excessive drinking. He left the party after the D.K.E. theatricals early and was just falling asleep when a crowd of his friends slammed into his rooms. Raymond protested that he was tired, so they undressed and piled into bed with him.

Vacation saved Raymond from being too studious. His club tacked mistletoe over the fireplace. The fine for being kissed under it was a bottle of champagne. Raymond with a pretense of innocence warmed himself before the fire. The girls flocked to him. He collected ten bottles of champagne.

"It was one of the cosiest and pleasantest afternoons I have ever spent," he decided.

His return home for Christmas was different from the triumphal visits Perry and August, Jr., used to make when Raymond was just a child. They had been so impressive: college men on holiday. The house had been so festive. Now, the fourth son back from school, he was welcomed without any special fuss; and on Christmas morning he and Oliver woke early and spent half an hour hunting for stockings, until they finally realized that "Santa Claus had left us out."

After his freedom during the past months Raymond found living with his parents hard. When he returned to 109 Fifth Avenue from an illegal New Jersey cockfight, he was closely questioned about where he had been and what he had been doing. Invoking his independence and dignity, he refused to answer. He enjoyed being with Oliver, who was beginning to be a good friend; together they raced sleighs through Central Park. But even Oliver's company did not compensate Raymond for the feeling that his days with his father and mother were ledgers that would be examined to make sure his time had been well invested.

A shooting expedition to Forked River, about halfway down the New Jersey coast from New York to Cape May, was a relief from his parents' scrutiny. Raymond and some friends shot a few quail; met two Frenchmen, brothers, who gave them homemade wine to sample; and visited the house of one of the locals. They arrived with bottles of beer and champagne under their arms, which they thought was a Forked River custom and which their new friends in Forked River thought was a New York City custom. After playing Authors they started a more serious card game: poker for forfeits, each forfeit a kiss.

"Then the fun began," Raymond said, "for we kissed the girls rabbit fashion, frog fashion, Chinese fashion, and every way that can be imagined; besides which we also 'crossed the cedar swamp,' 'gathered grapes,' and performed various other feats."

For his partner Raymond got the prettiest girl in the room, "a perfect beauty, tall, a stunning figure, and a mole on her upper lip just in the right place."

One of his friends was unlucky and for his partner got an old lady.

"Besides her ugliness," Raymond said, "it must have been doubly hard for the barkeeper remarked to me the next morning, 'It's too bad about the poor old lady, for she's a very nice woman, and it's only that catarrh that makes her breath so bad.' "

It seemed as though Oliver and Raymond treated nothing seriously, while Perry and August, Jr., treated everything seriously. Just as Oliver's fecklessness annoyed and Raymond's charmed, August, Jr.'s earnestness annoyed and Perry's at least commanded respect. Raymond and Perry ostensibly did not take either their pleasure or work personally; Oliver and August, Jr., did.

August, Jr., could not help feeling as though others were quick to take advantage of him. When F. Gray Griswold, the master of the Queen's County Hunt, strayed over the line into the Meadowbrook Hunt's territory, August, Jr., a founding member of Meadowbrook, reacted as though he had been assaulted. Confusing lack of tact with honesty, he was outspoken in his indignation.

"I hear you have made some remarks about my being unsportsmanlike," Griswold wrote to him. "I wish when you have anything disagreeable to say that you would come and say it to me and not behind my back."

August, Jr., immediately sent an angry letter to Griswold, detailing his complaints. Other members of the Meadowbrook Hunt—particularly Colonel William Jay, the club's vice-president, and Elliot Roosevelt—regretted August, Jr.'s rash and short-tempered defense of their territory. Feeling betrayed, August, Jr., attacked Jay and Roosevelt. When the rest of the club sided with them, August, Jr., apologized and then resigned both his stewardship and membership.

Frank Appleton congratulated August, Jr., for "what I and others must consider manly conduct" and granted that given the circumstances August, Jr.'s continued service as steward was impossible; but he warned that he would "oppose accepting your resignation as to membership. No one wants you to leave the club, and this unfortunate affair must be treated as a nightmare." He asked August, Jr., to withdraw his membership resignation.

August, Jr., refused.

Appleton placed the two resignations before the Meadowbrook Hunt's other stewards, who unanimously accepted August, Jr.'s apologies and his stewardship resignation but unanimously asked him to recall his membership resignation, since, as Appleton said in an official letter, "the board would be loath to entertain that."

"I don't believe you could be other than pleased with the feelings of the men on the board," Appleton added in a personal note he sent the same day. "Outsiders must be informed of the board's action, but I think and earnestly hope that the matter is of the past. I have acted as we all have from a feeling of necessity which has been anything but agreeable."

"You must not feel unhappy and friendless," Roosevelt wrote to August, Jr. "I am so delighted for old friendship's sake to be able to say that, after our talk yesterday and your letter, we can be just as before. Augie, I said you were a brave man and not afraid of acknowledging a mistake."

But within a year August, Jr.'s imperiousness got him in trouble again; the old quarrel was resurrected; and August, Jr., claiming the new tensions should have nothing to do with the previous "unfortunate affair," said, "if I did not atone sufficiently already for a half dozen hasty words, my friends are hard to please."

Both August, Jr., and Perry acted out of conviction; yet while August, Jr., often seemed to be defending his dignity, Perry seemed to be less concerned with what others thought of him than he was with his success in getting others to do what he wanted them to do. And what he wanted them to do was what he felt was best for the general good. His manner may have been abrasive, but he used it to smooth rough spots in the country's policies. Even his enemies admitted that his motives were above reproach.

Mistaking the trust created by honesty with the trust inspired by intimacy, people who had never met Perry wrongly assumed that he was easily approachable; and they flooded him with petitions for appointments, some of which Perry thought were "fantastic. . . . One active Democrat selected the legation at Rio de Janeiro as his particular reward for long activity in village politics. When the appointment was refused him, he considered that Cleveland's election had had negligible results," Perry recollected. "A woman living on Great South Bay asked to have her husband immediately appointed keeper of the Fire Island Light . . . because he was always too much about the house."

Disappointed with Perry's lack of enthusiasm for their causes, these office seekers may have been disgruntled; but most people thought Perry fair. In admiration for his political conduct a town in North Carolina and later an abbey located there were named after him.

During his third term Perry enhanced his reputation for principled if occasionally wrongheaded stands. He fought to increase the size of the navy and to defend United States waters against incursions by Canadian fishermen. When one hundred and fifty striking white miners at Rock Springs in Wyoming territory attacked their nonstriking Chinese coworkers, killing ten, wounding many more, and burning and looting their homes, Perry led the movement to pay the Chinese government an indemnity for the outrage. Undoubtedly he felt a historic and familial tie with the Orient because of his grandfather's mission to Japan. (Later he worked to reduce the immigration of poor Chinese into the United States. Although he was just when confronted with criminal activity against the Chinese immigrants, he apparently was culture-bound enough to feel that their presence had been a provocation.) He introduced a bill to base consular appointments on civil service examinations, the country presumably gaining in efficiency what it lost in cozy informality as posts were filled as a result of grades received instead of gifts given—or so Perry hoped. And, afraid of entanglements that might lead to war with European powers, he continued to oppose American involvement in a Berlin conference on the status of the Congo, a battle in which he was supported by the new President, who ended United States participation in the conference.

Cleveland sought Perry's opinion about various senators and representatives, "hardly any of whom were personally known to him," Perry later said. "I was somewhat surprised to discover how great was his lack of familiarity with national leaders of the Democratic Party." Cleveland sued for Perry's favor—inviting him to the White House, endorsing his suggestions for appointments—with a fervor no president had ever exhibited in appealing to August. Perry was like the man in the story Mark Twain would write almost a decade later, who because he had a £1 million note had virtually unlimited credit. His political influence to some extent was based on respect and fear of the politican he might one day become—all of which does not deny his real achievements.

In 1885 Perry was made chairman of the House Committee on Foreign Affairs, which infuriated the man being replaced so much that he quit the committee and refused any other appointment. The following year Perry squared his political miracle by being elected to a fourth consecutive term in a district where no one had ever served more than two.

Although pleased by Perry's victory, August was in general so disappointed by the off-year elections of 1886 that he wrote to Joseph Pulitzer:

"*À qui la faute?* Certainly not the rank and file of a great political party."

Years before when August had been politically powerful he had been inclined to trust the party leaders over the people; now, out of power, he was inclined to trust the people over the party leaders. Lack of influence had made him a better democrat.

In cultivating Pulitzer—dining with him, getting wine for his cellar, praising his wife as being "so much like Mrs. William Waldorf Astor when she was at her loveliest"—August was trying to cast Pulitzer, the current owner of the *New York World*, into the role played by Marble, the former owner. This attempt at friendship, like the return to racing represented by the Lexington stud, was a way of trying to recapture the past.

But August was a sculptor attempting to mold live clay; the present would not shape itself to the past. Although flattered by August's attention, Pulitzer did not become a close friend; and when in 1886 August reserved the directors' car of a railroad and went for the first time to see his Lexington stud, he was disappointed in that too—particularly since he had given up on both the Nursery and Oakland (which he finally sold, to a Vanderbilt for only $15,000). The past cannot be recaptured by mimicry.

"I was a fool," August said. "I made an ass of myself by going back to races."

He felt "old and very shaky." After recovering from an illness he still was not "quite right. It is the first time in my life that it has taken me so long to recuperate," he said. "I don't expect ever to see the day again when I am fully restored to strength and health."

He joked about his apprehension that his family did not appreciate him:

"Though I am a dreadful father, I will pay Oliver's and Perry's initiation fees and their year's dues to the Union Club." And he asked

August, Jr., "as a particular favor not to write [in his letters] anything disagreeable."

He did not want to hear about how one of their house cats, Ned, had been killed by one of August, Jr.'s dogs.

"Ned was such a beauty," August said, "and in his ways more like a pet dog than a cat."

He did not want to know about August, Jr.'s polo games.

"My opinion in regard to polo for a man who has a wife and child continues to be the same as before," he said, "especially when he takes the additional risk of following the hounds."

Most of all he did not want August, Jr. to differ with him about anything important, since he no longer had the energy or confidence—and certainly could not depend on his "poor old memory"—to hold his own against his son in any disagreement.

"I have *as usual* yielded my wishes to yours," August typically said in one conflict that year.

However, he resented his son for winning so many arguments; so when he was sure of his ground, August pounced.

"I cannot understand," August told August, Jr., "how you can still pretend that you were right and that you claim you would have won if I had bet."

Determined to prove his point, August even sought support from Oliver, who had been present during the initial discussion of the matter. And he was not above stooping to using his age to advantage: Weakness playing on compassion or guilt can be a powerful weapon. He said: "I consider it (and this I say in all kindness) a very questionable procedure to contradict an old man."

August had become so irritable that once, when he told August, Jr., that he was going to arrive for a visit earlier than they had agreed, he added, "Don't be alarmed. I shall try to be meek and patient and not worry others and make them unhappy whatever my own feelings may be."

His pleasures were few. He loved to take care of his grandson when August, Jr., and Caroline went on trips. He was tickled by how August III, on being given a telegram from his parents, "kept hold of it." He also liked August III's inquisitiveness, how he "must always know whom Caroline has been to see" once she returned from making calls. And he spent hours in Central Park watching a servant push August III on a sled through the snow.

He was proud of Raymond, who despite his carousing graduated "quite high" in his Harvard class and who was going on to study law at Columbia University. And not the least among his pleasures were his boars and pigs, which had among the best bloodlines in the country, and the trout and strawberries that he could not resist eating despite their effect on his digestion.

Toward the end of 1886 August fell down the stairs at 109 Fifth Avenue and was bedridden for weeks. With the egoism of the very young, the very old, and the very sick he projected his state onto the world, finding everywhere signs of disaster and decay. War, he was certain, was about to engulf Europe. In the United States, if the socialists did not take over the government, the monopolists would. Cleveland, betraying the Democrats, was truckling to the Republicans. New York City was filthier and more crowded than ever before. Slums had spread: the Jewish ghetto, where young men, caught between the orthodoxy of the Old World and the swagger of the New, wore derbies like yarmulkes and yarmulkes like derbies; Little Italy, where families used to the mild climates of Naples and Sicily spread into the streets during the summers (with what seemed to the old New Yorkers a lack of modesty) and went crazy in dark, airless, crowded tenements during winters that seemed to them endless; Chinatown with its rumors of opium dens, secret passageways, and underground labyrinths; Little Hungary with its candlelit tables at out-door cafés; and the Levant, where the streets smelled of spices, cooking lamb, and freshly ground coffee.

There were other slums that seemed to reproduce streets in not Europe or Asia but Hell: Mulberry Bend where packs of ragged, half-naked children slogged through foot-deep muck; the brothels on Thompson and Bleecker streets, where twelve- and thirteen-year-old girls worked with the blank professionalism that comes from never having considered any other possible life; the Gashouse district between Fourteenth and Twenty-seventh streets and First Avenue to the East River, where gangs of hoodlums prowled in the stench from the gas-tank leaks; Hell's Kitchen between Twenty-third and Fortieth streets and Seventh Avenue to the Hudson River, where other gangs prowled in the stink from the slaughterhouses; Corcoran's Roost, a shanty-and-tenement kingdom around East Fortieth Street with fiercely loyal subjects; and the Upper East Side between 96th and 125th streets and Lexington Avenue to the

East River. Here, where the Knickerbockers used to summer, was now one of the most sinister neighborhoods in the city, with the mists coming off the river and swirling around the trestle of the El.

Even August's New York, the world of the rich, was increasingly unfamiliar. Overshadowed by the Met, the Academy of Music was giving up opera. Theaters along the Rialto—Broadway between Madison Square and Forty-second Street—were lit with new incandescent lamps. Bartenders used noisy and vulgar cash registers. Businesses used equally noisy and vulgar typewriters. Everything seemed false. Actresses had press agents to promote them. Journalists, interested only in the sensational, distorted the news. Everyone, rich or poor, seemed morbidly obsessed with social position. New York no longer had time for the grace that August recalled from his early years in the city—although he forgot that when he was young the old Knickerbockers he used to mock had had the same complaints.

Newport had changed as much as New York. Like New York it had become crowded and its tempo had changed. Everyone seemed so desperate to have a good time, so competitive, and so formally casual. Almost every August morning, shortly before eleven o'clock, the first carriages would roll onto the beach in front of the yellow-painted casino, precipitating the flight of the Antiques.

"The Antiques are a queer collection of old ladies who come from nobody knows where . . . ," said *The New York Times*. "They wear bathing suits consisting of . . . horrible straw hats . . . , coats, . . . and knee breeches . . . made from bed ticking, a faded sofa cover, an old crazy quilt, or anything else that has no particular value. . . . They wear no stockings. Ugly? They are the ugliest things in the whole realm of zoology. . . . If one of them should come within the luminous circle of an electric light at night, the light would flare up wildly and then go out. They disappear . . . like witches . . . before the fairies come out."

After eleven o'clock the fairies, Newport's best society, rolled up in greater and greater numbers until the entire beach was crowded with carriages, the bright sun flashing off the polished wood, oiled leather, and silver of the tack. Men in white flannel and straw hats strolled from vehicle to vehicle; one of them might stop and, resting his foot on a wheel spoke, banter with a woman who according to custom had stayed in her carriage.

Most of the bathers who actually went into the water were middle-class. The socialites in the carriages tried to ignore them; and when they could not, they deplored them. Especially offensive were the women who did not wear stockings.

No one in August's set seemed to swim for the sake of refreshment as people had when August first summered in Newport. Even such a simple sport had become a battleground of competing social egos. There was so little fun in it, in everything, in life.

But who knew what fun was anymore?

Because of recent legislation, alcohol was outlawed in Newport—officially, that is. The cottagers "provided their own bottles," said the *New York Daily Tribune*. But chic women, bored with liquor and wine, did not care about the ban since the fashionable intoxicants were chloroform and chloral hydrate, chloroform being slightly more in vogue.

The resort was no longer a place to escape pressure but one to increase it. Even here privacy, that rock upon which life was built, was threatened. The telephone recently had come to Newport as it was coming everywhere with its surprising and unignorable demands. And it was as awkward to invade someone else's life as it was to have your own life invaded. Caroline, who had installed one of the first telephones in Newport, once called Thomas Cushing, who kept his telephone in his bathroom. At the ring Cushing leapt naked from the tub where he had been soaking and grabbed the receiver; but when he heard and recognized Caroline's voice, he said:

"Oh dear, I'm so sorry. I'm frightfully ashamed. I don't know how I can express—"

And dropping the receiver, he bolted for a bathrobe.

The new society dominating the resort appalled August as much as, decades before, he with his servants, balls, and dinners used to appall the Old Newport residents. But he would not abandon Newport. Family ties, the Perrys, had brought him to Newport; family ties would keep him there: Newport was where Jeannie was buried.

In November 1886 August, in honor of his daughter's memory, began building a memorial chapel in the Island Cemetery. No wood—except for the roof, domes, and around the windows, August ordered. Almost the entire structure, *The New York Times* reported, would be made of "a reddish brown sandstone from the Carlisle quarries in Springfield, Massachusetts." August wanted the chapel to last.

❦ *CHAPTER SIXTY-SIX* ❦

ON JANUARY 30, 1887, Raymond dined at the Knickerbocker Club with a friend from Boston; ran into his brother August, Jr., who thought him "well and cheerful"; and left relatively early. He arrived at 109 Fifth Avenue between twelve-thirty and one o'clock in the morning and according to one account "went direct to his room," where he "rang for the inside night watchman," told him that he "felt like having a little pistol practice," and asked for the guard's five-barrel .32 caliber pistol. "This was a common practice" of his, the report continued. Raymond followed the night watchman to the laundry, where the gun was hidden.

According to another account Raymond returned home in the company of "A private watchman, Leonard Behr, who is employed in the neighborhood" but not at 109 Fifth Avenue. Raymond "told Behr a story that something was wrong in the house and asked him to . . . help. . . . Behr consented, and they went inside. It is supposed that this story was given as a pretext to get Behr to go into the Belmont mansion, but the young man's reason for doing this is not known."

The two versions of that evening's events meet in the subcellar where Raymond led his companion (who, because the second version seems more authorative, probably was Behr, not the Belmonts' indoor night watchman). Raymond poked about for a few minutes "as if trying to find something that was causing trouble" and then asked if Behr had "good nerve."

Behr said yes.

"I am a pretty good shot with a revolver," Raymond said, plucking either a gold or pearl stud from his own shirt, "and I think I could hit a button between your fingers from across the cellar without hurting you. Will you let me try it?"

Hoping Raymond was joking, Behr said he was too fond of his fingers to risk losing them and suggested that Raymond shoot at the coal bin instead.

Raymond asked Behr to close the cellar door, because a draft was bothering him. Behr climbed the stairs. As he shut the door he heard a shot. Rushing down, he found Raymond "with blood and portions of his brain issuing from a hole in the right side of his head."

Behr called the outside watchman, who ran off to the New York Hospital. Rousing the other servants, he sent two to get Dr. William M.

Polk, the family physician, and another doctor, Morris J. Asch. Only then did Behr tell August, who, "completely prostrated" by the shock, "was unable to leave his room."

The police were not called until three o'clock in the morning.

Raymond was dead.

Perhaps, in Behr's presence, Raymond had said or done something of which he was so ashamed that in desperation he killed himself. Perhaps, as special editions of some New York newspapers suggested, he had been drunk. Or perhaps, as August claimed, Raymond simply had had an accident. Those who knew Raymond said that he "always turned the barrel of a pistol toward his head before taking sight."

"He was an expert horseman and a good shot," said William F. ("Buffalo Bill") Cody, a family friend, who had been expecting both Raymond and Oliver to visit his Nebraska ranch at the end of February.

But rumors continued to spread.

"I have just seen the unkind article of the *New York World*'s extra edition," August telegraphed Joseph Pulitzer some hours after Raymond's death. "My son was perfectly sober, as both the private watchman and the coroner testify."

"Coroner's inquest establishes conclusively that my poor boy's death was accidental," he said in a second telegram to Pulitzer. "The extra edition of your paper, selling in the streets does great wrong to his memory and is most cruel to his bereaved family."

To make sure the *New York Sun* did not pick up the scandalous version of Raymond's death, August, Jr., contacted its editor's son, Paul Dana, who answered that "of course your father's wishes would be respected and any unnecessary and unjustifiable theories will be guarded against. The edition of the *Sun* this morning describes your brother's death as accidental."

By the time Caroline and Perry, who both had been in Washington, D.C., reached New York, the rumors were, at least publicly, under control. When Pulitzer expressed his condolences, August responded, "I can only find strength for a line," and thanked him "from the bottom of my heart. It is a frightful blow, and I dread its effect upon my poor wife, whose pet Raymond was. God help her and me."

In the following days August, Jr., held the family together. He wrote to Raymond's friends at the Porcellian Club in Cambridge to make sure his brother's debts were paid and to have his effects—"quite a number of odd things, such as medals," said one of Raymond's friends, Charles Carroll—shipped to New York.

"The men in the club who knew him so well have but little heart for the February dinner, which will occur next week, as it will be full of sad memories," Carroll said. "There will be a vacancy at the table for me as long as I live and return here. Every chair and corner of the club is so connected with him in my mind."

When August, Jr., asked if there were any photographs of Raymond at the club, Carroll said, "Raymond never had many formal photographs taken, although he figured in a great many informal shots taken by fellows in the club who knew how to photograph." Raymond had been gregarious in life, so it was appropriate that in death his image would be preserved in group photographs. "I received a letter yesterday that he wrote to me when I was in England and which had just been sent over to me," Carroll added; "it was full of life and hope for this Winter."

Because of its delay the letter seemed like an incongruous message from the grave, a traveler's assurance that he had arrived safely and was settled happily in his new surroundings.

Raymond's funeral was held in the memorial chapel in Newport that August had built for Jeannie but that now was dedicated to both of his dead children. The service was crowded, but only the family accompanied the dark-blue casket to the cemetery.

As she had done before, Caroline sought escape from despair in Europe, which, however, had become for her more a symbol than a source of solace. She traveled because she could not bear to stay in America, not because she expected any relief. Drawn to her past she visited The Hague and was "rather disappointed with the old place." At Spa, she "took comfort" in long walks and drank "in small doses" of the waters that seemed to dilute her grief, "doing me good," she said. But she did not enjoy the resort because it "has changed, grown larger, and is crowded with Belgians." And her memory kept resurrecting the dead.

"I was very happy in years gone by," she told August, Jr., "when my children, *six* in all then, were here with your father and me."

She regretted, she told August, Jr., that she would not be "with you all to commemorate the birthday of our lost darling [Raymond]. It will be a trial for me when on the 19th July I shall find myself separated from the family and so far away from the spot where my sweet boy and darling Jeannie are laid and where you all will be congregated. The little chapel will look lovely, I know." She sent a memorial ribbon "for my dear Dolly," and she asked August, Jr., to place "a bunch of my geraniums" on Jeannie's grave. For Raymond she wanted geraniums mixed with pansies. "I don't care to have the bunches very large," she said. Raymond and Jeannie "were so dear, so young," she added; "when I think of how those two loved me, I can't help feeling that my cross is hard to bear; but I struggle with myself for the sake of all that is still left to me and try to be thankful."

Raymond's death disoriented August. Survival was loneliness. Old age was like the end of a party. One by one the guests leave. Charles O'Conor and Augustus Schell had died a few years before. Horatio Seymour, John Kelly, and Samuel Tilden had died the previous year. In March 1887, two months after Raymond's death, William Travers, who had gone to Bermuda for his health, began to fail. When someone with the insincerity of those who visit the dying tried to make optimistic small talk by saying that Bermuda was "a nice place for rest and change," Travers said:

"Y-y-yes, th-the waiters g-g-get th-th-the ch-change and th-the h-h-hotel k-k-keepers get th-the r-r-rest."

He died on March 19.

The other members of the old Belmont Clique, those who were not already dead, soon would follow Travers. They were all getting indecently old, hanging around, diehards who refused to admit that the party was over. Leonard Jerome, tall and bony, had become a virtual spectre haunting the Madison Club, which had been his own house before he had lost his fortune. And August. . . .

August had no illusions about himself: like Jerome he should have died long ago, when he could have made a dashing exit. At August's clubs the rooms were filled with new faces, his sons' generation. August even had trouble getting up whist games; now everyone played euchre.

In the summer of 1887 August III fell ill; apparently the doctor feared tuberculosis.

"Can I assist in any way?" August asked August, Jr.

The doctor urged August, Jr., and Bessie to take their son to Colorado or Switzerland. August recommended the south of France or the north of Italy; he did not trust doctors. And he urged August, Jr., to take advantage of the trip to enjoy himself. When they visited Paris, August,

Jr., should take August III to visit Rosa Bonheur, the painter, since "it will be a treat for August [III] to see her studio." Although she was "somewhat brusque," she was "a very understanding and nice person; and, as she has always been very fond of me, she will, I am sure, give you a cordial reception."

Because he did not want to leave the business, August, Jr., was hesitant to go with his wife and son.

"You could be of as much use for the House in Europe as in the United States," August reminded him.

August, Jr., agreed.

In England he found that doing business with the Paris branch of the House of Rothschild had had the expected effect on the London branch, whose members he found "loyal, kind, and very friendly." Nathaniel in particular "was truly and sincerely friendly to me personally apart from my mission," August, Jr., told his father, "and so were the clerks with whom we have to deal," including August's old nemesis Lorent, who was "very jealous of the Paris office. We will have a strong ally in him."

Without being "too pressing in my questions"—"I make them at intervals and then put the answers together"—August, Jr., tried to ascertain the current European reputation of August Belmont & Company. Carl Mayer Rothschild reported that Gerson von Bleichröder, the German banker, recently had snapped:

"We can do without Belmont."

Nathaniel thought that "perhaps Bleichröder expected more attention shown to his sons when they were in America."

August, Jr., told his father he "only listened and let that observation pass without going into a discussion about it."

Nathaniel also warned August, Jr., about how "hard" the Paris Rothschilds "are to do business with. If you write them long letters about cotton, petroleum stock, and Lord knows what and keep writing, they'll do business with you and will be very glad to," a useful tip, since as August Belmont & Company's relations with the London branch had improved, its relations with the Paris branch had deteriorated.

"The Paris House is not so kind," August, Jr., told his father, "and the reasons are many. The thing has to be fought inch by inch."

Keeping on good terms with both sets of Rothschilds was as tricky as straddling the middle of a seesaw that was being rocked by two vigorous children.

Gustave de Rothschild, of course, did not admit that August Belmont & Company's increased business with his English cousins had anything to do with his coolness toward United States investments. The French Rothschilds had "lost heavily in America in 1884," August, Jr., told his father; "and I could see by Gustave's conversation that he was sure that during all that decline we kept them very poorly informed."

Prompted by August, Jr.'s reports, August sent a cable that apparently placated Gustave, who grew warmer and more cordial. Edmond was even friendlier and more candid.

"He himself had great respect for tradition," August, Jr., told August, "and would like to see business done with us and added that he knew the heads of the House here were anxious to find a way back to activity with us. But he went on to say that he thought the partners here probably thought we hardly cared to work hard at business, that we had grown very rich and indifferent to the necessary efforts." From what he could learn, August, Jr., continued, this impression was generally held all over Europe—and, he added, the impression was correct.

"The grass has been allowed to grow under our feet a dangerously long time," he said, "and I feel a little doubtful with the short time before me of straightening out the difficulties. I know what we require at home. I can see that in every word of the discussions, whether with the heads of the houses or the clerks. We are not alive enough and do not work for our business sufficiently." August Belmont & Company could not ride piggyback on other houses. It had to lead as it used to and "maintain its individuality" in any joint venture that "might be contemplated," like the investment in Venezuelan rubber the Paris House had suggested. And it had to compete with new, hungrier, more aggressive firms, which meant that August would have to "consent to doing business, at times, for little or nothing. If we are shrewd and make some sacrifices, we can squeeze out the newer companies and gradually regain our lost ground." As for "stock gambling," August, Jr., added, "we can talk about that later."

August, Jr., doubted that August "can meet my views. But," he assured his father, "they are not wild. They are according to the requirements of the times." The "vastness of modern commerce and the immense fortunes being constantly accumulated attest the possibility of making money." One simply had to do business in the present. "The methods and kinds of trade" had changed, and "a house must change with them." August Belmont & Company had to modernize.

"On some subjects," August, Jr., told his father, "you must let me say it. You are very antiquated in your notions and go on the mistaken basis that it is only 'that miserable American way' of doing business, which differs from yours. You are quite as much out of time with European methods as with our own, and I must say that I think we have a little of that reputation abroad of *étants arrivés*. You will say I find a great deal of fault with ourselves, but all I can say is that if you were going into the subject as I am here, with your greater experience and business training, you would probably find much more."

August doubted that. And he distrusted August, Jr.'s analysis, no doubt wanted to distrust it. How could his son, who was just starting his career, pass judgment on him—who had just celebrated the anniversary of his fiftieth year in business? How could August, Jr., say he was not changing with the times? He was considering investing in a new underground railroad that was being planned for New York City. He simply did not want to take any risks. As he said when August, Jr., was flirting with one particularly doubtful deal:

"The name of Belmont must not be jeopardized."

However unwilling he was to admit that August, Jr., was right, August still was too good a businessman not to realize how bad a businessman he had become. Finally he confessed his "judgement has ceased to be of any use," and he agreed "fully" with August, Jr., about the problems facing the company. He suggested that August, Jr., find in Berlin or Frankfurt—"especially," he said, "in Frankfurt," where he had started his career—"some clever reliable German who knows English and German"— as he had when he was a boy—"and is fully equipped in regard to arbitrage," the specialty for which August had been famous. August wanted to find himself as a young man.

Leaving Bessie and his son in Europe, August, Jr., returned to New York to find his father trying very hard to be accommodating.

"I am always willing and anxious to do safe and pleasant business," he told August, Jr., *"and still more to please you in order to prove to you my confidence and affection."*

He was trying equally hard to maintain his dignity.

"Don't say that I am sick . . . ," he told August, Jr.

But it must have been obvious that he was sick. He almost never went into society anymore. He was at the office less and less frequently. And, after having been reelected as president and director of the Jockey Club, he resigned. He must have felt that there was no point in trying to pretend that he would ever be an active force on the track again, and he dwelled even more than before on the past, often recalling, for example, the race "of the century" between Kingfisher and Longfellow.

At the end of 1887 he had a wine-cellar report made up of "sundries remaining in the storeroom": 6,501 bottles of wine and liquor, more than 30 gallons of Commodore Perry's special Madeira, about 10 gallons of President Buchanan's special Madeira (from 1816), and 17 gallons of two other Madeiras from early in the century. He had always been a list maker, but his interest in cataloguing his possessions had become intense, as though he were desperately taking an inventory in preparation for a trip.

He was disappointed in his children and felt that, as August, Jr., had said three years before, the stones were dropping out of the family structure. Although Perry had made a reputation in Congress, his career had become—as the *New York Sun* quoted Perry as saying—"an expensive luxury." Perry later disclaimed that remark, but August apparently agreed with its sentiments, because, as Perry told Marble:

"My father is unwilling to give me an allowance sufficient for me to run again."

Perry, who had been traveling on vacation in Europe, was not unhappy with his father's decision. He wanted to "avoid all connection, direct or indirect, with the politics of my district this Autumn," he told his father. "I feel that I have other and better things to live for than those Congressional life can bring to me. I cannot tell you how anxious I am to get clear of all the detestable people I have had to deal with in that district and how glad I shall be to be done with it all."

Perry felt he had been badly used. One incident in particular became representative of all the painful humiliations that he had been forced to put up with in order not to alienate potential supporters. A political acquaintance named Hinckley had conned Perry into cosigning a loan for $15,000, which Perry when Hinckley defaulted had to pay. Like all of August's children Perry was kept on a tight allowance, so he had to ask his father for help. August agreed to cover $11,000 if Hinckley would take care of $4,000. Hinckley agreed but delayed and eventually asked Perry to cosign a second loan for $4,000, presumably so he could pay off his share of the first loan. Perry trustingly obliged, only to be stuck once more. Abashed, he again went to his father.

"Were it not for this unfortunate thing," Perry told August, "I would now be in the position I have so long wished for—clear of money troubles and not giving you pain." The whole affair, which went on for two years, was maddening. At one point he told August, "There must be an end of such use of my name, which, in fact, is *yours*."

Frederika, too, gave August cause for worry. She had been fighting with Mrs. Astor (the woman who had inherited Caroline's position as leader of New York's society). Mrs. Astor made her hostility to the Belmonts unignorable when she became godmother of Oliver's disowned daughter. At last, bored with and feeling superior to the struggle for social domination, Frederika abdicated any claim she, as Caroline's daughter, might have had to the social crown. She and Sam spent more and more time abroad, leaving Mrs. Astor to worry about how to make an exclusive society even more exclusive.

Oliver long ago had been lost to frivolity. Ever since his divorce he had aimlessly played. He had no ambition, few prospects, and felt no compunction about putting off any decision about his future career while he went for a year-long cruise to the Mediterranean on William K. Vanderbilt's new luxury yacht, the *Alva*. The ship, named for Vanderbilt's wife, was—at 285 feet long and 32 feet wide—the largest steam yacht in America. It had a reception room; a dining room with a piano; a library with a skylight and fireplace; a ten-room suite for Vanderbilt's family; and seven guest rooms, each with a canopy bed and private bathroom— as well as quarters for its fifty-three-man crew including a doctor, three cooks, and a man to work an ice maker. At a stopover in Monte Carlo, Oliver gambled more than August would have wished.

"He says that he lost at roulette," Caroline, who had gotten a rare letter from him, reported to August, "and that *33* had deserted him, that it would no longer be his lucky number."

But Oliver explained that "the last night I was there on the wheel's last spin of the evening, I said to myself, 'I'll try my old *33* and see if it has really forsaken me.' I backed it and won all I had lost during my whole stay and 1,500 francs to the good. So my faith is still in *33*."

During the trip Oliver and Alva Vanderbilt developed an affection for each other that was obvious by the time the yacht returned to New York in April 1888. August could well have feared that his son was about to become involved in a second divorce scandal.

Even August, Jr., the steadiest of the children, continued to get into so many controversies that August despaired of his ever being at peace with the world. August, Jr., tried to curb his temper and learn not to take himself so seriously. In chiding a friend who had gotten angry over a hunting matter, he admitted, "I am the last man to talk to another about flying off the handle." But no matter how hard he tried he could not avoid fights, which in his mind almost always—even the most trivial—became heroic struggles against dishonor.

On March 12, 1888, New York was hit by a blizzard that was the worst in the city's history and would keep that distinction for nearly a century. For three days the storm blew. Drifts piled up as high as a man. Telegraph and telephone poles toppled; communication was cut. One New Yorker's horse plowed out of the stable "on her hind legs," he said. "Under the evergreen tree she lunged, leaving the top of my buggy hanging in its branches. There it hung for three days." When the weather finally cleared, the city was paralyzed and muffled. New York was like the mind of a man suffering from amnesia: A few prominent landmarks remained, but almost all detail was gone.

As though the blizzard had blanked out the city's feuds as well as its features, four days later August, who had fought Tilden nearly all of his political life, was one of the friends and admirers of the late governor who gave a portrait of Tilden to the State of New York. Age, like politics, makes strange bedfellows.

Within a month August became reconciled with another political opponent, Roscoe Conkling, who having been caught out in the storm had fallen ill. August called on him and offered to send some wine to cheer him up.

"The wine," wrote Conkling after August had left, "yes. I shall like that very much for several reasons. Your visit has been a fragrant and consoling recollection."

The letter, which was the last Conkling would write to anyone, contained a few other rambling thoughts. He ended by promising, "When my senses return, if they ever do, I'll come to correct the shambles of this."

A few months later Allen G. Thurman, one of the Democratic party's greenback heretics, told August that, "No man living has rendered to his party so much service as you have" and admitted that "the very fact you took charge of the organization at a time when there was none other who would run the personal risk or could afford the expense seems to be the very reason why you in the hour of Democratic success are being ignored, except by a few who remembered the past and who looked to the future."

August was making friends with former enemies almost as often as he was making enemies of former friends.

August had been so much out of the public eye that when people spoke of him, as Ward McAllister did in an interview early that spring, they tended to eulogize him as though he were already dead.

"You see," said McAllister (who now—through Mrs. Astor—controlled New York Society), "there were not so many millionaires in those days [before 1873, when the Patriarchs started], and few people were spending their incomes. One of those was Mr. Belmont. I suppose he expended $60,000 or $70,000 a year on parties. He kept a chef at $60 or $70 a month, which was thought exorbitant in those days. . . . Mr. Travers used to be a princely entertainer and almost rivalled Mr. Belmont in hospitality. . . . I can remember some brilliant affairs when men like Belmont and Travers entertained."

However, August was not too moribund for McAllister to try to get his support for a ball he was throwing to spite some other social faction. But August declined to subscribe, "as I certainly prefer the good will of [those McAllister was trying to snub] to McAllister's," said August. McAllister was the symbol of the predatory social climbing August hated; and August even in retirement was one of the few wealthy New Yorkers, men or women, who dared cross McAllister—and could get away with it.

On the last day of May 1888 Bessie gave birth to another boy, whom she and August, Jr., named Raymond after August, Jr.'s dead brother. Weakened by the delivery, Bessie got sick. August, Jr., decided to send August III away—perhaps to visit Frederika, who was spending the summer in the mountains. Caroline thought that "an excellent idea." The mountain air "will brace him up before he comes here" to Bythesea. "This is a grand place for children," she added. Although Caroline preferred traveling by train, for memory's sake she suggested that August III come to Newport by boat.

"You remember that as a child you always came by that route," she wrote to August, Jr.

She and August looked forward to their grandson's arrival. He would fill their days. When they were alone they rarely went out except to walk along the cliffs or put flowers on Jeannie's and Raymond's graves. They tried to "get back home before the crowd begins to appear on the avenue," said Caroline. "I feel as if I did not want to meet anyone."

Except for family they needed no one else's company.

"We get along nicely in our quiet way together," Caroline said; ". . . by half past nine o'clock, we are ready to go to bed."

Later that summer August, Jr., and Bessie came to Bythesea for a month so that Bessie could rest, as Caroline said, "free of household cares." and August, Jr., could go fox hunting—which, possibly to counter growing public criticism, was advertised as a democratic sport.

"The poorest and the humblest resident is as welcome to the hunts as are the Astors, Vanderbilts, Belmonts, . . . Whitings, and others who are well up in the 'four hundred' . . . ," said a newspaper.

The first hunt of the season was rained out, so its democratic pretensions were not tested. In the second hunt, which was crowded, the rich rode and the poor walked. The humblest residents of Newport were welcome not to participate but to watch.

The attacks on hunting reminded August of the early attacks on racing. Hunting was European, aristocratic, un-American. Because the equipment involved was so expensive it reinforced class barriers. When later that year August, Jr., and some of his friends started a coursing club on Long Island, the public howled after them as viciously as the club members' dogs chased the rabbits. August, Jr., and "several of his assistants" were charged with cruelty to animals; and a *New York Times* headline asked:

"Why not try rats?"

August, Jr., could not understand such hostility. Those who objected to a sport could stay away. But, since the middle class could not join in the sports of the rich, they did not want the rich to enjoy them either. The public was meddlesome. His generation seemed more hampered than his father's had been; and no doubt in his lifetime it would get worse.

August, Jr., was discouraged, overtired, and overworked, trying to modernize August Belmont & Company and taking care of the financial affairs of not only his own family but his Aunt Belle's as well. When August saw how haggard his son looked, he became alarmed.

"Do take care of your health," he told August, Jr. "You cannot give me any greater satisfaction."

August would not be able to survive the loss of another child.

❧ *CHAPTER SIXTY-SEVEN* ❧

ONE FALL DAY IN 1888, August, caught in a crowd, watched a Republican parade pass.

"Their American flags and impudent boasts of being the protection of American labor and shipping," he said, "give me a sad foreboding of the disastrous results of the upcoming presidential election."

A *New York Post* editor asked him to "find an hour's time to write me a long chatty letter on political subjects," which the newspaper would "handsomely break up as a casual conversation with you." And August gave $10,000 to the Democratic National Committee. These involvements aside, he stayed in the background and did not go to the Democratic National Convention. He followed the campaign in newspapers, in whatever gossip he could pick up at his clubs, and in polite but not very informative letters from friends.

Some of the issues were familiar. August still thought "the Democratic Party is crushed between the weight of the billions of the monopolists and money kings and the socialistic heresies preached by unscrupulous demagogues." But other issues had been transformed so much that it seemed as though the politicians were in case after case missing the point—the point August would have made ten or fifteen years earlier. Once in a while August saw the name of an old acquaintance in the newspaper; but the person referred to was a son or nephew of the man August had known. So many politicians were new; for August they were merely names, no longer, as they had been in former days, antagonists or allies.

The Democratic ticket, Cleveland and Thurman, was defeated by the Republican. The president-elect, Benjamin Harrison, was a former Indiana senator, a curt idealist who approached politics as coolly and logically as if it were a branch of mathematics; and the vice-president-elect was Levi P. Morton, whose part in the Chile scandals Perry had exposed five years earlier.

"No American who has pride in his country or its institutions," said Perry, "can contemplate in silence and without protest the alarming possible contingency of a man of so little sensibility as Mr. Morton becoming President of the United States."

"What a fearful defeat we have suffered and how blind our leaders and managers must have been," August wrote to Daniel Sickles, who like August had been one of Buchanan's hot young diplomats in the 1850s. "I fear neither you nor I will ever see a Democratic administration again."

Before the election Cleveland had decided to give Perry a foreign mission —either Belgium, Spain, Chile, or Brazil. Thomas Bayard thought Belgium best, but Cleveland chose Spain. *The New York Times* reported that Perry's friends had said "he has long desired an appointment to a foreign court, that being his first political aspiration." But the *New York Sun* reported that Perry had no intention of applying for any foreign mission. Both were partially right. Perry wanted a mission but not a four-year assignment. His father was too old. Perry did not want to be across the Atlantic Ocean when August died. So he asked that his appointment be held up until after the election.

"If Cleveland had been reelected, I would not have accepted," Perry later explained. "Upon . . . his defeat, I accepted, knowing that my official term would end with the advent of the Republican administration."

When Perry's name was sent to the Senate, John Sherman, the chairman of the Committee on Foreign Relations, proposed that the appointment should be confirmed without sending it into committee. This atypical move would have betrayed more confidence in Perry if Sherman had not at the same time said—as Perry recalled—that he "hoped . . . Perry's instructions were in no way intended to bring about the acquisition of Cuba."

August may have retired from politics, but the ghosts of his political obsessions still haunted Congress.

That October, before Perry left on his diplomatic mission, the family congregated in Newport for the official dedication of the Belmont Memorial Chapel. The service was short: a processional hymn, then three psalms—"Out of the depths have I cried unto Thee, O Lord . . ."; "Lord, who shall abide in Thy tabernacle? . . . He that walketh uprightly. . . . He that backbiteth not. . . ."; "Help, Lord, for the godly man ceaseth; for the faithful fail from among the children of men. . . ." Grim but—August must have felt—appropriate sentiments. "He that backbiteth not"; that would exclude much of New York society. ". . . The faithful fail from among the children of men . . ."; August may well have felt that there was less goodness in the world now than when he had been young. For him, certainly, there was less joy.

The lesson, from Thessalonians, offered consolation: The dead and the living would meet again in Christ, ". . . comfort one another with these words." There was another hymn; responsive reading; a few other rituals—even a short service can seem long to a grieving parent.

When Perry sailed for Madrid in December 1888, Caroline accompanied him. The pomp of court life did not intimidate her as it had three and a half decades earlier when she had arrived at The Hague. And Perry was more impressed by "the complete absence of servility among Spaniards, particularly in small towns and villages," than he was by the pageantry that greeted him as minister. He was content to escape the queen's formal address, which had been canceled because the queen was in mourning over the death of her cousin, Crown Prince Rudolph of Austria, who had committed suicide with his mistress. But of course it was necessary for Perry to be presented at court.

He was called for by "two state carriages and a mounted guard," he said. Apparently on the way he told the official who would guide him through the maze of court etiquette that Mrs. Cleveland had asked for a photograph of the queen. The official doubted that the queen would give him one because, as Perry later explained, "Her unusual and great charm of expression, which was so marked a characteristic, was completely lost in a photograph." However, she and Perry talked for a longer than the usual time for such an occasion; and Perry must have pleased her, for she gave him the photograph for Mrs. Cleveland.

The next day during a military review a soldier fell from his horse and in the inexorable advance of the parade was run over by a gun cart that broke his leg. Perry jumped down, had the injured man lifted into his carriage, and drove him to a field hospital. The queen, who witnessed Perry's gallantry, was impressed. She had an aide-de-camp call Perry over so she could thank him.

Evidently Perry enjoyed being relatively casual—although always correct—within the diplomatic world. If he was not the cowboy in the ballroom he at times had seemed in Berlin in his youth, he still cultivated the American virtues—or liabilities, some thought—of openness and directness. His work did not take up a great deal of time. He was free to read the *Congressional Record*, he told his father, "much more carefully than when I was in Washington." And with Caroline he frequented the opera, which delighted him by being, unlike in America, "a relaxed, almost informal affair.

"Conversations were carried on during the performance in low tones, and were not considered interruptions in any way disrespectful to the artists," he said. "It was like a large drawing-room gathering in which audience and performers were expected to contribute to the general enjoyment." Perry thought "the Queen . . . would have understood" what was meant by a New York lady who once told Perry as the rising curtain of an opera interrupted their conversation:

"What a pity there is so much music."

In March 1889 Benjamin Harrison became President and James G. Blaine, Perry's former antagonist, became secretary of state. A rumor spread that Blaine had been rude to Perry and "very sharply" asked for his resignation. Any rudeness must have been unofficial; officially Blaine said, upon receiving Perry's resignation, that it was "accepted . . . with regret that your voluntary retirement deprives the service of a faithful and competent representative."

Caroline was ready to leave Spain. Oliver's former wife, Sallie, had arrived with her new—and, Caroline thought, "ungentlemanly"—husband, George L. Rives.

"You cannot imagine how unpleasant it is for us," Caroline told August, Jr., although she felt "sorry for Perry, who used to be on such good terms with Rives."

While waiting for his successor to relieve him, Perry took his mother to France, where at the opening ceremony of the exposition celebrating the one hundredth anniversary of the French Republic, Perry was the only foreign diplomat officially invited.

President Sadi Carnot of France asked to meet Perry, whom he called "that warm friend of France." After the introduction, he said:

"I am extremely glad to have made Mr. Belmont's acquaintance. He is one of the few men whom I have met who have refused the ribbon of the Legion of Honor"—an award France had offered to Perry as a further token of gratitude for his stand in Congress in favor of republicanism in Europe and which Perry had felt he could not accept as long as he held an official position in the United States government. Once Perry was formally replaced as minister to Spain, France again offered and this time Perry accepted the decoration.

When Perry returned to New York, the press hounded him for his views: What did he think about current politics in Europe? in the United States? In his answers Perry was conscientious and jovial. Always ready to give a vivid opinion on almost any important subject, he was regularly quoted in the newspapers. Retired from Congress and diplomatic service, he had become a reporter's dream: a reliable interview. Good copy.

August, Jr., suggested that his father build a new house at the farm in Lexington. The stud was worth it. Three of the year's leading horses had belonged to August.

"It is out of the question," August said.

Why spend $4,000 to $6,000 in construction costs when the house there, although admittedly neglected, was "substantial"? Anyway, the future of racing was unsettled. Jerome Park had lost $30,000 in operating costs during the past spring; the Fall Meet had to be postponed; and the city was going to replace the track with a reservoir. A new organization, the New York Jockey Club, had absorbed the old American Jockey Club for reasons *The New York Times* said were "numerous, chief of which is the fact that the American Jockey Club has seen its old prestige slowly vanishing since Mr. August Belmont retired from its presidency." The new club intended to build a track—which would be called Morris Park —in Westchester. August would miss the familiar grounds of the old track. But what must have been most galling was that the new club had elected Leonard Jerome president. After almost a quarter of a century Jerome finally was able to run a jockey club without August's interference.

For much of the winter August was too ill to go to the office. When he recovered he considered coming out of his social retirement to attend a certain dinner, until he learned it was being given for the new ministers to France and Russia, whom he had no desire to honor.

In the spring August, Jr., either broke or sprained one of his knees but insisted on going to work. August begged him, "if you love me," to stay home and recuperate.

"If you don't," he said, "you may repent it all your life."

Lamed ever since his duel, August did not want his son to suffer the same inconvenience and discomfort he had. So that August, Jr., would not feel uneasy taking a sick leave, August spent the summer of 1889 in New York covering for his son at the office. As a result he skipped his regular vacation to Bythesea, where Caroline, perhaps because of his absence, wanted to reduce the size of the staff.

"I know perfectly well that there is awful waste in our household," she told August, Jr. "But with so many servants and the way your father allows things to go on to save trouble, I can do little. It really makes me sick, because I am helpless to control or send away any servants, outside those in the house. The number that sit down to eat every day is appalling in a private house."

August III, who was spending the summer with Caroline, was "in fine spirits all the time," Caroline said. He was sleeping better than usual, "sometimes not waking up until nearly 8 o'clock in the morning," and his health was improved.

August must have been unhappy to miss what had become his grandson's customary stay at Bythesea. But August III wrote to him; and even though the letters were short—"I would like so much a box of two kinds of soldiers, because I have none with me in Newport. Hoping you are very well"—they surely amused August, who sent his grandson the soldiers and a butterfly net.

On weekends August went to the Nursery, where he fished, although he rarely caught anything; wandered about the farm checking the planting and the stock; and worked to improve his already extraordinary breed of boars, although even such a simple task seemed difficult.

"It is strange that everything I now try to undertake is uphill work and becomes a source of worry for me," he said.

He asked August, Jr., to help by sending a particular boar to the Nursery, which August, Jr., agreed to do. A few days later August wrote and reminded his son. August, Jr., accused his father of not trusting him. Why did he have to write? Did August think he would forget? He had in fact already taken care of it.

August defended himself.

"I am very sorry that I wrote to you about the boar," he said; "and my having done so ought to have proved to you how much my memory has deteriorated and how my age tells upon me. *If I had remembered that you had told me of your giving orders,* I certainly should not have *written to you.* I felt, as it is, quite ashamed when I found today at the Nursery that you had sent a boar. *Thanks cordially.*"

But August, Jr., had been more upset by the tone of the letter than by its implication that his father distrusted him.

"If I wrote '*dear* Augie' instead of 'darling' as I usually do, *it was entirely accidental,*" August told August, Jr. (As he got older August underlined in his letters more and more, as if he felt his voice were failing him even on paper and he had to rely on the written equivalent of a shout.) "I have no doubt I have done so often before to you and the other children. You wrong me deeply if you think that I would show my dissatisfaction in such an underhanded way. This is not and never has been my nature."

During the end of July and the beginning of August, Perry, August, Jr., Bessie, and Oliver went to Bythesea. Away from the office and his father's scrutiny, August, Jr., had invested $5,300 on his own in a risky venture, which August learned about only when he was going over the company books.

"Of course, you are perfectly at liberty to do with your money what you like," August told his son; "but I don't think it right for any partner of August Belmont & Company to have that kind of special transaction for his private account. I have never done it and would never do it without consulting or at least informing my partners. My dear boy, I don't want to find fault, but these things make me very unhappy. You have promised me not to speculate, and you know that you have always lost when you did it. Your share as partner of August Belmont & Company with your allowance ought to give you all the money you want, and I think you ought to have *love* and consideration enough for me to comply with my earnest and often repeated wishes."

August, as usual, confused obedience with love—just as August, Jr., as usual, confused rebelliousness with independence.

Whatever lapses of judgment August, Jr., might have, at least he had a career, which Oliver did not. He spent his days driving a new "fine team" through the streets of Newport.

"I am glad that he has some amusement and relaxation after his arduous work of the last year," August said sarcastically.

Indulging both his taste for travel and his infatuation with Alva Vanderbilt, Oliver had accepted an invitation to go on another European cruise in William K. Vanderbilt's yacht. Vanderbilt arranged for a private railroad car to carry his family and guests (Oliver and three others) from New York to Baltimore, where they boarded the *Alva* and waited for it to be provisioned.

"I feel very bad about Oliver, which I would not if I loved him less," said August. "He is preparing a very unhappy future for himself."

One dark night August, tired and leaning on his cane, was walking alone along Fifth Avenue. Between Nineteenth and Twentieth streets, where the arc lights were dim, someone almost running came abreast of him, peered into his face, and said:

"Good evening, Mr. Belmont."

Startled, August turned and, waving his cane over his head, said:

"Who are you, who are you? Why do you stop me like this? Who are you? You dare stop me in the street like this, me, August Belmont! You have no right to stop me like this. What do you mean, what do you mean by stopping August Belmont in the street?"

"I beg your pardon, Mr. Belmont, for giving you such a surprise," the stranger said, "and, if—"

"Who are you, who are you?" August kept shouting. "You dare stop me like this?"

"If you will permit me, I will introduce myself," said the stranger. "I am Mr.——of the *New York Daily Tribune*."

August dropped his cane; and half leaning on, half hugging the reporter, he said:

"Oh, my dear Mr.——, forgive me, forgive me. I am getting so old a man, and you at first frightened me. I beg your pardon. What can I do for you? I hope you are not angry."

One arm thrown around the reporter's shoulder, August walked to the Union Club, talking all the while about a race his horse Raceland had won the previous day.

"He would have talked an hour about Raceland," the reporter said, "he was so happy over winning. . . ."

In 1889 August's horses had done so well that his stable—which that year was possibly the best in turf history—led the country in earnings: $125,635, of which $76,288 was won by one horse, Potomac. It was the first time that August's winnings had covered his racing expenses.

He was severely disappointed in the results of only one race, the Oriental Handicap at Gravesend. He was sure Raceland was going to win; but the jockey, E. H. Garrison, who was called "The Snapper," pulled up in the stretch; and Raceland lost. August roared from the clubhouse balcony to the paddock.

"Now, Boss," Garrison said. "I couldn't—"

"Don't talk to me," August shouted. "Your stupidity or reckless riding lost . . . another race for me, too, and I don't propose to stand your work any longer."

"Please," Garrison said, "let me explain."

"Explanations are unnecessary," August shouted. "Your work doesn't suit me, and that's all there is about it. Remember you are not the only jockey alive."

As Garrison stared at the ground and fiddled with his moustache, August raged away, convinced that Garrison had thrown the race.

All afternoon and evening August fumed. At midnight he sent a courier to one of the country's most famous auctioneers, who was awakened and given August's note:

"Come to my house immediately."

The auctioneer dressed and hurried to 109 Fifth Avenue, where August told him to catalogue his "horses in training, yearlings, broodmares, stallions, and all." He was through with racing. And he wanted everything sold in ten days.

The auctioneer prepared the catalogue and brought it to August the next night. August, according to one account, "was in a better frame of mind—he could not remain long out of humor."

"You don't think I should retire, do you?" August asked.

The auctioneer said no.

"Then," said August, "I will wait awhile."

And he tossed the catalogue into the fire.

During the following week's races August invited Garrison to sit with him.

"The spectators . . . looked on in amazement," said one witness. "This was Mr. Belmont's way of informing all the world that he no longer believed his jockey guilty of pulling Raceland."

On New Year's Day, 1890, August told August, Jr., and Bessie that if they did not "come and dine with us, it would be a great disappointment, for there are not many New Years in store for your loving old father."

At the few dinners he attended that winter, August could not resist eating and drinking too much; but the pleasure was rarely worth the following day's agonies. His headaches were so bad he could "hardly hold my pen" to write letters, and the only way he could relieve his dyspepsia was by taking a medicine that gave him diarrhea so severe that he dared not leave his house. He constantly wrote notes to and telephoned August, Jr., keeping track of what was happening at the office and asking for help with the Nursery, which had become too much for him to handle. Everything seemed more complicated than it used to be. August wanted to buy some new cows for the farm so that his grandchildren "would have as good milk as possible," but the cows evidently were coming from New Jersey or Pennsylvania; and in order to get permission to transport them through the city, August needed "papers from the health board or some other rubbish." He also got into a fight with the postmaster at Babylon, who claimed that special delivery was limited to within a mile of the post office and service to the Nursery would cost a dollar extra per letter.

In the spring August, Jr., and Bessie went to Chicago for a vacation that was interrupted by a train wreck. August tried not to sound shrill in his concern; but as he became more feeble the world seemed more threatening. Neither his son nor daughter-in-law was hurt. But Frederika, who was now living in Mount Morris, New Jersey, was sick again. When August visited her he was shocked by how thin and "wretched" she looked. The doctors all said she would get better, but Frederika, taking after her father, did not trust them; and August thought "her morbid and desponding feelings and her dislike of her physicians" would delay her recovery.

"She was very sweet and glad to see me," August told August, Jr., "but she only talks of herself and her sufferings, which"—August caught himself; he did not want to sound critical—"is very excusable, poor child."

Oliver had returned from his European cruise and again taken up his aimless playboy ways in New York and Newport.

"What a useless life of self-indulgence he leads," August thought, "and how bitterly he will live to repent it in after years."

August sounded as though he were hoping, not just predicting; his paternal concern was part curse.

Fearing that Oliver—and Perry and August, Jr.—would squander time and money on racing, August stipulated in his will that after his death his stud should be sold. If he continued to race, it could be excused as an old man's well-earned folly—which in fact it was not. For the second year in a row his stable led the country in earnings, $171,350, breaking the previous record. And as August told August, Jr., his yearlings "are with few exceptions the best lot I ever had."

As he used to do, August woke early and prowled through his stables at the Nursery, where the horses that were running in the Northeast were kept. One morning the trainer, James Rowe, was absent; and the head stableboy was so thrilled to be taking August on the inspection tour that he did not stop talking.

"It is the only time I ever became thoroughly acquainted with my horses and the secrets of my stable," August kindly said. "If Mr. Rowe had taken charge of me, I should have seen and heard nothing. Oh, I wish I could run the stable as I pleased and that Mr. Rowe would take my place and pay the bills."

When August went to Long Branch for the Monmouth races, he spent his evenings playing cards and trying the gambling machines in the basement of the Hollywood Hotel.

"He might have lost a stake worth $20,000 at the track," said one observer; "but, if he won $1 on the toy horse that flies through a groove in a round table, he went to bed perfectly happy."

That year, perhaps because of how well his stable was doing, August was cheerful and energetic, eager for new enterprises. It was rumored that he was one of the new owners of the Saratoga Springs track; and when the mayor of New York appointed him to a rapid transit commission, he accepted, figuring, "I can always resign if I find it too tiresome." A politician from West Virginia asked for help in getting out of debt; August gave him a check. And when no one else would he bailed out George Westinghouse, the inventor and manufacturer, who had been hurt badly in the stock market.

For the first time in recent years he was not in conflict with August, Jr., over business. In fact, in one major deal August thought his son "deserved much credit for the energy and tact which you displayed."

"I am glad," he told August, Jr., a week later, "that you share my views about business in general."

This harmony did not last. For another venture, August, Jr., wanted to use a lawyer whom August admitted was "a smart and pushing fellow, anxious to make his fortune." But, August said, "I have no faith in him," since he had been "sanguine and crazy" about an ill-advised gas syndicate in which August Belmont & Company unfortunately had invested. Neither August nor August, Jr., knew anything about gas; and August said, *"it makes me utterly wretched to see my House connected in affairs, which we do not understand. I am too old to change my conservative course. I am rich enough for my children and myself not to wish to increase my fortune by business which will worry and fret me."*

As usual when August disagreed with his son about a risky investment, he had to beg August, Jr., who too often mixed emotion and finance, not to assume the difference of opinion implied a lack of confidence.

"Don't get angry with me, my dear boy, if I write you this in all candor and kindness," August said; "but, if you wish me, as I know you do, to have a few years more of at least a peaceful, if not a happy life, *stand by me in upholding the conservative and honorable reputation of the name you bear—no money, no profit could compensate for its loss.*"

In September Jacob, a former servant who had worked for the family ever since the boys were little, died. When August, Jr., wrote to his wife, Bessie, to say that he was going to the funeral, she replied that such consideration was "sweet in you, dear little Augie, as I used to call you." She signed her letter: "Nurse Betsy."

August was shaken. It was as though his world bit by bit were being erased. Every day another blank spot appeared; and it was harder and harder to bridge those spreading gaps. Every so often August might be hobbling along some street, a piece of old china he had just bought under his arm, his dachshund waddling behind, and he might be listening to the familiar neighborhood sounds—perhaps to children singing about Little Sally Waters, who spent her life sitting in the sun and turning east and west toward the one she liked best, as though she were a compass magnetized for love—when suddenly the city would seem strange to him, perhaps because of the vista up an avenue that never used to be quite so built-up or because of the telegraph wires festooned overhead as though they were dirty streamers from a long-ago party.

Early in October, August, atypically panicky, told August, Jr., that "the stockmarket looks very critical. I wish you would go over our securities to see that we are all safe." A few weeks later, in November, August went to Madison Square Garden to judge the coaching-stallion competition at a horse show. While he was there the show's sponsors learned that one of the judges of another event—the Hackney Class— had backed out. They asked August to fill in. August hesitated; but since he did not feel tired, he agreed. Throwing himself into his duties, he soon became sweaty. The hall was drafty; the floor of the show ring was damp. By the time August left, going out into the sharp night air, he had caught a slight cold, which he could not shake. He decided to stay in bed the following week; by Wednesday, November 20, he felt well enough to go to the office for two hours.

On Thursday, a sunny but bitterly cold day, August went for a drive through Central Park. The wind was strong but the carriage was closed; and feeling invigorated he stopped at an art dealer's shop to look at some pictures. From there he went to the Union Club, where he played some whist, after which he was in such good spirits that he decided to walk home.

At dinner his back began to hurt. Lumbago, he thought; and ignored it. After dinner he went again to the club for more whist. During the game he was bothered—as Raymond had been just before he shot himself—by drafts no one else noticed. He kept changing his seat but could not get comfortable. Finally, about eleven o'clock, he left, feeling ill.

Dr. Polk examined August and assured him that he only had a "simple cold." He should stay in bed for a few days and get some rest. By Saturday, August was in excruciating pain. A specialist who had been called in said that August had developed pleurisy; but still August was told he was in no danger. All day he was restless, talking incessantly about business and horses. He telephoned the office to make sure three barrels of apples were sent to Leopold Rothschild, his last order to August Belmont & Company.

That night he was found unconscious. On Sunday the doctors admitted that August had pneumonia; but if his heart held out he had a good chance of recovering. The family gathered around—Caroline, Perry, August, Jr., and Bessie, Frederika and Sam, and Oliver. At two o'clock on Monday morning, August, Jr., was told that his father's "pulse, temperature, and respiration evinced a sudden and decided change for the worse."

August's heart failed. At five minutes after three on the morning of November 24, 1890, August Belmont died.

"Puritan austerity, we doubt not, would have looked with sour-faced disapproval upon August Belmont as a man who got out of life too much pleasure himself and gave too much to others," said one of the many obituaries. "By persons of more joyous temperaments he will be remembered as a man who, combining solid business qualities with a noteworthy aptitude for the less serious affairs of life, contributed, certainly in as large a measure as any other of its citizens, to make the city of New York an agreeable place of residence."

As August had wanted, his horses were sold. He left the rest of his property and fortune—estimated at $10 million to $50 million—to Caroline and the children. Since everyone else was, as August, Jr., told Nathaniel Rothschild, "paralyzed," he took care of what had to be done, answering the telegrams and letters that arrived, cabling Germany to find out his grandmother's—August's mother's—name, which oddly neither Caroline nor any of the children knew.

The funeral was held at the Church of the Ascension, where August and Caroline had been married. Inside, friends, social acquaintances, politicians, and horse-racing cronies waited for the service to start; outside on Fifth Avenue, police fought to keep back the swarm of sight-seers. A few minutes after ten o'clock the "Funeral March" began. J. Pierpont Morgan, former president Grover Cleveland, the governor of New York, David B. Hall, and Manton Marble were among the twelve pallbearers. The coffin was covered with a black cloth and decorated with a single wreath of violets. There were no other flowers in the church. A special train carried the casket and mourners from New York City to Newport, where August was buried.

On New Year's Eve, Caroline wrote to August, Jr., to thank him "for all your kind attention to me and for looking after my affairs. I feel that time is so short, and the years roll by so quickly. It seems but yesterday that your dear father was with us well and satisfied that everything was looking so prosperous."

August, Jr., was now the head of the family.

On January 2, 1891, he wrote to his bank in Hempstead that "on and after this date" he would no longer be August Belmont, Jr.; he would be August Belmont.

Notes

August Belmont has been abbreviated as AB1 and August Belmont, Jr., as AB2. Frequently cited sources have been abbreviated as follows:

AAD	*An American Democrat,* Perry Belmont
AB4	August Belmont's Private Collection
AB5	August Belmont, Jr.'s Private Collection
CD	Caroline Belmont's Diary, Lineberry Private Collection
HSPL	Historical Society of Pennsylvania Library
LABHR	*August Belmont and the House of Rothschild,* Rahel Liebeschütz
LL	Rahel Liebeschütz's Private Collection
LOC	Library of Congress
LSB	*Simon Belmont, Gutsbesitzer, 1789/1859,* Rahel Liebeschütz
LWOC	*The Wind of Change,* Rahel Liebeschütz
NYHS	The New-York Historical Society
NYPL	The New York Public Library
SRL	Salomon de Rothschild letters
UCL	University of California Library
URL	University of Rochester Library

Chapter One

p. 4 "SINCE THERE WERE . . .": *Encyclopedia Judaica,* Vol. I, 481.

6 "JUST AS BEAUTIFUL . . .": *LSB,* 52.

7 "THE DESCRIPTION . . .": *LWOC,* Simon to Babette, April 30, 1852.

7 "I HAVE NEVER . . .": *LWOC,* Simon to Feist, July 5, 1873.

7 "THEY TREAT . . .": LL, Frederika to Simon, June 19, 1815.

8 "THE WAY I SEE . . .": *Ibid.*

8 "I ALSO GREET . . .": *Ibid.*

8 "IN THE DUST . . .": Howitt, 22.

9 "WANDS ADORNED . . .": *Ibid.,* 44.

9 "GARDEN, GARDEN . . .": *Ibid.,* 44.

9 "THE POPULAR . . .": Schwab, 207.

11 "I SCARCELY . . .": Browne, 216–217.

Chapter Two

p. 12–13 "THE CITY . . .": J. Russell, 23.

13 "OF THE FIFTY . . .": *Ibid.,* 25–26.

13 "WHAT FIRST . . .": Mrs. Trollope, 130–131.

14 "IF HE USES . . .": *LWOC,* Simon to Gertrude, February 25, 1828.

14–15 "YOUR INSISTENCE . . .": *LWOC,* Simon to AB1, February 25, 1828.

15–16 "I THANK YOU . . .": AB4, AB1 to Simon, September 22, 1828.

16 "IF THERE REALLY . . .": AB4, AB1 to Simon, October 15, 1828.

16 "SURELY, IT IS . . .": *Ibid.*

17 "I BEG YOU . . .": AB5, AB1 to Simon, June 17, 1829.

17 "DURING THE . . .": AB4, AB1 to Simon, September 15, 1830.

p. 17 "BOYS AND GIRLS . . .":
Browne, 220.
18 "THE RIOTS . . .": AB4, AB1
to Simon, September 15, 1830.
18 "WOULD BE A GREAT . . .": *Ibid.*
18 "THANK GOD . . .": *Ibid.*
18 "PRUSSIA AND AUSTRIA . . .":
Ibid.
18 "BY-PASSED THE DUKE . . .":
AB5, AB1 to Simon, n.d.
[1830].
20 "I AM PLANNING . . ." AB4,
AB1 to Babette, February 3,
1837.

Chapter Three

20–21 "PASS AND REPASS . . .":
Marryat, 26.
21 "SO THEY GO . . .": Strong,
April 30, 1837 (original manuscript).
22 "MIRACULOUS!": *Ibid.*, 113.
22 "UNCIVILIZED RACE . . .":
Browne, 135.
22–23 "PUBLIC AMUSEMENTS . . .":
Grund, 170–171.
23 "GO TO THE THEATER . . .":
Marryat, 29.
23 "SEVEN-EIGHTHS OF . . .": AB5,
AB1 to Babette, May 16, 1837.
23–24 "THE BANKS . . .": Dayton,
77–80.
25 "A MORE BEAUTIFUL . . .":
H. C. Brown, *Valentine's Manual, 1919*, 105.
26 "THE SUN'S . . .": Grund, 16–
17.
26 "THE WHOLE OF . . .": Hone,
80.
26 "THE CREATIONS . . .": Dayton,
120–121.
26 "WERE GLIDING . . .": Still, 108.
27 "SIT OR LIE . . .": Still, 101.
27–28 "WAS THERE EVER . . .":
Dickens, 80–81.
28 "INTERESTING PICTURES . . .":
Marryat, 35–36.

Chapter Four

29–30 "COMPLETELY CONCEALED . . .":
Dayton, 157.
30 "YOU SEE, SIR . . .": Grund,
225.
30 "THE RECOLLECTION . . .":
Dayton, 210.
33 "HIS AIR . . .": Grund, 272.
33 "HOW OUR . . .": *Ibid.*, 129.
33 "WE ARE HAPPY . . .": AB5,

Rothschilds to AB, April 27,
1838.
p. 33–34 "THE ARTS AND . . .":*Ibid.*,
AB1 to Babette, August 3,
1838.
34 "EVERYTHING TURNS . . .": *Ibid.*
34 "COST $6,000 EACH . . .": Hone,
183.
35 "LIBERAL VIEWS . . .": AB5,
AB1 to rabbi, October 1849.
36 "THE QUEEN . . .": Dayton,
331.
36 "AMERICAN WOMEN . . .":
AB4, AB1 to Babette, August
3, 1838.
36 "PROMINENT POINT . . .": Still,
87.
36 "AS REGARDS . . .": *Ibid.*
37 "DO YOU REALIZE . . .": AB5,
AB1 to Babette, April 30,
1839.
37 "I WISH . . .": *Ibid.*
38 "RATHER BAD . . .": *Ibid.*
38 "THIS UNTENDER . . .": *LWOC*,
Simon to Rothschilds, January
2, 1840.
38–39 "I THINK . . .": AB5, AB1
Babette, September 29, 1840.
39 "A MERE MISUNDERSTANDING
. . .": Bowmar, 47.
39 "A BEAUTIFUL HORSE . . .":
AB5, AB1 to Babette, April
30, 1839.
40 "THE MOST SPLENDID . . .":
Maurice, 37.
41 "FOR GOD'S SAKE . . .": Churchill, *The Upper Crust*, 54.
41 "THE WHOLE HOUSE . . .":
Minnigerode, *The Fabulous
Forties*, 39–40.
41 "HAS BEEN BOUGHT . . .":
Thomas, *Sam Ward*, 111.
42 "I HAVE BEEN INVESTIGATING
. . .": Wecter, 213.
42–43 "THE SON . . .": AB5, AB1 to
Simon, November 10, 1841.
43 "SHE FLIRTS . . .": Hone, September 3, 1841, 248–249.
43 "THEIR DEPORTMENT . . .":
New York Herald, August 30,
1841.
44 "I HOPE IN . . .": *New York
Herald*, August 28, 1841.
44 "ABANDONED THE SOCIETY . . .":
New York Herald, August 30,
1841.
44 "TWO FAMOUS . . .": *Ibid.*
44 "DURING HIS CONFINEMENT
. . .": *New York Herald*, September 1, 1841.
45 "GREAT HOSTILITY . . .": *New
York Herald*, September 11,
1841.
45 "GET WELL . . .": *Ibid.*, September 15, 1841.

Chapter Five

p. 46 "I DO NOT KNOW . . .": AB4, AB1 to Simon, November 11, 1841.

46 "IN FUTURE . . .": *Ibid.*

47 "I AM IMPROVING . . .": *Ibid.*

47 "I'M VERY GLAD . . .": *Ibid.*

47 "MISUNDERSTANDINGS . . .": *LWOC*, Simon to AB1, July 3, 1842.

47 "THE VARIOUS SLANDERS . . .": *Ibid.*

47 "AFTER A FEW . . .": *Ibid.*

48 "AS ONE SAYS . . .": *Ibid.*

48 "HOW COULD YOU . . .": *Ibid.*

48 "IN EACH . . .": *Ibid.*

49 "BOTH THE DOCTOR . . .": *Ibid.*

49 "LIMBS WHICH . . .": AB5, AB1 to Simon, November 10, 1841.

49 "IF ONLY I . . .": *LWOC*, quoted in Simon to AB1, July 3, 1842.

50 "LITTLE BY LITTLE . . .": *Ibid.*, Simon to AB1, March 26–27, 1844.

Chapter Six

51 "AT PUBLIC AUCTION . . .": AB4, McAllister & Cohen to AB1, July 21, 1845.

51 "VERY RELUCTANT . . .": *Ibid.*, AB Company to McAllister & Cohen, July 28, 1845.

52 "EVEN THOUGH THE AMERICANS . . .": *LABHR,* AB1 to Babette, October 24, 1848.

52 "THE STOCKS . . .": *LABHR,* AB1 to Feist, May 2, 1848.

53 "YOU HAVE SEEN . . .": Birmingham, *Our Crowd,* 58.

53 "I AM TOO 'GRAND . . .": *LABHR,* AB1 to Babette, March 5, 1849.

53 "IT IS TRUE . . .": *Ibid.*, AB1 to Feist, May 2, 1848.

53 "I CANNOT BELIEVE . . .": *Ibid.*

54 "TRYING TO ESTABLISH . . .": *Ibid.*, AB1 to Babette, June 11, 1849.

54 "SONS AND NEPHEWS.": *Ibid.*

54 "I HAVE BEEN INDEPENDENT . . .": *Ibid.*, AB1 to Babette, October 24, 1848.

54 "AT THIS POINT . . .": *Ibid.*

55 "IT IS NOW MORE . . .": *Ibid.*, AB1 to Babette, March 5, 1849.

56 "VERY ANGRY . . .": *Ibid.*, AB1 to Feist, May 2, 1848.

p. 56 "QUITE HONEST . . .": *Ibid.*, AB1 to Babette, March 5, 1849.

56 "HOPE THAT GOOD . . .": *Ibid.*, AB1 to Babette, June 11, 1849.

57 "I DO NOT FEEL . . .": *Ibid.*, AB1 to Babette, October 24, 1848.

Chapter Seven

59 "WORKING MEN . . .": Minnigerode, *The Fabulous Forties,* 197.

59 "TEAR IT DOWN . . .": *Ibid.*, 199.

59 "YOU CAN'T GO . . .": *Ibid.*, 202.

59 "WHO STYLE . . .": *New York Herald,* May 23, 1849.

60 "THE METRE . . .": Thomas, *Sam Ward,* 145.

61 "DEAR ANGEL'S . . .": AB5, AB1 to Babette, October, 1849.

63 "A VERY PRETTY . . .": *New York Herald,* August 19, 1849.

63 "FINE TACT . . .": Bowmar, 47.

63 "BELLE OF THE GRACEFUL . . .": *New York Herald,* August 2, 1849.

64 "IN ONE CORNER . . .": *Ibid.*, August 14, 1849.

64 "COMPOSED . . .": *Ibid.*

64 "RED CLOTH . . .": *Ibid.*, August 20, 1849.

65 "WAS DRESSED AS . . .": *Ibid.*

66 "ALTHOUGH SHE KNOWS . . .": AB5, AB1 to Babette, October, 1849.

66 "AN OUTSTANDING . . .": *LSB,* 69.

66–67 "MIGHT DESTROY . . .": *LWOC,* 231.

67 "DELUDING HIMSELF . . .": *Ibid.*, Simon to AB1, January 27, 1850.

67 "FULFILL THE OBLIGATIONS . . .": AB4, Creighton to Caroline, September 24, 1849.

67 "HAD POPPED . . .": *New York Herald,* November 9, 1840.

68 "CAROLINE WOULD MARRY . . .": AB4, Thomas Slidell to Commodore Perry, October 21, 1849.

Chapter Eight

71 "THE FIRST THING . . .": Bristed, 37.

*p.*71 "IT TASTED . . .": *LWOC,* Simon to AB1, January 27, 1850.

71 "WHICH IS NOT . . .": *LSB,* 47.

72 "COLONIZED IN . . .": Morison, 255.

72 "TO BE ABSENT . . .": AB5, AB1 to Babette, October 1849.

72 "YOU SLEPT . . .": AB4, AB1 to Caroline, n.d. [1850].

72 "MY DEAREST . . .": *Ibid.*

73 "NEVER LIFT . . .": Birmingham, *Our Crowd,* 62.

73 "I BOUGHT . . .": AB4, AB1 to Caroline, September 21, 1850.

73 "TAUGHT NEW YORK . . .": Churchill, *The Upper Crust,* 56.

73 "MY DEAR CAROLINE . . .": AB4, Jane Perry to Caroline, August 19, 1850.

74 "TALKED A GOOD DEAL . . .": *Ibid.,* AB1 to Caroline, March 20, 1850.

74 "THE FASHIONABLE . . .": Hone, Vol. II, 862–863.

74 "THE LARGE ORCHESTRA . . .": AB4, AB1 to Caroline, March 20, 1850.

75 "MAKE MY PRESENT . . .": *Ibid.*

75 "PLEASE . . .": *Ibid.*

75 "IN EVERY SENSE . . .": L. Morris, 25.

75 "WHEN YOU ENTER . . .": Churchill, *The Upper Crust,* 54–55.

75 "THERE'S A GOOD . . .": Birmingham, *Our Crowd,* 61.

75–76 "HIS WORLDLINESS . . .": Churchill, *The Upper Crust,* 55.

76 "THE OCCASION . . .": Belmont Papers, NYPL, Bedell to AB1, December 31, 1850.

Chapter Nine

77 "THE DEMOCRATIC . . .": W. Barrett, 81.

77 "THE CONSTITUTIONAL RIGHTS . . .": Nevins, *Ordeal of the Union,* 12.

78 "THE WILDEST SCHEMES . . .": Johannsen, 358.

78 "THE SENTIMENT . . .": Milton, *The Eve of Conflict,* 40.

79 "YOU MAY RELY . . .": Buchanan Papers, HSPL, Slidell to Buchanan, May 9, 1851.

79 "TO MAKE THEM . . .": *Ibid.,* AB1 to Buchanan, April 3, 1851.

79 "IT IS VERY DIFFICULT . . .": *Ibid.*

*p.*80 "COW-SKINNED . . .": Hone, II, 908.

80 "I SHOULD BE WELL . . .": *Ibid.*

80 "SHALL I . . .": Wecter, 262.

80 "DECLARATION OF . . .": *Ibid.,* 261.

80 "THE IMPORTANCE . . .": Buchanan Papers, HSPL, Slidell to Buchanan, October 16, 1850.

80 "WE HAD SEVERAL . . .": *Ibid.,* Slidell to Buchanan, August 8, 1851.

80–81 "EVERYTHING FOR THE ESTABLISHMENT . . .": *Ibid.,* AB1 to Buchanan, December 6, 1851.

81 "AT THIS PROPITIOUS . . .": Nevins, *Ordeal of the Union,* II, 13.

81 "IT WOULD HAVE BEEN . . .": Buchanan Papers, HSPL, AB1 to Buchanan, December 8, 1851.

81 "I HOPE I SHALL . . .": *Ibid.*

82 "FEELINGS OF INDECISION . . .": *Ibid.,* AB1 to Buchanan, April 3, 1851.

82 "WISH TO VISIT . . .": *LSB,* Caroline to Simon, April 18, 1852, 70.

83 "MAY I ASK . . .": *Ibid.*

83 "A VERY HONORABLE . . .": AB4, AB1 to Simon, n.d. [January 1852].

84 "FAIRLY AND FIRMLY . . .": Buchanan Papers, HSPL, AB1 to Buchanan, February 28, 1852.

84 "AND SAID THAT ALL . . .": *Ibid.*

84 "CONTROL OF A SMALL . . .": *Ibid.,* AB1 to Buchanan, April 15, 1852.

84 "THOUGHT BEST . . .": *Ibid.*

84–85 "YOU MAY RELY . . .": *Ibid.*

85 "ONLY OBJECT . . .": *Ibid.*

Chapter Ten

85 "VERY NEEDY INDEED . . .": AB4, AB1 to Townsend, September 4, 1852.

86 "CHILLING EFFECT . . ." Buchanan Papers, HSPL, AB1 to Buchanan, October 27, 1852.

86 "A RECEPTION . . .": AB1 to Buchanan, December 6, 1851.

86 "THE ORACLE . . .": Hone, 855.

86 "APT TO BE WILD . . .": *Ibid.,* 835.

87 "AUSTRIA AND THE MONEY . . . ": *New York Tribune,* October 26, 1852.

87 "VEXED AND GRIEVED . . .": Buchanan Papers, *HSPL,* AB1

to Buchanan, November 5, 1852.

p. 87–88 "I AM NATURALIZED . . .": *New York Evening Post*, October 27, 1852.

89 "WE CARE NOTHING . . .": *New York Tribune*, October 27, 1852.

89 "A HIGHLY CREDITABLE . . .": *New York Herald*, October 28, 1852.

89 "THE GROSSEST DISREGARD . . .": *New York Herald*, November 1, 1852.

89 "LOST NOT ONLY . . .": *New York Tribune*, October 29, 1852.

89 "RECKLESS SOCIALISTS . . .": *New York Herald*, November 1, 1852.

89 "THE SATANIC PRESS . . .": *New York Tribune*, October 29, 1852.

89 "IN HIS UNWASHED . . .": *New York Herald*, October 29, 1852.

89–90 "THE LAST NOTABLE . . .": G. T. Strong, II, 107–108.

90 "POOR SCOTT . . .": *Ibid.*, 109.

90 "GENERAL OPINION . . .": *Ibid.*

90 "I HAVE NO DOUBT . . .": Buchanan Papers, HSPL, AB1 to Buchanan, November 22, 1852.

91 "IN ORDER TO BRING . . .": *Ibid.*

91 "OFFICIAL POSITION . . .": *Ibid.*

92 "FROM NAPLES . . .": *Ibid.*

92 "HAVING RESIDED MYSELF . . .": *Ibid.*

92 "IS VERY ANXIOUS . . .": Buchanan Papers, HSPL, AB1 to Buchanan, November 30, 1852.

92 "IT SEEMS . . .": Marcy Papers, LOC, Staples to Marcy, November 26, 1852.

92 "IMMENSE WEALTH . . .": *Ibid.*

92–93 "WHO IS . . . NOT REMARKABLE . . .": *Ibid.*

93 "NOT LACK ABILITY . . .": *Ibid.*

93 "WHICH IS NOW . . .": Buchanan Papers, HSPL, AB1 to Buchanan, January 7, 1853.

93 "NUMEROUS ENGAGEMENTS . . .": *Ibid.*

94 "FROM FEAR . . .": *Ibid.*, AB1 to Buchanan, January 28, 1853.

94 "I DO NOT . . .": *Ibid.*

94 "PEASLEE URGES . . .": *Ibid.*

95 "WELL, THE AGONY . . .": *Ibid.*, March 5, 1853.

95 "WILL NOT . . . BE MUCH . . .": *Ibid.*

95 "ALMOST EVERY CANDIDATE . . .": *Ibid.*, March 7, 1853.

96 "MADE AN ABIDING . . .": *Ibid.*

96 "[I]T SEEMS TO BE VERY . . .": Sanders Papers, LOC, AB1 to Sanders, March 21, 1853.

p. 96 "DOUBT MY SINCERITY . . .": *Ibid.*

96 "WHAT COULD I GAIN . . .": *Ibid.*

96 "I DO NOT MEAN . . .": *Ibid.*

96 "FRENCHIFIED ALIAS . . .": *New York Tribune*, March 22, April 10, 1853.

97 "FOREIGN BORN . . .": *Ibid.*

97 "SAINT GREELEY['S] . . .": Buchanan Papers, HSPL, AB1 to Buchanan, April 15, 1853.

97 "NOW OR NEVER . . .": Marcy Papers, LOC, Peaslee to Marcy, May 9, 1853.

97 "WRITE A LINE . . .": *Ibid.*

97 "HIS INFLUENCE . . .": *The New York Times*, March 16, 1853.

98 "I AM VERY INDIFFERENT . . .": Buchanan Papers, HSPL, AB1 to Buchanan, April 4, 1853.

98 "I HAVE TOO MUCH . . .": *Ibid.*, April 15, 1853.

98 "I JUST AS LEAVE . . .": *Ibid.*, April 22, 1853.

98 "THE STEAMERS . . .": *Ibid.*, May 12, 1853.

99 "HUMBLE PETITIONER . . .": *Ibid.*, April 15, 1853.

Chapter Eleven

99 "ILLIBERAL IN THE . . .": Belmont Papers, NYPL, Marcy to AB1, August 8, 1853, No. 2.

99 "DURING YOUR RESIDENCE . . .": *Ibid.*, No. 1.

100 "THE MOST STUPENDOUS . . .": Brinnin, 184–185.

101 "VERY AGREEABLE . . .": CD, 2.

101 "CHARMING.": *Ibid.*

101 "AT THE TOP . . .": *Ibid.*

101 "AS FAT AS A . . .": AB4, Caroline to Jane Perry, October 5, 1853.

101 "ENJOYED VERY MUCH . . .": CD, 3.

101 "THE CENTER OF ALL PLEASURE . . .": *Ibid.*, 2.

102 "COULD BRING HIMSELF . . .": LWOC, Simon to Babette, June 19, 1853.

102 "A NICE GENTLEMANLY . . .": AB4, Caroline to Jane Perry, October 5, 1853.

102 "EXPECTED THEM TO . . .": *Ibid.*

102 "SPLENDID . . .": *Ibid.*

102 "VERY ATTENTIVE . . .": CD, 4.

103 "NOW TO HAVE . . .": *Ibid.*, 5.

103 "FROM MORNING . . .": *Ibid.*

p. 103 "DELICIOUS . . .": AB4, Caroline to Jane Perry, October 5, 1853.

103 "THE GERMANS . . .": *Ibid.*

103 "A VERY LIVELY . . .": CD, 5.

104 "A VERY STIFF PEOPLE . . .": *Ibid.,* 6.

104 "VERY GLAD . . .": AB4, Caroline to Jane Perry, October 5, 1853.

104 "THE HAGUE . . .": Benedict, 445.

104 "VERY ODD . . .": AB4, Caroline to Aunt Ann, October 16, 1853.

105 "THE CLEANLINESS OF THE DUTCH . . .": Bell, 49.

105 "THEY ARE VERY CLEAN . . .": AB4, Caroline to Aunt Ann, October 16, 1853.

105 "WERE TO RISE AGAIN . . .": Browne, Junius, "Holland and the Hollander," *Harper's,* January, 1872, 174–175.

105 "IN EVERYTHING ABOUT . . .": Buchanan Papers, HSPL, AB1 to Buchanan, November 18, 1853.

105 "VERY LARGE AND HANDSOME . . .": AB4, Caroline to Jane Perry, October 5, 1853.

Chapter Twelve

105 "GENERALLY DAMP . . .": AB4, Caroline to Aunt Ann, October 16, 1853.

105 "WE HAVE HAD BUT . . .": *Ibid.*

106 "MADE SUCH A FUSS . . .": AB4, Caroline to Jane Perry, November 6, 1853.

106 "IN VERY LITTLE NARROW . . .": AB4, Caroline to Aunt Ann, October 16, 1853.

106 "MANAGES . . .": *Ibid.*

106 "BEGINNING TO GET . . .": AB4, AB1 to Jane Perry, November 22, 1853.

106 "CRAZY TO GET . . .": AB4, Caroline to Aunt Ann, October 16, 1853.

106 "BUT LITTLE DISPOSITION . . .": AB4, AB1 to Jane Perry, November 22, 1853.

106 "YOU WOULD BE . . .": AB4, Caroline to Jane Perry, October 21, 1853.

107 "TO BE WITH WIFE . . .": Buchanan Papers, HSPL, AB1 to Buchanan, November 18, 1853.

107 "EVEN LITTLE PERRY . . .": AB4, AB1 to Jane Perry, November 22, 1853.

p. 107 "ONLY PRETTY WELL . . .": *Ibid.,* October 21, 1853.

107 "WILL . . . RESULT IN NO . . .": AB4, Commodore Perry to Jane Perry, June 24, 1853.

107 "WILL ALL ENJOY . . .": *Ibid.*

107 "ENGLISH SERVICE . . .": AB4, Caroline to Aunt Ann, October 16, 1853.

107 "RATHER A TIRESOME . . .": AB4, Caroline to Jane Perry, October 21, 1853.

108 "EVERYBODY SPEAKS . . .": AB4, AB1 to Jane Perry, November 22, 1853.

108 "I COULD HAVE INDUCED . . .": *Ibid.*

108 "A MOST TERRIBLE . . .": *AAD,* 33.

108 "RATHER TIRESOME . . .": AB4, Caroline to Jane Perry, October 21, 1853.

108 "A VERY INTELLIGENT . . .": AB4, Caroline to Aunt Ann, October 16, 1853.

108 "CALLED ON THE . . .": *Ibid.*

Chapter Thirteen

109 "THE SIMPLE DRESS . . .": Bemis, 264.

109 "THE KING WOULD . . .": Douglas Papers, UCL, AB1 to Douglas, November 15, 1853.

109 "LEFT THE MATTER . . .": Belmont Papers, NYPL, AB1 to Marcy, November 1, 1853, No. 5.

109 "TO WEAR . . .": *Ibid.*

109 "HAD BEEN RECEIVED WITH MUCH . . .": Belmont Papers, NYPL, AB1 to Marcy, November 1, 1853, No. 5.

109–110 "INSTRUCTIONS WERE . . .": *Ibid.*

110 "MY WEARING A . . .": *Ibid.*

110 "PLAIN AND NEAT . . .": Benedict, 446.

110 "ATTIRED IN GORGEOUS . . .": Douglas Papers, UCL, AB1 to Douglas, November 15, 1853.

110 "THE BAD UNDERSTANDING . . .": AB4, AB1 to Caroline, November 22, 1853.

110 "IS ALWAYS THE . . .": *Ibid.*

110–111 "ENTERING THE PALACE . . .": A. Rhodes, 73.

111 "THE GREAT BUSINESS . . .": AB4, Caroline to Jane Perry, November 6, 1853.

111 "I HOPE I SHALL . . .": *Ibid.*

111 "LOOKING VERY PRETTY . . .":

Chapter Fourteen

Chapter Fifteen

mont Papers, NYPL, AB1 to Marcy, December 6, 1854.

p. 127 "IT NOW ONLY . . .": *Ibid.*, AB1 to Marcy, September 23, 1854, No. 27.

128 "VERY FRANKLY . . .": Belmont Papers, NYPL, AB1 to Marcy, October 7, 1854.

Chapter Sixteen

130 "I HAVE INCURRED . . .": Belmont Papers, NYPL, AB1 to Marcy, December 23, 1853, No. 10.

130 "CLEVER, INFLUENTIAL . . .": Marcy Papers, LOC, AB1 to Marcy, May 31, 1854.

131 "DIRECT YOUR EFFORTS . . .": Manning, 175.

132 "BE JUSTIFIED IN . . .": U. S. Government, Executive Document 93.

132 "MANIFESTO OF . . .": *New York Tribune,* March 8, 1855.

132 "ATROCIOUS.": *New York Post,* March 6, 1855.

133 "I PREFER TO SEE . . .": *LWOC,* Simon to Stephan Feist, December 1, 1854.

134 "UNCOMMONLY WELL . . .": CD, 119.

134 "WHY DIDN'T YOU . . .": Morison, 291.

134 "PERFECTLY DELIGHTED . . .": AB4, Caroline to Aunt Ann, February 12, 1855.

134 "THE FIRST TIME . . .": AB4, AB1 to Marcy, February 26, 1855.

135 "I HAVE MISSED . . .": *Ibid.*, 135.

135 "SO HILLY . . .": CD, 132.

135 "TURNED OUT TO . . .": *Ibid.*, 135.

136 "I MAY PLAY . . .": Belmont Papers, NYPL, AB1 to AB Company, May 26, 1856.

136 "WITH MY USUAL LUCK . . .": *Ibid.*

136 "THE NEWS OF THE . . .": *Ibid.*, AB1 to Christmas and Matthiessen, March 4, 1855.

137 "HEAVY GOLD . . .": *Ibid.*, AB1 to Christmas and Matthiessen, October 30, 1855.

137 "I HOPE THAT THE CONTINUED . . .": *Ibid.*, AB1 to AB Company, November 27, 1855.

137 "I HOPE THAT THE PANIC . . .": Belmont Papers, NYPL, AB1 to Christmas and Matthiessen, November 13, 1855.

p. 137 "IT SEEMS AS IF . . .": *Ibid.*, November 27, 1855.

137 "ONE BAD LOAN . . .": *Ibid.*, November 13, 1855.

137 "MY YOUNGEST BOY . . .": *Ibid.*, April 3, 1855.

137 "I DO NOT WISH . . .": *Ibid.*, April 17, 1855.

138 "THE INCREASED . . .": *Ibid.*, AB1 to AB Company, January 19, 1856.

138 "NOT TO LEND . . .": *Ibid.*, AB1 to Christmas and Matthiessen, July 16, 1855.

138 "I STILL HAVE NOT . . .": *Ibid.*, September 2, 1857.

138 "THERE IS AN AMOUNT . . .": *Ibid.*, September 16, 1857.

138 "I REALLY AM AT . . .": *Ibid.*, September 20, 1857.

138–139 "A SALVATORE ROSA . . .": *Ibid.*, AB1 to Christmas and Matthiessen, June 23, 1855.

139 "A QUANTITY OF . . .": *Ibid.*, July 3, 1855.

139 "SOME OLD AND RARE . . .": *Ibid.*, July 15, 1855.

139 "SOME STEINBERG . . .": *Ibid.*, October 22, 1855.

139 "HAVE ALL MY . . .": *Ibid.*, July 3, 1855.

139 "RESTORE TO THEM . . .": *Ibid.*, July 15, 1855.

139 "DAMAGED WORKS . . .": *Ibid.*, January 22, 1856.

139 "AS REGARDS . . .": *Ibid.*, July 15, 1855.

139 "IT IS DISGRACEFUL . . .": *Ibid.*, July 3, 1855.

139 "MOTHER-OF-PEARL . . .": *Ibid.*, AB1 to AB Company, December 5, 1855.

140 "DEEP ENOUGH TO . . .": *Ibid.*, February 27, 1856.

140 "MAY APPEAR . . .": *Ibid.*, March 4, 1856.

140 "WOULD GIVE ME A CERTAIN . . .": *Ibid.*, April 21–23, 1856.

141 "PURCHASE A LARGE BLOCK . . .": AB4, AB1 to Commodore Perry, March 12, 1856.

141 "OUGHT TO SET 30 . . .": *Ibid.*

141 "CARE SHOULD ALSO . . .": *Ibid.*

141 "WILL BE PRETTY DIFFICULT . . .": *Ibid.*

142 "CLUB TOGETHER . . .": *Ibid.*

142 "I DO NOT WANT . . .": *Ibid.*

142 "THE TROUBLES WITH . . .": Houghton Library, AB1 to Commodore Perry, April 23, 1856.

142 "AS THE EXPOSURE . . .": *Ibid.*

142 "EITHER A PORTE COCHERE . . .": Belmont Papers, NYPL, AB1

to AB Company, February 27, 1856.
p. 142 "GOOD-SIZED ROOMS . . .": *Ibid.*
142 "VERY PLAINLY PAPERED . . .": *Ibid.*, April 3, 1857.
142 "A PICTURE GALLERY . . .": *Ibid.*, February 27, 1856.
142 "WAS LEFT FOR THREE . . .": Birmingham, *Our Crowd*, 60–61.
142 "THE GENERAL STYLE . . .": Belmont Papers, NYPL, AB1 to AB Company, August 25, 1857.

Chapter Seventeen

143 "HAS ASTONISHED EVERYBODY . . .": Belmont Papers, NYPL, AB1 to Marcy, November 7, 1855, No. 68.
143 "A UNION OF THE ABSOLUTE . . .": *Ibid.*, February 28, 1854.
143 "WARS ALWAYS CONCENTRATE . . .": *Ibid.*
144 "THE REMOTEST POSSIBILITY . . .": *Ibid.*, AB1 to Baron Lionel de Rothschild, December 1, 1855.
144 "TO THREE SHOOTING . . .": *Ibid.*, AB1 to Marcy, December 21, 1855, No. 70.
144 "NOT A TASTE . . .": AB4, Caroline to Bell Perry, January 6, 1856.
144–145 "I HAVE PLAYED FIVE . . .": AB4, Caroline to Bell Perry, January 6, 1856.
145 "AN IMMENSE BUNDLE . . .": *Ibid.*
146 "I HAVE RECEIVED YOUR . . .": Belmont Papers, NYPL, AB1 to Campbell, January 5, 1856.
146 "AS YOU STATE . . .": *Ibid.*
146 "I HAVE BEEN GUILTY . . .": *Ibid.*
147 "NO DOUBT THAT . . .": *Ibid.*
147 "YOUR OFFER TO PAY . . .": *Ibid.*
147 "THERE WAS . . . NOTHING . . .": *Ibid.*, January 9, 1856.
147 "DUTCH LADIES . . .": AB4, AB1 to Commodore Perry, April 23, 1856.
147–148 "UNDER THESE CIRCUMSTANCES . . .": *Ibid.*
148 "IT WOULD REALLY BE . . .": Belmont Papers, NYPL, AB1 to AB Company, January 15, 1856.
148 "GIVE ME THE FIVE . . .": Balla, 176–77.
150 "IN A MAGNIFICENT . . .": AB4,

The New York Times, n.d. [early 1857].

Chapter Eighteen

p. 151 "HAVE NOW SEEN . . .": Buchanan Papers, HSPL, AB1 to Buchanan, November 25, 1855.
151 "YOU MUST NOT FAIL . . .": AB4, AB1 to Commodore Perry, September 20, 1856.
151 "FILLMORE IS IN TOWN . . .": G. T. Strong, Vol. II, 281.
151 "A SECTIONAL NORTHERN . . .": *Ibid.*, 241.
151 "FRÉMONT WON'T BE . . .": *Ibid.*, 282.
152 "A LUCKY ADVENTURER . . .": AB4, AB1 to Commodore Perry, September 20, 1856.
152 "MAKE UP YOUR MIND . . .": Buchanan Papers, HSPL, Slidell to Buchanan, January 30, 1856.
152 "THE MASSES TAKE . . .": G. T. Strong, Vol. II, 281.
152 "WITH ALL HIS FORESIGHT . . .": Belmont Papers, NYPL, AB1 to Buchanan, October 31, 1856.
153 "THE MERCHANTS OF THE CITY . . .": *Journal of Commerce,* September 28–October 1, 1856.
153 "YOUR ALLUSIONS . . .": Belmont Papers, NYPL, AB1 to Schell, August 30, 1856.
153 "IT HAS BEEN THE FIRST . . .": AB4, Commodore Perry to AB1, November 7, 1856.
153–154 "IT IS A GREAT BLESSING . . .": Belmont Papers, Houghton Library, AB1 to Commodore Perry, November 15, 1856.
154 "TO FIND HER QUITE . . .": CD, 143.
154 "AGAINST TRUSTING THE . . .": AB4, Jane Perry to Caroline, December 29, 1856.
154 "LOOKING OUT FOR . . .": AB4, AB1 to Commodore Perry, September 20, 1856.
154 "LOOKS AS IF SHE . . .": *Ibid.*
154 "THE MOST DELIGHTFUL . . .": CD, 144–145.
154 "HOLDING ALL HANDS . . .": *Ibid.*
155 "TINY AND THE CHILDREN . . .": AB4, AB1 to Commodore Perry, December 21, 1856.
155 "HEALTH IS EXCELLENT . . .": *Ibid.*
155 "GRANDPA'S SHIP . . .": CD, 147.
155 "WE HAD EXCELLENT . . .": *Ibid.*, 151–152.

p. 155 "HE HAS . . . A VERY BENEVO-
LENT . . .": *Ibid.,* 161.

156 "WE WERE FORTUNATE . . .":
Ibid., 186.

156 "THE GUIDES . . .": *Ibid.*

156 "POOR LITTLE JEANNIE . . .":
Ibid., 188.

156 "WISELY . . .": *Ibid.,* 189.

156–157 "I HOPE . . . I MAY BE MIS-
TAKEN . . .": AB4, AB1 to
Commodore Perry, n.d. [spring,
1857].

157 "TELL HIM THAT I . . .": AB4,
AB1 to AB Company, July 5,
1857.

158 "MANAGED AFFAIRS . . .": *New
York Tribune,* May 7, 1857.

158 "I HAVE BEEN SHAMEFULLY
. . .": Belmont Papers, NYPL,
AB1 to Christmas, June 1,
1857.

158 "THE QUEEN HAS SENT . . .":
AB4, AB1 to Caroline, May 1,
1857.

158 "TELL PERRY . . .": *Ibid.,* May
3, 1857.

158 "RICKY, I HOPE . . .": *Ibid.,*
May 1, 1857.

158–159 "I CANNOT TELL YOU . . .":
Ibid.

159 "TO LIMIT MY BUSINESS . . .":
Belmont Papers, NYPL, AB1
to Christmas, July 12, 1857.

159 "WHICH . . . YOU WILL PLEASE
. . .": *Ibid.,* AB1 to AB Company, August 21, 1857.

Chapter Nineteen

163 "THE WESTERN BLIZZARD . . .":
Clews, 5.

164 "A MUCH GRANDER SCALE . . .":
New York Herald, June 27,
1857.

164 "IN ALL HUMAN PROBABILITY
. . .": *Ibid.,* August 23, 1857.

164 "TRANSFER BOOKS OF THE OHIO
. . .": Collman, 83.

165 "WALL STREET IS DEAD . . .":
G. T. Strong, Vol. II, 368.

166 "YOU OFTEN HAVE TO WAIT
. . .": Still, 125.

166 "WALKING DOWN BROADWAY
. . .": G. T. Strong, Vol. II,
367.

167 "LIKE A SOLUTION OF BAD . . .":
Ibid., 104.

169 "THE FIRST MAYOR . . .": *Ibid.,*
211.

170 "AS I HAVE NOW . . .": AB4,
AB1 to Commodore Perry, December 21, 1856.

170 "THE ELITE OF OUR LITER-

ARY . . .": NYHS scrapbook,
undated clipping.

p. 170 "WE HAVE NEVER BEFORE . . .":
Ibid.

170 "ONE CANNOT BUT . . .":
Ibid.

170 "THAT THE LIBERALITY . . .":
Ibid.

170–171 "PEOPLE WE MEET . . .":
Ibid. (*New York Leader*)

171 "ADOLESCENTS WHICH ARE NOT
. . .": *Ibid.,* item inferred,
"Mercy for the U.S.," no
paper identified.

172 "MAECENAS OF GASTRONOMY
. . .": Beebe, 371.

172 "OUR COOKING IS . . .": AB4,
Jane Perry to Caroline, November 12, 1855.

172 "WAS MISTRESS OF HERSELF
. . .": Gouverneur, 166.

172 "THE BEST HOUSES . . .":
Amory, *Who Killed Society?*
23–24.

172 "ALL THIS DAMNATION . . .":
Thomas, *Sam Ward,* 242.

172–173 "QUITE DISPOSED TO BE PLEAS-
ANT . . .": G. T. Strong, Vol.
II, 383–384.

173 "AS A GIRL . . .": Wolcott, 30.

173 "SHE WAS TALL . . .": *New
York Evening Post,* February
26, 1861.

173 "GOOD NIGHT, MR. BELMONT
. . .": Van Wyck, 67.

173 "ECCENTRICITY, COMFORT . . .":
NYHS, Belmont Papers, news
item, *New York Herald,* November 1860.

173 "AUGUST BELMONT RADIATED
. . .": Wolcott, 30.

174 "LIVING IN A PALACE . . .":
Ibid., 29.

174 "ONE REBUKE . . .": *Ibid.,* 31.

174 "BRUSQUE . . . ANYTHING . . .":
Bowmar, 51.

174 "IF HE CANNOT . . .": *Ibid.*

174 "LIKE A MAN ON THE BACK . . .":
Birmingham, *Our Crowd,* 61.

174–175 "HE WAS A GREAT BUSINESSMAN
. . .": AB4, clipping, n.d.

175 "HIS NATURE IS ESSENTIALLY
. . .": Bowmar, 51.

Chapter Twenty

176 "AMONGST MY CHILDREN . . .":
AB4, Commodore Perry to
AB1 and Caroline, May 26,
1856.

176 "TO HAVE SUCH A MEMORABLE
. . .": *Ibid.,* AB1 to Commodore Perry, July 1, 1856.

p. 176–177 "THE SUM OF FIVE . . .": *Ibid.,* memorandum of property and liabilities of service, M. C. Perry.

177 "A CHANGE OF AIR . . .": AB4, Alphonse de Rothschild to Caroline, March 31, 1858.

177 "WHENEVER I SEE . . .": R. Liebeschütz Private Collection, Simon to AB1, July 27, 1859.

178 "[A]LTHOUGH ALL YOUR LETTERS . . .": AB4, Simon to AB1, November 8, 1859.

178 "ONE DOES NOT NEED . . .": R. Liebeschütz Private Collection, Simon to AB1, July 28, 1859.

178 "THE EXCESSIVE FUNCTIONING . . .": AB4, Simon to AB1, November 8, 1859.

Chapter Twenty-one

179 "THE BARON, THOUGH . . .": G. T. Strong, Vol. III, 40.

179 "INTRODUCED INTO A ROOM . . .": SRL, 24.

180 "BELMONT IS QUITE . . .": *Ibid.,* 20.

180 "I HAVE ONLY ONE OBJECT . . .": Buchanan Papers, HSPL, AB1 to Slidell, December 8, 1857.

180 "MY APPOINTMENT . . .": *Ibid.,* AB1 to Slidell, June 5, 1858.

180 "PRESSED AUGUST'S CANDIDACY . . .": *The New York Times,* February 14, 1859.

181 "CONVERT THE GOVERNMENT . . .": Beard, Vol. II, 5–6.

181 "THE BAIT WHICH THE DEMOCRATIC . . .": Miles Papers, University of North Carolina, W. G. Simms to W. P. Miles, February 3, 1859.

181 "THE LITTLE JOKER . . .": *The New York Times,* February 14, 1859.

182 "THE TONE OF IT WAS . . .": Buchanan Papers, HSPL, Slidell to Buchanan, July 3, 1859.

182 "I HAVE HEARD . . .": *Ibid.*

182 "OUR FRIEND BELMONT . . .": *Ibid.*

184 "THE DOCTRINE THAT . . .": Foner, 158.

185 "THE SUBSTANTIAL . . .": AB4, Franklin Pierce to AB1, March 17, 1860.

186 "THE ONLY MAN IN THE . . .": Douglas Papers, UCL, West to Douglas, April 16, 1860.

187 "WE DO NOT MAKE . . .": AB4, AB1 to Caroline, April 25, 1860.

p. 188 "KID GLOVE, SCENTED, . . .": Mushkat, 318.

188 "NEVER MIND, . . .": Halstead, 38.

189 "SEND NO MESSAGES . . .": AB4, Douglas to AB1, May 8, 1860.

189 "IN A FORMER ARTICLE . . .": NYHS, scrapbook, *New York Leader,* May 1860.

189 "MUST OPEN . . .": Douglas Papers, UCL, AB1 to Douglas, May 18, 1860.

189 "YOUR CONDUCT . . .": AB4, Douglas to AB1, June 4, 1860.

Chapter Twenty-two

190 "ALL VERY UGLY . . .": SRL, 52.

190 "AT NIGHT MAKES . . .": Still, 167.

191 "SPLENDID HOUSE . . .": G. T. Strong, Vol. III, 36–37.

191 "PERFUMED HAIR . . .": SRL, 56.

191–192 "A RAGGED RAINBOW . . .": M. H. Elliott, 53.

192 "HUGE, YELLOW PAGODA . . .": Amory, *The Last Resorts,* 181.

192 "MR. BELMONT KEEPS . . .": Elliott, 47.

192 "BEAUTIFUL . . .": SRL, 67.

192 "A FOREIGNER . . .": SRL, 68.

193 "THERE IS NOTHING . . .": *Ibid.*

193 "THERE IS AT PRESENT . . .": Douglas Papers, UCL, AB1 to Douglas, July 28, 1860.

193 "FELT AS IF . . .": *Ibid.,* July 26, 1860.

193–194 "UNLESS WE CAN . . .": *Ibid.,* AB1 to Douglas, July 28, 1860.

194 "IT IS IMPOSSIBLE . . .": *Ibid.,* Taylor to Douglas, July 29, 1860.

194 "UNABLE OR UNWILLING . . .": *Ibid.*

194 "IT WILL NOT DO . . .": *Ibid.*

194 "A GREAT INJUSTICE . . .": *Ibid.,* August 13, 1860.

195 "THIS STATE MUST . . .": Bell Papers, LOC, AB1 to B. Duncan, August 19, 1860.

195 "IF WE COULD ONLY DEMONSTRATE . . .": *Ibid.,* AB1 to Douglas, July 28, 1860.

196 "I KNOW THAT MY SUGGESTION . . .": Douglas Papers, UCL, AB1 to Douglas, July 18, 1860.

196 "BOY LOST . . .": NYHS

scrapbook, *New York Evening Post,* October 1860.

p. 197 "POPULAR SOVEREIGNTY . . .": *The New York Times,* September 13, 1860.

197 "THE ORGY OVER . . .": SRL, 70.

197 "THOSE WHO WERE . . .": *Ibid.,* 71.

197–198 "BY MONDAY NEXT . . .": G. T. Strong, Vol. III, 45.

198 "I HAVE NEVER WITNESSED . . .": AB4, AB1 to unknown, n.d. [1860].

198 "SHONE AFAR . . .": *The New York Times,* October 13, 1860.

198 "FROM HIS CONNECTION . . .": NYHS scrapbook, *New York Leader,* October, 1860.

198–199 "IN LESS THAN FOUR . . .": *The New York Times,* November 4, 1860.

199 "MEN WHO CONFESS . . .": Sandburg, *The War Years,* Vol. I, 32.

199 "MONEY IS HOARDED . . .": SRL, 83.

199–200 "NEW YORK, IN SUCH A . . .": AB1, AB1 to J. Forsythe, December 19, 1860, *A Few Letters and Speeches,* 22.

200 "TO LEAVE TO MY . . .": *Ibid.*

200 "THE COUNTRY . . .": *Ibid.,* November 22, 1860.

200 "SHORT-SIGHTED . . .": AB1, AB1 to Pringle, November 26, 1860, *A Few Letters and Speeches,* 9.

200 "I FOR ONE . . .": *Ibid.,* 19.

200 "THE AMERICAN PEOPLE . . .": *Ibid.,* 24.

200 "THE IDEA OF SEPARATE . . .": *Ibid.,* 11.

200 "THE DISSOLUTION . . .": *Ibid.,* 8.

201 "A REIGN OF TERROR . . .": *Ibid.,* 26.

201 "THE SECESSION LEADERS . . .": *Ibid.,* 8.

201 "A MOST EFFICACIOUS . . .": *AAD,* 94.

201 "THE WISE AND CONCILIATORY . . .": AB1, *A Few Letters and Speeches,* 18.

202 "IN MY OPINION . . .": Douglas Papers, UCL, AB1 to Douglas, December 31, 1860.

202 "THE SELF-DENIAL . . .": *Ibid.*

202 "THE SECEDERS . . . ARE BEHAVING . . .": *Ibid.,* February 11, 1860.

203 "MARK AN EPOCH . . .": SRL, 90.

203 "ONE OF THOSE OLD . . .": *Ibid.*

p. 203 "ELEGANT . . .": W. H. Russell, 26.

204 "I HEARD IT DECLARED . . .": *Ibid.*

Chapter Twenty-three

204 "A QUESTION OF NATIONAL . . .": Foner, 299.

205 "IT IS THE FLAG . . .": *The New York Times,* May 16, 1861, *A Few Letters and Speeches,* 100.

205 "STEP TOWARD . . .": AB1, AB1 to Lionel de Rothschild, May 21, 1861, *A Few Letters and Speeches,* 32.

206 "YOU KNOW THAT . . .": AB1, *A Few Letters and Speeches,* 32–35.

206 "IT WOULD BE DIFFICULT . . .": *Ibid.,* 36.

206 "A HOME GUARD . . .": Seward Papers, URL, AB1 to Seward, June 18, 1861.

206 "IT IS CLEAR . . .": *Ibid.*

207 "BEFORE THE WAR . . .": *Ibid.,* June 6, 1861.

207 "A NATIONAL SUBSCRIPTION . . .": AB4, AB1 to Chase, June 14, 1861.

207 "BE NECESSARY TO LOOK . . .": Seward Papers, URL, AB1 to Seward, June 6, 1861.

207 "IT IS IMPOSSIBLE TO SAY . . .": Chase Papers, LOC, AB1 to Chase, July 3, 1861.

207 "OUR ARMY HAS . . .": AB4, AB1 to Chase, June 24, 1861.

208 "NO HARM WOULD . . .": Chase Papers, LOC, AB1 to Chase, July 3, 1861.

208 "ACTING . . . NOT AS . . .": *Ibid.*

208 "VOYAGE FROM NEW YORK . . .": SRL, 125.

208 "WITH ONE SHOE . . .": AB4, Perry Belmont to AB1, June 23, 1861.

209 "THERE WAS ONE . . .": *Ibid.,* Perry Belmont to AB1, June 23, 1861.

209 "OVER THE BRIDGES . . .": *Ibid.,* Military Pass, June 13, 1861, By order of General Joseph K. Mansfield, signed Drake De-Kay, Aide-de-Camp.

210 "MISCHIEVOUS RUMOR . . .": Chase Papers, LOC, AB1 to Chase, August 15, 1861.

210 "WHERE THE UNITED . . .": Seward Papers, URL, AB1 to Seward, July 30, 1861.

p. 210 "I suppose we . . ." Kohler Papers, American Jewish Historical Society, AB1 to Chase, August 15, 1861.

210 "enlist a few men . . .": *Ibid.*

210 "I have no purpose . . .": Foote, Vol. I, 39.

210–211 "we have nothing . . .": Kohler Papers, American Jewish Historical Society, AB1 to Chase, August 15, 1861.

211 "excuse . . . to break . . .": Seward Papers, URL, AB1 to Seward, July 30, 1861.

211 "we do not like . . .": *Ibid.*

211 "the general feeling . . .": *Ibid.*, August 16, 1861.

211 "our blockade . . .": *Ibid.*

Chapter Twenty-four

212 "a dangerous . . .": AB4, AB1 to Barlow, October 30, 1861.

212 "this is a time when . . .": *Ibid.*

212 "the influence of the administration . . .": Kohler Papers, American Jewish Historical Society, AB1 to Chase, August 15, 1861.

212 "your observations . . .": AB4, Chase to AB1, September 13, 1861.

212 "the remotest chance . . .": Chase Papers, LOC, AB1 to Chase, October 31, 1861.

212 "confident that, if . . .": AB4, Chase to AB1, September 13, 1861.

212 "restricted within . . .": *Ibid.*

213 "the Emperor . . .": Seward Papers, URL, AB1 to Seward, October 21, 1861.

213 "with three times . . .": Barlow Papers, Huntington Library, AB1 to Barlow, October 30, 1861.

213 "crafty and clever . . .": Barlow Papers, Huntington Library, AB1 to Barlow, October 30, 1861.

213 "would it be right . . .": *Ibid.*

214 "Goodbye, my dear . . .": Foote, Vol. I, 139.

214 "How enlightened . . .": Barlow Papers, Huntington Library, AB1 to Barlow, December 10, 1861.

214 "not a dozen . . .": AB4, AB1 to Seward, December 8, 1861.

p. 214 "strike a deadly . . .": *Ibid.*

214–215 "the retention of the . . .": Barlow Papers, Huntington Library, AB1 to Barlow, December 10, 1861.

215 "the President . . .": AB4, AB1 to Seward, December 8, 1861.

215 "on what an errand . . .": Barlow Papers, Huntington Library, AB1 to Barlow, February 10, 1861.

215 "all the resources . . .": *Ibid.*

215 "I could certainly . . .": *Ibid.*

Chapter Twenty-five

216 "what frightens me . . .": Seward Papers, URL, AB1 to Weed, July 20, 1862.

216–217 "at once establish . . .": *Ibid.*

217 "one of the wealthiest . . .": Seward Papers, URL, AB1 to Weed, July 24, 1862.

217 "say officially . . .": AB4, Lincoln to AB1, July 31, 1862.

217 "Broken eggs . . .": *Ibid.*

217 "my profound . . .": AB4, McClellan to AB1, December 7, 1862.

217–218 ". . . while the rebel . . .": Lincoln Papers, LOC, AB1 to Lincoln, August 10, 1862.

218 "they must become . . .": *Ibid.*

218 " 'imbicillity' . . .": Rhodes, *History of the Civil War,* 85.

219 "the appointment of Stanton . . .": AB4, AB1 to Barlow, n.d. [1862].

219 "right or wrong . . .": Lincoln Papers, LOC, AB1 to Lincoln, September 4, 1862.

219 "wisdom and moderation . . .": Barlow Papers, Huntington Library, AB1 to Barlow, February 10, 1862.

219 "while I fully . . .": *Ibid.*, October 1, 1862.

220 "like all money . . .": *Ibid.*, August 24, 1862.

220 "charming novel . . .": Marble Collection, LOC, AB1 to Marble, April 13, 1862.

220 "exchange is no . . .": *Ibid.*

220 "I have been . . . at the club . . .": AB4, AB1 to Marble, May 14, 1862.

*p.*220 "IN MY YOUTH . . .": Wolcott, 49.

220 "AMBITION FOR AVARICE.": Mitchell, Stewart, 231.

220–221 "THINK ME . . .": *Ibid.,* 246–247.

221 "MY NOMINATION WOULD . . .": Barlow Papers, Huntington Library, AB1 to Barlow, November, 27, 1862.

221 "IT WOULD HAVE GRATIFIED . . .": *Ibid.,* AB1 to Barlow, October 1, 1862.

221 "ALAS FOR NEXT . . .": G. T. Strong, Vol. III, 268.

221 "O ABRAHAM . . .": *Ibid.,* 256.

222 "IRREGULAR ARRESTS . . .": *Ibid.,* 268–269.

222 "TRAITORS AND SEYMOURITES . . .": *Ibid.*

222 "MISAPPREHENSION . . . WITH REGARD . . .": AB1 to Lionel de Rothschild, November 25, 1862, AB1, *A Few Letters and Speeches,* 10.

222 "WHY DID YOU NOT . . .": Barlow Papers, Huntington Library, AB1 to Barlow, August 24, 1862.

223 "A POWERFUL DEMONSTRATION . . .": Tilden Papers, NYPL, AB1 to Tilden, January 27, 1863.

223 "IF I TAP . . .": Foote, Vol. I, 245.

224 "ONE OF THOSE STUPID . . .": G. T. Strong, Vol. III, 300–301.

225 "IT WAS INTENTIONAL . . .": *Ibid.*

225 "I HAVE RECEIVED . . .": Barlow Papers, Huntington Library, AB1 to Barlow, October 12, 1869.

225 "HAD BEEN CONSORTING . . .": G. T. Strong, III, 301.

226 "WE WENT TO SOME . . .": AB1 to Lord Rokeby, May 7, 1863, AB1, *A Few Letters and Speeches,* 85.

226 "LET YOUR STATESMEN . . .": AB1 to Lionel de Rothschild, April 14, 1863, AB1, *A Few Letters and Speeches,* 81.

227 "AFTER THE CONVERSATION . . .": AB4, AB1 to Peters, May 1863.

227 "THE CHARGE CONVEYED . . .": *Ibid.*

227 "THERE WAS A PERIOD . . .": AB4, Peters to AB1, n.d. [May 1863].

227–228 "REFERENCE TO NEWSPAPER . . .": AB4, AB1 to Peters, May 25, 1862.

*p.*228 "I HONOR . . .": AB4, Peters to AB1, n.d.

228 "IN ORDER . . .": Seward Papers, URL, AB1 to Seward, May 18, 1863.

Chapter Twenty-six

228–229 "WHEN ARE YOU COMING . . .": AB4, Bancroft to AB1, October 20, 1862.

230 "FINE CASSEMERE PANTS . . .": McCague, 115.

231 "THE RINGLEADERS OF . . .": Seward Papers, URL, AB1 to Seward, July 20, 1863.

231 "IN A CITY LIKE . . .": *Ibid.*

231 "OUR DIFFERENT . . .": *Ibid.*

231 "THE BEST AND MOST . . .": AB1 to Seward, July 20, 1863, AB1, *A Few Letters and Speeches,* 90.

231 "IF I COULD SAVE . . .": Lincoln to Greeley, August 22, 1862, *Columbia Encyclopedia,* 862.

232 "FULL JUSTICE TO . . .": AB4, AB1 to Caroline, October 9, 1863.

232–233 "PERRY IS MORE . . .": *Ibid.*

233 "SHOW WELL OVER . . .": *Ibid.*

233 "A FEARFUL SIGHT . . .": *Ibid.*

233–234 "IF WE LIVE . . .": *Ibid.*

234 "I WAS DELIGHTED . . .": AB4, AB1 to Caroline, October 19, 1863.

234 "WE MUST NOT SHUT . . .": Seward Papers, URL, AB1 to Seward, November 29, 1863.

234 "I HAVE REALIZED . . .": AB4, AB1 to Caroline, October 9, 1863.

234 "I AM MORE AND MORE . . .": *Ibid.*

235 "THE PLACE IS FILLED . . .": AB4, AB1 to Caroline, October 23, 1863.

235 "I AM MAKING MYSELF . . .": *Ibid.,* AB1 to Caroline, October 29, 1863.

235 "OLD JAMES . . .": AB4, AB1 to Caroline, November 6, 1863.

235 "I HAVE NOT . . .": *Ibid.*

236 "THE BABY . . . IS OFF . . .": AB4, Caroline to AB1, n.d.

236 "TO COME HOME . . .": *Ibid.*

236 "YOUR REQUEST NOT . . .": AB4, AB1 to Caroline, November 13, 1863.

236 "BLACK LACE . . .": *Ibid.,* October 29, 1863.

236 "NOT TO SEND . . .": *Ibid.,* November 6, 1863.

*p.*236 "In fact . . .": AB4, AB1 to Caroline, November 6, 1863.

236 "If they are not pretty . . .": *Ibid.*, October 29, 1863.

237 "My room looks . . .": *Ibid.*, November 6, 1863.

237 "I am . . .": *Ibid.*, November 13, 1863.

237 "Oh, how I wish . . .": *Ibid.*, October 29, 1863.

237 "Hard customers . . .": *Ibid.*, November 13, 1863.

237 "They would not listen . . .": *Ibid.*

237 "Died . . .": SRL, 5.

238 "I think, my darling . . .": *Ibid.*, November 15, 1863.

238 "I feel old . . .": *Ibid.*

tion . . .": *New York World,* August 29, 1864.

*p.*246 "We are assembled . . .": *Ibid.*

246–247 "In your hands . . .": *Ibid.*

247 "Profoundly sad . . .": Brooks, 168.

247 "I have a most horrid . . .": Barlow Papers, Huntington Library, AB1 to Barlow, August 29, 1864.

247 "He supported Mr. Douglas . . .": *The New York Times,* September 4, 1864.

248 "I don't think . . .": Barlow Papers, Huntington Library, AB1 to Barlow, August 29, 1864.

Chapter Twenty-seven

238 "Bought and paid for . . .": Seward Papers, URL, AB1 to Seward, December 10, 1863.

239 "A malicious calumny . . .": AB4, AB1 to Corcoran, February 8, 1864.

239 "My own views . . .": *Ibid.*

239 "In my repeated . . .": *Ibid.*

240 "We must take in . . .": G. T. Strong, Vol. III, 336–337.

240 "The Committee on Flowers . . .": AB4, Document of Metropolitan Fair for the U.S. Sanitary Commission.

240 "One of the best . . .": NYHS scrapbook, from two clippings, March 1864.

240 "It is a comparatively . . .": *Ibid.*

242 "Out of chaos . . .": NYHS scrapbook, AB1 speech, September 1862.

242 "What can be expected . . .": Moore, Vol. XI, 353, Buchanan to John Blake, December 31, 1863.

244 "Urge postponement . . .": Barlow Papers, Huntington Library, AB1 to Barlow, June 15, 1864.

244 "I predict . . .": G. T. Strong, Vol. III, 477.

245 "A pledge . . .": Marble Papers, LOC, AB1 to Barlow, August 24, 1864.

245 "Seymour . . .": Barlow Papers, Huntington Library, AB1 to Barlow, August 29, 1864.

245 "All going well . . .": *Ibid.*, August 30, 1864.

246 "Gentlemen of the Conven-

Chapter Twenty-eight

249 "Five at a time . . .": *AAD,* 72.

250 "We have splendid . . .": *Ibid.*, 72–73, Perry Belmont to AB1, November 1, 1864.

250 "I like it pretty . . .": *Ibid.*, 72.

250 ". . . It has been raining . . .": AB4, AB2 to Caroline, November 8, 1864.

250 "What was Robert . . .": AB4, AB2 to Caroline, November 14, 1864.

251 "I hear you and . . .": *Ibid.*, AB2 to AB1, October 22, 1864.

251 "I have not received . . .": *Ibid.*

251 "I am sure . . .": AB4, AB2 to Caroline, November 4, 1864.

252 "It is absolutely necessary . . .": McClellan Papers, LOC, AB1 to McClellan, September 3, 1864.

252 "McClellan's letter . . .": G. T. Strong, Vol. IV, 482.

252 "Do not listen . . .": McClellan Papers, LOC, Vallandigham to McClellan, September 4, 1864.

253 "If we carry . . .": Marble Papers, LOC, AB1 to Marble, September 13, 1864.

254 "Boston . . .": *Ibid.*, April 28, 1864.

254 "Indeed if . . .": *The New York Times,* September 18, 1864.

254 "We are told . . .": AB1, *A Few Letters and Speeches,* 111.

255 "Finest possible . . .": G. T. Strong, Vol. III, 488–489.

p. 255 ". . . SOLDIERS WILL NOT . . .":
AB4, Chairman of the Demo-
cratic State Central Committee
to AB1, n.d. [1864].

255 "ANDREW JOHNSON . . .":
NYHS, "To the People,"
clipping, October 11, 1864.

255 "OPPOSE ALL ARMISTICES . . .":
Ibid.

256 "ARMY CAMPS . . .": NYHS
scrapbook, clipping, October
31, 1864.

256 "DOGGED AND EVERY . . .":
W. S. Myers, 460.

257 "SUPPORTING GENERAL . . .":
Sandburg, *The War Years,*
Vol. III, 296.

257 "LET US LOOK . . .": *The New
York Times,* October 9, 1864.

257 "THE QUESTION BEFORE . . .":
quoted in *The Israelite* XI, 99,
September 23, 1864.

257 "A SELLOUT TO WALL . . .":
Gray, 201.

257 "THEN THERE IS THE . . .":
The New York Times, November 2, 1864.

258 "WHAT A SCANDAL . . .":
Frothingham, 463–464.

258 "MCCLELLAN MAY POSSIBLY
. . .": U.S. Government Print-
ing Office, Halleck to Sherman,
November 16, 1864.

258 "BARLOW, BELMONT, . . .":
G. T. Strong, Vol. III, 486.

258 "JEW-PRESIDENT . . .": McClellan Papers, LOC, Langen-
schwartz to McClellan, June
27, 1864.

258 "THOUGH A JEW . . .": *The
New York Times,* November 6,
1864.

258 "REPUTED SON . . .": *New York
Evening Post,* October 6, 1864.

259 "IN HONOR OF THE AUSPICIOUS
. . .": *The New York Times,*
October 17, 1864.

259 "WE COMMEND . . .": *Ibid.*

259 "SPIRITLESS . . .": *Ibid.,* October 18, 1864.

259 "HAS HITHERTO BEEN . . .":
AB4, clipping from the *New
York Herald,* n.d. [October
1864].

259 "BELMONT WENT OFF . . .":
G. T. Strong, Vol. III, 510.

259–260 "IF ONLY MCCLELLAN'S . . .":
Ibid., 511.

Chapter Twenty-nine

260 "IF ONLY THE CONVENTION
. . .": AB4, AB1 to Marble,
November 30, 1864.

p. 260 "DECLARED IN FAVOR . . .":
Ibid.

260 "ALLOWED BARLOW . . .": G.. T
Strong, Vol. III, 511.

260 "THE DEMOCRATIC WORLD . . .":
NYHS scrapbook, *Mobile Reporter,* clipping, n.d.

261 "NO RHYME OR . . .": *Ibid.*

261 "HIS DEPARTURE . . .": Barlow
Papers, Huntington Library,
AB1 to Barlow, December 21,
1864.

261–262 "YOU CAN . . . IMAGINE . . .":
AB4, McClellan to AB1,
March 19, 1865.

262 "YOU DON'T KNOW HOW . . .":
AAD, 73, Perry Belmont to
AB1, November 20, 1864.

262 "I OWE YOU . . .": Marble
Papers, LOC, AB1 to Marble,
n.d. (at Union Club, 6:30).

262 "I HAVE BEEN MADE THE . . .":
Seward Papers, URL, AB1 to
Seward, February 21, 1865.

262–263 "POOR, PRETTY, LITTLE . . .":
G. T. Strong, Vol. III, 514.

263 "I WILL NOT WRITE . . .":
AB4, AB2 to Caroline, February 2, 1865.

263 "SHOULD NOT BE IMPATIENT
. . .": *Ibid.,* March 24, 1865.

264 "I HAVE MET . . .": *Ibid.,* AB2
to AB1, January 12, 1865.

264 "I AM . . . SORRY . . .": *Ibid.,*
AB2 to Caroline, February 7,
1865.

264 "PRIVATE ACCOUNT . . .": *Ibid.,*
February 2, 1865.

265 "I WANT A DECISIVE . . .": *Ibid.*

265 "MAMMA . . .": *Ibid.*

265 "BEING NOW AT LEISURE . . .":
Ibid., AB2 to AB1, May 11,
1865.

265 "HANG OUT YOUR . . .": *The
New York Times,* April 10,
1865.

265–266 "JUST BEFORE THE LAST . . .":
Ibid., May 3, 1865.

267 "THERE ARE HOPEFUL . . .":
G. T. Strong, Vol. III, 586.

266 "GENERAL MCCLELLAN . . .":
National Archives, Lincoln
Assassination Suspects File,
Microfilm Series M599, Frame
Numbers 1137–1139. Anony-
mous to Stanton, May 18,
1865.

Chapter Thirty

272 "I WANT TO . . .": O'Connor,
The Golden Summers, 98.

273 "W-H-Y Y-E-S . . .": Clews, 408.

275 "AFTER ALL . . .": Leslie, 53.

*p.*276 "AUGUST, . . . DO YOU . . .": *Ibid.*, 22.

276 "I CHANCED TO STOP . . .": AB4, Jerome to AB1, July 14, 1864.

276–277 "I SHALL ACCEPT . . .": AB4, Jerome to AB1, n.d.

277 "THIS COMMUNITY IS DEVOID . . .": G. T. Strong, quoted in O'Connor, *The German-Americans,* 247.

277 "PEOPLE LIKE BELMONT . . .": Martin, 26.

277 "THIS, THE SUMMER . . .": *AAD,* 74.

277 "PROFESSOR CHILD IS ONE OF THE MOST . . .": *Ibid.,* 130–131.

277 "AS TO MR. CHILD'S . . .": *Ibid.*

278 "PERRY, . . . WE HAD THE BEST . . .": AB4, AB2 to Perry, February 6, 1886.

278 "I SEE YOU HAVE . . .": AB4, AB2 to Caroline, February 11, 1886.

279 "I THANK GOD . . .": Sandburg, *The War Years,* IV, 338.

279 "THE ERRING MEMBERS . . .": *New York World,* July 11, 1865.

279 "TO EXPRESS . . . MY SINCERE . . .": Johnson Papers, LOC, AB1 to Johnson, March 24, 1866.

280 "TAKEN THE WIND . . .": Barlow Papers, Huntington Library, AB1 to Barlow, June 26, 1866.

280 "DEFUNCT . . .": Marble Papers, LOC, AB1 to Marble, February 18, 1866 (misdated 1867).

280 "SHABBILY TREATED . . .": *Ibid.*

280 "RICHLY DISGUISED . . .": *Ibid.*

281 "GIVING UP THE NATIONAL . . .": AB4, AB1 to Barlow, June 26, 1860.

281 "THINGS SEEM . . .": Marble Papers, LOC, AB1 to Marble, July 17, 1866 (misdated 1865).

281 "THE PRESIDENT BECAME . . .": Clews, 291–92.

282 "FORGET NOT . . .": AB1 Collection, NYPL, May 26, 1866.

282 "WE DID NOT GO . . .": AB4, Frederika to AB2, n.d. [1866].

Chapter Thirty-one

284 "A HANDSOME MODERN . . .": Bowmar, 53.

285 "I AM GLAD . . .": AB4, Mayer Rothschild to AB1, July 16, n.d.

*p.*285 "PROBABLY THE MOST . . .": Bowmar, 51.

285 "WHEN LEONARD . . .": *Ibid.*

285 "WHENEVER A MEMBER . . .": Glanz, 17.

286 "[W]HILE BARON ROTHSCHILD . . .": *The Turf, Field and Farm,* August 11, 1866.

286 "AS A MERE POPULAR . . .": *The New York Times,* September 26, 1866.

287–288 "AN ATTEMPT HAS . . .": *The Nation,* October 11, 1866.

288 "FANCY A MAN . . .": *The Turf, Field and Farm,* October 20, 1866.

288 "WHENEVER NEW YORK PEOPLE . . .": *Pittsburgh Daily Commercial,* November 7, 1866.

288–289 "BEFORE YOU COULD . . .": *The Turf, Field and Farm,* September 29, 1866.

289 "DO AS THOUSANDS . . .": *Ibid.*

289 "THE PRESTIGE OF JEROME . . .": *Ibid.*

289 "RACING . . .": Oral history, legendary quote.

290 "RIDICULOUS ONSLAUGHTS . . .": Marble Papers, LOC, AB1 to Marble, July 4, 1867.

290 "ONLY CHANNEL THROUGH . . .": *Ibid.*

290 "[T]HE SHEEP RUSH . . .": *Wilke's The Spirit of the Times,* June 22, 1867.

291 "WAS NOW DEAD AS . . .": *Ibid.,* June 29, 1867.

Chapter Thirty-two

292 "AGAIN COMPLAIN . . .": AB4, AB1 to W. H. Kemble, January 28, 1868.

292 "NO ARRANGEMENT . . .": *Ibid.,* W. H. Kemble to AB1, January 30, 1868.

292 "COARSE AND IMPERTINENT . . .": *Ibid.,* AB1 to House of Rothschild, February 4, 1868.

293 "LETTER DESERVED . . .": *Ibid.*

293 "HUNDREDS OF WIDOWS . . .": AB4, AB1 to W. H. Kemble, February 4, 1868.

293 "SHOW UP THE STATE . . .": *Ibid.*

293 "WE DESIRE TO CALL . . .": *Patriot and Union,* February 12, 1868.

p. 293 "AS USUAL, GENTLEMANLY . . .": NYHS scrapbook, clipping, "Ordinary Courtesy."

294 "I FEAR THAT . . .": AB4, John Hancock to AB1, May 17, 1867.

295 "IT CAN NEVER . . .": *Ibid.*

295 "THE WAR HAS REDUCED . . .": AB4, L. Hanes to AB1, April 16, 1867.

295 "I THINK IT WILL BE A GOOD . . .": Marble Papers, LOC, December 12, 1867.

296 "A DIFFERENT ARRANGEMENT . . .": AB4, Child to AB1, January 29, 1868.

296 "IF THERE IS ANYTHING . . .": *Ibid.*, AB2 to Caroline, November 1867.

296 "I KEEP CAREFUL . . .": *Ibid.*, AB2 to Jeannie Belmont, February 6, 1868.

296–297 "NOW IT WOULD HAVE . . .": AB4, AB2, to Caroline, October 20, 1868.

297 "IT SEEMS AS IF, SINCE . . .": AB4, AB2 to AB1, March 1, 1868.

297 "IF I SHOULD COME . . .": *Ibid.*

297–298 "RUGBY IS A NOBLE SCHOOL . . .": AB4, Everest to AB1, March 28, 1868.

298 "IT MAKES ME MAD . . .": *Ibid.*, AB2 to Caroline, April 2, 1868.

298 "YOU HAVE NOT GONE . . .": *Ibid.*, AB2 to Caroline, April 8, 1868.

298 "PLEASE WRITE BY FIRST . . .": *Ibid.*

298 "WILL YOU COME . . .": Marble Papers, LOC, AB1 to Marble, April 29, 1868.

298 "ACCORDING TO THEIR . . .": Locke, *The Struggles of Petroleum V. Nasby*, 681.

299 "RATHER CURTLY . . .": *The New York Times*, February 29, 1867.

300 "THE PRESIDENT WUZ . . .": Locke, *The Struggles of Petroleum V. Nasby*, 509–10.

300 "A NEWCOMER IN THE PARTY . . .": *AAD*, 135.

301 "COOL, FIRM, . . .": AB4, AB1 to Nathaniel Rothschild, February 4, 1868.

301 "THE MAN WHO DIDN'T . . .": Coleman, 175.

301 "PERHAPS, . . . WE MAY HAVE . . .": Marble Papers, LOC, AB1 to Marble, December 16, 1867.

p. 301 "ENTHRONED . . .": *Wilke's Spirit of the Times*, June 13, 1868.

302 "NOR HAS NEGRO . . .": AB4, unidentified newspaper clipping, n.d. [1868].

302 "TO WELCOME THE NEGRO . . .": *New York World*, February 23, 1868.

302 "RENDERING THE WHITE . . .": *Ibid.*, June 19, 1868.

302 "IN REGARD TO . . .": AB4, AB1 to Chase, May 29, 1868.

303 "THIS IS EQUIVALENT TO A . . .": G. T. Strong, Vol. IV, 217.

303 "WITH ALL MY . . .": Chase Papers, LOC, F. Aiken to Chase, June 25, 1868.

303 "POCKETS ARE OFTEN . . .": *The New York Times*, May 6, 1868.

303 "OUR MASTER, AS WELL . . .": *Cincinnati West and South*, February 29, 1868.

304 "PITY ME, HARVEY . . .": *Cincinnati Commercial*, August 31, 1868.

304 "IT IS IDLE TO TALK . . .": *New York World*, July 3, 1868.

305 "INTEND CONGRESSIONAL . . .": AB1, *A Few Letters and Speeches*, AB1 speech, July 4, 1868.

305 "I HAVE SPENT . . .": Marble Papers, LOC, AB1 to Marble, July 4, 1867.

305 "TO GIVE TO THE REPORTERS . . .": *Ibid.*, AB1 to Marble, May 1868.

305–306 "DWELL AS LITTLE . . .": *Ibid.*, AB1 to Marble, July 11, 1868.

306 "DO YOU THINK THERE . . .": *Ibid.*, July 19, 1868.

306 ". . . AS THY TINY . . .": AB4, Bachelor's Hall poem "To Mrs. Belmont," September 10, 1868.

306–307 "EVERY EFFORT . . .": Marble Papers, LOC, AB1 to Marble, July 1868.

307 "WE HAVE BEEN A LONG . . .": Tilden Papers, NYPL, Seymour to Tilden, July 20, 1868.

308 "I WANT TO GO . . .": Marble Papers, LOC, AB1 to Marble, August 17, 1868.

309 "I AM VERY GLAD . . .": *AAD*, 155.

310 "I HAVE SPENT . . .": AB4, AB1 to Marble, n.d. [1868].

Chapter Thirty-three

p. 310 "Daniel Drew . . .": Clews, 119.

311 "The difference between . . .": Sobel, 127.

311 "Hell has broken . . .": Warshow, 123–124.

313 "The price . . .": *Ibid.*

313 "Why, it was good . . .": *Ibid.*

314 "If this printing . . .": *Ibid.*

314 "Can't tell just . . .": Josephson, *The Robber Barons,* 127.

315 "Which said, 'Drew . . .'": Warshow, 128.

315 "The Erie war . . .": Josephson, *The Robber Barons,* 133.

316 "The Commodore was sitting . . .": Clews, 183.

316 "Sold ourselves to . . .": *Ibid.* 183.

316 ". . . I remember . . .": *Ibid.*

316 "There ain't nothin' . . .": Mott, 161.

319 "Then . . . I am a ruined . . .": *Ibid.,* 165.

319 "I swear I will . . .": *Ibid.*

321 "The aspect of Erie . . .": Barlow Papers, Huntington Library, AB1 to Barlow, April 30, 1869 (1).

321 "The whole affair . . .": Barlow Papers, Huntington Library, AB1 to Barlow, April 30, 1869 (2).

Chapter Thirty-four

322 "It will be three . . .": AB4, Caroline to Perry, Belmont, n.d. [winter 1868–1869].

322 "I do not wish . . .": *Ibid.,* Child to AB1, September 4, 1868.

323 "I scarcely dare . . .": *Ibid.,* AB2, to Caroline, December 17, 1868.

323 "Entertains us with . . .": *Ibid.,* AB2 to Caroline, September 22, 1868.

323 "She won't do . . .": *Ibid.,* AB2 to Caroline, January 1869.

323 "She is over-kind . . .": *Ibid.*

324 "I only wanted your . . .": *Ibid.,* AB2 to Caroline, January 19, 1869.

p. 324 "To begin with . . .": *Ibid.,* Perry Belmont to AB1, March 15, 1869.

324 "Was in the process . . .": *Ibid.*

325 "The 'Doctor' . . .": *Ibid.*

325 "You accuse me . . .": *Ibid.,* AB2 to Caroline, June 4, 1869.

325 "A place where you . . .": *Ibid.*

326 "He always cautioned . . .": *AAD,* 134.

326 "You know, gentlemen . . .": *Ibid.,* 133.

326 "I am very glad . . .": AB4. Caroline to Perry, n.d. [1869].

327 "Who has passed . . .": AB4. *AAD,* 136.

327 "My poor Rickie . . .": Barlow Papers, Huntington Library, AB1 to Barlow, April 30, 1869.

327 "To fulfill, at last . . .": Barlow Papers, Huntington Library, AB1 to Barlow, April 30, 1869.

328 "Pray destroy . . .": Marble Papers, LOC, AB1 to Marble, n.d. [1869].

328 "Manuscripts and scrapbook . . .": *Ibid.*

329 "Nine out of ten . . .": *The Spirit of the Times,* June 5, 1869.

330 "Glenelg's jockey . . .": Robertson, 106.

Chapter Thirty-five

330 "Done wonders . . .": Barlow Papers, Huntington Library, AB1 to Barlow, July 19, 1869.

330 "I trust . . . the business . . .": AB4, Alphonse de Rothschild to AB1, December 1, 1868.

331 "There are . . . about a hundred . . .": Marble Papers, LOC, AB1 to Marble, August 11, 1869.

331 "Have not even the merit . . .": *Ibid.*

331 "I hardly know a soul . . .": *Ibid.*

331 "Charming letter . . .": *Ibid.*

332 "Foreign born . . .": *The New York Times,* September 21, 1869.

p. 332 "HAS IN NO . . .": *Ibid.*

332 "IF HE SHOULD TAKE . . .": *Ibid.*

333 "SINS OF THE DEMOCRATS . . .": *Harper's Weekly,* September 11, 1869.

333 "A. BELMONT IS AN INEFFICIENT . . .": *Ibid.*

333 "I HAVE NO DOUBT . . .": Barlow Papers, Huntington Library, AB1 to Barlow, September 30, 1869.

333 "IF . . . SCHELL ONLY . . .": *Ibid.*

333–334 "IN FACT . . . AFTER TILDEN'S . . .": Marble Papers, LOC, AB1 to Marble, September 30, 1869.

334–335 "YOUR ADVICE IS VERY . . .": *Ibid.*

335 "FRIENDS, IF I HAVE ANY . . .": *Ibid.,* n.d. [1869].

335 "I SUGGEST IT TO YOU . . .": *Ibid.*

335 "ENLISTING SOME OF OUR . . .": Barlow Papers, Huntington Library, AB1 to Barlow, October 6, 1869.

335 "DISCREET AND DON'T TELL . . .": *Ibid.*

335 "BELMONT . . . IS REVENGED . . .": *New York Post,* September 23, 1869.

335 "THE STORM . . .": Barlow Papers, Huntington Library, AB1 to Barlow, September 30, 1869.

337 "HAVE YOU ANY TOBACCO . . .": AB4, AB2 to AB1, August 26, 1869.

337–338 "WE HAVE . . . A GREAT DEAL . . .": Marble Papers, LOC, AB1 to Marble, September 30, 1869.

Chapter Thirty-six

338 "I WANT YOU TO USE . . .": AB4, Caroline to AB2, October 28, 1869.

339 "I WILL CERTAINLY . . .": *Ibid.,* AB2 to Perry Belmont, November 14, 1869.

339 "INFLAMMATION OF THE BONE . . .": *Ibid.,* AB2 to Caroline, September 29, 1869.

339 ". . . PLEASE . . . DO WHAT . . .": *Ibid.,* AB2 to Perry Belmont, November 14, 1869.

339 "I AM ASHAMED . . .": *Ibid.,* AB2 to AB1, December 4, 1869.

p. 339 "GOD HAS GRANTED . . .": *Ibid.,* AB1 to AB2, December 20, 1869.

339–340 "UNDER THE CONDITION . . .": *Ibid.*

340 "YOU SEE, MY DEAR . . .": *Ibid.,* AB1 to AB2, December 20, 1869.

340 "I CANNOT TELL YOU . . .": *Ibid.,* AB1 to AB2, December 31, 1869.

340 "PERRY WAS NEGLIGENT . . .": *Ibid.*

340–341 "WILL COMPLY . . .": *Ibid.*

342 "LOTS OF FUNNY GOSSIP . . .": G. T. Strong, Vol. IV, 273.

343 "I TOLD YOU BEFORE . . .": Marble Papers, LOC, AB1 to Marble, March 1, 1870.

343 "I AM VERY MUCH OBLIGED . . .": *Ibid.*

344 "A SORT OF DRESSING . . .": AB4, AB2 to Caroline, February 28, 1870.

344 "SEND YOU WHAT HAS . . .": AB4, "Pig" to AB2, January 20, 1870.

344 "I TOLD YOU I WOULD . . .": *Ibid.,* AB2 to AB1, January 23, 1870.

345 "I HAVE NOT BEEN . . .": AB4, AB2 to Caroline, February 28, 1870.

345 "LADY LOVE . . .": *Ibid.,* AB2 to AB1, May 8, 1870.

345 "IT IS MUCH MORE . . .": *Ibid.,* AB1 to AB2, June 11, 1870.

345 "TO DO JUSTICE . . .": *Ibid.,* AB2 to AB1, April 28, 1870.

345 "AN AUCTION TOOK . . .": AB4, Caroline to AB2, April 23, 1870.

345 "A PAIR OF JAPANESE . . .": Belmont Papers, Houghton Library, Jane Perry to AB2, April 15, 1870.

345–346 "TELL PAPA . . .": AB4, AB2 to Caroline, April 28, 1870.

346 "TO SHUT YOURSELF . . .": AB4, AB1 to AB2, April 5, 1870.

346 "THERE IS NO COURSE . . .": *Ibid.,* AB1 to AB2, June 11, 1870.

346 "TURNING OVER A NEW . . .": *Ibid.,* P. Cummings to AB1, April 20, 1870.

347 "ALICK . . . PROVED . . .": *Ibid.,* Caroline to AB2, January 6, 1870.

347 "THEY SAY HE MUST . . .": *Ibid.,* Caroline to AB2, May 1, 1870.

347 "I blame myself . . .": *Ibid.,* AB2 to AB1, May 8, 1870.

Chapter Thirty-seven

p. 348 "EVERYBODY THINKS WELL . . .": AB4, Child to AB1, March 29, 1870.

348 "BOSTON, GAY BOSTON . . .": AB4, Perry Belmont to AB2, March 15, 1870.

348 "I SUSPECT THE ONLY . . .": AB4, Child to AB1, March 29, 1870.

348 "WE SHALL, OF COURSE . . .": AB4, AB1 to AB2, Wednesday morning, n.d. [summer, 1870].

349 "OUR TWO RAMS . . .": *Ibid.*

349 "I'M SORRY YOU HAVE . . .": AB4, Caroline to AB2, n.d. [summer, 1870].

349 "THE SAME CLEAR, CONCISE . . .": *AAD*, 143.

350 "SO GLORIOUSLY . . .": Muir, *The Writings of John Muir*, Vol. V, 127.

351 "AN ENERGETIC . . .": *AAD*, 140–141.

351 "ON A BEAUTIFUL EVENING . . .": *Ibid.*, 141.

351 "THE BRAVES WERE . . .": *Ibid.*

353 "I MADE HIM JUMP . . .": AB4, Jeannie to Caroline, April 30, 1870.

353 "WHERE I ALWAYS FEEL . . .": AB4, Caroline to AB1, June 24, 1870.

354 "ANXIOUS ABOUT MY BOOK . . .": Marble Papers, LOC, AB1 to Marble, May 2, 1870.

354 "YOU NEVER COME TO SEE . . .": Marble Papers, LOC, AB1 to Marble, May 12, 1870.

355 "WE WILL TREAT . . .": Marble Papers, LOC, AB1 to Marble, August 1, 1870.

355 "AN AMPLE REFUTATION . . .": AB4, R. C. Winthrop to AB1, October 10, 1870.

355–356 "IN SOME PLACES . . .": *Ibid.*, AB2 to Perry, October 7, 1870.

356 "I AM RATHER CURIOUS . . .": *Ibid.*, AB1 to AB2, October 15, 1870.

356 "YOUR GOOD AND LOVING . . .": AB4, AB1 to AB2, November 10, 1870.

356 "LIBERAL . . .": AB4, Chase to AB1, n.d. (August 1870).

357 "IF IT IS POSSIBLE . . .": *Ibid.*, Chase to AB1, September 1870.

357 "PRAY BE GOOD . . .": *Ibid.*, AB1 to AB2, October 3, 1870.

357 "REMEMBER . . . YOUR FATHER . . .": *Ibid.*, AB1 to AB2, October 15, 1870.

p. 357 "PERRY IS SITTING . . .": AB4, Caroline to AB2, October 18, 1870.

358 "I HAVE BEEN HERE . . .": AB4, AB2 to AB1, October 28, 1870.

358 "WE THINK THE TRIP . . .": *Ibid.* Caroline to AB2, October 27, 1870.

358 "IT REFLECTS BADLY . . .": *Ibid.*, AB2 to AB1, October 28, 1870.

358–359 "WHICH IS THE BEST . . .": *Ibid.*

359 "WE WERE AFRAID . . .": *Ibid.*, AB1 to AB2, November 1, 1870.

359 "CONTINUES TO SHOW . . .": *Ibid.*, Chase to AB1, December 22, 1870.

359 "TOO PAINFUL AND TOO . . .": *Ibid.*, AB1 to AB2, October 3, 1870.

359 "I HOPE AND PRAY . . .": *Ibid.*

359–360 "I TRUST THAT YOU . . .": *Ibid.*, Caroline to Perry Belmont, n.d. [fall, 1870].

360 "ALTHOUGH I WOULD LIKE . . .": AAD, 142–143.

360–361 ". . . INSTEAD OF BEING DRAGGED . . .": *The New York Times*, October 29, 1870.

361 "NEVER BEFORE . . .": *Ibid.*

361 "THREE TIMES A DAY . . .": Werner, *Tammany Hall*, 208.

361 "A MAN WHO WOULD . . .": *The New York Times*, October 29, 1870.

Chapter Thirty-eight

362 "A CAVE DWELLER . . .": Morris, *Incredible New York*, 112.

362 "THEY ARE ALL YOUNG . . .": Belmont Papers, Houghton Library, Oliver Perry to Caroline, July 25, 1870.

363 "READY . . . FOR REMOVAL . . .": *Ibid.*

363 "HIS NURSE SAYS . . .": Belmont Papers, Houghton Library, Jane Perry to Perry Belmont, February 9, 1871.

364 "I CANNOT URGE . . .": AB4, AB1 to Perry Belmont, March 26, 1871.

364 "IF THEY WISH TO MAKE . . .": *AAD*, 144.

365 "YOU HAVE . . . A TERRIBLE WEEK . . .": AB4, Perry Belmont to AB2, March 26, 1871.

p. 366 "HAVE YOU BEEN . . .": *Ibid.*, AB2 to AB1, December 1870.

366 "WHEN I GOT UP . . .": *Ibid.*, AB2 to Perry Belmont, February 7, 1871.

367 "AS THE FIRE WAS MAKING . . .": *Ibid.*, AB2 to Perry Belmont, February 12, 1871.

367 "A PITCHER IN ONE . . .": *Ibid.*

367 "IT SEEMS TO ME . . .": AB4, AB2 to Perry Belmont, March 28, 1871.

367 "I SUPPOSE . . .": *Ibid.*, AB2 to Caroline, January 11, 1871.

368 "MAMA . . . WRITES SO SELDOM . . .": *Ibid.*, AB1 to Perry Belmont, March 28, 1871.

368 "I WOULD ADVISE . . .": *Ibid.*

369 "NONSENSE . . .": *Ibid.*, AB2 to AB1, May 14, 1871.

369 "LIKE PACKING MY BAGS . . .": *Ibid.*, AB2 to Perry Belmont, March 28, 1871.

369 "BY THE TIME . . .": *Ibid.*, AB2 to Perry Belmont, February 7, 1871.

369 "LET US KNOW . . .": *Ibid.*, AB2 to Perry Belmont, n.d. [spring, 1871].

370 "HE HAD A DEPRESSING . . .": *Ibid.*, Chase to AB1, October 5, 1871.

370 "I AM VERY SORRY . . .": *Ibid.*, Caroline to AB2, July 6, 1871.

Chapter Thirty-nine

370 "KINGFISHER IS A HIGH-FLY . . .": Perkins, 14.

370 "STARTS OFF LIKE . . .": *Ibid.*, 8–9.

370 "A BATTLE OF . . .": NYHS scrapbook, "Kingfisher," January 16, 1876.

371 "AN ANIMATED GHOST . . .": Perkins, 2.

371 "WHAT IS THE BEST . . .": *Ibid.*

371 "ALMOST BREATHLESS . . .": *Ibid.*, 8.

371 "TOO MUCH BELLY . . .": *Ibid.*

372 "WHO IS TO RIDE . . .": *Ibid.*, 12–13.

373 "IT WAS A GREAT DISAPPOINTMENT . . .": AB4, Caroline to AB2, July 15, 1871.

375 "FOR THE TROUBLE OF . . .": *The New York Times*, August 15, 1871.

375 "COLD ARGUMENT . . .": AB4, AB2 essay, "Does Writing for the Press Vitiate a Man's Style?" for Forensic III (Prof. Palmer).

376 "THE GOOD FIGHT . . .": Tilden Papers, NYPL, AB1 to Tilden, November 1, 1871.

p. 376 "IF . . . HE WILL THROW . . .": Marble Papers, LOC, AB1 to Marble, September 1871.

377 "WITHOUT A MAYOR . . .": *Ibid.*

378 "I HAVE JUST CALLED . . .": AB4, Hall to AB1, n.d. [September 1872].

378 "FROM MY KNOWLEDGE . . .": Marble Papers, LOC, AB1 to Marble, n.d. [September 1870].

379 "BELMONT IS GOING ABOUT . . .": *The New York Times*, December 13, 1871.

379 "BELMONT FIGHTS HARD . . .": G. T. Strong, Vol. IV, 402.

379 ". . . THE MAYOR HAS FOUND . . .": *The New York Times*, December 13, 1871.

379 "A MAN WHO WOULD NOT . . .": *Ibid.*, October 29, 1870.

379 "NOW . . . IF MR. AUGUST BELMONT . . .": *Ibid.*, December 13, 1871.

380 "[W]E ARE UNABLE . . .": *Ibid.*, September 14, 1871.

380 "BELMONT AND TWEED . . .": *Ibid.*, December 22, 1871.

380 "MR. BELMONT'S IDEAS . . .": *Ibid.*, September 14, 1871.

380 "I WOULD LIKE . . .": Marble Papers, LOC, Caroline to Marble, n.d. [September 1871].

380 "I DON'T MUCH MIND . . .": *Ibid.*, AB1 to Marble, December 20, [1871].

380 "MY TRANSACTION WITH . . .": *Ibid.*, AB1 to Marble, January 3, 1872.

380 "MUCH GOOD . . .": AB4, Caroline to Perry, December 11, 1871.

381 "ALL THE CHARGES, . . .": *The New York Times*, December 22, 1871.

381 "MR. BELMONT'S . . .": *Ibid.*

381 "BECAUSE MR. AUGUST . . .": *Ibid.*, December 24, 1871.

381 "TO BE A 'LEADER . . .": *Ibid.*, December 31, 1871.

381 "WE HAVE BEEN INFORMED . . .": *Ibid.*, January 22, 1872.

382 "IT IS WITH FEELINGS . . .": AB4, Hall to AB1, December 28, 1871.

382 "BELMONT'S ENTHUSIASM . . .": G. T. Strong, Vol. IV, 405.

Chapter Forty

383 "THE KU KLUX . . . ARE NO MYTH . . .": AB4, Severance

to AB2, November 10, 1870.

p. 383 "I CANNOT UNDERSTAND . . .": AB4, clipping, n.d.

383 "WE DO WANT . . .": *Ibid.*

384 "NOBODY KNOWS IT . . .": *Ibid.*

385 "THE ORGANIZERS AND MANAGERS . . .": U.S. Congress, Report into the Condition of Affairs in the Late Insurrectionary States, 233.

385 "WE DO NOT INTEND . . .": *Ibid.*, 292.

385 "WE DENY . . .": *Ibid.*

386 "FORGIVE ME . . .": AB4, AB1 to Bayard, n.d.

386 "WHEN . . . AUGUST STARTS . . .": *Ibid.*

386 "YOU BEGAN THE BUSINESS . . .": *Ibid.*, Caroline to Perry Belmont, March 25, 1872.

387 "A REPETITION OF THE OLD STORY . . .": *Ibid.*, AB1 to Perry Belmont, February 14, 1872.

387 "ALL OF YOUR SON'S . . .": *Ibid.*, E. W. Gurney to AB1, April 24, 1872.

387 "I HEAR THAT THERE . . .": *Ibid.*, AB1 to AB2, June 7, 1872.

387–388 "BETWEEN THE QUESTION . . .": *Ibid.*, AB1 to Perry Belmont, February 21, 1872.

388 "THE DEVELOPMENT . . .": *AAD*, 145.

388 "THAT WILL REQUIRE . . .": *Ibid.*

388 "THE GERMS OF THE SYSTEM . . .": *Ibid.*

389 "AGAINST MY BETTER . . .": AB4, AB1 to Perry Belmont, February 6, 1872.

389 "I FIND IT . . .": *Ibid.*

389 "I HARDLY BELIEVE . . .": *Ibid.*

390 "I HOPE . . . THAT . . .": *Ibid.*

390 "ILLUSTRISSIMUS DOCTOR . . .": *AAD*, 138–139.

390–391 "WELL, BELMONT . . .": *Ibid.*, 149.

391 "I HAD TAKEN DOLLY . . .": AB4, AB1 to AB2, June 7, 1872.

Chapter Forty-one

392 "DISLOYALTY AND COPPERHEADISM . . .": Marble Papers, LOC, AB1 to McCook, June 5, 1871.

392 "I HAVE NOT . . . ONE DOLLAR . . .": *Ibid.*

393 "IT SEEMS TO ME . . .": *Ibid.*,

AB1 to Marble, September 14, 1871.

p. 393 "EVEN GRANTING . . .": *Ibid.*, September 19, 1871.

394 "PERSONALLY . . .": *Ibid.*

395 "IF THE LIBERAL . . .": AB1 Papers, LOC, AB1 to J. R. Doolittle, n.d.

395 "MANY REPUBLICANS . . .": *Ibid.*

395 "BY FAR THE STRONGEST . . .": Schurz Papers, LOC, AB1 to Schurz, April 23, 1872.

396 "THE PAPERS HAVE MADE . . .": AB4, AB1 to Perry Belmont, May 2, 1872.

396 "IT IS THE GENERAL BELIEF . . .": NYHS scrapbook, n.d. [1872].

396 "MR. ADAMS, . . .": NYHS scrapbook, n.d. [1872].

396 "IT WOULD BE BAD . . .": AB4, AB1 to Perry Belmont, May 2, 1872.

397 "TIMES HAVE CHANGED . . .": NYHS scrapbook, n.d. [1872].

397 "TOWARDS NOON . . .": NYHS scrapbook, n.d. [1872].

397 "MY CONVICTION . . .": AB4, AB1 to Perry Belmont, May 2, 1872.

398 "SPEECH IS SILVERN . . .": *New York Tribune,* May 6, 1872.

398 "SO MUCH AM I . . .": AB4, AB1 to Woolley, May 21, 1872.

398 "WHATEVER . . .": Marble Papers, LOC, AB1 to Marble, June 10, 1872.

399 "I HAVE PRETTY MUCH . . .": *Ibid.*

399 "THE THINKING MEN . . .": AB4, AB1, Speech to the Baltimore Convention, pamphlet, July 9, 1872.

399 "HURRAH FOR GREELEY . . .": *The New York Times,* July 10, 1872.

400 "MR. GREELEY . . .": AB4, AB1, Speech to the Baltimore Convention, pamphlet, July 9, 1872.

400–401 "AND NOW . . . PERMIT ME . . .": *Ibid.*

401 "GOOD, GOOD . . .": Marble Papers, LOC, AB1 to Marble, n.d. [1872].

401 "PERHAPS . . . BECAUSE . . .": *Ibid.*

401 "CONFIDENTLY . . .": Office of the Proceedings of the Democratic Convention held at Baltimore, July 9, 1872, Boston, 1872.

401–402 "THE NEW YORK DELEGATION

. . .": Marble Papers, LOC, AB1 to Marble, n.d. [1872].

p. 403 "MY FUTURE NAVAL . . .": Ibid., May 1872.

403 "ARE GROWING AND LEARNING . . .": Ibid.

403 "A LITTLE ASS . . .": AB4, Frederika to AB2, July 22, 1872.

403 "MADE BLOOD . . .": Marble Papers, LOC, AB1 to Marble, n.d. [1872].

403 "LIFE LOOKS STRANGELY . . .": AB4, Marble to AB1, August 13, 1872.

403 "YOU WILL TELL . . .": Ibid.

403 "WE ARE . . . VERY QUIET . . .": Marble Papers, LOC, AB1 to Marble, n.d. [1872].

403 "I FELT VERY BADLY . . .": AB4, Caroline to AB2, October 29, 1872.

Chapter Forty-two

407 "I ANSWERED IN MY . . .": AB4, Fredericka to AB2, November 24, 1872.

407 "LIKE ONE OF THE PERSUASION . . .": Ibid., Caroline to AB2, November 24, 1872.

408 "I WISH THERE WAS . . .": Ibid., Oliver Belmont to AB1, n.d. [December 1872].

408 "UP AT THE DEATH . . .": Ibid.

409 "HARDLY ANYONE . . .": Ibid.

409 "SKATING ON ALL . . .": Ibid., Frederika to AB2, January 30, 1873.

409 "LOOKS SO . . .": Ibid.

410 "A WEALTHY FOREIGNER . . .": Golden Age, II, November 29, 1872.

410–411 "I HAVE NOT CASHED . . .": AB4, E. M. Davison to AB2, January 27, 1873.

411 "A MAN WITHOUT PROFESSION . . .": Ibid., AB1 to AB2, n.d. [1873].

411 "I DO NOT THINK . . .": AAD, 148.

411–412 "THE FIRST THING I . . .": Ibid., 146.

414 "WE DINE, EIGHT . . .": Ibid., 150.

414 "I NEVER WAS . . .": Lineberry Collection, Perry Belmont to AB1, November 22, 1873.

414 "I NEVER GO . . .": Ibid., November 30, 1873.

414–415 "THE PASSION . . .": AAD, 148–149.

p. 415 "AN EXCELLENT JUMPER . . .": Lineberry Collection, Perry Belmont to AB1, November 22, 1873.

415 "ALL THIS TIME . . .": Ibid.

415–416 "TWO MEMBERS OF THE HUNT . . .": AAD, 112.

416 "AS I WAS THE ONLY . . .": Lineberry Collection, Perry Belmont to AB1, November 22, 1873.

416 "I WAS OBLIGED . . .": Ibid.

417 "NOTHING SAID ABOUT . . .": Lineberry Collection, Perry Belmont to AB1, November 30, 1873.

417 "ALL THE DIPLOMATIC . . .": AAD, 153.

417 "STANDS IN THE MIDDLE . . .": Ibid., 154.

Chapter Forty-three

419 "I HAD BEEN WONDERFULLY . . .": Clews, 152–153.

419 "BUT GENTLEMEN . . . IT IS . . .": Fiske, 200.

419–420 "I HAVE BEEN MORE CAREFUL . . .": Marble Papers, LOC, AB1 to Marble, October 30, 1873.

420 "NOBODY PAYS . . .": Ibid., November 15, 1873.

420 ". . . EVERYTHING LOOKS . . .": Ibid., October 30, 1873.

420 "PRINTS BOTH SIDES . . .": AB4, Marble to AB1, n.d. [1873].

421 "IT WOULD HAVE SEEMED . . .": Ibid., Marble to AB1, October 28, 1873.

421 "I HAVE GREAT CONFIDENCE . . .": AB4, Marble to AB1, n.d. [fall, 1873].

421 "TO INSPIRE YOU . . .": Marble Papers, LOC, AB1 to Marble, October 9, 1873.

421–422 "IT MAKES LIFE . . .": AB4, Marble to AB1, October 9, 1873.

422 "BY THE BEGINNING OF DECEMBER . . .": Marble Papers, LOC, October 22, 1873.

422 "YOU CANNOT IMAGINE . . .": AB4, AB1 to AB2, February 4, 1874.

423 "$500 TO CELEBRATE . . .": AB4, AB2 to Jeannie Belmont, January 18, 1874.

423 "I HAVE WRITTEN TO . . .": Ibid., AB1 to AB2, January 18, 1874.

p. 423 "The best thing you can . . .": *Ibid.*, AB1 to AB2, January 18, 1874.

424 "I almost ran . . .": *Ibid.*, AB2 to Jeannie Belmont, January 18, 1874.

424 "reliable horse . . .": *Ibid.*, AB1 to AB2, January 20, 1874.

424 ". . . I can only repeat . . .": *Ibid.*, AB1 to AB2, January 26, 1874.

424 "I cannot command . . .": *Ibid.*, AB1 to AB2, February 10, 1874.

424 "It is of the utmost . . .": *Ibid.*, AB1 to AB2, March 19, 1874.

424 "urgent personal . . .": *Ibid.*

425 "Such ideas are . . .": *Ibid.*, AB1 to AB2, April 9, 1874.

425 "You will never know . . .": *Ibid.*, AB1 to AB2, March 19, 1874.

425 "I can hardly get . . .": *Ibid.*, AB1 to AB2, June 20, 1874.

425 "the literary swells . . .": Marble Papers, LOC, AB1 to Marble, December 7, 1874.

425 "I feel more uneasy . . .": AB4, AB1 to AB2, January 18, 1874.

426 "peculiar ways . . .": *Ibid.*, AB1 to AB2, February 27, 1874.

426 "My nieces tell me . . .": Marble Papers, LOC, Marble to Caroline [added to a note from Caroline to Marble, n.d., January 1874].

427 "if I have really any . . .": AB4, Perry Belmont to Caroline, January 31, 1874.

427 "It really looks as if . . .": *Ibid.*, Perry Belmont to AB1, April 28, 1874.

427 "may do something . . .": *Ibid.*

427 "terribly impatient . . .": *Ibid.*, Perry Belmont to Caroline, April 27, 1874.

427–428 "lithographed on an ordinary . . .": *Ibid.*

428 "Jeannie is very . . .". *Ibid.*, Perry Belmont to AB1, May 17, 1874.

428 "I never thought . . .": *Ibid.*

428 "Nobody was near . . .": AB4, AB1 to Perry Belmont, n.d. [spring, 1874].

429 "old and valued . . .": *Ibid.*

p. 429 "a better accommodation . . .": *Ibid.*

429 "two nice umbrellas . . .": AB4, AB1 to Perry Belmont, n.d. [summer, 1874].

429 "The time of your return . . . .": *AAD*, 155.

Chapter Forty-four

430 "if he succeeds . . .": Marble Papers, LOC, AB1 to Marble, March 3, 1874.

430 "Hullo, Seligman . . .": Birmingham, *Our Crowd*, 129–130.

430 "I have lost my confidence . . .": AB4, AB1 to AB2, February 4, 1874.

431 "What has become . . .": *The New York Times*, November 4, 1873.

431 "willing and anxious . . .": Marble Papers, LOC, AB1 to Marble, February 2, 1874.

431 "one of the earliest . . .": *New York Tribune*, August 8, 1874.

431–432 "not to make you . . .": Marble Papers, LOC, AB1 to Marble, August 25, 1874.

432 "When the World . . .": *The New York Times*, August 4, 1874.

432 "I care not one . . .": Marble Papers, LOC, AB1 to Marble, August 11, 1874.

433 "I should think . . .": AB4, Caroline to AB2, September 20, 1874.

433 "cut me deeper . . .": *Ibid.*, AB1 to AB2, October 21, 1874.

434 "Your father . . .": *Ibid.*, Caroline to AB2, October 27, 1874.

434 "I have but a few . . .": *Ibid.*, November 17, 1874.

434 "a great specialty . . .": *Ibid.*

434–435 "eating his head off . . .": *Ibid.*, February 27, 1875.

435 "I am perplexed . . .": *Ibid.*, Caroline to AB2, October 27, 1874.

436 "Five and twenty . . .": *Ibid.*, Anonymous poem.

436 "What with paying . . .": *Ibid.*, AB1 to AB2, November 11, 1874.

436 "Altho' . . .": *Ibid.*, Caroline to AB2, November 23, 1874.

p. 436 "You will have your . . .":
Ibid.

437 "the Hercules who slew
. . .": Marble Papers, LOC,
AB1 to Marble, November 4,
1874.

437 "Not Hercules Tilden . . .":
Ibid.

437 "nomination . . . the best
. . .": Marble Papers, LOC,
AB1 to Marble, September 19,
1874.

437 "I hope sincerely . . .":
Ibid.
"I am delighted . . .": *Ibid.*

437 "You are the most pugnacious . . .": *Ibid.*

438 "political revolution . . .":
AB4, AB1 to AB2, November
11, 1874.

438 "If Tilden becomes . . .":
Marble Papers, LOC, Marble
to AB1, November 4, 1874.

438 "His amiability . . .": Bowmar, 57.

438 "nefarious . . .": NYHS
scrapbook, clipping, "Democratic Rejoicing," 1874.

439 "I shall certainly . . .":
Marble Papers, LOC, AB1 to
Marble, November 4, 1874.

439 "I desire to remove . . .":
The New York Times, October 30, 1874.

440 "How is the mighty . . .":
Marble Papers, LOC, AB1 to
Marble, December 30, 1874.

440 "put in type . . .": *Ibid.,*
January 11, 1874.

440 "I am glad your present
. . .": AB4, Jeannie Belmont
to Jane Perry [December 1874
or January 1875].

441 "I feel about . . .": *Ibid.*

Chapter Forty-five

441 "Nobody knows . . .": AB4,
AB1 to AB2, February 12,
1875.

441 "Late! tired! . . .": *Ibid.,*
AB2 to Jeannie, February 17,
1875.

442 "so that you could . . .":
Ibid., AB1 to AB2, February
17, 1875.

442 "Mamma's and Rickie's . . .":
AB4, Jeannie Belmont to Jane
Perry, October 13, 1875.

442 "preached . . .": AB4, Marble
to Caroline, n.d. [1875].

442 "invitations . . . are always . . .": AB4, Unidentified

newspaper clipping [probably
New York World, 1875].

p. 443 "we regret . . . the caps . . .":
Ibid.

443 "I think . . . the caps . . .":
AB4, Frederika to AB2, n.d.
[1875].

444 "I cannot consistently . . .":
AB4, AB2 to Jeannie Belmont,
February 17, 1875.

444 "You cannot back . . .":
AB4, Frederika to AB2, n.d.
[March 14, 1875].

444 "in an azure satin . . .":
NYHS scrapbook, "Fancy
Dress Ball," March 29, 1875.

445 "I have a bone . . .": Marble Papers, LOC, AB1 to
Marble, April 7, 1875.

445 "married a favorite . . .":
Ibid., AB1 to Marble, March
3, 1875.

445 "You ought to know . . .":
Ibid., AB1 to Marble, April
12, 1875.

445 "I was very sorry . . .":
Ibid., AB1 to Marble, n.d.
[Tuesday, 1875].

446 "You are really . . .": *Ibid.,*
AB1 to Marble, n.d., Sunday
evening [1875].

446 "You must make daily . . .":
Bayard Papers, LOC, AB1 to
Bayard, January 24, 1875.

446 "great speech . . .": Marble
Papers, LOC, AB1 to Bayard,
February 7, 1875.

446 "What you want to . . .":
Hoar, Vol. I, 208.

447 "there was a general . . .":
Marble Papers, LOC, Bayard
to AB1, March 25, 1875.

448 "God . . . does . . .": *Ibid.,*
AB1 to Marble, February 3,
1875.

448 "I'd be damned . . .": *Ibid.,*
AB1 to Marble, n.d., Sunday
[1875].

448–449 "She . . . is becoming . . .":
AB4, AB1 to AB2, February
12, 1875.

449 "a great undertaking . . .":
Ibid., Caroline to AB2, April
8, 1875.

449 "It is a hard trial . . .":
Ibid., Caroline to AB2, May
3, 1875.

449 "Come and dine . . .": Marble Papers, LOC, AB1 to Marble, June 21, 1875.

450 "Faithless creature . . .":
Ibid., Caroline to Marble, June
9, 1875.

450 "damned bad . . .": *Ibid.,*
AB1 to Marble, July 2, 1875.

450 "PAY MY DEBTS . . .": AB4, Marble to AB1, June 30, 1875.

*p.*450 "YOU AND I DON'T . . .": Marble Papers, LOC, AB1 to Marble, June 30, 1875.

450 "I WISH TO THE LORD . . .": AB4, Marble to AB1, September 11, 1875.

451 ". . . UTTERLY IMPOSSIBLE . . .": Marble Papers, LOC, AB1 to Marble, September 11, 1875.

451 "YOUR TELEGRAM . . .": AB4, Marble to AB1, September 11, 1875.

451 ". . . IT IS VERY GOOD . . .": *Ibid.*, Jeannie Belmont to AB1, n.d. [August 1875?].

451 "MY RHEUMATISM . . . IS VERY . . .": *Ibid.*, Jeannie Belmont to AB1, n.d., [August 1875?].

451 "THERE WAS NO PHYSICAL . . .": *Ibid.*, AB1 to Babette, November 10, 1875.

451 "IT WAS THE FIRST . . .": *Ibid.*

Chapter Forty-six

452 "JEANNIE WAS SUCH . . .": Liebeschütz Private Collection, AB1 to Babette, November 10, 1875.

452 "WERE THERE EVER . . .": AB4, Marble to AB1, n.d. [May 1876].

452 "WE HAVE TASTED . . .": AB4, Van Buren to AB1, October 20, 1875.

452 ". . . LET ME JUST . . .": AB4, Edmond de Rothschild to AB1, October 1875.

452 ". . . FOR AUGUST'S . . .": *Ibid.*, Babette to Caroline, December 2, 1875.

453 "OLIVER IS VERY . . .": Marble Papers, LOC, AB1 to Marble, n.d. [August 1876].

453 ". . . AT HIS AGE . . .": AB4, Rodgers to Caroline, October 20, 1875.

453 "THE THOUGHT IN THE SECOND . . .": *Ibid.*, Hurlbert to AB1, December 26, 1875.

454 "THE HOUSE IS VERY . . .": *Ibid.*, AB1 to Raymond, January 24, 1876.

454 "SOMETHING HAVING . . .": *Ibid.*

454 "PAPA AND I . . .": *Ibid.*, AB2 to Raymond, January 27, 1876.

455 "THIS MADE IT MY . . .": AB4, AB2 to Raymond, February 9, 1876.

*p.*455 "I GO AND PLAY . . .": *Ibid.*, AB2 to Raymond, January 27, 1876.

455 "THE JUDICIAL TEMPER . . .": *Ibid.*, Bayard to AB1, September 15, 1876.

455 "IN READING THE ACCOUNTS . . .": AB4, Perry Belmont to Bayard, January 11, 1875.

456 ". . . THE SPIRIT WHICH . . .": Marble Papers, LOC, Perry Belmont to Bayard, February 1876.

456 "MY FATHER IS STILL . . .": *Ibid.*, Bayard Papers, January 11, 1876 [misdated 1875].

456 "AS HE IS A MUCH OLDER . . .": AB4, AB1 to AB2, January 3, 1876.

457 "WHEN COMMODORE PERRY . . .": *New York Herald,* January 26, 1876.

457 "NEVER BEEN . . .": *Hannibal* (Mo.) *Clipper,* September 28, 1875.

457 ". . . I WROTE . . .": *New York Sun,* October 2, 1875.

458 "CAN YOU TELL . . .": *The New York Times,* January 11, 1876.

458 "DO YOU THINK THE CONFIRMATION . . .": *Ibid.*

458 "KNOWN TO BE A FRIEND . . .": NYHS scrapbook, clipping, January 11, 1876.

458 "THERE IS NO REASON . . .": *The New York Times,* January 11, 1876.

458 "IT WAS A GROSS . . .": *New York Herald,* January 12, 1876.

459 "MY FATHER'S TRIP . . .": Bayard Papers, LOC, Perry Belmont to Bayard, February 18, 1876.

459 "YOU WILL BE PLEASED . . .": AB4, AB1 to Raymond, January 24, 1876.

459 "THINGS LOOK VERY . . .": Marble Papers, LOC, AB1 to Marble, February 14, 1876.

460 "I FEAR THE DEMOCRATS . . .": *Ibid.*

460 "HOW ANY MAN . . .": *Ibid.*, AB1 to Elijah Ward, March 2, 1876.

460 "I AM AFRAID . . .": *Ibid.*, AB1 to Marble, n.d. [May 1876].

460 "PLEDGE THEMSELVES . . .": *Ibid.*

460–461 "WE HAVE BATTERING . . .": *Ibid.*

461 "BOGUS BILL . . .": *Ibid.*, AB1 to Marble, n.d. [June 1876].

p. 461–462 "WHILE THE DEMOCRATIC PARTY . . .": *New York World,* June 21, 1876.

462 "TO IDENTIFY HIM . . .": *The New York Times,* June 29, 1876.

462 "THE HARD MONEY . . .": *Ibid.,* June 22, 1876.

463 "I WISH HE HAD . . .": Marble Papers, LOC, AB1 to Marble, n.d. [1876].

463 "AS OFTEN AS I . . .": Marble Papers, LOC, Perry Belmont to Marble.

463 "THE ARTICLE IS . . .": AB4, Marble to AB1, n.d. (2 A.M.).

463 "THIS DIRTY BUSINESS . . .": Marble Papers, LOC, AB1 to Marble, March 3, 1876.

463 "THE WORST TRAIT . . .": Bayard Papers, LOC, Perry Belmont to Bayard, March 9, 1876.

464 "MIGHT BE INSTRUMENTAL . . .": Marble Papers, LOC, AB1 to Marble, March 6, 1876.

464 "I WISH . . . IF YOU THINK PROPER . . .": *Ibid.,* AB1 to Marble, n.d. [April 1876].

464 "OUR CANDIDATE . . .": *Ibid.,* n.d. [April 1876].

464 "OF COURSE, I SHALL . . .": *Ibid.,* AB1 to Marble, n.d. [Library listing: May 1876; probably April 1876].

465 "UPON REFLECTION . . .": *Ibid.,* AB1 to Marble, April 28, 1876.

465 "ON RETURNING . . .": *Ibid.,* AB1 to Marble, May 23, 1876.

465 "I HAVE DESIRED . . .": AB4, S. E. Church to AB1, May 20, 1876.

465–466 "A GOOD MAN TO SOME . . .": *Ibid.,* S. E. Church to AB1, May 29, 1876.

466 "I AM SURE IT WILL . . .": Marble Papers, AB1 to Marble, n.d., 1876.

466 "YOUR CREDULITY . . .": Marble Papers, LOC, AB1 to Marble, June 19, 1876.

466 "I SHALL BARRICADE . . .": *Ibid.,* AB1 to Marble, May 5, 1876.

467 "I AM NOT AWARE . . .": *Ibid.,* AB1 to Marble, May 1876.

467 "I AM DELIGHTED . . .": *Ibid.,* Marble to AB1, June 11, 1876.

467 "DON'T LET US . . .": *Ibid.,* AB1 to Marble, June 12, 1876.

467 ". . . I CONFESS . . .": Bayard Papers, LOC, Perry Belmont to Bayard, June 20, 1876.

p. 468 ". . . I CAN UNDERSTAND . . .": *Ibid.*

468 "WHO IS HAYES? . . .": Gouverneur, 381.

468 "THAT COCK WON'T . . .": AB4, Eaton to AB1, June 14, 1876.

469 "COME THIS WAY . . .": *AAD,* 192.

Chapter Forty-seven

470 "A DASHING, ATTRACTIVE . . .": AB4, Bayard to AB1, September 15, 1876.

470 "THE ONLY GOOD . . .": *AAD,* 158.

470 ". . . IN REPLY TO SOME . . .": *Ibid.*

470 "THE WRONG INFLICTED . . .": *Ibid.*

470–471 "THE PEACE AND GOOD ORDER . . .": AB4, Bayard to AB1, September 15, 1876.

472 "HIS REMARKABLE ABILITY . . .": *AAD,* 163.

472 "TO SATISFY HIMSELF . . .": *Ibid.,* 164.

477 "WE WERE ON THE MOST . . .": *Ibid.,* 168.

477 ". . . OUR PEOPLE ARE VERY WRONG . . .": *Ibid,* 169.

477–478 "ANOTHER MONTH AMONG . . .": *Ibid.*

478 "MOURNFUL GRANDEUR . . .": *Ibid.,* 173.

479 "IT WAS SIMPLER . . .": *Ibid.,* 175.

479 "SUDDENLY . . . AN HOUR AFTER . . .": Turenne, 251–252.

481 ". . . IT SEEMED TO US . . .": *AAD,* 178.

481–482 "IT HAS BEEN ALLEGED . . .": *AAD,* 170–171.

Chapter Forty-eight

482 "I HAVE BEEN IN THE DEPTHS . . .": AB4, AB1 to Perry Belmont, October 22, 1876.

482 "FAR FROM BEING . . .": AB4, AB1 to AB2, July 18, 1876.

483 "I AM MORE THAN GRIEVED . . .": *Ibid.*

483 "I WOULD SHOOT . . .": *Ibid.,* AB1 to AB2, August 14, 1876.

484 "THE GRASS IS ALL . . .": *Ibid.,* AB1 to AB2, July 10, 1876.

484 "SO THAT THERE IS . . .": *Ibid.,* AB1 to AB2, July 18, 1876.

*p.*484 "TO PLAY HIGH LIFE . . .":
Ibid., AB1 to AB2, July 23,
1876.

485 "I THINK YOU WILL . . .":
Ibid., AB1 to AB2, August 11,
1876.

486 "SO . . . I HAMMERED . . .":
Ibid., AB1 to AB2, July 23,
1876.

486 "IN FACT . . . MOST OF THE
RACING . . .": *Ibid.,* AB1 to
AB2, August 11, 1876.

486 "MORE CURT . . .": *Ibid.,* AB1
to AB2, July 18, 1876.

486 "SO SICK AND TIRED . . .": *Ibid.*

487 "HIS HAND TREMBLES . . .":
Ibid., AB1 to AB2, July 18,
1876.

487 ". . . BUSINESS IS AS USUAL
. . ." *Ibid.,* AB1 to AB2,
August 11, 1876.

487 ". . . GOLD AND MONEY . . .":
Ibid., AB1 to AB2, July 23,
1876.

487 "HAD TO TAKE ALL . . .": *Ibid.,*
AB1 to AB2, n.d. [summer
1876].

487 "DOING VERY WELL . . .": *Ibid.,*
AB1 to AB2, July 18, 1876.

487 "MY DARLING BOY . . .": *Ibid.*
487-488 "NOW, I WANT YOU . . .":
Ibid., AB1 to AB2, August 8,
1876.

488 "ON RECEIVING HIS WAGES . . .":
Marble Papers, LOC, AB1 to
Marble, July 2, 1876.

488 "THE SENTENCE VERY . . .":
Marble Papers, LOC, AB1 to
Marble, July 2, 1876.

488 "BUT MADE A DREADFUL . . .":
AB4, AB1 to Caroline, n.d.
[1876].

488 "MAMMA . . . WILL BE . . .":
Ibid., AB1 to AB2, September
6, 1876.

489 "I WISH MAMMA'S WISH . . .":
Ibid., AB1 to AB2, July 18,
1876.

489 "TODAY I HAD THE FIRST . . .":
Ibid., AB1 to AB2, August 18,
1876.

489-490 "I COULD NOT WELL . . .": *Ibid.*
490 "I HAVE ALREADY . . .": *Ibid.,*
AB1 to AB2, August 4, 1876.

490 "THOSE WHO CLAIM . . .":
New York World, July 14,
1876.

490 "A DAMNED LIE . . .": Marble
Papers, LOC, July 12, 1876.

490 ". . . NO MAN OF SENSE . . .":
New York World, July 14,
1876.

490 "THE BANKER SEEMS . . .":
New York Herald, July 15,
1876.

*p.*490 "I THINK MY POSITION . . .":
AB4, AB1 to AB2, August 4,
1876.

491 "EXERT YOURSELF . . .": *Ibid.,*
AB1 to Caroline, n.d. [1876].

491 "COMMAND ME IN ANY . . .":
Ibid., AB1 to Marble, May 3,
1876.

491 "I FORGOT TO TELL . . .":
Marble Papers, LOC, AB1 to
Marble, September 8, 1876.

491 "MARBLE . . . IS MOVING . . .":
AB4, AB1 to AB2, September
6, 1876.

491 "IF YOU COULD SECURE . . .":
Marble Papers, LOC, AB1 to
Marble, September 7, 1876.

492 "ALBANY FRIEND . . .": Marble
Papers, LOC, September 9,
1876.

492 "OLD USUFRUCT TILDEN . . .":
Rhodes, *History of the United
States,* 216.

492 "STILL, . . . SO GREAT . . .":
AB4, AB1 to AB2, August 4,
1876.

492-493 "MY HEART IS NOT . . .": AB4,
AB1 to AB2, September 22,
1876.

493 "I DID MY BEST . . .": Marble
Papers, LOC, AB1 to Marble,
July 25, 1876.

493 "LOCAL FINANCE COMMITTEE
. . .": AB4, E. Cooper to AB1,
August 23, 1876.

493 "WILL YOU READ . . .": Marble Papers, LOC, AB1 to
Marble, n.d. [September 1876].

493 "NOT A VERY BRILLIANT . . .":
AB4, AB1 to AB2, September
22, 1876.

493 "DO . . . FOR MY ENLIGHTENED
. . .": Marble Papers, LOC,
AB1 to Marble, n.d. [August
1876].

494 "CONTROL OF UNITED . . .":
Hayes Papers, Hayes Memo-
rial Library, J. Livingston to
Hayes, November 11, 1876.

494 "I AM BOILING . . .": Marble
Papers, LOC, AB1 to Marble,
July 29 [1876].

494 "IT WAS MY CUSTOM TO . . .":
NYHS scrapbook, clipping,
September 30, 1876.

494-495 "OUR FRIEND SEEMS . . .":
Marble Papers, LOC, AB1 to
Marble, October 2, 1876.

495 "BROODING . . . OVER . . .":
Ibid., AB1 to Marble, October
3, 1876.

495 "YOU MUST NOT . . .": *Ibid.*
495 "I SEND YOU ENCLOSED . . .":
Tilden Papers, NYPL, AB1 to
Tilden, October 3, 1876.

Chapter Forty-nine

*p.*496 "IF YOU DON'T CARE . . .": Marble Papers, LOC, AB1 to Marble, October 6, 1876.

496 "COMMON SENSE . . .": *Ibid.*, AB1 to Marble, n.d. [October 1876].

496–497 "THAT I SHOULD RATHER . . .": *Ibid.*, AB1 to Marble, Tuesday morning, n.d. [October 1876?].

497 "YOUR . . . SOUND, WITTY . . .": AB4, S. Ward to AB1, October 31, 1876.

497 "AN EMPHATIC DENIAL . . .": Marble Papers, LOC, Simon Sterne to AB1, October 19, 1876.

497 "LIKE MUCH THE IDEA . . .": *Ibid.*, AB1 to Marble, October 19, 1876.

497 "NO SUCH LETTERS . . .": NYHS scrapbook, *New York World,* October 19, 1876.

498 "THE SAFETY AND WISDOM . . .": *Ibid.*

498 "WE HAVE REASON . . .": *New York Tribune,* October 21, 1876.

498 "MR. AUGUST BELMONT . . .": *The New York Times,* October 21, 1876.

498 "THIS CURIOUS CONTEST . . .": *Ibid.*, October 25, 1876.

498 "HE HAS BEEN THE . . .": *New York Tribune,* November 1, 1876.

499 "NATURAL ON THE PART . . .": Marble Papers, LOC, AB1 to Marble, n.d. [October 1876].

499 "I WILL SEE . . .": *Ibid.*, AB1 to Marble, October 26, 1876.

499 "BUCKLE ON YOUR . . .": *Ibid.*, AB1 to Marble, October 31, 1876.

499 "WE DO NOT THINK . . .": *The New York Times,* November 7, 1876.

499 "VAGUE RUMORS . . .": *New York World,* November 1, 1876.

500 "NEVER SINCE . . .": *New York Herald,* October 31, 1876.

501 "DON'T YOU THINK . . .": Marble Papers, LOC, AB1 to Marble, November 6, 1876.

501 "THE ONLY FEAR . . .": *Ibid.*

501 "I HAVE TAKEN . . .": Lineberry Collection, AB1 to Perry Belmont, October 22, 1876.

502 "IF LOUISIANA CAN . . .": Tilden Papers, NYPL, AB1 to Tilden, November 9, 1876.

p. 502 "I AM AS MUCH INTERESTED . . .": *Washington Star,* November 29, 1890.

502 "WALL STREET . . .": Tilden Papers, NYPL, AB1 to Tilden, November 8, 1876.

503 "I SUGGEST A PUBLIC . . .": *Ibid.*, AB1 to Tilden, November 9, 1876.

503 "I WOULD ADVISE . . .": *Ibid.*

503 "WOULD YOU LIKE MY . . .": *Ibid.*, AB1 to Tilden, November 10, 1876.

504 "CAN YOU MAKE . . .": Bayard Papers, LOC, AB1 to Bayard, November 10, 1876.

504 "SITUATION . . . BECOMING . . .": *Ibid.*

504 ". . . THE TRIBUNE VILIFIES . . .": AB4, Marble to AB1, November 13, 1876.

505 "NO OTHER SOLUTION . . .": to Tilden, n.d. [Sunday morning].

505 "THE AGONY IS OVER . . .": *Ibid.*

505 "MADE IT ALL . . .": *Ibid.*, AB1 to Tilden, Thursday, n.d.

506 "THE CRITICAL MOMENT . . .": Bayard Papers, LOC, Perry Belmont to Bayard, December 11, 1876.

506 ". . . WE'LL VOTE THE DEMOCRATIC . . .": *AAD,* 193.

506 "CLEAR DISTINCTION . . .": Marble Papers, LOC, AB1 to Marble, Friday morning, n.d.

506 "IT MAY BE PRESUMPTION . . .": *Ibid.*

507 "WITH . . . TELEGRAPHS . . .": *Ibid.*, AB1 to Marble, Saturday evening, n.d.

507 "MY WINGS FEEL . . .": AB4, Bayard to AB1, December 21, 1876.

507 "MADE A VERY FAVORABLE . . .": Marble Papers, LOC, AB1 to Marble, December 24, 1876.

507 ". . . I SHOULD LIKE HIM . . .": *Ibid.*

507 "FRIGHTEN . . .": *Ibid.*

507 "I DON'T SEE WHY . . .": Bayard Papers, LOC, Perry Belmont to Bayard, December 31, 1876.

508 "HAVING THE WHOLE . . .": *Ibid.*, AB1 to Bayard, January 17, 1877.

508 "MR. BELMONT, INDIVIDUALLY . . .": *Ibid.*

508 "HAVE NO FEAR . . .": *Ibid.*, Bayard to AB1, January 18, 1877.

p. 508 "I AM AFRAID . . .": Marble Papers, LOC, AB1 to Marble, January 18, 1877.

509 "I BEGIN TO THINK . . .": Bayard Papers, LOC, AB1 to Bayard, January 19, 1877.

509 "IS, OF COURSE . . .": Marble Papers, LOC, AB1 to Marble, Sunday morning, n.d.

509 "ALLOWING THEMSELVES . . .": Bayard Papers, LOC, Perry Belmont to Bayard, January 18, 1877.

509 "I DO NOT . . .": AB4, Bayard to AB1, January 27, 1877.

509 "It will be a struggle . . .": Marble Papers, LOC, AB1 to Marble, n.d. [January 1877].

510 "I CERTAINLY THOUGHT . . .": *Ibid.*

510 "WHAT IS GOING . . .": *Ibid.*, AB1 to Marble, n.d. [February 1, 1877].

510 "THE REPUBLICAN RADICALS . . .": *Ibid.*

510–511 "PROBABLY A GREAT STUDENT . . .": *AAD,* 1980.

511 "BEST BE IN ADVANCE . . .": Tilden Papers, NYPL, AB1 to Tilden, February 15, 1877.

511 "IF THE DEMOCRATIC . . .": Marble Papers, LOC, AB1 to Marble, February 28, 1877.

511 "VIGOR AND FIRMNESS . . .": *Ibid.*, AB1 to Marble, February 11, 1877.

511–512 "HOODWINKED . . .": *AAD,* 200–202.

512 "THE INFAMOUS PLAY . . .": Marble Papers, LOC, AB1 to Marble, February 28, 1877.

512 "FROM ALL I CAN . . .": Bayard Papers, LOC, AB1 to Bayard, February 28, 1877.

512 "HAYES WILL COME . . .": AB4, Bayard to AB1, March 1, 1877.

512 "UNPRECEDENTED WRONG . . .": Bayard Papers, LOC, AB1 to Bayard, March 9, 1877.

512 "YOU WERE THE LEADER . . .": *Ibid.*, AB1 to Bayard, March 9, 1877.

512 "I ONLY WISH . . .": *AAD,* 202.

Chapter Fifty

513 "RECKLESS AND WILD . . .": AB4, AB1 to AB2, September 8, 1876.

514 "WHY DON'T YOU COME . . .": Marble Papers, LOC, AB1 to Marble, February 23, 1877.

p. 514 "I DON'T SEE . . .": *Ibid.*, AB1 to Marble, March 9, 1877.

514–515 ". . . NOBODY ELSE . . .": *Ibid.*

515 "ANNOYANCES . . .": *Ibid.*, AB1 to Marble, May 4, 1877.

516 "I HAD BARELY . . .": *Ibid.*, AB1 to Marble, June 6, 1877.

516 "I HAVE CONTRIBUTED . . .": *Ibid.*, AB1 to Marble, May 1, 1877.

516–517 "HE DELIGHTS . . .": *New York Sun,* February 4, 1877.

517 "POOR BELOVED BABETTE . . .": AB4, Stephen Feist to AB1, April 20, 1877.

517 "MY PRODIGAL . . .": Marble Papers, LOC, AB1 to Marble, May 17, 1877.

517 "HAS GOT HIS NOTIONS . . .": *Ibid.*, AB1 to Marble, June 13, 1877.

517–518 "I SHOULD THINK . . .": *Ibid.*, AB1 to Marble, n.d. [1877].

518 "WOULD YOU ADVISE . . .": *Ibid.*

518 ". . . I AM REALLY . . .": *Ibid.*, AB1 to Marble, June 13, [1877].

518 "I AM CRAZY . . .": Marble Papers, LOC, AB1 to Marble, June 25, 1877.

518 "THIS IS SO GRAVE . . .": *Ibid.*, AB1 to Marble, July 4, 1877.

519 "I HAVE NEVER SEEN . . .": Bayard Papers, LOC, Perry Belmont to Bayard, August 7, 1877.

519 "IMPRUDENT . . .": AB4, Johnny to Frederika, August 7, 1877.

519 "ONE OF THE LOVELIEST . . .": *New York World,* September 19, 1877.

520 "A SECOND IN A PEACEFUL . . .": F. H. Hall, 161.

520 "WHICH . . . WAS A VERY NOTICEABLE . . .": *Boston Herald,* September 19, 1877.

520 "HIS FRIENDS REMARKED . . .": *New York Herald,* September 19, 1877.

521 "A GIFT . . . OF A VERY . . .": *Ibid.*

521 "NOT A VERY APPROPRIATE . . .": AB4, J. Hone to Frederika, September 7, 1877.

Chapter Fifty-one

522 "THE AUTHORITIES . . .": AB4, AB1 to AB2, July 25, 1877.

522 "I HAVE OFTEN . . .": Bayard

Papers, LOC, Perry Belmont to Bayard, June 30, 1877.

p. 522 "ARE SO BESET . . .": *Ibid.,* Perry Belmont to Bayard, October 2, 1877.

523 "PARTY MEN . . .": *Ibid.*

523 "THE VERY FACT . . .": Marble Papers, LOC, Perry Belmont to Marble, November 21, 1877.

523 ". . . AS HIS FATHER . . .": AB4, Bayard to AB1, July 7, 1877.

523 "THERE IS NOT A MORE . . .": Bayard Papers, LOC, Perry Belmont to Bayard, August 7, 1877.

524 "THE SYMPATHY OF THE COMMERCIAL . . .": Marble Papers, LOC, n.d. [December 1877].

524 "EVERY DOLLAR OF GOLD . . .": AB4, AB1 to Bayard, November 18, 1877.

524–525 "THE DISASTROUS CONSEQUENCES . . .": *Ibid.*

525 "I SHOULD HAVE LIKED . . .": *Ibid.*

525–526 "IT IS RATHER . . .": AB4, AB1 to Bayard, November 18, 1877.

526 "IT WAS JUST AS WELL . . .": *Ibid.,* Bayard to AB1, March [14 or 18], 1877.

526 "I COMPREHEND PERFECTLY . . .": *Ibid.,* Bayard to AB1, November 29, 1877.

526 "ABOUT SOME INTRIGUES . . .": Marble Papers, LOC, AB1 to Marble, n.d. [1877].

526 "THE STAUNCHEST DEFENDER . . .": Bayard Papers, LOC, AB1 to Bayard, March 9, 1877.

526 "TREATED ME . . .": AB4, AB1 to Sherman, June 14, 1877.

526 "LITERARY CURIOSITY . . .": Marble Papers, LOC, n.d. [June 1877].

526 "THE THREATENING POSITION . . .": AB4, AB1 to Sherman, November 7, 1877.

527 "INIQUITOUS . . .": Bayard Papers, LOC, AB1 to Bayard, December 30, 1877.

527 "EUROPEAN SHYLOCKS . . .": *Ibid.,* clipping, *Washington Telegram,* n.d. [late January 1878].

527 "THE WESTERN FARMER . . .": Garfield Papers, LOC, AB1 to Garfield, February 1, 1878.

527 "MEMORIALS FROM BANKERS . . .": AB4, T. Randolph to AB1, February 5, 1878.

p. 527 "I AM NOT AT ALL . . .": *New York World,* December 5, 1879.

527–528 "THE INTELLIGENT AND WELL-MEANING . . .": *Ibid.*

528 "NAILS HENDRICKS . . .": *New York Commercial Advertiser,* February 9, 1878.

528 "DISORGANIZED AND DISAFFECTED . . .": *The New York Times,* January 28, 1878.

528–529 "INSTEAD OF BATTLING . . .": *Ibid.*

529 "THE BEST TIME . . .": *Ibid.*

529 "BAD TASTE . . .": Marble Papers, LOC, AB1 to Marble, June 19, 1878.

529 "OH, FOR A RICHELIEU . . .": Marble Papers, LOC, AB1 to Marble, June 19, 1878.

530 "SOLID TURRETS . . .": Tennyson, 299–300.

530 "OLD SIR THOMAS . . .": AB4, Roger A. Pryor to AB1, January 31, 1878.

530 "BELMONT . . . FEARS . . .": C. R. Williams, Vol. |II, 123.

530 "WE . . . HAD THE ASSURANCE . . .": *New York World,* December 5, 1879.

530 "UNDERSTOOD THE PRINCIPLES . . .": AB4, H. W. Blair to AB1, February 11, 1878.

530–531 "MAY NOT COME . . .": *Ibid.*

531 "A WEDGE DRIVEN . . .": Garfield Papers, LOC, AB1 to Garfield, March 2, 1878.

Chapter Fifty-two

531 "IT IS A WONDER . . .": AB4, AB1 to AB2, September 28, 1878.

532 "SO MISERABLE AND BEDEVILLED . . .": AB4, AB1 to AB2, August 2, 1878.

532 "FELT VERY BADLY . . .": AB4, AB1 to AB2, October 1, 1878.

532 "BELIEVE ME, . . .": AB4, AB1 to AB2, November 26, 1878.

532 "THERE IS SOME DEVILTRY . . .": AB4, AB1 to AB2, September 20, 1878.

532 "I HAVE SUCH AN AWFUL . . .": AB4, AB1 to AB2, September 25, 1878.

533 "I HAVE COME TO THE FIRM . . .": *Ibid.*

533 "A GOOD WAY . . .": AB4, AB1 to AB2, August 2, 1878.

p. 533 "AT FIRST HE WAS UTTERLY . . .": AB4, Bayard to AB1, September 24, 1878.

533–534 "IN STRICT CONFORMITY . . .": AB4, B. Taylor to AB1, September 15, 1878.

535 "FOR MR. BELMONT . . .": Rives, 19.

535 "I SLEEP VERY . . .":*Ibid.*, 26.

535 "THE TRANSIT OF MERCURY . . .": *Ibid.*, 29.

536 "I GIVE YOU FAIR . . .": AB4, AB2 to Lincoln, February 1, 1878.

537 "PRAY DO WHAT . . .": AB4, AB1 to Oelrichs, September 5, 1878.

537 "SPASM OPERA . . .": Goldin, 48.

538 "THE DISTINCT UNDERSTANDING . . .": Belmont Papers, NYPL, AB1 to Morton, May 7, 1878.

538 "ONE OR TWO OF THE GREAT . . .": *Ibid.*

538 "NO DECENT ARTIST . . .": Belmont Papers, NYPL, AB1 to Ullman, June 2, 1878.

538 "A GREAT MANAGER . . .": *Ibid.*, Ullman to AB1, August 27, 1878.

539 "HE . . . IS A GOOD-NATURED . . .": *Ibid.*

539 ". . . BEING THE OFFICIAL . . .": *Ibid.*, Ullman to AB1, June 2, 1878.

539 "SERVED UP . . .": *Ibid.*, AB1 to Morton, May 7, 1878.

539 "A CONCEITED ASS . . .": *Ibid.*, Ullman to AB1, August 27, 1878.

540 "AMOUNTING TO A LARGER . . .": *Ibid.*, Ullman to AB1, July 1, 1878.

540 "MAPLESON IS SMART . . .": *Ibid.*

540 "NOTHING GREAT . . .": *Ibid.*

540 "$250 A NIGHT . . .": *Ibid.*, AB1 to Morton, May 7, 1878.

541 "HIS DESIRE SEEMS . . .": *Ibid.*, Morton to AB1, June 6, 1878.

541 "SHE EITHER LOVES . . .": *Ibid.*, Bennett to Ullman, June 20, 1878.

541 "I HAVE BEEN RUNNING . . .": *Ibid.*, Mapleson to Morton, June 1, 1878.

541 "HAS BEEN IN LONDON . . .": *Ibid.*, Mapleson to Morton, June 4, 1878.

541 "I HAD BREAKFAST . . .": *Ibid.*, Mapleson to Morton, June 8, 1878.

542 "THERE IS NOT A MOMENT . . .": *Ibid.*, Mapleson to Morton, June 11, 1878.

p. 542 "AUTHORIZE CONTRACT . . .": AB4, AB1 to Morton, June 13, 1878.

542 "GERSTER IS A VERY . . .": Belmont Papers, NYPL, Morton to AB1, June 19, 1878.

542 ". . . HER ATTRACTIVE POWERS . . .": *Ibid.*, Mapleson to Morton, June 4, 1878.

542 "RUIN ALL THE OTHER . . .": *Ibid.*, Mapleson to Morton, June 11, 1878.

542 "A MOST ADMIRABLE . . .": *Ibid.*

542 "EQUAL TO EITHER . . .": *Ibid.*, Mapleson to Morton, June 8, 1878.

542 "THE PRINCIPAL PRIMA . . .": *Ibid.*, Mapleson to Morton, June 11, 1878.

542 "I MAY ADD . . .": *Ibid.*, Mapleson to Morton, June 8, 1878.

542 "I KNOW BY EXPERIENCE . . .": *Ibid.*

542–543 "WILL WORK WELL . . .": AB4, AB1 to Morton, June 18, 1878.

543 ". . . STRAKOSCH . . .": Belmont Papers, NYPL, Mapleson to Morton, June 29, 1878.

543 "IS MOST DESIROUS . . .": *Ibid.*, Mapleson to AB1, June 29, 1878.

544 "I SEE . . . THAT IT WAS . . .": *Ibid.*, Phelps to AB1, July 7, 1878.

544 "REQUIRED A RENTAL . . .": *Ibid.*

544 "STROKE OF A HARLEQUIN'S . . .": *Ibid.*, Kingsland to AB1, n.d. [1878].

545 "TERMS ARE REASONABLE . . .": *Ibid.*, AB1 to Phelps, September 4, 1878.

545 "FURNISHED HIM . . .": *Ibid.*, Kingsland to AB1, n.d., [1878].

545 "THE MESSAGE FROM MR. FOX . . .": *Ibid.*, Phelps to AB1, August 29, 1878.

545 "IN FACT, . . . WE DO NOT . . .": *Ibid.*

545 "SEE THAT HE HAS . . .": *Ibid.*, Phelps to AB1, September 1, 1878.

545 "A MERE UTILITY . . .": *Ibid.*, Ullman to AB1, September 10, 1878.

546 "BUT SUCH IS THE MAN . . .": *Ibid.*, Ullman to AB1, August 27, 1878.

546 "YOU MUST . . . BE PREPARED

. . .": *Ibid.,* Ullman to AB1, July 12, 1878.

p. 546 "I HOPE FOR THE SAKE . . .": *Ibid.,* Phelps to AB1, July 14, 1878.

546 "WHAT HE, BROKEN . . .": *Ibid.,* Ullman to AB1, September 6, 1878.

546 "THE PREPARATION . . .": *Ibid.,* Mapleson to AB1, August 24, 1878.

546 "THERE IS NOT A GHOST . . .": Phelps to AB1, September 5, 1878.

547 "I FEAR . . . IT WILL . . .": *Ibid.,* AB1 to Mapleson, September 4, 1878.

547 "UPON HER . . .": *Ibid.,* Ullman to AB1, September 10, 1878.

547–548 "THE PEOPLE ARE PERFECTLY . . .": AB4, AB1 to AB2, November 26, 1878.

548 "OVERFLOWING HOUSE . . .": AB4, AB1 to AB2, November 26, 1878.

548 "TRAINED TO DANCE . . .": *The New York Times,* November 24, 1878.

549 "SEVERAL OF THE DIRECTORS . . .": *Ibid.,* December 12, 1878.

549 "MR. PHELPS . . .": *Ibid.*

Chapter Fifty-three

550 "HENDRICKS AND PENDLETON . . .": Bayard Papers, LOC, AB1 to Bayard, August 13, 1878.

550 "I CANNOT BECOME . . .": *Ibid.*

551 ". . . BENNETT . . . WOULD BE VERY GLAD . . .": Marble Papers, LOC, AB1 to Marble, August 4, 1878.

551 "UTTERLY DISGUSTED . . .": *Ibid.*

551 "YOU ARE REALLY . . .": *Ibid.,* AB1 to Marble, n.d. [1877 or 1878].

552 "WITH THE GREATEST ATTENTION . . .": *Ibid.,* AB1 to Marble, August 4, 1878.

552–553 "I SHALL, OF COURSE, ASSIST . . .": AB4, AB1 to AB2, September 20, 1878.

553 "PERRY FINDS THE NOMINATION . . .": *Ibid.,* AB1 to AB2, September 25, 1878.

553 "POOR FELLOW . . .": *Ibid.,* AB1 to Marble, September 25, 1878.

p. 553 "I HAVE THIS MATTER . . .": *Ibid.,* AB1 to Marble, September 25, 1878.

553 "I WAS AFRAID . . .": AB4, AB1 to AB2, October 18, 1878.

553 "A VERY EXPENSIVE . . .": *Ibid.,* October 22, 1878.

554 "I SEE TOO PLAINLY . . .": *Ibid.,* Bayard to AB1, September 12, 1878.

554 "IT IS A GREAT MISTAKE . . .": *Ibid.*

554 "THE PARTIES . . . ORGANIZED . . .": *Ibid.,* Bayard to AB1, August 31, 1878.

554 "WHAT HAS BECOME . . .": *Ibid.,* AB1 to Bayard, September 15, 1878.

555 "THE DEMOCRATIC PARTY . . .": *Ibid.,* AB1 to AB2, October 22, 1878.

555–556 "ONE COULD HEAR . . .": *New York Tribune,* October 12, 1878.

556 "WHAT DO YOU WANT . . .": *New York Tribune,* October 12, 1878.

556 "BELMONT . . . SHOULD AT LEAST . . .": *Ibid.,* October 14, 1878.

556 "HIS FOOD HANDED . . .": *Ibid.*

556 "SOMEBODY SHOULD WRITE . . .": *Ibid.,* October 12, 1878.

556 ". . . I NEVER MENTIONED . . .": McJimsey, 209.

557 ". . . NEXT SUMMER, IF WE . . .": Bayard Papers, LOC, AB1 to Bayard, September 3, 1878.

557 "I AM DREADFULLY . . .": AB4, AB1 to AB2, October 18, 1878.

557 "SUCH A STRAIN . . .": AB4, AB1 to Bayard, September 15, 1878.

557 "WERE SO AFRAID . . .": *Ibid.,* AB1 to AB2, October 22, 1878.

558 "WE SHALL NOT . . .": *Ibid.*

558. "THE FIRST TIME . . .": *Ibid.,* AB1 to AB2, October 14, 1878.

558 "THERE IS NOT A HOUSE . . .": *Ibid.*

558 "ON THE 8 OF SEPTEMBER . . .": *Ibid.*

558 "I CANNOT REFRAIN . . .": . . .": *Ibid.,* AB1 to Rothschilds (London), October 22, 1878.

558 "CONTINUATION OF BUSINESS . . .": AB4, AB1 to AB2, October 11, 1878.

558 ". . . I WILL GIVE . . .": *Ibid.*

. . .": *Ibid.*, AB1 to Marble, n.d., [February 1880].

*p.*573 "MIND . . . AFFECTED . . .": *Ibid.*, Marble to AB1, n.d. [February 1880].

574 ". . . NOTHING QUITE . . .": *New York Tribune,* January 6, 1880.

575 "HALF WAY ACROSS . . .": *Ibid.*

575 "YOU FIND OUR POOR . . .": Bayard Papers, LOC, AB1 to Bayard, November 9, 1879.

575 "INSTINCT OF SELF-PRESERVATION . . .": *Ibid.*, AB1 to Bayard, November 10, 1879.

575 "NUMEROUS . . . STUPID . . .": AB4, Bayard to AB1, November 19, 1879.

575 "BUT I AM RATHER TO . . .": *Ibid.*

575–576 "A FRENCH COUNTRY . . .": *Ibid.*, Bayard to AB1, December 13, 1879.

576 "IT HAS BEEN VERY . . .": Bayard Papers, LOC, Perry Belmont to Bayard, December 24, 1879.

577 "THURMAN IS UNDOUBTEDLY . . .": *Ibid.*, AB1 to Bayard, March 11, 1879.

577 "THE SOUTH IN THE LAST . . .": *Ibid.*, B. T. Johnson to AB1, November 6, 1879.

577 "I WAITED FOR . . .": *Ibid.*, AB1 to Bayard, March 8, 1880.

578–579 "HE CANNOT GET . . .": *Ibid.*, AB1 to J. Hunter, February 19, 1880.

579 "IT WOULD BE WORSE . . .": *Ibid.*, AB1 to Perry Belmont, February 19, 1880.

579 ". . . OUR ONLY CHANCE . . .": AB4, Perry Belmont to J. Hunter, n.d. [1880].

579 "POLITICAL RIVALS . . .": Bayard Papers, LOC, AB1 to Bayard, March 8, 1880.

579 "THE TILDEN PEOPLE . . .": *Ibid.*, Perry Belmont to Bayard, March 24, 1880.

580 "WENT AWAY . . .": *Ibid.*, Perry Belmont to Bayard, April 23, 1880.

580–581 "OUR PARTY LEADERS . . .": *Ibid.*, AB1 to Bayard, February 1, 1880.

582 "THE OFFICE OF THE VICE . . .": Morgan, 95.

582 "STRAIN EVERY NERVE . . .": AB4, O'Conor to AB1, June 10, 1880.

582 "I AM QUITE . . .": *Ibid.*, AB1 to AB2, June 23, 1880.

582 "CANNOT YOU INDUCE . . .":

Marble Papers, LOC, AB1 to Marble, June 24, 1880.

*p.*582 "YOUR TELEGRAM . . .": *Ibid.*, Marble to AB1, June 24, 1880.

582–583 "UNDER THE PRESSURE . . .": Bayard Papers, LOC, AB1 to Bayard, June 27, 1880.

583 "MOMENTARY DISAPPOINTMENT . . .": *Ibid.*

583 "TWO YEARS TO WAIT . . .": AB4, AB1 to AB2, July 17, 1880.

583–584 "AS YOU GROW OLDER . . .": *Ibid.*

584 "IF YOU WANT . . .": Amory, *Who Killed Society?,* 454.

Chapter Fifty-six

584 "THE ESPECIAL FRIENDS . . .": AB4, W. A. Wallace to AB1, July 17, 1880.

585 "STUPIDITY OR WANT . . .": Bayard Papers, LOC, AB1 to Bayard, Friday morning, n.d. [September 24, 1880].

585 ". . . KELLY WILL NOT . . .": *Ibid.*

585 "PREFERRED . . . PARTICULARLY . . .": Marble Papers, LOC, AB1 to Marble, n.d. [1880].

585 "I SHALL BE PERSONALLY . . .": *Ibid.*, AB1 to Marble, October 6, 1880.

585–586 "THE 'BARREL' HAS . . .": *The New York Times,* September 24, 1880.

586 "WELL, WE'LL BUST . . .": *Ibid.*

587 "UNSOUND POLICY . . .": AB4, AB1 to Bayard, January 28, 1881.

587 "THIS POLICY . . .": *Ibid.*

588 "FOR THE BENEFIT . . .": *Ibid.*

588 "IN THE STABILITY . . .": *Ibid.*

589 "RENDERED VALUABLE . . .": *New York World,* June 28, 1881.

590 "TRUSTS, MONOPOLIES . . .": *The New York Times,* June 11, 1908.

590 "HOUSE AND PARTICULARLY . . .": AB4, AB1 to Bayard, January 28, 1881.

590 "THE INCOMING ADMINISTRATION . . .": *Ibid.*, Bayard to AB1, January 31, 1881.

Chapter Fifty-seven

591 "I WANT YOU TO TELL . . .": AB4, AB1 to AB2, April 4, 1881.

p. 591 "BUT LITTLE FAITH . . .": *Ibid.,* AB1 to AB2, March 30, 1881.

592 "SOMEWHAT STORMY . . .": *Ibid.,* AB1 to AB2, May 9, 1881.

592 "A SHORT VISIT . . .": *Ibid.,* Caroline to AB1, April 21, 1881.

592 "TOO YOUNG . . .": *Ibid.,* AB1 to Caroline, March 30, 1881.

592 "HAS GROWN QUITE . . .": *Ibid.,* AB4, Caroline to August, March 19, 1881.

592 "TO GO ABOUT . . .": *Ibid.,* AB1 to Caroline, March 30, 1881.

592–593 "MANY THANKS . . .":*Ibid.,* Caroline to AB1, April 21, 1881.

593 "I AM A PERFECT . . .": *Ibid.,* Caroline to AB1, March 31, 1881.

593 ". . . ALTHOUGH I WEAR . . .": *Ibid.,* Caroline to AB1, April 21, 1881.

594 "NEVER TO GO . . .": *Ibid.,* Caroline to AB1, April 16, 1881.

594 "I CANNOT GET . . .": *Ibid.,* Caroline to AB1, April 25, 1881.

594 "THIS MAY SEEM . . .": *Ibid.*

594 "THE FACT IS . . .": *Ibid.*

594 "I WOULD RATHER . . .": AB4, Caroline to AB1, April 21, 1881.

594 "YOU MUST NOT WORRY . . .": *Ibid.,* Caroline to AB1, May 9, 1881.

594 "I HOPE . . . THE SERVANTS . . .": *Ibid.,* Caroline to AB1, April 30, 1881.

595 "I HAVE DONE . . .": *Ibid.,* AB1 to AB2, May 23, 1881.

595 ". . . I SHALL REGRET . . .": *Ibid.,* Lawton to Caroline, April 11, 1881.

595 "CALLED MY ACTION . . .": *Ibid.*

596 "RAYMOND HAS . . .": AB4, Caroline to AB1, April 13, 1881.

596 "TOOK THE FIRST . . .": *Ibid.,* Caroline to AB1, April 16, 1881.

596 "I do not wish . . .": *Ibid.*

596 "CURT AND DISRESPECTFUL . . .": *Ibid.*

596 "I REGRET EXTREMELY . . .": AB4, Caroline to Lawton, n.d.

596 ". . . HE HAS A MOST . . .": *Ibid.,* Caroline to AB2, May 11, 1881.

596 "RAYMOND CAN STAY . . .": *Ibid.,* AB1 to AB2, May 23, 1881.

p. 596 "IN THIS GAY . . .": *Ibid.,* Caroline to AB1, April 23, 1881.

596–597 ". . . HE FEELS OUT . . .": *Ibid.,* Caroline to AB2, May 11, 1881.

597 "HE WILL GO . . .": *Ibid.,* Caroline to AB1, April 23, 1881.

597 "RAYMOND IS GOOD . . .": *Ibid.,* Caroline to AB1, May 9, 1881.

597 ". . . IF YOU KNEW . . .": *Ibid.,* Oliver to AB1, n.d. [1881].

597 "HIS FIRST VISIT . . .": *Ibid.,* Caroline to AB1, April 21, 1881.

597 "I HOPE NOW . . .": *Ibid.,* Caroline to AB1, May 9, 1881.

598 "I SOMETIMES THINK . . .": *Ibid.*

598 "AMONG THE FACES . . .": M. H. Elliott, 127.

598 "COULD CRACK . . .": *Ibid.,* 200.

598 "IS AMIABLE AND . . .": AB4, Caroline to AB1, February 3, 1882

598 "HALF-ENGAGED . . .": *Ibid.,* Oliver to Caroline, July 29, 1881.

598 "MY DEAR LITTLE . . .": *Ibid.*

598–599 "I DON'T ASK . . .": *Ibid.*

599 "IF AT THE END . . .": AB4, AB1 to Oliver, n.d.

599 "THESE YOUNG . . .": *Ibid.,* AB1 to AB2, April 4, 1881.

600 "UNSCRUPULOUS . . .": *Ibid.,* AB1 to AB2, March 9, 1881.

600 "HAS BEEN VERY GOOD . . .": *Ibid.,* AB1 to AB2, April 4, 1881.

600 "TO REPAY IN A MEASURE . . .": *New York Tribune,* February 25, 1881.

601 ". . . I WOULD GIVE . . .": *Ibid.*

601 ". . . YOU ARE A VERY LONG . . .": *Ibid.*

601 "I AM SO PLEASED . . .": AB4, Caroline to AB2, August 9, 1882.

601 ". . . BESIDES . . . HE DOES NOT . . .": *Ibid.*

602 ". . . HE HEREAFTER . . .": *New York Herald,* January 7, 1882.

602 "WAS RECEIVED WITH REGRET . . .": *New York World,* January 9, 1882.

602 "BEAUTY . . .": AB4, Caroline to AB2, August 25, 1881.

602 "KNOWING HIS DISCRETION . . .": *Ibid.,* AB1 to AB2, August 19, 1881.

603 "YOUR STRICTURES . . .": *Ibid.,*

AB1 to AB2, August 26, 1881.

*p.*603 "DEAR BESSIE . . .": *Ibid.*

603 "I AM VERY GLAD . . .": AB4, AB1 to AB2, August 21, 1881.

603–604 "HE HAD JUST RETURNED . . .": *Ibid.*, AB1 to AB2, August 12, 1881.

604 "IT WAS A REAL . . .": *Ibid.*, Bennett to "cher ami" (AB1?), n.d.

604 "I THINK IT IS ABSOLUTELY . . .": *Ibid.*, Caroline to AB2, August 25, 1881.

605 ". . . I SHALL HAVE MORE . . .": *Ibid.*, Caroline to AB2, September 12, 1881.

605 "BE A VERY PLEASANT . . .": *Ibid.*, Caroline to AB2, September 3, 1881.

605 "I HOPE I SHALL FIND . . .": *Ibid.*, Caroline to AB2, November 15, 1881.

605 "I WILL BE GLAD . . .": *Ibid.*, Caroline to AB1, November 24, 1881.

605 "WHAT A PITY . . ." *Ibid.*, Caroline to AB1, November 20, 1881.

605 "I HAVE TRIED . . .": *Ibid.*, Caroline to AB1, November 24, 1881.

605–606 "WE HAVE BEEN . . .": *Ibid.*, Caroline to AB2, September 12, 1881.

606 "IF YOU COULD . . .": *Ibid.*, Caroline to AB1, November 15, 1881.

606 "THE TROUBLE YOU HAVE . . .": *Ibid.*, Caroline to AB1, November 24, 1881.

606 "I HAVE NEVER . . .": *Ibid.*, Oliver to AB2, August 27, 1881.

606–607 "THE PEOPLE ARE AWFULLY . . .": *Ibid.*

607 "THE MOST LARGELY-ATTENDED . . .": *New York Tribune*, November 30, 1881.

607 "THE MOST BRILLIANT . . .": *New York Commercial Advertiser*, November 30, 1881.

607 "GETTING AHEAD . . .": *American Queen*, December 3, 1881.

607 ". . . THE BRIDAL CARRIAGE . . .": *Ibid.*, December 3, 1881.

607 "WILL BE GENERALLY . . .": *The Town*, Saturday, November 26, 1881.

607 "THE LARGEST AND MOST . . .": NYHS scrapbook, clipping, November 30, 1881.

607 "WAS PERFORMED WITHOUT . . .": *New York Herald*, November 30, 1881.

Chapter Fifty-eight

*p.*608 ". . . IN A FEW MORE TURNS . . .": AB4, Raymond Diary, 15.

608–609 "TWO BEAUTIFULLY . . .": *Ibid.*, 21.

609 "MINIATURE STREET . . .": *Ibid.*, 28.

609 "BEAUTIFUL . . . GOLDEN . . .": *Ibid.*, 37.

609 "IT IS EVIDENT . . .": AB4, Lawton to Drexel (Drescel?), January 21, 1882.

609 "I AM SORRY . . .": *Ibid.*, Raymond to AB1, n.d.

609–610 "CONFIRMED THE STORY . . .": AB4, Raymond's Diary, 89–90.

610 "AWFULLY HANDSOME . . .": *Ibid.*, 50–51.

610 "IF I AM GOOD . . .": *Ibid.* (page in diary), n.d.

611 "MORE LOVING AND AFFECTIONATE . . .": AB4, Caroline to AB1, November 24, 1881.

611 "I CAN'T SAY . . .": *Ibid.*, Caroline to AB1, November 15, 1881.

611 "IT IS JUST NINE . . .": *Ibid.*, Caroline to AB1, December 2, 1881.

611 "A SHEET AND PILLOWCASE . . .": AB4, Raymond's Diary, 124–125.

612 "THE GUIDEBOOK . . .": *Ibid.*, 128–133.

612 "MORE INTERESTING . . .": AB4, Caroline to AB1, December 4, 1881.

612 "A MOST EXTRAORDINARY . . .": AB4, Raymond's Diary, 163–165.

612 "ONE OLD MAN . . .": AB4, Caroline to AB1, December 9, 1881.

613 ". . . NO MAN . . .": AB4, Raymond's Diary, 126.

613 "COULD NOT HELP LAUGHING . . .": *Ibid.*, 136–137.

613 "WAS MORE CROWDED . . .": *Ibid.*, 151–152.

613 ". . . I ARRIVED RATHER . . .": *Ibid.*, 157–158.

613–614 "GOING THROUGH WHAT . . .": *Ibid.*, 147.

614 "MY HEADGEAR . . .": *Ibid.*, 171.

614 "AN EXCELLENT MAN . . .": AB4, Caroline to AB1, December 13, 1881.

614 "OUR DAHABEAH . . .": LaPorte, 7–8.

615 "RAYMOND HAS ALREADY . . .":

AB4, Caroline to AB1, December 13, 1881.

p. 615 ". . . I SHOT A POOR . . .": AB4, Raymond's Diary, 174.

615 "BANGED . . . AWAY . . .": *Ibid.*

615 "I WENT ON SHORE BEFORE . . .": *Ibid.*, 195–196.

616 "I WENT ASHORE . . .": *Ibid.*, 198–199.

616 "MONOTONOUS . . .": AB4, Caroline to AB1, December 18, 1881.

616 "I CAUGHT MAMA'S . . .": AB4, Raymond's Diary, 176–177.

616–617 ". . . TEA IS BEING SERVED . . .": AB4, Caroline to AB1, December 25, 1881.

617 "HOW WELL YOU TIMED . . .": *Ibid.*, Raymond to AB1, December 25, 1881.

617 "AUNT JULIA WROTE . . .": *Ibid.*, Caroline to AB1, December 25, 1881.

617 "WAS NOT VERY LIVELY . . .": AB4, Raymond's Diary, 201.

617 "WE PASSED A MERCHANT . . .": *Ibid.*, 194.

617 "YOU HAVE GIVEN HER . . .": AB4, AB1 to Raymond, February 20, 1882.

617 "RICA'S WILL BE . . .": AB4, Raymond's Diary, 201.

618 "SKIPPING VERY SUCCESSFULLY . . .": *Ibid.*, 205.

618 "A LARGE BUFFALO . . .": AB4, Caroline to AB1, December 25, 1881.

618 "IT IS NOW SUNSET . . .": *Ibid.*

618 "MAMA AND RICA . . .": AB4, Raymond's Diary, 207–210.

619 "SOME OF THEIR SONGS . . .": *Ibid.*

619 "QUEER LOOKING . . .": *Ibid.*, 211.

619 ". . . AFTER I HAD TAKEN . . .": AB4, Caroline to AB1, January 2, 1882.

620 "MY OLD ENEMY . . .": *Ibid.*, AB1 to Raymond, January 30, 1882.

620 "AND FOR THAT PURPOSE . . .": *Ibid.*

620 ". . . OUR CLOTHES . . .": AB4, Caroline to AB1, January 23, 1882.

620–621 "MAMA TAKES GREAT . . .": *Ibid.*, Raymond to AB1, January 8, 1882.

621 "NOTHING SHORT . . .": *Ibid.*, Caroline to AB1, January 7, 1882.

621 "ALL GOT THE ARTISTIC . . .": AB4, Raymond's Diary, 215.

621 "RICA'S LITTLE . . .": *Ibid.*

p. 621–622 "I COULD NOT FIND . . .": *Ibid.*, 221.

622 "AS BOYS DO . . .": AB4, Raymond to AB1, January 16, 1882.

622 ". . . EVEN THE CORRECTIONS . . .": *Ibid.*

622 ". . . THE COLORS . . .": *Ibid.*

622 "WAS INFESTED WITH . . .": *Ibid.*

622 "THE VERY LIBERAL . . .": AB4, Raymond to AB2, February 3, 1882.

622 "I MUST STUDY . . .": *Ibid.*, Raymond to AB2, February 6, 1882.

622 "I WISH THAT I . . .": *Ibid.*, Caroline to AB1, January 26, 1882.

622–623 ". . . IN THE FUTURE . . .": *Ibid.*, Caroline to AB1, January 23, 1882.

623 "YOU ARE A GOOD . . .": *Ibid.*, Caroline to AB1, January 13, 1882.

623 "IT IS JUST . . .": *Ibid.*

623 "IT DELIGHTS ME . . .": *Ibid.*

623–624 "AH ME! . . .": *Ibid.*

624 "HE MAY WANT TO GIVE . . .": AB4, Caroline to AB1, January 18, 1882.

624 "YOU MUST NOT . . .": *Ibid.*, Caroline to AB1, January 28, 1882.

Chapter Fifty-nine

625 "WE ARE THUS . . .": AB4, AB2 to AB1, February 6, 1882.

625 "POOR MAMA . . .": *Ibid.*, AB2 to AB1, April 9, 1882.

625 "HAVE BEEN SELFISH . . .": *Ibid.*

625 "SAM HAS HIS WEAKNESSES . . .": AB4, AB1 to AB2, April 4, 1882.

626 ". . . I CANNOT POINT . . .": *Ibid.*, AB2 to AB1, April 9, 1882.

626 "IT IS NOT OFTEN . . .": *Ibid.*, AB2 to AB1, February 16, 1882.

626 "CITIZENS . . .": *Ibid.*

626–627 "A SHAMEFUL AND INHUMAN . . .": *Ibid.*

627 "SHE IS VERY SWEET . . .": AB4, Caroline to AB1, March 2, 1882.

627 "WE MAY FEEL . . .": *Ibid.*, Caroline to AB1, March 20, 1882.

*p.*627 "I THINK SHE . . .": *Ibid.,*
Raymond to AB1, March 10,
1882.

627 "NICE . . . , MANLY . . . ,":
Ibid., AB2 to AB1, April 9,
1882.

628 "I AM HAVING A MUCH . . .":
Ibid., Raymond to AB1,
March 10, 1882.

628 "THEY ACKNOWLEDGE, . . .":
Ibid.

628 "AUGIE HAS SHOWN . . .":
Ibid.

628 "I HAVE . . .": *Ibid.,* AB2 to
AB1, April 9, 1882.

628 "SECOND VISIT . . .": *Ibid.,*
Raymond to AB1, March 10,
1882.

628 "THIS DANCE . . .": AB4,
Caroline to AB1, March 2,
1882.

628 "TO PLEASE . . .": *Ibid.*

628 "THEIR PRINCIPAL EFFECT
. . .": AB4, Caroline to AB1,
March 20, 1882.

628 "YOU NEED NOT . . .": *Ibid.,*
Caroline to AB1, March 2,
1882.

628 "I AM TOLD . . .": *Ibid.,* Caroline to AB1, March 13, 1882.

629 "WE HAD TO SCRAMBLE . . .":
Ibid., Caroline to AB1, March
30, 1882.

629 "SO . . . I WENT IN . . .":
Ibid.

629 "I WISH YOU . . .": *Ibid.*

629 ". . . IT REMINDED ME . . .":
Ibid.

629 "OTHER MORE DISGUSTING
. . .": AB4, Caroline to AB1,
March 27, 1882.

629–630 "I SAW OUR STEERSMAN . . .":
Ibid.

630 "A COMFORT . . .": AB4, Caroline to AB1, March 30, 1882.

630 "LEAN UPON US . . .": *Ibid.,*
Caroline to AB1, April 10,
1882.

630 "CRAZY ON THE . . .": *Ibid.,*
Caroline to AB1, April 3,
1882.

630 "I DON'T FEEL . . .": *Ibid.,*
Caroline to AB1, March 22,
1882.

Chapter Sixty

631 "THE . . . RIGHT TO WITHDRAW
. . .": AB4, AB2 to AB1,
February 16, 1881.

631 "I CHARGE YOU . . .": *Ibid.*

631 "OLIVER DOESN'T . . .": *Ibid.*

631 "HE WILL DROP . . .": *Ibid.*

*p.*631 "NOW, . . . THE QUESTION
. . .": AB4, AB2 to AB1,
February 16, 1882.

631–632 "THE TIME OF THE ENGAGE-
MENT . . .": *Ibid.,* AB2 to
AB1, April 9, 1882.

632 "CHEER UP, WE WILL . . .":
Ibid., AB2 to AB1, February
16, 1882.

632 ". . . IF OLIVER . . .": *Ibid.,*
Caroline to AB1, February 3,
1882.

632 "I HAD INTENDED . . .": *Ibid.,*
Oliver to AB1, January 22,
1882.

633 "AT LAST, AFTER . . .": *Ibid.,*
AB1 to Oliver, February 24,
1882.

633–634 "I APPEAL TO YOUR . . .":
Ibid., AB1 to Oliver, April
8, 1882.

634 "WHY NOT QUIETLY . . .":
Ibid.

634 "I KNOW VERY . . .": *Ibid.,*
Oliver to AB1, May 26, 1882.

634 "YOU WILL FIND . . .": AB4,
AB1 to Oliver, February 24,
1882.

634 "SHE WILL . . . SOON BE . . .":
Ibid., AB1 to Oliver, April 8,
1882.

635 "CAUGHT A GLIMPSE . . .":
Ibid., Caroline to AB1, April
26, 1882.

635 "I DODGED . . .": *Ibid.*

635 "BEFORE I COULD . . .": *Ibid.*

636 "I AM SO HURRIED . . .": AB4,
Caroline to Oliver, May 1,
1882.

636 "HE HAS BECOME VERY STRONG
. . .": *Ibid.,* Frederika to AB1,
May 15, 1882.

636 "HE IS THE SAME EASY . . .":
Ibid., Caroline to AB1, May
14, 1882.

636 "SALLIE . . . ACCEPTED . . .":
Ibid.

637 "HE APPROVES OF ALL . . .":
Ibid.

637 "PLEASANT FOR VISITORS . . .":
Ibid.

637 "THERE IS NO . . .": AB4,
Caroline to AB1, May 18,
1882.

637 "MAIN IDEA . . .": *Ibid.,* Caroline to AB1, May 25, 1882.

637 "HE WILL ONLY . . .": *Ibid.,*
Caroline to AB1, May 14,
1882.

637 "THEY HAD BETTER . . .":
Ibid., Caroline to AB1, May
18, 1882.

637 "YOU DON'T SEE . . .": *Ibid.,*
Caroline to AB1, May 31,
1882.

p. 637 "IF I HAD ONLY . . .": *Ibid.*, Caroline to AB1, April 30, 1882.

638 "FAGGED AND WORN . . .": *Ibid.*, Caroline to AB1, May 5, 1882.

638 "DRESSING AND UNDRESSING . . .": *Ibid.*, Caroline to AB1, May 25, 1882.

638 "A NICE LITTLE MAN . . .": *Ibid.*, Caroline to AB1, May 18, 1882.

638 "DELIGHTED . . . PREVAILED . . .": *Ibid.*, Frederika to AB1, May 15, 1882.

638 "PETITE APPEARANCE . . .": *Ibid.*, AB2 to AB1, May 19, 1882.

638 "PLAY THE PIANO . . .": *Ibid.*, Caroline to AB1, May 28, 1882.

638 "AT FIRST . . .": *Ibid.*, Caroline to AB1, May 25, 1882.

639 "NAGGING . . . IMAGINARY LOSSES . . .": *Ibid.*, AB1 to AB2, March 31, 1882.

639 "I SHALL PAY . . .": *Ibid.*, AB1 to AB2, May 19, 1882.

639 "NO POSSIBLE EXCUSE . . .": *Ibid.*, AB1 to AB2, April 4, 1882.

639 "I HAVE MORE FAITH . . .": *Ibid.*, AB1 to AB2, March 31, 1882.

639 "THEY WANT . . . TO EXASPER-ATE . . .": *Ibid.*

639 "UNDOUBTEDLY AT THE BOT-TOM . . .": AB4, AB1 to AB2, April 21, 1882.

639 "LORENT IS AN 'INTRIGANT' . . .": *Ibid.*, AB1 to AB2, May 23, 1882.

639 "THERE WAS . . . MORE FAULT-FINDING . . .": *Ibid.*, AB1 to AB2, April 21, 1882.

639–640 "I DON'T MEAN . . .": *Ibid.*, AB1 to AB2, April 4, 1882.

640 "THIS STATE OF THINGS . . .": *Ibid.*, AB1 to AB2, May 9, 1882.

640 "IS THE LAST PRIVATE . . .": *Ibid.*, AB1 to AB2, May 19, 1882.

640 "I SHALL PUT ASIDE . . .": *Ibid.*, AB1 to AB2, May 23, 1882.

640 "I WANT YOU TO MAKE BE-LIEVE . . .": *Ibid.*, AB1 to AB2, April 4, 1882.

640 "FROM WHOM . . .": *Ibid.*

640 "DOES NOT KNOW OR CARE . . .": AB4, AB1 to AB2, April 21, 1882.

640 "GET HIM ALONE . . .": *Ibid.*, AB1 to AB2, April 4, 1882.

p. 640 "YOU WILL HAVE TO PLAY . . .": *Ibid.*, AB1 to AB2, April 21, 1882.

640 "BEST . . . NOT TO SAY . . .": *Ibid.*

640 ". . . NATHANIEL WILL LIKE MUCH . . .": AB4, AB1 to AB2, May 9, 1882.

641 ". . . AS LONG AS . . .": *Ibid.*, Caroline to AB1, May 18, 1882.

641 "BECAUSE I SEE SO . . .": *Ibid.*

641 "IT IS HARD . . .": AB4, Caroline to AB1, May 14, 1882.

641 "IT IS QUITE STRANGE . . .": *Ibid.*, Caroline to AB1, May 20, 1882.

642 "I SHALL WANT . . .": *Ibid.*, Caroline to AB1, May 31, 1882.

642 ". . . I PRAY . . .": *Ibid.*, Caroline to AB1, May 14, 1882.

Chapter Sixty-one

643 "THEY WANT TO SHELVE . . .": *AAD*, 219.

643 "JURISDICTION OVER . . .": *Ibid.*, 216.

643 "MY POLITICAL STRENGTH . . .": *Ibid.*, 217.

644 "THERE WILL HAVE TO BE . . .": *Ibid.*, 220.

644 "GO THE WHOLE . . .": *Ibid.*

644 "YOU WILL TAKE SPECIAL . . .": House of Representatives, 47th Cong., 1st Sess., Report No. 1790, 17, Blaine to Hurlbert, August 4, 1881.

644 "INSTEAD OF ACTING . . .": *AAD*, 237.

645 "PRETTY FISHY . . . WILL NOT GET . . .": AB4, AB1 to AB2, May 9, 1882.

645 "I INTEND TO GIVE . . .": *AAD*, 255.

645 "FIRST BLOOD . . .": Marble Papers, LOC, Marble to Perry Belmont, April 25, 1882.

645 "I FEAR MY BOY . . .": *Ibid.*, AB1 to Marble, April 25, 1882.

645 "I HOPE PERRY . . .": AB4, Caroline to Oliver, May 1, 1882.

646 ". . . WHILE YOU CANNOT . . .": Perry Belmont, Public Record, Chile-Peru Investiga-tion, 17.

646 "WHY . . . NINE SECRETARIES . . .": *Ibid.*, 426.

647 "RELIEVES ME . . .": *Ibid.*, 447.

p. 647 "WHEN YOU HAVE . . .": *Ibid.*, 452.

647 "MR. BELMONT . . . HAS, DURING . . .": *Ibid.*, 477–479.

648 "UNTRUTH IS NOT . . .": *The New York Times*, April 28, 1882.

649 "CANNOT YOU COME . . .": Marble Papers, LOC, AB1 to Marble, April 28, 1882.

649 "I MAY RANSACK . . .": *Ibid.*

649 "EVEN THE IDEA . . .": *Ibid.*

649 "SO UTTERLY WRETCHED . . ." *Ibid.*

649 "A VERY BRIGHT . . .": *Ibid.*

649–650 "IN THE EXAMINATION . . .": AB4, Perry Belmont to House Committee on Foreign Affairs, April 28, 1882.

650 "IT IS EXCELLENT . . .": Marble Papers, LOC, AB1 to Marble, n.d. [April 29, 1882].

650 "MR. BELMONT'S MOVEMENTS . . .": *New York Tribune*, April 29, 1882.

650 "AN UNFORTUNATE MANNER . . .": *Ibid.*, April 27, 1882.

650 "A VERY STUPID MAN . . .": *Ibid.*, May 2, 1882.

651 "KEPT UP A RATTLE . . .": *The New York Times*, April 27, 1882.

651 "THERE IS A GENERAL BELIEF . . .": *New York Tribune*, April 27, 1882.

651 "BIG BROTHER . . .": *AAD*, 271.

651 "I SHOULD LIKE MYSELF . . .": AB4, Caroline to AB1, May 14, 1882.

651 "IS AS TOUGH . . .": *Ibid.*, Frederika to AB1, May 15, 1882.

651 "SUCCESS IS NOW . . .": *Ibid.*, AB2 to AB1, April 19, 1882.

652 "THE SONS OF OUR . . .": *Knickerbocker*, December 20, 1882.

652 ". . . IT'S ABOUT TIME . . .": *New York Daily Tribune*, August 24, 1882.

652 "HOW MANY YOUNG . . .": *Ibid.*

652–653 "WHETHER PERRY . . .": *Ibid.*, October 3, 1882.

653 "THIS FACT WAS STATED . . .": *Ibid.*, September 30, 1882.

653 ". . . IF PERRY DID NOT INHERIT . . .": *Ibid.*, June 12, 1883.

653 ". . . AS ONE WHO . . .": Marble Papers, LOC, Marble to Perry Belmont, February 8, 1882.

653 ". . . I HAVE DONE ALL . . .":

The New York Times, June 16, 1882.

p. 654 "I LEAVE IT TO YOU . . .": AB4, Nathaniel de Rothschild to AB1, November 28, 1882.

655 "YOUR ZEALOUS . . .": *Ibid.*, AB1 to Nathaniel de Rothschild, December 11, 1882.

655 "A SLENDER MILITARY . . .": *AAD*, 303–4.

655 "A MYSTERIOUS, BUT . . .": *Ibid.*

656 "A WALKOVER . . .": *Ibid.*, 267.

Chapter Sixty-two

656 "FRIENDS REMARK . . .": AB4, Caroline to AB1, September 15, 1882.

656–657 "I DON'T KNOW WHAT . . .": *Ibid.*, Caroline to AB1, July 22, 1882.

657 "I LONG FOR HOME . . .": *Ibid.*, AB2 to AB1, May 19, 1882.

657 "TO STRAIGHTEN . . .": *Ibid.*, AB2 to AB1, February 16, 1882.

657 "FURNISHED APARTMENTS . . . I SUPPOSE . . .": *Ibid.*, AB1 to AB2, July 21, 1882.

657 "DO AS MUCH DAMAGE . . .": *Ibid.*

658 "IS BRUSQUE BUT . . .": AB4, AB1 to AB2, October 14, 1883.

658 "WE HAVE TO WAIT . . .": *Ibid.*, AB1 to AB2, April 21, 1882.

658 "WE WOULD PUT . . .": *Ibid.*

658 "A LONG AND SERIOUS . . .": AB4, Purdy to AB1, n.d. [October 1882].

658 "I MOST HEARTILY . . .": *Ibid.*, AB1 to Purdy, October 5, 1882.

659 "IF YOU HAD NOT GONE . . .": *Ibid.*, AB1 to AB2, July 26, 1882.

659 "SAY NOTHING . . .": *Ibid.*, Caroline to AB2, July 7, 1882.

659 "ON ANY ACCOUNT . . .": *Ibid.*, AB1 to AB2, July 1, [1882?].

659 "I DO NOT WISH . . .": *Ibid.*

659 "FOR HIM TO LIVE . . .": AB4, AB1 to AB2, July 21, 1882.

659 "GOOD ORDER . . .": *Ibid.*

659 "DON'T MENTION . . .": *Ibid.*

659 "MY DEAREST PETITE . . .": AB4, Sallie to Caroline, March 29, 1883.

p. 659–660 "THE GREAT PERSONAL . . .": *Ibid.*, Sallie to Oliver, May 20, 1883.

660 "I CAN DO ABSOLUTELY . . .": *Ibid.*, Sallie to Caroline, March 28, 1883.

660 "PAST LISTENING TO . . .": *Ibid.*, Sallie to Caroline, March 29, 1883.

660 "I WISH I WERE . . .": *Ibid.*, Sallie to Frederika, March 28, 1883.

660 "YOU DON'T KNOW . . .": *Ibid.*, Sallie to Caroline, March 29, 1883.

660 "A FEW DAYS . . .": *Ibid.*

660 "I HOPE HE WILL . . .": *Ibid.*

660 "I HOPE THE CHANGE . . .": AB4, Mrs. Whiting to Oliver, March 29, 1883.

660 "SORRY TO HEAR . . .": *Ibid.*, Mrs. Whiting to Oliver, April 4, 1883.

660 "FLYING AROUND . . .": *Ibid.*, Sallie to Frederika, April 14, 1883.

661 "FORGOTTEN . . . NOTHING . . .": *Ibid.*, Mrs. Whiting to Oliver, April 20, 1883.

661 "THREE THOUSAND . . .": *Ibid.*, Caroline to Sallie, April 18, 1883.

661 "SALLIE'S LETTERS . . .": *Ibid.*, Caroline to Oliver, April 14, 1883.

661 "TAKE INTO CONSIDERATION . . .": *Ibid.*

661–662 "HAVE PATIENCE . . .": AB4, Caroline to Sallie, April 18, 1883.

662 "CAN BE ACCOUNTED FOR . . .": *Ibid.*, Sallie to Caroline, April 22, 1883.

662 "I LEAVE FOR LONDON . . .": *Ibid.*, Sallie to Oliver, May 2, 1883.

662 "DO NOT COME . . .": *Ibid.*, Sallie to Oliver, May 2, 1883.

662 "EVERYTHING AT AN END . . .": *Ibid.*, Sallie to Oliver, May 2, 1883.

662 "I NEVER CAN . . .": *Ibid.*, Sallie to Caroline, May 15, 1883.

663 "OVERCOME WITH HORROR . . .": *Ibid.*, Sallie to Caroline, May 19, 1883.

663 "YOU CANNOT BE MORE . . .": *Ibid.*, Caroline to Sallie, May 22, 1883.

663 "SURPRISE AND . . . DEEP REGRET . . .": *Ibid.*, Oliver to Sallie, n.d. [May 1883].

663 ". . . IN MY PRESENT . . .":

Ibid., Sallie to Oliver, May 20, 1883.

p. 663 "WHICH I PRONOUNCE . . .": *Ibid.*, Oliver to Sallie, May 23, 1883.

664 "SUCH GREAT CHANGES . . .": Marble Papers, LOC, Perry Belmont to Marble, June 3, 1883.

664–665 "HE DOES NOT SEEM . . .": AB4, L. L. Schuyler to AB1, July 26, 1883.

665 ". . . I KNOW HOW MUCH . . .": *Ibid.*, L. L. Schuyler to Perry Belmont, November 29, 1883.

665 "I AM TOLD . . .": *Ibid.*, Caroline to AB2, June 6, [1887].

665 "WHAT MORE CAN . . .": *Ibid.*, Caroline to AB2, September 26, [1884].

665 "YOU SAY YOU GRUMBLED . . .": *Ibid.*, Caroline to AB2, September 28, [1884].

666 "MR. BELMONT, WILL . . .": *New York Tribune*, July 1, 1883.

666 "PLEASE DO NOT ALLUDE . . .": AB4, AB2 to J. Pulitzer, January 24, 1884.

667 "THAT HORRIBLE . . .": *Ibid.*, Caroline to Mrs. Cushing, n.d. [winter, 1883].

667 "OUR MISNAMED . . .": Marble Papers, LOC, AB1 to Marble, December 21, 1884.

667 "BEAUTIFUL BRIDE . . .": AB4, Nathaniel de Rothschild to AB1, April 4, 1884.

667 "BLACK VELVET . . .": *Ibid.*, C. Louis Heck to AB1, February 4, 1884.

667 "IF WE COULD KNOW . . .": *Ibid.*, Daily Journal [by Mrs. Foster Fly Lockport], August 25, 1884.

667–668 "MY NERVOUSNESS . . .": *Ibid.*, AB1 to AB2, July 1, 1883.

668 "SINCERE REGRETS . . . I SHOULD . . .": Marble Papers, LOC, Marble to AB1, February 20, 1884.

668 "IF ANYTHING . . .": *Ibid.*, AB1 to Marble, February 20, 1884.

668 "I WILL FOLLOW . . .": *Ibid.*, Marble to AB1, n.d. [February 1884].

668 "I CAME FOR ATONEMENT . . .": *Ibid.*, Marble to AB1, n.d. [February 1884].

668–669 "BEEN FOOL ENOUGH . . .": AB4, AB1 to Marble, November 25, 1884.

669 "ONE MUST FORGET . . .":

Ibid., Marble to AB1, Sunday night, n.d. [1884].

*p.*669 "MY FEELINGS TOWARD . . .": Marble Papers, LOC, Marble to AB1, April 27, 1885.

669 "NOT WHAT I EXPECTED . . .": *Ibid.*, AB1 to Marble, May 14, 1885.

669 "LOOKED FOR IT . . .": AB4, Marble to AB1, August 28, 1885.

670 "COME! MY DEAR . . .": *Ibid.*

670 "DEEPLY MORTIFIED . . .": Marble Papers, LOC, April 21, 1885.

Chapter Sixty-three

670 "IT MUST BE SAD . . .": AB4, Caroline to AB2, n.d. [1884].

671 ". . . YOU MUST NOT LET . . .": *Ibid.*, AB1 to AB2, July 25, 1884.

671 "BRIGHT AND LIVELY . . .": *Ibid.*, AB1 to AB2, July 23, 1884.

671 "STRONG LACE . . .": *Ibid.*

671–672 "EXTREME CAUTION . . .": *Ibid.*

672 "I WILL NOT TOUCH . . .": AB4, AB1 to AB2, August 21, 1884.

672 "THE TIME WILL COME . . .": *Ibid.*

672 "SIMPLY BUTCHERED . . .": AB4, AB1 to AB2, June 23, 1884.

673 "DON'T LET HIM FORGET . . .": *Ibid.*, Caroline to AB2, October 9, 1884.

673 "A VERY PRETTY GIRL . . .": AB4, Raymond's Cambridge Diary, 6.

673 "I . . . HAD ALL THE TROUBLE . . .": *Ibid.*, 7.

673 "SINGLED OUT A TURKISH . . .": *Ibid.*, 8.

673 "TO TRAMP THROUGH . . .": *Ibid.*, 16.

673–674 "WE RAN INTO . . .": *Ibid.*, 17.

674 "ENOUGH OF A MISHAP . . .": *Ibid.*, 18.

674 "BUT WHY DID WE . . .": *Ibid.*, 19.

674 "DELIGHTED TO GET . . .": *Ibid.*, 21.

675 ". . . I GULPED IT . . .": *Ibid.*, 30.

675 "I TREATED HIM COLDLY . . .": *Ibid.*, 35.

675–676 "WE JUMPED FENCES . . .": *Ibid.*, 47.

676 "THE DAMNED BRUTE . . .": *Ibid.*, 53.

*p.*676 "VERY PRETTY HOUSE-KEEPER . . .": *Ibid.*, 54.

676 "ALL OVER . . .": *Ibid.*, 56.

676 "MR. PERRY BELMONT HAS . . .": *New York Tribune,* February 23, 1884.

677 "THE PRICE OF LIBERTY . . .": *Ibid.*, June 11, 1883.

677 "SUCH THINGS MIGHT . . .": *The New York Times,* June 11, 1883.

677–678 "IN SELECTING THE . . .": Fiske, 26–27.

678 "TOO CLEAN . . .": Morgan, 189.

69 "THE IRISH WERE SO DEEPLY . . .": AB4, AB1 to AB2, July 29, 1884.

679 "TERRIBLY GLOOMY . . .": AB4, AB1 to AB2, July 29, 1884.

679 "HOW LUCKY . . .": Marble Papers, LOC, AB1 to Marble, Thursday, n.d. [1884].

679 "WILL DO MY BEST . . .": *Ibid.*, AB1 to AB2, October 10, 1884.

679–680 "I THANK YOU . . .": *Ibid.*

680 ". . . AM I NOW . . .": *Ibid.*

680 "I NEVER WAS HARD . . .": AB4 to AB2, October 12, 1884.

680 "WELL MEANT . . . I THINK . . .": *Ibid.*

681 "OF COURSE . . .": AB4, AB1 to Gorman, October 17, 1884.

681 "THIS OUGHT . . .": *Ibid.*

681 "IT IS THE FIRST TIME . . .": AB4, AB1 to AB2, August 21, 1884.

681 "THE TICKET SUITS . . .": Marble Papers, LOC, AB2 to Marble, July 14, 1884.

681 "A FLAG-RAISING . . .": AB4, Raymond's Cambridge Diary, 49.

682 "I HAD THE PLEASURE . . .": *Ibid.*

682 "WENT IN FOR . . . DISREPUTABLE . . .": *Ibid.*, 68.

682 "BUT THEY DID NOT LAST . . .": *Ibid.*, 66.

682 ". . . BUT SOMEBODY . . .": *Ibid.*, 67.

682 "BOOMING FOR . . .": *Ibid.*, 69.

682 "A GENERALLY WELL . . .": AB4, AB1 to Gorman, November 10, 1884.

683 "THE FALLING OFF . . .": *Ibid.*, AB1 to Cleveland, November 13, 1884.

683 "STAUNCH AND TRUE . . .": *Ibid.*

683 "THANK GOD, . . .": *Ibid.*

683 "DELIGHTED TO HAVE LIVED . . .":

AB4, AB1 to McHenry, April 27, 1885.

p. 683 "THE RICH AND POWERFUL . . .": AB1, *Letters, Speeches, and Addresses,* 230–231.

683 "SOME EIGHT OR TEN . . .": AB4, AB1 to Nathaniel de Rothschild, January 5, 1883.

683–684 "WILL HAVE TWENTY . . .": *Ibid.,* AB1 to Nathaniel de Rothschild, November 18, 1884.

684 ". . . I AM SURE . . .": *Ibid.,* AB1 to Bayard, February 20, 1885.

684 "HEALTH, TIME, . . .": *Ibid.*

684–685 "I DO NOT WISH . . .": *Ibid.*

685 ". . . YOU KNOW THE COUNSEL . . .": AB4, Bayard to AB1, February 22, 1885.

685 "IF I DON'T AGREE . . .": *Ibid.,* AB1 to H. D. McHenry, April 28, 1885.

685 "ANOTHER INSTANCE . . .": *Ibid.,* AB1 to Cleveland, May 1885.

Chapter Sixty-four

686 ". . . THE MISCREANT'S . . .": Marble Papers, LOC, AB1 to Marble, December 21, 1884.

686 "TO HAVE A LONG . . .": AB4, Bayard to AB1, July 27, 1885.

686 ". . . THE STONES ARE DROPPING . . .": *Ibid.,* AB2 to AB1, December 15, 1884.

686 "TO INDULGE IN THIS . . .": *Ibid.,* AB1 to AB2, July 23, 1884.

687 "THE PEOPLE ALL AROUND . . .": *Ibid.,* AB1 to AB2, July 18, 1884.

687 "ALMOST BREAKING . . .": AB4, Raymond's Cambridge Diary, 73.

688 "VERY CLOSELY SEARCHED . . .": *Ibid.,* 79.

688 "THEY NEVER TAKE . . .": *Ibid.*

688 "JOHN L. SULLIVAN . . .": *Ibid.,* 88.

688 "IN 'FRAGRANT . . .": *Ibid.,* 91.

688 "SEIZED A FRENZY . . .": *Ibid.*

688 "I'M A PRETTY . . .": *Ibid.,* 92.

689 "BROTHERS WINTHROP . . .": *Ibid.*

689 "WORSHIPED WITH ALL . . .": *Ibid.,* 93.

689 "IS A HELL . . .": *Ibid.,* 95.

689 "ENACTED A MIRACLE . . .": *Ibid.,* 97.

p. 690 "QUITE STRAIGHT . . .": *Ibid.,* 128.

690 "IT WAS ONE OF THE COSIEST . . .": *Ibid.,* 131.

690 "SANTA CLAUS . . .": *Ibid.,* 135.

690–691 ". . . THEN THE FUN . . .": *Ibid.,* 145.

691 "BESIDES HER UGLINESS . . .": *Ibid.,* 146.

691 "I HEAR YOU HAVE . . .": AB4, Griswold to AB2, November 4, 1885.

691–692 "WHAT I AND OTHERS . . .": *Ibid.,* F. Appleton to AB2, November 5, 1885.

692 "THE BOARD WOULD BE LOATH . . .": *Ibid.,* F. Appleton to AB2, November 6, 1885.

692 "I DON'T BELIEVE . . .": *Ibid.*

692 ". . . YOU MUST NOT FEEL UNHAPPY . . .": AB4, E. Roosevelt to AB2, November 6, 1885.

692 "UNFORTUNATE AFFAIR . . .": *Ibid.,* AB1 to Appleton, n.d. [1885].

692–693 "FANTASTIC . . . ONE ACTIVE . . .": *AAD,* 306.

693 "HARDLY ANY OF WHOM . . .": *Ibid.,* 307.

693 "I WAS SOMEWHAT . . .": *Ibid.*

694 ". . . À QUI LA FAUTE . . .": AB4, AB1 to Pulitzer, November 4, 1886.

694 "SO MUCH LIKE MRS. . . .": Swanberg, *Pulitzer,* 108.

694 "I WAS A FOOL . . .": AB4, AB1 to AB2, September 13, 1886.

694 "I MADE AN ASS . . .": *Ibid.,* AB1 to AB2, June 27, 1886.

694 "OLD AND VERY SHAKY . . .": *Ibid.,* AB1 to AB2, January 27, 1886.

694 "QUITE RIGHT . . .": *Ibid.,* AB1 to AB2, January 11, 1886.

694–695 "THOUGH I AM A DREADFUL . . .": *Ibid.*

695 ". . . NED WAS SUCH A BEAUTY . . .": AB4, AB1 to AB2, July 7, 1886.

695 "MY OPINION IN REGARD . . .": *Ibid.,* AB1 to AB2, June 26, 1886.

695 "POOR OLD . . .": *Ibid.,* AB1 to AB2, June 22, 1886.

695 "I HAVE . . . AS USUAL . . .": *Ibid.,* AB1 to AB2, January 11, 1886.

695 "I CANNOT UNDERSTAND . . .": *Ibid.,* AB1 to AB2, June 22, 1886.

695 ". . . I CONSIDER IT . . .": *Ibid.*

695 "DON'T BE ALARMED . . .":

AB4, AB1 to AB2, October 15, 1886.

p. 695 "KEPT HOLD OF . . .": Ibid.

696 "QUITE HIGH . . .": AB4, AB1 to AB2, June 27, 1886.

697 "THE ANTIQUES ARE A QUEER . . .": The New York Times, August 5, 1887.

698 "PROVIDED THEIR OWN . . .": New York Tribune, July 18, 1886.

698 "OH DEAR, I'M . . .": Van Rennselaer, The Social Ladder, 231.

698 "A REDDISH BROWN . . .": The New York Times, November 4, 1886.

Chapter Sixty-five

699 "WELL AND CHEERFUL . . .": AB4, AB2 to Pulitzer, January 31, 1887.

699 "WENT DIRECT . . .": The New York Times, February 1, 1887.

699 "A PRIVATE WATCHMAN . . .": New York Tribune, January 31, 1887.

699 "AS IF TRYING . . .": Ibid.

699 "WITH BLOOD AND PORTIONS . . .": Ibid.

700 "COMPLETELY PROSTATED . . .": The New York Times, February 1, 1887.

700 "ALWAYS TURNED . . .": Ibid.

700 "HE WAS AN EXPERT . . .": Ibid.

700 "I HAVE JUST SEEN . . .": AB4, AB1 to Pulitzer, January 31, 1887.

700 "CORONET'S INQUEST . . .": Ibid.

700 "OF COURSE YOUR FATHER'S . . .": AB4, P. Dana to AB2, n.d. [January or February 1887].

700 "I CAN ONLY FIND . . .": Ibid., AB1 to Pulizer, n.d. [January or February 1887].

700–701 "QUITE A NUMBER . . .": Ibid., C. Carroll to AB2, February 16, 1887.

701 "RAYMOND NEVER . . .": Ibid., C. Carroll to AB2, February 22, 1887.

701 "RATHER DISAPPOINTED . . .": Ibid., AB1 to AB2, August 31, 1887.

701 "TOOK COMFORT . . .": Ibid., Caroline to AB2, August 27, [1887].

701 "I WAS VERY HAPPY . . .": Ibid.

701–702 "WITH YOU ALL . . .": Ibid.,

Caroline to AB2, June 19, 1887.

p. 702 "A NICE PLACE . . .": Clews, 420.

702 "CAN I ASSIST . . .": AB4, AB1 to AB2, August 30, 1887.

703 "IT WILL BE A TREAT . . .": Ibid., AB1 to AB2, n.d. [1887].

703 "SOMEWHAT BRUSQUE . . .": Ibid.

703 "YOU COULD . . . BE OF . . .": AB4, AB1 to AB2, August 30, 1887.

703 "LOYAL, KIND, . . .": Ibid., AB2 to AB1, September 2, 1887.

703 "WAS TRULY AND SINCERELY . . .": Ibid., AB2 to AB1, September 8, 1887.

703 "WE CAN DO WITHOUT . . .": Ibid.

703 "HARD . . . ARE . . . TO DO BUSINESS . . .": AB4, AB2 to AB1, September 2, 1887.

703 "THE PARIS HOUSE . . .": Ibid.

704 "LOST HEAVILY . . .": AB4, AB2 to AB1, September 8, 1887.

704 "HE HIMSELF HAD GREAT . . .": Ibid.

704 "THE GRASS HAS BEEN AL-LOWED . . .": AB4, AB2 to AB1, September 2, 1887.

704 "MAINTAIN . . . ITS INDIVID-UALITY . . .": Ibid., AB2 to AB1, September 8, 1887.

704–705 "CONSENT TO DOING BUSINESS . . .": Ibid.

705 "THE NAME OF BELMONT . . .": AB4, AB1 to AB2, n.d. [1887].

705 "JUDGMENT HAS CEASED . . .": Ibid.

705 "I AM ALWAYS WILLING . . .": AB4, AB1 to AB2, March 1888.

705 "DON'T SAY . . .": Ibid., AB1 to AB2, January 24, 1888.

706 "SUNDRIES REMAINING . . .": Ibid., Ledger, December 14, 1887.

706 "AN EXPENSIVE LUXURY . . .": New York Sun, June 24, 1888.

706 "MY FATHER IS UNWILLING . . .": Marble Papers, LOC, Perry Belmont to Marble, n.d. [1887].

706 "AVOID ALL CONNECTION . . .": AB4, Perry Belmont to AB1, September 1, [1888].

706–707 "WERE IT NOT FOR . . .": Ibid., Perry Belmont to AB1, Feb-ruary 10, 1889.

707 "THERE MUST BE AN END . . .": Ibid., Perry Belmont to AB1, September 1, [1888].

p. 707 "HE SAYS THAT HE LOST . . .": *Ibid.*, Caroline to AB1, April 16, [1888].

707 "THE LAST NIGHT . . .": *Ibid.*

707–708 "I AM THE LAST MAN . . .": *Ibid.*, AB1 to F. Appleton, November 29, 1886.

708 "ON HER HIND LEGS . . . UNDER THE EVERGREEN . . .": Van Wyck, 383.

708 "THE WINE . . . YES . . .": AB4, Conkling to AB1, April 5, 1888.

708 "NO MAN LIVING . . .": *Ibid.*, Thurman to AB1, September 2, 1888.

709 "YOU SEE . . . THERE WERE . . .": *New York Tribune*, March 25, 1888.

709 "AS I CERTAINLY PREFER . . .": AB4, AB1 to AB2, May 4, 1889.

709 "AN EXCELLENT IDEA . . .": *Ibid.*, Caroline to AB2, July 7, 1888.

709 "THIS IS A GRAND . . .": *Ibid.*

709 "YOU REMEMBER . . .": *Ibid.*

709 "GET BACK . . .": AB4, Caroline to AB2, July 4, 1888.

710 "WE GET ALONG . . .": *Ibid.*, Caroline to AB2, July 7, 1888.

710 "FREE OF HOUSEHOLD . . .": *Ibid.*, Caroline to AB2, July 4, 1888.

710 "THE POOREST AND THE HUMBLEST . . .": *The New York Times*, August 7, 1888.

710 "SEVERAL OF HIS ASSISTANTS . . .": *Ibid.*, December 11, 1888.

710 "WHY NOT TRY . . .": *Ibid.*

710 "DO TAKE CARE . . .": AB4, AB1 to AB2, October 17, 1888.

Chapter Sixty-seven

711 ". . . THEIR AMERICAN . . .": AB4, AB1 to Sickles, n.d. [1888].

711 "FIND AN HOUR'S . . .": *Ibid.*, F. A. Aiken to AB1, April 30, 1888.

711 "THE DEMOCRATIC PARTY . . .": *Ibid.*, AB1 to Sickles, n.d. [1888].

711 "NO AMERICAN WHO . . .": *Ibid.*, (newspaper clipping in letter), Perry Belmont to Cleveland, July 8, 1888.

711–712 "WHAT A FEARFUL . . .": *Ibid.*, AB1 to Sickles, n.d. [1888].

712 "HE HAS LONG DESIRED . . .": *The New York Times*, November 18, 1888.

p. 712 "IF CLEVELAND HAD BEEN . . .": *AAD*, 377.

712 "HOPED . . . PERRY'S INSTRUCTIONS . . .": *Ibid.*, 378.

712–713 "OUT OF THE DEPTHS . . .": I Thess. 4:18.

713 "THE COMPLETE ABSENCE . . .": *AAD*, 381.

713 "TWO STATE CARRIAGES . . .": *Ibid.*, 379.

713 "HER UNUSUAL AND GREAT . . .": *Ibid.*, 380.

713 "MUCH MORE CAREFULLY . . .": AB4, Perry Belmont to AB1, February 10, 1889.

714 "CONVERSATIONS WERE CARRIED . . .": *AAD*, 385.

714 "VERY SHARPLY . . .": *New York Herald*, April 12, 1889.

714 "ACCEPTED . . . WITH REGRET . . .": AB4, Blaine to Perry Belmont, March 11, 1889.

714 "UNGENTLEMANLY . . .": *Ibid.*, Caroline to AB2, April 22, 1889.

714 "YOU CANNOT IMAGINE . . .": *Ibid.*

714 "THAT WARM FRIEND . . .": Perry Belmont, *Public Record*, Vol. 4, 137.

715 "IT IS OUT . . .": AB4, AB1 to AB2, September 28, 1888.

715 "SUBSTANTIAL . . .": *Ibid.*

715 "NUMEROUS, CHIEF . . .": *The New York Times*, December 5, 1888.

715 "IF YOU LOVE . . .": AB4, AB1 to AB2, June 26, 1889.

715 "IF YOU DON'T . . .": *Ibid.*

716 "I KNOW PERFECTLY . . .": AB4, Caroline to AB2, August 6, 1890.

716 "IN FINE SPIRITS . . .": *Ibid.*

716 "I WOULD LIKE SO . . .": AB4, AB3 to AB1, July 23, 1889.

716 "IT IS STRANGE . . .": *Ibid.*, AB1 to AB2, July 22, 1889.

716 "I AM VERY SORRY . . .": *Ibid.*, AB1 to AB2, July 25, 1889.

716–717 "IF I WROTE . . .": *Ibid.*

717 "OF COURSE, YOU ARE . . .": AB4, AB1 to AB2, August 5, 1889.

717 "FINE TEAM . . .": *Ibid.*, AB1 to AB2, July 30, 1889.

717 "I AM GLAD . . .": *Ibid.*

717 "I FEEL VERY BAD . . .": AB4, AB1 to AB2, July 30, 1889.

718 "GOOD EVENING . . .": *New York Tribune*, December 1, 1890.

718–719 "NOW, BOSS . . .": *The New*

York Times, September 18, 1889.

p. 719 "COME TO MY HOUSE . . .": *New York Tribune,* December 1, 1890.

719 "HORSES IN TRAINING . . .": *The New York Times,* December 1, 1890.

719 "WAS IN A BETTER . . .": *Ibid.*

719 "THE SPECTATORS . . . LOOKED . . .": *Ibid.*

719 "COME AND DINE . . .": AB4, AB1 to AB2, January 1, 1890.

719 "HARDLY HOLD . . .": *Ibid.,* AB1 to AB2, April 17, 1890.

720 "WOULD HAVE AS GOOD MILK . . .": *Ibid.,* AB1 to AB2, June 25, 1890.

720 "PAPERS FROM THE HEALTH . . .": *Ibid.,* AB1 to AB2, June, 25, 1890.

720 "WRETCHED . . .": *Ibid.,* AB1 to AB2, July 8, 1890.

720 "HER MORBID AND DESPONDING . . .": *Ibid.*

720 "SHE WAS VERY SWEET . . .": *Ibid.*

720 "WHAT A USELESS . . .": *Ibid.*

720 "ARE WITH FEW EXCEPTIONS . . .": AB4, AB1 to AB2, July 6, 1890.

721 "IT IS THE ONLY TIME . . .": *New York Tribune,* December 1, 1890.

721 "HE MIGHT HAVE LOST . . .": *Ibid.*

p. 721 "I CAN ALWAYS . . .": AB4, AB1 to AB2, April 11, 1890.

721 "DESERVED MUCH CREDIT . . .": *Ibid.,* AB1 to AB2, August 8, 1890.

721 ". . . I AM GLAD . . .": *Ibid.,* AB1 to AB2, August 13, 1890.

721 "A SMART AND PUSHING . . .": *Ibid.,* AB1 to AB2, August 14, 1890.

721 "IT MAKES ME UTTERLY . . .": *Ibid.,* AB1 to AB2, August 29, 1890.

722 "DON'T GET ANGRY . . .": *Ibid.*

722 "SWEET IN YOU . . .": AB4, Betsy to AB2, September 10, 1890.

722 "THE STOCKMARKET LOOKS . . .": *Ibid.,* AB1 to AB2, October 9, 1890.

723 "SIMPLE COLD . . .": *Ibid.,* AB2 to Lord Rothschild, December 2, 1890.

723 "PULSE, TEMPERATURE, AND RESPIRATION . . .": *Ibid.*

723 "PURITAN AUSTERITY . . .": *The New York Times,* November 25, 1890.

724 "PARALYZED . . .": AB4, AB2 to Nathaniel de Rothschild, December 2, 1890.

724 "FOR ALL YOUR KIND . . ." *Ibid.,* Caroline to AB2, December 31, 1890.

724 "ON AND AFTER . . .": *Ibid.,* AB2 to Hempstead Bank, January 2, 1891.

Bibliography

I. MANUSCRIPT SOURCES

Albemarle Ledgers, University of Virginia Library

Samuel Latham Mitchill Barlow Papers, Henry E. Huntington Library

Thomas Francis Bayard Papers, Library of Congress

John Bell Papers, Library of Congress

August Belmont Papers, Houghton Library, Harvard University

August Belmont Papers, Library of Congress

August Belmont Papers, AB4 Private Collection

August Belmont Papers, AB5 Private Collection

August Belmont Papers, Collections of The Massachusetts Historical Society

August Belmont Papers, New York Public Library

August Belmont Papers, Rahel Liebeschütz Private Collection

Belmont Papers Scrapbook, Collections of The New-York Historical Society

Belmont Stock Farm Papers, University of Virginia Library

Caroline Slidell Perry Belmont Diary and Perry Belmont Papers, Lineberry Private Collection

Eleanor Belmont Papers, Columbia University Library

Blair Family Papers, Library of Congress

George Bliss Papers, Collections of The New-York Historical Society

James Buchanan Papers, Historical Society of Pennsylvania Library

Salmon Portland Chase Papers, Historical Society of Pennsylvania Library

Salmon Portland Chase Papers, Library of Congress

Grover Cleveland Papers, Library of Congress

Samuel Sullivan Cox Papers, Brown University Library

John Givan Davis Papers, Indiana Historical Society

Stephen Arnold Douglas Papers, Illinois State Historical Library

Stephen Arnold Douglas Papers, University of Chicago Library

Henry Francis DuPont Collection, Winterthur Manuscripts, Eleutherian Mills Historical Library

William Hayden English Papers, Indiana Historical Society

James Abram Garfield Papers, Library of Congress

Arthur Doe Gorman Papers, Maryland Historical Society

Simon Gratz Collection, Historical Society of Pennsylvania Library

Rutherford Birchard Hayes Papers, Hayes Memorial Library

Philip Hone Diary, Collections of The New-York Historical Society

Andrew Johnson Papers, Library of Congress

Herschel Vespasian Johnson Papers, Duke University Library

Oral History, Frances Kane

Max James Kohler Papers, American Jewish Historical Society

Daniel Scott Lamont Papers, Library of Congress

Abraham Lincoln Assassination Suspects File, Microfilm Series M599

Abraham Lincoln Papers, Library of Congress

George Brinton McClellan Papers, Library of Congress

Manton Malone Marble Papers, Library of Congress

William Learned Marcy Papers, Library of Congress

W. P. Miles Papers, University of North Carolina Library

George Nicholas Sanders Papers, Library of Congress

Carl Schurz Papers, Library of Congress

William Henry Seward Papers, University of Rochester

Horatio Seymour Papers, Collections of The New-York Historical Society

Henry Hastings Sibley Papers, Minnesota Historical Society

Samuel Jones Tilden Papers, New York Public Library

Oral History, Mrs. Harold B. Tinney

Thurlow Weed Papers, University of Rochester

Henry Benjamin Whipple Papers, Minnesota Historical Society

Matilda Young Papers, Duke University

II. NEWSPAPERS AND MAGAZINES

The Albion
American Heritage
American History Illustrated
American Mercury
American Queen
Architecture Record
Boston Herald
Broadway
Business History Review
Cassier's Magazine
Cincinnati Commercial
Cincinnati Enquirer
Cincinnati West and South
Collier's
Contemporary Review
Coronet
Cosmopolitan
Current History Magazine
Current Literature
Daily Graphic
Evening Express
Golden Age
Hannibal (Mo.) *Clipper*
Harper's
Harper's Weekly
The Historical Outlook
International Studies
The Israelite
Jewish Social Studies
Journal of Commerce
Journal of the Illinois Historical Society
Knickerbocker
Literary Digest
The Lorgnette
Magazine of History and Biography
Munsey's Magazine

Nassau County Historical Journal
The Nation
New York Commercial Advertiser
New York Herald
New York Leader
New York Morning Journal
New York Post
New York Sportsman
New York Sun
New York Telegram
New York Telegraph
The New York Times
New York Tribune
New York World
Newport Herald
The Newport (R.I.) *Mercury*
The New-York Historical Society Quarterly
Omaha Herald
Patriot and Union
Pittsburgh Daily Commercial
Review of Reviews
Scribner's Magazine
Sports Illustrated
The Times (London)
The Town
Town Topics
The Turf, Field and Farm
Van Norden Magazine
Vanity Fair
Washington Star
Washington Union
Wilke's Spirit of the Times (title changed in 1868 to *The Spirit of the Times*)
World's Work

III. BOOKS AND ARTICLES

ADAMS, GEORGE WORTHINGTON, ed. *Mary Logan: Reminiscences of the Civil War and Reconstruction.* Carbondale, Ill.: Southern Illinois University Press, 1970.

ALBION, ROBERT G., and POPE, JENNIE

B. *The Rise of New York Port, 1815–1860.* New York: Charles Scribner's Sons, 1939.

ALEXANDER, DEALVA STANWOOD. *Four Famous New Yorkers: The Political Careers of Cleveland, Platt, Hill and Roosevelt.* Port Washington, N.Y.: Ira J. Friedman, 1969.

————. *A Political History of the State of New York,* Volumes II–IV. Port Washington, N.Y.: Ira J. Friedman, 1969.

ALTROCCHI, JULIA COOLEY. *The Old California Trail.* Caldwell, Idaho: The Caxton Printers, 1945.

AMORY, CLEVELAND. *The Last Resorts.* New York: Harper and Row, 1948.

————. *Who Killed Society?* New York: Harper and Row, 1960.

ANDREWS, ALLEN. *The Splendid Pauper: Jerome.* London: Harrap, 1968.

ANDREWS, WAYNE. *The Vanderbilt Legend: The Story of the Vanderbilt Family, 1794–1940.* New York: Harcourt, Brace and Company, 1941.

ANONYMOUS. *Saratoga Illustrated, The Visitors' Guide.* New York: Taintor Brothers and Company, 1976.

AUCHAMPAUGH, PHILIP G. "The Buchanan-Douglas Feud." *Journal of the Illinois State Historical Society,* XXV (April 1932).

BAILEY, THOMAS A. *A Diplomatic History of the American People.* New York: Appleton-Century-Crofts, 1964.

BAILEY, VERNON HOWE. *Magical City: Intimate Sketches of New York.* New York: Charles Scribner's Sons, 1935.

BAKER, GEORGE AUGUSTUS. *Bad Habits of Good Society.* New York: F. B. Patterson, 1876.

BALES, WILLIAM ALAN. *Tiger in the Streets.* New York: Dodd, Mead Company, 1962.

BALLA, IGNATIUS. *The Romance of the Rothschilds,* New York: G. P. Putnam's Sons, 1913.

BALSAN, CONSUELO VANDERBILT. *The Glitter and the Gold: An Autobiography.* New York: Harper and Brothers, 1952.

BAMBURGER, LUDWIG. *Erinnerungen.* Berlin: G. Reimer, 1888.

BARINGER, WILLIAM ELDON. *A House Dividing.* Springfield, Ill.: The Abraham Lincoln Association, 1945.

BARNES, MRS. MARGARET (AYER), and FAIRBANK, JANET AYER. *Julia Newberry's Diary.* New York: W. W. Norton and Company, 1933.

BARNES, THURLOW WEED. *The Life of Thurlow Weed.* Vol. III, *Memoir.* Boston: Houghton Mifflin Company, 1884.

BARRET, RICHMOND. *Good Old Summer Days.* Boston: Houghton Mifflin Company, 1952.

BARRET, WALTER. *The Old Merchants of New York City.* New York: George W. Carleton, 1862.

BARRY, PATRICIA C. *August Belmont: New York Financier and Chessman of Politics in the Mid-Years of the Nineteenth Century.* Historical Studies Institute, Saint Francis College, 1971.

BARUCH, BERNARD M. *Baruch: My Own Story.* New York: Henry Holt and Company, 1957.

BASLER, ROY P., ed. *The Collected Works of Abraham Lincoln,* 8 vols. New Brunswick, N.J.: Rutgers University Press, 1953.

BATTERBERRY, MICHAEL. *On the Town in New York: 1776–the Present.* New York: Charles Scribner's Sons, 1973.

BATTERSEA, LADY CONSTANCE DE ROTHSCHILD. *Reminiscence.* London: Macmillan and Company, 1922.

BAYLES, W. HARRISON. *Old Taverns of New York.* New York: Frank Allaben Genealogical Company, 1915.

BEACH, MOSES YALE. *Wealth and Biography of the Wealthy Citizens of New York City.* 6th ed. New York: The Sun Office, 1845.

BEARD, CHARLES A., and BEARD, MARY R. *The Rise of American Civilization.* Vols. I–II. New York: The Macmillan Company, 1930.

BEEBE, LUCIUS. *The Big Spenders.* Garden City, N.Y.: Doubleday and Company, 1966.

BELL, ROBERT. *Wayside Pictures Through France, Belgium, and Holland.* London: Richard Bentley, 1849.

BELMONT, AUGUST. "Address of the National Democratic Committee to the People of the United States." Democratic National Committee, 1860–64.

―――. *The Belmont Gallery on Exhibition for the Benefit of the U.S. Sanitary Commission, Monday, April 4 to Saturday, April 9, 1864.* New York: J. A. Gray and Green, Printers, 1864.

―――. *A Few Letters and Speeches of the Late Civil War.* New York: Privately printed, 1870.

―――. *Letters, Speeches and Addresses.* New York: Privately printed, 1890.

―――, comp. *The Presidential Election of 1884 and August Belmont's Part in It: Newspaper Clippings from the New York* World, *the New York* Herald, *the New York* Tribune, *the New York* Sun, *and the New York* Evening Post, *July 18–October 7, 1884.*

―――. Supreme Court, City and County of New York, August Belmont and Ernest B. Lucke, Plaintiffs, Against the Erie Railway Company, Jay Gould, James Fisk (and others), Defendants, 1868.

BELMONT, ELEANOR. *The Fabric of Memory.* New York: Farrar, Straus and Cudahy, 1957.

BELMONT, PERRY. *An American Democrat.* New York: A.M.S. Press, 1967.

―――. *Public Record of Perry Belmont, A Member of the House of Representatives in the 47th, 48th, 49th, 50th Congresses.* Albany: Printed for Private Circulation by J. B. Lyon, 1898–1902.

BEMIS, SAMUEL FLAGG, ed. *The American Secretaries of State and Their Diplomacy.* New York: Cooper Square Publishers, 1963.

BENEDICT, ERASTUS C. *A Run Through Europe.* New York: D. Appleton and Company, 1860.

BERLET, EDUARD. *Aus der Geschichte der Judischen Gemeinde zu Alzey.* Alzeyer Geschichtsblatter, Heft 8, 1971.

―――. *Ein Alzeyer Einwohnerverzeichnis aus dem Jahre 1803.* Alzeyer Geschichtsblatter, Heft 8, 1971.

BINKLEY, ROBERT C. *Realism and Nationalism, 1852 to 1871.* New York: Harper and Brothers, 1935.

BIRD, FREDERICH SPENCER. *A Sketch of Holland and the Dutch.* Rotterdam: M. Wyt and Zoner, 1874.

BIRMINGHAM, STEPHEN. *Our Crowd: The Great Jewish Families of New York.* New York: Harper and Row, 1967.

―――. *The Grandees: America's Sephardic Elite.* New York: Dell Publishing Company, 1971.

BLACK, MARY. *Old New York in Early Photographs: 1853–1901.* New York: Dover Publications, 1973.

BLAINE, JAMES G. *Twenty Years of Congress: From Lincoln to Garfield.* 2 vols. Norwich, Conn.: The Henry Bill Publishing Company, 1884–1886.

BLUM, JOHN M., et al. *The National Experience.* New York: Harcourt, Brace and World, 1963.

BOTKIN, B. A., ed. *New York City Folklore.* New York: Random House, 1956.

BOWEN, CROSWELL. *The Elegant Oakey.* New York: Oxford University Press, 1956.

BOWERS, CLAUDE G. *The Tragic Era: The Revolution After Lincoln.* New York: Blue Ribbon Books, 1929.

BOWMAR, DAN M. III. *Giants of the Turf.* Lexington, Ky.: The Bloodhorse, 1960.

BRADLEY, HUGH. *Such Was Saratoga.* New York: Doubleday, Doran, and Company, 1940.

BREEN, MATTHEW P. *Thirty Years of New York Politics.* New York: Matthew Breen, 1899.

BRINNIN, JOHN MALCOLM. *The Sway of the Grand Saloon: A Social History of the North Atlantic.* New York: Delacorte Press, 1971.

BRISTED, C. ASTOR. *The Upper Ten Thousand.* New York: Stringer and Townsend, 1852.

BROOKS, NOAH. *Washington in Lincoln's Time.* New York: Rinehart, 1958.

BROWN, DEE. *The Year of the Century: 1876.* New York: Charles Scribner's Sons, 1966.

BROWN, HENRY COLLINS. *Brownstone Fronts and Saratoga Trunks.* New York: E. P. Dutton and Company, 1935.

―――. *Delmonico's: A Story of Old New York.* New York: Valentine's Manual, 1928.

———. *Fifth Avenue Old and New, 1824–1924.* New York: Official Publication of the Fifth Avenue Association in Commemoration of the One Hundredth Anniversary of the Founding of Fifth Avenue, 1924.

———. *In the Golden Nineties.* New York: Valentine's Manual, 1927.

———, ed. *Valentine's Manual of Old New York, 1916–1917.*

———, ed. *Valentine's Manual of Old New York, 1919.*

———, ed. *Valentine's Manual of Old New York, 1925.*

———, ed. *Valentine's Manual of Old New York, 1926.*

BROWN, ROLLO WALTER. *Harvard Yard in the Golden Age.* New York: Current Books, 1948.

BROWN, WILLIAM GARROTT, ed. *Official Guide to Harvard University.* Cambridge, Mass.: Harvard University Press, 1899.

BROWNE, J. ROSS. *An American Family in Germany.* New York: Harper and Brothers, 1866.

BROWNE, JUNIUS. "Holland and the Hollanders," *Harper's,* January, 1872, 174–175.

BRYANT, ARTHUR. *The Age of Elegance, 1812–1822.* New York: Harper, 1951.

BUCKHAM, GEORGE. *Notes from the Journal of a Tourist.* Vol. I. New York: G. Houston, 1890.

BUCKINGHAM, JAMES SILK. *America: Historical, Statistic, and Descriptive.* New York: Harper and Brothers, 1841.

BURT, NATHANIEL. *The Perennial Philadelphians: The Anatomy of an American Aristocracy.* Boston: Little, Brown and Company, 1963.

BURTON, RICHARD F. *The City of Saints.* New York: Alfred A. Knopf, 1963.

BUTLER, WILLIAM ALLEN. *A Retrospect of Forty Years: 1825–1865.* New York: Charles Scribner's Sons, 1911.

CALLENDER, JAMES HODGE. *Yesterdays in Little Old New York.* New York: Dorland Press, 1929.

CALLOW, ALEXANDER B., JR. *The Tweed Ring.* New York: Oxford University Press, 1966.

CATTON, BRUCE, ed. *The American Heritage Picture History of the Civil War.* New York: American Heritage Publishing Company, 1960.

CHAFETZ, HENRY. *Play the Devil. A History of Gambling in the United States.* New York: Bonanza Books, 1960.

CHILD, LYDIA MARIA. *Letters from New York.* New York: C. S. Francis Company, 1845.

CHURCHILL, ALLEN. *The Splendor Seekers, An Informal History of America's Multimillionaire Spenders: Members of the 50 Million Dollar Club.* New York: Grosset and Dunlap, 1974.

———. *The Upper Crust: An Informal History of New York's Highest Society.* New Jersey: Prentice-Hall, 1970.

CLEWS, HENRY. *Twenty-Eight Years in Wall Street.* New York: J. S. Ogilvie Publishing Company, 1887.

COCHRAN, HAMILTON. *Noted American Duels and Hostile Encounters.* New York: Chilton Books, 1963.

COCHRAN, THOMAS C., and MILLER, WILLIAM. *The Age of Enterprise.* New York: The Macmillan Company, 1942.

COHEN, HENRY. *Business and Politics in America from the Age of Jackson to the Civil War.* Westport, Conn.: Greenwood Publishing Company, 1971.

COHEN, LUCY. *Lady de Rothschild and Her Daughters, 1821–1931.* London: J. Murray, 1935.

COLE, ARTHUR C. *The Irrepressible Conflict 1850–1865.* New York: The Macmillan Company, 1934.

COLEMAN, CHARLES H. *The Election of 1868.* New York: Octagon Books, 1971.

COLEMAN, J. WINSTON, JR. *Famous Kentucky Duels.* Frankfort, Ky.: Roberts Printing Company, 1953.

COLLINS, FREDERICK L. *Money Town.* New York: G. P. Putnam's Sons, 1946.

COLLMAN, CHARLES ALBERT. *Our Mysterious Panics, 1831–1930.* New York: William Morrow and Company, 1931.

COOK, FREDERICK FRANCIS. *Bygone Days in Chicago.* Chicago: A. C. Mclurg and Company, 1910.

COREY, LEWIS. *The House of Morgan: A Social Biography of the Masters of Money.* New York: Grosset and Dunlap, 1930.

CORTI, COUNT EGON CAESAR. *The Rise of the House of Rothschild.* BRIAN and BEATRIX LUNN, trans. New York: The Cosmopolitan Book Corporation, 1928.

CRAIG, W. W., and GORE, CHALLISS. *House of Belmont: A Banking Family's First Hundred Years.* 3d rev. November 5, 1937. New York: Challiss Gore Financial Sales Counsel.

CROWNINSHIELD, FRANK. "The House of Vanderbilt." *Vogue,* November 15, 1941.

CURTIS, GEORGE TICKNOR. *The Life of James Buchanan.* New York: Harper and Brothers, 1883.

DANA, ETHEL NATHALIE. *Young in New York.* Garden City, N.Y.: Doubleday and Company, 1963.

DAY, A. GROVE, and MICHENER, JAMES. *Rascals in Paradise.* New York: Random House, 1957.

DAYTON, ABRAM C. *The Last Days of Knickerbocker Life in New York.* New York: G. P. Putnam's Sons, 1897.

DEDMON, EMMETT. *Fabulous Chicago.* New York: Random House, 1953.

DELLENBAUGH, FREDERICK S. *A Canyon Voyage.* New Haven: Yale University Press, 1926.

DEVOTO, BERNARD. *The Year of Decision, 1846.* Boston: Little, Brown and Company, 1943.

DIAMOND, SIGMUND, ed. and trans. *A Casual View of America: The Home Letters of Salomon de Rothschild, 1859–1861.* Stanford: The Stanford University Press, 1961.

DICKENS, CHARLES. *American Notes.* London: Oxford University Press, 1957.

EARLY, ELEANOR. *New York Holiday.* New York: Rinehart and Company, 1950.

ELIOT, ELIZABETH. *Heiresses and Coronets: The Story of Lovely Ladies and Noble Men.* New York: McDowell, Obolensky, 1959. (Published earlier under the title *They All Married Well.*)

ELLIOTT, MAUD HOWE. *This Was My Newport.* Cambridge: The Mythology Company, A. Marshall Jones, 1944.

ELLIS, EDWARD ROBB. *The Epic of New York City.* New York: Coward-McCann, 1966.

EMERSON, EDWIN, JR. *A History of the Nineteenth Century, Year by Year.* New York: P. F. Collier and Son, 1900.

ENCYCLOPEDIA JUDAICA. Vols. I and II. New York: Funk and Wagnalls Company, 1916.

ETTINGER, AMOS A. *The Mission to Spain of Pierre Soulé, 1853–1855: A Study in the Cuban Diplomacy of the United States.* New Haven: Yale University Press, 1932.

EWEN, DAVID. *Music Comes to America.* New York: Thomas Y. Crowell Company, 1942.

FAIRFIELD, FRANCIS GERRY. *The Clubs of New York.* New York: H. L. Hinton, 1973.

FAULKNER, HAROLD UNDERWOOD. *Politics, Reform, and Expansion: 1890–1900.* New York: Harper and Row, 1959.

FAY, THEODORE SEDGEWICK. *Views in New York.* New York: Peabody, 1831.

FEDER, ERNST, ed. *Bismarcks Grosses Spiel.* Frankfurt-am-Main, Societäts-Verlag, 1932.

FIELD, H. M. *From Egypt to Japan.* New York: Charles Scribner's Sons, 1886.

FISKE, STEPHEN. *Offhand Portraits of Prominent New Yorkers.* New York: George Lockwood and Sons, 1884.

FLICK, ALEXANDER, G., ed. *History of the State of New York.* 10 vols. New York: Ira J. Friedman, 1962.
———. *Samuel Jones Tilden: A Study in Political Sagacity.* Port Washington N. Y.: Dodd Mead Company, 1939.

FONER, PHILIP S. *Business and Slavery: The New York Merchants and the Irrepressible Conflict.* Chapel Hill: The University of North Carolina Press, 1941.

FOOTE, SHELBY. *The Civil War: A Narrative.* Vol. I: *Fort Sumter to*

Perryville. New York: Random House, 1958.

———. *The Civil War: A Narrative*. Vol. II: *Fredericksburg to Meridian*. New York: Random House, 1963.

———. *The Civil War: A Narrative*. Vol. III: *Red River to Appomattox*. New York: Random House, 1974.

FORBES, SIR JOHN. *Sight-Seeing in Germany and the Tyrol in the Autumn of 1855*. London: Smith, Elder and Company, 1856.

FORD, WORTHINGTON CHAUNCEY. *A Cycle of Adams: Letters 1861–1865*. Vols. I and II. Boston: Houghton Mifflin Company, 1920.

FRANCIS, JOHN W. *Old New York: or Reminiscences of the Past Sixty Years*. New York: Charles Rowe, 1858.

FREEMAN, LEWIS R. "The Dutch in Malaysia." *Contemporary Review* 105: 548–555 (1914).

FROTHINGHAM, PAUL R. *Edward Everett: Orator and Statesman*. Boston: Houghton Mifflin Company, 1925.

FULLER, ROBERT H. *Jubilee Jim: The Life of Colonel James Fisk, Jr.* New York: The Macmillan Company, 1928.

FURNAS, J. C. *The Americans: A Social History of the United States, 1587–1914*. New York: G. P. Putnam's Sons, 1969.

FURNIVALL, J. S. *Netherlands India*. Cambridge, England: Cambridge University Press, 1944.

GARRATY, JOHN A. *The New Commonwealth: 1877–1890*. New York: Harper and Row, 1968.

GAVRONSKY, SERGE. *The French Liberal Opposition and the American Civil War*. New York: Humanities Press, 1968.

GIBSON, WALTER M. *The Prison of Weltevreden*. New York: J. C. Riker, 1856.

GILDER, RODMAN. *The Battery*. Boston: Houghton Mifflin Company, 1836.

GILLE, BERTRAND. *Histoires de la Maison Rothschild*. Geneva: Li Droz, 1965.

GLANZ, RUDOLPH. "The Rothschild Legend in America." *Jewish Social Studies*, XIX: 3–28 (January-April 1957).

GOLDIN, MILTON. *The Music Merchants*. London: The Macmillan Company, 1969.

GOTTHEIL, RICHARD JAMES HORATIO. *The Belmont Family, A Record of Four Hundred Years*. Norwood, Mass.: Plimpton Press, 1917.

GOUVERNEUR, MARION. *As I Remember: Recollections of American Society During the Nineteenth Century*. New York: D. Appleton and Company, 1911.

GRAETZ, H. *History of the Jews*. Vol. 5. Philadelphia: The Jewish Publishing Society of America, 1895.

GRAFTON, JOHN. *New York in the Nineteenth Century*. New York: Dover Publications, 1977.

GRAY, WOOD. *The Hidden Civil War: The Story of the Copperheads*. New York: The Viking Press, 1942.

GRINSTEIN, HYMAN B. *The Rise of the Jewish Community of New York: 1654–1800*. Philadelphia: The Jewish Publishing Society of America, 1945.

GRUND, FRANCIS J. *Aristocracy in America*. London: Richard Bentley, 1839.

GUEDELLA, PHILIP. *The Hundred Years*. Garden City, N. Y. Doubleday and Company, 1936.

HALL, CLIFTON R. *Andrew Johnson: Military Governor of Tennessee*. Princeton: Princeton University Press, 1916.

HALL, FLORENCE HOWE. *Social Customs*. Boston: Estes and Lauriat, 1887.

HALSTEAD, MURAT. *Caucuses of 1860: A History of the National Political Conventions of the Current Presidential Campaign*. Columbus, Ohio: Follett, Foster and Company, 1860.

HARRIS, CHARLES TOWNSEND. *Memories of Manhattan in the Sixties and Seventies*. New York: The Derrydale Press, 1928.

HARRIS, THOMAS L. *The Trent Affair*. Indianapolis: The Bobbs-Merrill Company, 1896.

HASWELL, CHARLES H. *Reminiscences of New York by an Octogenarian, (1816–1860)*. New York: Harper and Brothers: 1896.

HAUK, MINNIE. *Memoirs of a Singer*. London: A. M. Philpot, 1925.

HAVENS, CATHERINE E. *Diary of a Little Girl in Old New York.* New York: H. C. Brown, 1919.

HAWTHORNE, NATHANIEL. *English Note-Books.* Boston: J. R. Osgood and Company, 1872.

HEADLEY, JOEL TYLER. *The Great Riots of New York, 1712–1873.* New York: E. B. Treat, 1873.

HEIMER, MEL. *Fabulous Bawd: The Story of Saratoga.* New York: Henry Holt and Company, 1952.

HEMSTREET, CHARLES. *Nooks and Corners of Old New York.* New York: Charles Scribner's Sons, 1899.

HERSHKOWITZ, LEO. *Tweed's New York—Another Look.* Garden City, N.Y.: Anchor Books, 1978.

HICKS, FREDERICK C., ed. *High Finance in the Sixties.* New Haven: University Press, 1929.

HOAR, G. F. *Autobiography of Seventy Years.* Vols. I and II. New York: Charles Scribner's Sons, 1903.

HOLBROOK, STEWART H. *The Age of Moguls.* Garden City, N.Y.: Doubleday and Company, 1953.

HOOGENBOOM, ARI and OLIVE, eds. *The Gilded Age.* Englewood Cliffs, N.J.: Prentice-Hall, 1967.

HONE, PHILIP. *The Diary of Philip Hone.* Manuscript. New York: The New-York Historical Society.

———. *The Diary of Philip Hone.* Ed. by Allan Nevins, Vols. I and II. New York: Dodd, Mead and Company, 1927.

HORN, STANLEY F. *Invisible Empire: The Story of the Ku Klux Klan: 1866–1871.* Montclair, N.J.: Patterson-Smith, 1969.

HOWARD, M. W. *The American Plutocracy.* New York: Holland Publishing Company, 1895.

HOWE, JULIA (WARD). *Reminiscences, 1819–1899.* Boston: Houghton Mifflin Company, 1899.

HOWE, WILLIAM WIRT. *The Pasha Papers: Epistles of Mohammed Pasha.* New York: C. Scribner's Sons, 1859.

HOWITT, WILLIAM. *The Rural and Domestic Life of Germany.* Philadelphia: Carey and Hart, 1843.

HOYT, EDWIN P. *The Vanderbilts and Their Fortunes.* New York: Doubleday and Company, 1962.

HUGHES, ROBERT. *The Real New York.* New York: Smart Set Publishing Company, 1904.

HUGHES, THOMAS. *Vacation Rambles.* New York: The Macmillan Company, 1895.

HUNGERFORD, EDWARD. *Men of Erie.* New York: Random House, 1946.

HYMAN, HAROLD M. *A More Perfect Union: The Impact of the Civil War and Reconstruction on the Constitution.* Boston: Houghton Mifflin and Company, 1975.

IRVING, ROBERT. *The Story of Wall Street.* New York: Greenburg, 1929.

JAMES, HENRY. *The American Scene.* London: Chapman and Hall, 1907.

———. *The Art of Travel: Scenes and Journeys in America, England, France and Italy from the Travel Writings of Henry James.* MORTON DAUWEN ZABEL, ed. New York: Doubleday and Company, 1958.

———. *English Hours.* BEWLEY MARIUS, ed. New York: Horizon Press, 1968.

———. *Henry James: Autobiography.* FREDERICK W. DUPEE, ed. New York: Criterion Books, 1956.

———. *Portraits of Places.* Boston: J. R. Osgood and Company, 1884.

JOHANNSEN, ROBERT W., ed. *The Letters of Stephen A. Douglas.* Urbana: University of Illinois Press, 1961.

———. *Stephen A. Douglas.* New York: Oxford University Press, 1973.

JOHN, EVAN. *The Atlantic Impact, 1861: England vs. America in the Civil War.* New York: G. P. Putnam's Sons, 1952.

JOHNSON, ROBERT UNDERWOOD, and BUEL, CLARENCE CLOUGH, eds. *Battles and Leaders of the Civil War.* Vols. I–IV. New York: Thomas Yoseloff, 1951.

JONES, HOWARD MUMFORD. *The Age of Energy: Varieties of American Experience, 1865–1915.* New York: The Viking Press, 1970.

———. *America and French Culture: 1750–1898.* Chapel Hill: The University of North Carolina Press, 1927.

JOSEPHSON, MATTHEW. *The Politicos:*

1865–1896. New York: Harcourt Brace and World, 1966.

———. *The Robber Barons: The Great American Capitalists, 1861–1901*. New York: Harcourt, Brace and Company, 1934.

KATCHEN, LEO. *The Big Bankroll*. New York: Harper and Row, 1959.

KATZ, IRVING. *August Belmont: A Political Biography*. New York: Columbia University Press, 1968.

KAVALER, LUCY. *The Astors: A Family Chronicle of Pomp and Power*. New York: Dodd, Mead and Company, 1966.

KIRKLAND, EDWARD CHASE. *The Peacemakers of 1864*. New York: The Macmillan Company, 1927.

KLEIN, MAURY. *History of the Louisville and Nashville Railroad*. New York: The Macmillan Company, 1972.

KLEIN, PHILIP SHRIVER. *President James Buchanan: A Biography*. State College: The Pennsylvania State University Press, 1962.

KLERCK, EDUARD SERRAAS DE. *History of the Netherlands East Indies*. Rotterdam: W. L. and J. Brusse, 1938.

KOENIG, LOUIS W. *Bryan: A Political Biography of William Jennings Bryan*. New York: G. P. Putnam's Sons, 1971.

KOUWENHOVEN, JOHN A. *The Columbia Historical Portrait of New York: An Essay in Graphic History*. New York: Doubleday and Company, 1953.

LANDHEER, BARTHOLOMEW. *The Netherlands*. Berkeley: The University of California Press, 1943.

LAPORTE, LAURENT. *Sailing on the Nile*. VIRGINIA VAUGHAN, trans. Boston: Roberts Brothers, 1872.

LEARNED, HENRY BARRETT. *William Learned Marcy, Secretary of State*. Reprinted from *American Secretaries of State and Their Diplomacy*. Vol. VI. SAMUEL FLAGG BEMIS, ed. New York: Alfred A. Knopf, 1929.

LEECH, MARGARET. *Reveille in Washington, 1860–1865*. New York: Grosset and Dunlap, 1941.

LEHR, ELIZABETH DREXEL. *"King Lehr"*

and the Gilded Age. Philadelphia: J. B. Lippincott Company, 1935.

LESLIE, ANITA. *The Remarkable Mr. Jerome*. New York: Henry Holt and Company, 1954.

LETTS, MALCOLM. *A Wayfarer on the Rhine*. London: Methuen and Company, 1930.

LEWIS, R. W. B. *Edith Wharton: A Biography*. New York: Harper and Row, 1975.

LIEBESCHÜTZ, RAHEL. Yearbook XIV, Leo Baeck Institute. *August Belmont and the House of Rothschild: Four Letters from the Years 1848 and 1849*.

———. *Simon Belmont, Gutsbesitzer, 1789–1859*. Sunderdruch aus Alzeyer Geschichtsldatts: Heft 9, 1977.

———. Yearbook VII, Leo Baeck Institute. *The Wind of Change*, 227–256.

LINCOLN, ABRAHAM. *The Collected Works of Abraham Lincoln. Vol. V: 1861–1862*. New Brunswick, N.J.: Rutgers University Press, 1953.

LINK, ARTHUR. *Woodrow Wilson and the Progressive Era: 1910–1917*. New York: Harper and Row, 1954.

LINTON, WILLIAM JAMES. *The House that Tweed Built*. Cambridge, Mass.: W. J. Linton, 1871.

LIVINGSTON, BERNARD. *Their Turf: America's Horsey Set and Its Princely Dynasties*. New York: Arbor House, 1973.

LOCKE, DAVID R. *Nasby in Exile, or Six Months of Travel in England, Ireland, Scotland, France, Germany, Switzerland, and Belgium*. Boston: Locke Publishing Company, 1882.

———. *The Struggles (Social, Financial, and Political) of Petroleum V. Nasby*. Boston: Lee and Shepard, 1893.

LOCKWOOD, CHARLES. *Manhattan Moves Uptown*. Boston: Houghton Mifflin Company, 1976.

LOGAN, ANDY. *The Man Who Robbed the Robber Barons*. New York: W. W. Norton and Company, 1965.

LONGSTREET, STEPHEN. *Win or Lose: A Social History of Gambling in America*. New York: The Bobbs-Merrill Company, 1977.

LOWE, DAVID. *New York, N.Y.* New York: American Heritage Publishing Company, 1968.

LOWELL, ABBOT LAWRENCE et al. *The History and Traditions of Harvard College.* Cambridge, Mass.: Harvard Crimson, 1929.

LOWENTHAL, MARVIN. *A World Passed By.* New York: Harper and Brothers, 1933.

LUHAN, MABEL DODGE. *Intimate Memories.* New York: Harcourt, Brace and Company, 1933.

LUNDBERG, FERDINAND. *America's Sixty Families.* New York: Vanguard Press, 1937.

———. *The Rich and the Super-Rich: A Study in the Power of Money Today.* New York: Bantam Books, 1969.

LUTHIN, REINHARD, H. *The First Lincoln Campaign.* Gloucester, Mass.: Peter Smith, 1964.

LYNCH, DENIS TILDEN. *"Boss" Tweed: The Story of a Grim Generation.* New York: Blue Ribbon Books, 1927.

———. *Grover Cleveland: A Man Four-Square.* New York: Horace Liveright, 1932.

———. *The Wild Seventies.* New York: D. Appleton-Century Company, 1941.

LYNES, RUSSELL. *The Tastemakers.* New York: Grosset and Dunlap, 1949.

LYON, PETER. *To Hell in a Day Coach.* Philadelphia: J. B. Lippincott Company, 1967.

MCALLISTER, WARD. *Society as I Have Found It.* New York: Cassell Publishing Company, 1890.

MCCABE, EDWARD WINSLOW. *The Secrets of the Great City.* Philadelphia: National Publishing Company, 1868.

MCCABE, JAMES D. JR. *Lights and Shadows of New York Life, or The Sights and Sensations of the Great City.* Philadelphia: National Publishing Company, 1872.

———. *New York by Sunlight and Gaslight: A Work Descriptive of the Great American Metropolis.* New York: Union Publishing House, 1886.

MCCAGUE, JAMES. *The Second Rebellion: The Story of the New York Draft Riots of 1863.* New York: The Dial Press, 1860.

MCCULLOUGH, ED. *Good Old Coney Island.* New York: Charles Scribner's Sons, 1957.

MCJIMSEY, GEORGE T. *Genteel Partisan: Manton Marble, 1834–1917.* Ames: The Iowa State University Press, 1971.

MCVICKAR, HARRY WHITNEY. *The Greatest Show on Earth: Society.* New York: Harper and Brothers, 1892.

MALONE, DUMAS, and RAUCH, BASIL. *The New Nation, 1865–1917.* New York: Appleton-Century-Crofts, 1960.

MANNING, WILLIAM RAY. *Diplomatic Correspondence of the United States: Inter-American Affairs 1831–1860.* Vol. XI. Washington, D.C.: Carnegie Endowment for International Peace, 1932–39.

MARCUS, JACOB RADER. *Memoirs of American Jews, 1775–1865.* Vol. III. Philadelphia: The Jewish Publication Society of America, 1955.

MARCUSE, MAXWELL F. *This Was New York!: A Nostalgic Picture of Gotham in the Gaslight Era.* New York: Carlton Press, 1965.

MARKS, EDWARD B. *They All Had Glamour: From the Swedish Nightingale to the Naked Lady.* New York: Julian Messner, 1944.

MARRYAT, FREDERICK. *A Diary in America.* New York: Alfred A. Knopf, 1962.

MARTIN, RALPH G. *Jennie: The Life of Lady Randolph Churchill; The Romantic Years, 1854–1895.* Englewood Cliffs, N.J.: Prentice-Hall, 1969.

MARTINEAU, HARRIET. *Society in America.* Vols. I–III. London: Saunders and Utley, 1837.

MASTERSON, V. V. *The Katy Railroad and the Last Frontier.* Norman, Okla.: The University of Oklahoma Press, 1952.

MATHEWS, JAMES MCFARLANE. *Recollections of Persons and Events.* New York: Sheldon and Company, 1865.

MAURICE, ARTHUR BARTLETT. *Fifth Avenue.* New York: Dodd, Mead and Company, 1918.

MAYER, GEORGE H. *The Republican Party, 1854–1964.* New York: Oxford University Press, 1964.

MAYER, GRACE M. *Once upon a City.* New York: The Macmillan Company, 1958.

MILLER, FRANCIS TREVELYAN, ed. *The Photographic History of the Civil War.* 10 vols. New York: The Review of Reviews Company, 1911.

MILTON, GEORGE FORT. *The Eve of Conflict.* Boston: Houghton Mifflin Company, 1934.

MINNIGERODE, MEADE. *Certain Rich Men.* New York: G. P. Putnam's Sons, 1927.

———. *The Fabulous Forties, 1840–1850: A Presentation of Private Life.* New York: G. P. Putnam's Sons, 1924.

MITCHELL, LUCY (SPRAGUE), and LAMBERT, CLARA. *Manhattan: Now and Long Ago.* New York: The Macmillan Company, 1934.

MITCHELL, STEWART. *Horatio Seymour of New York.* Cambridge, Mass.: Harvard University Press, 1938.

MOORE, JOHN BASSETT, ed. *The Works of James Buchanan, Comprising His Speeches, State Papers, and Private Correspondence.* 12 vols. Philadelphia: J. B. Lippincott Company, 1908–1911.

MORGAN, H. WAYNE. *From Hayes to McKinley: National Party Politics, 1877–1896.* Syracuse, N.Y.: Syracuse University Press, 1969.

MORISON, SAMUEL ELIOT. *"Old Bruin"–Commodore Matthew C. Perry, 1794–1858.* Boston: Little, Brown and Company, 1964.

MORRIS, CHARLES, ed. *Makers of New York.* Philadelphia: L. R. Hamersly and Company, 1895.

MORRIS, LLOYD. *Incredible New York: High Life and Low Life of the Last Hundred Years.* New York: Random House, 1951.

MORTON, FREDERIC. *The Rothschilds, A Family Portrait.* New York: Curtis Publishing Company, 1961.

MOTLEY, JOHN L. *The Correspondence of John L. Motley,* Vol. XV. GEORGE W. CURTIS, ed. New York: Society of English and French Literature, 1889.

MOTT, EDWARD HAROLD. *Between the Ocean and the Lakes: The Story of Erie.* New York: Ticker Publishing Company, 1907.

MOWRY, GEORGE E. *The Era of Theodore Roosevelt and the Birth of Modern America: 1900–1912.* New York: Harper and Row, 1952.

MUIR, JOHN. *The Mountains of California.* New York: Century Company, 1894.

———. *Steep Trails.* Boston: Houghton Mifflin Company, 1918.

———. "The Yosemite," in *The Writings of John Muir,* Vol. V. Boston: Houghton Mifflin Company, 1916.

MUSHKAT, JEROME. *Tammany: The Evolution of a Political Machine, 1789–1865.* Syracuse, N.Y.: Syracuse University Press, 1971.

MYERS, GUSTAVUS (MEYERS, GUSTAV). *History of the Great American Fortunes.* New York: Random House, 1937.

———. *The History of Tammany Hall.* New York: Boni and Liveright, 1917.

MYERS, WILLIAM STARR. *A Study in Personality: General George Brinton McClellan.* New York: D. Appleton-Century Company, 1934.

NEVINS, ALLAN. *Abram S. Hewitt, with Some Account of Peter Cooper.* New York: Harper and Brothers, 1935.

———, ed. *America Through British Eyes.* New York: Oxford University Press, 1948.

———. *The Emergence of Lincoln.* Vols. I and II. New York: Charles Scribner's Sons, 1950.

———. *Frémont.* New York: Longman, Green and Company, 1955.

———. *Ordeal of the Union.* Vols. I and II. New York: Charles Scribner's Sons, 1947.

———. *The War for the Union.* Vols. I–IV. New York: Charles Scribner's Sons, 1959–71.

NICHOLS, ROY F. *The Democratic Machine: 1850–1854.* New York: Columbia University Press, 1923.

———. *The Disruption of American Democracy.* New York: The Macmillan Company, 1948.

———. *Franklin Pierce: Young Hickory of the Granite Hills.* Philadelphia: University of Pennsylvania Press, 1931.

O'CONNOR, RICHARD. *The German-Americans: An Informal History.* Boston: Little, Brown and Company, 1967.

———. *The Golden Summers: An Antic History of Newport.* New York: G. P. Putnam's Sons, 1974.

———. *The Scandalous Mr. Bennett.* New York: Doubleday and Company, 1962. Official Proceedings of the National Democratic Convention . . . Different Cities, 1856–1884.

PERINE, EDWARD. *Here's to Broadway!* New York: G. P. Putnam's Sons, 1930.

PERKINS, ELI. *Saratoga, 1901.* New York: Sheldon and Company, 1872.

PHISTERER, FREDERICK, comp. *New York in the War of the Rebellion, 1861 to 1865.* Albany, N.Y.: Weed, Parsons, and Company, 1890.

PILAT, OLIVER RAMSAY, and RAMSON, JO. *Sodom by the Sea.* New York: Doubleday, Doran and Company, 1941.

PINEAU, ROGER, ed. *The Japan Expedition, 1852–1854: The Personal Journal of Commodore Matthew C. Perry.* Washington, D.C.: Smithsonian Institution Press, 1968.

POST, WALDRON KINTZING. *Harvard Stories: Sketches of the Undergraduate.* New York: G. P. Putnam's Sons, 1893.

POWELL, E. ALEXANDER. *The End of the Trail: The Far West from New Mexico to British Columbia.* New York: Charles Scribner's Sons, 1916.

PRIME, SAMUEL IRENACUS. *Life in New York.* New York: R. Carter, 1847.

———. *Travels in Europe and the East.* New York: Harper and Brothers, 1855.

RADDOCK, CHARLES. *Portrait of a People.* New York: The Judaica Press, 1965.

RAPPORT, SAMUEL, and SCHARTLE, PATRICIA, eds. *America Remembers: Our Best-Loved Customs and Traditions.* New York: Hanover House, 1956.

RAUCH, BASIL. *American Interest in Cuba, 1848–1855.* New York: Oxford University Press, 1948.

RAVAGE, MARCUS ELI. *Five Men of Frankfort: The Story of the Rothschilds.* New York: The Dial Press, 1934.

RAWLEY, JAMES A. "Financing the Freemont Campaign." *Magazine of History and Biography,* LXXV: 25–35 (January 1951).

REDLICH, FRITZ. *The Molding of American Banking: Men and Ideas.* 2 vols. New York: Hafner, 1947.

RHODES, ALBERT. "A Court Brief at The Hague." *Harper's,* February 7, 1973.

RHODES, JAMES FORD. *History of the Civil War: 1861–1865.* New York: The Macmillan Company, 1917.

———. *The History of the United States from the Compromise of 1850 to the Final Restoration of Home Rule in 1877.* New York: The Macmillan Company, 1906.

RIESBECK, THE BARON. *Travels through Germany in a Series of Letters.* Vol. III. London: T. Codell, 1787.

RIVES, REGINALD. *The Coaching Club: Its History, Records and Activities.* New York: Privately printed, 1935.

ROBERTSON, WILLIAM H. P. *The History of Thoroughbred Racing in America.* Englewood Cliffs, N.J.: Prentice-Hall, 1964.

ROSS, ISHBEL. *Crusades and Crinolines.* New York: Harper and Row, 1963.

———. *Silhouette in Diamonds: The Life of Mrs. Potter Palmer.* New York: Harper and Brothers, 1960.

ROSS, JOEL H. *What I Saw in New York, or A Bird's Eye View of City Life.* New York: Derby and Miller, 1851.

ROTH, CECIL. *The Magnificent Rothschilds.* London: R. Hale, 1939.

———. *A Short History of the Jewish People.* London: East and West Libraries, 1953.

RUSSELL, JOHN. *A Tour in Germany.* Boston: Wells and Lilly, 1925.

RUSSELL, WILLIAM HOWARD. *My Diary North and South.* Boston: Burnham, 1863.

SANBORN, ALVAN F., ed. *Reminiscences of Richard Lathers: Sixty Years of a Busy Life in South Carolina,*

Massachusetts and New York. New York: The Grafton Press, 1907.

SANDBURG, CARL. *Abraham Lincoln: The Prairie Years,* Vols. I–II. New York: The Pictorial Review Company, 1925.

————. *Abraham Lincoln: The War Years,* Vols. I–IV. New York: The Pictorial Review Company, 1925.

SATTERLEE, HERBERT L. *J. Pierpont Morgan: An Intimate Portrait.* New York: The Macmillan Company, 1939.

SAUNDERS, FREDERICK. *New York in a Nut-shell; or, Visitors' Hand-book to the City.* New York: T. W. Strong, 1853.

SCHAPPES, MORRIS U., ed. *A Documentary History of the Jews in the United States: 1654–1875.* New York: The Citadel Press, 1950.

SCHWAB, HERMANN. *A World in Ruins.* London: Edward Goldston, 1946.

SCOVILLE, JOSEPH A. *The Old Merchants of New York City.* 5 vols. New York: Carleton, 1864–1870.

SCUDDER, HORACE ELISHA. *James Russell Lowell: A Biography.* Vols. I and II. Boston: Houghton Mifflin Company, 1901.

SEAMAN, L. C. *From Vienna to Versailles.* London: Methuen and Company, 1955.

SEARS, LOUIS MARTIN. "August Belmont: Banker in Politics." *The Historical Outlook,* XV: 151–154 (April 1924).

————. *John Slidell.* Durham, N.C.: Duke University Press, 1925.

SEITZ, DON C. *Famous American Duels.* New York: Books for Libraries Press, 1929.

SELDES, GILBERT. *The Stammering Century.* New York: The John Day Company, 1928.

SHERMAN, JOHN. *John Sherman's Recollections of Forty Years in the House, Senate and Cabinet.* Vol. II. Chicago: The Werner Company, 1895.

SICHEL, PIERRE. *Jersey Lily.* Englewood Cliffs, N.J.: Prentice-Hall, 1957.

SILVER, NATHAN. *Lost New York.* New York: Schocken Books, 1967.

SMITH, GENE. *High Crimes and Misdemeanors: The Impeachment and Trial of Andrew Johnson.* New York: William Morrow and Company, 1977.

SMITH, JOSEPH. *Reminiscences of Saratoga.* New York: The Knickerbocker Press, 1897.

SMITH, JUSTIN H. *The War with Mexico.* New York: The Macmillan Company, 1919.

SOBEL, ROBERT. *Panic on Wall Street: A History of America's Financial Disasters.* London: Collier-Macmillan, 1968.

SPENCER, IVOR DEBENHAM. *The Victor and the Spoils: A Life of William L. Marcy.* Providence, R.I.: Brown University Press, 1959.

SPRAGUE, JOHN FRANKLIN. *New York: The Metropolis, Its Noted Business and Professional Men.* New York: The New York Recorder, 1893.

STEBBINS, HOMER A. *A Political History of the State of New York, 1865–1869.* New York: Columbia University Press, 1913.

STILL, BAYRD. *Mirror for Gotham: New York as Seen by Contemporaries from Dutch Days to the Present.* New York: New York University Press, 1956.

STOKES, I. N. PHELPS. *Stokes's Iconography of Manhattan, 1498–1909.* New York: R. H. Dodd, 1915–1928.

STRONG, GEORGE TEMPLETON. *The Diary of George Templeton Strong.* Ed. by Allan Nevins and Milton Halsey Thomas. Vols. I–IV. New York: The Macmillan Company, 1952.

STRONG, SAMUEL MEREDITH, comp. *The Great Blizzard of 1888.* Brooklyn: Arrangement by Marion Overton, 1938.

SWANBERG, WILLIAM A. *Pulitzer.* New York: Charles Scribner's Sons, 1967.

————. *Sickles the Incredible.* New York: Charles Scribner's Sons, 1956.

SWEENY, PETER B. *Peter B. Sweeny on the "Ring Frauds" and Other Public Questions.* New York: J. Y. Savage (For Private Circulation Only), 1894.

TEBBIL, JOHN. *The Inheritors.* New York: G. P. Putnam's Sons, 1962.

TENNYSON, ALFRED, LORD. *Poems and Plays.* London: Oxford University Press, 1967.

THARP, LOUISE HALL. *Mrs. Jack: A Biography of Isabella Stewart Gardner.* Greenwich, Conn.: Fawcett Publications, 1965.

———. *Three Saints and a Sinner.* Boston: Little, Brown and Company, 1965.

THOMAS, AUGUSTUS. *The Print of Remembrance.* New York: Curtis Publishing Company, 1921.

THOMAS, LATELY. *Delmonico's: A Century of Splendor.* Boston: Houghton Mifflin Company, 1967.

———. *Sam Ward: "King of the Lobby."* Boston: Houghton Mifflin Company, 1965.

TOWNSEND, REGINALD T. *Mother of Clubs: Being the History of the First Hundred Years of the Union Club of the City of New York, 1836–1936.* New York: The Printing House of W. E. Rudge, 1936.

TRAIN, GEORGE FRANCIS. *Young American in Wall-Street.* New York: Derby and Jackson, 1857.

TRUMAN, BEN C. *The Field of Honor: Being a Complete and Comprehensive History of Dueling in All Countries.* New York: Fords, Howard Hulbert, 1884.

TULLY, ANDREW. *The Era of Elegance.* New York: Funk and Wagnalls Company, 1947.

TURENNE, LOUIS DE. *Quatorze Mois dans l'amérique du Nord (1875–1876).* Tomes I et II. Paris: A. Quantin, 1879.

ULMAN, ALBERT. *New Yorkers from Stuyvesant to Roosevelt.* Port Washington, N.Y.: Ira. J. Friedman, 1969.

United States Congress. Report of the Joint Select Committee to Inquire into the Condition of Affairs in the Late Insurrectionary States. Washington, D.C.: U.S. Government Printing Office, 1872.

United States Government. Executive Documents; 33d Cong., 2d Sess., Vol. 5-1854-55. Washington, D.C.: A. O. P. Nicholson, 1855.

———. *War of the Rebellions; Official Records of the Union and Confederate States.* Series I and II. Washington, D.C.: U.S. Government Printing Office, 1880–1901.

VALENTINE, F. C., trans. *Gotham and the Gothamites.* London: Field and Tuer, 1887.

VAN ALSTYNE, RICHARD W. *The Rising American Empire.* New York: Oxford University Press, 1960.

VAN DEUSEN, GLYNDON G. *William Henry Seward.* New York: Oxford University Press, 1967.

VAN RENSSELAER, MRS. JOHN KING. *Newport: Our Social Capital.* Philadelphia: J. B. Lippincott Company, 1905.

———. *New Yorkers of the XIX Century.* New York: F. T. Neely, 1897.

———. *The Social Ladder.* New York: Henry Holt and Company, 1924.

VAN WYCK, FREDERICK. *Recollections of an Old New Yorker.* New York: Liveright, 1932.

VANDERBILT, CORNELIUS J. *The Vanderbilt Feud.* London: Hutchinson, 1957.

WALLER, GEORGE. *Saratoga: Saga of an Impious Era.* Englewood Cliffs, N.J.: Prentice-Hall, 1966.

WALLING, GEORGE WASHINGTON. *Recollections of a New York Chief of Police.* New York: Caxton Book Concern, 1887.

WARREN, JOHN H. *Thirty Years' Battle with Crime, or The Crying Shame of New York, as Seen Under the Broad Glare of an Old Detective's Lantern.* Poughkeepsie, N.Y.: A. J. White, 1874.

WARSHOW, ROBERT IRVING. *The Story of Wall Street.* New York: Greenberg Publisher, 1929.

WECTER, DIXON. *The Saga of American Society: A Record of Social Aspirations, 1607–1937.* New York: Charles Scribner's Sons, 1937.

WERNER, M. R. *Barnum.* New York: Harcourt, Brace and Company, 1923.

———. *It Happened in New York.* New York: Coward-McCann, 1957.

———. *Tammany Hall.* Garden City, N.Y.: Garden City Publishing Company, 1932.

WERSTEIN, IRVING. *The Blizzard of '88.*

New York: Thomas Y. Crowell Company, 1960.

———. *The Draft Riots: July, 1863.* New York: Julian Messner, 1971.

WHARTON, EDITH. *A Backward Glance.* New York: D. Appleton-Century Company, 1934.

WHEELER, GEORGE. *Pierpont Morgan and Friends.* Englewood Cliffs, N.J.: Prentice-Hall, 1973.

WHITE, WILLIAM ALLEN. *Masks in a Pageant.* New York: The Macmillan Company, 1928.

WILLIAMS, C. R. *The Life of Rutherford B. Hayes.* Boston: Houghton Mifflin Company, 1914.

WILLIAMS, MYRON R. *The Story of Phillips Exeter.* Exeter, N.H.: Phillips Exeter Academy, 1957.

WILLIS, N. PARKER. *The Prose Works of N. P. Willis.* Philadelphia: Henry C. Baird, 1855.

———. *Rural Letters and Other Records of Thought at Leisure.* New York: Baker and Scribner, 1849.

WILSON, JAMES GRANT, ed. *The Memorial History of the City of New York.* New York: New York History Company, 1893.

WOLCOTT, FRANCES M. *Heritage of Years–Kaleidoscopic Memories.* New York: Minton, Balch and Company, 1932.

WOLFE, GERARD R. *New York: A Guide to the Metropolis.* New York: New York University Press, 1975.

WOODWARD, C. VANN. *Reunion and Reaction: The Compromise of 1877 and the End of Reconstruction.* Boston: Little, Brown and Company, 1951.

WORDEN, HELEN. *Society Circus.* New York: Covici, Friede Publishers, 1936.

WRIGHT, MABEL OSGOOD. *My New York.* New York: The Macmillan Company, 1926.

ZIFF, LARZER. *The American 1890s: Life and Times of a Lost Generation.* New York: The Viking Press, 1966.